ZIONISM: THE FORMATIVE YEARS

ZIONISM:
THE
FORMATIVE YEARS

DAVID VITAL

CLARENDON PRESS · OXFORD

1982

Oxford University Press, Walton Street, Oxford OX2 6DP

LONDON GLASGOW NEW YORK TORONTO
DELHI BOMBAY CALCUTTA MADRAS KARACHI
KUALA LUMPUR SINGAPORE HONG KONG TOKYO
NAIROBI DAR ES SALAAM CAPE TOWN
MELBOURNE AUCKLAND

AND ASSOCIATE COMPANIES IN
BEIRUT BERLIN IBADAN MEXICO CITY

*Published in the United States by
Oxford University Press, New York*

© *Oxford University Press 1982*

British Library Cataloguing in Publication Data

Vital, David
    Zionism.
    1. Zionism—History
    I. Title
    956.94′001   DS149

ISBN 0 19 827443 2

*Typeset by Latimer Trend & Company Ltd Plymouth
Printed in Great Britain
at the University Press, Oxford
by Eric Buckley
Printer to the University*

Preface

THE moral and material crisis into which the Jewish people were plunged in the nineteenth century and in which they were all but crushed forever in the century that followed was of shattering proportions. That there is a connection between the mounting catastrophe that overtook Jewry and the rise of Zionism is evident, but much of its precise nature and import are unclear. Certainly, there are no grounds in general, and none here in this particular case, for concluding that disasters tend naturally to breed ultimate triumph. The only ascertainable consequences of the disasters that overtook the Jews of Europe in recent times have been moral anguish, pain, and untimely death, not success, nor, in the most positive sense of the term, progress. The disasters were the ground out of which the movement sprang and the eventual triumph was real enough. But it was a reduced and bitter triumph in that there were only survivors to enjoy it. What marks the history of the Zionist movement is, therefore, the prodigious disparity between the dimensions of the problem with which it had originally wished to cope and the dimensions and quality of the solutions it ended up offering—or even striving for. It remains true that at the heart of the matter of Zionism was the idea of change. Herzl had conceived of the Problem of the Jews as one to be dealt with not palliatively, but surgically, as a problem to be *solved* and solved permanently. The great evacuation of the Jews of eastern Europe that he envisaged and their resettlement elsewhere as a politically autonomous society were to be the means whereby the nation's condition was to be transformed. And the change was to be so profound and to touch so many features of people's private and collective lives that no term but 'revolutionary' is adequate to describe it and direct attention to its essential nature. Moreover, in the promise of change lay the ultimate justification for the entire enterprise—at any rate, for Herzl and his school.

But even under Herzl's leadership and certainly, ever more rapidly and decisively, under his successors, the idea of inducing change by means of a single, radical stroke faded. The terms of the social transformation sought for the Jews were moderated. The great impatience with the exilic condition which was always at the root of Zionism softened. Above all, the scale of the enterprise on which the Zionists conceived of themselves as having embarked came to be drastically reduced. A revolution had indeed been begun. The establishment of the movement at Basel in 1897 had undoubtedly precipitated a process whereby the Jewish scene and the thinking of some, at any rate, of the Jews themselves were transformed; and the consolidation of the movement did ensure that the process would be sustained. There was no retreat from the tremendous, basic step taken towards the remaking of the Jews as a political nation and re-equipping them with national purposes and a national government to pursue them. The proponents of Zionism could still say that they were keeping and nourishing ideas—and an organization to embody them—that stood in clear contrast to the fatalism and national self-abnegation that were at the bottom of all other views of how the Jews should meet the pressures of the age. But even so conceived, Zionism, by its second decade, had been reduced to a cause—pious, rather than entirely practical, possibly something to be taken up again in earnest when the time was ripe, but barely, at best marginally, of direct, material significance to the wretched Jews of eastern Europe in the mass. The revolution had been diminished.

But of course the time had been (and continued to be) ripe all along. The condition of the Jews never ceased to deteriorate. Was there therefore some flaw in Zionism such that, having first drawn so many towards the belief that the need to transform the condition of Jewry was of the utmost gravity and urgency, it then drew them away from it? Or was the flaw—if that is the right word—in the Jews themselves, eternal underlings; so that it would be more appropriate to say that, while the Zionist diagnosis was right—at all events, more perceptive than any other that was offered—the audience, the constituency, to which its proponents addressed themselves was in no condition to accept and act upon it?

Or, again, was it that the external obstacles to progress were so great that Zionism, unless conceived of in diminished terms, was doomed to failure, and that, accordingly, the contrast between what the movement appeared to have stood for in 1897 and what it was preoccupied with a decade later merely reflected the realism and wisdom of its leaders?

No serious consideration of the phenomenon of Zionism can fail to elicit such questions as these and the answers to them must be sought, in the first instance, in the movement's formative years. Within the decade subsequent to the calling of the First Congress the Zionist Organization acquired something very like its definitive institutional and political shape. It discovered most of the major obstacles to further progress. It underwent the experience of discarding policies and modes of action that had proved, or been thought to have proved, unworkable. It weathered its greatest internal crisis. It set its collective mind finally and irrevocably on Erez-Israel/Palestine as the proper locus of its major endeavours. It implicitly took up an attitude—still broad and somewhat ambivalent and a matter for dispute—to the national cultural and historical tradition from which it itself constituted so radical a deviation. Finally, it was in these years that most of the men and women who were to form its central cadres and to direct its affairs well into the middle of the twentieth century first appeared on the scene and made their initial mark. It is with this period and with the analysis of these developments that this book is concerned.

Acknowledgements

So many people gave me of their time and attention while this book was in preparation that I cannot hope to acknowledge all of them. But I do particularly want to thank Dr Michael Heymann, the director of the Central Zionist Archives, Jerusalem, and other members of his staff; Mr Moshe Schaerf and his colleagues of the Herzl Papers Editorial Committee, Jerusalem; and the staff of the Public Record Office, London, who were all exceptionally helpful to me over a very long period. I have also to thank Frau Hofrat Dr Anna Benna, director of the Haus-, Hof-, und Staatsarchiv, Vienna; Mrs Trude Levi of the Mocatta Library, University College London; Mr Joseph Neville of the Jewish Colonization Association, London; Mgr. Terzo Natalini, Vice-Prefect of the Archivo Segreto Vaticano, City of the Vatican; and members of the staffs of the British Library, London; the Bodleian Library, Oxford; the Haifa University Library; the Diplomatic Archives at the Ministry of Foreign Affairs, Paris; the National Archives, Washington; the National and University Library, Jerusalem; and, of course, the staff of the library of my own Tel-Aviv University.

A number of scholars and experts in various fields were kind enough to help me either by calling my attention to sources that I might otherwise have neglected to consult, or by reading parts of the manuscript and letting me have the benefit of their comments: Dr S. Z. Abramov; Dr P. A. Alsberg, director of the Israel State Archives; Mr Richard Dalby; Dr Eli'ezer Don-Yihye of Bar-Ilan University; Dr Yoram Friedman of Tel-Aviv University; Professor James Joll of the London School of Economics and Political Science; Professor Jacob M. Landau of the Hebrew University, Jerusalem; Professor Bernard Lewis of the Institute for Advanced Studies, Princeton; Professor D. A. Low of the Australian National University, Canberra; Dr Meir Mendes;

Mr Bülent Mim Kemal Öke of Istanbul University; Dr Giorgio Romano; Dr Anita Shapira of Tel-Aviv University; Professor Rina Shapira of Tel-Aviv University; Professor Chone Shmeruk of the Hebrew University, Jerusalem; Professor ʿAzriel Shoḥat of Haifa University; and Professor Tarik Zafer Tunaya of Istanbul University.

Mr Joseph Rochev, Tel-Aviv University, gave me invaluable assistance in the often tedious work of putting together the statistical appendix. Mr D. Ben-Horin, Mrs R. Erez, Mrs B. Freundlich, Mrs E. Goodman, Mrs Y. Hershkowitz, Miss Y. Horowitz, Mrs R. Langbart, Miss M. Oren, Mrs S. Palmor, Mrs M. Shiloh, Miss B. Stern, Mr H. Wasserman, Mrs S. Weinberg, and Mrs Dorit Yaniv all gave me valuable assistance at one stage or another of the preparation of the book.

For a great many years now I have had the benefit of the professional skill and the unfailing courtesy of the members of the staff of the Oxford University Press, some known to me personally, some not. But if I cannot thank them all by name, I do at least want to express my particular thanks to Mr Peter Sutcliffe for his patience and good advice over a very long period; and to Ms Hilary Feldman for her meticulous work on the present volume.

Mrs Ruth Nijk, who typed the whole of a difficult manuscript with great devotion and in circumstances that were far from easy for her, participated in the making of this book from beginning to end. I am exceedingly grateful to her.

The book was put into final shape during a stay at the Villa Serbelloni, Bellagio (Como). I am very grateful to the Trustees of the Rockefeller Foundation for their invitation to the Study Centre they maintain there and to the Administrator and the staff of the Villa for their great friendliness and kindness to my wife and to me while we were their guests.

Finally, I must note that it is unlikely that this book would have been completed—or perhaps even begun—without the encouragement and counsel of Sir Isaiah Berlin. I owe him an exceptional debt of gratitude, not for the first time.

September 1980

Contents

List of Maps

A note on transliteration and translation

IT is extremely difficult to render Hebrew in Latin characters with accuracy, but without pedantry. But I have thought it sufficient to give such rough phonetic equivalents as will be plain to the English reader and only in a few cases to indicate those sounds for which no readily understood equivalent is available. Thus I have not distinguished between the two *ts* in Hebrew, *tav* and *tet*; and I have rendered the *pe degusha* as *p* and the *pe refuya* as *f*. But the guttural *'ayin* has been indicated (by *'*); the two gutturals *ḥet* and *khaf* (both roughly equivalent to *ch* in 'loch') have been written as *ḥ* and *kh* respectively; and the *zadi* (equivalent to the *ts* in 'cots') has been written as a single letter *z*. *Alef* has been indicated (by *'*) only where the transliteration would otherwise suggest a diphthong (as in *Shemu'el*, for example).

I have not always thought it necessary to be consistent where the English of a term is very familiar and written in a manner tolerably close to what accurate transliteration would require. So, for example, Israel rather than Yisrael; *Zion* rather than *Ziyyon*. Where the English is specifically called for, however, I have written Zion, Zionist, Zionism, for example (but *Zioni*, *Zionut*, if it is the Hebrew that is intended).

In the case of place-names, I have used the familiar English ones where appropriate (not Yerushalayim and Moskva, but Jerusalem and Moscow) and where local usage has changed over the years I have generally preferred the practice of the time, namely the late nineteenth and early twentieth centuries (Constantinople not Istanbul, St. Petersburg not Leningrad, Kattowitz not Katowice, Lemberg not Lvov).

Names of persons are more difficult. The common Jewish surname Rabinovitch can be spelt in at least two dozen different ways. I have used the spelling preferred and used by the person in question where known to me. Otherwise, I have followed the new *Encyclopaedia Judaica* or the most reliable alternative source available.

Dates have generally been given according to western (Gregorian calendar) usage. In a few cases, Julian calendar dates have been indicated—by the addition of (O[ld]. S[tyle].). The full Jewish year, which runs from September/October to September/October, has in most cases, and where absolute precision is not important, been given as the Gregorian year parallel to the last nine months of the Jewish year. Thus 5740 would be given as 1980 although, strictly, it runs from 22 September 1979 to 10 September 1980.

Responsibility for the translation of source material in the various languages into English is mostly mine. In the few cases where reliable translations into English already exist, as with Herzl's diary and some of his speeches and articles (very successfully translated by Harry Zohn), full use has been made of them, with only rare and slight changes where an alternative rendering seemed preferable.

There remained, as always, the question of the name of the Land itself—to some the Holy Land, to others Palestine, to the Jews, by and large, Erez-Israel. 'Palestine' was a Roman invention which fell into local disuse until the arrival of the British, but here and there, where the context, or fidelity to the source, so required, I have used it. However, this is a book about Jews and the modern Jewish revival. For the most part, therefore, I have used the term that makes best sense in the context of Jewish history: *Erez-Israel*.

Abbreviations

CZA   Central Zionist Archives.

Diaries   *The Complete Diaries of Theodor Herzl*, edited by Raphael Patai, translated by Harry Zohn (5 vols, New York, 1960).

EAC   Engeres Aktions-Comité (Smaller Actions Committee).

GAC   Grosses Aktions-Comité (Greater Actions Committee).

Heymann   *The Minutes of the Zionist General Council [GAC]; The Uganda Controversy*, edited with introductions by Michael Heymann (2 vols, Jerusalem, 1970, 1977).

ICA   Jewish Colonization Association (Hirsch Fund).

Igrot AH   *Igrot Aḥad Ha-ʿAm [The Letters of Aḥad Ha-ʿAm]*, second edition, edited by Arye [Leon] Simon with Yoḥanan Pograbinsky (6 vols, Tel-Aviv, 1956–60).

Igrot Herzl   *Igrot Herzl [The Letters of Herzl]*, edited by Alex Bein et al., vol. ii (1895–7) translated by Dov Sadan, vol. iii (1897–9) translated by Ḥ. Izak (Jerusalem, 1957–8). (Vol. iv, comprising letters for 1899–1901, was in preparation as the present book went to press; letters known to be included in it have been so indicated, but no serial or page numbers could be given.)

ITO   Jewish Territorial Organization.

OFMA   Ottoman Foreign Ministry Archives.

Origins   *The Origins of Zionism*, by David Vital (Oxford, 1975).

PRO   Public Record Office.

Protokoll I, II, III, etc.	*Stenographisches Protokoll der Verhandlungen des I. [II., III., etc.] Zionisten-Kongresses* (verbatim reports of debates at the First, Second, Third, etc., Zionist Congresses).
R.	Rabbi.
Tagebücher	*Theodor Herzls Tagebücher* [*Theodor Herzl's Diaries*] (3 vols, Berlin, 1922–3).
Weizmann Letters	*The Letters and Papers of Chaim Weizmann, Series A, Letters*, general editors Meyer W. Weisgal and Barnet Litvinoff (23 vols, London and Jerusalem, 1968–80).

PART ONE

Praxis

I

After the Congress

i

THE history of Zionism as an effective political movement begins with the First Congress of Zionists in Basel (29–31 August 1897). Prior to the Congress the spectacle is largely one of disunity, incoherence, painfully slow progress—or none at all—confusion of ideas, dearth of leadership, and, above all, no set policy and no forum in which a set policy can be hammered out and formally adopted. Before the Congress there is, as it were, proto-Zionism.[1] Thereafter there is Zionism proper. But in essence, the Congress itself was a public demonstration. So it was intended to be by its maker, Herzl. And so it was understood to be by all who attended. It had no powers and no resources. There was no man or thing subject to its immediate control. Its status as a representative body was questionable. Some participants had been chosen, with greater or lesser formality, to represent their communities or local Zionist societies, but the majority, perhaps two-thirds, represented no one but themselves. Looked at coldly, even its one formal act, the formulation and approval of what came to be known as the Basel Programme, bore a pale fruit. There had been a good debate on the Programme, contributing some tension to what would otherwise have been largely an affair of set speeches and declarations; but the result, to the relief of the prudent majority and to the disgust of the radical minority, was a victory for caution. The ill-expressed but powerful desire for Jewish political autonomy which was at the bottom of the entire enterprise had been thinned out by a little masterpiece of moderate, not to say

[1] Discussed in detail in the author's *The Origins of Zionism* (Oxford, 1975) (henceforth *Origins*).

ambiguous phrasing: 'Zionism aims at the creation of a home for the Jewish people in Palestine to be secured by public law.'[2] And there were other ways in which the weaknesses of the movement which was being launched were apparent at this decisive stage—both in absolute terms and in terms relative to the human and material resources that the Jewish people were capable of mustering had they a mind to do so. The Congress was marked by the almost total absence of the notables of Jewry, secular as well as religious, eastern as well as western, European as well as oriental.

The view of the contemporary Jewish condition represented at the Congress, and of which the Zionist movement was henceforth to be the spokesman, could under no circumstances be described as anything but a minority view in Jewry, and a small minority at that. The Zionists themselves were not yet a coherent group. There was no Zionist *Party*. There was, as yet, no comprehensive organization. The convening of the Congress itself had been the work of a single and extraordinarily passionate individual with a mere handful of followers. To some he was a hero; to others barely more than an enthusiast. But either way it was plain from the beginning that while the other participants, along with their own lesser followers, particularly in eastern Europe, were to be the rock on which the movement must be founded, Herzl alone was capable of giving the enterprise a rational design and an agreed direction. In a word, the Congress provided less *direct* evidence of the revolutionary change that was implicit in what the Zionists were occupied with than of the enormous practical and psycho-

---

[2] The full Basel Programme, which remained the Zionist movement's official statement of purposes down to the establishment of the state of Israel in 1948, and for some years after, read as follow:

'Zionism aims at the creation of a home for the Jewish people in Palestine to be secured by public law.

To that end, the Congress envisages the following:

1. The purposeful advancement of the settlement of Palestine with Jewish farmers, artisans, and tradesmen.

2. The organizing and unifying of all Jewry by means of appropriate local and general arrangements subject to the laws of each country.

3. The strengthening of Jewish national feeling and consciousness.

4. Preparatory moves towards obtaining such governmental consent as will be necessary to the achievements of the aims of Zionism.'

logical obstacles to setting the wheels of social and mental revolution among the Jews turning in earnest.

The Zionists sought a change in both the condition and the status of the Jews. Unlike most Jews—and virtually all non-Jews—they refused to regard the pressures and humiliations to which the Jewish people were subject in their Dispersion as part of the natural order of things. They wished to extricate the Jews from a rhythm of national history such that the quality of their life at all levels was determined in the first instance by the treatment meted out to them by others, in which 'toleration' carried with it the indignities which they, the Zionists, could not stomach, and persecution meant pain and death beyond reason or decency. There was, indeed, a Jewish Question, as the anti-Semites were saying. But the disturbance, if any, which the Jews caused the gentiles was as nothing compared with the moral and physical injury which the status of an alien minority caused the Jews. The answer to the Question, the solution to the Jewish Problem, was therefore for the Jews to cease to be aliens and members of a minority, and this they could only do when they had concentrated in sufficient numbers to constitute a majority in a country of their own. Civil emancipation in gentile society, the steady extension of liberal feeling and liberal institutions from west to east and from north to south, the rise of scientific and enlightened attitudes to social questions of all kinds—in none of these was it sensible to place real hope. If, in the progressive countries of the West, the condition of the Jews was generally tolerable, it was also in many ways unpleasant. As for the East, there it was entirely intolerable. The hoped-for wave of liberalism and amelioration had only lapped around the borders of the Russian Empire and never reached Romania at all. The five or six million Jews entrapped in Russia and Romania could see it receding definitively and would do well to put it out of sight and mind. The Jewish people would therefore be wrong to put its trust in others; it should learn to solve its Problem for itself. The Jews had not merely to see to their defences as best they might, but to learn all over again what they had long forgotten: how to order their common affairs by collective action. Jewry had to cease to be object and become subject. The Jews had to be taught more than mere norms of conduct for coexistence with the non-Jews in good times and methods of intercession and pleas for quarter in bad times. They must be equipped with recognized leaders and national institutions. And these must operate on the basis of a programme of action which, in turn, would be the source of their popular support. Support would legitimize both the leaders and the institutions through which this programme was expressed. Only then would the quality of relations with the non-Jewish peoples be transformed. And, finally, the initial condition of this transformation was the public announcement of what was intended. On all this, in varying degrees of clarity and explicitness, the Zionists were at one.[3] The desire to shatter the ancient conventions of action and thought on the matter of the Jews tugged at their hearts and softened—if it did not dissolve—the doubts of those most sceptical of Herzl the man and of Herzl the potential statesman. And if they were agreed on very little else than this, they did now have a leader, if they wanted one; they did have a programme of sorts; and they did have the basis for a parliament due to reconvene with properly elected members in a year's time. Above all, the public statement of intent had been made with all the force of which their new leader and his closest associates were capable.

In the aftermath, seen in this light, the Congress could be judged not unsuccessful. Israel Zangwill, the one English Jew of repute to attend, noted that 'There is a good deal about Zionism in the French papers and I think the movement has done at least the good of showing that the Jew is not ashamed to stand up seriously for his race.'[4] The *Jewish Chronicle* of London was at first torn between an urge to put the upstarts in their place (for not having 'even risen to the rank of a Hyde Park Demonstration, for while the latter is at least representative, there is a yawning gulf between prominent speakers at

[3] Dr Ya'akov Bernstein-Kohan of Kishinev, who had been chosen by the Russian delegates to speak for them in the sessions of the Congress, summed up before the caucus when it reassembled before leaving Basel. The main thing to carry back with us, he said, was that the Congress had taken place, that 'Jews from all parts of the Exile had gathered in a single city to consult each other and to seek to improve their lot not through the graces of others or the charity of their neighbours, but by their own efforts' (*Ha-Magid*, 9 September 1897).

[4] Letter to Salvina Schloss, 4 October 1897. CZA, A 120/61.

the Congress and the earnest, believing Jews whose cause Dr Herzl's friends imagine themselves to represent') and a measure of real, if grudging admiration ('Dr Herzl's movement has not been altogether fruitless. It has demonstrated that after all Judaism is a real, living force.').[5] But a week later, faced with the evidence, its leader-writer had to admit that 'In one respect the Zionist Congress will stand as a landmark in the history of the Jews of Europe. It has called forth, in the English and Continental Press, fuller and more sympathetic comment on the position of the Jews of Europe than any event of our history.'[6]

This was true enough, even if not all the comment was sympathetic. *The Times*, the *Daily News*, the *Daily Mail*, the *Spectator*, and the *Pall Mall Gazette* in England, all but one of the Berlin dailies, not excluding those that were openly anti-Semitic, virtually all the major German provincial newspapers including the important *Kölnische Zeitung* and *Frankfurter Zeitung*, influential newspapers in Hungary, Russia, Poland, Switzerland, the United States, and France—all these carried reports, often followed up by comment and letters to the editors. So did the foremost organ of systematic European anti-Semitism, Drumont's *Libre Parole*, which had sent a correspondent to Basel and published a long, not unperceptive analysis of the event. This and much else was duly picked up and quoted at length in the Jewish press, especially in the Hebrew daily and weekly newspapers of Russia and Poland, which were closest to the movement in spirit and whose correspondents and editors were often prominent within it. Their own representatives had attended in force; and long and detailed reports on the Congress, leading articles, second thoughts, and extensive coverage of the activities of the new organization throughout Europe filled their pages for months thereafter. 'In the Zionist Movement' made its appearance as a standard rubric. Much of the comment was sceptical. But the attention Herzl seemed to be being paid in the world outside Jewry impressed the Jewish journalists in spite of themselves, and, like the actual participants in the Congress, they tended to be caught by the sense of the special and historic

---

[5] *Jewish Chronicle*, 3 September 1897.
[6] Ibid., 10 September 1897.

nature of the occasion, sometimes at the expense of their
judgement. An editorialist in *Ha-Meliz* (St. Petersburg)
wrote: 'Who would have believed ten years ago that the elder
of the Rabbis of Israel [Rabbi Shemu'el Mohilever] and that
most brilliant among the writers of Europe [Herzl] would be
brothers at heart?!'[7]

Earlier in the year, depressed by the condition of the Jews
and by what he judged to be the poor response to the call to
the Congress, the finest Hebrew poet of the age had written
of a 'Withered nation . . . Even were the trumpet to sound . . .
would the dead wake?'[8] Now Bialik published a triumphant
poem to celebrate the Congress[9] and from his isolation in a
small town in southern Poland watched the scene in the
larger centres with envy. 'When I read what the Hebrew
periodicals have to say about the revival and excitement in
Jewry, then even after deducting ninety per cent for exaggeration it still pains me to see myself a stranger, distant and removed from it all.'[10]

ii

His Congress achieved and support for his person manifest,
Herzl felt free to turn once more to high politics, namely the
attempt to gain the co-operation of Turkey and the support of
the major European Powers. These efforts he would continue
to conduct himself by means, and according to strategies,
which he himself had already set. He gave little thought to the
role the new movement would play in these matters, nor to
its internal structure. The fact of its existence and the support
and applause it gave him were what mattered most. He was
thus provided, he thought, with the credentials he needed to
appear authoritatively before princes and statesmen and with
a position of influence within the Jewish world which would
enable him to treat with its notables on an equal footing.
Beyond that, he saw the movement as the living link between
himself and the Jewish masses on whose behalf he had taken

[7] *Ha-Meliz*, 10 September 1897.
[8] 'Akhen ḥazir ha-'am'. Cf. Isa. 40:7.
[9] 'Mikra ha-ẓionim', *Ha-Shilo'aḥ*, January 1898.
[10] Letter to Yehoshu'a Rawnitzki, 23 January 1898. *Igrot Ḥayyim Naḥman Bialik*, i
(Tel-Aviv, 1937–9), no. 47, p. 110.

it upon himself to act. In brief, he conceived of the movement first and foremost as an instrument, not as an end in itself, as a half-way house between the invertebrate, semi-anarchic condition of contemporary Jewry and the orderly, properly structured national life which lay at the end of the Zionist rainbow. He did not think, as his predecessors of Ḥibbat Ẓion[11] had thought, that because progress was necessarily slow, and the culmination was impossibly distant, the movement in all its manifestations should be the more carefully cultivated and, indeed, enjoyed as a form of national and social activity that was inherently superior to anything else on the Jewish scene. Herzl's optimism at this early stage and his conviction that very great things could be done in a very brief space of time were immense. His interest in the detail of Zionist activity at the lower level was correspondingly small. He did not seek to come to terms even with the better-known and more influential figures who had emerged out of Ḥibbat Ẓion to join him, except at the formal Congresses and, broadly speaking, in so far as the proceedings of the Congresses dictated. He did not seek to impose himself institutionally at the regional level. And the upshot was that the greater part of the new Zionist movement, the east European branch, that which was in all essential respects continuous with Ḥibbat Ẓion and which had provided most of the men and virtually all the ideas that had gone into the making of the movement up until the advent of Herzl himself less than two years earlier,[12] was left to evolve under its indigenous leadership and under the influence of local pressures and

---

[11] Ḥibbat Ẓion ('Love of Zion')—proto-Zionism, as it might be called—was a somewhat inchoate movement devoted to the resettlement of the Jews in Ereẓ-Israel/Palestine. It arose in the immediate aftermath of the first wave of pogroms in Russia (1881–4) and the onset of the great migration of the Jews westwards and then spread slowly throughout the Jewish world. Institutionally it was weak. In character and ethos it was philanthropic rather than political. Its most influential local chapter was that of Odessa; and the Odessa Committee was the only one in Russia to enjoy a legal existence. The members of Ḥibbat Ẓion termed themselves Ḥovevei Ẓion ('Lovers of Zion'). See *Origins*, pp. 65–229.

[12] Herzl began to make his views known, but in a limited circle, at the end of 1895. The first public statement of his views appeared in the *Jewish Chronicle* in January 1896. His famous pamphlet, *Der Judenstaat: Versuch einer modernen Lösung der Judenfrage* [*The Jews' State: An Attempt at a Modern Solution of the Jewish Question*], was published in Vienna a month later. See *Origins*, pp. 246–66.

considerations much as before, rather than subject to a fresh and commanding influence from Vienna.

It is true that Herzl had managed to get the Russian, Polish, and Romanian wings of Hibbat Zion represented at the Congress in sufficient numbers and at a sufficiently impressive level for it to have been legitimate for him to feel that a union between the old and the new forms had been concluded. But in some respects the result, for the time being, was less a union than an alliance. Attitudes to him and to his doings tended to remain ambivalent in almost all quarters, as we shall see. Few of the established figures in Russian and Polish Hibbat Zion had accepted his primacy in the movement without hesitation. Some did not accept him at all, nor would in the future. He himself had only begun to grasp the fundamental importance of eastern Jewry as not merely, and obviously, the most numerous branch of the people and the branch most sorely beset and therefore, in effect, the true subject of immediate Zionist concern and the pool out of which the population of the future Jewish territory would be drawn, but also as that branch of Jewry which was culturally and psychologically the most unequivocally and most unaffectedly national in its attitudes towards social questions of all kinds, and therefore the one with the strongest and most natural tendency to Zionism itself. 'Our Russian Zionists', Herzl wrote shortly after Basel, '. . . possess that internal unity which has long been lost among most European Jews. They feel themselves to be national Jews . . . They are troubled by no thought of assimilation; their existence is simple and unbroken.'[13] But Herzl was still very far from considering whether and how the presence of his new associates in the movement might effect what could and should be done with it, what policy should be pursued, what tactics adopted. And thus, for a number of years to come, the movement at its apex and the movement at its base would be relatively free to follow recognizably distinct lines of development—ultimately with momentous consequences for the character and fortunes of Zionism as a whole.

---

[13] 'The Zionist Congress', *Contemporary Review* (London), October 1897, p. 595. The article was translated and widely disseminated throughout eastern Europe.

iii

It has been estimated that at the end of the nineteenth century there were between ten and eleven million Jews in all parts of the world. Slightly over five million, half of the total, were subjects of the Russian Emperor. Russian Jewry was therefore far and away the largest of the Jewish communities. The persecution of the Romanian Jews was in many respects more savage than that suffered by the Russians. The economic condition of the Jews of Austrian-ruled Poland (Galicia) was hardly better. The Jews of the Islamic lands, notably those of Morocco, Yemen, Mesopotamia, and Syria, were, for the most part, still subject to the rigours and humiliations of the treatment which the law and custom of Islam had prescribed for them almost from its beginnings. None the less, the great focus of such concern as there was about the condition of Jewry was on Russia. This followed from the anxiety which stemmed from the immense international importance and the looming presence of the Russian state itself, as well as from the unique combination of obscurantism and modernism-at-second-hand which informed its political system. But it had still more to do with the sheer size of the Russian-Jewish community and its pre-eminence in the Jewish world as much at the modernist level as at the traditional. In many minds the destinies of Russian Jewry were hardly differentiated from the destinies of the entire Jewish people. Particularly among the more fortunate Jews of western Europe, the *Judennot*—the contemporary distress and misery of Jewry as a whole—was chiefly seen in terms of the distress and misery of the Russian Jews. It was therefore of the Russian Jews principally that western Zionists thought when they sought to relieve the misery and transform the condition which generated it; and it was the public support and approval of the Russian Jews—or, at the very least, the Russian Zionists—that they required if they were to act to that end. This was as true of Herzl as it had been of the western Hovevei Zion who had preceded him. But Russian Zionism had evolved in Russia before it had evolved elsewhere. The Russian Zionist movement was much the largest and most important of the country groupings of Zionists both before the advent of Herzl and after. And Jews from the Russian Empire were the largest contingent among the new settlers in Erez-Israel. As the principal *object* of Zionism, as the indispensable component of the movement, and as a great autonomous reservoir of men, money, and ideas on which the movement might, in certain circumstances, rely, Russian Jewry thus accounted for much of the foundation of the entire edifice. By the same token, its weaknesses explain many of the movement's disabilities. Some would reveal themselves only in the course of time. Others were apparent from the start. The direction and tone of Zionism would at first be Herzlian—or, one might say, Viennese. This represented an imbalance, but it followed, of course, from such easily observed circumstances as the lack of a commanding figure in Russia itself, the mental and material constraints imposed by the Russian governmental system, and long-standing commitments to a certain view of what the content of Zionism might be—to name but three. But deeper and more compelling than any of these was a certain fundamental tension in the Zionists' thinking, the effect of which was to enfeeble them in action. A decade and a half after the first outbreak of pogroms and the adoption of a frankly anti-Jewish policy by the Russian Government (1881) there was little disagreement among them on the diagnosis of the ills of Jewry, of what Aḥad Ha-'Am called *ẓarat ha-yehudim*.[14] Nor was there much disagreement on what might, ideally, constitute a cure: the concentration of the Jews in an autonomous territory of their own. But this was no more than a target, the final stage of a process, the intermediate stages of which they were incapable of setting out clearly and specifically. The terms of the diagnosis on which they were agreed were too general for a precise prescription for action to emerge from them. And treatment could not be limited to the Jews alone. A radical transformation of the conditions of Jewish life required corresponding changes outside Jewry. Zionism had to impinge on factors that were external to Jewry and functionally independent of it. Hope of inducing the Jews to rally to the new cause were slim enough; what hope could there be of inducing the states and nations in whose hands

[14] On Aḥad Ha-'Am (Asher Zevi Ginsberg) see *Origins*, pp. 187–200; and below, pp. 24–34 and *passim*.

most available power was concentrated and to whom the Jews, in most cases, were *subject* to make the great change possible? Small wonder that despair tugged at the hearts of even the hardiest and most determined.

What enfeebled Russian Zionists was not, then, simply a sense of the enormous obstacles to progress. It was their inability to conjure up a programme of action suggesting plausibly how they might begin to overcome them. But what they had failed to do Herzl had just done. Here lay their main weakness and his main strength.

iv

The organization agreed upon by the Basel Congress was no more than rudimentary. It was laid down that the Congress was to be the chief and sovereign institution and that there was to be an executive committee—the Actions Committee—of twenty-three members. Five of these, all resident in Vienna and all elected directly by the full Congress, were to form an Inner or Smaller Actions Committee (EAC—Engeres Aktions-Comité) charged with responsibility for the day-to-day management of affairs. The rest, constituting the Greater Actions Committee (GAC—Grosses Aktions-Comité), were chosen by their country associations on a basis that reflected, without strictly representing, the demographic map of Jewry: two for Austrian Poland (Galicia), one for Bukovina, two for Romania, one for the Jews of the Islamic world, and so on. In the event, not all country associations proceeded to elect representatives and not all those elected served. Nor was it clearly worked out how the fifteen members who were chosen and did agree to serve could perform their duties efficaciously. Long and infrequent journeys to Vienna, communication by letter-post, and the casting of proxy votes—for all of which provision was made—were a recipe for giving the men in Vienna a free hand. And, appropriately, the presiding member of the Smaller Actions Committee in Vienna was Herzl himself, while the other four were decidedly lesser figures, assistants to whom Herzl could delegate matters of secondary importance, rather than true colleagues whom he would wish—and be morally and politically obliged—to consult.

The country representatives on the GAC were, for the

most part, men of greater weight and public standing, especially in eastern Europe. Max Nordau had refused to serve as the member for France. The English representatives elected no one for the time being. But the German members, Rabbi Isaac Rülf and Dr Max Bodenheimer, were far from being nonentities, either in the terms of contemporary German-Jewish society or in those of the movement itself.[15] The Romanians, Karpel Lippe and Samuel Pineles, were similarly prominent at home. Professor Zevi Belkowsky of Bulgaria was, in fact, a Russian Jew with close ties with the Russian Ḥibbat Zion who had played an important role in establishing ties between Herzl and the Russian and Polish Ḥibbat Zion before the First Congress.[16]

The personal standing of the four Russian-Polish members was as great if not greater. The most notable was Rabbi Shemu'el Mohilever of Bialystok, a prestigious figure in the world of traditional (non-Hasidic) orthodoxy in his own right and its only truly prominent representative in the movement in either its earlier or its later forms. He had been a central figure in Ḥibbat Zion from its earliest days. He had attended the founding meeting at Kattowitz in 1884 and had competed with Pinsker for the leadership. In recent years there had developed around him in Bialystok an organization which took upon itself tasks of communication and propagation within the Empire and outside it which the men of the Odessa Committee, the legal, officially authorized 'Society for the Support of Jewish Farmers and Artisans in Syria and Palestine', were too cautious to execute themselves lest they lose their legal status. And to this must be added the value that those of the much more numerous secular or semi-secular tendency attached to his support as a figure of the highest prestige within the orthodox world to which the great majority of east European Jewry still belonged. It was through Bialystok that the initial ties with Herzl had been maintained (so as not to compromise Ḥibbat Zion in Russia before more was known about the new man). And Herzl showed the same

---

[15] On Rülf see *Origins*, pp. 136–7, 271, n. 15; on Bodenheimer see ibid., pp. 228–9, 271–3, and *passim*.

[16] Belkowsky later returned to Russia where he played a prominent role on the local Zionist scene until well after the First World War.

desire to ensure Mohilever's support that Pinsker, the convinced secularist, had shown years earlier. He made the most of the earnest declaration of support that the Rabbi had sent the Congress (he had been too unwell to make the journey himself). Mohilever's death in the following year was an early and acute loss to the new movement.

The second member for Russia was Dr Max Mandelstamm, a distinguished ophthalmologist from Kiev and another of the original leaders of Ḥibbat Ẓion in Russia. Mandelstamm had played a crucial role in propelling Pinsker into its leadership and thus setting the original organization in motion. The third member for Russia (or, more strictly, Poland) was a Warsaw lawyer, Yisrael [Isidor] Jasinowski, a lesser figure, but similarly active in Ḥibbat Ẓion from the first. The fourth, Dr Ya'akov Bernstein-Kohan, a physician in Kishinev, Bessarabia, was a younger man than the others (Mohilever, the oldest, was then seventy-three years of age, Mandelstamm and Jasinowski were in their late fifties, Bernstein-Kohan was thirty-eight). Like them he had been a member of, if less prominent in, Ḥibbat Ẓion. But unlike them he was socially radical in his views. Bernstein-Kohan had been involved in the Russian populist movement as a very young student just before the onset of the great anti-Semitic wave of the late 1870s and early 1880s and had been expelled from his university for his pains. His brother, more deeply implicated than he, had been killed in a Siberian prison. Mandelstamm, Jasinowski, and Bernstein-Kohan had all attended Herzl's Congress. Mohilever had been represented by his grandson. Bernstein-Kohan, as already indicated, had served as the spokesman for the Russian delegation.

These four did not constitute the whole of the leadership of pre-Herzlian Zionism in the Russian Empire, nor were any of them to be in the very first rank of the new movement. But it is worth noting that by virtue of an ingenious arrangement laid down at Basel, the role they were called upon to play was one of genuine substance none the less. It had been provided that country members of the Greater Actions Committee, as opposed to members of the Smaller Actions Committee in Vienna, would exercise executive authority in their own country associations. The members of the GAC were thus, from the start, simultaneously territorial delegates to the Committee itself and proconsuls representing it in the various communities. This was only wise, for considering the differences between the various Jewish communities and between the political systems to which they were subject, there could be no uniformity of organization or behaviour in any case. It had therefore been expressly laid down at Basel that 'The organization and agitation of the Zionists . . . shall conform to the requirements and laws of their respective countries.'[17] In the Russian Empire the Zionist movement, as the national movement of what the authorities saw as an alien and suspect minority, was necessarily illegal. Now that its political character, hitherto latent, would be pronounced, it was bound to become an object of active interest and periodic (if, in the event, never excessively harsh) persecution by the police. Neither in Herzl's mind nor in anyone else's was there therefore any question but that caution had to be exercised.

V

The first working party of leading Russian Zionists to meet after Basel gathered in Bialystok on 16 and 17 November 1897. The meeting was not as dramatic as Hibbat Zion's founding conference at Kattowitz (November 1884) had been, let alone the Basel Congress itself. The participants seem to have been slightly uncertain of themselves and doing their best to make it a business-like affair. Mohilever was the host; he was joined by Jasinowski and Bernstein-Kohan; Mandelstamm did not attend, but was represented by Leo (Arye Leib) Motzkin. At Basel Motzkin had led the radical demand for a clearer statement of Zionist aims.[18] There were some two score lesser figures present—one from Erez-Israel, the rest from major centres in Poland, Lithuania, Latvia, Byelorussia, the Ukraine, and Russia proper. It seems that few or none of those attending had been systematically selected, let alone elected (apart, of course, from the three GAC delegates and Mandelstamm's proxy). There is a hint in the report of the proceedings sent to Vienna that for the matters the delegates were most anxious to discuss they felt they were insufficiently prepared and

[17] *Protokoll I*, p. 174.
[18] See *Origins*, especially pp. 224–5 and 367–9.

insufficiently representative. They made the point that the conference was not entitled to resolve anything binding on the local societies and that it derived such formal authority as it might have had from the presence of the GAC delegates. With one exception, the topics they attended to were organizational. But the exception, the question of general policy as debated and agreed upon, was cardinal: the participants resolved that 'action for the benefit of the settlements in Erez-Israel accords with the programme of the Basel Congress and that it is the duty of all Zionists to contribute to its success'.[19] Strictly speaking, there was no contradiction between this statement and the Basel Programme, as formulated and accepted at the Congress. But, in spirit and intention, the Bialystok resolution, as those attending well knew, ran entirely counter to Herzl's political purposes and his chosen *modus operandi*—the handwritten report sent to Vienna specifically making the point that the resolution had been adopted unanimously; and the actual wording of the resolutions being both underscored *and* written out in especially large characters! There is no evidence that, in the event, the men in Vienna were suitably impressed; but in any case the main concern of the easterners, for the time being, was with how the movement within Russia was to be run in practice, that is to say, with money matters, with the 'propagation of the Zionist idea among the people', and with the division of authority and the distribution of functions between the four elected delegates.

The working party confirmed the system agreed upon at Basel whereby membership of the movement and the right to vote in elections to the Congress was conditional on payment of a small fee, the *shekel* (40 copecks in Russia, 1 mark in Germany, 1 franc in France, and so forth), the sum of the fees constituting the movement's income. But they also decided to retain 50 per cent of the income derived from the *shekalim* to cover 'the costs of agitation and propaganda' within Russia itself. The Russian contribution to the expenses of the centre in Vienna was thus to be severely limited for many years to come. On the propagation of Zionism nothing new or ingenious was proposed. It was to be pursued in all relevant

[19] CZA, Z 1 384/127, n.d.

languages (Hebrew, Yiddish, Russian, and Polish) by word of mouth and in print, by travelling speakers, through sympathetic Jewish periodicals, by pamphlets, and by periodicals which the movement would found if the authorities permitted.

The responsibilities of the four delegates would be as follows: Rabbi Mohilever would continue to preside over his propaganda centre in Bialystok; Mandelstamm in Kiev would be responsible for finances; Jasinowski's centre in Warsaw would be responsible for preparing written material for publication and dissemination; Bernstein-Kohan in Kishinev would run what came to be called the 'correspondence office' through which communication between the local societies was to be maintained. No effective tie with the long-established centre in Odessa seems to have been contemplated and, geographically speaking, the distribution of the four offices was lopsided: two in Poland, only one in the Ukraine—and that in Kiev, the access of Jews to which was restricted—none in the important Jewish centres of Lithuania and White Russia, and the key function, the 'correspondence office', in Bessarabia on the periphery of the Empire. It was not long before the inadequacy of the arrangement was apparent. Mohilever's death within some months of the meeting put an end to Bialystok as a major centre of activity. Responsibility for the regular distribution of information to the branches in all parts of Russia then gravitated to Kishinev and into the hands of the energetic Bernstein-Kohan for a while. Jasinowski's centre was of little consequence from the start. In 1901 the system was thoroughly revamped.

That more attention should have been paid to details of organization, rather than the broad lines of policy, at this early stage is less surprising than might appear. The question how the movement—revivified or new, depending on one's outlook—was to function was a real one. The first effect of the advent of Herzl, the heroic figure, confirmed and virtually canonized in many simple minds by the Congress over which he had presided, was to give a great boost to hopes for a rapid advance towards large-scale and radical changes in the condition of the Jews of eastern Europe. And the immediate consequence of this for the movement was the rapid increase in local Zionist societies, new ones being formed and old ones being revived. At its peak, in the middle of the 1880s, Ḥibbat Zion had had some 15,000 members in, perhaps, 150 localities. A decade later it had declined almost by half. In 1897 Mohilever's office in Bialystok held a list of no more than 85 active local societies, all but 12 of which were, in fact, mere outlying branches of the Odessa Committee. But now over 300 new societies came into existence and were entered in Bernstein-Kohan's list by the time the Second Zionist Congress convened in the following year.[20] All these local groups and their members had to be serviced. From this time on the institutions of Zionism, as they were set up, steadily, one after the other in the years to come in Russia as elsewhere—the Congress, the Smaller and the Greater Actions Committees, the journals, the publishing house, the outlying offices established in later years in Constantinople and Jaffa—all began to take on a life of their own, absorbing the mental and physical energies of ever more members of the movement, and collectively illustrating Robert Michels's dictum that 'mechanism becomes an end in itself'.[21] Moreover, as time passed and as debate on long-term and larger purposes intensified and the prospect of their attainment in the short term receded from view, submission to the pressures and logic of institutional activity and absorption in its minutiae became an ever more welcome source of solace and satisfaction in the interim.

But there was a larger reason for the political inaction of the movement there where it was strongest. It had been understood at Basel that for the time being it was for Herzl, and virtually for him alone, to act. All others, unless specifically called upon to help him, were to remain for all practical purposes passive. At all events, it was clear what was not wanted of them. They were to do nothing that might interfere with the implementation of the central policy, of Herzl's diplomacy. The Russian state, for example, was not to be publicly criticized, nor were the Turks. The practice of systematically circumventing Turkish restrictions on the immigration of Jews into Ereẓ-Israel and on the purchase of land there by Jews, even at inflated prices, was to be discontinued. And, more generally,

[20] *Protokoll II*, p. 52. And cf. ibid., p. 47.
[21] *Political Parties* (New York, 1962), p. 190.

the central thesis of the proto-Zionists of Ḥibbat Ẓion, namely that the resettlement of Ereẓ-Israel was a proper objective in itself, however small the scale and however tenuous the legal (let alone the political) status of the settlers, was to be abandoned lest hands and energies be diverted from Zionism's ends as now defined anew. Herzl's new supporters were thus being invited to do little more than remain in readiness, witnesses to his own furious activity. They were being asked to accept both a subordinate role for themselves and a change of direction so far as the movement as a whole was concerned. Indeed, more than a change of direction: a change of character and ethos. Not unnaturally, no sooner had the euphoria engendered by the Congress waned than an extended debate on the true aims of the movement, and the means it should choose to attain them, began.

Elements of this debate were to be perpetual in Zionism. What is noteworthy about it at this initial stage was its relatively abstract and academic nature—a consequence, no doubt, of two salient facts: the participants were cut off, for the time being, as we have seen, from the actual making of central policy for the Zionist movement; and the question whether or not to return to Basel for the *Second* Congress of Zionists was never seriously raised. True, it was one thing to go to Basel for a first, necessarily experimental Congress and quite another to return to Basel to attend a second, and so commit oneself to the new organization and publicly accept, with whatever private reservations, the ideas and methods of its leader. Even Aḥad Ha-'Am, the one powerful voice from within the movement to be raised, as we shall see, against Herzl's ideas and Herzl's methods *in toto*, and who was listened to by all in the East with close attention, refrained from proposing that the Herzlian initiative be explicitly rejected. It followed that the battle for the full accession of Russian Zionism, on which depended the conversion of a small grouping of like-minded individuals around Herzl into a genuine mass movement with grass roots in the great centres of Jewish population, had been won by Herzl before it had really started—and without Herzl himself being involved in it or even being properly aware of it being about to break out. Even the first, clear defection from the ranks the Russian

Zionists were shortly to suffer (that of an important wing of the small orthodox contingent) hinged only very indirectly on the issue of support for Herzl. Indeed, the orthodox Zionists, as will be seen, tended to support him a good deal more readily than they did their own secular countrymen from Russia.

This easy, initial success of the new western Zionists owed something to the fact that theirs had been just such a *western* initiative as Pinsker, the first leader of Ḥibbat Ẓion, had hoped for fifteen years earlier;[22] and the men and women cooped up within Russia were not disposed to reject it lightly. 'You will yourselves understand that if the *yishuv*[23] is not to fail utterly', one of Pinsker's successors, Menaḥem Ussishkin, wrote early in 1895, 'there must be a great awakening . . . in the cities of western Europe and America, there where the question of the *yishuv* can and must be put on a political basis.'[24] Moreover, many had, after all, come away impressed by what they had seen at Basel: Naḥum Sokolov, for a notable example, who, with characteristic caution, had gone to the First Congress as a journalist and was to return a year later as a delegate. But perhaps the more important reason for this surrender of authority by men who had devoted half a lifetime to public work on behalf of the resettlement of Ereẓ-Israel and were (and remained) quite fixed in their view that what was done there, on the ground, was much more important than diplomacy and 'politics', was that they could not allow themselves to ignore the change of popular mood that had occurred, the tremendous expectations that Herzl had aroused. There was now a common feeling in the ranks of the movement that nothing need ever be, or could ever be, the same—an almost overpowering sense of great events being in the offing.

This highly charged atmosphere was repulsive to men who habitually prided themselves on the sober view they took of things. It smacked of Sabbatianism, of the false prophecy of imminent release from the slavery of the Diaspora that the Jews of eastern Europe had been taught for generations to regard with nothing but horror. And the prudent *'askanim*

---

[22] See *Origins*, pp. 126–32.

[23] *Yishuv* (=settlement): the term used to denote the Jewish community in Ereẓ-Israel.

[24] S. Schwartz, *Ussishkin be-igrotav* (Jerusalem, 1949), p. 61.

(activists and office-holders) of Ḥibbat Ẓion noted with alarm the rapidity with which Herzl the Viennese journalist was evolving into a legendary figure in the eyes of folk whom they regarded as simpler than themselves.[25] But they could not deny the enthusiasts' claim that 'the attitude to Zionism has now entirely changed everywhere',[26] nor that there was a good deal more interest and sympathy for Zionism among non-Jews than had been known before.[27] And they reckoned that, this being the public mood, a decision to stay away from the Congress, indistinguishable, in practice, from a decision to boycott it, would have been incomprehensible to all but the most sophisticated—and therefore a decision that was politically impossible to contemplate. They themselves had little to offer beyond more of the deathly-slow 'infiltration' of Jewish settlers into Ereẓ-Israel that Herzl condemned as both hopelessly disproportionate to the dimensions of the Problem and undignified as a public policy for a people bent on regaining a place for itself within the society of nations.

The majority of sceptics were therefore moved to join Herzl after all. They could still hope to swing the movement in time towards purposes more akin to those which they favoured. Many argued, quite possibly with conviction, that in any case Zionism and Ḥibbat Ẓion, properly understood, were no more than synonymous terms for an identical tendency.[28] Some took comfort in Herzl's resounding declaration at the Congress that Zionism was the return to Judaism and hoped (not entirely without cause) to see him in the vanguard of a return of the assimilated to the fold.[29] 'Herzl has become a Jew', a correspondent to Sokolov's *Ha-Ẓefira* wrote in triumph.[30] Others noted with approval that Herzl had

[25] For a sentimental but graphic description of Herzlian Zionism penetrating a small townlet in the Pale of Jewish Settlement, see Shelomo Salzmann, *Min he-ʿavar* (Tel-Aviv, 1943), pp. 136–9.

[26] Leib Jaffe to Yosef Klausner, 22 September 1897. Leib Jaffe, *Be-sheliḥut ʿam* (ed. Benjamin Jaffe, Jerusalem, 1968), p. 21.

[27] e.g. *Ha-Meliẓ*, 8 October 1897; *Ha-Ẓefira*, 11 November; 8 December 1897.

[28] e.g. 'Ha-ḥovevim ve-ha-ẓionim', *Ha-Meliẓ*, 19 December 1897; Sh. P. Rabbinowitz ('Shefer'), 'Mak'helat ẓion asher be-bazel', *Aḥiasaf*, V (1897), pp. 347–63; and 'Ein keẓ', *Ha-Meliẓ*, 26 May 1898.

[29] Cf. 'Ze leʿumat ze', *Ha-Meliẓ*, 23 December 1897.

[30] 'Ẓion be-bazel', *Ha-Ẓefira*, 14 September 1897.

avoided dangerous talk of a Jewish state,[31] and agreed implicitly with the observation that the essential programme of the Congress was the Congress itself,[32] by which was meant both that the Basel Programme had been cast in terms too general for objections to be raised to it and that the main thing had been, and would be, the gathering of all Zionists together. So all might come right in the end.

There remained [wrote a veteran figure in the movement, Sh. P. Rabbinowitz ('Shefer'), shortly after the Congress] the thin line which divided Hibbat Zion from the Zionism of Herzl and his party: what the Hovevei Zion wanted before all else was a well-structured *yishuv* in Erez-Israel, while what Herzl and his people wanted was the evacuation of Europe by its Jews to put an end to anti-Semitism. This is why he is unhappy about piecemeal settlement ('infiltration'). Yet surely he too would admit that even if we got our heart's desire we would not all be free men in the Land of Israel next year for a thousand reasons which everyone understands; and he would also admit that it would take time for the immigrants to turn into proper farmers on arrival at their destination—years, no doubt. In which case all this division of opinion is to no purpose.[33]

In brief, even the profoundest sceptics were impelled to concede that Hibbat Zion had been visited with a *fait accompli* which it was pointless to regret. It was better to look forward to co-operation with the 'men of Vienna' with as much optimism as one could muster, while abandoning no principles that mattered and retaining, in the face of all the clamour, that wary attitude to all that was new and untried that came so naturally to unemancipated Jewry. So much for the general tendency among those who could neither bring themselves to go over to Herzl whole-heartedly, nor were prepared to reject him.

There was, however, another, minoritarian view of the matter, the importance of which lay partly in the very precision of its formulation and partly in the exceptional status within eastern Hibbat Zion—and within the intelligentsia of eastern European Jewry generally—enjoyed by its ex-

---

[31] 'Aharei ha-ra'ash', *Ha-Magid*, 9 September 1897.
[32] R. A. Braudes, 'Ha-kongres ha-zioni be-bazel', ibid.
[33] 'Mak'helat zion', p. 363.

pounder. Characteristically, it was Aḥad Ha-ʿAm who broke the spell of Basel and turned a still desultory and somewhat complacent discussion of recent achievements and future prospects into a debate on ultimate aims and basic principles.

vi

Aḥad Ha-ʿAm had had doubts about the Congress before it assembled and had disliked much of what he saw when he attended it. Nordau had impressed him. The Congress, as 'a great public statement before all the world that the Jewish people was still alive and wished to go on living', was welcome— not, indeed, 'so that other nations hear it and grant us our desire, but, before all else, so that *we ourselves* hear the echo of our voice in the depths of our soul which might then awake and shake off its degradation'.[34] But otherwise nothing of importance had been accomplished, nor could have been accomplished by the assembly, most of whose members were no more than boys, while even the older men followed herd-like after the leader. 'We have destroyed a great deal more than we have built', he wrote with uncharacteristic fury and haste (but privately) as soon as the Congress ended. '. . . Who knows if this was not the last gasp of the dying nation!'[35] A week later he regretted the harshness of his language; but in essentials his opinion did not change. He distrusted and disliked Herzl from the start; and he rejected the aims and modes of the new Zionism as incompatible with the true diagnosis of the ills of Jewry and as irrelevant to its real needs.

The two men met twice at Basel. Herzl left no record of the meeting. Aḥad Ha-ʿAm noted a general impression immediately[36] and recounted both conversations in some detail a year later—with a clarity that suggests that they were well embedded in his memory.[37] It is clear that Herzl shocked him by what he, Aḥad Ha-ʿAm, took to be the superficiality—the '*feuilleton*-character', as he put it—of Herzl's thinking on the

[34] 'Ha-kongres ha-ẓioni ha-rishon', first published in *Ha-Shiloʾaḥ*, September 1897. *Kol kitvei Aḥad Ha-ʿAm* (Tel-Aviv, 1947), pp. 275–6. Emphasis in original.

[35] Letter to Y. H. Rawnitzki, 1 September 1897. *Igrot AH* (revised edition, Tel-Aviv, 1956), vol. i, pp. 251–2.

[36] Ibid.

[37] Letter to Tchlenov, 7 October 1898. Ibid., ii, pp. 146–8.

major issues and Herzl's disingenuous and misleading account
of his political achievements. 'I had a brief conversation with
[Herzl] after the meeting and I came to the conclusion that
his allusions to his doings in Constantinople are all worthless.
No promise was made to him and there is no doubt that from
now on the Government of Turkey will come down upon us
with a much heavier hand than before.'[38] Herzl, for his part,
had not taken kindly to Aḥad Ha-ʿAm's questioning at their
first encounter and had sought to avoid a second. But having
failed to do so, he appears to have done his best to win his
interrogator over and 'the springs of "diplomacy" opened',
as Aḥad Ha-ʿAm put it.[39] However, Herzl achieved nothing
except to confirm Aḥad Ha-ʿAm's suspicions. His considered
objections to what Herzl was intent upon were then summed
up in a short article, 'The First Zionist Congress', in the first
issue of *Ha-Shilo'aḥ* (which he edited) to follow the event.
When this raised a furore—or, as he himself put it, 'my small
comment on the Congress was judged discordant'—he published a longer piece in December in which there was further
explication, but no retreat. Other articles followed as the
debate continued. A single argument ran through all.

The foundation of Aḥad Ha-ʿAm's outlook on Zionism at
this moment of transition was his extremely pessimistic view
of what could be done in practice to advance the movement in
either mode, whether by piecemeal settlement as before, or by
high-level political and financial negotiation as was now proposed. In part this was because he took the external political
obstacles—the hostility of the Ottoman Government and all
that derived from it—very seriously indeed. But he also considered the enterprise too great and too complex to be plausible
—at any rate at the speed with which the Herzlians hoped to
implement it. The Jews were too poor a people to be capable
of amassing the vast resources needed. The process of creating
a viable economy in which very great numbers would find a
livelihood was far more intricate and likely to be far less rapid
than most people realized. It was therefore mad to think that
millions of Jews could enter the country and settle in it satis-

---

[38] Letter to Rawnitzki, 1 September 1897. *Igrot AH*, i, pp. 251–2. For details of
Herzl's first venture in diplomacy in June 1896, see *Origins*, pp. 280–98.

[39] Letter to Tchlenov, 7 October 1898. *Igrot AH*, ii, pp. 146–8.

factorily even if a state were established and entry were free. If they did enter they would soon 'turn and flee from their state before the most terrible enemy of all . . . hunger'. International political and legal guarantees would be of no avail. And that was not all.

The truth is bitter, but with all its bitterness it is better than illusion. We must bring ourselves to admit that the ingathering of [all] the exiles is beyond nature. It may be that in the natural course of things we shall have a Jewish state and it may be that the Jews will become so numerous and strong there that they will fill the country; but even then the greater part of the nation will remain scattered and separated in foreign lands.[40]

It follows that however matters turned out the *material* problems of the Jews, their poverty and the legal and illegal oppression to which they were subject, would be little affected by the foundation of a state, or indeed by Zionism generally. On the other hand, while Zionism could offer the Jews little materially, there was much it could offer them morally. But not *political* Zionism and not a state for the Jews as such. Even if all the obstacles were swept away and the state were founded in circumstances as good as any that could be imagined, it would still be a poor thing if represented as the realization of the national ideal.

'According to the suffering so is the reward.'[41] It cannot be that after thousands of years of untold evil and affliction the people of Israel will rejoice upon attaining, at long last, to the rank of a small and mean nation, its state a plaything in the hands of great neighbours and incapable of survival except by the machinations of diplomacy and perpetual abasement before whomever fortune happens to have smiled upon; an ancient people which was a light unto the gentiles cannot be satisfied with no more than this as a reward for its hardships—when many other nations, of unknown origins and without culture, have achieved it in short order without first suffering a fraction of what it had undergone.[42]

[40] 'Medinat ha-yehudim ve-"ẓarat-ha-yehudim"' ('The Jews' State and the "Jews' Affliction"'), published in *Ha-Shiloʾaḥ*, January 1898. *Kol kitvei Aḥad Ha-ʿAm*, p. 136.

[41] Aḥad Ha-ʿAm is quoting the *Mishna*, Avot, v. 23.

[42] 'Ha-kongres ha-ẓioni ha-rishon', p. 275.

But again the matter went deeper. Western Jews, despondent in their realization that they were unacceptable to the peoples among which they lived, were sometimes drawn to the Land of their fathers. Why? Because they believed that if a Jewish state arose there once again and was a state like the states of all other nations, then they could, after all, live as full a life among their own people as they could conceive of living among others. And even if not all could go to Erez-Israel, the very reappearance of a Jewish state would redound to the honour of the nation and transform the attitude of other nations to them. The Jews would be treated with respect, 'not as degraded slaves waiting at the tables of others'. Even mere attachment to the idea of such a state and the effort to achieve it served to enhance the western Jews' self-respect and sense of well-being. Therein lay the secret of the power of Zionism to draw the Jews of the West.

In the East it was otherwise. There it was not the individual who was afflicted morally—his affliction was material—but the entire nation. And not as a consequence of anti-Semitism, but because of an involvement with an ancient culture so powerful as to be unaffected even if all the troubles of the Jews and all the anti-Semitism were to vanish everywhere and the Jews found they could earn a decent living and be received kindly by their neighbours. The moral affliction lay in their culture. 'It is not only Jews who have emerged from the ghetto; Judaism has too.' Its old defences are down. It can no longer exist apart.

The spirit of our people seeks to develop, to take in the foundations of the general culture that come to it from outside, to digest them and turn them into a part of itself as it had done at other times. But this the conditions of life in the Diaspora do not favour. Everywhere in our times, culture assumes the national spirit of the indigenous people and the stranger who approaches it must set his own identity at naught and allow himself to be absorbed by the spirit that is dominant. It follows that Judaism will be unable to develop in its own individual way so long as it is in the Diaspora. When it leaves the walls of the ghetto behind it is in danger of losing its independent life or, at best, its national unity, breaking up into many kinds of Judaism, each with its special character and life, as many kinds as

there are countries in which the Jews are scattered. And seeing this . . .
Judaism seeks to return to its *historic centre* to live a life of natural
development, to apply its powers to all components of human culture,
to develop and complete its national heritage, and so once more to
contribute a great national culture to the storehouse of humanity,
the fruit of the free labour of a nation that lives according to its own
spirit, as in the past.[43]

For a purpose such as this, Aḥad Ha-ʿAm argued, the Jews
could make do with less than a state of their own in Ereẓ-
Israel. What they needed there was a community of just such
sufficient size as to comprise people who could labour un-
disturbed in all branches of learning, on the land, and in
crafts. In time such a community would become the centre of
the Jewish people, there where its 'spirit would be realized
in all its purity'. Out of it, when the time was ripe, would come
men who were capable of founding a state—'not merely a
state of Jews, but truly a Jewish state'.[44]

Of all this, of the problem of the content and the direction
of Judaism in the modern world in the face of the new secular
and scientific culture, Herzl and his 'political Zionists' understood little or nothing, or else they paid mere lip-service to
questions about the Jewish national culture. Typically,
they had relegated the discussion on the subject—this, the
heart of it all—to the fag-end of the Congress, while spending
all their energies on the trivialities of the precise wording of the
Basel Programme.

Reviewing Herzl's own pamphlet on the Congress, Aḥad
Ha-ʿAm summed up thus. Herzl himself cautioned us that it
might ultimately prove impossible to come to an agreement
with the Turkish Government and that, despite all expectations, the Eastern Question might remain unresolved and
that, in that event, the nation would have to endure and wait,
perhaps for generations. But then, says Aḥad Ha-ʿAm, would
it not be more becoming and more useful to the Jews if they
employed their time on work, however limited, in Ereẓ-Israel
instead of leaving the improvement of the country to others

[43] Ibid., pp. 137–8. Emphasis in original.
[44] Ibid., p. 138.

on the churlish grounds that the 'political price' to pay might rise with its economic value?[45]

It is characteristic of Aḥad Ha-ʿAm's very deliberate self-discipline in these matters that he made no move to persuade Zionists in Russia to stay away from the Second Congress even after he had himself finally made up his mind, late in June or early in July 1898, not to attend. On the contrary, he continued to encourage them to take an active part in its preparation. He pressed them to seek to get the Second Congress to deal with what, in his view, the First had neglected: an open and frank consideration of the essential idea that united Zionists along with the questions of theory and practice that divided them.[46] He played a small part in a minor committee (on the Hebrew language) set up by the First Congress. And when it was resolved that the delegates from Russia and Poland would meet in Warsaw to co-ordinate their views for the coming Congress, he asked to attend. He was well aware, he explained, that opinion ran against him; but he wished to 'lay the truth (as I understand it, of course,) before those whose devotion to our affairs is *whole-hearted*'. Others, he implied, he would do his best to ignore.[47]

The others were numerous, however, and his reputation as the inventor and leader of the minoritarian 'spiritual' Zionists, as they now came to be called in contradistinction to the majoritarian 'material' and 'political' Zionists, was soon established. Much of the ensuing criticism of Aḥad Ha-ʿAm was harsh. There was mock surprise: he, the modernist and secularist, seemed now to be telling the Jews that they had a divinely ordained mission to wander from country to country heralding the Kingdom of Heaven. There was much irritation: for whom precisely was he claiming to speak with his pontifical 'It was not to found a Jewish state today or tomorrow that we came to Basel'? Who were 'we'? More than a tiny handful of the educated and the privileged? And would not the culture by which he set such store be alien to the great majority only a generation after our own, one writer asked.

[45] 'Ha-kongres ve-yoẓro' ('The Congress and its Creator'), *Ha-Shilo'aḥ*, January 1898.

[46] Letter to Bernstein-Kohan, 15 April 1898. *Igrot AH*, ii, pp. 63–4.

[47] Letter to Bernstein-Kohan, 12 July 1898. Ibid., p. 105. Emphasis in original.

And what then? Did Aḥad Ha-ʿAm not understand that for
the secular Jews of the West who rejected both the content and
the burden of the tradition there was only the idea of a Jewish
state to pull them into the Zionist camp?[48]

None of this writing was as distinguished as his own. The
only figure to lend real lustre to the company of the attackers
was Moshe Leib Lilienblum. It had, after all, been he who had
first put the case for a territorial solution to the problem of the
Jews in clear and modern terms. He had been a founder-
member of the Odessa circle of Ḥovevei Ẓion and, with
Pinsker dead and Mohilever dying, was now the last major
figure of the original movement left. And while of smaller
talent than Aḥad Ha-ʿAm, less polished, and of narrower
scope, he was none the less a writer of attested courage and
great intellectual integrity.[49] Lilienblum had welcomed Herzl
and his Congress with a combination of goodwill and mild,
somewhat weary scepticism—with his mind, as it were, rather
than his heart. If little had been accomplished at Basel, he
did not think that more could have been expected. If what
emerged looked Utopian, why, matters accepted today as
part of the natural order of things had been judged Utopian
a hundred years ago. Good men had now been brought into
the movement who would otherwise never have entered it.
So he was not ungrateful.[50] But there was no mildness in his
criticism of Aḥad Ha-ʿAm, rather the same impatience and
irritation that underlay what other critics had said and wrote
and would continue to colour the views of opposing schools of
thought during Aḥad Ha-ʿAm's lifetime and posthumously
as well.[51]

The trouble with Aḥad Ha-ʿAm's thesis, wrote Lilienblum,
was that in the nature of things few members of the nation

[48] 'Heyllel ben Shahar', 'Or yekarot ve-kipa on' ('Clear Light and Dark'), *Ha-Magid*, 28 October 1897; A. Segal, 'Shomrei ruʾaḥ u-vaʿalei maḥshava' ('Guardians of the Wind and Philosophers'), *Ha-Meliẓ*, 2 December 1897.

[49] See *Origins*, pp. 111–22.

[50] Letters to Kaminka, 20 September 1897. CZA, A 147/23/3; and to S. P. Rabbinowitz ('Shefer'), 11 November 1897. CZA, A 27/8/1.

[56] Lilienblum's considered views were contained in an article 'Bein ha-dimyon ve-ha-efshar' ('Between the Imagination and the Possible') published in instalments in *Ha-Meliẓ*, 29, 31 October, 1 November 1897; reprinted in *Kol kitvei Moshe Leib Lilienblum*, iv (Odessa, 1913), pp. 247–55.

were as concerned as he was with spiritual and intellectual matters. Most were, on the contrary, 'swept by the current of the material aspect of life'. Overwhelmingly, they lived in misery and pauperdom and were correspondingly deaf to 'songs of inner pride and greatness'. If our fathers had that sense of inner pride it was because they were concerned more with faith than with matter. In their days, the Jew in his poverty, seeing the oppressor ride by in his carriage, thought, 'He will die like a dog, while I shall have eternal life', and was consoled. But the modern Jew was not so easily consoled. It was his external and material condition that concerned him first and foremost and 'the idea of uprooting these evil values without a transformation of the condition of our life was more fantastic than the fantasy of the state of Jews. [The foundation of] a state required the agreement of a few statesmen; to breathe a new spirit into our nation required acting upon millions of people whose situation taught them otherwise.' As for the people of Israel's recompense for the long centuries of misery, 'it was not a reward the unfortunate nation sought, but rest'. And if the state could not be a great one like England or Germany, then let it be a small one; better a small one that was ours than none at all. A small state need not be 'a plaything'; there were neutral states like Belgium and Switzerland. We were weak and we were few. But was it better to remain scattered? Aḥad Ha-ʿAm tells us that our first task is to prepare ourselves morally and culturally for the future—the very distant future presumably. Then he tells us that 'a state of Jews will only be at peace when universal justice reigns.' But consider, says Lilienblum, who the neighbours of Ereẓ-Israel are: not Europeans, but Persians, Arabs, and Druzes. 'It would have been more proper to say, briefly, that the state of the Jews can never rise, at least until the coming of the Messiah.'

That this was not a fully accurate summary of Aḥad Ha-ʿAm's views mattered less, for the time being, than the fact that this was what he was commonly taken to have been driving at.[52] Lilienblum reflected a common mood: impatience,

[52] Cf. Aḥad Ha-ʿAm's indignant letter to Ehrenpreis, 22 December 1897. He had never said, he claimed, that the Jews should wait in the Diaspora until their qualities

willingness to take a risk, satisfaction at the appearance of free western Jews who had come to join the easterners on their own initiative and with evident devotion to the national interests and needs as they understood them—and, on the other hand, fear of the alternative, of a second descent into the black despair that had begun to eat into their hearts as Hibbat Zion stood still and then declined in the years before the advent of Herzl. What had Ahad Ha-ʿAm, with his impossibly high standards, to offer ordinary men in actual practice, except to put all present considerations away and prepare for an infinitely remote future? Was that Zionism? And if so, who would be the Zionists? Therefore better to follow Herzl to see what he could do.

None the less, Ahad Ha-ʿAm's every word was read by the *cognoscenti* and the unpopularity of his views had no effect on his general standing in the movement itself. More than one local Zionist society wanted him to represent it at the Second Congress. He was asked to provide a statement of his views for transmission to the Congress and he was granted the unique status of an officially invited private person at the preliminary meeting of the Russian caucus in Warsaw late in August 1898.

How so? It is not easy to account for Ahad Ha-ʿAm's unique position in the movement. He held no offices of significance or power and he sought none. He appears to have been devoid of political and social ambition of the ordinary kind. He wrote for an audience which he assuredly wished to influence, but the results he aimed at were intellectual and impersonal. He drew distinctions, he corrected errors of judgement and fact, he showed familiar things in a fresh light. No doubt he wished to inculcate a way of thinking about public affairs which was like his own, but nothing suggests that he wished other men to identify themselves with him personally. If he craved approval and applause, he never showed it. He knew very well how unpopular he had become. 'The Zionists here [in Russia] think me a very dangerous

---

changed. What he had said was that for their qualities to change there had to be a Jewish centre in Erez-Israel. He had said nothing about a mission to the gentiles. What he had said about the era of universal justice was that until it arrived the Jewish state would not solve the Jewish Problem *completely*. *Igrot AH*, i, p. 291.

enemy', he observed in August 1898.[53] And it is likely that he derived a dour satisfaction from the indignation and objections which were common reactions to his essays on contemporary affairs. But if so, even that small satisfaction was kept well below the hatches of his conscious mind. What absorbed him was the Problem itself, the argument, the truth as he saw it— along with the rigid literary and moral standards to which he was equally devoted. And since he cultivated a marvellously astringent and succinct style of writing and was forever seeking to lay bare the bones of the matter in hand, his essays and letters were like so many judgements handed down politely, but pitilessly, in a court of the utmost probity—a court which laymen learned to regard with great respect, if, inevitably, with small affection. People were therefore wary of Aḥad Ha-'Am. Many misunderstood him. Some feared him. But none ignored him. So it had been almost from the first when he burst upon the scene in Odessa in 1889 with his devastating critique of the aims and methods of Ḥibbat Ẓion—all the more painful because it was from the inside, from a man totally committed to the Jewish national revival and a devoted Ḥovev himself.[54] Since those days his reputation and moral authority had only grown. Now, at the turn of the century, in his early forties, he was at the height of his powers.

On the matter of Zionism, Aḥad Ha-'Am wrote to analyse, never to celebrate. What he had to say positively he derived from what he had to say critically; and what he tried to show his audience was, more than anything else, an *alternative*—to foolishness or danger or misconception or whatever else it was that he was intent on exposing at the heart of what the current claimants to the vacant leadership of the Jews had to say. But as he himself disclaimed any such leadership, and as the severe form and elevated content of his argument were not of a nature to appeal to, let alone be understood by, any but his own social and intellectual equals or near-equals, he had no followers in the political sense of the term, but only pupils— and some disciples.

Aḥad Ha-'Am was not unpractical or other-worldly. For much of his life he earned his living as a salaried manager

---

[53] Letter to Neumark, 1 August 1898. Ibid., ii, p. 121.
[54] *Origins*, pp. 191 ff.

in a firm of traders in tea. At business he seems to have been at least adequate. He was a great deal better than adequate at applying his formidable intelligence to public affairs. His political judgement was acute. He had something penetrating to say about virtually every issue of consequence to come before the movement—from that of relations with the Arab population of Erez-Israel to the hidden implications for the future of the loose wording of the Balfour Declaration. The historian is more than repaid by reading him today. By his contemporaries he was often consulted and always listened to. There is indeed a temptation to classify him as the sage of the Zionist movement. It is not for nothing that we have it from so distinguished and cautious a historian as Leonard Stein that Chaim Weizmann (a political animal of almost sublime egotism) 'felt respect [for Aḥad Ha-ʿAm] bordering on reverence'.[55] Yet it would not be quite right to think of him in such terms. He was business-like, not oracular. He was prepared to be co-opted onto working parties and committees, provided only he thought they were likely to be to some practical purpose. He was severe, not pompous. Above all he was in no sense remote from, or above, the fray.

The effect Herzl had had on the movement was, as has been seen, to present it, for the first time, with a focus and a centre: his own person and the institutions he established. To reject Herzl was therefore tantamount to rejecting Zionism, at least in its organized form: and Herzl, as we have seen, was accepted because that was precisely what he was manifestly able to provide. But he was not accepted, not in the main body of the movement in eastern Europe, not, at all events, completely and whole-heartedly, as the *ideological* leader; and so long as he lived these reservations persisted and the movement remained somewhat less than organically unified. Aḥad Ha-ʿAm did not create this fissure, but he contributed a great deal to preventing it from ever being sealed. He did this by presenting the adepts of Zionism with a fully formulated, alternative outlook that was Zionist, yet non- (or even anti-) Herzlian. He did not offer an institutional alternative. He did not entirely reject the institutions that Herzl established or which were

[55] *Weizmann Letters*, vii, Introduction, p. xxiii.

established under Herzl's aegis. But he did offer a different
position, a different perspective and therefore, in the realm of
ideas and opinions, he emerged as the natural focus (and in
some respects the source) of opposition to Herzl within
Zionism as a whole.

At this early stage, it was, after all, ideas and opinions that
were the principal stuff of Zionism and members of the intelligentsia predominated in its ranks.[56] These were precisely the
people who were, at any rate potentially, most amenable to
the influence of such a man as Aḥad Ha-ʿAm, a man of ideas,
not of action. So while Herzl was accepted as the effective
leader of the movement for all immediate practical purposes,
and the authority of the institutions he established was
acknowledged, the reservations in respect of his methods, his
ideas, and his goals—and therefore in respect of his ultimate
personal authority—remained very much alive in the minds
of great numbers of people who played, or were about to play,
not unimportant roles.

vii

Aḥad Ha-ʿAm had unsettled the Russian Zionists by criticism
so trenchant that the debate on the new, political mode
threatened to turn into a fundamental reconsideration of
Zionism as a whole. Herzl, remote in Vienna and only dimly
aware of the row, further unsettled it by his silence.

The Zionist movement in Russia [wrote Ussishkin] goes from
strength to strength. Societies appear in every town, speakers ex-
pound, books are printed, *shekalim* are collected, members multiply;
but everyone asks the same question: what news from Vienna?
What is the Actions Committee doing, what *real* activity has been
begun? Unfortunately we can only reply in the negative: [from
Vienna] not a word. I am greatly afraid that if the Committee
does not strengthen its position soon, if it does not show people just
what it is doing, despair will grow and the movement weaken.[57]

Moreover, the news that did filter out from Vienna, or
was formally communicated, was received with reserve,
and some of it with disbelief. Personal contact was rare and to

---

[56] See below, pp. 452–3.

[57] Letter to Wolffsohn, 4 December 1897. Schwartz, *Ussishkin*, p. 64. Emphasis in
original.

little purpose. There were no emissaries from Herzl to Russia. There was only one of any significance from Russia to Herzl; and he was not encouraging. Bernstein-Kohan had set out an enthusiast and had returned with doubts about the sanguine picture of affairs that Herzl had painted for him.[58] One way or another, as the date for the Second Congress approached, the mood in Russia and Poland became one of uncertainty: minds had still to be made up finally about the new movement. The Russian members of the Greater Actions Committee therefore decided to bring together the prospective delegates to the Congress in Warsaw—on home ground—to formulate and co-ordinate their position before setting off for Basel.

The meeting lasted four days, from 19 to 22 August, but sessions were not continuous because the 20 August was a Sabbath on which not all the participants were willing to meet. Some delegates to the Congress ignored the summons and travelled directly to Basel. Some of those present in Warsaw were not delegates at all, or were elected delegates who would not, in practice, be travelling to the Congress. But effective delegates were in the great majority. All told some 160 people from just under 100 cities and towns in the Russian Empire participated.

The Warsaw meeting was thus the first large-scale representative gathering of the Russian wing of the movement ever held. It was held in secret for fear of police intervention, the participants moving from one private apartment to another as it proceeded. For many years after, the only published report on it was that contained in a pamphlet written early in the following year by Yeḥiel Tchlenov in which Warsaw was referred to as a 'summer resort near the Austrian border' and the major speakers (with the exception of Aḥad Ha-ʿAm) were all indicated by their initials alone.[59] The atmosphere was mostly one of great tension and excitement, to which the frequent crowding of scores of delegates into

[58] Bernstein-Kohan to Aḥad Ha-ʿAm, 22 April 1898. *Sefer Bernstein-Kohan*, eds. Miriam Bernstein-Kohan and Y. Korn (Tel-Aviv, 1946), pp. 230–2.

[59] 'Ha-kongres ha-ẓioni ha-sheini ve-ha-veʿidot she-kadmu lo', in S. Eisenstadt (ed.), *Yeḥiel Tchlenov* (Tel Aviv, 1937), pp. 101–69. What follows is based chiefly on Tchlenov's account and on additional material in A. Rafaʾeli, 'Veʿidot arẓiot shel ẓionei rusiya', *Kaẓir* [i] (Tel Aviv, 1964), pp. 43–59; and E. ʿA. Rabinovitz, *Sefer ẓion be-mishpat* (Warsaw, 1899).

rooms which could hold no more than a fifth of the number in any comfort greatly contributed. This was also the first occasion on which veterans and newcomers could take stock of each other and, more particularly, the veterans see the change in the composition of the movement which had been wrought—not without a sense of disquiet at their having been reduced to a minority by new men who struck them as less experienced, less tolerant, and altogether more volatile than themselves, to say nothing of being much more fervent supporters of the new mode. There was also a handful of ortho-dox rabbis, perhaps ten in number, who formed a group that was sharply distinguished from the others by their calling, by their dress, by their cohesion and, above all, by the principal subject of their concern, as would soon become evident.

There were four main items of business. The first was an attempt to iron out differences between the adepts of the new movement and those of the old, particularly of its stronghold, the Odessa Committee. The Committee was suspected not merely of being unco-operative, but of having tried to stir up opinion against the new Zionism. A representative of the Committee, 'Mr A.G.' (presumably Avraham Greenberg, the Committee's chairman), came to Warsaw to deny the charges, explain its members' belief in caution, particularly with an eye on the Russian police authorities, and to make peace. This seems to have been achieved without much trouble on a live-and-let-live basis, and the upshot was that a certain duality was thereupon instituted in Russian Zionism. On the one hand there would remain a small, legal, non-political, philanthropically minded centre in Odessa committed to organizing direct support for settlements in Erez-Israel. On the other hand there was now a relatively large, illegal, mass movement, integrated into the World Zionist Organiza-tion and subordinate to it. In time the line dividing the two would grow indistinct. But the formal differences would persist until the Revolution.

The second major item was what might be termed the Ahad Ha-ʿAm thesis. His proposal that he attend as an officially invited guest to put his views having been accepted, he now rehearsed the arguments he had set forth in his articles—making some effort to soften their impact without diluting

their content. All present must have been familiar with their
terms. None the less, his appearance aroused enormous interest and the evidence suggests that he was heard with respect
—and here and there with a little sympathy—throughout
the five hours devoted to the debate with him. There is no
record of anyone having gone so far as to support him fully;
and on at least two cardinal points all disagreed with him.
All were of the view that an autonomous Jewish centre in
Erez-Israel was indeed a matter of fundamental need—not
because they thought it could contain all Jewry (and so solve
the Jewish Problem mechanically, as it were), but because the
restoration of political autonomy would radically and instantly change the *status* of Jews in all countries. The other
point was equally characteristic of the differences between
him and them. 'I do not think there was anyone', Tchlenov
noted, 'who assessed the material future of our nation with the
same cold and terrible despair as did Aḥad Ha-'Am.'[60]

The third main topic at the conference lay at the heart of
the differences between the two major schools of thought:
what was to be the approach to the settlement of Erez-Israel
in the interim period, that is to say, while the new political
school sought to bring new forces to bear upon the problem
and before it succeeded? Were all resources to be devoted to
the main political effort; or should 'practical' settlement work
remain Zionism's chief concern, both in its own right and
because 'politics' in any case was dangerous and inappropriate
and therefore had to be proceeded with, if at all, with great
caution? Into this debate was intercalated the new, but related
question of the project for a Bank which Herzl was proposing
to launch and which was to be debated at the coming Congress.
What exactly were to be the Bank's functions—and were they
to be political, that is to say, providing financial support for
the political arm of the movement; or practical, that is, providing direct support for the settlements? Beyond that, who was
to control its activities once it had been established; and how
was it intended to ensure that this new instrument of national
and popular policy would be prevented from falling into
selfish, plutocratic hands?[61]

[60] Op cit., p. 115.
[61] In the event, there was never any danger of this happening. Subscriptions were

There was much heated argument and some confusion. (At one point contradictory resolutions were passed successively, thanks to an excess of zeal by the 'political' chairman— and a terminological compromise had to be worked out.) On the cardinal issue the delegates took refuge in ambivalence. It had been laid down in the Basel Programme *inter alia* that the movement would promote 'The purposeful advancement of the settlement of Palestine with Jewish farmers, artisans, and tradesmen.' This could be interpreted, it was pointed out, as dissolving the purported distinction between the settlement Zionists and the politicals. On the other hand, in the light of Herzl's known position, it could also be dismissed as something very close to humbug. If one took it more or less literally, and seriously, and no one seems to have gone so far as to suggest otherwise, everything turned on the word 'purposeful' (*zweckdienlich*). The compromise with which the Russians agreed to go armed, but united, to Basel therefore took the form of a gloss on 'purposeful'. 'Purposeful settlement', it was formally resolved, 'shall be understood to be settlement undertaken under licence granted beforehand by the Turkish Government and in accordance with the plans and instructions of the relevant body chosen by the Congress.' The politicals could now be reasonably content, because further settlement had been made conditional upon a formal arrangement of some kind with the Turkish Government. The settlement-firsters were entitled to feel that by dropping all allusion to a full-scale, essentially political, at least quasi-internationalized agreement with the Turks, they had gone some way towards forcing a retreat from the pretentions of the Basel Programme and all that was being read into it. And they won an additional point by having appended to the gloss a 'remark' of extreme ambiguity to the effect that Jews 'already resident in Turkey' could form the basis of initial settlement activity. This, in turn, could be taken to mean that, whatever else was decided, the most should be made of whatever foothold had already been gained in the constant petty warfare of settlers

---

overwhelmingly of single shares—it was literally the common people who backed the Bank—while the Jewish plutocracy, taken as a class, soon showed that it was not interested.

and would-be settlers with the Turkish authorities over
entry into the country and the purchase of land.

So far as the Bank was concerned, none were opposed to
trying to ensure its effective subordination to the Congress.
It was also agreed that the scope of its activities should specifically include the purchase of unoccupied land in Erez-Israel
and that, generally, its affairs be restricted to matters relating
directly or indirectly to Erez-Israel and Syria. In effect this
was another victory for the pro-settlement wing, although
approval of the Bank project itself was in the nature of support
for Herzl. Finally, a vote was taken on the full set of resolutions,
which were passed by 59 votes to 40.

All these were matters with which the participants could
deal in much the same spirit in which they had been debating
them in public and in private in the course of the year between
the two Congresses. Both large issues and specific projects
(like the Bank) could be considered more or less *a priori*, in
the light of general principles and views relating to the condition of Jewry and some very general and untested notions
of what might or might not be practicable for the movement to
undertake. In no case did the participants anticipate assuming
direct responsibility for putting the resolutions into effect,
for breaking them down and translating them into action. In
part, the exercise upon which they had embarked in Warsaw
was an act of coming together and beginning to perform as
an organized body. In part, it was one of seeking to clear their
own minds on what they judged to be the great issues of the
day. But more than anything, they were seeking to introduce
an element of constraint and influence over Vienna by arriving
at the Congress as an organized and indispensable body
equipped with an articulated philosophy, 'programme' being
too strict a term to ascribe to what they had formulated. It is
true that there is no firm evidence that they were persuaded
they would succeed in establishing a true partnership with
Herzl. But one is drawn to the conclusion that at least they
wished to formulate their opinions and discipline themselves
in such a way as to be capable of functioning satisfactorily
at the Congress—not, that is to say, as a mere audience, or
worse a claque, but as a body of men of independent mind
whom Herzl and his inner circle would have no choice but to

take at something like the Russians' own estimate of their value.

The fourth item of business had little to do with relations between the eastern and western wings of the movement and everything to do with how Zionism would be situated in Jewry as a whole and hence with its fundamental quality and strength. It raised issues which relatively few were disposed to debate without inhibition, because none could doubt that the longer one argued and the further one probed, the more painful the argument would be and the more surely hope of compromise and consensus would evaporate.

The quarrel between Jewish religious orthodoxy and Zionism in all its forms had been in evidence from the very beginning of the movement, even if it had never been as clearly articulated as it now would be. Its ultimate source lay in the resistance of the orthodox leadership to the advance of secularism in its inner, native, non-assimilationist form—the *haskala* or Enlightenment. They correctly judged Ḥibbat Ẓion to be a movement which, if not identical to, drew its strength from much the same sources as the *haskala*. There was the same desire to reform Jewish society and culture by the adaptation, so far as possible, of resources taken from the storehouse of the Jewish past and the same insistence that the Jews must begin to take their destiny in their own hands—or, at the very least, begin to cast about seriously for means to do so. Since this entailed a clear threat to traditional ways and traditional authority, the rabbis divided into two camps. The great majority were rigidly—and some hysterically[62]— opposed to Zionism. They knew danger when they saw it and took a fundamentalist line on all the tricky theological and historiosophical issues it raised.[63] There were other grounds for opposition, notably the deeply ingrained reluctance to cross the governmental authorities for insufficient cause. But defensive theological grounds and resistance to loss of communal authority were uppermost. Against the majority were arrayed a few, such as Mohilever, of more independent mind,

---

[62] See the argument between the leading rabbi of Lodz, R. Eliyahu Ḥayyim Meisel, and Mohilever's erstwhile lieutenant, R. Yiẓḥak Nissenboim. Y. Nissenboim, *'Alei ḥeldi* (Warsaw, 1929), pp. 145–7.

[63] See below, pp. 210–13.

who were not wholly unsympathetic to the *maskilim*, who
believed that a threat such as this was best contained by
co-operation, and who thought it likely that the Zionist
movement in one or other of its forms did indeed offer a basis
for co-operation and, possibly, for social control. They wished
to take the movement over, if they could. But if they could not,
they did at least want to position themselves on or very near
its commanding heights. However, now, with Mohilever
dead and no one of comparable stature to replace him, a
clear fight and a definitive identification of Zionism with
secularism was once again in prospect, the more so as a
contingent of rabbis of impeccable orthodoxy turned up at the
Warsaw conference and then at the Congress that followed.

Herzl had appealed to the orthodox rabbinate to express
public support for the movement and, if possible, to attend the
Congress.[64] Tchlenov noted cautiously that while he did not
think that Herzl's appeal had 'caused' the rabbis to attend the
Warsaw meeting, he was sure they had been flattered and that
it had helped.[65] But the real source of interest being displayed was the new, 'political' character that Herzl had
given the movement. The rabbis may not have been any less
sceptical about Herzl's prospects than were the Hovevei Zion.
But they believed that the shift of attention to 'politics' would
help steer people away from excessive concern with 'culture'
and cognate matters, all of which served to promote the
disposition to religious reform. Herzlian Zionism, with its
relatively superficial interest in the inner life of Jewry, was a
great deal safer, in the orthodox view, than Hibbat Zion
and its child, 'practical' Zionism, to say nothing of 'spiritual'
Zionism in terms such as Aḥad Ha-ʿAm conceived of it.

Nevertheless, no meeting of minds was possible. After a
preliminary skirmish over modernized infants' schools (*hadarim
metukanim*) and public libraries, the rabbis met privately to
consider their position. Later they set out their demands.
They wanted a special rabbinical council, set up independently
under the highest rabbinical authority, and charged with
supervising all Zionist Cultural and propaganda activities.
The freedom of the Zionist Actions Committee to act in the

---

[64] *Igrot Herzl*, iii (Jerusalem and Tel-Aviv, 1957), no. 581, pp. 167–8.
[65] Op. cit., p. 107.

political and economic spheres would not be impaired, they were careful to state. But the Actions Committee might take no step in the sphere of culture and education that had not first been submitted to the rabbis for approval. The latter would duly examine it to ensure its accordance with the Law, in matters of which their judgement would be final. To the question what their attitude to the movement would be if their demands were turned down, Rabbi Leib Zirelson, their leader, replied that they would leave it. Questioned further, he made it clear that while the rabbinical council they proposed would no doubt consult the laymen on the Zionist Actions Committee, in general 'you would have to obey our instructions'. This was met with shouts of 'A Jewish inquisition!' and 'No, no, we shan't go to Canossa'; and after more heated exchanges the show-down was postponed to the last day of the conference.[66]

The rabbis then submitted a carefully drafted, moderately phrased resolution in which the idea of a supervisory rabbinical council was recapitulated, but now justified theoretically on the grounds that there were two forms of nationalism in question here. One was the form that had 'maintained us for three thousand years . . . and which had impressed us with a special stamp'. The other was 'a nationalism which purports to exist independently of our heritage', which therefore repelled most Jews, and which, being excessively influenced by the spirit of that nationalism which was now common in Europe and therefore foreign to the Jews, was liable to fail. Zionism had 'to be founded on our Holy Law, that which was our original and natural nationalism . . . Only then would it be solidly founded.' The function of the rabbinical council was to ensure just that. The rabbis' draft resolution was put to the vote after minimal debate and overwhelmingly rejected.

Their discussions over and the air cleared somewhat, most of those present at the Warsaw meeting then moved off in a body to

[66] It was Rabbi Zirelson himself, however, who had begun talk of 'inquisitions'—in his case, talk of the 'liberal inquisition' which he feared would be set up in the Jewish state. He had also made his proposal for a rabbinical supervisory council public and seen it discussed in the Hebrew press well before the Warsaw conference. The confrontation was therefore less than entirely spontaneous and all the more deserving of attention. See leading article, *Ha-Meliz*, 26 May 1898.

Basel for the Second Congress. They had fortified themselves for the short term. In the long term it remained to be seen whether Herzl's plan of action was well founded. If it proved not to be, the movement's centre of gravity would shift once more to the East and the governing influence within it would be constituted once again of the specific character and circumstances of Russian Zionism. To some this might be a more comfortable prospect; but to none, as yet, did it positively beckon. Meanwhile, Herzl had a free hand.

2

The New Model Zionism

i

For six years, between 1897 and 1903, Herzl dominated the Zionist movement, virtually without challenge. His ability to do so owed something to his person, the figure he cut, the impression he made. It owed more to the simple fact that the movement, as it emerged in 1897, was, in its formal structure and in its public aspect, largely his own creation—a movement in which others, new Zionists and old, had joined *him*. But it owed most of all to the particular direction which he gave the movement and to the particular role which he allotted to himself. So long as the response to his performance in that role, when it was not applause, was nothing more obstructive than doubt or irritation, he remained free to pursue it virtually unchecked. Zionist external or 'foreign' policy in those years, and in its essentials, was thus neither more nor less than Herzl's policy, the sum of what Herzl thought should be done and what he himself sought to do about it. Accordingly, it is possible to see these six years from two, partly contradictory points of view. On the one hand, they may be regarded as, in some sort, Zionism's finest hour, the time when Zionism in its purest form, uncluttered by doctrinal irrelevancies and virtually unaided by external forces, was injected into the world arena. This was a time when what was achieved *for* Zionism was achieved *by* it and when it was in its failures that the just measure of its weakness could be taken. Alternatively, the six years of Herzl's supremacy may be regarded as an interlude between two much more extended periods, an interlude of peculiarity and abnormality in which the true nature of the movement and the real wishes of its adepts were temporarily swept out of sight and mind

by the extraordinary man who had placed himself so unexpectedly at its head—and who then, after a single but
tremendous quarrel with his most important followers, and
with what one is tempted, inevitably, to see as his characteristic sense of the theatrical, quickly died.

Herzl, in other words, was the champion of his movement.
More: in his own mind and in the minds of many of his followers
he was the champion of all Jews. Appropriately, he rode
onto the battlefield alone, his direction dimly perceived, the
details of his action lost to sight—the more so because he
subscribed willingly to an extreme form of the contemporary
code of diplomatic secrecy whereby there were such as were
rightly privy to high politics and such as were not. He was
anxious, understandably enough, to establish himself in the
eyes of the great men in the chancelleries of Europe as a man
who could be trusted, as an *interlocuteur valable*—in some sense
as one of their own kind, at any rate for practical, if not social
purposes. Yet beyond the rational grounds which he could and
did adduce for keeping his own counsel so far as was practicable
and in all the matters that he himself regarded as most important, there can be little doubt that it suited him temperamentally to do so. There is no mistaking the peculiar thrill he
derived from his political and diplomatic negotiations with
the great men *outside* Jewry. It was then that his attention to
every aspect of his own dress, speech, and gesture was at its
peak and that his recording of it all—with that combination of
care for detail and touches of gaiety and self-deprecation that
makes his diary and some of his letters so splendid and important a documentary record of his progress—was most meticulous. It was in the theatre of international politics that Herzl
felt he was fulfilling himself. All the rest was necessary—the
committees of the Organization, the followers, the petitioners,
the journalism, the interminable preparations to set up the
national Bank that was to be the financial instrument of the
movement, even the Congresses themselves after a while,
when the initial elation had given way to routine and to
its inevitable concomitants, boredom and irritation. To
all he tried to pay their due. But they could not often be
enjoyed and would never be a source of triumph. They were
of a weekday world. There is something grim and deliberate

about his application to these grey areas of his work, his inner eye remaining fastened on the uplands where the really great matters would be resolved and where he would play out the role he had written for himself to the full. To that end his patience and his self-control were immense, as was his capacity to apply himself entirely and without distraction to the immediate purpose in view. And there, of course, on that centre stage, his associates from Vienna, Cologne, London, Kiev, Libau, or wherever it might be, rarely had any role of consequence to play and chiefly he need rely on no one but himself. Besides, they belonged, essentially, to that same weekday world. A few were despised, many were valued, one or two were loved. But what was demanded of all of them, and before all else, was to fall into the pattern of activity which he had devised. Since he was disinclined to reveal all he was doing and since he tended to take scepticism hard and mistake honest disagreement for jealousy and rivalry, differences on policy frequently turned into issues of loyalty. The effect was to convert the truest loyalists into something like a coterie—which outsiders naturally resented. Yet, so long as it was not evident that he was leading the movement where it might not wish to go and progress of some kind seemed, on the thin evidence available, to be being made, Herzl had a very free hand.

Diplomacy not only suited Herzl: it was the whole of his policy. Temperament and set purpose nourished each other. 'Political Zionism' could as well have been called 'diplomatic Zionism'; and the implications were profound. It is of the essence of diplomacy that for those who practise it the dominant reality is external. It is the forces which escape the diplomat's (or the statesman's) authority—rivals of the force for which he himself acts, as well as enemies, allies, or neutrals, actual and potential—that loom largest for him, while the cause for which he acts and over which he may claim authority tends to be relegated to the back of his mind and to be thought of, if at all, in terms that are relatively abstract. So with Herzl. Chiefly, the Jews were in the back of his mind and in abstract form. In the forefront was the world external to Jewry. It was there that he sought to act and it was upon it that his real attention was concentrated. It was there that he was best able to perceive his own mistakes and correct them, to learn.

There is in this tendency to concentrate attention on external forces a possible clue to his lack of interest in the living people to whom he was manifestly devoted—as opposed to the abstraction that he had formed of them in his own mind; and possibly a clue to the paradox that so sensitive and at times brilliant an observer of the world of the gentiles remained so ill informed and so misguided in respect of the nation he regarded as his own. When Herzl told people, as he was fond of doing, that he was not a 'professional politician' (invariably he used the English phrase to make his point) he meant that he despised intrigue, chicanery, and the use of public office for private benefit and that he himself had entered the public arena only for a great purpose and with no profit to himself. All of this was true. But he was no 'politician' in a deeper and less obviously pejorative sense. Herzl formed no party. He was liable to meet opposition head on. He was not an especially good judge of men. Instead of a circle of intimates he had allowed a court to form. Above all, he was not devoted heart and soul to the achievement and maintenance of power and authority within his new movement. What he wanted was a diplomatic success, the movement serving primarily as an instrument; and the results were paradoxical. By the time the Second Congress was convened in the summer of 1898, it was already plain that his internal political achievement was greater than his diplomatic. The Zionist Organization was alive and functioning. For his efforts in diplomacy there was much less to show.

ii

The rock on which everything broke was the absolute refusal of the Ottoman Government to accept that the goals of Zionism might be consistent with the interests of Turkey. Its policy on Zionism had been established, however, long before Herzl appeared on the scene and therefore well before the movement had adopted a political form, let alone explicit political ends. It was to the still numerically insignificant, ill- or unorganized movement of Jews from Russia and Romania in 1881 that the Turks had reacted when they recognized, or thought they recognized, in it signs of an old and familiar enemy, albeit in an unexpected quarter. They then drew their conclusions so swiftly that by the following year the main elements of their policy in the matter of the desire of Jews from eastern Europe to settle in Erez-Israel in numbers had all been formulated and put into effect. And, on the whole, they remained consistent in its application to the end of their rule in the country. Thus, for over thirty years, throughout its formative period and for some time beyond it, the Zionist movement was constrained to live under the long shadow cast by the Ottoman Government. The Turks not only blocked off the road to Herzl's Zion, the territorial state, but the road to the infinitely milder and less ambitious, rehabilitating, non-political *social* Zion at which the men of Hibbat Zion and their heirs had aimed. By the same token, of all Herzl's diplomatic campaigns, the attempt to breach the walls of Constantinople was potentially the one of greatest intrinsic importance. It was also the most painful and frustrating, the least fruitful, and the most costly in time, money, and nervous energy expended; and its impact on Herzl's thinking and on Zionist policy generally, in Herzl's time and beyond, was to be immense.

The sources of this hostility to the Zionist endeavour, even in its mildest form, are not hard to seek. The Jews constituted a recognized religious community (*millet*) in the Ottoman scheme of things with a well-understood, firmly subordinate role within it—as was ordained by Muslim doctrine and Muslim practice for Jews and Christians alike. But the differences between the Jews and the Christians were substantial. The Jewish communities (with some exceptions, as in Salonika) were small and scattered. The Jews, unlike the Christians, had no natural champions among the foreign states. The long, grim experience of the Diaspora had habituated them to compliance, at any rate so long as the external pressures of the State were not excessive and the inner life of the communities was left relatively free. And again, unlike most Christians, the downfall of the Ottomans was not a cause in which the Jews, as a community, could have an interest: the Turks, it could be assumed, would be succeeded by other masters under whose rule the lot of the Jews might be a good deal worse. So it had proved to be the case in Romania; so it would prove to be in

Syria and Mesopotamia. Thus geography, demography, and
the deeply ingrained mental habits of all concerned combined
to keep the Jews in political impotence and give the Turks
good reason to regard them as safe and tame, least likely of all
the ethnic groups of which the Empire was composed to set
their minds on national autonomy, liberation, and rebellion.

The arrival of east European Jews in Erez-Israel in 1881[1]
confronted the Turks with people of whom no such comfortable
assumptions could be made; and with the rapidity and
astuteness which were characteristic of them in matters such
as these, the Turks grasped the danger the men of Ḥibbat
Zion might present—not for the present, to be sure, but in the
distant, but still foreseeable future. True, nothing was further
from the minds of the members of the First ʿAliya[2] than purposes
subversive of the Ottoman Empire. Their small numbers,
their poverty, and, not least, the effect on their minds of the
circumstances that had precipitated their departure from
Europe all dictated total concentration on the hard business of
re-creating lives in new surroundings. But potentially, under
the surface, and to some extent without the settlers themselves
being fully conscious of it, things were a good deal more
complex. Their attitude to the country itself, as that of all
Jews, from time immemorial, was, as the Turks well knew,
intimate and possessive. The journey from Odessa or Constanza
to Jaffa or Haifa was in one sense merely parallel to the journey
to New York or Baltimore. In another sense it was totally
unlike it—not a journey to a new part of the Dispersion, but a
return home. In their minds the fact of presence, of daily life
in Erez-Israel was, or ought to be, of deep and far-reaching
significance; and first and foremost it implied, however
vaguely, a species of liberation in itself and led rapidly to a
dropping-away of habitual inhibitions of thought and conduct
in relation to non-Jews. Moreover, those who came did see
themselves as the vanguard of a larger army. However ill-
defined their ideas on the final political status of the Jews in
Erez-Israel/Palestine, there is no question but that the early
Zionists, like the later, hoped for a large and compact com-

---

[1] See *Origins*, pp. 65–108.

[2] On the ʿAliyot, the successive waves of immigration into Erez-Israel by which the
new *yishuv* was built up, see below, pp. 384–5.

munity—for that territorial concentration of the Jews which
was the corner-stone of their common philosophy and their
recipe for the solution of the Jewish Problem. Finally, they
were Jews of Europe and in some respects and for certain
purposes indistinguishable from other Europeans. They lacked
the habit of submission to the Muslims and, no less disturbing
to the Ottomans, when pressed hard by the local authorities,
were ready enough to invoke their rights as subjects of European Powers under the Capitulation agreements, the foreign
consuls, in some cases, supporting them. In sum, they appeared
to the Turks as a category of people who, if allowed to multiply,
could end up being almost as troublesome to the tranquillity
of the regime as the Bulgarians and the Armenians—with the
added evil that the country in question was the Holy Land and
the Return of the Jews in force could not but mean a diminution of the Muslim preponderance in it. Finally, there was
irritation at having to cope with what appeared to be a *European*
problem. 'Why should we accept Jews whom the civilized
European nations do not want in their countries and whom
they have expelled', 'Abd al-Hamid wrote to his ministers on
one occasion, summing up: 'It is not expedient to do so,
especially at a time when there is Armenian subversion
[*fesad*].'[3] Thus, considerations of internal security, vigilance
in the face of foreign encroachment, the maintenance of the
specifically Muslim character of the Ottoman state, the
supremacy of the Muslims within it and the prestige of the
Caliph-Sultan himself as their leader all led to a single operative
conclusion. The number of Jews entering and settling in the
country must be very severely limited and the progress of
those already there impeded as thoroughly as could be managed
without scandal.

It is worth stressing that the attitude of the Turks was not
entirely negative. They knew perfectly well what pressures the
Jews were subject to in eastern Europe. If some among them
assumed that the Jews owed their troubles to their own evil
characteristics and believed that the *émigrés* included great
numbers of revolutionaries and 'nihilists', others, fewer

[3] Imperial instruction addressed to the Grand Vezir, 28 June 1890. Quoted in
C. R. Itilhan, *Ittihat ve Terâkkinin Suikastleri* (Istanbul, 1973), p. 199. The book cited
is virulently anti-Semitic, but the document is genuine.

probably, knew better. But in either case the decisive question was whether the immigrant Jews would conduct themselves as tamely as did the members of the existing Jewish communities in the Empire and play as useful an economic role. If so, the Ottoman Government was prepared to extend to them a cautious welcome—somewhat in the spirit of the generous reception accorded the Jews expelled from Spain four centuries earlier—and to that end it set down precise conditions. 'His Majesty's Council of Ministers . . . had decided affirmatively that the Jews from whatever parts could come and settle in Turkey', the Foreign Minister informed the United States Minister in Constantinople in June 1882; and 'they could come when they pleased'. However, they would be settled only in groups of 200 or 250 families and 'on any unoccupied lands in Mesopotamia, about Aleppo, or in the regions of the Orontes river; . . . they could not establish themselves in Palestine.' Furthermore, foreign nationality would have to be relinquished, Ottoman nationality adopted, and the immigrant would have to undertake to seek no special rights or privileges.[4] To this offer, however, there was virtually no response. Those Jewish emigrants from Russia, Poland, and Romania who were set upon escape from present miseries and were concerned with their own private pain and individual salvation—the great majority—looked not east or south, in any case, but *west*. The minority, the men of Ḥibbat Ẓion, and the Zionists proper, with larger purposes in mind, had their eyes set exclusively on Ereẓ-Israel. None the less, the Turkish offer of settlement in Syria and Mesopotamia in small and scattered groups was never rescinded but, on the contrary, reiterated from time to time, as we shall see.

What ensued in Ereẓ-Israel itself was an endless game of wits and force. The Turks instituted a total ban on entry, but retreated somewhat when they found they were up against the opposition of the foreign Powers on the grounds that such a ban was an infringement of their (and their subjects') rights under the Capitulations. They then sought to draw a distinction between Jews intending to settle and Jews arriving

[4] Wallace to Frelinghuysen, 11 July 1882. Department of State, Despatches from United States Ministers to Turkey, 1818–1906, no. 107. National Archives Microfilm M 46.

as pilgrims or business men, the latter being admitted for a very limited period, the former prohibited. Under fresh foreign pressure the period was extended from one month to three. Later still (1901), under new regulations, Jewish travellers of all kinds, Ottoman subjects as well as foreigners, were required to surrender their passports on entry. In return they were issued with a temporary residence permit, specially printed on red paper and good for three months, at the end of which they had to leave or risk arrest. Part of the new plan was to keep a register of arrivals and departures and check compliance with the law regularly. Other measures, instituted and reinstituted, were warnings to the shipping companies not to provide passage and strong police control at the ports themselves.

The proclaimed grounds for these prohibitions were often specious: 'overcrowding', 'safeguard of public health'. The entire exercise entailed an unmistakable and embarrassing departure from the picture of itself which the Government wished to have projected abroad, to say nothing of its formal undertakings at the Congress of Berlin,[5] as the ambassadors in Constantinople were ready to point out. But on the whole, the Turks were frank enough about their purpose.

In a recent conversation which I had with the Mutessarif, [the British consul in Jerusalem reported in 1899] I gathered from H[is] Ex[cellency] that the Regulations issued by the Porte for preventing the entry, for purposes of settlement, of all foreign Jews into Palestine, emanate from political motives rather than a desire to adopt measures of a temporary nature to protect the country from the evils of pauper immigration and there seems to be little doubt that the so-called 'Zionist Movement' for the establishment of Jews in Palestine has induced the Porte to enforce with greater stringency the Regulations against Jewish immigration. The Mutessarif gave me to understand that these Regulations were aimed quite as much against the rich as against the poor, and he further stated that he had rec[eive]d

---

[5] Article 62 of the Treaty of Berlin, 13 July 1878, stated: 'The Sublime Porte having expressed a wish to maintain the principle of religious liberty and to give it the widest scope, the contracting parties take note of this spontaneous declaration.

In no part of the Ottoman Dominions shall difference of religion be alleged against an individual as a ground for exclusion or incapacity as regards the discharge of civil and political rights, admission to the public service, functions and honours or the exercise of different professions and industries.'

no instructions from the Porte to modify them. He, therefore, felt that he w[oul]d have to continue to enforce them ag[ains]t all foreign Jews without distinction of nationality.[6]

It should be added that parallel measures to prevent Jews from purchasing land in Erez-Israel were promulgated and regularly modified and their enforcement repeatedly tightened up to keep up with attempts to circumvent them. For the problem which faced the Turks in both cases, namely that of the barriers to entry and residence and that of the barriers to striking economic roots, was not simply the one set them by the intervention of the foreign consuls in Jerusalem, backed, when necessary, by their ambassadors in Constantinople, but the actions of the would-be settlers themselves. Most would-be immigrants were in any case unable to invoke such aid, or only to a very limited degree: the Russians, for example, because of the intense hostility of the Russian Government to Jews as such, the Romanians because they were denied the rights of citizenship in their country of birth. The problem was that while the barriers facing the settlers were severe and constituted a deterrent and a nuisance, they were not impenetrable. The Ottoman administration was no more consistently efficient in this sphere than in any other. Rigour alternated with laxity. Orders were not invariably carried out. Registers were not kept up. The planning was bad and the holes in the net consequently large. When control of movement through the ports happened to be severe, it was often possible to enter the country overland unhindered. Determined young men and women thought very little of the loss of their passports in exchange for the 'Red Slip' and were prepared to take their chances with the police later. Administratively, there was no such unit or entity as 'Palestine'. The southern half of the country, including Jerusalem, was an independent governorate (*mutasarriflık*). The northern half

---

[6] Dixon to O'Conor, 9 February 1899. PRO, FO 78/5479. In 1897 the German consul in Jerusalem reported a very similar conversation with the governor of Jerusalem, adding that the explicit reference to 'political' grounds for restrictions on the acquisition of real estate had first been brought up in 1893. Tischendorf to Hohenlohe, 19 June 1897. AA/Juden in der Türkei, K 175 847/65. Text in Mordechai Eliav (ed.), *Ha-yishuv ha-yehudi be-Erez-Israel be-re'i ha-mediniut ha-germanit 1842–1914*, Te'udot (Tel-Aviv, 1973), no. 163, pp. 233–8.

of the country formed part of the *vilayet* of Beirut. The land east of the Jordan formed part of the *vilayet* of Damascus. Such rigour as did obtain was to be found, naturally enough, in the *mutasarrıflık* of Jerusalem; in the north attitudes to the entire issue were more serene. Finally, the people upon whom the execution of the laws devolved in practice were not, as a class, famous for their integrity: a British vice-consul in Haifa concluded a report on the *yishuv* in the northern part of the country with the observation that 'Foreign Jews are not supposed to be allowed to settle in this country, but Jewish settlers from Europe often arrive in Haifa where there seem to be exceptional facilities for their admission by pecuniary arrangement with the local officials.'[7] Of course, for conscientious senior officials, and they were not rare, the situation was intolerable and *their* reaction to the spectacle was liable to be hot. 'What we are concerned with', wrote the district officer in Jaffa in 1907, summing matters up and outlining proposals for action, 'is an important and dangerous element which, in the future, will hold out the threat of most serious injury to the District of Jaffa, the country of Palestine, and, by extension, to the exalted Government in its entirety. These are the foreign Jews who stream here in their hundreds each week and, possibly, each day.'[8] His numbers were exaggerated,[9] his prophecy of gloom uncalled for, the picture of semi-criminal elements implied in his report absurd, but the *kaymakam*'s detailed account of crowds of people set upon entering the country by hook or by crook was fair enough. This, indeed, was how the *yishuv* had been built up; these were the techniques which the Hovevei Zion and the Zionists had learned to employ over the years—with little pleasure, but with the conviction that they were necessary and justified; and this, in a word, was the 'infiltration' into Erez-Israel which Herzl detested and which he was intent on bringing to an end.

Herzl was opposed to 'infiltration' because it was demeaning,

[7] Monahan to Drummond Hay (Consul-General in Beirut), 5 February 1900. PRO, Foreign Office Confidential Print, 19 March 1900, section 2, enclosure 2 in no. 1.

[8] The *kaymakam* of Jaffa to the *mutasarrıf* of Jerusalem, 26 June 1907. Israel State Archives, 'Teʿudot mi-tokh arkhion ha-mutaẓarif bi-Yerushalaim 1906–1908' (Jerusalem, 1962).

[9] Total Jewish immigration between 1882 and 1914 amounted to 55 70,000 or some 2,000 a year on average.

because it could only work on a very small scale and was therefore irrelevant to the vast problem *he* was intent on dealing with, and finally because he judged it must be poisoning relations with the Turks. He wanted to work with the Turks, not against them. It was true that when he paid his first visit to Constantinople in June 1896[10] they had rejected his fundamental idea, namely that in exchange for the grant of autonomy to the Jews in Erez-Israel Jewish financial resources would be used to relieve the Turks of the humiliating arrangement whereby a large part of the national revenues was collected by foreigners and devoted to the servicing of Turkey's foreign creditors. And later, from time to time, there were private, but also public denunciations of his plan.

There seems to be a prevailing idea in this country that only a monetary consideration is involved in this plan now being agitated in high Hebrew circles over the proposed purchase of Palestine [the Turkish Minister in Washington stated in 1899, following guidance from home]. I can assure the American people that such is not the state of affairs. The Sublime Porte does not desire to sell any parts of its Arabian country and no matter how many millions of gold are offered this determination will not be altered.[11]

The effect of such statements as these was, of course, to alarm the old-school Zionists who thought it an error to raise fundamental questions in Constantinople—the effort being doomed to failure from the start—and who pointed out, correctly, that the screws had only been tightened since the appearance on the scene of Herzl, the Congress, and political Zionism generally. Better to keep to the quieter, incrementalist ways of Ḥibbat Ẓion, they thought: there would at least be something tangible to show for one's pains at the end of the day's work—and the Turks had grown accustomed to it all, or would end up being so. But Herzl took comfort in the fact that there had been no overt hostility towards him when he was at the Porte and at the Palace. He had been treated politely. And there had been a promising ambivalence in the terms of the rejection of his central idea: the notion that a Jewish

[10] See *Origins*, pp. 280–98.
[11] *Jewish Chronicle*, 12 May 1899.

autonomous province should be set up in Erez-Israel had indeed been turned down flat, but its complement, the idea that Jewish financial resources be mobilized in the Ottoman interest, had not been so entirely. His right to speak on behalf of the Jews (a full year before the First Congress), in fact the right of anyone at all to speak on their behalf, or of the Jews themselves to have legitimate collective interests and purposes, had not been questioned. In Turkey it did not seem unnatural. And moreover, certain officials at the very heart of affairs, in the Sultan's personal establishment at the Yildiz Kiosk as well as in the Government proper, the Sublime Porte, had indicated that they were prepared to help if suitably rewarded and Herzl, for his part, had grimly accepted the prospect of oiling the machinery of state with bribes. All in all, it seemed reasonable to him to judge the journey as something better than a plain failure. He was sure he was free to return to Constantinople to try again. He was equally sure, however, that there was no point in returning without something substantial to offer.

The Turks had not reacted publicly to the convening of the Congress and the foundation of the Zionist Organization. But they had taken careful note of it; and henceforth, at the Foreign Ministry's demand, received fairly regular reports on the Zionists—and on their Congresses, in particular—from Turkish diplomatic missions abroad. In the course of time a considerable dossier on the 'question of Zionism', as it was labelled, accumulated. The dispatches, based partly on press reports and partly on informants, were generally well founded. Some were hostile in tone; most were matter-of-fact. Occasionally a nice appreciation of the character, ultimate purposes, and immediate weaknesses of the new movement was shown. Since their Congress at Basel the Zionists seemed to have redoubled their efforts to put their project into execution, the Ottoman Ambassador in London reported early on. Just what they intended was still unclear, he pointed out; there was much that was 'vague and indeterminate' about their programme. They evidently had in mind a sort of autonomous, tributary state in Palestine under the Sultan's suzerainty, but under international legal safeguards as well. And they believed, with the example of the existing, flourishing Jewish settlements in the country before them, that a large injection of funds and an adequate use of modern economic techniques would ensure sufficiently rapid development for the expected influx of great numbers of European Jews to be catered for. However, whether the enormous sums of money they needed would be available to them was doubtful, the Ambassador thought. The Zionists themselves admitted that their most hostile opponents were neither Muslims nor Christians, 'but Jews themselves, especially those who are rich and have not the slightest inclination to exchange their comfort, their habits, their contact with all that is most brilliant and elevated in the great capitals of Europe for a restricted and modest existence in Palestine. Thus far, not a single big Jewish bank has agreed to help them.'[12]

In this he was correct. It had been Herzl's hope to persuade the plutocracy of Jewry to put up the funds with which to pursue negotiations with the Turks. The hope was soon dashed;[13] whereupon he reverted to the broad plan of campaign outlined in his programmatic pamphlet *Der Judenstaat*. First he called a Congress of Zionists and set up the Zionist Organization as a mass movement—as a stick with which to beat the rich men who had turned him down and as just that public demonstration of Jewish unity and national purpose which they feared. It was also the 'Society of Jews' which he had envisaged in *Der Judenstaat*. There then remained the 'Jewish Company', the financial arm of the movement, the national Bank of the Jews. Once set up, funds would flow into it from all sources, Herzl was sure, from the little people in small amounts and, in due course, from the great men in large. And so to it, first named the Jewish Colonial Bank, then re-named the Jewish Colonial Trust, he now devoted much of his time and a good part of his own fast-dwindling private resources. His files for the years 1898–1902 are crammed with letters which instruct and cajole and argue with his associates about the Bank and its affairs, to the great irritation of those among them who were real business and banking professionals and to the impatience of those who were not. Herzl's Bank

[12] Anthopoulos to Tevfik Pasha (Foreign Minister), 8 June 1898. OFMA, file C/332–D/17, 23598/216.
[13] *Origins*, pp. 299–308.

would end as a modest affair. Not until 1902 was it able to show the quarter of a million pounds sterling it needed finally to open its doors;[14] and there was never to be any question of its providing funds on a sufficient scale to ease the Turks' financial dependence on the European Powers.

Herzl's persistence was due to his belief that to drop Turkey was to drop everything and that the ultimate key to Turkey had to be of gold. Equally, he continued to press for a personal interview with the Sultan (denied him on his first visit to Constantinople, when he had to be satisfied with the Grand Vizier). And he did not relax his opposition to 'infiltration'. He only softened it by becoming firmer in public on the principle that Zionism referred solely to Erez-Israel[15] and by proposing a joint technical mission of inquiry with the Odessa Committee and other settlement societies to take a systematic look at the country's agricultural, industrial, and commercial potential. The formula for what was asked of Turkey underwent change: not a state nor, necessarily, an autonomous territory. It could be settlement by formal Charter to be granted by the Sultan, a public act by which the civil and military duties, but also the rights, of the settlers would be specified. But that at least. He would not have it whittled down further. A mere *ferman*, he explained to Tchlenov, would not do. A *ferman* was one-sided, an edict which could be revoked or amended. In contrast, a Charter was in the nature of a contract and was not susceptible to change except by agreement of both sides.[16] There *had* to be an element of public guarantee. There had to be a special relationship, founded on mutual advantage, between the Government and the Company. The political quality of what was proposed to Turks as well as to Jews could not and would not be entirely dissolved. But since this was precisely what the Turks would not allow, the question how, if at all, they could be persuaded to change their

---

[14] The Trust's authorized capital was £2,500,000. Two years after its incorporation in 1899 paid-up capital was still less than £200,000.

[15] For example: Herzl refused to support a scheme for Jewish settlement in Cyprus because it ran counter to the letter of the Basel Programme. (Herzl to Heinrich Rosenbaum, Jassy, 22 or 23 October 1899. *Igrot Herzl*, iv.)

[16] Herzl to Tchlenov, early January 1900, *Igrot Herzl*, iv. The model in Herzl's mind was Cecil Rhodes's Chartered Company. Herzl to Bodenheimer, 5 September 1899, ibid.

minds echoed and re-echoed down the corridors of Herzl's mind—and of the minds of his successors for years to come.

iii

Herzl's diplomacy at this early stage may be seen as an instance of the effect produced when the clarity and strength of the statesman's purposes are so great as to diminish his ability to perceive and assess his real political possibilities. The effect was the sharper for there being embodied in him at this time virtually all the decision-making and decision-implementing functions that in conventional and orderly diplomatic machinery—even where dominated by exceptionally powerful individuals—are commonly divided up amongst many: those who gather information, those who examine it, those who formulate recommendations for policy, those who decide, and those who execute decisions and then report back on the immediate consequences of their having been taken. True, it is rarely the case that particular politicians or functionaries are limited, or limit themselves, to single, narrowly defined functions. But it is rarer still for all, or even for a great many of the significant functions to be performed by a single, unaided person. A consequence in Herzl's case was that while some of the functions were performed well, and even brilliantly, others were neglected—because their importance was never grasped, or because Herzl was temperamentally unsuited to their performance, or because no man acting virtually alone could have performed them adequately, or, finally and perhaps decisively, because, faced with the eternal political tension between means and ends, it was to the ends that Herzl's thinking was best geared. It was in the definition of ends—of goals and purposes for the people he proposed to lead—that he was at his most original and effective and, indeed, impressive.

To the selection of means, to the appreciation of the environment in which he sought to operate, and to the assessment of the forces with which he would necessarily have to contend, to this duller, often depressing, ostensibly harder, but almost equally vital political work he tended to apply himself less assiduously—at all events at this initial stage of his career—certainly less systematically, and with results that betrayed him as an amateur in an arena dominated by professionals. There is, for example, no evidence to suggest that after his initial, admittedly somewhat delicate rebuff in Constantinople in 1896 he paused to consider what there might have been in it to teach him. He did not apply himself to a study of the Ottoman system. He did not even make a thorough search for new sources and contact men within it. There is a fleeting reference in his diary to the possibility that his entire grand strategy might have to be revised (because 'the poor masses need immediate help, and Turkey is not yet so desperate as to accede to our wishes');[17] but the idea is not pursued, let alone acted on seriously for several years. And in any case the fundamental thesis that a deal could be concluded with the Sultan remained unexamined. For the time being, his response to the initial set-back was, as it were, tactical. The movement had to be expanded, the Jewish communities of the Diaspora 'captured' for Zionism, and the opposition within Jewry won over, or neutralized, or shamed into silence. Zionism had to be established as a recognized and constituent element of the world of high politics. Political support to help tip the balance of the calculation in Turkey in his favour was to be hunted. And these three, mutually reinforcing lines of activity were to be pursued in tandem with the fourth: his contacts in Turkey and his effort to prize the gate to Ereẓ-Israel open by frontal attack. Herzl's policy, it can be said, was to try everything that was, or might conceivably be, useful and to keep up the momentum at all costs. Zionism must be made to appear as confident and representative and strong as possible. Weakness and poverty had to be overcome; and, until overcome, so far

---

[17] *Diaries*, ii, p. 644. The full entry is as follows:
'I am thinking of giving the movement a closer territorial goal, preserving Zion as the final goal.

The poor masses need immediate help, and Turkey is not yet so desperate as to accede to our wishes.

In fact, there will probably be hostile demonstrations against us in Turkey in the immediate future. They will say that they have no intention of giving us Palestine.

Thus we must organize ourselves for a goal attainable soon, under the Zion flag and maintaining all of our historic claims.

Perhaps we can demand Cyprus from England, and even keep an eye on South Africa or America—until Turkey is dissolved.

C'est encore à creuser profondément. [This is still to be thoroughly explored.] Discuss with Nordau before the Congress.'

as possible, hidden.[18] The Zionists had to begin to be accepted
as natural and legitimate members of the international
community, politically *salonfähig*, real potential partners for
serious business.

Accordingly Herzl pressed for an entrée to any circle or to
any public figure who might ultimately serve as the Archimedean point on which the final and successful effort would
turn. He sought the aid of the Poet Laureate of England to
obtain an interview with Lord Salisbury. He tried to put the
Zionist case before the Vatican. He asked the Grand Duke of
Hesse to try to get him received by his brother-in-law, the
Emperor of Russia. The catalogue is long and varied, the particular cases often odd, the over-all logic clear and simple. But
there were internal contractions too in all this activity. How
could the Zionists offer themselves as allies to the Turks in
Turkey's campaign of defence against the political and
economic encroachment of the Powers and at the same time
seek a relationship with one or more of the Powers in the
interests of applying pressure, however friendly, however
innocent of design, against Turkey, on Turkey itself? Could
the attempt to recruit Russian diplomatic support be squared
with the plainest of all facts of the contemporary Jewish scene:
that it was Russian internal policy that was the prime cause of
the great migration of Jews that made the restoration of the
Jewish state a sensible plan, rather than merely a pious thought?
In the event, the paradox was only apparent and Herzl's
intuition turned out to have some basis in fact. But there remains an unmistakable touch of the nervous and the compulsive
in the constant, restless pressure to which Herzl subjected
himself and others in this quest for any increment of influence
and power, however small, that would make the difference
for him and help complete the structure.

---

[18] It is characteristic of the difference between Aḥad Ha-ʿAm and Herzl that when
the former queried the plan to set up a financial institution on the grounds that the
funds available would very likely be so small as to disgrace the movement, the latter
replied, 'Well, what of it? If the sum is very small we will tell no one, and it will
remain our secret.' Aḥad Ha-ʿAm was shocked. Letter to Tchlenov, 7 October 1898.
Igrot AH, ii, p. 146.

3

Seeking an Ally (I)

i

In form, the Second Congress of Zionists (at Basel, 28–31 August 1898) was much like the First: the same attention to detail, the same effort (as the local French consul reported to Paris) to 'impart consequence and a degree of pomp to [its] sessions',[1] the set-piece opening with a programmatic speech by Herzl and a review of the Jewish condition by Nordau, and, once more, some moments of high emotion as hope for revolutionary change in that condition gripped the delegates.

The scale was larger. The number of delegates (349) was close to double that of the previous year. The number of journalists attending was put at 150. A larger hall had been taken for the sessions.

The composition of the assembly too was much as before. There was a handful of new, notable faces from the West of the kind by which Herzl set such store, among them Bernard Lazare, one of the heroes of the campaign to vindicate Dreyfus, Moses Gaster, the Ḥakham (Chief Sephardi Rabbi) of Great Britain, and Richard Gottheil, a Professor of Semitics at Columbia University in New York who was later to lead the Zionist movement in America. There was also the small group of orthodox rabbis from the East, set apart from the others by their fundamental outlook, much sharpened by the disgruntled mood in which they had arrived after the clash in Warsaw. But, broadly, it was the elements which had formed the ranks of Ḥibbat Zion in Russia and Russian Poland, in Austrian Poland (Galicia), and in Romania before Herzl and which

---

[1] Audisio (?) to Delcassé, 1 September 1898. Ministère des Affairs Étrangères, Archives. Correspondence Politique. Turquie, nouvelle série, vol. 136.

had already appeared in force at his First Congress that
dominated: the modernist, but non-assimilationist wing of
contemporary east European Jewry. The difference was that
this time the delegates had been chosen by a process of local
election by the newly formed local Zionist associations throughout the world; and the Second Congress was thus a representative body in a sense (the formal sense) in which the First had
not been.

The results were soon evident. The delegates, the Russians
most notably,[2] were less inhibited about participating in
open debate than before. Many had come determined from
the start, as we have seen, to bring their views and influence to
bear. Those who were of like mind on particular topics
showed a will and some capacity to work together. And one
result of all this was that the full diversity of opinion within the
Zionist camp was in evidence as never before. When to this is
added the external impact of the Congress on the city of Basel,
of some hundreds of delegates with their distinctive lapel-
badges, along with their hangers-on and with the flags and
the posters in the streets, Herzl's immediate purpose—to
confirm and make visible the vitality and authenticity of his
movement and so renew his own mandate—may be said to have
been achieved handily.

The main business of the movement at this stage was not
up for public discussion: external, diplomatic policy was
only alluded to in very general terms. Indiscreet 'people who
always want to be kept up to date on just what the Actions
Committee is doing' had been warned off by Herzl even
before the Congress assembled.[3] The main items on the
agenda were matters internal to the movement and, by extension, to Jewry and to the activity of the Zionists within Jewry.
Apart from the project to establish a Bank as the movement's
financial arm, there was nothing here that greatly interested
Herzl, except where he feared the results might obstruct his
diplomacy, but there was much to interest other delegates.
The upshot was that the Second Congress, unlike the First,
was free to be inward-looking—as many had anticipated and

[2] The Russians had been generally silent the year before, not being sure of their
ground, or of Herzl's, and fearing trouble with the state police on their return.
[3] 'Der Congress', *Die Welt*, 26 August 1898.

some had explicitly desired.[4] Questions of ethos and general principle, rather than tactics, were to the fore almost throughout. And as the world outside receded in the delegates' minds (although never in Herzl's), and as they grew accustomed to, and began to enjoy, the parliamentary situation, and as the tide of debate swept them along, the contrast between the complexity of the Zionist scene and the simplicity of Herzl's original design became fully apparent.

Herzl's opening address[5] was cast in terms that were typically brief and clear. In part it was an answer to critics of Zionism and a restatement of his conception of the logic which underlay it.

From that emancipation, which cannot be revoked, and from anti-Semitism, which cannot be denied, we were able to draw a new and important conclusion. It could not have been the historical intent [*der geschichtliche Sinn*] of emancipation that we should cease to be Jews, for when we tried to mingle with the others we were rebuffed. Rather, the historical intent of emancipation must have been that we were to create a homeland for our liberated nation. We would not have been able to do this earlier. We can do it now, if we desire it with all our might.

In part, too, it was a restatement of the argument that only advantages would accrue to the Turks, on the one hand, and to the Powers, on the other, by the return home of 'the most unfortunate of peoples' to a land that, 'by reason of its geographical position, [was] of immense importance to the whole of Europe'. The Turks, for all their virtues, 'do not possess the qualities that are needed to cultivate and industrialize a country'. The Powers, for their part, have a common interest in its not falling into the hands of one of their number.

But his principal theme was a call for action within Jewry itself. Zionism had met internal hostility, notably from the rabbis. 'It will always be one of the great curiosities of our period', Herzl told the Congress to loud applause, 'that these gentlemen should be praying for Zion and working against it

---

[4] For example: Mordechai Ehrenpreis, *Ra'ayonot 'al devar ha-kongres ha-zioni ha-sheini* (pamphlet) (Berlin, 1898).

[5] *Protokoll II*, pp. 3–11. English translation by Harry Zohn in *Zionist Writings*, ii (New York, 1975), pp. 14–23.

at the same time.' But the Zionist idea could not remain dependent upon the sympathies of the present secular leaders of the various Jewish communities and on 'the utilitarian considerations of their spiritual leaders'. The communities were formed of masses, he declared, the masses almost everywhere supported Zionism. Agitation against Zionism within the communities was therefore intolerable and had to be ended—but by methods that were honourable, legal, and democratic, by fair debate, and through the ballot box. The communities must be 'won' for Zionism. 'It is not enough that we alone should know the extent to which the Zionist idea has gripped Jewry; the facts must be demonstrated.'[6]

These were fair points; and 'the winning of the communities' for Zionism was a good slogan. But the notion that 'almost everywhere the great masses are for us' was, to put it no more strongly, untested. No figures were published then (or later) to show how many members of the rank and file the some 350 delegates represented. In Russia orderly records could not be kept for fear of the police. Without the Russians the figures, even if they could have been collated, would have been misleading. The most reliable guide to strength, up to the outbreak of the First World War, was the movement's income from the *shekel*—the small membership-fee which entitled whoever paid it to vote in the elections to the Congress. But at this Congress Herzl refused to allow the full financial statement of the movement for the year to be published, for fear the poverty of its resources and the thinness of its ranks be revealed. The entirely decent treasurer was embarrassed. Many delegates were dismayed. But Herzl held firm, as he generally did when matters likely to affect his political work were in question. All he was prepared to have made known was the number of local associations world-wide: 913 in all; and the breakdown by country: 373 associations in Russia, 250 in Austria-Hungary, 127 in Romania, and so forth, down to 1 in Denmark.[7] These were encouraging figures so far as they went, but there was no way of knowing whether a particular local association numbered hundreds of members or half a dozen; and, accordingly, the number of delegates to the

[6] Ibid.
[7] *Protokoll II*, p. 47.

Congress was an equally unreliable clue to total membership in these early years. The only firm figures were financial—confidential at the time, but even on later inspection difficult to interpret. Income from the *shekel* membership-fees for the year 1897/8 was recorded as Kr. 80,000.[8] But allowance has to be made for the fact that the Russian country association kept back half of its income, for distortions due to the variety of currencies in which the fees were collected, and to such minor anomalies as the fact that no payment was recorded from some minor country associations, Greece and Turkey among them. Taking all this together, however, and comparing it with estimates of membership in Ḥibbat Ẓion in earlier years, it seems likely that the movement's total membership at the time of the Second Congress was well under 100,000, or roughly 1 per cent of all Jewry.[9] Herzl's reluctance to publish figures is then readily understandable, as is his insistent wooing of the orthodox (more insistent than his attacks on them); for, without the rabbis' sanction or, at the very least, their benevolent neutrality, the Zionists' capacity to 'win' the communities was in doubt. Meanwhile, as the ensuing debates showed clearly, it would be hard enough to win the avowed Zionists themselves for ideas and plans—Herzl's or anyone else's—on which all could agree.

The first division in the ranks, not much more than a crack at this early stage, was between those who were already, or were in process of becoming, Herzl loyalists and those in whom Herzl aroused disquiet, even a slight measure of distrust, but who, being unwilling and unable to deny him either their grudging admiration or the commanding role he had assumed, were subject to repeated bouts of half-conscious irritation. Herzl's own growing self-confidence, his efficient, but lordly way of acting through assistants, his refusal to take even the veterans completely into his confidence, and his totally secular, non-Jewish culture, alienated him from many delegates. His very success at handling the Congress in its noisiest

[8] CZA, Z 1/444.

[9] A correspondent for the *Jewish Chronicle* (2 September 1898) reported 'on the authority of one who knows' that the movement's income for the year was £12,000 and the number of adherents therefore about 250,000. This seems extremely unlikely. The latter figure is not credible. On the further, numerical growth of the movement in its early years, see below, p. 413 n. 1.

moments—but at the price of stopping debate before all had
had their say in the admittedly exhausting, untidy, but more
generous manner to which the easterners were accustomed—
and the fact that the debates were in German, the translations
inadequate, and the Yiddish and Russian speakers (and the
French and English speakers with them) therefore at a disadvantage, these too were points of surface friction. In conjunction, they encouraged a just-perceptible tendency of the
irritated to see themselves cast for the role of an opposition. The
tone of *private* debate within the Russian caucus was often
furious: 'They wish to avoid us, to trick us . . . They treat us as
children. We are responsible before those who elected and
sent us. What shall we tell them [when we return]?'[10] In the
plenum there was more restraint. Herzl was prepared to
retreat gracefully when necessary; and the opposition, such
as it was, remained loyal and always amenable, in the last
resort, to arguments against rocking the boat. The result was
a series of pacifying victories for the Ḥibbat Zion school in
line, more or less, with what the Russians among them had
resolved on in Warsaw—but minor victories and, for the most
part, formal victories, some of which Aḥad Ha-'Am, from a
distance, severe as ever, was quick to judge as being tainted
with 'sophistry'.[11]

The issues on which the Herzlians and the embryonic
opposition were divided were formidable, as we have seen.
On the question of further settlement in Ereẓ-Israel and whether
it should be entirely subject to progress at the political level,
that is to say, postponed until the Jews were able to settle
there as of right and by formal agreement, the answer given
was unclear. The Congress resolved that settlement would
indeed continue (a formal victory for the Ḥibbat Zion school),
but only subject to permission being granted by the Turkish
Government and in line with plans laid down by a committee
of the Congress (a *de facto* victory for the Herzlian, anti-
'infiltration' school).

[10] Yeḥiel Tchlenov, 'Ha-kongres ha-ẓioni ha-sheini ve-ha-ve'idot she-kadmu lo',
in S. Eisenstadt (ed.), *Yeḥiel Tchlenov* (Tel-Aviv, 1937), p. 150. This, Tchlenov's
detailed and balanced report on the Congress, was written while its events and atmosphere were fresh in his mind.
[11] Aḥad Ha-'Am to Tchlenov, 19 September 1898. *Igrot AH*, ii, p. 137.

On the question of Erez-Israel itself, its absolute primacy in the Zionist scheme of things was reaffirmed and latent suspicion of Herzl on this score largely allayed by a change in the wording of the draft Charter for the Bank. It had been originally laid down that the Bank would operate in the 'Orient'. But, led by Menaḥem Ussishkin, delegates from the East pressed for the sphere of operations to be defined specifically as 'Erez-Israel and Syria'. With Turkish sensibilities in mind, Herzl had wanted a looser wording, but he accepted the change.

Formally, the Congress resolved on a programme of mass, modern education and re-education, very much in the spirit of Aḥad Ha-ʿAm's conception of intellectual and moral renewal as the condition of political and social advance. The problem of Jewish orthodoxy and rabbinical authority was thus brought to a head, as it had come to a head in Warsaw, and the results were just those that the Herzlians had wished to avoid. The Congress refused to accept rabbinical authority and supervision in matters of education and culture. The rabbis from eastern Europe (who were the ones who counted for these purposes) thereupon left Basel in a bitter mood, their bitterness compounded by the belief that they had been led at an early stage of the proceedings into thinking that things would be moved in their direction after all.[12] On their return to Russia they launched a public counter-attack and the process whereby the orthodox began to make up their minds about Zionism finally, with the great majority evolving an increasingly clear-cut and hostile stand against it, was begun. The modernist majority had not in fact precipitated the break deliberately. There was nothing to suggest that they had thought the issue through and made up their minds on the basis of what they judged possible and desirable in relations between their own movement and orthodoxy. They wanted their own way, of course. They offered mutual toleration. They did not want a quarrel. There were few among them who could bring themselves to contemplate separation from what almost all of them still accepted as the supreme embodiment of the Jewish tradition. Fewer still wished to burn what they believed, half-intuitively, to be the bridge

[12] Israel Klausner, *Opoziẓia le-Herzl* (Jerusalem, 1960), pp. 29–34.

over which the Jewish 'masses' would eventually march over to their side. On what should be done in the face of the rabbis' refusal to accept mutual toleration as a basis for relations (for fear of erosion of their own straightforward, fundamentalist position, whence, as they knew, their moral and social authority derived) they were confused and divided. And what this meant in practice was that most were for patience and muddling through. Some, following Herzl's lead, thought that action for 'culture' was best postponed, that the rabbis must not be antagonized, and that once the state was won, the problem would be settled as elsewhere, with the 'Church' acquiescing to the superior authority of the secular government. 'We shall keep our priests within the confines of their temples', Herzl had written in his original manifesto, 'in the same way as we shall keep our professional army within the confines of their barracks.'[13] Until then, the Zionists must keep from breaking up into parties, from being deflected from the *political* purpose they had set themselves.

Among the very few, however, who did favour an uncompromising line with the orthodox were the socialists. Doctrinaire secularism governed their theoretical view; so far as tactics were concerned, they were sure they could construct a stronger, broader bridge to the people than any the orthodox could provide. But as ideologues they came up against Herzl's opposition to all that he judged to be extraneous to the central purposes of Zionism and to his own loose, but rather grand conception of the movement. As Nordau had put it in his address at the opening, 'The Zionists are not a party; they are Jewry itself.'[14] Besides, while the problem of religious orthodoxy versus modernism was internal to Jewry, class politics were not. Herzl wanted the movement to steer clear of any involvement in the domestic politics of any of the states in which it functioned. He believed strongly in the efficacy of the argument he constantly employed, that Zionism would help divert the Jewish working classes and the Jewish intelligentsia away from revolutionary movements and was therefore deserving of support from the Powers. True, his own ideological bent was markedly towards social reform and there

[13] *Der Judenstaat*, Chapter V.
[14] *Protokoll II*, p. 27.

was an unmistakable populist strain in his dislike of the Jewish plutocracy and his attacks on them. Moreover, in practice, the direction in which he proposed to lead the nationalist tendency in Jewry was designed to bring massive, thoroughgoing help for the impoverished and the miserable—the Jewish 'masses' of eastern Europe. There was thus much here, and in him, to attract such populists and socialists as had lost confidence in the promise of orthodox socialism and the goodwill of orthodox internationalist socialism to deal with the problems of the Jews. Yet there was also much to disappoint them.

Among the men of the Left at the Congress the best known by far was Bernard Lazare. In some respects he was of the type Herzl himself represented. Lazare had moved from a position of doctrinaire assimilationism, not untouched by hostility to some elements of Jewry, especially the east European,[15] to a demand for Jewish national salvation based on self-respect and specific treatment for specific ills.[16] Like Herzl he had become a nationalist by clear decision. His Zionism was explicit, passionate, and imbued with an overwhelming sense of urgency and profound commiseration for the unfortunates of eastern Europe. But there were differences. He saw the Jews as a broken people to be *re-created*, scarcely a people at all. He had brought his social outlook, anarchist as much as socialist, with him into the Zionist camp and sought, no doubt unconsciously, to adapt his newly developed views on Jewry to it. When he broke with Herzl soon after the Congress it was partly because he disliked Herzl's authoritarian ways and partly because he had perceived, correctly, that whereas his own populism was fundamental and intrinsic to his feeling on both the national and the social questions, Herzl's, in essence, was tactical. The Zionist movement was unalterably middle-class, in Lazare's view.

You are bourgeois in your thinking, [he wrote to Herzl,] bourgeois in sentiment, bourgeois in your social outlook. Being such, you wish to guide a people, our people, which is a people of the poor,

[15] *Origins*, p. 210.
[16] On Lazare's views on Jewish problems see especially Edmund Silberner, 'Bernard Lazare ve-ha-ẓionut', *Shivat Ẓion*, ii–iii (1951–2), pp. 328–63; Robert S. Wistrich, *Revolutionary Jews from Marx to Trotsky* (London, 1976), pp. 133–52; and the posthumous collection of Lazare's essays, *Job's Dungheap* (New York, 1948).

of the unhappy, a people of proletarians. You can only do so in an authoritarian manner, or wishing to direct them towards that which you think is best for them. Thus you act outside them and above them: you wish to herd them along. Before creating a people you set up a government, you act financially and diplomatically and so, like all governments, you are at the mercy of your financial and diplomatic set-backs. Like all governments, you wish to gloss over the truth, to be the government of a people that makes a good impression, and it becomes your highest duty 'not to display national disgraces'. But I want them displayed so that poor Job may be seen on his dunghill scratching his sores with a piece of broken bottle. We are dying of having concealed our disgraces, of having hidden them away in deep cellars, instead of taking them out into the clean air where the great sun will purify and cauterize them. Our people is embedded in the meanest mire: we must roll up our sleeves and set out to look for them there where they moan, there where they suffer. Our nation must be re-created, that is what I would judge to be a solid enterprise, a strong enterprise, and above all the enterprise to be undertaken first. They must be taught, shown what they are, caused to grow in their own esteem so that they grow in the esteem of others, and their hearts and their spirits are raised. Then they will be able to take their place. Jewish schools, that is what the prime enterprise of the Zionist should be, and schools where our proletariat are brought up democratically. That is what I think, what I want, what you do not do, what you do not want.[17]

He had particularly detested the Bank project and had tried to persuade the Congress to reject it or, at the very least, postpone a decision on it for a year. In public, he had limited himself to the argument that the project had been ill prepared; that it was improper and undemocratic to take such important decisions hastily; and that the Jewish people should be given time to consider it.[18] In private, he wrote to Herzl:

Your mistake is to have wanted to make a bank the engine of your enterprise; a bank is never, will never be an instrument of national recovery and how ironic to make a bank the founder of the Jewish nation! Ezra and Nehemiah and Zerubbabel took the blade and the law, the word and the sword with them, and they had the [strong] arms of the poor, for they had left the rich behind in Babylon.[19]

[17] Lazare to Herzl, 4 February 1899. CZA, H VIII 479/11. Text also in Silberner, p. 358.
[18] *Protokoll II*, p. 175.
[19] Lazare to Herzl, 4 February 1899, Silberner, ibid.

However, the intellectual journey travelled by Lazare's fellow socialists from *eastern* Europe had been in the opposite direction. It was socialism they had discovered, not the people-hood of the Jews. The latter was in their bones. It did not occur to them to think it due for re-creation—as distinct from reform. When they came to socialism they sought to apply its categories and characteristic forms of analysis to the Jewish condition. What they did in fact, and did best, as we shall see, was to subject socialism itself to a new critique and, in time, to provide it with new models of action. That was in the future. Mean-while, at this Congress they wearied Herzl and his closest followers with their protests and loud interjections. They attacked the rabbis; they attacked the Bank project (where they were at one with Lazare); and they attacked Herzl himself for having dared to suggest that the Jews' great and undoubted enemy, the Russian Emperor, be congratulated on having proposed an international peace conference at The Hague (and were, for once, at one with all the easterners and many others too). They demanded representation for the Jewish proletariat *per se* in the institutions of the movement and comprehensive discussion of workers' conditions in the Con-gress. Their most brilliant representative, Naḥman Syrkin, stated the view (amid loud protest) that the new society to be built in Ereẓ-Israel should be collectivist.

Throughout, Herzl deflected the socialists with skill, without loss of nerve, and with great care to avoid a break. When, during the long, final, late-night session, one of their number (S. R. Landau) brought up the 'class question' Herzl pounced on him. 'We are ready to sacrifice the night to talk of Zionism, but even if we were to remain awake all night we would fail to solve the social question', he said and was rewarded with cheers and laughter in the hall.[20] But when Mandelstamm lost his patience and demanded the 'exclusion of all socialists' from the Congress, Herzl merely remarked, to renewed cheers, that 'of course, I shall not take Professor Mandelstamm's proposal into consideration'.[21] Finally, at half past four in the morning of 31 August, it was over. Herzl had approval for his Bank; and his own personal

[20] *Protokoll II*, p. 224.
[21] Ibid., p. 226.

mandate as leader of the movement had been renewed without question or dissent. What else, if anything, had been settled remained unclear.

The Congress, in the final analysis, was an assembly of men of goodwill and roughly similar views. In their vast majority they regarded their coming together as the fact of greatest significance. None doubted that the divisions within the movement were no less than reflections of the problems of Jewry itself and of the lines of conflicting schools of thought within it. Only the orthodox at one end of the scale and the socialists at the other were sure, each in their way, that they knew what was to be done and what choices were to be made. The rest wavered; and, wavering, were willing, if not content, to see what Herzl could do for them. If his diplomacy succeeded, the terms of Jewish life would be recast dramatically. If it did not, there would be no choice but to avert their gaze from the future and their attention from plans to attain it; and to reconsider the bitter, painful, and intractable present.

ii

Immediately after the Congress Herzl left Basel for Lake Constance where, at Mainau Castle, he was to meet the Grand Duke of Baden. The irritations and frustrations of the Congress were behind him. The exhaustion dropped away. There is no mistaking his sense of release and exhilaration as he reassumes his role of champion. His recording of the Congress in his diary is almost laconic. In contrast, his notes on his talk with the Grand Duke are detailed and studded with observations on his own state of mind, and on such details as the appearance of the lackeys and officers who inhabited the castle, the Grand Duke's dress, and precisely how he and the Grand Duke were seated during the conversation. The enormous satisfaction with which he records the ambience is plain.

The conversation was downright grandiose, highly political. If I were to publish it today, it would be a sensation for all of Europe. The Grand Duke conversed with me in the most candid manner about all of world politics, and from each of his kindly words there shone benevolence toward me and good will for the cause. But he also gave me a magnificent demonstration of his confidence by discussing with me the most secret German political matters and speaking unreservedly about the intentions of the Kaiser.[22]

This was Herzl's second meeting with the Grand Duke Friedrich I. His meeting with him two years earlier, at Karlsruhe, had been his first confrontation in the Zionist interest with a figure of real political and social note. It had been before his decision to call a Congress and form a movement: he appeared as a private individual. The meeting had been arranged by William Hechler, the chaplain at the British Embassy in Vienna, but half-German in origin and a former tutor to the Grand Duke's children. Hechler was a crank who had long before calculated that the Restoration of the Jews to Erez-Israel was nigh and had seen in Herzl's appearance on the scene early in 1896 first evidence of the truth of his prediction. He talked a certain amount of nonsense and was often a source of mild embarrassment to Herzl. But he was genuine, well-meaning, and no fool (when all was said and done). He knew his way around eminent circles in Germany. He was glad to try to introduce Herzl to his former master and succeeded in doing so without much difficulty.[23]

Friedrich I (1826–1907) was the nominally sovereign ruler of the Grand Duchy of Baden. As such he was not without some real authority in one of the more important German states. But his importance in Herzl's eyes owed more to the fact that he was married to the daughter of the first German Kaiser, Wilhelm I—whose assumption of that title in Versailles in 1871 he himself had been the one to proclaim. The Grand Duke was a man of liberal views by the standards of the times and after the fashion of his brother-in-law, Wilhelm I's son, the Kaiser Friedrich. Nevertheless, he managed to establish cordial relations with his nephew Kaiser Wilhelm II soon after the latter's ascent to the throne in 1888 and the consequent dashing of the hopes of the liberal tendency at court. 'Fritz of Baden especially has completely changed in politics, and sails with William (i.e. the young Kaiser)', Wilhelm II's mother, the widowed Empress, complained to

---

[22] *Diaries*, ii, p. 656.
[23] For details, see *Origins*, pp. 283–6.

her mother, Queen Victoria, not long after the short reign of her husband, Friedrich III, came to an end.[24] But he kept his views to himself and did not change them much. And on the Question of the Jews he did not hide his views at all. Unlike most men of his time and class he was no anti-Semite and detested anti-Semitism. He was thus a perfect candidate for bringing Herzl's ideas, if not Herzl himself, before the Kaiser.

At first, when he had had no clearly defined purpose—apart from wanting support in such exalted quarters for the impression it would make on the public, particularly the German public—Herzl was careful not to press too hard. But after his journey to Constantinople the idea of gaining the Kaiser for the Zionist cause took on some urgency. In the summer of 1896 he 'venture[d] to . . . ask Your Royal Highness point-blank [*geradezu*] to induce His Majesty the German Kaiser to give me a hearing'.[25] Friedrich advised him to ask for one directly. Reluctant to do so, Herzl tried other avenues. When all failed him, he applied once more to the Grand Duke and through him, in an accompanying letter, to the Kaiser. In December 1897 he was informed that the Kaiser would not see him, but was prepared to read his written account of the Congress. Only in the summer of 1898, after more false attempts, did things pick up. In July the Grand Duke wrote directly to Wilhelm, speaking favourably of 'this interesting movement' and of the 'consistent and diligent work [that] is being done towards the founding of an Israelite State'. He proposed that Count Philipp zu Eulenburg, the German Ambassador in Vienna, be instructed to inform himself on the subject and he suggested a connection between Zionism and the Kaiser's coming journey to Jerusalem.[26] The Kaiser's response was friendly, but non-committal. Eulenburg would be instructed to look into the question and report back; but he thought the Zionist movement too new for its future to be relied upon and he reminded the Grand Duke that 'a large and particularly

[24] Frederick Ponsonby (ed.), *Letters of the Empress Frederick* (London, 1928), p. 351.

[25] Herzl to Grand Duke Friedrich, 1 August 1896. *Herzl, Hechler, the Grand Duke of Baden and the German Emperor 1896–1904, Documents found by Hermann and Bessi Ellern* (Tel-Aviv, 1961), no. 5, p. 20. English translation of the entire set by Harry Zohn in *Herzl Year Book*, iv (New York, 1961–2), pp. 207–70.

[26] Grand Duke Friedrich to the German Emperor, 28 July 1898. *Herzl, Hechler, etc.*, no. 12, pp. 32–5.

influential segment of Jewry is offering spirited opposition to [it]'.[27] This was the immediate background to Herzl's meeting with Friedrich of Baden after the Second Congress and it, in turn, must be seen in the context of the general character and direction of contemporary German foreign and imperial policy.

Wilhelm II's journey to the Near East in October 1898 was one of a number of spectacular manifestations of Imperial Germany's new *Weltpolitik*. It may be classed with such incidents as the affair of the Kruger telegram (1896), the seizure of the Chinese port of Kiao-Chow (1897), and a second thrust in the Far East designed to establish the Germans in the Philippines which nearly brought the ships of Admiral Dewey into action against the German squadron sent after him into Manila Bay (1898).[28] It expressed the same consciousness of power and more than a little will to use it. But in contrast to the certainty of Germany's growing material and military resources, the political ends to which its great force might be applied were, for the most part, still somewhat vague and impermanent, ill-thought-out, or extravagant, or both, pursued erratically, or else trivial and out of all reasonable relation to the main interests and concerns of Germany itself. Germany was already what Eyre Crowe, some years later, was to call 'the leading, if not, in fact, the foremost Power on the European continent'.[29] And 'everywhere Germany's presence implied conflict'.[30] Yet its presence was not always and everywhere unwelcome.

Germany's special relationship with Turkey had begun to form under Bismarck. The first German military mission left for Turkey in 1882, specifically to 'provide us', in Bismarck's words, 'with influence and informants'.[31] On the Turkish

---

[27] Wilhelm II to Grand Duke of Baden, 29 August 1898. Alex Bein, 'Zikhronot v-teʿudot ʿal pegishato shel Herzl ʿim Wilhelm ha-sheini' in *Sefer ha-yovel li-khvod N. M Gelber* (Tel-Aviv, 1963), no. 5, pp. 18–19. English translation in *Herzl Year Book*, vi (New York, 1964–5), p. 62.

[28] Nathan Sargent, *Admiral Dewey and the Manila Campaign* (Washington, D.C., 1947), pp. 67–76.

[29] G. P. Gooch and Harold Temperley (eds.), *British Documents on the Origins of the War, 1914–1918*, iii (London, 1928), p. 404.

[30] Fritz Fischer, 'World Policy, World Power and German War Aims', in H. W. Koch (ed.), *The Origins of the First World War* (London, 1972), p. 82.

[31] Marginal note by Bismarck to dispatch from Constantinople, 6 July 1880. Quoted

side, its origins lay in Turkey's military weakness, as revealed in the Russo-Turkish War of 1877–8, and Germany's prestige as the foremost military Power in Europe. On the German side, the military and economic penetration of Turkey was at one and the same time object and vehicle of policy. But it was pursued with restraint at first. Only upon the departure of Bismarck and the young Kaiser Wilhelm II's assumption of a cardinal role in the making of German policy did the penetration of Turkey begin to be pursued with energy. Constantinople was a station in the Kaiser's first journey abroad in 1889. German holdings in the Ottoman Public Debt grew, outranking the British and second only to the French. German investments in the Empire, most notably for railway construction, grew even more rapidly.

By the outbreak of the First World War Germany was the pre-eminent European Power in Turkey both economically and militarily. In contrast, British influence in Constantinople had been in decline since the time of Disraeli, rapidly so after the British occupation of Egypt and the repeated expressions of public disapproval in England of Turkish treatment of subject peoples in the 1880s. Nor was this greatly regretted in London. Salisbury thought little of Turkish progress towards political and administrative reform and hence of the long-term prospects of the Ottoman Empire. In any case, the focus of British strategic interest in the Near East had moved from the Straits to the Suez Canal; and besides, the major centres of active Great-Power rivalry were then in Africa and the Far East. All this was well understood by the contemporary diplomatic community as was the fact that Turkey's friend in Europe was now Germany. Proof of the latter's support and interest was visible and abundant: trade, money, excellent military and civilian technicians on attachment, a good ambassador (Marschall von Bieberstein), senior generals as advisers for extended periods (von der Goltz, Liman von Sanders), and a second visit by the Kaiser in 1898 during which Wilhelm followed up a pious visit to Jerusalem as a Christian monarch with a declaration in Damascus that he

---

in Jehuda L. Wallach, 'Bismarck and the "Eastern Question"—a re-assessment', in J. L. Wallach (ed.), *Germany and the Middle East, 1835–1939* (Tel-Aviv, 1975), p. 27.

was the faithful friend of all 300 million Muslims. Even so, German policy in the Levant was not absolutely consistent. It was dynamic and ambitious, but often badly focused and capricious. There was an incessant danger of the horses pulling in different directions. Among some at least of the professionals of German diplomacy there was fear lest excessive German involvement in what was unquestionably an area of secondary importance lead to dangerous consequences in the area of prime importance. It was perfectly sound to favour the pre-servation of the Ottoman Empire, the better to continue to draw material benefits from Turkey, was the Foreign Minis-try's response to an over-enthusiastic dispatch from the military attaché in Constantinople. But to go so far as to press the Sultan —and assist him—to strengthen Turkish defences against Russia was 'to overlook Germany's perilous geographical situation between France and Russia and to fail to take account of the meaning the benevolent neutrality of Russia would have for us in the event of a European conflict'.[32]

The general outlines of German policy were familiar to Herzl, but his was not systematic or detailed knowledge. His grasp of the world of high politics, even of central Europe and the Balkans, was not much better than superficial. It is worth recalling that Herzl's professional competence was that of a fashionable playwright and journalist-littérateur. He was, indeed, an excellent journalist, highly prized by his employers and a perennial candidate for an editor's chair. His particular talent was for writing clever, usually light, sometimes cutting *feuilletons*; but he had learned a great deal about a great many things in the course of time, as do all good newspaper-men. His work as a correspondent in Paris had gained him a good grasp of French politics. His first-hand knowledge of politics in Vienna was good enough for him to have been on excellent terms with two Austrian Premiers, one (Koerber) going so far as to recruit him for a while as a kind of back-stairs political adviser. This was not extraordinary. The Jews held a pivotal position in the Empire of many nationalities and there was a notable contingent of Jews in the influential Austrian press. The (still very limited) passage

---

[32] Richthofen to Bülow, 9 August 1898. *Die Grosse Politik der Europäischen Kabinette 1871–1914*, xii (Berlin, 1924), no. 3343, p. 573.

of Jews out of the familiar spheres of trade and finance and into spheres that bore directly on government was more or less accepted by the central government—with resignation, if not with pleasure. And as Jews became participants, however marginal, in political life, so they acquired familiarity with it. All this pertained to politics only in the ordinary sense of the term.

On the other side of the traditional divide between the internal affairs of the state and its external relations, the traditional exclusion of the Jews (as of other classes of subjects newly arrived on the political scene) from what were conceived of as the higher and, so to speak, the true affairs of state still remained firmly in force. Accordingly, it was a great deal rarer for a Jew to acquire a first-hand knowledge of those matters and Herzl was no exception. But Herzl's mental picture of the world of power politics was not simply incomplete. His thinking was impulsive, not systematic, that of a man who was ever ready to form judgements rapidly, on the basis of immediate and patchy information as it came his way. He would learn a great deal, as time went on, but since the formulation of his purposes had preceded his experience of the resistant environment in which he had to do battle, he learned slowly and at high cost. The result (of which he himself was not always aware) was to keep him for some years groping in the dark, grateful for any chink of light that might help him find his bearings.

The Kaiser's response to the Grand Duke of Baden's letter of recommendation amounted to written permission to pursue matters with Herzl; and Herzl's long interview with Friedrich on 2 September followed within days. The Grand Duke talked very freely, as Herzl noted. He said that Berlin had had it from its own sources in Constantinople that the Zionists were 'viewed . . . with favour' there. So, since 'German influence in Yildiz was now unlimited', while 'England has been crowded out completely, to say nothing of the other Powers . . . if our Kaiser drops a word to the Sultan, it will certainly be heeded.' Of course, one still had to be careful. The Kaiser had better receive Herzl on his return from the Near East, not before. But in any event, the prospects were very favourable. And the

Zionists themselves? 'Do you intend to found a state?', he asked; 'I believe that would be the only right thing to do, if you wish to have legal security.' The Grand Duke told Herzl that Count Eulenburg was to draw up a report on the Zionist movement for the Emperor. Herzl repeated his request for an audience with the Kaiser before he left for Jerusalem. They also talked of Zionism in general, of anti-Semitism, of the problem of nationalities in Austria, and of Hechler's ideas on the location of the Ark of the Covenant.[33] Things now moved rapidly. On 16 September Herzl saw Eulenburg in Vienna, as agreed.

Count (later Prince) zu Eulenburg was at this time one of the most influential men in Germany. He was an intimate of the Kaiser, who had confided his Napoleonic ambitions to him, and he, for his own part, regarded himself as the 'steersman' of 'the ship we may call the Emperor's Reign'.[34] He was, however, a man of greater culture and intelligence than his master. Of Herzl, Eulenburg later recorded that he was 'undeniably one of the most interesting personalities I ever met . . . extraordinarily gifted . . . the prototype of a militant Jewish leader from the age of the Jewish kings, without a particle of the type we call "trading Jew". My association with this high-minded, *selfless*, distinguished man will remain in my memory forever.'[35] Eulenburg himself struck Herzl as 'a tall, elegant man, on life's downward slope', completely self-possessed:

You have a man before you who is locked tight like an iron safe. He looks you full in the face, and yet there is nothing to be read in his cold, blue eyes, in his wrinkled face with its grey, pointed beard. Suddenly the iron safe opens, although he has not moved a muscle. The change lies only in the expression of his hard, blue eyes, which can become soft. And on bidding me farewell, while a moment before he had given me a full and friendly look, he suddenly locked himself up again.[36]

[33] *Diaries*, ii, pp. 655–60.
[34] Johannes Haller, *Philip Eulenburg: the Kaiser's Friend*, ii (New York, 1930), p. 39.
[35] Bein, 'Zikhronot etc.', no. 4, pp. 15–16; English translation in *Herzl Year Book*, vi, pp. 59–60.
[36] *Diaries*, ii, pp. 662–3.

The talk between the two men went well and was to the
point. What exactly was it that Herzl wanted the Kaiser to
do for him in Constantinople? Herzl replied that he only
wanted Wilhelm to recommend that the Sultan negotiate
with him. But the Germans must know that the matter was
complicated. It was not simply permission to immigrate that
was being asked, it was autonomy. No doubt, sooner or later,
one of the Powers would offer the Zionists support. At first
he had expected England to do so, he told the Ambassador.
But if it was Germany, so much the better. 'The Jews of today',
Herzl said, 'are predominantly German in culture. I am not
saying this because I am at the German Embassy right now,
but because it is true. Proof: the official language of the two
Basel Congresses.'[37] Eulenburg told Herzl that Bülow, the
German Secretary of State for Foreign Affairs, was in Vienna
and advised him to talk to the Minister too. This was very
encouraging. All told, Herzl wrote to his wife, it had been a
'tremendous' conversation.[38]

The meeting with Bülow took place next day. The Foreign
Secretary was smooth and superficially friendly. He showed
that he knew something of Zionist affairs and took the trouble
to flatter Herzl by kindly references to his writings. Herzl
rehearsed the arguments for a Zionist solution to the Jewish
Problem and spoke of its advantages to the Jews and to others
as an alternative to socialism and revolution. Bülow did not
question the idea of Germany assisting the Zionists in Constantinople. He only expressed concern lest 'others' find out
about it and Herzl later noted that both Bülow and Eulenburg
had 'expressed themselves about the Jews in such a way that
if their words were made public they [feared they] would get
the reputation of being philo-Semites'.[39] And he found the
conversation disturbing in another way. Bülow had been
altogether too amiable, too courteous, too slick. Herzl 'knew
even on the stairs that nothing was going to come of it—either
because I had committed some blunder, or because he [Bülow]
did not consider it expedient'.[40] So once again he pressed for

---

[37] Ibid., p. 664.
[38] 16 September 1898. *Igrot Herzl*, iii, no. 605, p. 183.
[39] *Diaries*, ii, p. 667.
[40] Ibid., p. 668.

an interview with the Kaiser *before* the departure for Constantinople. Writing to Eulenburg, he summoned up all the relevant arguments: the benefits European society would derive from the departure of the 'superfluous' Jews, the benefits to Turkey from the 'influx of an intelligent, economically energetic national element' and 'a large payment of money on our part', 'the restoration to health of this neglected corner of the Orient' and the 'civilization and order' that the Return of the Jews would bring with them, and, finally, the role the Jews could play in the building of a great railroad from the Mediterranean to the Persian Gulf—'which, if undertaken differently, might call forth the most serious rivalries'. 'The journey to the Holy Land', he concluded, 'is now grandly conceived as a pilgrimage on the part of His Majesty. But it can turn out to be more; it can attain to the significance of a historic turning-point in the Orient, if the return of the Jews is initiated.'[41]

Herzl's letter to Eulenberg was written from Paris. On 30 September he left for Holland on the affairs of the Bank. Eulenburg had been informed of his expected movements for the coming fortnight. There was nothing to do but wait.

Herzl had also observed that for all his unctuousness, Bülow did really know a thing or two about the Zionist movement. Up to this point, official German interest in Zionism had been minute. Even a year or so later, when the Berlin Police-President was asked for an assessment of the movement (in particular, on the question whether Zionism was not a 'cloak' [*Deckmantel*] for socialist agitation) it took him almost two months to formulate a reply—a sure sign in the circumstances of an initially empty dossier.[42] But the German consulate in Jerusalem reported on Zionist affairs from its local angle from time to time and the German Legation in Bern had reported,

[41] Herzl to Eulenburg, 24 September 1898. *Igrot Herzl*, iii, no. 618, pp. 189–92. English translation in *Diaries*, ii, pp. 669–72.

[42] The reply, when it came, was a brief, but shrewd list of the forces of opposition to Zionism within German Jewry and an accurate estimate of Zionism's thin ranks within the Empire; and Police-President von Windheim did not think there was anything to be concerned about, on the socialist score or on any other. Windheim to Recke, 23 June 1899. Text in Alex Bein, 'Al ha-yaḥasim bein ha-tenu'a ha-ẓionit u-vein germania ha-keisarit be-tekufat Herzl', *Shivat Ẓion*, ii–iii (1951–2), pp. 386–7.

as a matter of routine, on the first two Zionist Congresses of
1897 and 1898.[43] It is conceivable that Bülow had read the
dispatches; but what neither he nor anyone else in the German
administration had done until now was to trouble themselves
with the question what their policy towards the movement
should be. And there was no reason why they should have
done so until the Kaiser, at his uncle's behest, took an interest
in it.

That interest now grew very rapidly—before it faded more
rapidly still. After Eulenburg had reported to Wilhelm, evidently in favourable terms, on his talk with Herzl, the Kaiser,
in his impulsive way, decided there and then to adopt the
Zionist cause. Yes, he would receive Herzl. More: he would
receive him at the head of a delegation in Jerusalem itself.
And he would indeed intercede with the Sultan on the Zionists'
behalf. He was convinced, he wrote to his uncle Friedrich in
a letter tingling with excitement, that 'we are dealing with a
question of the most far-reaching significance', that the 'settlement of the Holy Land by the financially strong and diligent
people of Israel will soon bring [it] undreamt-of prosperity
and blessing', and that the resulting 'millions into Turkish
money-bags' would lead to a gradual curing of the Sick Man
and the solution of the Eastern Question. Then the energy
and talents

of the tribe of Shem would be directed to worthier goals than the
exploitation of Christians . . . Now, I realize that nine-tenths of all
Germans will be horrified and shun me if they find out at some later
date that I am in sympathy with the Zionists and might even place
them under my protection if they call upon me to do so. I should
[therefore] like to state the following: that the Jews killed our Saviour,
the Good Lord knows better than we do, and he has punished them
accordingly. But neither the anti-Semites nor I nor anybody else
has been instructed or authorized by Him to ill-treat these people in
our own way *in majorem Dei gloriam*! . . . And from the point of view
of secular *Realpolitik*, we must not disregard the fact that, considering
the tremendous power represented by international Jewish capital
in all its dangerousness, it would surely be a tremendous achievement
for Germany if the Hebrew world looked up to our country with

[43] Tattenbach to Hohenlohe, 24 September 1897; Rotenhan to Hohenlohe, 16
September 1898. Ibid., pp. 368–74.

gratitude. Everywhere the hydra of the crudest, most hideous anti-Semitism is raising its horrible head, and, full of anxiety, the Jews, ready to leave the lands where they are in danger, are looking for a protector. All right, then, those who return to the Holy Land shall enjoy protection and security, and I shall intercede with the Sultan on their behalf, for Scripture says: 'Make to yourselves friends of the Mammon of unrighteousness' and 'Be ye wise as serpents and harmless as doves.'[44]

'I now see the matter as assured', the Grand Duke telegraphed to Herzl,[45] his message backed up by authoritative letters from Eulenburg which were waiting for Herzl in Amsterdam. 'I have only *good news* to report to you', Eulenburg began. He had twice spoken to the Kaiser who 'showed a full and profound understanding of the movement'. He himself had been 'a zealous advocate . . . My friend Bülow feels the same way.' Then came an explicit pledge. Eulenburg stated that Wilhelm 'was ready to intercede with the Sultan very exhaustively and as *urgently* as possible' (*hat Seine Majestät sich bereit erklärt in sehr eingehender und—so weit dieses möglich sein wird—dringender Weise bei dem Sultan*). An audience before departure was undesirable, but a Zionist deputation would be received in Jerusalem: 'that would be the very best opportunity to state your wishes to His Majesty in person'. Meanwhile, Herzl was asked to keep the contents of the letter 'in absolute secrecy'.

A second letter, written after further talk with the Kaiser the following day, was in still plainer terms:

His Majesty will discuss the matter with the Sultan most emphatically (*in nachdrücklichster Weise*), and he will be pleased to hear further details from you in Jerusalem.

The Kaiser has already given orders that nothing is to impede the reception of the deputation.

Finally, His Majesty wishes to inform you of his *readiness* to assume a possible protectorate. In making this disclosure, His Majesty naturally counts on your discretion.

It is a pleasure to be able to give you this information, and I hope

---

[44] Kaiser to Grand Duke of Baden, 29 September 1898. *Herzl, Hechler, etc.*, no. 16, pp. 48–53; English translation in *Herzl Year Book*, iv, 236–8.
[45] Bein, ''Al ha-yaḥasim', p. 374.

that you will manage to arrive in Jerusalem in time. Your failure to do so would disappoint His Majesty. I leave it to your discretion whether you want to arrive in Constantinople at the same time as His Majesty.[46]

It was, Herzl reflected in his diary, a 'colossal achievement'. 'J'étais littéralement bouleversé', he was moved to write in French. He worried about losing his post on the *Neue Freie Presse* if he went off to Erez-Israel at the end of his leave instead of reporting for work, but there could be no question of disregarding the Kaiser's wishes. 'C'est l'engrenage. I cannot do otherwise.' As he sailed from Holland to England he recalled his state of mind the day before after reading what Eulenburg had written to him.

I rode my bicycle, alone, to Scheveningen, relaxed through the physical exercise and the view of the beautiful sea. A sunset in reddened clouds, some cloud-drama of unknown melody and plot which was taking place between the lustreless sky and the shimmering sea, in bloody catastrophes, unintelligible, but gripping. . . .

And he went on to write: 'What obscure, indescribable battles I have had to fight over every little step I took will never be suspected or appreciated by the ungrateful Jews, who will show enmity toward me soon after success has come.' Finally, he wrote, 'One effect of [Eulenburg's] letter is that tomorrow evening in the East End I shall speak more moderately, because unfortunately the participation of the moneyed Jews will be necessary after all. I was planning to lash out at them.'[47]

iii

The disappointment to come was the greater for the great hopes that had been engendered.

Returning to the continent Herzl saw Eulenburg once more at the latter's estate near Berlin. Arriving there he was profoundly conscious of having penetrated into a milieu in which his own kind were characteristically despised and he noted

---

[46] Eulenburg to Herzl, 27 and 28 September 1898. CZA, HS 2. English translation in *Herzl Year Book*, vi, pp. 63–5. Emphases in original.

[47] *Diaries*, ii, pp. 675–7.

that his host did 'seem to acknowledge the fact that one can associate with the Jew Herzl'. The Prussian aristocrat, for his part, was, as before, friendly without lowering his reserve. Eulenburg confirmed all that he had written. He emphasized his own role in convincing the Kaiser and winning over Bülow (his 'best friend and a most outstanding statesman') and he met Herzl's thanks by remarking that 'perhaps the moment will come when I shall claim favours from you'.[48] He also repeated what he had already written to the Grand Duke: Herzl should first go to Constantinople ('to be available during the Kaiser's sojourn there, since this would be particularly helpful in the negotiations with the Sultan'[49]) and only then to Jerusalem for the grand audience. They discussed the composition of the Zionist delegation and the probable attitudes of the Powers to the scheme as a whole. Russia presented no problem, they thought. On that Eulenburg was categorical: the Tsar's intentions were of the best; and, if necessary, the Kaiser could always win him over. England, on the other hand, might present difficulties and France too—although, as Herzl pointed out, it was now a country enfeebled by internal crisis. As for Turkey, 'the Kaiser', said Eulenburg, 'did not doubt that the Sultan would receive his advice favourably.'

All in all, Herzl could conclude from both the content and the atmosphere of the talk that the German decision to support Zionism held firm. True, the establishment of a German protectorate of some kind over the movement was immeasurably far from his and other Zionists' original intentions; many of his followers would disapprove: it was not true independence; it was not clear what it would imply for their own relations with the Turks. On the other hand, it was a great advance and ought to be accepted gratefully.

To live under the protection of this strong, great, moral, splendidly governed, tightly organized Germany [he reflected next day] can only have the most salutary effect on the Jewish national character. Also, at one stroke we would obtain a completely ordered internal and external legal status. The suzerainty of the Porte and the pro-

[48] *Diaries*, ii, pp. 686–90.
[49] Grand Duke to Herzl, 5 October 1898. Bein, 'Zikhronot etc.', no. 11, p. 25; English translation in *Herzl Year Book*, vi, p. 66.

tectorate of Germany would certainly be sufficient legal pillars. The
only question is whether it should be 'and' or 'or', suzerainty and/or
protectorate? We shall see how this develops.

Adding later: 'Strange ways of destiny. Through Zionism it
will again be possible for Jews to love this Germany to which
our hearts have been attached despite everything!'[50]

But when he met the Imperial Chancellor, Prince Hohenlohe,
and Bülow two days later (9 October 1898) the atmosphere
was different again. Hohenlohe was a great Catholic aristocrat,
much older than Bülow, more independent of mind and more
frankly hostile and anti-Semitic. 'Do you think that the Jews
are going to desert their stock exchange and follow you?'[51]
was one of his opening questions. What precisely were Herzl's
intentions and what was the Turkish attitude, he wanted to
know. Bülow was now cool and unhelpful. Of the influence of
Eulenburg there was no sign; and the conversation ended
abruptly and inconclusively with the two ministers rushing
off to lunch and leaving Herzl to puzzle over the contradictions between the Kaiser's attitude as Eulenburg had reported
it and the hostility with which the Chancellor and the Foreign
Secretary evidently regarded the entire project. But in any
event, the journey to Constantinople and Jerusalem had to be
made and there was very little time left to prepare for it.

Herzl returned to Vienna. There was the agreement of his
employers at the *Neue Freie Presse* to be gained for another
absence, the delegation for presentation to the Kaiser to be
formed, contact with the Turks to be established, if possible,
as a preliminary to his arrival in Constantinople, and money
for the long and expensive journey to be procured. Everything
was difficult. The delegation would not be the powerful one
he would have liked; Nordau, in particular, could not join
him. The Turkish Ambassador in Vienna was unhelpful.
The money (6,000 gold crowns sent post-haste by Mandelstamm from Kiev) arrived only an hour before the group's
departure on the Orient Express.[52] And when they arrived in

[50] *Diaries*, ii, pp. 693–5.
[51] *Diaries*, ii, p. 701.
[52] Max Bodenheimer, 'Daf zikaron', in Henriette Hannah Bodenheimer (ed.),
Be-reishit ha-tenuʻa (Jerusalem, 1965), p. 73.

Constantinople on 15 October and Bodenheimer was sent to the German Ambassador, Marschall, to announce their arrival and arrange for Herzl to meet him, the response was that Dr Herzl was unknown. After two days of fretting Herzl tried again. Time was pressing: they had still to take passage for Jaffa if they were to arrive in Jerusalem in time for the Kaiser's visit and the formal audience. This time all went well; Wolffsohn found his way through Turkish and German retinues to make contact with the Kaiser's party and Herzl was duly summoned (18 October) to the Kaiser's quarters at the Yildiz. It was the occasion he had tried for ever since his letter to Bismarck, over three years earlier, when he wrote that he believed he had found the solution to the Jewish Question. 'Not *a* solution', he had written, 'but *the* solution, the only one.'[53]

Herzl arrived for the audience in a mood to be impressed and the German Emperor did impress him greatly: 'I felt as though I had entered the magic forest where the fabulous unicorn is said to dwell . . . He has truly Imperial eyes. I have never seen such eyes. A remarkable, bold, inquisitive soul shows in them.' Wilhelm was polite to Herzl and listened to him 'magnificently'. He then explained his own interest in Zionism in his turn: 'There are elements among your people whom it would be a good thing to settle in Palestine. I am thinking of Hesse, for example, where there are usurers at work among the rural population.' Herzl, irritated and offended, spoke up against anti-Semitism—upon which Bülow, ever the courtier, and cautiously hostile throughout the talk, chimed in to point to the debt Jews owed the House of Hohenzollern. The conversation shifted to France: Prince Napoleon, the Gap in the Vosges, the French Army, Dreyfus, the form of government, the national character. Then back to Zionism: he, Wilhelm, had no doubt that it would make an impression on the Turks if the German Kaiser concerned himself with it. In conclusion: 'Just tell me in a word what I am to ask of the Sultan.' 'A chartered company', Herzl replied, 'under German protection.' 'Good! A chartered company!', said the Kaiser[54] and departed.

Nothing came of it. After being kept waiting for four days in

[53] *Diaries*, i, p. 118.
[54] *Diaries*, ii, pp. 722–34.

Jerusalem the Zionist delegation was granted the audience
as planned (2 November 1898), but the reception accorded it
was cool and formal in the extreme. The Zionists' public
address to the Emperor had had to be rewritten under the
supervision of a middle-rank foreign-service officer to exclude
all traces of political content;[55] and Herzl, weak from ill health
during most of his stay in Jerusalem and unhappy about what
he saw of the Jewish community, old and new, of Erez-Israel,
swallowed the humiliation without resistance. The conversation itself consisted of banalities and observations on the climate
and agricultural prospects of Erez-Israel. There were no
politics. The Charter was not mentioned. Nothing was said
about the Kaiser's promised intercession with the Sultan.
The official communiqué issued by the Emperor's party
reduced the Actions Committee of the Zionist Organization
to 'a Jewish deputation which presented [the Kaiser] with
an album of pictures of the Jewish colonies in Palestine'.
Herzl was unnamed—merely described as 'the leader of the
deputation'. And the brief announcement concluded with the
statement that in his reply, 'His Majesty remarked that he
viewed with benevolent interest all efforts directed toward the
improvement of agriculture in Palestine as long as these
accorded with the welfare of the Turkish Empire and were
conducted in a spirit of complete respect for the sovereignty
of the Sultan.'[56] The communiqué had been approved by
Bülow and possibly drafted by him. Herzl could (and in the
event would) cast about for crumbs of comfort: the private and
public audiences had taken place; the promises had not been
explicitly withdrawn; the disadvantages of too close an association with Germany would no longer loom so large. But however
one looked at it, the fruit of the long journey to Jerusalem was
exceedingly meagre. It was plain that the German Government had reversed its position—substantially, if not totally.
What had gone wrong?

---

[55] Among the excisions were references to the Zionist Congresses and to the Basel
Programme and the phrase 'we bespeak the protection of the German Emperor for
this Company'—i.e. for the Jewish Chartered Company. Text with the corrections in
Alex Bein et al., *Theodor Herzl, Bifnei ʿam ve-ʿolam*, i (2nd edn., Jerusalem, 1976),
pp. 273–5; English translation in *Zionist Writings*, ii (New York, 1975), pp. 30–2.

[56] Alex Bein, *Theodore Herzl* (Philadelphia, 1940), p. 307.

'The ruler of the Ottoman empire harbours a certain distrust of your co-religionists', the Grand Duke of Baden wrote
to Herzl to explain. It was a letter of consolation in which
Friedrich was at evident pains to make his points gently.
He had spoken to the Kaiser and the effort to get him to see
Zionist intentions 'as I know them and in their true light'
would continue, he assured Herzl. One great difficulty, however—one which the Kaiser himself had mentioned—was
'the way your co-religionists live and carry on in the City of
Jerusalem'. The impression had been 'repulsive' and it had
harmed Herzl's cause.[57] Political calculation, the old man
seems to have been trying to tell the Zionist leader without
giving offence and without implying criticism of his overlord,
was inextricably bound up with a fundamental hostility to the
Jews. From another, less expected and somewhat less reliable
source Herzl had it that the gist of the argument the Kaiser had
put to the Sultan was that while the Zionists were no danger to
Turkey, everywhere else the Jews were a nuisance to be got
rid of, and further that the Empress, for her part, had said
that the only disagreeable thing about the otherwise agreeable
journey in prospect was that she would have to see so many
Jews.[58] The official German record confirms that the Kaiser
did raise the matter of a Chartered Company with the Sultan
and that ʿAbd al-Hamid's short response was that he did not
like it; but that as there could be no question of the German
Emperor backing a project liable to cause the Turkish people
harm, he would none the less have his ministers examine it.[59]
Thereupon the Germans took the hint and dropped the subject.[60] In other words, as soon as the Kaiser's fantasy of a
Jewish exodus from Europe so ordered that the Jews would
thank rather than blame him collided with the reality of
Turkish policy and with living Turkish statesmen, it collapsed

---

[57] Grand Duke of Baden to Herzl, 5 December 1898. Bein, 'Zikhronot etc.', no. 12,
p. 26. English translation in *Herzl Year Book*, vi, pp. 67–8.

[58] *Diaries*, ii, p. 770. The source was Newlinski, Herzl's (and many others') agent in
Constantinople. But it had all been published a month before Herzl heard it, in the
Jewish Chronicle for 11 November 1898 which Herzl evidently had not seen.

[59] D. Yisraeli, *Ha-raikh ha-germani ve-Erez-Israel* (Ramat-Gan, 1974), pp. 27–8.

[60] Eulenburg later (1901) told Herzl that 'the Sultan rejected the Kaiser's suggestion
regarding the Zionists so brusquely that it was not possible to pursue the matter
further.' *Diaries*, iii, p. 1021.

—to the great relief of Turkish and German officialdom alike. Writing to Bülow some time later and in another connection, Eulenburg remarked on the Kaiser being an 'explosive being' whose 'individuality prevails over the effects of experience'. 'When so markedly eccentric a nature dominates a realm', Eulenburg went on, 'there cannot but be convulsions, and we are heading straight for a period which will decide whether the age or the Emperor is the stronger. I am afraid that it will not be he, for at the moment his strength consists chiefly in the skill of his advisers, especially you.'[61] This was too flattering to Bülow, but Eulenberg's proposition about the convulsions that must occur when 'experience' and 'the age' prevailed over the Kaiser's 'individuality' was appropriate to the present case.[62]

Contemporary German Near-Eastern policy was founded on the proposition that the Ottoman Empire could be strengthened and preserved more or less intact. Germany had no direct territorial designs on the Empire—unlike Russia or, if to a lesser extent, France. Where German activities, private or public, appeared to be in conflict with this proposition, or were thought liable to appear so in the eyes of the Turks themselves, it was the firm priority which Berlin attached to the special relationship with Constantinople that came consistently to the fore—very notably so in relation to Erez-Israel/Palestine. Outside those areas of the Ottoman Empire, such as Anatolia, in which Germany did have economic and (latent) military interests, even the ethnic, self-consciously German evangelical sect of Templars, who founded seven colonies in Palestine between 1869 and 1907, fared ill at the hands of the Wilhelmstrasse—almost as ill as the Zionists—when the promotion of their affairs clashed with considerations of high policy.[63] Despite Herzl's periodic fits of warm feeling for Ger-

---

[61] Haller, pp. 61–2.

[62] 'The Kaiser', wrote Friedrich von Holstein, the influential senior counsellor in the German Foreign Office, 'has, at least up till now, the unfortunate habit of talking all the more rapidly and incautiously the more a matter interests him. Hence it happens that he has generally already committed himself, or at least that the entourage persuades him that he has already committed himself, even before the responsible advisers, or the experts, have been able to submit their opinion to him.' N. Rich and M. H. Fisher (eds.), *The Holstein Papers*, iii (Cambridge, 1961), p. 612.

[63] Alex Carmel, 'The political significance of German settlement in Palestine 1868–1919', in Wallach (ed.), pp. 45–71.

many and the undoubted prestige of German science and language among the Jews of central and eastern Europe of the time, the Zionists were in no sense a pro-German or Germanophil movement (let alone one of *Germans*). Herzl himself was not a German subject, nor were there more than a handful of German subjects who were Zionists, as the German Foreign Ministry took note and later pointed out to the Grand Duke. In a considered review of the entire issue, probably in response to pro-Zionist representations by Friedrich, the German diplomatists were firm on their failure to see what special German interests might be involved in the matter of Zionism. Nor could they see why it should be expected that Herzl be granted in one corner of the Ottoman Empire what the European Powers had been denied with 'stubbornness and desperation' in another—the 'Macedonian provinces'. They also wanted the Grand Duke to know that in their estimate a German protectorate over the Zionists would do neither the Zionists nor the Jews of Turkey any good. The realization of the former's aim would be delayed. The latter would 'fare much like the Armenians who were treated well until the Sultan was made apprehensive by the interests of foreign states in their [i.e. the Armenians'] political aspirations'. But in any event, the Wilhelmstrasse summed up, 'intervention by Germany in favour of Herzl's "Jewish State" would inflict irreparable damage on all our other interests in Turkey.'[64] Of the fact of Turkish hostility to Zionism the German specialists in Ottoman affairs were never in doubt. The consulate in Jerusalem knew all about the silent struggle over entry and land between the Turkish administration and the Jewish settlers and had reported on it in detail.[65] And there were additional reminders of it in Constantinople, if only as a by-product of Herzl's periodic visits. On one occasion, in February 1902, a German diplomat happened to observe Herzl at the Yildiz Kiosk. Herzl, he reported, had dictated a long note to the Court Chamberlain and the German

---

[64] *Aide-mémoire* submitted by the Prussian envoy in Karlsruhe, 26 January 1904. *Herzl, Hechler, etc.,* no. 47, pp. 101–3. English translation in *Herzl Year Book,* iv, pp. 268–70.

[65] Tischendorf to Hohenlohe, 19 June 1897. AA/Juden in der Türkei K 175 847/65. Text in M. Eliav (ed.), *Ha-yishuv ha-yehudi etc.,* no. 163, pp. 233–8.

had then asked Ibrahim Bey what Herzl had wanted. 'Des
choses impossibles', was the laconic reply, duly reported to
Berlin.[66]

A great weakness of the diplomatic campaign mounted by
Herzl (and his successors) was that the idea of a thoroughgoing
political rehabilitation of the Jewish people was never entirely
credible to any but the very few who were thoroughgoing
converts to it. The problem for the initiated was therefore to
provide arguments and evidence of its plausibility so striking
as to induce conversion; and if not outright conversion, then
at least a suspension of disbelief. The circle was vicious: for
lack of converts in sufficient numbers and quality, such evidence was hard to provide. But to bridge the gap with *argument*
was harder still.

Contemporary diplomacy was still Cabinet diplomacy,
dominated by members of the traditional (and the traditionally
minded) governing classes of the major European states.
Among these people, and quite apart from explicit and vulgar
anti-Semitism (which was common enough), there was a
deep-seated resistance to the very idea of change in the Jewish
condition. Or if change there was to be, then the preference
was for it to be in a retrogressive and restrictive direction,
designed, so far as possible, to keep the Jews down and in
what was believed to be their proper place: anything but total
liberation. Moreover, the romantic and nostalgic elements of
Zionism, the idea of a Return to the ancestral Land and to the
ancient status, the Jewish Risorgimento—these were ideas
which fitted ill with the minds of men who were accustomed
to thinking through their problems with self-confident and
mildly cynical calculation. Besides, they were habituated to
dealing with their own kind, namely with officials and chancelleries and with what was well established and of a known

---

[66] Marschall to Bülow, 19 March 1902. Alex Bein, ''Al ha-yaḥasim', pp. 402–3.
After Herzl's death Bülow said, in an interview, that he had admired Herzl as a
writer and recognized the misery of eastern European Jewry. But he thought little of
Zionism. Palestine was a poor land for settlement and the German Jews who, 'by their
whole history and the assiduity with which they have identified themselves with the
German economic, spiritual and artistic life', were best suited to settle there were
unlikely to plunge into such an experiment. *Jewish Chronicle* (quoting the *Neue Freie
Presse*), 21 October 1904.

and well-tried category. On this count too the Zionists were ill
suited to them. They fitted into no familiar slot. They were not
a state. They were not even a non-sovereign colonial nation—
had they been, they might have been somewhat better off
because then their affairs would normally have been the responsibility of some less exalted, but less impenetrable, branch
of government than that comprising the sovereigns, foreign
ministers, and ambassadors whom Herzl was always seeking
out. Finally, protocol still counted for something in this
world; and it counted against Zionism because it reflected
routine thinking and because it served as a defence against
outsiders.

Herzl knew this and was intensely aware of the formal
disadvantages under which he laboured. He was quick to note
each skirmish and reckon each minor victory as an augury of
greater victories to come. But the disadvantage could not
be lifted. It followed that, as a rule, the more conventional and
unimaginative the statesmen and officials with whom contact
had been established, the less chance there was of breaking
through their bureaucratic—in practice, their psychological
and intellectual—defences. With original minds, or the adventurous, or the more 'irresponsible', his chances were
better. Hence, indeed, the ephemeral success with Eulenburg
and the Kaiser. And hence the later success with Joseph Chamberlain, the English Colonial Secretary. But on the whole,
this was a time when the affairs of the European Powers were
governed by men whose thinking was cautious, whose moves
were calculated and crab-like, and who instinctively resisted
what was radical and novel. It is true, there were cracks in the
wall. Wilhelmine Germany did not quite fall into this category,
certainly not in respect of its policy in the Near East. And
generally the somewhat cold intricacy of European politics
in the strictly European sphere was not always in evidence in
the conduct of the same Powers' affairs in Asia and Africa.
These tended to be less balanced, more impulsive in their
origins, more easily and more directly influenced by individuals.
But the cracks were thin and, from the Zionists' point of view,
not quite in the right places. Nor was Herzl himself well
equipped to enlarge them. The Zionists could not and did not
appear on the scene as a tangible political, let alone military,

factor in their own right. They possessed little or no usable power. They did not lead more than a fraction of the Jews they claimed to represent. They did not command any significant fraction of Jewish wealth. Zionism was *for* the impoverished of Jewry; but it was also largely *of* them. It was led by members of the Jewish intelligentsia, not the Jewish plutocracy, which was aloof or hostile.

Finally, the Zionists were not in *conflict* with any of the Powers. The Jews as such were in no sense and in no place in rebellion, actual or potential. Their case was therefore not really analogous to that of the other submerged peoples of eastern and southern Europe, let alone, say, of the American Indians, then in the last throes of their resistance to the encroachment of the white men, or even of the unfortunate Armenians. These were peoples the dominant Powers had either to make peace with, or circumscribe, or destroy. In no case could they be, or were they, ignored. The Jews could be ignored, the more so as the Zionists, at this early stage, were profoundly reluctant to raise the spectre of Jewish 'disloyalty' within the lands of the Dispersion. When, in August 1914, German attention was on the Russian territories which were heavily populated by Jews the attitude changed somewhat. But for the time being Jews as such, Zionists or others, did not constitute a political problem for any but the Turks, potentially, and in a special sense, as we shall see, for the Russians; they certainly did not seek to fight any of the Powers, not even Turkey; and it did not occur to any one of the Powers to incite the Jews against any other. The Zionists, in any event, for their part, sought the co-operation of the great states. Doing so they had to couch their arguments in terms of the self-interest of those to whom they applied for support, as well as that of their own people. But it was not easily done and the chain of argument had to be a long one, no small weakness in itself.

iv

Herzl had been careful to keep his promise to Eulenburg; and for that he paid a price. The letters the Ambassador had written to him at the end of September were kept secret—

the fact that they had been written no less than their contents—from all but a handful of intimates. But immediately
after receiving them and before the cold douche administered
to him by Hohenlohe and Bülow in Potsdam, he had allowed
himself one oblique reference to great things to come. He said,
in the course of a public speech in the East End of London
(3 October 1898), 'I can assure you: the time is no longer far
off. I know quite well what I am saying; never before have I
spoken with so much assurance. Today I declare to you that I
regard the time not far off when the Jewish people will start
to move.'[67]

The audience was overwhelmingly east European. The effect
was a sensation. Then came the equally sensational journey to
Erez-Israel; then the seemingly dramatic meeting of the
Zionist delegation with the Kaiser; then the chilling German
communiqué, anticlimax, and then, in effect, silence.

Uncertain whether to give more weight to his second interview with the Kaiser than to his first, but obliged to say and
write something, Herzl now hedged. 'We did not go to Palestine as tourists or as explorers but with a definite political
purpose', he wrote in *Die Welt* upon his return. 'After our aim
had been achieved, we immediately started on our trip home.'
His only reference to that 'definite political purpose' and to
what had actually been 'achieved' was elliptical. 'We have
unfurled our flag: it is already fluttering above the heads of
people. We are full of good cheer and firm confidence. And
people will understand that we have sufficient reason for this,
for we have succeeded in arousing the interests of two rulers in
our just cause.'[68] But this was not nearly enough to make up for
the deafening silence from Germany; and rumours and counter-
rumours about what had or had not occurred in Constantinople
and Jerusalem now circulated, adding confusion and moral
indignation to the disappointment. It was rumoured that he
had been received by the Sultan; then the rumour was denied.
The Jerusalem correspondent of the *Jewish Chronicle* reported,
probably in good faith, that the local German consulate knew
nothing of Herzl and his colleagues having been received by
the Kaiser; and that what was known was that a deputation

[67] *Bifnei 'am ve-'olam*, i, p. 269. English text in *Zionist Writings*, ii, p. 28.
[68] *Die Welt*, 18 November 1898. English translation in *Zionist Writings*, ii, pp. 33–7.

that *had* been presented to Wilhelm and *had* presented him with an album of pictures of local settlements had been composed of German Templars.[69] This was then picked up and circulated among the *cognoscenti* in eastern Europe and doubts about Herzl's integrity were now mingled with doubts about his prudence. Even after the essential outline of events had become clearer, the entire affair of the journey to Erez-Israel seemed to many, especially to the veterans of Hibbat Zion in eastern Europe, to encapsulate all the features of Herzl's policy and activity which most irritated and frightened them: the secrecy — and hence the impossibility of their forming their own considered judgement on the great affairs of the movement; Herzl's bland assumption of authority to act in the movement's name; the danger to the existing settlements in Erez-Israel that followed from the identification in Turkish minds of Zionism with a predatory European Power; what they took for bombast, if not dishonesty: the scattering of hints and promises with little or no substance to them; and, above all, the raising of false hopes among the people in their misery.

I have never doubted Dr Herzl's diplomatic talents [wrote Ahad Ha-'Am]. My only regret is that he employs his talents not only in the outward direction, but *inwardly* too, in his attitude to us. Take, for example, the matter of his journey to Erez-Israel and his interview with the Emperor of Germany. No doubt, in itself, it makes a good impression; although what benefit may result from it is far from clear to me. But what need was there to deceive us and assure us that the Emperor told [the deputation] that he is prepared to support the *yishuv*, etc., when the truth (as it now emerges from the *Jewish Chronicle*) is that it was not his response to us, but to *the German colonists*.[70]

'Was there any real, political value to the interview in Jerusalem?', Re'uven Brainin, a correspondent for *Ha-Meliz*, asked Herzl bluntly. 'Why we all know that Wilhelm is easily enthused and fired . . . and that what the Kaiser says is one thing and that politics are another. . . .' Then there was the

---

[69] 'Dr. Herzl in Jerusalem: the Truth about the Emperor's Speech', *Jewish Chronicle*, 25 November 1898.

[70] *Ahad Ha-'Am to Tchlenov*, 22 December 1898. *Igrot AH*, ii, p. 188. Emphases in original.

question of Herzl's methods. The foreign ministers of enlightened countries were subject to criticism and to removal from office if they lost the public's confidence, his interviewer insisted. But 'there is not one of us . . . who knows what your political method is and what path you intend to follow in the future.' Herzl's response was to repeat that secrets had to be kept if the confidence of statesmen was to be retained and to remark that the Kaiser would hardly have summoned the delegation to Jerusalem merely to tell it that he disapproved of Zionism. Wilhelm himself, when all was said and done, was 'one of the makers of politics in our times'. As for the promise made in London, it was merely a reference to the meeting due to take place in Jerusalem.[71] He said nothing of Eulenburg. He was not greatly discomposed by the critical thrust of the questions.

But it was another matter when the criticism was embodied in an article by Nordau, 'The Tasks of Zionism', which appeared in December in a Hebrew annual much favoured by the Jewish intelligentsia of eastern Europe. Written long before the journey to Jerusalem, its publication could not have been better timed to reflect ill on Herzl's methods, his judgement, and, in sum, on the foundation of his policy. And from no one could criticism have been more painful than from his greatest recruit to the movement. The nub of Nordau's argument was that it was an error to suppose, as most did, that a handful of leaders 'in Vienna and elsewhere' would negotiate with statesmen and that then, when all had been neatly arranged, and they had conveniently and immediately found a vast sum of money, it would be time for them to turn to the Jewish people and tell them to 'rise, go, take over your Land, and be blessed'. The real state of affairs, Nordau insisted, was quite different. The powers of the leaders of a nation are a function of the strength and will of its people. As individuals the leaders had nothing to offer the Powers. And it was not the custom of governments to give lands and rights away for nothing. Charity, mercy, love of justice, and ideals—all these played no role in politics. The rule of politics was *do ut des*. And even if the Zionists were, by way of a miracle, told by Turkey and the Great Powers that Ereẓ-Israel was open to us

[71] *Ha-Meliẓ*, 28, 29, 31 January; 1, 2, 9, 15 February 1899.

and that we did have the right to manage our own affairs
there, it would then immediately be seen that we were un-
prepared for what would have to be undertaken immediately.
Then the damage done our movement would be irreparable.
For all these reasons, Nordau argued, the task of the movement,
before all else, was to employ its time as Moses had employed the
forty years Israel spent in the desert: to bind the nation
together and to prepare it and Ereẓ-Israel for the great exodus
that was in the making.[72]

To Herzl this line of argument was 'utterly incredible' and
'basically incorrect'. Besides, although both he and Nordau
knew it had been written half a year before the journey to the
Kaiser, it would inevitably be taken by the public as an attack
stemming from that event.[73] However, Herzl only remonstrated
with Nordau gently. He reminded him that he had not acted
as a private person, that no one so regarded him, and that it
was Nordau who had written to him after the First Congress,
'Consider yourself a Government!'[74]

Generally, Herzl's feelings about the affair of the Kaiser's
promise and the failure to redeem it were never clear-cut.
In time he regretted his incaution in London: 'There were . . .
moments in which one despaired and moments in which one
hoped again. [It was in one of the good moments] in the
autumn of 1898 that I told my brethren in the East End of
London that I held the realization of our hopes to be nigh.
I ought not to have said that. People fell on me as on a char-
latan.' Adding, 'The final judgement, however, will be spoken
by a later age which will have before its eyes all the evidence.'[75]
But on the substance he was reluctant, typically, to draw firm
conclusions. In Bülow he recognized an enemy. But he failed
to see what all the German diplomats had seen—the hostility
of the Turks, no less implacable for being softly and indirectly
expressed. 'In Constantinople, in the end, everything will
boil down to money', he wrote in the draft of a letter to the
Grand Duke. Prudently he erased the sentence from the

[72] 'Te'udat ha-ẓionut', *Aḥiasaf*, vi (1898).

[73] *Diaries*, ii, entry for 24 December 1898, p. 779.

[74] Herzl to Nordau, 24 December 1898. *Igrot Herzl*, iii, no. 692, pp. 234–5.

[75] Address (in English) to the Maccabean Club, 11 June 1901, *Zionist Writings*, ii,
pp. 165–70.

finished letter, along with other speculations on the causes of the reversal;[76] but it reflected his thinking well enough. He persisted in regarding the Eulenburg letters as a 'colossal' achievement and in demanding of his closest followers that they take his word for it that achievements there had been even if he could not be more specific about them.[77]

Herzl never entirely gave up the idea of restarting official German interest in Zionism. Two years later he was still turning the reasons for the failure over in his mind. Five years later, newly back from Russia and after a chance and very friendly encounter with Eulenburg, he day-dreamed briefly of 'revived relations'[78] with the German Empire. These, of course, were episodes. It was not long before the direction of German policy was clear to him almost beyond a doubt. A request for a fresh interview with the Kaiser having been turned down, Herzl was sober enough to reject a counter-proposal that he ask to see Bülow.[79] But sobriety induced depression, until depression, characteristically, gave way to a fevered casting-about for new avenues to explore. He tried to gain an audience with the Tsar. In June 1899 he set off for The Hague, then the scene of the Peace Conference, to look for new contacts in high places. Then, neither totally unsuccessful nor yet effectively successful, he fell back on his original tactic, a direct approach to Turkey.

At the beginning of April 1899 his agent, Philipp de Newlinski, set off for Constantinople on his behalf. It was Newlinski who had gained access to the Porte for him on his own first journey to Constantinople three years earlier.[80] It was reasonable to suppose that he might succeed in doing so again. Newlinski's relations with the Turks were excellent. He had served as their regular agent for a considerable period and had established himself as their informant on the affairs of the Zionists. 'In case Your Excellency wishes someone to attend the debates of Second Congress at Basel . . . and to furnish us

---

[76] 18 November 1898. *Igrot Herzl*, iii, no. 653, fn. 7, p. 208.

[77] Herzl to Kellner, 21 November 1898. *Igrot Herzl*, iii, no. 658, p. 212. See also Herzl to Nordau, 29 November 1898. Ibid., no. 662, p. 215; and Herzl to Gottheil, 25 December 1898. Ibid., no. 694, p. 236.

[78] *Diaries*, iii, p. 981; iv, p. 1546.

[79] Herzl to Friedrich of Baden, 10 March 1899. *Igrot Herzl*, iii, no. 780, p. 296.

[80] See *Origins*, pp. 291–2.

with comprehensive information on its deliberations and on the resolutions taken there, then', wrote the Ottoman Ambassador in Vienna to his Minister, 'Monsieur de Newlinski, who has connections with the principal members of the Zionist movement and who has told me of the long reports on the subject he has submitted in high quarters, seems to me to be entirely indicated.'[81] Equally, he had spoken up for the Zionists. In a memorandum 'Concerning the Foundation of a Jewish State in the Land of Palestine' submitted to Nuri Bey at the Ottoman Foreign Ministry just prior to the First Congress, he had argued that the welfare of the Ottoman Empire might depend on the transactions of the Congress because it was impossible to correct the finances of the Empire without the help of the Jewish people.[82] But Newlinski died very shortly after arrival in Constantinople. And Herzl, knowing nothing certain of Newlinski's double role, although sometimes dimly suspecting one, rightly judged it a set-back. Virtually, he felt, he would now have to start from scratch. Besides, to disappointment and frustration there was added a debt of honour the Zionists could ill afford. The body had to be brought back for burial and financial provision made for Newlinski's 'clear-headed and covetous' widow.

Herzl's own followers presented problems of a different order. They were the more restless now for his having committed a public and undeniable error. At the Third Congress (15–18 August, in Basel) the reckoning could not be avoided and the attack was general. There were complaints about poor administration, about unanswered letters, about failure to maintain regular contact with the country organizations of the movement and to grant their committees proper authority to act on their own account. A change in the wording of the Bank's Charter which had the effect of loosening the Second Congress's resolution that its activities be restricted to support for settlement in Erez-Israel and its geographical vicinity was denounced. The twin issues of culture and religion came

[81] Mahmoud Nedim to Tevfik Pasha, 21 July 1898. OFMA, file C/332–D/17, 23600/182.
[82] 28 July 1897. OFMA, file TS 129/1.

up once more,[83] this time in the form of a charge that the leadership had neglected the 'cultural work'.

The central thrust was formulated by Leo Motzkin, who led the opposition now, as he had led it in the debate on the Basel Programme at the First Congress two years before.[84] Motzkin was surprised, he said, to find that certain events that had occurred between the Congresses had passed, thus far, without mention and that resolutions of the last Congress were not being fulfilled. Generally, there was the unsatisfactory way in which the Smaller Actions Committee in Vienna was conducting affairs: and the manner in which the ideas and programme of the movement were being propagated was a case in point. Two years before, Motzkin pointed out, we had said, over and over again, that we could not offer Erez-Israel to the people immediately, that it would take time, and that he who thought otherwise could not be a true Zionist, but merely one who was impelled by his material condition to agree with us. But in this past year our propaganda has been rash and over-hasty. The people had been told authoritatively such things as to imply that, on the contrary, Erez-Israel could be gained for them right now. Consider the danger to our movement, said Motzkin, if nothing of the kind occurred. Moreover,

Ladies and gentlemen, if one of our speakers, in his enthusiasm, promises more than he should, it is no great matter. But we know very well that this was not said by [ordinary] speakers. In September or October a speech was delivered in London, a speech which gave rise . . . to such enthusiasm as I should have been glad to succumb to it too . . . But the form, the hints . . . the expression 'Never before have I spoken with such assurance', and the like—all stamped the propaganda [campaign] with such precipitateness that it was absolutely necessary to bring the matter up with due emphasis. I asked myself, can it be true? . . . If it is, then after such a statement Erez-Israel must be given us! . . . And we hear the same tune in other speeches. Why? Do you think that in this way the Jewish people will be the sooner won [for our cause]?

[83] See above, pp. 69–70.
[84] See *Origins*, pp. 367–9.

He had brought this up, Motzkin said, to plead for caution in our affairs, for with caution the disharmony and heartbreak that had been borne in the course of the past year could be avoided in the future. And there was a related matter, which had already been brought up in the debate: responsibility and authority had to be shared and the members of the Greater Actions Committee had to be treated as partners and with the respect due to their representative function.

There are moments [said Motzkin] when dictatorship is necessary and in such a case I too would support one. But it is always a passing, temporary thing. There can be no dictatorships in long-lasting movements; for if there were, the movements could not exist. (Stormy applause.) Therefore, with all the respect I feel for Dr Herzl . . . I want the Congress to declare that responsibility does not rest on Dr Herzl alone, but on all members of the Actions Committee, who must all possess equal rights. The confidence that Dr Herzl enjoys, as one who gave such an impetus to our movement, will no doubt give him a preponderance, but the preponderance must be constitutional, for otherwise we cannot act, as we should like to, sacrificing our lives for the movement. (Stormy applause.)[85]

The attack was not violent or rude. Herzl's primacy was never in question.[86] For his part, he responded to his critics at very great length, but with wit and goodwill. He tried to show that despite minor and technical errors the record was a good one, if all the circumstances were taken into account. To Weizmann's charge that Vienna ignored the Greater Actions Committee he replied by pointing to the huge correspondence which Vienna handled: 5,115 letters dispatched up to the time of the Congress, not counting 43 circular letters in the past year to members of the Greater Actions Committee. Most of the other specific charges were dealt with as smoothly.

[85] *Protokoll III*, pp. 68–71.

[86] Motzkin wrote: 'I protested more than once at this Congress against certain steps taken by Herzl . . . but despite [everything] there is something great, sensitive, even noble in him.' Klausner, p. 39. The young Chaim Weizmann, already a member of what he himself termed 'the opposition at the Congress', marked its end by sending Herzl a postcard with Herzl's own picture. Weizmann wrote on the back, 'This is the picture which is ever in our mind's eye and which we always carry and shall carry in our hearts.' *Weizmann Letters*, i, no. 38, p. 74. And cf. ibid., Weizmann to Motzkin, 11 September 1899, no. 40, pp. 75–6.

To the accusation that the country associations had not been granted authority to act his reply was that it was not a question of granting them authority, but of their assuming it for themselves.

On the matter of the Bank's Charter he could show, he said, that Vienna was formally in the clear, the change having been made locally in London by the Bank's governors, their attention having been especially called to the content of the Congress's resolutions by the Smaller Actions Committee in Vienna. Herzl denied that the East End speech had caused harm and he poked gentle fun at Motzkin (a mathematician): 'The words I spoke in London, fell, fortunately, on fruitful soil and put some fire into our friends' zeal; it cannot, perhaps, be kept warm with mere speeches and mere mathematical expositions.' But he refrained from responding directly to the central charge of dictatorial conduct and in the end was rewarded with prolonged and warm applause from the public gallery as well as from the body of the assembly, as the stenographers noted for the record.[87] Herzl was not greatly affected by the criticism. His inner sense of integrity was untroubled. His unshared knowledge of all the details of his most spectacular diplomatic venture thus far fortified him. For the moment, his mind was set on the Bank and it was final authorization for it that he wanted from the Congress, and which he got. There was little else in Basel to interest him and much to bore him. His final judgement on the Third Congress was that it had gone well enough and had ended on a note of harmony after all.[88] Back in Vienna he noted, 'And having tasted the feeling of freedom and been a lord for one week, I must return again to my vile servitude at the *Neue Freie Presse* where I am not allowed to have an opinion of my own.'[89]

[87] *Protokoll III*, pp. 71–83.
[88] *Diaries*, iii, p. 862.
[89] Ibid., p. 863.

4

The Insurmountable Obstacle

The logic underlying Herzl's reversion to his original tactic, the direct approach to Turkey, was typically clear and simple. The indirect approach through Germany had failed; the first encounter with the Turks in 1896 had been inconclusive. His old argument that the Jews could do something for the Turks which the Turks were unable to do for themselves— namely, liberate them from the chains of indebtedness in which the Europeans held them—had not, he felt, been disproved. But it did have to be put before the Sultan himself, directly; it was futile to try to pierce the walls of interlocking and conflicting bureaucracies with which ʿAbd al-Hamid had surrounded himself, except for the express purpose of reaching the Master himself. Herzl's experience with the Germans had tended, if anything, to confirm his belief in the supreme value of the face-to-face interview with the man at the apex of the structure of power. He had, after all, made headway with the Kaiser and been undone by the men around him. In Turkey, the sovereign was ruler in a deeper sense and to a greater degree than even Wilhelm II. Moreover, much had happened since his first visit to Constantinople in June 1896. The movement had been formed and had grown. His own status as a national spokesman had been established. Once in the presence of the Sultan he would, he was sure, know how to draw on his powers of persuasion, on his tact, and on his moral authority to make that impact on ʿAbd al-Hamid's thinking on which all depended and from which all would subsequently flow. And, indeed, the period of Herzl's maximum effort to reach an understanding with the Turks— between the summer of 1899 and the summer of 1902—fell clearly into two well-defined parts. In the first he devoted himself to reaching the Sultan; in the second to building on what appeared to have been accomplished in and by the meeting. Here, once again, Herzl's practice of noting and, if possible, testing every likely opening may be seen in operation. But so too may his growing flexibility in the definition of targets in the interest of making progress towards them.

There was no Grand Duke of Baden to smooth his way to the Sultan. Herzl had to make do with intermediaries of lesser standing, two in particular. The first was Mehmed Nuri Bey, whom he knew from his first visit to Constantinople[1] and whom he met once more at the Peace Conference at The Hague in 1899. Nuri doubled as chief official of the Foreign Ministry and as a principal spy for the Palace within the Ministry. He was friendly to Herzl and very free with comment and advice. The dead Newlinski he dismissed as 'une sale canaille'[2] (a term that might have been applied, and with better reason, to Nuri himself). Herzl was counselled not to try directly for Erez-Israel. He should attack the problem 'sidewise' by buying land in the regions of Aleppo and Beirut and then waiting for an opportune moment before making the demand for Erez-Israel explicit. And to that, or to a similar end, Nuri was prepared to form a syndicate of Turkish notables with which Herzl and his friends would deal. Furthermore, for a fee of 40,000 francs, he would undertake to have Herzl received in audience by the Sultan. Nuri's business proposals were ignored, but his offer to bring Herzl before the Sultan was accepted. The 10,000 francs Nuri wanted paid on account were raised, with some difficulty, and paid over. A new character, one Eduard Crespi, was named by Nuri as *his* agent and contact man and Herzl, after drafting a formal request for an audience, settled back to wait. But the succession of disappointments he had suffered, the irritations at the *Neue Freie Presse* (where he sometimes felt he was treated as 'a servant or an office-boy'[3]), his inability to suffer the fools around him gladly, the inroads his heart disease was making on his health—all these made the long wait difficult to bear. The autumn passed without

---

[1] See *Origins*, p. 294.
[2] *Diaries*, iii, p. 847.
[3] *Diaries*, iii, p. 919.

development; only an occasional, irrelevant letter from Crespi. 'Nothing from Constantinople', he wrote in his diary on 27 December, 'nothing, nothing.'[4] Early in 1900, when he learned that Nuri had passed through Vienna without a word to him he began to fear that he had been made a fool of. But it was hard for him to tell. It could still be that the Turks were serious. In March he was asked to write formally to the Palace once more explaining the purpose of the audience 'more clearly'.[5]

Four years earlier Herzl had thought nothing of beginning in Constantinople with explicit talk of a Jewish state. He was now no longer ignorant of the Turks' official position; and the Basel Programme permitted great flexibility. The year before, at the Third Congress (15–18 August 1899), he had outlined a modified approach and redefined the target. It amounted to a retreat even from the Programme of 1897.

Naturally, it is very important for us to emphasize and demonstrate our honourable character, particularly in our relations with the Turkish government. We shall not take any step which might even remotely arouse justified suspicion in the sovereign owner of Palestine. We will and can offer the greatest benefits to the Ottoman Empire, and hence we can act quite openly.

The old immigration by stealth, he went on, was misguided because it could only arouse distrust. Whereas our

great goal is so reasonable and sensible that no one will search for ulterior motives therein. Why, then, should we not come right out and say so? In this way our entire plan will be comprehensible all at once. There will be no further mistrust. We are entering upon negotiations which sooner or later will lead to results—provided that we proceed with unity and keep our forces together.

This unity, Herzl told the Congress, would assuredly follow upon the achievement of results. At what result should the Zionists aim?

Let us express it in a single word: A Charter! Our efforts are directed at obtaining a Charter from the Turkish government, a Charter

[4] Ibid., p. 898.
[5] Ibid., p. 917.

under the sovereignty of His Majesty the Sultan. Only when we are in possession of this Charter, which will have to include the necessary guarantees under public law, will we be able to begin large-scale practical settlement. In return for granting us this Charter we shall secure great benefits for the Turkish government.[6]

One delegate, Siegmund Werner, a member of Herzl's own circle in Vienna and sometime editor of *Die Welt*, did raise the question whether the target, so defined, was compatible with the Basel Programme. What of the original insistence on settlement under public (by implication international) law, he wanted to know. Was this not a 'narrowing' of the original Programme?[7] Werner had to press for an answer and when it came it was evasive. His opening address had been approved in advance by the Greater Actions Committee, Herzl told him, so there could be no question of a narrowing of the Basel Programme, 'our Magna Charta'. What was intended was simply a practical step in the right direction, one which 'held within it what we understand by the term guarantees under public law'.[8] For his part he sincerely hoped it would succeed. No one else objected, the old-school Zionists least of all. Tchlenov himself, as the rapporteur for the settlement committee, proposed the resolution of approval, in which was incorporated the idea of a Charter granted by the Turkish Government as one of several tasks for the new Bank to undertake.[9]

Now in March 1900, setting out once more the grounds for requesting an audience with the Sultan, Herzl took another cautious step backwards. The purpose of the audience, he wrote, was to explain the Zionist plan whereby Jewish immigration into Erez-Israel and 'the financial services we wish to render His Majesty's government' were linked. The details had to be set forth orally, if only because of the great sums of money involved. If the Sultan had any doubt about his character or about the benefits to be derived from the plan, 'let His Majesty the Sultan deign to learn about me from his powerful

---

[6] *Protokoll III*, pp. 6–7. English translation by Zohn in *Zionist Writings*, ii, pp. 104–6.
[7] *Protokoll III*, p. 57 and p. 140.
[8] Ibid., p. 140.
[9] Ibid., pp. 229–30.

friend [the Kaiser]'. Meanwhile, time was growing short; his own people were beginning to be impatient; other projects, such as one of settlement in Cyprus, were being advanced; emigration to America was continuing.[10] But the sole response, two months later, was a request for a fresh memorandum. And meanwhile there was Crespi warning him that in Constantinople 'Palestine and Zionists sound bad'.[11]

The other intermediary through whom Herzl hoped to reach the Sultan was not a Turk at all, but a man who was in some respects of his own kind. Arminius Vámbéry was an orientalist of distinction, a great traveller, a master linguist, a particular expert on the peoples and languages of Central Asia, and an occasional adviser to 'Abd al-Hamid with whom he had been on unusually close terms for a great many years. He had been, at various times, tailor's apprentice, compiler of dictionaries, tutor in European languages at the court in Constantinople, explorer for the Hungarian Academy, and Professor of Oriental Languages at the University of Budapest. He was a Hungarian patriot, an enemy of Russia, and an admirer of England which he served diligently as a secret agent. Gladstone had thought highly of his services. Queen Victoria had received him at Windsor.[12] Born Hermann Wamberger, of orthodox Jewish parents, he had passed for a Muslim dervish in Central Asia and briefly, and vaguely, for a Protestant back in Europe. He had been an adventurer in religion as in virtually everything else. But insofar as he troubled to define a basic identity for himself, there was never any doubt in his mind, nor in anybody else's, that it had to be defined in terms of his origins. He was well versed in Jewish lore, knew Hebrew, had—at any rate professed—a profound sympathy for the Jews of eastern Europe in their misery, and took a position on Jewish assimilationists in the West not far from that of the Zionists. 'It is surprising', he once wrote, 'that the Jew, treated like a stranger everywhere in Europe, still persists in ingratiating himself into the national bond. Why does he not

[10] Herzl to Tevfik (Minister of Foreign Affairs), mid-March 1900. *Igrot Herzl*, iv. *Diaries*, iii, pp. 917–18.
[11] Crespi to Herzl, 8 April 1900. CZA, H VIII/162.
[12] Lory Alder and Richard Dalby, *The Dervish of Windsor Castle* (London, 1979), *passim*.

accept the fact and simply say, "Since you want none of me I remain a Jew, and you can brand me as a cosmopolitan if you like."[13] Herzl had known about Vámbéry for a long time (probably from Nordau) and had made contact with him at least as early as September 1898.[14] But he had not followed it up, probably because of the intensity of his chase after the Kaiser. When they finally met, in June 1900, Herzl thought 'this limping, 70 year-old Hungarian Jew who doesn't know whether he is more Turk than Englishman' one of the most interesting men he had ever met[15] and Vámbéry was clearly impressed by Herzl the leader and Herzl the man of total dedication. They took to each other at once; they exchanged political intimacies—Vámbéry freely, Herzl, it seems, at Vámbéry's insistence; and they struck a note in their relationship in which affection, respect, some slight artificiality, pecuniary interest (on Vámbéry's part), and outrageous flattery (on Herzl's) were all comfortably combined.

Vámbéry was prepared to help, but refused to be hurried. He agreed eventually with Herzl that it was pointless to go on setting things out before the Sultan in *writing*. 'That *mamzer* [bastard] has to be spoken to, if anything is to be accomplished', but only when he (the Sultan) was in dire straits, he wrote. One should not press too hard. In the Orient one must be patient in the oriental manner.[16] Herzl pressed none the less and in August Vámbéry informed him that he had written to the Sultan and had had 'a not unfavourable reply'.[17] Herzl continued to press, Vámbéry, unhurried, to reassure. His relations with the Sultan were excellent; something had to be done and would be done: 'patience and shrewdness—that is what I advise you'.[18] But it was difficult advice to take. Besides, Vámbéry having failed to swing the gates of the Yildiz Kiosk open for him, Herzl had his other contacts to worry about. To cover his

---

[13] Arminius Vámbéry, *Story of My Struggles*, ii (London, 1904), pp. 423 f.

[14] Vámbéry to Herzl, 21 September 1898. CZA, H VIII/870.

[15] *Diaries*, iii, p. 961. Vámbéry was in his 68th year in 1900, not his 70th. Oddly, the diary does not reflect the shadow of a doubt in Herzl's mind: 'He loves you', Herzl wrote to Nordau after the first meeting. 'And I believe I won him. But can he be relied upon?' 22 June 1900. *Igrot Herzl*, iv.

[16] Vámbéry to Herzl, 19 June 1900. CZA, H VIII/870.

[17] Vámbéry to Herzl, 24 August 1900. Ibid.

[18] Vámbéry to Herzl, 30 August 1900. Ibid.

flank in the meantime, he informed Nuri that he was looking for another route to the Sultan, but that in any event Nuri and his friends were not to worry: they would be paid whichever route turned out to be the more successful.[19] In September Vámbéry and Herzl met again. The old man, Herzl noted in his diary,

gave me his word of honour that the Sultan would receive me by May.

To be sure, I don't quite understand how he can give me his word about something that doesn't depend upon himself. But I must be satisfied with anything. For the rest, I am quite weary.[20]

The months that followed were passed in futile correspondence with Nuri and Crespi and in chasing after schemes for proving the uses of the Zionists to the Ottoman Government: an offer by Herzl to participate in the building of the Hejaz railway (ignored), an invitation by the Turks (through Crespi[21]) to arrange an urgent £T7–800,000 loan (raised with immense pain by Herzl and then not taken up by the Turks), fresh assurances that Herzl would, indeed, be called to the Palace, warnings (mostly from Crespi) of actual and potential deals-in-the-making with European, mostly German, financial groups, and attempts by Herzl to interpret hopelessly incomplete and often conflicting bits of information.[22] In the end, it was all to no purpose. Herzl's own contacts were

[19] Herzl to Nuri, 2 August 1900. *Igrot Herzl*, iv.

[20] *Diaries*, iii, p. 979.

[21] The invitation came in the form of a letter from Crespi to Herzl, in Crespi's hand and on his private writing-paper. The operative part of the letter gives the flavour and style of the correspondence as a whole:

'Monsieur

Le Gouvernement a un besoin pressant de 7 à 800000 £tq qu'il veut qu'on lui avance. La garantie est de première ordre: les recettes des douanes; l'interêt 6 même 6½%.

C'est donc une belle opération financière.

Arrivez comme le "Deus ex machina", faites cette avance avec laquelle il n'y a aucun risque, entrez dans les bonnes grâces de Sa Majesté, faites vous connaître, prouvez qu'en tout temps, toutes circonstance[s], Elle peut compter sur vous, rendez-vous indispensable et une fois que vous serez entré dans les bonnes grâces du Souverain, du Gouvernment, du pays vous aurez *tout, tout, tout.*'

Crespi to Herzl, 12 October 1900. CZA, H VIII/162.

[22] See especially Herzl to Nuri, 1 October 1900. *Diaries*, iii, p. 980; Crespi to Herzl, 12 October 1900; 18 February; 13; 15; 18 March 1901. CZA, H VIII/162. Also *Diaries*, iii, pp. 985–1077 *passim*.

infinitely unreliable, as Vámbéry had warned him from the start,[23] their inner purposes difficult to discover, the danger of losing sums which the movement and its supporters could ill afford very great, and he himself out of his element.

That you are a *gentleman from top to toe*, I have no doubt [the Professor wrote to him] . . . What I fear is that despite your role as leader of the Zionists and therefore [by rights] a thoroughbred Oriental, you are nevertheless too much of an Occidental to know how to escape the danger presented by the Levantines. The rascality of that rabble is immeasurable and Mr N[uri] Bey, behind whom will be found [the Sultan], is notorious for his little affairs. So once again, take care! Take care![24]

Not until mid-April 1901 did Vámbéry make the journey to Constantinople to ask the Sultan point-blank to receive Herzl. Several more weeks of insufferable tension followed, filling Herzl with gloom. Had the Professor really left Budapest? Was there danger for him if he ever got as far as following Vámbéry to Constantinople? What disappointments were yet to come? To which were added dismal thoughts of his own rapidly approaching death in this, the forty-first year of his life and the sixth year of 'this movement which has made me old, tired, and poor'.[25]

However, early in May, first Crespi, then Vámbéry informed him that he would be received in audience after all. Limiting conditions had been set. Vámbéry himself would not be allowed to participate, but would have to leave Constantinople before Herzl arrived.[26] A court official, Ibrahim Bey

[23] Vámbéry to Herzl, 2 October; 22 October; 18 December 1900. CZA, H VIII/870.
[24] Vámbéry to Herzl, 29 December 1900. Ibid. The phrase in italics is in English in the original.
[25] *Diaries*, iii, pp. 1086–9.
[26] 'In most cases I was unable to discover the motive of his fear and precaution', Vámbéry wrote of 'Abd al-Hamid much later, after the 1908 revolution. 'When I decided to introduce the late Dr. Herzl, the head of the Zionists, I had to use every kind of pretext to disarm the Sultan's apprehension. He was fond of the Jews, he knew the Jewish colonization in Palestine would serve as a counterpoise against the steadily intruding inimical Christians and would strengthen his rule in Syria. But it nevertheless cost me days and days of persuasion, and when he ultimately acceded to my wish and agreed to receive Dr. Herzl, he did it under the condition that I must leave Constantinople at once, which I also did. Now I am quite at a loss to discover the reason of his command, and I shall probably never know it.' 'Personal recollections of Abdul Hamid II and his court', *Nineteenth Century and After* (June 1909), p. 987.

would serve as interpreter instead. Herzl would not be received as a Zionist, but as a Jewish leader and as a prominent journalist; the matter of Zionism *per se* was not to be brought up. But Herzl was in no mood to dwell upon these restrictions and reservations. The opportunity to talk to the Sultan was all he had asked for. The condition and the resources of the movement, he told himself, were such that if he were offered Ereẓ-Israel there and then it would be an embarrassment anyway. So he lost no time, arrived in Constantinople on 11 May 1901, had a brief, cool meeting with Tahsin Bey, the Sultan's First Secretary, and settled down in his hotel to await the call and consider precisely what he would say to the Sultan 'so that the fabulous moment of my desire might not go by unused'.[27]

The talk with the Sultan took place six days after his arrival, on Friday 17 May. It was a long one, lasting over two hours, and was superficially cordial.[28] In some ways it was an odd affair. The contrast between the two men was striking and ironic. The Jew was a remarkable individual, in externals as in everything else. A self-declared 'non-Zionist' observer described him at about this time as one who struck him

as a perfect model of Chaldean biblical beauty: slim, fine, pure Viennese, 'fesch und elegant' [smart and elegant], a gentleman from head to toe, an enchanting and witty talker . . . His languorous and deeply set eyes, the quality of his voice, the perfect style of his German—all exercised the attractive force of a lover, hypnotizing, electrifying. His entire personality reflected nobility of spirit and thought.[29]

The Caliph was a man of a totally different order. Contemporary descriptions of ʿAbd al-Hamid, mostly hostile, are legion and Herzl's initial, two-line portrait was typical:

[27] *Diaries*, iii, p. 1106.

[28] The only known contemporary record of the interview is Herzl's own in his diary (*Diaries*, iii, pp. 1110–18). ʿAbd al-Hamid disliked committing himself to paper, but the question whether a parallel Turkish version exists cannot be settled until free access is granted to the relevant Yildiz Palace archives. The Turkish Foreign Ministry files on the Zionist movement contain no such document. Cf. Bülent Mim Kemal Öke, 'Ottoman Policies towards Zionism (1880–1908)' (unpublished M.Phil. thesis, Cambridge University, 1979).

[29] Léon Baratz, *Réalités et Rêveries de Ghetto* (Geneva, 1934), p. 9.

'"The Monster" stood before me exactly as I had pictured him: short, skinny, with a large hooked nose, a full dyed beard, a small tremulous voice.'[30] Later, recapitulating his recollections of the interview, on board ship after leaving Constantinople, he drew a sharper picture: 'Small, shabby, with his badly dyed beard which is probably freshly painted only once a week for the *selamlik*. The hooked nose of a Punchinello, the long yellow teeth with a big gap on the upper right . . . The feeble hands in white, oversize gloves, and the ill-fitting, coarse, loud-coloured cuffs. The bleating voice, the constraint in every word, the timidity in every glance. And *this* rules! Only on the surface, of course, and nominally.'[31]

Herzl underestimated ʿAbd al-Hamid, as did many other Europeans. His portrait of the man is almost identical with the one drawn by the noted contemporary expert, Sir Edwin Pears.[32] It had much in common with Vámbéry's and may well have been influenced by him. The latter, reporting to the Foreign Office in London on what he had learned during his stay in Constantinople in April 1901 (when he had arranged for Herzl's audience with the Sultan), drew a dark picture of the future of the Empire and argued that a major cause of its trouble was the decline of the Sultan.

Abdul Hamid is decidedly mentally and physically broken, he is no longer the supreme lord in the palace who is able to impose and to command his greedy, dishonest and cunning servants; he does not unite and keep in his hands any longer the threads of the varied plots, tricks and foul games upon which his rule was founded. On the contrary, he is now an instrument in the hands of the leading court officials, who exploit him in the interest of their personal affairs, and of whom he is much afraid. Nothing is more interesting than to watch from near the machinations of Tahsin Bey and Izzet Bey, his first and second secretaries, who are in furious enmity against each other, and who, considering the puppet character of the leading statesmen, are his real hands and ministers. The former, a hardworking man from nine in the morning till 1 or 2 after midnight, is so to say his pen, whilst the latter may be called his brain, i.e. chief adviser; for Izzet knows french [*sic*] and has been in Europe, whereas Tahsin

---

[30] *Diaries*, iii, p. 1112.
[31] Ibid., p. 1128.
[32] *Life of Abdul Hamid* (London, 1917), pp. 340–1.

does not know any European language. This Izzet, a shrewd Arab, is a bitter enemy to every Christian, he is cruel and reckless in the extreme and all the evil deeds of the latter rule of the Sultan are his own diabolical inventions. Of course the Sultan is quite helpless in the hands of these two servants and manages his affairs only by inciting one against the other and by giving occasionally presents to both of them.[33]

Still, as Vámbéry knew himself, nothing could be done in direct defiance of the Sultan, nor could there be any radical move or change without his approval. Within the system, it was he who held the balance of power. Herzl's instinct to press for an audience was therefore correct, as far as it went; and in Vámbéry's undertaking to help arrange one may be seen his ultimate appreciation of the way in which power in Constantinople was distributed.

The tenor of the conversation matched the scene formed by the protagonists. Herzl was at his best: strong, self-confident, successful in striking the note he had desired; and the Sultan seemed receptive. He allowed Herzl to take the lead, he asked no searching questions, he voiced no disagreement with anything Herzl had to say. His every word and gesture implied, so it seemed, trust in Herzl and, beyond him, in the Jewish people, along with goodwill and a disposition to see the Jews as allies, a source of much needed help in times of difficulty. But in terms of content, matters were otherwise.

Obedient to repeated warnings and bound by the terms of his introduction to the presence, Herzl said nothing of Zionism specifically. To the condition of the Jews he alluded only indirectly. Of their ultimate hopes in Ereẓ-Israel he did not speak. The Charter went unmentioned; so, of course, did the possibility of international guarantees for the returning Jews. He felt obliged to limit himself to no more than paving the way to the greater matter by speaking repeatedly and meaningfully of the services the Jews could render the Ottoman state and by dwelling on the traditional protection and hospitality which Jews had found in Ottoman territory. He did say that

---

[33] 12 May 1901. PRO, FO 800/33. Vámbéry's letter has no clear addressee, but is marked 'Ack[nowledge]d' and 'Seen by Sir N. O'Conor' (the British Ambassador at Constantinople at the time).

the services he and his friends would perform required the Sultan's corresponding support. And, 'when the time came, this support would have to take the form of some measure particularly friendly to the Jews, and it must be proclaimed in an appropriate manner.' When the Sultan, blandly, offered to say something favourable about the Jews to his court jeweller, a Jew, and instruct him 'to put it in the papers', Herzl turned the offer down, politely, but refrained from specifying just what he himself had in mind. His immediate, limited aim was to gain acceptance of the offer of financial assistance and of the *principle* that it would be met in the future by some still undefined measure of support for him and his friends on the part of the Turkish sovereign. In the event, the offer was accepted; and the principle of a quid pro quo was not questioned. And thus, ostensibly, the basis—in fact, the idea—of co-operation was established. For the rest, the details and the modalities of the relationship were to be worked out with the staff of the Yildiz—in great secrecy, as the Sultan and Herzl had agreed. Herzl's aim had been a restricted one, but it appeared to have been achieved. And the ordeal over, he emerged 'calm', as he noted in the diary, 'as always in success'.

None the less, these were slender foundations on which to build. The mixing of economic and political elements in the proposed relationship had its logic and its tactical advantages. But the problem Herzl had now burdened himself with was how to bring about a change in the original proportions of the mix—in which the economic element was dominant and the political barely more than implicit. To this end everything depended on the validity of his fundamental assumptions that economic co-operation could be transmuted into political and that through close economic ties the sources of Turkish suspicion of, and hostility to, the Zionists could be dissolved.

But this assumed, in turn, that the traditional line of thought dividing the economic from the political was less than clear-cut and that there was some interchangeability between the two, and that matters economic and matters political could be weighed one against the other. These were all nice assumptions. Their flaw, and one source of Herzl's errors in his dealings with the Turks, lay in their neglect of the inherent primacy of the *political*, the sphere of ultimate control. The economic difficulties of the Turks were real, the Debt was a burden, and its administration by a European Commission humiliating.[34] All this was undeniable. Almost as difficult to deny was the argument that in the abstract and in the very long term economic strength and development appear to be conducive to political efficacy. In one sphere, that of the external politics of states, the evidence tends to support this argument by reason of the direct functional connection between economic progress and military technology. But whether the thesis can be as easily applied to the internal political context is less clear; and still less clear is the question whether it was applicable to the particular case of the Ottoman Empire in its years of decline and in the *short* term. Everything suggests that in the minds of the Sultan and the members of his entourage strictly political considerations, that is to say, those pertaining to internal social control and the continuation of their own rule and government as they understood it, were absolute; and the arguments for or against a particular measure had to be cast in matching political terms if they were to be allowed to count at all. The weight of the Debt in their minds was simply not comparable with that of such perceived and familiar dangers to their rule as independently and politically minded ethnic groups, particularly non-Muslim groups, were known to constitute. In the case of the Jews, and of Palestine, there were, as already suggested, additional considerations to reinforce the opposition to what the Zionists intended. And in a society in which the political and the religious were not separable ultimately (as the political and the economic were) these were very weighty considerations and formidable overt and covert obstacles to Herzl's purposes.

So all in all, it is not surprising that, surface changes apart, the sum total of Herzl's achievement at the interview did not

[34] At the accession of ʿAbd al-Hamid the external debt of the Ottoman State amounted to some £T190,000,000, an immense sum at the time. Incapable of meeting payments, Turkey was, in principle, bankrupt—if a sovereign state may ever be said to be 'bankrupt'. In 1881, following foreign pressure and hard negotiations, state revenues from tobacco, salt, spirits, stamps, silks, and fisheries were 'ceded' to a specially set-up Council of Administration of the Ottoman Public Debt, six members of which represented the European creditors and only one, without voting rights, the Imperial Ottoman Bank. The Turks also lost their right to impose tariffs freely: an 8% tax on imports was levied uniformly.

amount to much more than a repetition, in admittedly grander circumstances, of the result of his first visit to Constantinople five years earlier. Then too his claim to speak for Jewry had not been questioned and his formulation of the principle that Jewish financial resources would be at the disposal of the Turks in exchange for political concessions had been implicitly accepted.[35] Indeed, there had been no change in Turkish policy. In its most visible aspect—on the ground in Erez-Israel itself—it was as firm as ever. Herzl's first visit to Constantinople had been followed by a tightening of the entry and settlement restrictions. This, his third visit, had been preceded by another bout of restrictive measures (the 'Red Slip') and was to be followed within a month by the dispatch of an inspector in the secret police to set up a branch of the service in Palestine.[36] Yet although the tension between what the Zionists wanted, even at a minimum, and what the Turks would allow them had not been relaxed in any degree, the denouement was long delayed. Fourteen months passed in more tiresome exchanges in writing and irritating and futile negotiations during a fourth visit to Constantinople in February 1902 and a fifth and last visit in July of that year before the only reasonable inference from the accumulated evidence had finally been drawn. This was a long period for a man consumed with impatience, who believed that it would be by a great and dramatic stroke that the condition of the Jews would be transformed, and who was now sure that he had not long to live. But it is not difficult to account for.

In the first place, the Turks, in their dealings with Herzl, were clear and firm in some respects, but vague and shifting in others. They spoke with different voices at different times, literally as well as figuratively. Herzl was unable to see the Sultan again,[37] but was repeatedly invited to communicate

---

[35] *Origins*, pp. 296–8.

[36] N. J. Mandel, 'Turks, Arabs and Jewish Immigration into Palestine: 1882–1914' (D.Phil. thesis, Oxford, 1965), p. 88.

[37] Evidence purporting to establish that Herzl was in Constantinople in *June* 1902 (as well as in July) and that he was received by the Sultan for a second time, through the intercession of the Ḥakham Bashi, or Chief Rabbi of the Empire, has been published (Abraham Galanté, 'Abdul Hamid II et le Sionisme', *Hamenora*, xi, 1–3 (January–March 1933), pp. 2–15). But there is no trace of such a second audience in any of Herzl's own papers and his movements in Europe in June of that year make it

with him in writing. The response was almost always verbal and came through the Sultan's men—principally through Tahsin, the First Secretary, and Izzet, the Second Secretary, but also through Said Pasha, the Grand Vizier, and Ibrahim, the *Introducteur des Ambassadeurs*. Herzl knew that each represented a distinct source of influence over the Sultan and in the Government and that Tahsin and Izzet counted for most; but it was impossible for him to distinguish between what these two men said and did on the Sultan's behalf and what they said and did for their own private and corrupt gain, particularly when they contradicted each other. At one point Herzl was asked to deposit the considerable sum of three million francs as a preliminary to the granting of *fermans* authorizing strictly economic concessions. The invitation came through Izzet. But when Herzl, with much pain and effort, had succeeded in arranging the necessary credits, the money was abruptly refused by Tahsin and the deal cancelled. Had the Sultan had second thoughts? Had he been consulted at all; and if so at what stage? Or had Herzl tripped on wires laid for the unwary by rival Palace camarillas? And how much weight was it right to attach to the affair and how drastic a conclusion ought he to draw from it? To none of these questions were there clear answers.

What Herzl did perceive in the course of time was that the revival of Turkish interest in him in 1902 which had led to his being summoned to Constantinople twice in that year coincided with the Turks' entry into negotiations with a powerful French financial group. The subject of negotiations was precisely that which Herzl had initially proposed: the consolidation of the Public Debt. Plainly, the Turks had found it useful to bring him on to the edge of the stage as a spur to the French. But in itself, the probability that they were manipulating him

---

exceedingly improbable that he could have gone to Constantinople and back (in the age of steam) without being in two places at the same time. Besides, the Ḥakham Bashi was known for his hostility to Herzl, to whom it had been reported (not necessarily correctly) that he had gone so far as to write to the Sultan of his opposition to Zionism. (Crespi to Herzl, 14 August 1901. CZA, H VIII/162.) Nor does the story fit the known outlines of Herzl's relations with the Yildiz and the Porte. Its confirmation will therefore depend on the discovery of supporting documentation in the Turkish archives.

could lead him to no firm, operative conclusion, only to the further question whether they were prepared to fall back on him if the prospective deal with the French fell through or if he, in the meantime, made a better offer.[38] Once again, this was a question he had no way of answering; and for lack of an answer it was difficult for him to decide what to do.

The objective difficulty for Herzl in dealing with the Ottoman Government was constant. He moved perforce in a fog of disconnected and frequently false bits of information, barriers of language, and incomprehensible signals from well-wishers and ill-wishers alike—a fog that was the more difficult to penetrate for its being disseminated by, and in the vicinity of, a regime that was itself fed by an army of spies and informers whose product was too great to be digestible. During his visits to Constantinople Herzl was subject, moreover, to the disorienting effects of an unfamiliar rhythm of action and reaction, of endless waiting, of the physical discomfort (especially in summer) of the obligatory formal dress for court, and of the 'snake food'[39] he was obliged to eat. To this must be added the mental discomfort which stemmed from the distasteful dual role into which he had felt he must fit himself—of national leader and international financier.[40] The result was constant mental stress and a loss of ability to predict the likely outcome of his or anyone else's actions. It was a loss, in a word, of some part of his power of judgement—manifest, for example, in his inclination to underrate the Sultan.

The second reason why negotiations with the Turks were so prolonged was that Herzl's ability to play the role of financial saviour of Turkey to the full was vitiated by his failure to mobilize the great sums of money required for the operation. 'We are perhaps on the eve of the Charter!', he had written to

---

[38] In the event, negotiations for the consolidation of the Ottoman Debt were completed in September of the following year, 1903, with the setting-up of an international consortium led by Maurice Rouvier, a former French prime minister. Details in Louis Delaygue, *Essai sur les finances ottomanes* (Paris, 1911), pp. 140–52.

[39] *Diaries*, iv, p. 1339.

[40] There could be no question of his getting a commission on the Turkish loan, he wrote to Wolffsohn on one occasion; and Jacobus Kann, the Dutch-Jewish banker who was arranging it, *must* know this. Kann might take a commission; Wolffsohn might too, Herzl wrote. 'Aber ich als Führer darf an keinem Geschäft theilnehmen.' Herzl to Wolffsohn, 14 November 1900. *Igrot Herzl*, iv.

Mandelstamm in glee after the audience.[41] But the achievement
in Turkey, such as it was, changed nothing in Europe. Major
Jewish figures in the world of finance, the Rothschilds and the
Pereires among them, would have no more to do with him
now than before; among the lesser figures there were at best
one or two who would go as far as promising help, but only
when the Charter had been granted. It was infuriating.
'I would so much like to proclaim', he wrote to Mandelstamm
a few months later, 'Jews! Look how I, a poor journalist, have
brought negotiations with [the Sultan] to such a point single-
handedly and now you let me down. Well, to Hell with you!
But I cannot [cease].'[42] And, indeed, Herzl had no choice
but to play for time in the hope that a substantial gesture by
the Turks would bring the plutocrats round. The Turks
themselves seem to have sensed what he was doing; in any
event, no great gesture was forthcoming. Later, when he was
able to put a fair sum on the table (admittedly for a less
dramatic purpose than the consolidation of the full Public
Debt), it was, as has been said, turned down. But had there
been a moment when a deal might have been concluded and
the moment missed for lack of funds? That, approximately,
was his own view. It is not entirely inconceivable: but it remains
improbable.

The Ottoman Government, Herzl was told (not for the first
time or the last) at the high point of negotiations in February,
was prepared to open the Empire to settlement by Jewish
refugees from all countries. The Jews must renounce their
original nationality and accept the Ottoman; and they must
accept all the normal obligations that nationality implied,
including military service. They could settle in Anatolia or
Mesopotamia. But they could only settle in very small clusters;
and they must not settle in Erez-Israel at all. In exchange,
he was to 'form a syndicate for the consolidation of the Public
Debt, which is currently under discussion, and to assume the
concession for the exploitation of all the mines in the Empire,
those already discovered and those yet to be discovered'.[43]
The principle of Ottoman nationality presented no difficulty

[41] Herzl to Mandelstamm, 18 May 1901. CZA, A 3/46.
[42] Herzl to Mandelstamm, 18 August 1901. Ibid.
[43] *Diaries*, iii, pp. 1218–19.

and was immediately accepted. But dispersed-settlement in general, and *a fortiori* outside Erez-Israel, was out of the question. It removed the concession from the political plane to the philanthropic. It nullified the fundamental thesis of territorial concentration as the key to national rehabilitation and national safety. It was, of course, no more and no less than what the Turks had offered just under twenty years ago. In that sense, it was hardly a concession at all, although Herzl does not seem to have realized this. There could hardly have been better proof of the Turks' fixity of purpose, the strength and length of their institutional memory, and their mastery of diplomatic cunning.

Herzl, for his part, was cautious at first and pressed for a change obliquely. There had to be a *link* between Jewish settlement and the financial operation for the Debt. That much had been conceded. The proper form for such a link, he argued, was 'a great Ottoman-Jewish company for colonization' (in other words: a Charter). To apply restrictions on the settlement would only alienate the scheme's potential backers. That would endanger the link. The Sultan's response (through Izzet) then weakened it at another point: the idea of an Ottoman-Jewish company was implicitly accepted, but the prohibition on Jewish settlement in Erez-Israel was explicitly reiterated. The locus of disagreement was now outlined sharply and Herzl was forced to tell the Turks (in February 1902) that a 'Charter without Palestine' was out of the question.[44] To avoid a break he then fell back on the plan to involve the Zionists in economic activity in Turkey without any political quid pro quo whatsoever being specified, but merely as a means to garner strength and influence for the future. This had been Nuri's original advice. It was now Izzet's. Was it the Sultan's too? There was no way of knowing; but the longer Herzl turned it over in his mind, the more he was inclined to accept it. There followed the plan to issue *fermans* authorizing economic concessions, the deposit of the three million francs the Turks had requested, the subsequent withdrawal of the Turkish invitation, and, after an interval, a fresh summons to Constantinople plainly linked to the concurrent negotiations with the French.

[44] *Diaries*, iii, pp. 1221–2.

Herzl now tried again. He and his friends, he told the Turks when he arrived in Constantinople towards the end of July 1902, were prepared to undertake anything the French group had undertaken—or had been asked to undertake—and to go one better. 'In exchange, the imperial government would grant us a charter or concession for Jewish colonization in Mesopotamia, as Your Imperial Majesty deigned to offer me last February, adding the territory of Haifa and its environs in Palestine.'[45] The retreat was substantial. Areas other than Erez-Israel would be considered, in spite of the Basel Programme and the overwhelming sentiment in the movement and beyond it; and the country itself, for present purposes, had been reduced to 'Haifa and its environs'. Lastly, if the Sultan did not 'deem it proper to accept Herzl's views on the usefulness of Jewish colonization to the Empire' in *any* form, the alternative of purely economic services was still available. A week of further interviews, clarifications, translations and retranslations, and interminable waiting passed. As he waited, Herzl reflected on his own recurring thoughts—'the feeling while speaking with them that they aren't really serious about it after all. They are like sea foam. Only their expressions are serious, not their intentions. And it kept occurring to me suddenly while deep in conversation: Why, all of that is just talk. They wanted nothing in reality.'[46] But the reply that reached him on 2 August 1902 and was *dictated* to him (in French) to leave no room for doubt was clear enough.

The Jews can be admitted and established in the Ottoman Empire on condition that they are settled ununited [non réunis], that is to say dispersed, in such places as are judged suitable by the Government, their numbers fixed beforehand by the Government. They will be accorded Ottoman citizenship [la sujétion ottomane] and charged with all civic duties, including military service, and as Ottomans be subject to all the laws of the land.[47]

This was the policy that had been laid down in 1882. It meant then, and continued to mean, no special status or rights, no

---

[45] French original in *Tagebücher*, iii, pp. 242–5. English translation in *Diaries*, iv, pp. 1314–16.

[46] *Diaries*, iv, p. 1334.

[47] *Tagebücher*, iii, p. 274.

Charter, no Ottoman-Jewish land company, no settlement (by clear implication) in any part of Erez-Israel. It allowed, at best, for some relief for hard-pressed people in one part of the Jewish Dispersion by their transfer in small, dispersed, and vulnerable groups to other parts of the Dispersion, some old and familiar, some new and forbidding. The Turkish machinery of government had held absolutely firm—as well it might in the face of so puny an effort to shift it to a fresh position. A year later, reporting on the Sixth Congress, a senior Ottoman diplomat wrote as a matter of course of the imperial Government's urgent need

> to draw up special laws prohibiting the purchase of land in Palestine by the Zionists under any name whatsoever, so preventing the colonization of that country, the purpose of which colonization is first to attain autonomy and [then], employing all political or other means, form an independent state there.
>   That is the essential aim of the Zionists.[48]

Tahsin's own recollection of the affair in his memoirs is summary, substantially inaccurate in detail, and hostile, but instructive as a reflection of his and his colleagues' approach in its unvarnished form to the matter of Zionism.

> ʿAbd al-Hamid's policy, founded on suspicion, was particularly evident in the matter of Zionism. The establishment of a Jewish country within Turkey had always been one of the great aims of the Zionist world. The Zionists acted several times to reach their goal, but never succeeded. Each time Sultan ʿAbd al-Hamid suspected [or: was fearful of] the purpose and the outcome and evaded it. On one occasion there came to Istanbul an Austrian Jew who was one of the Zionist leaders. He saw the Dragoman Munir Pasha and asked for permission to found a Jewish state in Jerusalem . . . Behind the matter was the famous banker Rothschild . . . Both because of the importance of the Jew from Vienna and because of the seriousness of the proposal concerning the [Public] Debt I informed His Majesty. The Jew was received into the presence of His Majesty after the Friday ceremony. The Jew from Vienna explained the matter in detail to Sultan ʿAbd al-Hamid. However Sultan ʿAbd al-Hamid saw certain faults in the matter. The Palestine region was in any

---

[48] Ahmed Tevfik (Ambassador in Berlin) to Tevfik Pasha (Foreign Minister), 31 August 1903. OFMA, file C/332–D/17, 3309/178.

case a subject of [foreign] political aspirations because of its holy places . . . Besides, the Jewish aspect was not liked by the Sultan. The Zionist from Vienna returned to his country without achieving anything.[49]

A third reason why the effort to win over the Turks lasted so long and took so convoluted a form may be surmised: the alternative was a bitter one to contemplate. Failure here seemed to imply failure on the whole broad front of political, Herzlian Zionism. In the autumn of 1901, when Herzl was still fairly confident that the Turks would eventually grant him the Charter, he addressed the Greater Actions Committee on what he saw then as the harder problem—raising the money to activate it. Everything and everyone would be tried, the City of London, the communities, public pressure and campaigns, even a journey to America in which he would be joined by Nordau and Zangwill. But, 'If everything fails, Zionism will have turned into a theoretical movement. We will then have done everything of which we were capable. Zionism in its Basel form will have ended.'[50] Reporting to the GAC once more, a year later (October 1902), he dwelt on the 'pitiful' results of the appeal for money (chiefly in London) immediately after the interview with the Sultan and the consequences of 'our present financial impotence'. He argued, sticking to his guns, that had matters been otherwise, better things could have been obtained from the Turks. 'We have laid out the wires, but the energy has not been forthcoming.' And since the movement's poverty was unlikely to be relieved in the foreseeable future, it followed that if there was to be a change in its relations with the Turks, the change would have to be on the Turkish side—such as 'could occur only if Turkey were suddenly to become involved in a war or if she were to get into some international difficulty'.[51]

Herzl's analysis of the causes of his failure was superficial even on the bais of his own experience and the information available to him at the time. The Turkish Government had

---

[49] Tahsin Paşa, *Abdülhamit ve Yıldız Hatıraları* (Istanbul, 1931), p. 80.

[50] GAC session, 10 October 1901. CZA, Z 1/191.

[51] GAC session, 29 October 1902. CZA, ZB 1 168. English translation of Herzl's political report by Zohn in *Zionist Writings*, ii, pp. 216–20.

been undeviating in its refusal to countenance the growth of a modern Jewish community in Erez-Israel and hostile in the extreme to any hint of political autonomy for the Jews there or anywhere else. The terms on which Jewish immigration would be tolerated had been laid down early and had been stuck to rigidly. Co-operation with Herzl even in principle was acceptable only provided that these same rules of policy remained unimpaired. And even then there was nothing to indicate that the Turks were really prepared to proceed from principle to practice and much to suggest that they were not. On this showing, the money which Herzl so badly wanted would have been of little help. More generally, his basic thesis, as formulated at the very beginning of his decision to act in the Jewish interest, had proved unfounded. The harsh language of the Turkish Ambassador in Washington in 1899 was a more accurate reflection of the fundamental Turkish position than he or almost any of the new men he had brought with him to the movement had realized.[52] Richard Gottheil, his principal ally in the United States and a Professor of Semitics at Columbia University, wrote to him some months later that 'The question is—what sort of Charter *can* a Muhammedan power grant?' Gottheil had been looking into it in all its legal and conceptual complexity, but had no answer. 'But it seems to me', he added, 'that we ought to know exactly what to ask when we get to the asking', and he recommended that Ignaz Goldziher be consulted.[53]

There is no evidence that Gottheil's query or line of thought was ever followed up. Yet Herzl's operative conclusion, as put to the GAC in October, that there was nothing to be done before Turkey underwent internal or external change was in itself impeccable. He did now see the rock which blocked the road to progress for the great obstacle it was and recognized his inability to shift it—for all that he still failed to understand its quality and structure. And his powerful instinct for action, for anything but repose—'I do not want to wait any longer. More precisely: I cannot', he wrote to one of his contact men

[52] See above, p. 56.
[53] Gottheil to Herzl, 6 September 1899. CZA, H VIII/289. Goldziher was one of the foremost Islamic scholars of his day; but he had no sympathy for Zionism and it is unlikely that he would have been helpful if he had been approached.

in Constantinople[54]—was evident in another respect. He did not now proclaim that Zionism in its 'Basel form' was at an end, as he had promised. On the contrary: 'I am naturally not of the opinion that our movement will have to close up shop or that we should be disheartened',[55] he told his Committee, and went on to outline new developments and fresh lines of thought and action.

[54] Letter to Crespi, 24 August 1902. CZA, HN III/207.
[55] GAC session, 29 October 1902. Loc. cit.

5

Seeking an Ally (II)

i

Herzl did not break with the Turks. He kept the mounting
irritation, bordering on revulsion, that he had come to feel
for Constantinople, that 'den of Ali Baba, and the forty
thieves',[1] to himself. He was careful to do nothing or say anything that might spoil the tenuous relationship that he had
set up on his very first visit there in 1896 and which he had
nursed so devotedly and expensively ever since. For if there was
nothing to be done with the Turks, neither was there any way
of circumventing them. There was simply no alternative to a
policy of self-control, patience, and alertness to the slightest
change in the wind. 'They have grown accustomed in Yildiz
and the Porte to looking upon me as someone interested in the
vilayet of Beirut', he noted in his diary on the train carrying
him back to Europe for the last time. 'Some day—when they
are *dans la dèche* [reduced to beggary], as the Jew Daoud
Effendi told me as early as 1896—they will suddenly send for
me in their need, and throw the thing in my lap.'[2] Meanwhile,
he would revert to Europe and the indirect approach.

The force of the tactical logic underlying this shift of Herzl's
resources of time and nervous energy was strengthened
by an unmistakable sense of relief at leaving Turkey behind
him and by an accession of ease and confidence in his relations
with the men of office and established position with whom he
now had to treat. There followed a brief and fruitless attempt
to re-heat German interest. There was a more serious and
more elaborate effort to convert Russian hostility to the Jews
within Russia into support for Zionism outside it—of which

---

[1] *Diaries*, iv, p. 1342.
[2] Ibid., p. 1344.

more will be said, as of his audiences with the Pope and with
the King of Italy towards the end of his career and life. And
there were other, minor soundings with the Americans and
the Portuguese. Herzl never wavered in his fundamental rule
of trying everyone and everything and probing every crack in
the wall that barred the Zionists' way to free movement inside
the political arena. But his main business from now until his
death in the summer of 1904, and almost exclusively between
the autumn of 1902 and the summer of 1903, was with Great
Britain; and it may be taken as a tribute to the validity of his
methods that, as we shall see, the groundwork for what was to
turn into his one undoubted diplomatic success had been laid
well before he was forced to admit defeat in Constantinople
and impelled to turn elsewhere—if only to keep up the momentum by which he had always set such store.

Herzl, in brief, remained consistent in his aims and methods.
In his diplomacy he kept his own counsel. His reports on it in
the sessions of the Greater Actions Committee were cast in
general terms only; in the Smaller Actions Committee they
were perfunctory; before the Congresses they were, in essence,
proclamatory, not to say rhetorical. On the very rare occasions
when he consulted his colleagues it was almost invariably on
questions of minor tactics or points of information. Where they
could be helpful and where they fell into line with him smoothly,
they earned his praise and affection. Where they showed
signs of independence they caused irritability, even rage.
But those consulted were few and those actively involved, if
only as his representatives and messengers, were no more than
a handful.

All this added to the strain between Herzl and the main
body of his captains in the East; and the tension was fast
becoming irresolvable. Its remoter source lay, as we have
seen, in his having won them to his side on a basis that was never
other than incomplete and conditional. They had come to
him with hope, but also resignation. Their regard for him was
high, but inextricable from his not being one of their own.
They were aware that the old forms and the old methods had
lost whatever validity they had had, but (with some exceptions) they remained incompletely convinced of the validity
of the new. They found it difficult to argue against the logic of

his diplomacy and the grounds on which Herzl justified the secrecy of his operations; but they chafed under them. They granted him votes of confidence at successive Congresses because the alternative was to disown him and to fend for themselves, when it was plain that there were no rival candidates for his role and functions and that, moreover, his appeal reached beyond their own circle and committed activists. At the apogee of his career, towards its end, Herzl had acquired just that position in Jewry to which he had aspired from the first and which he had assumed—brazenly, as some thought— long before it was objectively justified. For by 1902, or thereabouts, it was plain to all that Herzl was much more than a formally elected parliamentary leader of the Congress and therefore of the Zionist movement as a whole. He was the preeminent national figure in contemporary Jewry, the man to whom ever greater numbers of Russian, Polish, and Romanian Jews turned in their anonymous misery and upon whom their hopes were placed. More: he had entered into the tiny class of Jews to whom the great men of the world were willing, from time to time, to pay attention. And thus, now, towards the end of his life, he was indeed in the process of becoming what his warier followers and many of his enemies had feared from the first: a Prince of the Jews, a personage enveloped in a semi-Messianic aura, virtually a latter-day Shabbetai Zevi, a *popular* leader, owing less to the due process of election by which his own movement periodically reconfirmed its support for him and more to general acclamation. Had the Jews had their state, he could have been their King—except that, almost certainly, he would not have chosen to be one. Along with his insistence on playing a lone and autocratic hand, he had a profound and, in some ways, sentimental regard for established, orderly political institutions, parliamentary institutions above all. In this respect, as in so many others, he was no more than a man of his place, social class, times, and original professional training in the law. There can be no doubt that he had been intent all along to imbue the Zionist movement— and, by extension, the Jewish people—with just such permanent, authoritative national institutions as were on view for general admiration in *western* Europe. When faced with the alternative of pursuing his policy in defiance of the organized parliamentary opposition to it or of preserving the unity and authority of the movement and the Congress he had himself created, even at the cost of beating a retreat, he opted, as we shall see, for retreat—virtually without hesitation.

ii

The British census of 1871 had listed some 10,000 Russian and Russian-Polish resident aliens. The census of 1911 was to list approximately ten times as many resident aliens as being of Russian, Russian-Polish, and Romanian nationality. All these, apart from a few thousand Polish miners and factory hands, were Jews[3]—a by-product of the great migratory wave out of Russia, Poland (Austrian as well as Russian), and Romania that was bringing so large a number into the United States at the end of the nineteenth century and the beginning of the twentieth. Some had made for England (and to a lesser extent Scotland and Wales) of free choice; some because they could not afford passage to more distant and seemingly more promising lands; some had arrived in England in transit and then judged they would do well, or well enough, to remain; others had been cheated by the owners or masters of the ships in which they had travelled and had been landed against their will in London or Liverpool long before arrival in New York or Philadelphia or Baltimore. Just how many such immigrants there were can now be estimated from the census figures. But at the time no one could say—not, at all events, with anything approaching precision. Government inspection and control of immigration at the ports and the keeping of official figures were conducted under a hopelessly incomplete and antiquated system originally set up under the authority of an Act of Parliament passed in the reign of William IV in 1836 and based upon the lists of non-British passengers which shipmasters were required to submit on entry. But such lists were not collected at all ports. At some of those ports where they were collected only deck passengers were counted. The important distinction between passengers in transit and passengers entering for extended or permanent stay was not always made. Positive verification of the shipmasters' lists by customs

[3] Lloyd P. Gartner, 'Notes on the Statistics of Jewish Immigration to England 1870–1914', *Jewish Social Studies*, xxii (1960), 2, pp. 97–102.

officers (there were no specially appointed and trained immigration officers) actually boarding the ships in question was chiefly on a spot-check basis; at best, it was done for ships known in advance to be carrying large numbers of migrants;[4] and the staff available were hopelessly inadequate: in the Port of London, through which most migrants passed, there were only two officers specially assigned to the immense task. They were zealous enough: one officer had gone so far as to learn enough Yiddish to be able to interrogate the migrants in their own language.[5] But the scale of the enterprise defeated them.

Largely for these reasons, the wildest estimates of the size of the recent settlement of 'aliens'—in practice, east European Jews—were current and proclaimed with confidence even by spokesmen for the Government in Parliament. In 1904, introducing an Aliens Bill to authorize rigorous inspection and control of the traffic, the Home Secretary spoke of over 80,000 immigrants in each of the years 1901 and 1902; and part of a subsequent Committee debate in Parliament revolved around the belief that the grand total for the past decade had been no less than 750,000.[6] Those agitating publicly against immigration outside Parliament cited similar or greater figures. But chiefly they relied on arguments of a different order. 'I don't ask what are the statistics. I say, what are the facts', was the characteristic note struck by Arnold White, a leading opponent of alien immigration, at a rally in London early in 1902 at the height of the campaign to stop free entry. His 'facts' were the social injuries allegedly inflicted by the foreign immigrants on English society, notably crime, dispossession, overcrowded housing, lowered rates of wages, unclean habits, sweat-shops, and their bringing with them into the country children whose education had then to be paid for out of public funds.[7]

While the fight to restrict or, if possible, stop their entry was mostly conducted to the accompaniment of hot denials of

[4] Evidence given before the Royal Commission on Alien Immigration by H. Llewellyn Smith of the Board of Trade, 24 April 1902. Royal Commission on Alien Immigration, *Minutes of Evidence*, Cd. 1742 (London, 1903), pp. 1–15.

[5] Evidence of Thomas Hawkey, 1 May 1902. Ibid., p. 39.

[6] *Hansard, Parliamentary Debates*, 4th Series, vol. 148, 3 July 1905, cols. 794–876.

[7] Report on a public meeting organized by the British Brothers' League at the People's Palace in the East End of London. *Jewish Chronicle*, 17 January 1902.

ordinary and explicit anti-Semitic intent and motivation, the fundamental element of the controversy was none the less the Jewish one and so it was understood to be by all concerned. Accordingly, the primary focus of interest and indignation oscillated between the East End of London, where so many of the new and indigent Jewish immigrants had congregated, and the West End where there was a small but visible sprinkling of their affluent brethren. One Liberal Member of Parliament (Henry Norman) who had joined Arnold White on a platform in the East End spoke of 'the scum of Europe' being dumped in England, here 'in the heart of the Empire [instead of in] the dustbin of Austria and Russia' where they belonged; another Liberal Member of Parliament (John Burns), speaking in the House of Commons, asked the President of the Board of Trade if he would inform the House whether 'the promised inquiry [into alien immigration] will extend to the district of Park Lane?'[8] There were Conservatives too who were prominent among the restrictionists and it was a Conservative-Unionist Government which finally legislated against free entry. Nevertheless, what gave the campaign against alien immigration its special flavour and force was its overlap with a certain anti-Semitic undercurrent in the radical wing of contemporary British politics and the converging drives for social and political reform at home and against imperial expansion abroad.

Within Great Britain new Jewish wealth did not amount to much either in aggregate or as a proportion of the total; and it did not count for a great deal politically. But it had acquired notoriety; and it did count for a great deal, both in straight financial terms and politically, in South Africa. Jews formed a substantial fraction of the non-Afrikaner element in the Transvaal, the Uitlanders, whose rights and privileges were one of the issues upon which the conflict between the Boers and the British had turned. Some were in close relations with Milner and, more dangerously, with Rhodes. And all this had been picked up by the radicals at home as the crisis in southern Africa mounted and became a war. In his *The War in South Africa; its Causes and Effects*, J. A. Hobson, on his way to becom-

---

[8] Ibid.; and *Hansard, Parliamentary Debates*, 4th Series, vol. 101, 29 January 1902, col. 1290. Norman was later appointed a member of the Royal Commission on Alien Immigration. Burns was the outstanding working-class leader in the Liberal Party.

ing the most effective intellectual critic of British imperial policy of the day, pointed to the 'small group of international financiers, chiefly German in origin and Jewish in race', who 'by superior ability, enterprise and organization . . . out-competing the slower-witted Briton, have attained a practical supremacy which no one who has visited Johannesburg is likely to question'.[9] In private Hobson went much further in tone and content.

The bulk of the Uitlanders excepting the actual miners I believe to be Jews . . . German Jews who have been in England and figure as British subjects. Many of them are the veriest scum of Europe. The entire mining industry, with the partial exception of the Consolidated Gold Fields (Rhodes), is in their hands, the Dynamite Monopoly, the illicit Liquor Traffic are theirs, they and Rhodes own or control the press, manipulate the slave market, and run the chief commercial businesses both in Johannesburg and Pretoria. These men will rig the politics when they have the franchise. Many of them have taken English names and the extent of the Jew power is thus partially concealed. I am not exaggerating one whit. I think I can prove this.[10]

Some years before, in his *Problems of Poverty*, Hobson had ascribed the willingness of the Jewish immigrant to accept abysmal conditions of labour and bad pay to the 'fact' that 'The Jew craves the position of a sweating monster, because that is the lowest step in a ladder which may lead to a life of magnificence, supported out of usury.'[11]

In this atmosphere, those pressing for an end to the free entry of alien Jews were not above insinuating that the failure of Salisbury's Unionist Government to follow their advice could be traced to the counter-pressure of the Jewish pluto-cracy. Politically embarrassed, fearful of the electoral con-sequences of inaction, faced with a genuine problem of principle (that of free entry into the country) as well as evidence of real and possibly growing social tensions, and genuinely uncertain of the facts of the case, the Government resorted to

[9] (London, 1900), p. 189.
[10] Letter to C. P. Scott, editor of the *Manchester Guardian*, who had sent him out to South Africa as a correspondent, 2 September 1899. Quoted in Bernard Porter, *Critics of Empire* (London, 1968), pp. 201–2.
[11] Quoted in Bernard Gainer, *The Alien Invasion* (London, 1972), p. 85.

the classic tactic of setting up a Royal Commission of inquiry. In composition it included neutrals and the most prominent Jew in the kingdom, Lord Rothschild; but the balance of its membership was restrictionist from the start. None the less, the Commission, in its researches, did an honest and, so far as possible, thorough job.

The facts, as the Commission very soon discovered on the basis of an analysis of the returns of the population census of 1901, turned out to be a great deal less sensational than had been believed and subsequent research has more than confirmed their findings.[12] We now know that the total number of Jews in London at the time was about 55,000, most of them in the borough of Stepney. Thus, proportionately, London had the smallest Jewish population of any of the great cities of Europe, with the exception of St. Petersburg to which Jews were normally denied access by law. Net immigration at its peak (that is, after deducting the transmigrants) had never been more than 10–15,000 annually in any year and was usually at an annual rate of 3,000. The absence of entirely reliable and detailed statistics certainly made the problem of computation an extremely difficult one, but there was thus no question of the Jewish population of Great Britain, let alone the net immigration into the country in any period of ten years, ever having reached three-quarters of a million. The 1911 census, taken after the passing of the Aliens Act (1905), gave the total number of 'Russian', 'Russian-Polish', and 'Romanian' aliens in England and Wales as 99,263. It is reasonable to conclude that if Scotland were added, and allowance made for Jews of German and Austrian nationality, the total figure would not be greater than 120,000.[13]

However, what mattered most in the long term was that along with the immigrants themselves there had come over from the Continent 'the Jewish Question'. The Problem of the Jews had become a subject of public discussion and examination—at a level of seriousness and authority, moreover, which in Great Britain it had never before been thought to merit and which on the Continent of Europe, for all its severity

[12] See especially, Lloyd P. Gartner, *The Jewish Immigrant in England, 1870–1914* (Detroit, 1960).
[13] Ibid., p. 45.

there, it had never been granted.[14] Here, therefore, was the opening into the British political world that the Zionists had sought from the beginning, but without results.

iii

Herzl's first public statement of his views (in 1895) had been in London. It was the London *Jewish Chronicle* that had first published the gist of the argument to be elaborated in his manifesto *Der Judenstaat*. Again, it was in London, in its East End, that he had first come face to face with *eastern* European Jewry and he had had, ever since, a loyal following in England. Some of the notables of English Jewry too had given him a hearing, a better hearing than the notables of Jewry in other countries, even though their leader, Lord Rothschild, had denounced and avoided him.[15] But that was all. The Zionist Congress (the Fourth, in 1900) was transferred from Basel to London. But while it promised to be, as the *Jewish Chronicle* pointed out, 'the most important Jewish gathering—having regard to the remote and varied Jewries it will focus—that has ever been held in this country',[16] it failed to become the 'turning-point' in the Zionists' relations with the English, hope of which Herzl had held out to his followers.[17] Established English Jewry was not much interested and Herzl sought to reach beyond them to the 'gentile English public outside', as he put it.[18] In the event, the response of the English press was good: the Congress was widely reported on and editorial comment was generally favourable, if tinged with scepticism.[19]

---

[14] See I. Finestein, 'Jewish Immigration in British Party Politics in the 1890's', *Migration and Settlement* (Jewish Historical Society of England, London, 1971), pp. 128–43.

[15] Herzl's last attempt to see Lord Rothschild (in February 1901) had reduced him to falling back, as at the beginning of his political career, on what can best be described as muttered threats: that he would rally the Jewish masses against Rothschild; that he would turn the Congress 'into a splendid demonstration against him and his clan'. The banker's enemies would then support the Zionists—who, if they must suffer the disadvantages of Rothschild's hostility, might as well have its advantages. Herzl to Cowan, 4 February 1901. *Igrot Herzl*, iv.

[16] *Jewish Chronicle*, 1 June 1900.

[17] Circular letter to GAC, 18 June 1900. *Igrot Herzl*, iv.

[18] *Jewish Chronicle*, 17 August 1900.

[19] Benjamin Jaffe, 'The British Press and Zionism in Herzl's Time (1895–1904)', *Transactions of the Jewish Historical Society of England*, xxiv (1970–3), pp. 95–7.

But as a tactic to make a political mark in England it was no more successful than any other he had tried. Attempts to meet statesmen of ministerial rank and members of the royal family failed as regularly as they were made. So with the decision to establish the Bank (the Jewish Colonial Trust) in London. On the surface of things, it made good business sense to set it up in the financial centre of the world; in fact it changed nothing commercially and politically it remained without effect. There was a fair response when the case for Zionism was put to candidates in the parliamentary election of 1900 with a request for expressions of support, but no consequences of direct political use followed. The idea of putting up a Zionist candidate in an East End constituency fizzled out. Twelve Jewish Members of Parliament (eight Unionists and four Liberals) were indeed returned in the general election of that year, but without the benefit of any systematic Jewish support, least of all Zionist. This last fact could be taken as demonstrating that the rise of anti-Jewish feeling had had little or no effect at the level of general party politics and that there was no cause for the esteem in which England was held by the Zionists, as by virtually all European Jews, to be impaired by the continuing agitation over 'aliens'. 'England the mighty, England the free, the England that looks out over all the seas, will understand us and our endeavours', Herzl had told the Fourth Congress with unmistakable sincerity and to stormy applause.[20] But what mattered was that there was no response to his call and that all these efforts were to no avail—until in March 1902 Herzl's leading follower in England, Leopold Greenberg, grasped the tactical use to which the official inquiry into alien immigration could be put.

Greenberg, once an active radical in the politics of his native Birmingham, approached the city's greatest political son, Joseph Chamberlain, and through him proposed to the Commission that Herzl be invited to give evidence. Late in May (over Lord Rothschild's objections) the formal invitation to attend went out. Early in June Herzl travelled to London, only to be recalled almost immediately to Vienna upon the death of his father. This was a hard blow on any account.

[20] *Protokoll IV*, p. 5.

Relations between the two had been close and his father had given him strong and generous moral and financial support from the very beginning of his adoption of the Jewish national cause—in striking contrast to his wife's resentful attitude to all that disturbed the even flow of domestic life. Herzl was now a more isolated man than before and for a moment the political race in which he had entered himself, virtually as a lone runner, stopped short. A month passed before he had pulled himself together and was back in London. There followed in short order a long, tense, but not entirely unfriendly talk with Nathaniel Mayer (Lord) Rothschild, the formal appearance before the Royal Commission in public session, and a private talk on the day after with its chairman, Lord James of Hereford. James was a distinguished public figure in his own right, a Liberal Unionist like Joseph Chamberlain, due shortly to retire from his seat in the Cabinet and from active politics.

Herzl's own major preoccupation was still with Turkey; and shortly after arrival in London, he was summoned to Constantinople by the Yildiz.[21] But it was to be the last of his visits and his own unspoken estimate of his chances there being now very sober, his mind turned ever more frequently to thought of alternatives, albeit partial and temporary alternatives.

The idea of settling a territory adjacent to Erez-Israel, if formal rights of settlement in Erez-Israel could not be had, was an old one and was not peculiar to Herzl. Cyprus had been chiefly in mind, its chief promoter Davis Trietsch, a German Jew who had lived in the United States for some years. Trietsch had brought it up repeatedly, virtually from the day the movement was founded. Herzl himself had toyed with it as 'the *ultima ratio* in case we failed, and a concomitant arrangement (*eine mitlaufende Combination*) in case we succeeded'.[22] However, when Trietsch presumed to raise it publicly at the Third Congress in 1899 he was shouted down and the best Herzl could do for him was to put the question whether he should be allowed to proceed with his speech to an immediate vote. The vote went against Trietsch[23] and so far as that Con-

---

[21] See above, p. 120.

[22] Herzl to Trietsch, 3 December 1898. *Igrot Herzl*, iii, no. 679, p. 227.

[23] *Protokoll III*, pp. 232–3. Trietsch's ideas on Cyprus had already come before the

gress and the immediately subsequent ones were concerned,
the issue was as good as dead. Herzl did nothing further to
encourage Trietsch directly. 'You cannot expect us to support
a proposal that to the best of our understanding and conscience
[*Wissen und Gewissen*] is impracticable', he wrote to him a year
later.[24] But he used the incident in the Congress to suggest to
the Turks that the Zionists might eventually tire of the long
wait for Ereẓ-Israel and turn to Cyprus 'which is under English
rule and always accessible to us';[25] and thoughts of Cyprus—
as a possible jumping-off place for the real goal, Ereẓ-Israel, or
at any rate as a potential lever or quid pro quo for use in a
political and territorial arrangement in a future too distant to
be delineated—continued to recur in his mind. The Turks,
who had only just been compelled to complete their withdrawal from the island, maintained their interest in it. There
had been rumours of the Germans coveting it. It was certainly
near Ereẓ-Israel. And it was now in British hands, as was the
territory immediately to the south of Ereẓ-Israel in Sinai.
Something, sometime, might be made of all this. There had
even been several independent, but feeble attempts by groups
of Jews from eastern Europe, chiefly Romania, to settle in
Cyprus on their own account.[26] They had done so without
Zionist support and contrary to Zionist policy, but that in itself
did not preclude reconsideration of that policy. A great
Jewish settlement there, or indeed almost anywhere in the
east Mediterranean region, would have the effect of strengthening the prospects for the ultimate attainment of Ereẓ-Israel,
Herzl had begun to think.[27] At the very least, it would provide
a talking-point with the British, as should any genuine project
for the 'settlement of destitute Jews', that is to say, their diver-
sion from England itself. The great thing was to obtain a
Charter. If it could not be had of the Turks, it might be granted
by the British. And if by the British, the support that the Jewish

Smaller Actions Committee in Vienna, where Herzl had stated his opposition to
them. EAC Minutes, 28 February 1900. CZA, Z I/171.

[24] Herzl to Trietsch, 20 June 1900. *Igrot Herzl*, iv.

[25] Letter to Nuri Bey, 7 November 1899. *Igrot Herzl*, iv.

[26] John M. Shaftesley, 'Nineteenth-Century Jewish Colonies in Cyprus', *Transactions of the Jewish Historical Society of England*, xxii (1968–9), pp. 88–107; *Jewish
Chronicle*, 20 April, 14 September, and 12 October 1900.

[27] Letter to Rothschild, 12 July 1902. *Diaries*, iv, p. 1302.

plutocracy had refused him thus far might be forthcoming after all. Then the Turks would look differently at the enterprise and the terms of the problem would be transformed. Given a Jewish Eastern (Chartered) Company, 'I would be a serious but friendly neighbour to the sanjak of Jerusalem, which I should somehow acquire at the first opportunity, as the Bulgarians did with Eastern Rumelia.' Thus Herzl, reflecting in his diary at the end of his final round of talks in Constantinople at the beginning of August 1902.[28]

Lord James had been friendly when Herzl saw him after giving his evidence before the Commission, but warned him that he had better gain Rothschild's support if he hoped to make real progress. Rothschild, in turn, had told him that it would all have to be discussed with Chamberlain and promised to see what could be done in that direction. But the meeting with Chamberlain did not materialize and the renewed summons from Constantinople had forced Herzl to leave London before anything had been concluded one way or the other.

That Rothschild was no longer hostile was pure gain in itself; but the main effect of the correspondence that followed between the millionaire and the journalist, while friendly enough, was to reveal that the difference of outlook between them remained profound.

I tell you very frankly [Rothschild wrote] that I should view with horror the establishment of a Jewish Colony pure and simple; such a Colony would be Imperium [in] Imperio; it would be a Ghetto with the prejudices of the Ghetto; it would be a small petty Jewish State, orthodox and illiberal, excluding the Gentile and the Christian. And what would be the result; ten, fifteen or fifty thousand Jews would live in comparative happiness and ease, their habits and their example would be quoted and their co-religionists and breth[ren] at home would be more oppressed and more ground down on the principle of 'Do unto others as you would be done by'.

My aim and object must always be a different one from yours. I wish the Jew wherever he lives to be a prosperous and good citizen, and you can not attain that object by establishing a few orthodox communities in scattered parts of the world. By all means encourage emigration. Find new homes for the Jews, but let them live amongst

<hr />

[28] *Diaries*, iv, p. 1344.

their Christian breth[ren], by the streams of Babylon or elsewhere, but let one and all of us beware of the impossible.[29]

Herzl replied without heat. He did not agree that the Jewish commonwealth would have to be small, orthodox, and illiberal and he would be sending Rothschild a copy of his novel *Altneuland* to make clear what he did have in mind. He did not think that the original founders of the great contemporary states had been

mightier, cleverer, better educated, wealthier than we Jews of today . . . In our own time, Greeks, Rumanians, Serbs, Bulgarians have established themselves—and should *we* be incapable of doing so? . . . We have just had no self-confidence up to now. Our moral misery will be at an end on the day when we believe in ourselves. . . . The coming into being of the Jewish commonwealth, the Jewish colony—call it what you will at the beginning—will not be regarded by the Powers with repugnance or mistrust. For this I have much and sufficient proof.[30]

But in any event, Herzl had already resolved on a direct approach to the British Government and had asked Greenberg to try to arrange the meeting he wanted with Chamberlain. This, after some initial hesitation on Chamberlain's part, was agreed to and in October Herzl disappeared from the editorial offices of the *Neue Freie Presse* once again and returned to London.

iv

The new venture in political Zionism that was now under way rested on a foundation that was in part, as has been seen, domestic. The Jews had come to be judged a source of social and economic tension; and the public effort to examine the problem and trace it to its origins had led to greater understanding and better knowledge of the forces pushing the Jews of eastern Europe westwards. From there to the beginnings of a grasp of what the Zionists wanted was a short step.

Nothing will meet the problem the [Royal] Commission is called upon to investigate and advise upon [Herzl had told it in his opening

---

[29] Rothschild to Herzl, 18 August 1902. CZA, H VIII/708.
[30] Herzl to Rothschild, 22 August 1902. *Diaries*, iv, pp. 1347–8.

statement] except a diverting of the stream of migration that is bound to go on with increasing force from Eastern Europe. The Jews of Eastern Europe cannot stay where they are—where are they to go? If you find that they are not wanted here, then some place must be found to which they can migrate without by that migration raising the problems that confront them here [in England]. These problems will not arise if a home be found them which will be legally recognised as Jewish.[31]

No one in a position of influence had questioned the logic of this argument.[32] And it was not long before it was seen that there were both moral and political advantages in adopting it. To restrict free entry into the country was to break sharply with an ancient liberal tradition in these matters—one still valued in Edwardian England. The criticism which the restrictive measures put up by the Unionist Government were now to arouse could be blunted, however, by a show—and more than a show—of some serious interest in a cure of the problem at its source.[33] But although vital, in that it provided Herzl with his entrée to Whitehall, the domestic nexus was insufficient for his larger purposes. It was no more than a point at which British and Zionist affairs touched tangentially and ephemerally. A solid foundation of long-term coincident interests—on which alone a true working partnership between Great Britain and the Jewish national movement might be based—could only be sought, or constructed, in the external sphere, in the realm of British foreign and imperial policy. Better advised than he had been in earlier years, Herzl knew that the central figure in that realm was the Colonial Secretary, Joseph Chamberlain. He was not the 'master of England'—as Herzl thought of him, half seriously[34]—but he was the pre-

---

[31] 7 July 1902. *Minutes of Evidence*, p. 212.

[32] Summed up with admirable compression by one of the members, Sir Kenelm Digby: 'I understand the point of his [Herzl's] evidence to be that in order to deal satisfactorily with the Jewish problem it is desirable that they shall be diverted elsewhere than to countries where they will be aliens.' Ibid., p. 214. Digby, shortly to become Permanent Under-Secretary at the Home Office, joined Lord Rothschild in opposing the Commission's majority recommendation to restrict immigration into Great Britain.

[33] See Balfour's defence of the second Aliens Bill in the House of Commons, 10 July 1905. *Hansard*, vol. 149, col. 178. The first Aliens Bill, submitted in 1903, had been defeated.

[34] *Diaries*, iv, p. 1360.

eminent politician of the day, 'the one who made the weather', as Winston Churchill put it.[35] Chamberlain stood out among the members of Balfour's Government as a self-made man of quick mind, passionate in pursuit of the cause that interested him most at any moment, an excellent administrator, a first-rate public speaker in an age which had to make do without microphones and amplifiers, a master of grass-roots politics, but equally at home in 'the great game' of high politics, and imperial strategy, a man of broad ideas, flexible when necessary, and extremely tough. His enemies tended to say of him, with some justice, that he was ruthless and, with something less than justice, that he was a demagogue. No man was his master, not even Gladstone, in opposition to whom he had split and largely wrecked the Liberal Party in 1886 (on the issue of Home Rule for Ireland), still less Salisbury, into alliance with whom he had led his Liberal Unionists. The great Conservative Prime Minister Salisbury acquiesced in the unusual freedom of action and speech which Chamberlain assumed under the old man's formal leadership. Salisbury's successor, Balfour, conscious that Chamberlain was the bigger political figure in his Cabinet, did not assert his Prime-Ministerial authority either.

Chamberlain had chosen the Colonial Office for himself in 1895 and he remained its head until his resignation from the Cabinet in September 1903—the longest-serving Colonial Secretary ever. But although his main business was squarely in the colonial domain, the influence he sought and exercised extended far beyond the normal departmental bounds. He has rightly been seen as one of the leaders, if not the leader, of the contemporary movement to take Great Britain out of its long-standing ('splendid') diplomatic and military isolation. His policies and his ideas for the development of the Empire derived to no small degree from his concern with the decline of British strength relative to that of the other Great Powers. And here, most probably, was his central political purpose in the last part of his political life to which all the rest, in the final analysis, bore an instrumental relationship. To this end—crudely: the fortifying and the invigorating of imperial Great

[35] Winston S. Churchill, *Great Contemporaries* (London, 1962), p. 63.

Britain—he applied himself without mental reservation, whence his continual openness to fresh ideas and possibilities, the absence of bureaucratic traits, the extra margin of power that accrued to him in all his doings, and, not least, the opportunism. Whence, too, the attention which the best-placed foreign observers paid to him and their own mixed feelings about him. 'The most important politician in England', wrote the German Ambassador, Metternich.[36] 'But it must not be forgotten', the French Ambassador, Cambon, had occasion to note some months after Balfour's Cabinet had been formed, 'that Mr. Chamberlain has no political principle, that he is a man of the present moment, and that he changes opinions with incredible facility; he is not in the least troubled by his own statements and contradicts himself with prodigious ease.'[37]

That said, nothing in Chamberlain's background or personal philosophy predisposed him to a special and warm regard for the Jews. He shared the commonplace anti-Semitic prejudices of his time. He was, in general, a firm believer in 'race', in the sense that he attributed vast political importance to the fundamental culture of societies and to the traits of national character and behaviour as they are passed from generation to generation. These, he thought, were—or should be—the essential building-blocks on which national policy should be based and out of which great international alliances should be formed. He had no doubt that the races fell into a natural hierarchy, at the head of which was the 'Anglo-Saxon' (the English and the Americans), with the 'Teutonic' (the Germans) close by and differing from them only slightly. The Jews were far below, virtually out of sight. At the same time, this did not preclude, in a man who all through his political life had pressed for liberal social reform, a dislike of systematic oppression of the kind to which the Jews of eastern Europe were subject. And the very tendency to apply large and loose ethnic categories to political issues and, by extension, to think in terms of ethnic balance and manipulation, made him peculiarly receptive, as we shall see, to what Herzl had to tell him.

---

[36] Metternich to Bülow, 19 November 1901. *Holstein Papers*, iv, no. 785, p. 237.
[37] Quoted in Julian Amery, *The Life of Joseph Chamberlain*, iv (London, 1951), p. 205.

V

The Zionists' negotiations with the British Government fall
naturally into two periods. The first opens with Herzl's first
face-to-face encounter with Chamberlain on 22 October 1902
and a briefer meeting on the following day; the second with
his third and last meeting with the Colonial Secretary six
months later, on 23 April 1903. During the first period the
initiative and the ideas on which the talks and the action turn
are Herzl's. The British listen, consider, and respond and it is
their response that is decisive for the outcome. In the second
period the roles are largely reversed. The British propose, the
Zionists consider; and, in the final analysis, it is the Zionists'
response that is decisive for the outcome. This latter was without
precedent; and if only for this reason (there were, as will be
seen, others), it is the second period that invites attention and
is certainly the more dramatic. Still, it is the period between
October 1902 and April 1903 in which each side takes the
other's measure, in which something of the tone of the relationship is set, and in which, on the one hand, Zionist expectations
are raised to unaccustomed heights and, on the other hand, a
certain idea of Zionism begins to sink into the British political
mind—at any rate, into Joseph Chamberlain's: Zionism as a
force that can be usefully fitted into the political and territorial scheme of things for which the British Government of the
day was pressing overseas.

Herzl saw Chamberlain twice on this first occasion, on 22
and 23 October 1902. He found the atmosphere in Whitehall
and Downing Street a world away from Potsdam and the
Yildiz: vastly less posturing and fuss, no uniforms and medals,
no flunkeys, no nastiness, no lies. Chamberlain was polite,
attentive, and business-like. He disclaimed hostility to the
Jews. He accepted Herzl's analysis of the Jewish Question and
approved of the Zionist prescription for solving it. When Herzl
spoke of the three British-controlled territories in which Jews
could be settled under special arrangements—to discuss
which he had come to see the minister—he drew a distinction,
however, between those administered from Cairo on the one
hand (El Arish and other, unstated parts of the Sinai Peninsula) and the island of Cyprus on the other. The former were

the responsibility of the Foreign Office. The latter was Chamberlain's own. But Cyprus, Chamberlain thought, was unsuited to Herzl's purposes. An influx of Jews would be resisted by the native Greeks and he himself would be bound to support them. It would be the East End of London all over again. The conversation shifted back to El Arish. This, perhaps, held out a little promise. The land was virtually vacant. Its appropriateness as 'a rallying point for the Jewish people in the vicinity of Palestine'[38] was evident. Yes, for his part, Chamberlain concluded, he would agree to the founding of a Jewish settlement there. But there were two provisos. Lord Cromer, the British governor, in all but name, of Egypt must approve; and as departmental responsibility for Egypt was the Foreign Office's, Herzl would have to see Lord Lansdowne. If Herzl returned the following day, a meeting with the Foreign Secretary would be arranged.

From then on things moved with the sure rhythm of a well-organized bureaucracy that believed in dealing with affairs, if it was to deal with them at all, coolly, but with dispatch.

I was interviewed yesterday by Dr. Hertzel [*sic*], an Austrian Jew who is interested in the Zionist movement [Lansdowne wrote to Cromer]. He had made the acquaintance of Chamberlain who asked me to see him. I am told he is respectable, and he impressed me favourably.

His idea is to get hold of a tract near El Arish and there to establish a colony of carefully selected Hebrews. I suggested, but without much effect, that they were not likely to make very good settlers and that El Arish might not be exactly the spot upon which to dump Jews from the East End of London or from Odessa.

He told me that he and his friends were sending out at once to Cairo one Mr. Gruneberg [*sic*] to collect information and I promised that I would mention the matter to you and explain the nature of Gruneberg's mission.

I think he should be civilly received by the authorities, although it is impossible for me to express any opinion as to the merits of his scheme, which seems to be very visionary.

Pray forgive me for troubling you.[39]

[38] *Diaries*, iv, p. 1362.
[39] Lansdowne to Cromer, 24 October 1902. Lansdowne Papers, Egypt 7 (277). Text in O. K. Rabinowicz, 'Herzl and England', *Jewish Social Studies*, xiii (1951), pp. 25–6.

The Foreign Office soon learned the correct spelling of Herzl's and Greenberg's names. But otherwise Lansdowne's letter set the tone for the manner in which his department would be dealing with the exercise Chamberlain had set it: correct, non-committal, moderately sceptical, willing (as Chamberlain had been) to leave Cromer to handle it to the best of his understanding, but (unlike Chamberlain) fundamentally uninterested in Zionism, in the Jews in general, or even in the Jews in England in particular—uninterested, in a word, in the *rationale* of that same exercise.

Like Chamberlain, Lansdowne had been one of the Liberal leaders who had broken with Gladstone over the issue of Home Rule for Ireland and then joined the Conservatives as a Liberal Unionist. But he was unlike Chamberlain in almost every other respect. The fifth Marquis of Lansdowne was a Whig aristocrat and a great Irish landlord. His chief interests and ministerial experience had been almost exclusively in the foreign and military spheres, at the War Office, as Governor-General of Canada, as Viceroy of India, and now as Foreign Secretary. He was a decent, somewhat colourless minister and an indifferent practical and parliamentary politician. Balfour, his Prime Minister, said of him in retrospect, 'I shouldn't call him very clever. He was—I don't quite know how to put it—better than competent.'[40] It took the Great War to rouse him to a truly daring and unconventional act: his famous letter to the *Daily Telegraph* (29 November 1917) proposing a negotiated peace with the Central Powers. Now he acted true to form in passing the matter to Cromer.

Lord Cromer (Evelyn Baring), British Agent and Consul-General in Cairo, was in his twentieth year at the post. He was still more remote from the domestic concerns and politics of Great Britain than Lansdowne and of a tougher and more self-confident nature. His *de facto* rule of Egypt was characterized as much by his impregnable authority *vis-à-vis* the British Government in all matters that pertained to Egypt as by his overlordship within Egypt itself. And since, in the course of time, after its occupation by the British in 1882, Egypt had gradually become one of the great fixed points around which British strategic and diplomatic thinking

[40] Blanche E. C. Dugdale, *Arthur James Balfour* (London, 1936), i, p. 335.

turned,[41] Cromer's influence on larger issues than those he was nominally charged with was very great. He played a role of first importance, for example, in the negotiations leading to the Anglo-French Entente of 1904. Yet he did so more as a function of his own obsession with Egypt than out of direct concern for the greater questions. Cromer, before all else, was an administrator—both in his practice and in his outlook. He was a very able, if rigid administrator (increasingly rigid as the years passed) and sincerely devoted, in the manner of the best colonial administrators of the day, to two well-defined—and, as he thought, equal and compatible—purposes: the domestic welfare of the inhabitants of his proconsulate and the thorough entrenchment of over-all British control.

Thus the outlook from both London and Cairo—but especially Cairo—was bureaucratic in its essentials. Nothing was ruled out, the question (like all questions, once they had leaped the introductory hurdle) would be looked at carefully and with system; system meant that it was difficulties and obstacles that would be looked for first and with the most energy; but, above all, anything likely to disturb the status quo would be resisted as a matter of professional instinct and routine. It was not long before difficulties were duly uncovered and the narrow limits within which the project was to be judged in Egypt—and hence in London—were soon evident.

Greenberg went out to Egypt for a brief, preliminary reconnaissance, was received by Cromer and by Boutros Ghali, the Egyptian Foreign Minister (a Copt), and returned to Europe to report to Herzl. Together they drafted a memorandum on the entire subject for submission to the Foreign Office in London. Zangwill, Nordau, and two lesser figures in Herzl's inner circle of Zionist *dirigenti* were also involved in the preparation of the draft. This was a sharp departure from

---

[41] The strategic dogma at this time was that Egypt had to be held in the ultimate interests of continued British control of India. If it was 'true that Egypt is an anxiety, and a burden', the Director of Military Intelligence had put it some years before, 'the former is not serious, so long as we maintain naval supremacy in the Mediterranean; and the latter is light in comparison with the valuable interests involved'. This was his answer to the question 'What is the strategical value to England of—(a) Egypt; (b) the Suez Canal.' 'Memorandum on Naval Policy', 13 October 1896. Text in Arthur J. Marder, *The Anatomy of British Sea Power: A History of British Naval Policy in the Pre-Dreadnought Era, 1880–1905* (New York, 1940), pp. 571–4.

Herzl's practice of single-handed action; but then Herzl was aware that neither his command of the English language nor his familiarity with the ways and style of the British Government were adequate to the task. The result was a change from the usually lively, always highly personal style of Herzl's letters to great men, in which an attempt to strike at the recipient's imagination always figured. A smooth and lucid statement of purposes and probable advantages to both Great Britain and the Jews was put together. The broad brush-strokes of Herzl's first draft ('At one stroke England would get ten million secret but faithful subjects . . .') were carefully wiped away and replaced by copperplate ('My proposition . . . while reflecting fresh honour upon England, may also benefit her materially.'). The British and Egyptian Governments' approval of 'the general Scheme' was requested and it was proposed that once that had been granted, a technical commission of inquiry to investigate the area would be sent out.[42]

London and Cairo now had a document before them and it was read with care. A phrase alluding to a special status for the settlement ('colonial rights'—wherein would lie its 'powerful attraction for the Jewish people') was promptly pounced upon in both capitals and Cromer lost no time in setting forth additional grounds for doubt. There was the question of the view likely to be taken by the Sultan, the nominal suzerain of Egypt. There was the problem of the eastern frontier of Egypt upon which there was still no agreement with the Ottomans. Since the region in question was unlikely, in Cromer's judgement, to be suitable, it would be right if a small commission of inquiry went out to the spot before, not after, commitments of any kind had been made. And to make sure its findings were reliable, it should include non-Jewish experts. Then there were security questions: the settlers would have to be protected from the Beduin 'whose lawless habits are well known'; but a security force would be expensive. Finally, there was the question of the precise status of the settlement and of the settlers. It and they would have to be 'wholly governed

---

[42] Text of memorandum (12 November 1902) in Alex Bein, 'Ha-masa u-matan bein Herzl le-vein britania ha-gedola be-'inyan el-'arish', *Shivat Ẓion*, i (Jerusalem, 1950), pp. 200–24. Herzl's first draft is in *Diaries*, iv, pp. 1364–7.

by Egyptian law'. Otherwise, Cromer wrote, 'I do not think that the project should be entertained'.[43]

All this was accepted in London without argument and transmitted to Herzl for his information. The Foreign Office added the rider that before the commission of inquiry set out there would have to be assurances that the conditions the Egyptian Government was likely to lay down in respect of the settlers' status would be complied with.[44] This was a bad beginning; but the assurances were provided. Something, Herzl thought, could be worked out with the Egyptians— perhaps payment of an annual tribute in exchange for 'the governor of the Egyptian province of Judea being elected by the colonists for ten or seven years and only confirmed by the Khedive—or nominated by the English government and appointed by the Khedive'.[45] In any event, as a further visit to the Foreign Office (16 January 1903) made clear, it was on Cromer that everything depended, not on the Khedive or his Government.

Greenberg returned to Cairo at the end of January 1903 and the expedition of experts to El Arish followed soon after. The Egyptians were unexpectedly difficult. Concessions of real substance to the settlers were refused out of hand. They would grant them the same rights in matters of personal status that other non-Muslims enjoyed in Egypt and, as a sop, their wishes and interests would be taken into account by the Government in the choice of local judges and officials 'as far as possible'.[46] Nordau thought that this was as much as was likely to be conceded 'in an official agreement',[47] but Herzl was now alarmed and thoroughly dissatisfied—the more so as he had been chafing all along under the unfamiliar restraint of someone having to act for him and had begun, without much real justification, to doubt Greenberg's loyalty. In contrast—and more vexing to him still—an interim report

[43] Cromer to Lansdowne, 29 November 1902. Text in Rabinowicz, 'Herzl and England', pp. 33–6.

[44] Sir Thomas Sanderson (Permanent Under-Secretary) to Greenberg, 6 January 1903. Text in Rabinowicz, ibid., pp. 40–1.

[45] *Diaries*, iv, p. 1382.

[46] Boutros Ghali to Greenberg, 22 February 1903. Text in Raphael Patai, 'Herzl's Sinai Project', *Herzl Year Book*, i (New York, 1958), pp. 114–15.

[47] *Diaries*, iv, p. 1427.

from the leader of the Sinai expedition seemed to suggest that Cromer's pessimism about the prospects for settlers from Europe was misplaced. In the middle of March Herzl could stand the tension no longer and embarked for Egypt to take the operation over. His hopes that the 'Archimedean point' by which the entire enterprise would be levered home was at last to be won were still high.[48] But he got no further than Greenberg had with either the British or the Egyptians. His first meeting with Cromer was a failure. 'The most disagreeable Englishman I have ever faced', Herzl noted in his diary and never overcame his distrust of him;[49] while Cromer wrote to Sanderson that Dr Herzl 'is a wild enthusiast. Be careful not to pledge yourself *to anything* in dealing with him.'[50] When it became evident to Herzl that Cromer 'wishes to deal with Englishmen', Colonel Goldsmid, who had been a member of the expedition, was deputed to act for him.[51] Herzl's meeting with Boutros Ghali was easier, but to even less purpose. Herzl may not have been aware of Ghali's reputation as a pliant instrument of the British.[52] What he did note was that it was the atmosphere of Constantinople all over again: 'Too many servants idling about in spacious waiting rooms. . . . He kept agreeing with me while we drank coffee alla turca.'[53]

For a while it was the text of the draft agreement—the 'act of concession', as Cromer termed it in his correspondence with the Foreign Office—that was the immediate subject of the debate in which Cromer, his officials, the Egyptians, and a local Belgian lawyer whom Cromer himself had recommended were all involved. But then the commission of engineers and other specialists returned from northern Sinai and interest shifted to their technical report (dated 26 March 1903). It was thorough, detailed, and of impeccable honesty. Its conclusions were fatal.

---

[48] Herzl to Mandelstamm, 20 March 1903. Text in Heymann, i, no. 19, p. 62.

[49] *Diaries*, iv, p. 1446; H. H. Bodenheimer, op. cit., p. 225.

[50] Cromer to Sanderson, 28 March 1903. Patai, op. cit., p. 116.

[51] *Diaries*, iv, p. 1450. Colonel A. E. W. Goldsmid, an officer in the British regular army, had been a leader of Ḥibbat Ẓion in England and an early recruit of Herzl's. See *Origins*, pp. 227–8 and *passim*.

[52] Samir Seikaly, 'Prime Minister and Assassin: Butrus Ghali and Wardani', *Middle Eastern Studies*, xiii (1977), 1, pp. 112–23.

[53] *Diaries*, iv, p. 1447.

The result of the Commission's research has been, that in their opinion, under existing conditions, the country is quite unsuitable for settlers from European countries; but from what they have seen on the spot, and from the experience of individual members of the Commission, they can confidently state that were a sufficient water supply forthcoming, the conditions of soil, hygiene and climate are such, that part of what is now desert, would be capable of supporting a considerable population. In short, the whole question is one of water supply, the furnishing of which would involve great capital expenditure.[54]

The great snag about this conclusion lay in the fact that the entire question of a Jewish settlement of some sort could now be shifted out of the political realm where argument was free and tended to be inconclusive to the technical realm where, seemingly, facts were facts, argument was rigorous, and expert opinion could be treated by the non-experts as infallible. The commission itself had proposed methods for bringing water to the regions marked out for potential settlement, but these were rejected by the Egyptian Government and, more significantly, by Cromer's own chosen expert, Sir William Garstin. And for Cromer himself, the combination of Egyptian dislike of the project in principle and the technical objections to its implementation in practice more than sufficed. He informed Lansdowne that he was

convinced that nothing can be done in the direction of carrying out Dr. Herzl's wishes without the exercise, on the part of His Majesty's Government, of a far stronger pressure than the circumstances of the case would in any degree justify . . . In conversation with Colonel Goldsmid, I have strongly urged him to allow the negotiations to drop altogether, and I venture to express a hope that similar language should be used to Dr. Herzl should he, as is not improbable, apply to Your Lordship.[55]

For a while, as Cromer anticipated, there ensued further debate—now, of necessity, technical. But Cromer was unyielding. He had never much liked the project. He could recall what must have seemed to him a similar project a decade

---

[54] Text in Patai, op. cit., pp. 128–35.
[55] Cromer to Lansdowne, 14 May 1903. Text in Patai, op. cit., p. 119.

earlier—a private plan to settle east European Jews in southern Sinai—which had achieved nothing beyond irritating the Turks.[56] He could see no advantage in what Herzl intended to *Egypt* or to British interests there. He sensed, on the contrary that there might be encapsulated in it all kinds of political unpleasantness. To cap it all, it would have to lead to unconventional use of water-supplies in a country in which water was so obviously life's blood itself. And the great proconsul's position being so clear-cut, the Foreign Secretary did not hesitate to back him. 'Lord Cromer has evidently been much impressed by these objections to the scheme', Herzl was informed in June, when he persisted, 'and they appear to Lord Lansdowne to be of so cogent a nature that he is constrained to tell you that in his opinion no favourable result can be expected from the further reference which is now being made to Cairo.'[57] By a final letter a month later, in still firmer language,[58] the Foreign Office brought the matter to an end.

vi

As the prospect of the Foreign Office, Cromer, and the Egyptians all agreeing to the Sinai project faded, the Zionists naturally looked to Chamberlain once more. But Chamberlain had left England for a tour of Africa at the end of November 1902 and did not return before the middle of March 1903. Apart from a brief meeting with Cromer *en route*, he was therefore in no position to follow up his own initiative. By the time he had returned minds were already made up and there could be little or no question of his intervening to real effect. British constitutional and bureaucratic etiquette tended strongly (as it still does) to the maintenance of clear boundaries between ministers' respective departmental fiefs: ministers rarely poached on neighbours' territory because all functioned devotedly as gamekeepers of their own. The issue was not of such weight in British eyes as to justify its being brought up

---

[56] See Jacob M. Landau, 'Te'udot min ha-arkhionim ha-britiim 'al nesayon ha-hityashvut ha-yehudit be-midyan be-shenot 1890–1892', *Shivat Zion*, i (1950), pp. 169–78; and Oskar K. Rabinowicz, 'A Jewish State in Midian', in D. J. Silver (ed.), *In the Time of Harvest* (New York, 1963), pp. 284–319.

[57] Sanderson to Herzl, 19 June 1903. Text in Bein, 'Ha-masa u-matan', p. 219.

[58] Sanderson to Herzl, 16 July 1903. Ibid., pp. 219–20.

in Cabinet for discussion, let alone a showdown and, possibly, a row—even if Chamberlain had been convinced that the Foreign Office was in error—and what evidence there is suggests that it did not occur to him to quarrel seriously with Cromer's assessment. There only remained the question of what could be done, with tact, to ensure that the Zionists received a fair hearing. When Herzl returned from Egypt and met Chamberlain for the third and last time (23 April 1903) the Colonial Secretary was friendly, listened to him sympathetically, and did promise to speak to Lansdowne.[59] He may well have done so; he may later have thought better of it. But, as he made clear when Greenberg went to see him on 20 May to press him to use his influence, he refused to *interfere*. He would promise no more than to mention the matter to Lansdowne 'as opportunity arises'.[60] And he repeated to Greenberg what he had already told Herzl, that while in Africa he had formed ideas of his own of 'a land for Dr. Herzl'.[61]

The object of Chamberlain's journey to Africa (a 'momentous' journey, his biographer called it[62]) was, after the violence and bitterness of the Boer War, to pull South Africa firmly into the imperial scheme on a basis of conciliation and co-operation between the Afrikaners and the British. It was also a visit of inspection: the first such visit by any British Colonial Secretary. It was a long journey by sea and land. On the way, after passing through the Suez Canal, he stopped in Mombasa and spent some ten days travelling on the newly completed Uganda railway through what would later be called Kenya to Nairobi, and then on to the Kikuyu lands and the Mau escarpment. Riding on a seat specially constructed for him on the engine-buffer, Chamberlain could see the country improve in climate and possibilities as the train moved up from the coast. 'The whole country', he wrote of the Kenya Highlands, 'bears considerable resemblance to the Sussex Downs, and, in parts, to an English park. Throughout this district English children live and thrive and the settlers speak with the utmost confidence of their experiments in cultivation. English roses bloom pro-

---

[59] *Diaries*, iv, p. 1475.
[60] Greenberg to Herzl, 20 May 1903. CZA, H VIII/292.
[61] *Diaries*, iv, p. 1473.
[62] Amery, op. cit., p. 283.

fusely, and all English fruits and vegetables can be cultivated.'[63]

The British East Africa Protectorate, of which Kenya was a part, was still, anomalously, under Foreign Office jurisdiction, although due to pass before long to the Colonial Office.[64] Government and administration, in so far as they were not tribal, were British. The beginnings of European settlement were already strongly in evidence, as Chamberlain had noted. It is clear from the topics he discussed with the High Commissioner and other officials and with members of the settler communities that Chamberlain's approach was entirely business-like and developmental, that here, to his mind, was another 'imperial estate' to be improved.[65] The railway was a beginning. Agriculture had now to be put on a scientific basis. Administration had to be expanded. The last vestiges of slavery done away with. Above all, the population—the non-indigenous population—had to be increased.

Policy on population was fundamental to the underlying approach of both the practitioners and the theorists of contemporary British colonialism. It derived in part from the then virtually universal, 'Darwinian' tendency to think in, and ascribe enormous importance to, ethnic categories. The 'races' could be distinguished one from the other, it was thought. The members of each tended to run true to type, the salient characteristics of which could be reliably delineated. The relative place of each nation or people in a hierarchy of quality could be established. And thus behaviour could, broadly, be predicted and, in sum, solid and verifiable grounds on which to base large-scale political and economic action adduced. Some races, it was believed, could gradually be made over into something more like others—the Indians, perhaps, into fair replicas of Englishmen, for example. Others could not; at all events, not without immense pains being taken over immense periods of time. It was thought, accordingly, that the 'opening-up' of the territories normally inhabited by those placed low in the ethnic hierarchy by the conventional wisdom of the

[63] 'Notes on Mombasa and East Africa Protectorate by the Right Honourable J. Chamberlain', Ladysmith, 2 January 1903, pp. 2–3. PRO, FO 2/722.

[64] As it did in 1905.

[65] Joseph Chamberlain, *Foreign and Colonial Speeches* (1897), p. 136; J. L. Garvin, *The Life of Joseph Chamberlain* (London, 1934), iii, pp. 19–20, 175–7.

times depended upon the introduction of a class of people of a higher rating who alone would be capable of building up the necessary economic and educational infrastructure—the condition of any progress whatsoever. 'The Negro', wrote Sir Harry Johnston, a contemporary authority on Africa (who later joined in the ensuing public debate on Jewish settlement in East Africa), 'seems to require the intervention of some superior race before he can be roused to any definite advance from the low stage of human development in which he has contentedly remained for many thousand years.'[66] And for his own good, as a governor of Kenya 'state[d] definitely', 'we desire to make of the native a useful citizen and . . . we consider the best means of doing so is to induce him to work for a period of his life for the European.'[67] In this way, the interests of all would be met: the 'civilized' would not be denied the economic progress they wished for and deserved; the 'primitive' would gradually gain promotion.

But there were two snags about the Europeans as prime developmental movers. One was that not all areas had a climate which was attractive to them and not all kinds of labour were thought appropriate. Hence the introduction of Indians into East Africa, initially to build the great railway. Their place in the hierarchy was seen as intermediate between black and white and they were thought well suited to work in the tropics. The other snag was that Europeans were liable to be less docile than others, as the conflict in South Africa had so plainly demonstrated. Now that the Afrikaners had been beaten, it was British policy to conciliate them. But no one, least of all Chamberlain, supposed that they would now easily convert into faithful subjects of the Crown. So those who offered the best prospects as developers and the least promise of political and administrative trouble were the British themselves. But South Africa, for all its attractive riches, drew nothing like so many emigrants from Great Britain as formed the great river of people to the United States and Canada running at the rate

---

[66] 'The Development of Tropical Africa under British Auspices', *Fortnightly Review* (November 1890), p. 705. Quoted in D. A. Low, *Lion Rampant* (London, 1973), p. 65.

[67] Sir Henry Belfield, *Proceedings of the East Africa Protectorate Legislative Council*, 1st Session 1917, p. 3. Ibid., p. 66.

of several hundred thousands annually throughout the 1900s.[68] As for East Africa, which had much less to offer than South Africa and in which virtually everything had to be built up from scratch, the problem of finding suitable settlers was acute. Experienced farmers with enough capital to set themselves up on large holdings seemed most needed; and the British settlers already there wanted more of their own kind. But, in the nature of things, there were not many to be had.

Chamberlain's view on the entire subject was pragmatic. One of the conclusions that he seems to have drawn from the way the South African war had gone and from the promise, as he saw it, of a decent Anglo-Dutch *modus vivendi* in the aftermath was that even the self-governing half of the Empire could not be composed exclusively of colonies of Englishmen. A composite racial structure was already in being; why not build on it and derive maximum benefit from what it had to offer? When in Mombasa he lectured the British settlers on the indispensability of Asians if the country was ever to be fully opened up.[69] And it was perfectly natural, in all the circumstances, that it should have occurred to him that the east European Jews might serve the overarching imperial purpose as well or better. 'If Dr. Herzl were at all inclined to transfer his efforts to East Africa', he noted after leaving Mombasa, 'there would be no difficulty in finding land suitable for Jewish settlers. But I assume that this country is too far removed from Palestine to have any attraction for him.'[70] The Jews were bound to serve the economic interests of the territory well. Politically they would be harmless—entirely unlikely to form a troublesome, independently minded community, let alone a rebellious one like the Afrikaners. Back in England, there was the other, undesirable stream of immigration and the prospect of having to cope shortly with the unpleasantness of a Bill to be introduced into Parliament to bring it to a halt. And further to the east, the primary source of the trouble was intensifying. The great massacre of Jews at the hands of the mob in Kishinev in Bessarabia[71] took place a few days before Herzl's meeting

[68] See W. A. Carrothers, *Emigration from the British Isles* (London, 1965), Appendix I, pp. 305–6.

[69] Amery, op. cit., p. 291.

[70] 'Notes on Mombasa', p. 7.

[71] See below, pp. 239–42.

with Chamberlain (23 April 1903), but neither seems then to have been aware of what had happened. However, when Greenberg was received by the minister a month later it was Chamberlain himself who brought it up—'as evidence', Greenberg wrote, 'that you [Herzl] have been all along right as to the necessity of finding Jews a settled home and bringing them away from Eastern Europe. In fact and in short [Chamberlain] is a convinced Zionist!'[72]

At their meeting in April, therefore, Chamberlain proposed a tract in East Africa for Jewish settlement. Herzl, however, turned it down. The Zionists had to build on a 'national foundation', he told the Secretary; 'our base must be in or near Palestine'. Of course, there were masses of people wishing to emigrate and 'later on we could also settle in Uganda [*sic*]'.[73] But it was El Arish he wanted and it was on El Arish that he dwelt in his talk with Chamberlain. Later, back in Vienna, it occurred to him that there might be something in Africa for the Zionists none the less—as yet another point of pressure, or as 'an object of barter'[74] in some still ill-defined three-cornered deal, to help induce the British to approve the El Arish project after all. Thus it came to be his thinking at this stage that, if in Africa at all, the concession had to be outside the British territories; and he set about, none too confidently and with less than his customary energy, to see whether the Portuguese would discuss a Charter for Jewish settlement in Mozambique. It was one more turn in the endless road along which strength and influence had to be gathered in penny packets. So, in essentials, was another move taken at this time.

Herzl now reverted to his old idea of opening a dialogue with the Russian enemy himself. This he did with a practised

---

[72] Greenberg to Herzl, 20 May 1903. CZA, H VIII/292.

[73] *Diaries*, iv, p. 1473. Chamberlain never reached Uganda and it was soon obvious, to Herzl and to others, that the territory in question was in Kenya. But the term 'Uganda' stuck and the great crisis in the Zionist movement which arose as a later consequence of Chamberlain's offer has gone down in its history, unrectifiably, as the 'Uganda affair'. There is now no telling whether Chamberlain had called it Uganda when the topic was first brought up, or had merely mentioned his travels on the Uganda railway and been misunderstood by Herzl. In the present study an effort has been made to avoid the old error, but since much of the contemporary debate revolves around 'Uganda' and virtually all of the literature employs the term, the reader must bear with its use from time to time.

[74] *Diaries*, iv, p. 1487.

hand and familiar arguments and vastly greater determination than was evident in his approach to the Portuguese. There were also other, urgent reasons, as we shall see, for an approach to the Russians. But the political purpose was always uppermost with Herzl and his reasoning here was plain. There could be no government for whom the Problem of the Jews was more evident than the Russian. And none, in their sober moments, who could be more interested than the Russians in its solution. Who, then, should be more willing to help the Zionists deal with it once and for all, so ridding themselves of a continual source of social tension and revolutionary ferment? What, as a first step, would do more to calm the 'desperate mood of our poor people', Herzl wrote to the Russian Minister of the Interior, than a personal audience with the Tsar at which he would give 'all desired information about our movement and . . . request . . . future aid'.[75] Meanwhile he continued to press the British, but with rapidly failing confidence in success as Cromer's views hardened and the Foreign Office, as we have seen, fell in with them. On 20 May Greenberg saw Chamberlain and heard the Secretary reiterate his reluctance to intervene in Egypt and his refusal to consider Cyprus and then repeat the offer of land in East Africa. This time Herzl (when he received Greenberg's long report on the conversation) did not dismiss it out of hand.

The territory in question, Chamberlain had told Greenberg,

was on very high ground with fine climate and every possibility for a great colony which could support at least a million souls. 'I did not press it upon Dr. H[erzl]', [Chamberlain] said 'because I sympathised with his desire to satisfy the sentimental idea in regard to Palestine, and I quite saw that the [El Arish] plan to some extent did so. But, if that comes to nothing, I do hope Dr. H[erzl] will consider very seriously the suggestion. At the moment there is nothing in the way of his having the place, but it will not be long vacant as there are undoubtedly large mining prospects, apart from all else.'

I asked him [Greenberg continued] if it w[oul]d be possible, providing you considered the scheme[,] for us to have local self government and he replied 'Certainly'. He said it would be necessary

[75] Herzl to Plehve, [–?] May 1903. *Diaries*, iv, pp. 1493–4.

to send out a Governor—'Who would be a Jew?' I asked. 'Who could be a Jew', he replied. Anyway, he said, let Dr. H[erzl] consider this and I shall be glad to hear further upon it.[76]

Chamberlain was careful to point out that East Africa was still under Foreign Office jurisdiction, but he made it clear that if things were to get under way he would propose to the Government that he take it over himself.

Greenberg's response was cautious, promising only to report to Herzl. Chamberlain pressed. He had read Zangwill's speech at Shoreditch the week before in which the best-known English Zionist of all had said that the lesson of the great Kishinev pogrom was that the Jews must be found a centre. For this, Chamberlain thought, a settlement in East Africa 'would be an admirable beginning'. He was sure it would be successful.

Greenberg's private recommendations to Herzl were equally marked by a desire to be prudent before all else. Pressure in the matter of El Arish should not be relaxed, regardless of the prospect of something new, if only because to drop El Arish was to risk making a poor impression on the British Government. As for East Africa itself, the essential question, Greenberg thought, was whether it would 'get us nearer or take us further from [Erez-Israel]'—and on that he wanted to hear Herzl's view before expressing his own. For his own part, he was careful to point out, he was an Erez-Israel man, 'thoroughly'. And yet

it occurs to me that from the political point of view it would be no mean thing to [be able to] say that [the British Government] had offered us a refuge[;] and I think [East Africa] could be used in the nature of a drill ground for our national forces. . . .

In any case I think it would be well to pay some close attention to [Chamberlain's] plan—not, I mean, to reject it 'off the reel'. For he is a strong-headed man and holds opinions very tenaciously. Consequently he is likely to feel vexed if he thinks his opinion slighted. Even if ultimately you do not fall in with his plan you should show great attention to it. I am of course assuming you think nothing of

[76] Greenberg to Herzl, 20 May 1903. CZA, H VIII/292.

it—it may be you think a great deal and I am not sure you would be wrong.[77]

Herzl agreed. It was now clear, he telegraphed to Greenberg, that nothing could be done about El Arish for some years and that Chamberlain's proposition must therefore be taken 'into serious consideration, provided it is really advantageous'.[78] The point about the general political benefit to the movement that would derive from the very fact that such an offer had been made by the British Government was well taken. Greenberg should therefore return to the Colonial Office and take the matter up. As for the larger issues of strategy and principle which the offer raised, he failed to declare himself. These, his silence implied, could be left for the time being in abeyance. The great thing was still to find the vital Archimedean point.

[77] Ibid.
[78] Herzl to Greenberg, 23 May 1903. *Diaries*, iv, p. 1498.

PART TWO

Ferment

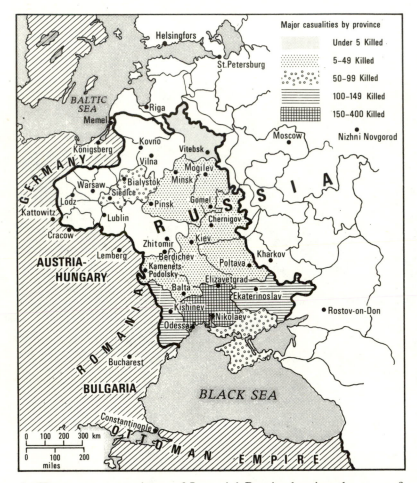

A. The western provinces of Imperial Russia showing the area of permitted residence to Jews (the Pale of Settlement) and the provinces in which Jews were hardest hit in the pogroms of 1905.

6

The Pressures of Here and Now

We now know that the fate of Russian Jewry was decisive for the structure, distribution, and—if so vague a term may be applied to so vast a subject—the *quality* of Jewry in our own times. Virtually all the salient threads (the German being the great exception) lead back to Russia—more precisely to the material condition of Russo-Polish Jewry in the final decades of the Autocracy, to the psychological and political effects upon the Jews of Russian policy towards them, and to the great up-heavals which overtook the Jews (along with the other peoples of the Empire) as successive wars, revolutions, and a system of government of unique rigour and ferocity beat upon them in turn. Both the drive to escape from Russia, namely the great migration westwards, and the drive towards a positive, lasting, and beneficent solution to the Jewish Problem derived the greater part of their force in energy and numbers from Russian Jewry. In consequence, Russian Jews (and their descendants) came to the fore in Jewish life virtually everywhere in the course of time. In contrast, but not in contradiction, the sealing-off of one great part of Russian Jewry after the First World War and the destruction of the other half during the Second changed the character and potentialities of the Jewish people forever.

These are reasons enough to suggest that it is in Russia, equally, that the keys to the evolution of Zionism in its forma-tive years should be sought. Indeed, consistently, the greatest *underlying* influence within and on the Zionist movement throughout its some fifty years of prime activity was that of Russian Zionists; and through them, directly and indirectly, there were reflected in the movement the condition and the crises and, in the course of time, the amputation of Russian

Jewry as a whole. This may not always have been apparent on the surface of things; and it was not always so in actual fact in the short term. Herzl and his men, the 'diplomats of Vienna' of whom Aḥad Ha-'Am and many others complained, did hold the stage, as we have seen, for some years; and doing so, their immediate influence on the movement was tremendous and in certain, if limited ways—technical and organizational *modi operandi*, for example—lasting. But this leadership from the periphery was exceptional, of relatively brief duration, and always somewhat anomalous. The grudging trust which the Russian Zionist leadership had granted Herzl in 1897 was as much a function of their temporary loss of nerve as of the Herzlian brilliance and dynamic. It was therefore inherently revocable and the question when the centre of gravity would shift back to the East was always one of time. But while it was in Russia and for Russian Jewry, above all, that Zionism had arisen as a coherent movement, conditions were far from being straightforwardly hospitable to its growth and internal strength. Over and above its own internal divisions on issues of general policy, Zionism in pre-revolutionary Russia was caught on the horns of two dilemmas. One issued from the question whether the Zionists' concern with a lasting, but future solution to the Problem of the Jews was, or could be shown to be, compatible with concern with the condition of the Jews here and now. The other, a corollary of the first, amounted to the question of what attitude Zionists should adopt towards the Russian state, its masters, and its servants.

The effect of almost two decades of direct repression, along with the general rise in political tension and revolutionary temperature in the Empire, had been to complete, for all practical purposes, the alienation of Russo-Polish Jewry from the regime and to establish them as one of the great—indeed, relative to its size, the greatest reservoir of actual and potential revolutionaries in the country. For Jews were now prominent (as they had not been in the 1870s) at all levels of the revolutionary movement, in the rank and file no less than among militants.

These pariahs [as Plekhanov put it in a much quoted passage of a report to the 1896 congress of the International] who do not even have the paltry rights the Christian inhabitants possess, have shown so much staunchness in the struggle with their exploiters and such keenness in understanding the sociopolitical tasks of the contemporary workers' movement that in some respects they may be considered the avant garde of the workers' army in Russia.[1]

This development was entirely contrary to Jewish tradition, which had always favoured prudent non-involvement in the internal political life of the countries of the Exile. It naturally sharpened the hostility of the authorities, although, briefly, as we shall see, there were divided counsels on how rebellious Jews were best handled. And it offered abundant evidence of a new tendency in Jewry of tremendous and lasting potency, a formidable rival not only to the forces of tradition, but to the radical, modernist, forward-looking force of Zionism itself. For the Jews did not only appear in large numbers in the two great all-Russian wings of the revolutionary movement, the Marxist Social Democrats and the populist Socialist Revolutionaries; they were present in the arena in autonomous and indigenous Social-Democratic, revolutionary Parties of their own. The most important of these was the *Bund*, 'the General Jewish Workers' Party of Lithuania, Poland, and Russia', which had been founded, as it happened, in the year in which the First Congress of Zionists had been held, 1897. It was for many years by far the largest component of the Social-Democratic movement: at the outbreak of the first Russian revolution of 1905 its membership (of some 23,000) was almost three times as great as that of Lenin's all-Russian Social-Democratic Party.[2] It had been a founding constituent of that Party; and for many Jewish Social Democrats as individuals it was the staging post, so to speak, on their journey into it.

The salient reasons for this unprecedented combination of revolutionary sentiment and aptitude for organized revolutionary activity are not hard to find. An ever greater proportion of the Jews of the Empire were in the process of being reduced

---

[1] Henry J. Tobias, *The Jewish Bund in Russia* (Stanford, 1972), p. 61.
[2] Leonard Schapiro, *The Communist Party of the Soviet Union* (London, 1966), p. 22. Cf. Tobias, op. cit., p. 239.

to extreme, *urban* poverty; a high proportion of the Jewish population—as compared, that is, with the general, still largely peasant society around them—was of the artisan class; and Jewish artisans, or proletarians, were, by virtue of certain sociological characteristics, peculiarly adapted to syndicalist activity.

Out of the host of details available[3] a few examples will serve to illustrate these general propositions. The move to the towns and cities was common to all sections of the population, but took place at a higher rate among the Jews, chiefly as a consequence of a government policy designed to evacuate them from the countryside by direct regulation and by deprivation of means of employment. In 1897 the Jews constituted 11·6 per cent of the total population of the Pale (ten Polish provinces and fifteen provinces in Lithuania, White Russia, south-west Russia, and 'new', southern Russia); but they formed 50 per cent of the urban population (as officially defined) in Lithuania, 55·2 per cent in White Russia, 35·9 per cent in south-west Russia, 28·2 per cent in southern Russia, and 37·7 per cent in Poland. Figures for the larger urban centres were generally higher still. The Jewish Colonization Association estimated in 1898 that of the 4,900,000 Jewish inhabitants of the Pale (94 per cent of all Jews in Russia) 3,800,000, or about 78 per cent, were to be classed as urban. And despite the high rate of emigration (some 400,000 Jews left Russia for the United States in the course of the six years from the beginning of 1901 to the end of 1906) and a lower

[3] There is a good contemporary compendium (based principally upon the Russian imperial census of 1897 and on figures collected by the U.S. Commissioner of Immigration and by Jewish philanthropic organizations) in a report prepared by I. M. Rubinow for U.S. Bureau of Labor: published as *Economic Conditions of the Jews in Russia*, U.S. Bureau of Labor, Bulletin v. 15 (Washington, D.C., 1907; reprinted by Arno Press, New York, 1975). Other important sources are the *Evreiskaya Entsiklopediya*, 16 vols (St Petersburg, 1906–13); and the long, detailed, and regular reports in the *Jewish Chronicle* (London) for the period in question usually headed 'The Jews of Russia'. For an instructive contemporary account see Ḥ. D. Horowitz, 'She'elat ha-kalkala u-mekoma bi-tenu'ateinu ha-le'umit: (7) ha-maẓav ha-kalkali shel ha-yehudim bi-zemaneinu', *Ha-Shilo'aḥ*, x (1903), pp. 57–72. Among modern studies see especially Ezra Mendelsohn, *Class Struggle in the Pale* (Cambridge, 1970); and Bina Garncarska, 'Ba'ayot maẓava ha-ḥomri ve-ha-ḥevrati shel ha-ukhlusiya ha-yehudit be-varsha ba-shanim 1862–1914', in M. Mishkinsky and others (eds.), *Gal-'Ed*, i (Tel-Aviv, 1973), pp. 101–34 (a detailed socio-economic study of Warsaw Jewry).

birth rate than the non-Jews',[4] the proportion kept rising.

Three-quarters of all those engaged in commerce in the Pale were Jews and a little under a third of all Jews in the Pale were engaged in commerce. But 'commerce' was a grand term for what was often a very small affair. A self-employed owner of a street-stall counted as a 'trader' for statistical purposes. So with craftsmen: a third of all artisans and factory-hands in the Pale were Jews; 38 per cent of all employed Jews in the Pale were artisans; but most were either self-employed or were journeymen working for a master hardly better off than themselves.[5] The chief fields of occupation were the garment, food, wood, and metal trades, in that order.

The combination of artificially restricted residence and abnormal concentration in certain sectors of the economy (a traditional feature in Jewish life, but much exacerbated by official restrictions on the occupations Jews might engage in) was catastrophic for the morale, the social stability, and the livelihood of all these people. The annual income of a shoe-maker in Grodno would be something between £15 and £20 *annually*, when the estimated minimal annual family budget was a little over £30 (300 roubles). Tailors in southern Russia earned between £25 and £40. Carpenters in Volhynia between £10 and £30. The wages of women, children, and unskilled workmen (agricultural labourers, teamsters, dockers, and the like) were lower still. Conditions of labour were often appalling. The hours were long, commonly twelve to fourteen, even sixteen hours a day. The workshops were often in the homes, the rooms small, crowded, ill-lit, cold, and damp—in keeping, it may be said, with the generally grim picture which the Jewish quarters of the major cities of the Pale presented. Vilna was notorious. A member of the Royal Commission on Alien Immigration who had taken the trouble to see for himself 'the causes which lead to the large emigration from Eastern Europe' wrote that

[4] The death rate was lower too.

[5] According to figures gathered by the Jewish Colonization Association (ICA) in 1898, of 500,986 Jewish artisans in the Pale 51·8 per cent were masters, 28 per cent journeymen, and 20.2 per cent apprentices. A. Ruppin, *The Jews in the Modern World* (London, 1934), p. 188.

There are probably few better places than Vilna in which to study a Jewish ghetto in all its original picturesque squalor and poverty. In many parts the streets are so narrow that only one vehicle can pass at a time. They are crowded with foot-passengers and the shops and stores on either side form a truly Oriental bazaar. At intervals along these narrow streets there are arched gateways leading into court-yards, round which the miserable dens and cellars in which the people live are clustered, and it is here that the housing conditions of the Jewish poor may be seen. I spent a whole day in visiting them . . . The walls of the houses were blistered and rotting, as if poisoned by the pestilent atmosphere within. Two and three families would be found in one miserable room or cellar rented at 45 roubles a year. They were mixed up together, regardless of age and sex and health. In one room I found a lunatic as a lodger among a family of young children.

During my walks through the ghetto I was surrounded by a crowd of gaunt, curious, anxious faces—sad, careworn, hungry-looking people. Many openly begged alms. Some had trifles for sale. Others seemed to spend most of their time in the synagogues reading and rocking themselves into oblivion of their troubles.[6]

One of the important features of this evolution of a large and growing class of Jewish town-dwelling artisans was the perpetuation of the social separateness that had always been characteristic of Jews within a given economic category in parallel with the separateness of Jews among the non-Jews generally. It was rare for Jews and gentiles to be employed together in the same workshop or factory and, if they were at all, then it was chiefly in the larger enterprises. Jews and non-Jews were divided not only by faith, culture, and language, but by different rates of literacy (the rate among the Jews tended to be double that of the non-Jews, when not higher), by differing attitudes to secular authority, and, on the whole, by differing social and economic notions and ambitions. Jewish workers, notably the skilled amongst them, might be described as petty bourgeois at heart and were at any rate far removed psychologically and sociologically from the Christian peasants newly arrived in the cities, or even from the first generation of city-born who formed the bulk of the new Russian

[6] Evidence of Major W. E. Evans-Gordon, MP, 26 February 1903, Royal Commission on Alien Immigration, ii, *Minutes of Evidence*, p. 456.

working class. Most Jewish artisans were to be found, as has
been said, in small workshops; these made for, and required,
an intimacy that was unattainable between Jews and others
in any but the rarest of cases. In the larger enterprises other
factors made for separation. The Jews, in their majority,
insisted on observing the Sabbath and the prospect of closing
down factories for two days in each week to accommodate
them as well as the Christians was normally resisted by owners,
whether Jews or Christians themselves. Many employers—
Jews as well as non-Jews—judged Jewish workers to be either
inherently less competent to operate modern machinery, or
weaker physically than gentiles, or at any rate more difficult
and troublesome, or rebellious, or, worse still, liable to be
familiar with their employers, particularly if they themselves
were Jews. In fact, the physical unsuitability of the Jews for
labour in modern factories was a myth; whatever physical
disabilities Jewish workmen—skilled and unskilled—in Minsk,
Vilna, and Warsaw may have suffered from, they were functions of the miserable conditions of life and labour to which
they were subject and soon cured by warmth, light, and
better food. But there was more than a little truth in the view
that the Jews were less docile, more argumentative, and keener
on what they perceived to be their rights and their dignity
and, perhaps above all, more liable to form cohesive groups for
common action. Jewish workers, notably in Lithuania, had a
tradition of self-help and pooling of resources in bad times.
And they had, of course, another natural meeting place
besides the work-floor, namely the synagogue. Moreover, by
the end of the century they had acquired no small experience
of strike action for strictly economic, trade-union purposes
such as shorter working hours. Some of it was successful and
encouraged repetition, as did the occasional spectacle of the
police standing aside when the employers too were Jews on
the grounds that no harm could come to the state or to public
order from one class of Jews quarrelling with another. In sum,
Jewish artisans, particularly in north-west Russia and eastern
Poland, were strong and natural candidates for membership
in the ranks of the revolutionary movement, especially its
Social-Democratic wing—that which sought to rely on the
proletariat as the crucial vehicle by means of which power was

to be seized and a new social and economic order imposed and then secured.

The only drawback to this fine reservoir of revolutionary material lay, as the Social Democrats soon found, in the *fons et origo* of their suitability and availability for revolutionary action: their ethnic differentiation from the surrounding population. The Jewish proletariat was prepared to embrace new and bold ideas for action in their own direct interest and, more remotely, against the hated Russian state. They were not to any significant degree willing or even capable (at any rate in the short term) of sweeping the tensions between them and their non-Jewish fellows out of their minds, nor of shedding their indigenous culture and social practices. As the thoroughly Russified young agitator Iulii Martov (né Tsederbaum) soon found when he was exiled to the Pale in time to join in the first moves towards the forming of what came to be the Bund, the Jewish workers of Vilna had to be spoken to in their own language, Yiddish. And addressed, moreover, in terms of their own condition as they understood it:

As workers we suffer under the yoke of capital; as Jews we suffer under the yoke of the absence of rights. These disabilities oppress us, enslave us, keep us down, and made the struggle against the capitalists difficult. They prevent us from selling our labour under the most favourable conditions, force us into the Pale of Settlement, cause hectic competition. They made every policeman our overlord and thus again prevent us from improving our position.[7]

The purpose of the Bund, in Martov's words (of which he was later to repent), was 'to create a separate Jewish workers' organization which would lead and educate the Jewish pro-letariat in the struggle for its economic, civil, and political emancipation'.[8] Its view, in a nutshell, was that 'like all nations, the Jewish nation too has to have equal political, economic, and national rights'.[9]

At the first, founding congress of the Russian Social-Demo-cratic Workers' Party (1898) the Bund had been recognized

[7] Israel Getzler, *Martov* (Cambridge and Melbourne, 1967), p. 25.
[8] Ibid.
[9] *Der yidisher arbayter*, 6 March 1899.

as autonomous in Jewish matters on the principle that only a free Jewish organization could effectively defend Jewish interests. (The Polish Socialist Party had refused to recognize a separate Jewish labour movement and had fought the Bund from the start.) But then this ran counter to the powerful centralist tendency within the Party, where the pervasive view of Bolsheviks and Mensheviks alike was that there was no room for what might be termed a federal relationship, with the Bund having the monopoly of access to, and organization of Jewish workers. It also ran counter to the internationalist, anti-particularist approach of the great majority of Social-Democratic activists of the time, of which Jewish activists were frequently the principal and most strident spokesmen. When the issue came to a head at the second Party congress in 1903 it was the same Martov, who had long since left Vilna and the Bund, who led the attack; and in this he was backed by Trotsky in exceptionally bitter and violent terms. The Bund, Trotsky claimed, was out to undermine the structure of the party by its insistence on autonomy. Its position implied distrust of non-Jews as such (for why else should it insist on a monopoly of access to Jewish workers?). It was separatist in outlook and intention (whereas socialism was set on sweeping all barriers between races, religions, and nationalities away, and socialists held that all such ties were due to dissolve anyway). In sum, in this cardinal, national respect, it was no better than Zionism.[10]

The Bund lost the fight for special status within the Party (and by withdrawal helped unwittingly to tip the balance of votes against the Mensheviks at the same congress). But their position within Jewry, notably in their stronghold in the north-west of the Empire, was unaffected. And, *pace* Trotsky, they were not the allies or dupes or pupils of the Zionists, but their rivals. Much of the strength of Zionism in eastern Europe lay in its combination of a clear appeal to national sentiment with a plausible formula for national salvation and renewal. But salvation through territorial concentration, the heart of the Zionist creed, was necessarily contingent upon political arrangements which even the most loyal and optimistic of

---

[10] Isaac Deutscher, *The Prophet Armed; Trotsky: 1879–1921*, i (New York, 1954), pp. 74–5.

Herzl's supporters knew to be distant in time and contingent too on logistic arrangements which, as the most simple-minded believers could be shown, would have to be on a truly massive scale. And even then it was a fair question how many of Russia's five million Jews could be transferred to the Jewish territory, to say nothing of well over a million candidates for resettlement from Romania and Austrian-ruled Galicia. Thus the Diaspora might turn out to be interminable after all. Writing in 1898, the historian S. M. Dubnov, highly sceptical of, but not hostile to Zionism, calculated that on (what he regarded as) the most optimistic of assumptions it would take a hundred years for the Jewish population of Erez-Israel to reach half a million, or a little more than the existing (1897) Jewish population of the province (*guberniya*) of Kiev.

Of course [Dubnov argued], the hope that the beginning of the twenty-first century would see half a million of our brethren settled in our ancient fatherland is very dear to us. But would this solve the problem of the ten million Jews who are, and will remain scattered all over the earth? Zionist doctrine has it that these scattered millions are doomed to destruction through either assimilation or socio-economic degeneration. What do you say of this original [plan for a] settlement of the Jewish Question which sentences the whole of the people, with the possible exception of a twentieth part of it, to national extinction? I doubt that the boldest of Zionists can cherish the hope that *every* unassimilable Jew will move to Palestine. The process would have to be a very gradual one and in the end immeasurably more Jews will have remained in the Diaspora than will have moved to Palestine. As for the view that the govern-ment of the future Jewish state would be able to protect its co-religionists in other countries by diplomatic means—it is a naïve self-deception; we know only too well what significance attaches to the voice of a little state in the councils of the 'Great Powers'. In the best of cases, they would then be able to say to the protesting Jews of the Diaspora, 'If you don't like it here, why don't you go away and live in your own state?'

Thus, political Zionism represents a threefold Utopia: the dream of the establishment of a Jewish state secured by international law, the dream of transferring to it a significant part of the Jewish people, and the dream of thus deciding the fate of all Jewry.[11]

[11] S. M. Dubnov, 'Utopicheskoe i real'noe v sionizme', *Pis'ma o Starom i Novom Evreistve* (St. Petersburg, 1907), pp. 171–2.

Meanwhile the immediate pressures on Russo-Polish Jewry were mounting and with them impatience for relief—or, at the very least, for a clear programme of action in some other, more promising direction. By seeking to act within the immediate arena of Jewish experience and in terms of what appeared a reasonable time-scale—ever more reasonable as the sense of impending upheaval grew from year to year down to the explosion of 1905 and continuing beyond it—the Bund had a considerable psychological and dialectical advantage over the Zionists. The Bundists said and felt with some (if limited) justification that they were part of a larger movement of peoples, yet did no violence to Jewish national feeling. They argued, again with some justification,[12] that the Zionists were in essentials an outcrop of the Jewish middle class, led in practice and dominated in ethos by the men and notions and even, to some extent, the needs of the bourgeoisie. Habitually they hammered away at the iniquities of the Jewish middle class ('the most wretched and the meanest in the world', Martov had called it in his Vilna days[13]). They stressed the Zionists' emphasis on the revival of (scholarly) Hebrew, in contrast to their own insistence on (popular) Yiddish, and the Zionists' ambivalent, yet genuine affection for the Jewish tradition, arguing that there was evidence of the incorrigibly reactionary, non-popular, crypto-clericalist, and narrowly nationalist nature of the rival movement. They claimed that the Zionists were doing nothing for the Jewish worker. And they resolved at their fourth congress in 1900 that under no circumstances were Zionists to be allowed membership in the Bund's economic or political organizations.[14] In 1904 they informed the International that Zionism was 'the most evil enemy of the organized Jewish proletariat'.[15]

The tone and content of the Bund's denunciation of the Zionists was well within the tradition inaugurated by Marx and continued by Lenin of drawing the sharpest possible lines between yourself and those near you but not of you; but it did less than justice to the complexity of the situation.

---

[12] See below, pp. 452–3.
[13] Getzler, p. 25.
[14] Tobias, pp. 128–9.
[15] Ibid., p. 251.

The problem for the Zionists in determining their attitude to the regime was partly one of principle and partly one of practice. Their detestation of the Russian state was not a whit slighter than that of the Bundists; if anything, its sources and implications ran deeper. For it was of the essence of Zionism that even reform of the Russian state would avail the Jews little or nothing. Hence their call to remove the Jews elsewhere; and hence the pessismism with which they judged the notion—to which the Bundists subscribed (with whatever qualification), along with liberals and assimilationists—that within Russian (and Polish) society at large there were allies to be found for a common cause. The Jews, the Zionists had argued from the very beginning, must learn to apply their energies and resources to their own affairs first and foremost, otherwise there would never be an end to their troubles. Common causes, if there were any, would have to wait. So while all sympathized with the reformist tendencies, and many among them with the revolutionary, the governing view from the start in Odessa in the early 1880s[16] had always been that conflict with the authorities must be avoided if possible. There was a common feeling that the fully dedicated and active members were in any case too few and that the movement as a whole was too weak to cope with so vast an enterprise as the amelioration of the Jews' *material* condition in Russia itself. When Herzl proposed that the matter be discussed at the Fifth Congress at the end of 1901 Ussishkin objected. If the '*true* activists, those who say little and do much', were given so great an additional task, he wrote to Vienna, their main responsibilities towards the movement itself would suffer. And failure would be damaging to the movement's reputation. But his main point was fear of trouble in St. Petersburg.

If you say: new activists will join us to undertake the new task, then I greatly fear them, for they would be socialists mostly, such as the Russian Government looks at with a jaundiced eye. If they [joined us] the Government would look at us and our doings and it could end with the total destruction of all Zionism in Russia. That this is the true state of affairs I can prove: there have already been

---

[16] See *Origins*, p. 175.

demands from on high for information on new people joining the Zionist societies.[17]

There was in this some expression of an ancient, entrenched tradition in Jewry, such as can be found in other weak and scattered minority peoples, that it is wise to keep friction with the state very low. In part, it followed from the truth, as they perceived it, that the Russian state was too vast and dangerous a target for them to think of tackling it directly. But chiefly, it was bound up with the circumstance that their minds were set on other things and other places and that what concerned them *in Russia* was no more than all possible freedom to go about their business within the confines of the Jewish communities without the interference and opposition of the authorities. To this end they judged regularization of their status desirable—without being willing to sacrifice anything of importance if it proved to be unobtainable. In practice, therefore, the problem for every Zionist group and militant was reduced to keeping as low a profile and sailing as close to the wind as was commensurate with efficient management of affairs on the one hand and avoiding the attentions of the police on the other. The rule was a certain amount of subterfuge and conspiracy, most of it crude, much of it ineffective, such as disguising meetings as wedding celebrations, using code-words in written correspondence and avoiding committing certain matters to paper altogether, bribing local policemen when they became too inquisitive, and maintaining a loose and decentralized organization, as has been shown.

But the effort to maintain the movement in a state of suspended, but *tolerated* illegality—for there was no disguising its existence, nor its general aims and major activities—required of the Russian Zionists that they avoid being finally registered in the books of the police as a movement actually, or even potentially, subversive to the Russian state. And here, given the set Russian policy on nationality, lay a certain contradiction. Whatever the Zionists' attitude to the state might be, there was no question but that they constituted a Jewish national movement and that as such they had, from the first, been

[17] Ussishkin to the EAC, Vienna, 14 August 1901. Schwartz, *Ussishkin be-igrotav*, pp. 69–70.

an object of official suspicion and were therefore, potentially, an object of official repression. Their saving grace in the eyes of the police lay in their objectives being notionally and geographically external to Russia; and as a group promoting the exit of Jews from Russia they merited, in the eyes of the authorities, nothing less than applause. Still, the balance was a delicate one. The police remained suspicious and the policies of the Zionist movement, grounded as they were on a desire to avoid upsetting the balance, required of its members too high a degree of self-control and denial to be successful. The issue could not have been more highly charged. The Russian state remained the brutal enemy. The same Russian Zionists who wished all references to the persecution of Jews in Russia to be avoided at the Congresses—in itself an absurdity, seeing that the condition of the Jews was regularly reviewed and that the persecution was a central cause of their miserable condition —were outraged (as has been noted[18]) when Herzl proposed a resolution applauding the Tsar's initiative in convening the Hague Peace Conference in 1899. Indeed there were none more upset by this policy of self-control than its own proponents and supporters; and thus it carried within it the seeds of its own collapse. Yet it was not entirely without profit, while it lasted. For briefly (1901–2), the Zionists were granted a degree of freedom in the conduct of their affairs which, in the circumstances of Russia, was no less than remarkable.

The background to this uncharacteristic toleration by the authorities was the protracted experiment in accommodating and manipulating dissident forces in general known as the *Zubatovshchina*, after its chief promoter and operational director, Colonel S. V. Zubatov, commander of the *Okhrana*, or political police, in Moscow. His purpose was to contain the forces of subversion and revolution by deflecting their greater part into channels that were benign, or at any rate less dangerous than outright opposition to the Autocracy, while limiting direct repression to the anticipated rump of irreconcilables. Zubatov believed, somewhat in the fashion of Russian Social Democrats of the 'economist' school, that the spheres of economics and politics were, and should be, kept distinct, at any rate in Russia. It was only in the former that the proletariat were truly

[18] See above, p. 73.

involved. What really worried the workers was the state of their stomachs and pockets, not the institutions and practices of government. So far as they were concerned, the class struggle was therefore reducible to trade-unionism. And thus reduced, the workers, Zubatov argued, did have a case which it was both right and politic for the Autocracy to support: right, because their condition was miserable and their employers often unconscionable exploiters; politic, because the masses in the towns, no less than in the country, were fundamentally loyal to the Tsar. The dedicated hard-core revolutionaries should be given no opportunity to exploit the workers' just economic grievances in their own subversive political interest. The sensible policy for the authorities was to wean the workers away from the revolutionaries by helping them to take politically neutral industrial action. Since such action was bound to benefit from the covert, or even overt, support of the state, the end result would be a fruitful and soundly based alliance between the Tsar and his subjects. Other advantages would accrue: state-sponsored trade unions would be subject to a degree of control and manipulation by the authorities that could never be reached in any other way; and such rival, illegal unions and parties as would remain in being would be open to lateral observation and penetration as never before.

This 'police socialism', as it came to be called by its critics, was directed, of course, first and foremost at the general population; but it did have its Jewish variant, notably in Minsk where the local chief of the *Okhrana* was Zubatov's ally in the operation. The rise of the Bund, as the strongest and most coherent single component of the Social-Democratic movement, had brought Jews into the ken of the political police not merely as individuals, or as a reservoir of potential dissidents, but as a category in which all three sources of danger to the regime could be identified: the national, the socialist, and the revolutionary. The authorities' initial reaction, with the first arrests of Bundists, had been to threaten dire consequences for all Russian Jewry if they persisted. But the logic underlying police socialism (that 'the police are obliged to be interested in the same thing as the revolutionary'[19]) was evidently

---

[19] General D. F. Trepov, head of the Police Department in the Ministry of the Interior, in 1898, quoted in Lionel Kochan, *Russia in Revolution* (London, 1970), p. 48.

applicable to the Jews as well; and in 1901 a group of former Bundists and a number of Zionists inclined to socialism were interrogated by Zubatov and sufficiently impressed by his arguments in favour of legality to allow themselves to be induced to form the Independent Jewish Workers' Party.[20] In the event, the experiment was short-lived. It foundered on the contradiction inherent in a profoundly antidemocratic and anti-Semitic government seeking to foster an authentic, voluntary mass movement of Jewish workers, even one of limited targets for immediate action. For one thing, it could not fail to lead to its official sponsors putting forward a plea for some extension of the Jews' civil rights, if only so as to demonstrate their good faith to their Jewish clients; and since such proposals cut right across the grain of general policy on the Jews as defined and promoted in St. Petersburg, they were refused by higher authority.[21] For another, the experiment of a *modus vivendi* between a sector of the bureaucracy and the Jews was vitiated from the start by the latter's now deeply ingrained distrust of the Russian state and all its works and by the taint of provocation and betrayal that adhered to all who were minded to try it. However, the temporary lull in the long war of attrition which the Russian Government was conducting against its Jewish subjects did have one positive, short-term result, the grant of permission to hold an all-Russian conference of the Zionist movement at Minsk—freely and openly, with the press in attendance, and complete with a group photograph at the close. True, the *Okhrana* watched the proceedings carefully, in line with their now closer interest in Zionist affairs, and resolved when it was over that they had not liked what they had seen. But, for the internal evolution of the movement the conference at Minsk was of first importance. It provided a unique opportunity for the affairs of the movement to be discussed at length, in considerable depth, and exclusively in terms set by its own participants—that is to say, in terms of their own surroundings and experience and far from the

---

[20] For a full discussion, see M. Mishkinsky, 'Ha-"soẓialism ha-mishtarti" u-megamot ba-mediniut ha-shilton ha-ẓaari le-gabei ha-yehudim (1900–1903)', *Ẓion*, xxv, 3–4 (1960).

[21] Jeremiah Schneiderman, *Sergei Ẓubatov and Revolutionary Marxism* (Ithaca, N.Y., 1976), pp. 278 ff.

magic influence of the great man in Vienna. It was therefore one of the rare occasions on which the central issues and leading personalities of the Russian wing of the movement were free to surface and on which its principal components were caught like fish in an aquarium, readily available for inspection.

7

Within the Movement:
High Principles and Party
Politics

i

The all-Russian conference of Zionists held in Minsk 4–10 September 1902 (22–8 August, O.S.) was characteristic of contemporary Russian Zionism: huge energies, much individual talent, and great strength in numbers were all in abundant display along with an invertebrate institutional structure, deep ideological divisions, and an absence of first-rate (as opposed to very good second-rate) leadership. There was much good feeling and a sense of great occasion. It was indeed an occasion without precedent. The assembly was very large, with over 500 elected delegates and hundreds more invited guests, journalists representing both the Russian and the Jewish press, and assorted hangers-on.[1] Almost all the notables of Russian Zionism were present, beginning with the father of them all, the venerable Moshe Lilienblum,[2] who had come to deliver the greetings of the Odessa Committee and lecture on its work. The debates were generally intense, well-attended, and, on at least two occasions, a source of such excitement that the number of those signing up for an opportunity to speak ran into three figures and had to be cut down ruthlessly. The atmosphere was a world away from the rather decorous manner in which Herzl ran his Congresses. Things were looser at

---

[1] Several estimates of the number of delegates attending were current; none tally. The police count, possibly the most reliable, was 526. (Ministry of the Interior, *Sionizm* (St. Petersburg, 1903), p. 132. CZA, K 14 a/13. See below, pp. 232–5.)

[2] On Lilienblum, see *Origins*, pp. 111–22.

Minsk, less tidy; the conference was less of a parliament, more of a town-meeting. For the delegates themselves it was more like home. Hebrew, Yiddish, and German were used, but the chief language of debate was Russian. Even Aḥad Ha-ʿAm employed it. Again, unlike the Congresses, the conference was inward-looking. The topics of debate and the lines along which opinion was divided were indigenous. The absent Herzl, when his name was respectfully recalled, once at the beginning and once at the end, and when his personal message to the delegates was read out, was warmly cheered. But none spoke for him;[3] and except that much of what was said plainly ran counter to his known ideas and policies, he was virtually ignored. Altogether it is not difficult to see why a great number of delegates came away from Minsk convinced that Russian Zionism had come into its own and why, in a limited sense, it had. Henceforth Russian Zionists would be infused, as never before, with a measure of self-awareness and self-confidence born, it seems, partly of their numbers, partly of fresh recognition of shared values and concerns that generally counted for more than their divisions, and, most keenly, of what might be termed a profound sense of their own special worth and quality.

However, this mood of good feeling bore no easily discernible relationship to what was actually transacted. Russian Jewry's relations with the Russian state, the central topic of political and social concern, were not discussed, or even alluded to, except in very veiled and indirect terms. Of course things could not be otherwise at a public gathering in contemporary Russia. And, besides, the circumstances had to be borne in mind in which permission to hold the conference had been granted. The permit had been obtained through the good offices of one of Zubatov's principal recruits to the 'Independent Jewish Workers' Party' he had sponsored as a rival to the Bund. This was Manya Vilbushevich, a young woman in her early twenties, in whom socialist and Zionist convictions were combined. She had already induced Zubatov to press his superiors to legalize the movement and had herself been invited

---

[3] Mandelstamm, closest of all the Russian leaders to Herzl, was absent, possibly because one of his children had been arrested for revolutionary activity and he was afraid of compromising her.

to put the case for legalization before the new Minister of the Interior, V. K. Plehve, a few months earlier, in May 1902. She had failed in this larger purpose, but her subsequent intervention in the matter of the conference was successful and could not but appear auspicious to those who knew of it. The last thing the notables of Russian Zionism wanted was to compromise the chance of a thoroughgoing regularization of the movement's status. In the event, the formal permit, as granted by the Minsk police, was made subject to several conditions: the conference was to last for no more than a week, there were to be no more than 300 delegates, the agenda was to be submitted to the authorities beforehand for their information (not their approval), a verbatim report of the debates was to be submitted at the conference's end, and Manya Vilbushevich herself was to be present at all the sessions.[4] Only the first and last conditions appear to have been kept; but the fact that they had been set at all cannot but have helped to reinforce the organizers' ingrained political caution and inhibitions— further strengthened when two officers of the gendarmerie turned up, sat through the opening session in the front row of the assembly, and took notes.[5]

The matter of the economic and social state of Russian Jewry was raised by a single speaker: Hayyim Dov Horowitz, one of a growing number of professionals and intellectuals, all activists in the movement, mostly from eastern Europe, who were dissatisfied with the existing leadership, but, unusually, an economist by training. Horowitz was the author of what is reputed to be the first modern treatise on a theoretical topic in economics to be written in Hebrew, *Ha-Mamon* ('Money', 1900). He also differed from most members of his own class of students and young graduates in that he was sceptical of their ability to take over the direction of the movement themselves and was more sensitive to the condition of the masses than to problems of national culture and destiny. He was correspondingly less critical of the Bund than were most of his associates. Horowitz argued that the success of Zionism was necessarily linked to an improvement in the

---

[4] Israel Klausner, Introduction, in M. Nurock, *Ve'idat zionei rusiya* (Jerusalem, 1953), pp. 25–6.

[5] Yosef Eliash, *Zikhronot zioni me-rusiya* (Tel-Aviv, 1955), p. 105.

economic condition of the people. And he drew the operative conclusion that the Zionists must assume some direct responsibility in that sphere.[6] This was his theme at Minsk. Concern with final goals and with the cultural and moral conditions of Jewry was well enough, he said, but the Zionists must not avert their attention from the Jews' pressing material needs. Horowitz reviewed the steady process of their pauperization and argued that failure to join the social and economic battle being mounted on their behalf brought Zionism into ill repute. Philanthropy and charity were to no purpose. What was required was mutual help. But this was not sufficiently understood; and the Zionists should therefore help by founding co-operative loan and friendly societies, co-operatives for marketing and for bulk buying of raw materials, traders' associations, and mutual insurance groups. Data on the occupational structure of Russian Jewry should be collected; labour exchanges should be set up; and the migratory current should be guided, as far as it was possible to do so. All this would go far to help the Zionists assert their leadership and lay a solid and healthy base for the attainment of their greater purposes.

There was no discussion of these ideas. There were sympathizers, but for the most part the topic was regarded as eccentric in the Zionist context and incompatible in principle with the fundamental Zionist approach—one which invited all energies to be concentrated on obtaining a territorial solution to the Jews' problems *outside* Russia. Moreover, as a proposal for a kind of 'going to the people', Horowitz's plan was judged likely to arouse the wrath of the authorities. Yet there was much in it that was incontestable. It was resolved therefore that local Zionist societies would be under no obligation to undertake such activities as Horowitz had proposed, but that individual members would be free to follow their private bent.[7]

A great deal more attention was paid to the question of the internal structure of the movement. The debate was led by Menaham Ussishkin (1863–1941), one of the twelve Russian

---

[6] Horowitz's views are set out in elaborate detail in a series of articles, 'She'elat ha-kalkala u-mekoma bi-tenu'ateinu ha-le'umit', *Ha-Shilo'ah*, ix (1902), pp. 17–32, 130–49, 305–20; x (1903), pp. 57–72, 110–27, 328–37, 401–12.

[7] A. Rafa'eli, 'Vei'idot arziot shel zionei rusiya', *Kazir* [i] (Tel-Aviv, 1964), pp. 69–70.

members of the GAC and, as the delegate based in Ekaterinoslav, effectively chief of Zionists for all southern Russia. But
Ussishkin was more than a regional leader. He was an authentic
veteran of the movement whose activism dated from its very
beginnings in 1881/2. With Pinsker dead, Lilienblum frail,
and Aḥad Ha-ʿAm consistent in his refusal to undertake
institutional responsibility, Ussishkin remained the most considerable figure on the scene, at any rate so far as the organized
movement went, and the very embodiment of its continuity.
He shared with Yeḥiel Tchlenov of Moscow (who presided
with his usual tact over the Minsk assembly) a certain informal,
but generally recognized primacy in Russian Zionism. But
he was a stronger man than Tchlenov and vastly more determined to assert himself, the great powerhouse among a host of
weaker spirits, the organization man *par excellence*. Ussishkin
was an exceptionally systematic and clear-minded man of
enormous energy and of considerable administrative and
organizational gifts, in the application of which his professional
training as an engineer was fully evident. He was also somewhat
insensitive; he was domineering and self-important; and he
was inordinately vain. But above all, he was single-minded.
The bull-like manner in which he brought his energies to bear
on the issues of the day was a source of perpetual irritation and
amusement, in about equal parts. 'I must begin by congratu-
lating you on your office', Aḥad Ha-ʿAm wrote to him on his
election to the GAC as member for southern Russia, 'as really
it [the office] is greater than that of your provincial governor.
For he only does as he is instructed from "on high" while you,
I think, are sole judge of affairs within your borders and there
is none to tell you what to do.'[8] But his devotion, body and soul,
to the cause of Jewish national Redemption was absolute and
it commanded genuine, if often somewhat reluctant respect
all round.

He is not as 'solid' and hard as people say [Bialik wrote of him].
Those who know him well find in him a good measure of emotion
and sentimentality. There is a little bit of fantasy in him too. His
eyes tend to fill with tears. His supposed hardness stems more from
stubbornness and inflexibility. His thoughts move as heavily as a

---

[8] Aḥad Ha-ʿAm to Ussishkin, 29 September 1898. *Igrot AH*, ii, pp. 140–1.

bear and when he is set on an idea he cannot easily move away from it or turn right or left in the slightest degree. He is by nature and in spirit limited; he is straight. Very conservative. One-sided and one-faced. A monist. A trumpet that plays a single note . . . He recognizes no colours or shadings. He knows only black and white. Whence his primitive clarity. The force of his actions derives from the force of his thinking. In sum: a man who is not very complicated—but nevertheless a man whose greatness is in his simplicity, his primitivity, and in all his impulses, small as well as big.[9]

Ussishkin was appalled by the inefficiency, the slackness, and the poor use of meagre resources that he judged, with reason, to be characteristic of the Zionist Organization in Russia. Membership-fees were collected late, or not at all; there were demands upon the time of the most loyal of the activists, always few in number, which could not possibly be met; and these were expected to take decisions on a variety of matters too great for them to be competent to deal satisfactorily with them all. There was duplication of effort and therefore waste, much dilettantism, and no clear line dividing the true and the loyal adherents from the occasional, the half-hearted, and the self-seeking. There were too many idlers and windbags, and there was no discipline. What Ussishkin wanted, he told the assembly, was order and system: a rational division of labour and responsibility, the separation of wheat from chaff, a preference for quality over quantity, the removal of those who, while unwilling to work, none the less demanded equality of status and influence with those who were willing. He wanted inspection and control and an account of their stewardship by the officers of the movement as a matter of duty. Above all, he wanted

Strict discipline. What is strict discipline, you will ask? I shall tell you: strict discipline is complete and absolute submission to such laws as we ourselves lay down. Democratic freedom pertains only to the ways and means of making such laws as we ourselves freely establish. Once established, they must be submitted to, the submission being to our own selves and our own will.[10]

[9] Letter to David Rothblum, 1 September 1933. *Igrot Ḥayyim Naḥman Bialik*, ed. P. Laḥover (Tel-Aviv, 1939), v, no. 1457, p. 281.
[10] 'Organizazia', in R. Binyamin [Yehoshu'a Radler-Feldmann] (ed.), *Sefer Ussishkin* (Jerusalem, 1934), p. 72.

Ussishkin, in sum, wanted to convert the movement into something like a party with established cadres and vertical lines of organization and authority. Membership, in the elaborate plan he brought before the assembly, would be subject to certain tests, the leadership organized on a clear geographical-hierarchical basis with elections at each stage, but with clear authority within its stated sphere. There would be a central leadership group which would hold the reins collectively, but divide the work of its members by subject, with proper places found for women, for the young, and for workers—but always on the basis of good order, loyalty, and personal merit.

The workers too have begun to tend towards our movement. We must pay attention to them and to the populist movement generally. It has been suggested that a worker be elected to the Greater Actions Committee; and on that I have only this to say: if there shall be found amongst us a diligent worker who is, truly, devoted to our cause and sufficiently intelligent to understand and know all that is required of a member of the Greater Actions Committee, then I assure you that I myself shall be the first to grasp his hand and [see to] his election. But if there are other considerations . . . then I shall be the first to oppose it.[11]

Lastly, he wanted the formation of a corps of young pioneers, a sort of 'Zionist Guard', all unattached and free to devote a year or two entirely to the purposes of the movement, either in the Diaspora itself or in Erez-Israel.

Much time and energy were devoted to this matter of internal organization. Ussishkin himself spoke for three hours and 120 delegates asked to address the conference on the subject. But while some of his points struck home, on the whole there was little sympathy for his conception of a thoroughly integrated, tightly run ship of a movement. So a committee was formed, without much enthusiasm, to study his proposals and report back. It sat for two days, but as both it and, later, the full conference itself were about equally divided on the only one of the twenty-one items on Ussishkin's list to be put to a formal vote,[12] the whole matter was finally left over for a fresh

---

[11] Ibid., p. 75.

[12] This concerned the basic building-block of the movement, the local association.

committee to look at more closely still and report back to the next conference of Russian Jewish Zionists to be held.

There were other matters of organization besides those which Ussishkin had brought up: the Bank, on which the delegates wanted more information and over which they wanted more control, and the proposed Jewish National Fund for land purchases in Erez-Israel, which they wanted set up without delay and very strictly limited to its stated purpose. Actual settlement activities in Erez-Israel were reported on amply, Tchlenov himself lecturing on the subject at length, joined by Lilienblum and representatives of the *yishuv* itself. But here there was no debate, no disagreement. The central business of the conference, in any case, was in a different sphere. The matter to which the conference devoted most of its time and almost all of its passions was that of *culture*, by which was meant, in the first place, education for Zionism and education in general, but which led back, by an inevitable process of reduction, to primary views on society, religion, culture in its broader sense, politics, and the state of the nation. This being the sphere of principle and ideology, debate was long and disagreement sharp and fundamental.

ii

The question of culture was a perennial item on the agenda of Russian Zionism. In it were reflected both the long-standing pressures to modernize Jewry and Judaism, associated, most notably, with the nineteenth-century Jewish Enlightenment (the *haskala*),[13] and the corresponding counter-pressures which emanated from those who stood by the orthodox tradition. These had all been sharpened by the new circumstances: by the rise of Zionism and other radical tendencies, by modernists and orthodox finding themselves together in the Zionist camp, by the turn which Zionist policy had taken since Herzl's assumption of leadership (away from the direct concern with 'culture' and towards other matters which appeared irrelevant

---

Ussishkin wanted it re-formed in a rigorous manner by requiring, in each case, the election of a five-man committee by members whose purchase of the *shekel* would not be a form of charity, but an expression of full adherence to the principles of Zionism.

[13] See *Origins*, pp. 43–8.

or premature to many of the old hands), and by the irritating need for the leaders of the movement in eastern Europe to devise tasks with which to occupy themselves while Herzl occupied the arena. The question of culture was thus, from the first, a subject for indirect dispute with Herzl and his 'political' school and, by stages, a topic—in fact, a banner—around which opposition to him, overt and covert alike, tended to muster. And the debate having become political, at least in part, to the natural acerbity of argument on ideology and principle there came increasingly to be added the force of private feeling and ambition.

In the vanguard of the double rebellion against Herzl— against his strong methods as the movement's leader and his weak position on 'culture'—was a small and remarkably coherent group. They were mostly students or fresh graduates of central and western European universities, German and Swiss for the greater part, but their origins, with a few exceptions, were in Russia. Their language of debate in the early stages was Russian. They had ties with groups of similar composition, but somewhat more radical social views, in Russia itself. The influence of many years in central and western Europe was apparent, however. They were not excessively doctrinaire. Their main bent, it may be said, was towards science and system. In matters of politics and society they were egalitarian in the sense current at the time which emphasized equality of opportunity rather than equality of achievement. Some were mildly populist in tendency, but all were strong believers in political democracy, by which they meant, in essence, representative government on the contemporary English or French model. They were firm modernists and free thinkers, and were hotly opposed to what they termed 'clericalism'.

Their views on the specific question of socialism were less well defined. They tended to sympathize with the aims of the socialists, while being, on the whole, opposed to doctrinal, especially Marxist socialism, and, more deeply, to class as the fundamental category of analysis and the primary basis for political and social activity. To Jewish Marxists they were hostile. For the Bund, accordingly, they had no use whatsoever. But they tended to resist attempts to marry Zionism with milder forms of socialism (after the manner of Nachman Syrkin[14]) too. This was partly on the familiar pragmatic grounds that it was impolitic to attract the hostile attentions of the Russian police, but chiefly because they believed, with most other Zionists, that the common, central task of the movement was the achievement of national independence and the precipitation of national social and cultural revival, above and also before all else.

In sum, they may be thought of as early twentieth-century liberals of distinct, yet entirely mild national persuasion, who would have been comfortable in, say, the radical wing of the contemporary Liberal Party in Great Britain.

Zionism [they laid down when they assembled in Heidelberg in June 1902 to formulate their programme] is the striving for the liberation of the Jewish nation from historical pressure, the solution of the problem of the Jewish individual, and thus also of the economic problem of the Jewish nation and the political Jewish problem. . . . [It rests on the general principle] that the development of mankind can proceed only through the development of viable nations; that social and cultural progress can be achieved only by utilizing all national energies; and that this utilization of national energies can be achieved only if a nation is able to chart its own destinies on a territory of its own . . .

The introduction of religion into the argumentation for, and the programme of, Zionism is inconsistent with the national character of Zionism. . . .

The purpose of the liberation of the Jewish nation is the regeneration [and] the restoration of the Jewish people as an organic entity which, thus regenerated, should be enabled to unfold its authentic natural tendencies and to create cultural and social values of high quality.

Their programme, long, detailed, and painfully earnest in intent, was the most serious attempt thus far to lay down a clear and binding and, so far as possible, complete platform for the movement. It sought to define the matter and rationale of Zionism in general, and in relation to the Jewish people and individual Jews. It dealt elaborately with the question of Zionism's antithesis, assimilation, and touched upon the

---

[14] See below, pp. 394–6.

economic problem of the Jews ('for the most part a result of
the exceptional position of the Jewish people'), upon Jewish
cultural values, upon ways and means of realizing the movement's aims and mobilizing the Jewish masses in its interest,
and upon the central role of 'cultural activity' and education
in that very context. Its operative and also its sharpest part
was a critique of the Zionist Organization as it stood and as
it was being managed, along with a defence of that action of
which the programme was the crowning step, namely the setting up of a party (*Fraktion*, in the contemporary terminology)
within the larger movement.

'The division of Zionists into fractions and groups is an
inevitable result of the existing differences within the movement', the rebels declared. The unity of the Jewish people
and 'the necessity for joint practical work' notwithstanding,
there were 'among the Zionists a variety of elements which
differ sharply in their political, economic and cultural views'.
It was proper, they claimed, for these differences to be articulated. The formation of parties would only enrich the composition of the Congresses and improve their working by ensuring
that the very best-qualified spokesmen for the various view-
points were heard. For their part, the founders of the Democratic Party[15] wished to 'combat and eliminate' such 'phenomena' as the 'superficiality' of Zionist propaganda, 'opportunism in regard to religious prejudices and personal or public
tendencies and powers', 'Byzantinism and religious hypocrisy,
personality cults and petty place hunting for Zionist honours',
and 'violation of democratic principles' in the composition
and management of the Congresses.

A typical case in point [they emphasized] is the 'cultural question',
one of the most important issues in the national movement, which
haunts the Congresses like a spectre. Despite the longtime efforts
of individual delegates at the Congress, this question has never come
to a clear-cut decision because many of the members do not even
understand it and most of them do not properly appreciate its
significance. The economic question [too] was raised as a problem
[but] was buried in a committee that was a monstrosity if for no

---

[15] The familiar term 'Democratic Fraction', a questionable translation of the original
Demokratische Fraktion anyway, plays down the party-political content of the initiative.

other reason but that it was composed of elements with opposing economic views. The entire question of 'improvement' [of the condition of the Jews], to cite one instance, did not fare better last year; in this case there was not even a debate although six reports had been delivered on the subject.[16]

Their reference here was to the Fifth Congress of Zionists (26–30 December 1901 at Basel) where the Democratic Party had appeared in public for the first time as a coherent and identifiable group and had with calculated drama, at a tense moment in a procedural argument with Herzl, walked out in a body from the hall. The surface issue in dispute had been the placing of the debate on 'culture' on the agenda of the Congress; the underlying issue was the place of culture on the agenda of the movement. Herzl was reluctant to back the promoters of yet another debate on the subject for fear, as has been said, of an irreparable quarrel with the orthodox. The members of the Democratic Party were encouraged to persist in the effort to force a decision by their conviction that what divided them from Herzl was a fundamental disagreement on the nature and content of Zionism itself, which they conceived in broader terms than those which they ascribed to Herzl. They judged his views to be simplistic in his reliance on diplomacy as a method and in his confidence in the future Jewish state as the prime engine of national revolution and revival. They had no time or taste for compromise with orthodoxy, resented Herzl's tendency to seek it, and discounted his belief in the 'power of the rabbis' over the Jewish masses. And besides all this, they were prey to that general discomfort and that frustration and disapproval of Herzl and his ways that have already been alluded to, and which they themselves so plainly evinced in their manifesto (drafted six months later) in its references to 'Byzantinism and religious hypocrisy, personality cults and petty place hunting . . . [and] violation of democratic principles'—language that for its harshness was unprecedented thus far in the movement.

[16] 'Programm und Organisationsstatut der Demokratisch-zionistischen Fraktion', Heidelberg, 22 June 1902. Published in Hebrew at the time of the Minsk conference in *Ha-Ẓefira*, 3 September; 4 September; 7 September; 9 September 1902. English translation by Harry Zohn, Documentary History of Zionism Project (Jerusalem, n.d.).

But why the emphasis on culture? In the first place, disapproval of Herzl as leader was more difficult to argue than a substantive issue of policy: for lack of knowledge of the details of Herzl's affairs, they were poorly placed to meet him on the primary ground of high politics. It may be said that they had little choice, in fact, but to bring their guns to bear on what for Herzl, at any rate, was a flank. Then, their guns were very few: the Democrats were never more than a tiny group within the movement (37 delegates out of 358 at the Fifth Congress). Lastly, they were to the end too unsure of themselves and too mixed in their feelings about either the man Herzl or his policies to mount a really hard attack. Even to his harshest critics, Herzl was unquestionably the awesome and indispensable leader, the man who, single-handed, had brought the movement together and founded its central institutions and now stood head and shoulders above the ruck, its greatest single asset, its veritable symbol.

When Herzl asked Chaim Weizmann, who, with Leo Motzkin and some others, was trying to organize a foundation conference of the group in July 1901, *not* to hold it, on the grounds that it would embarrass him in his negotiations in Turkey—because there were bound to be strong statements about Erez-Israel and the Turks were sure to pick them up—Weizmann fumed, but eventually submitted to Herzl's call to 'discipline'.[17] For a while Weizmann toyed with the idea of breaking away from the 'unhealthy' official Zionist movement altogether and setting up a new 'youth organization'. 'I have no doubt', he wrote to Aḥad Ha-'Am, 'that its basic principle will indeed be complete independence of the general Zionist Organization, and that there will be no concessions in this respect.'[18] But again he changed his mind. 'As to the existing Zionist Organization', he wrote to Leo Motzkin just before the Congress, 'our attitude must be positive, in the sense of

[17] Herzl to Weizmann, 2 and 18 July 1901, cited in Gedalia Yogev, 'Weizmann ke-manhig si'at opozizia (1901–1904), in Y. Gorni and G. Yogev (eds.), *Medinai be-'itot mashber* (Tel-Aviv, 1977), pp. 20–1. Weizmann to Catherine Dorfman, 5 July 1901; and to Herzl, 22 July 1901. *Weizmann Letters*, i, no. 103, p. 151 and no. 107, pp. 157–8. Herzl eventually agreed to the conference being convened just prior to the main Zionist Congress in December 1901 when, he expected, it would be all but lost to sight among the many other preliminary group discussions.

[18] Weizmann to Aḥad Ha-'Am, 9 June 1901. *Weizmann Letters*, i, no. 86, p. 124.

taking part in it and working on behalf of its institutions.'[19] Later still, after the Fifth Congress, when Aḥad Ha-ʿAm himself advised the young men to cut loose from Herzl's movement,[20] Weizmann avoided a direct response. Motzkin, the older of the two leaders of the group, does not appear ever to have considered breaking clear of the parent movement. He had himself been one of the more important of Herzl's original recruits to the movement, even if he had also been, from the first, Herzl's boldest and most outspoken critic. He was rather more aware of the lasting significance of such a step as the forming of a *party* within the larger Organization and more sensitive, it seems, than Weizmann and many others to criticism on that score. Speaking at the December conference and writing the text of the group's manifesto, he was at pains to justify the step as much on pragmatic grounds as on grounds of principle. In any event, it was not political activities he opposed; as with Weizmann and so many others, it was Herzl's monopoly of them that he objected to.

There has been preserved a photograph of the group taken at the same Fifth Congress at which they made their mark. Almost all of the members of the Democratic Party are present: Leo Motzkin, Chaim Weizmann, Martin Buber, Berthold Feiwel, and some thirty others, all carefully dressed and posed, all intensely serious. In the centre, arms folded, head bent slightly forward, glowering at the camera, sits Herzl. The opposition, it might be said, is draped around him. The picture is characteristic of the time, the place, and the ambivalence of their attitude to him.

Here then was an opposition, but a loyal opposition; at all events, tractable. Short-lived too. After the splash it made at the Fifth Congress and a reappearance in Minsk, it faded rapidly, swallowed up in the greater oppositional movement that rose against Herzl upon his presentation of the East Africa scheme at the Sixth Congress in 1903. The Democratic Party was, perhaps, too specialized in the themes it took for its own, too remote, in spite of the origins of its members, from the actual east European scene, and, with one fateful exception, composed of men who were too intellectual in cast

---

[19] Weizmann to Motzkin, 23 November 1901. Ibid., no. 144, p. 206.
[20] Aḥad Ha-ʿAm to Weizmann, 17 March 1902. *Igrot AH*, iii, p. 136.

of mind and too fastidious in taste to make a thoroughgoing stab at power or power-sharing—even if such a thing had been feasible in the years of Herzl's supremacy. Finally and fatally, there were great differences and tensions dividing its two leading personalities, Motzkin and Weizmann. These put a brake on progress and coalescence at every stage.

On the face of it Motzkin and Weizmann had much in common. Both had emerged from the Pale of Settlement, both had studied in Germany, both were men of the exact academic disciplines (Motzkin was a mathematician, Weizmann a chemist), and both were devoted heart and soul to the national cause. Each applied enormous resources of energy to relevant activities in their respective, but not dissimilar milieux, Motzkin still in Berlin, Weizmann now in Geneva. But otherwise they were chalk and cheese. Motzkin was older (by seven years), at an age in life when such a margin can matter. He had lived in Germany since his adolescence and was rather more 'European' than Weizmann. He had, as we know,[21] played a role in the movement before, as well as upon, the advent of Herzl and his moral authority among the young Zionist intelligentsia was the greater for it. He was extremely bright and brave, a man of absolute principle to the end of his life, gentle, unassuming, essentially unambitious, of extremely modest habits, hard-working. He was disorganized, a poor manager of others, and entirely incapable of holding his public and private lives in comfortable and productive balance. He never took his degree. It may be said of Motzkin that there was something in him of the secular saint. He was a man whose life was truly and decisively influenced by the precepts to which he adhered; and he was a puritan.

The young Weizmann (just turned twenty-seven at the time of the Fifth Congress) was of different stuff: strong, somewhat more self-indulgent than Motzkin, given to irritability and violence in thought and language, habitually and enormously critical of others, but especially of his equals and inferiors, less thoughtful than Motzkin, less concerned with doctrine, with more drive and a practical bent, vastly more efficient and effective in matters of organization, and superb at keeping both halves of his life in balance. Weizmann found it possible

[21] *Origins*, pp. 224–5, 367–9.

not merely to complete his studies, but to obtain academic appointments at the Universities of Geneva and Manchester; and if he never attained the Chair of Chemistry he had always coveted, he did distinguish himself in research. Both men were perhaps in character when their most intense quarrel, after a period of great friendship, turned on Weizmann's having jilted his mistress, a member of the Democratic circle itself. Motzkin, regarding Weizmann's behaviour as dishonourable, does not seem to have hesitated to allow moral judgement to influence his attitude to his political colleague. Weizmann, thereafter, tended to vent his spleen on Motzkin in wildly inappropriate language when further disagreement erupted between them. Motzkin was 'repulsive', and his behaviour was 'foul',[22] he wrote to his new fiancée from the conference at Minsk, where he and Motzkin, both in attendance, had failed to see eye to eye on some question, however obscure.

None the less, the Democratic Party did leave a mark. It helped to make open, vocal opposition to Herzl somewhat more respectable than it might otherwise have been. It was the means whereby a handful of new, competing figures came to the fore. It inaugurated the political party as a regular institution within Zionism, where there had only been country organizations before; and by doing so it put an end to Herzl's concept of a monolithic, undifferentiated movement. It helped to polarize opinion on main Zionist policy by encouraging the view that political Zionism was not so much mistaken in principle as inadequate in practice and by promoting the idea that there was much value in activities that were not purely political, but such as would directly serve the central political effort. Thus the results of the Democratic Party's brief appearance on the scene were more marked in the realm of hearts and minds than in immediate and perceptible influence on the major affairs or institutions of the Zionist Organization[23]— apart, that is, from the precedent set by its actual formation.

---

[22] 3 and 6 September 1902. *Weizmann Letters*, i, nos. 308 and 313, pp. 394 and 398.
[23] The Jewish University which some of the members of the Democratic Party pressed for was not established until very much later and then in Erez-Israel, not Europe. But a publishing house, the Jüdischer Verlag (with which Martin Buber was prominently associated), did materialize and lasted until 1938 when the Gestapo shut it down.

In sum, the members of the Democratic Party served as cata-
lysts. They helped to break the spell under which Herzl had
held his movement since 1897 and they did much to start the
process whereby the general tendency of Zionism shifted away
from attachment to the idea of a rapid and radical solution to
the Problem of the Jews back to a less dramatic conception of
the means and likely instruments of change.

iii

The debate on culture at the Fifth Congress had been concluded
with a final resolution declaring that 'the cultural advancement,
namely the education of the Jewish people in a national sense,
was one of the essential elements of the Zionist programme and
it was the duty of all Zionists to contribute to it.'[24] Under
one of its operative clauses a commission on culture was to be
set up and after further argument Herzl had agreed to Aḥad
Ha-ʿAm being appointed to it. Herzl was entirely aware of the
distance Aḥad Ha-ʿAm was so careful to keep from the Congresses and from the organized movement generally and of his
now well-established public position as the arch-critic (*within*
the camp) of the leading (Herzlian) trend in Zionism. But
the case for the co-option of the foremost spokesman for a
massive and thoroughgoing, yet entirely non-assimilationist
cultural revival among the Jews was incontrovertible. In the
event, the commission failed to achieve anything of substance
and had managed, moreover, by excess of ambition, to bring
its relations with the Russian members of the GAC almost to
the level of its relations with Herzl's circle in Vienna. None the
less, once it had been decided to debate the subject of culture
all over again at Minsk, the call to Aḥad Ha-ʿAm was as
inevitable and incontestable as ever. But whereas he had only
loomed over the debate at the Congress in Basel without being
present in the flesh, at Minsk he was the central figure in the
debate itself; and since culture was the issue of greatest concern
at Minsk, he was second to none in his personal impact on the
conference as a whole.

As so often in the past, the slight, schoolmasterly figure, so
much less of a physical presence than Herzl or Nordau or
Ussishkin, or even Pinsker or Mohilever in their time, quite

[24] *Protokoll V*, p. 427.

dominated his surroundings. He did this, so it must be supposed, by the sheer weight of his unique moral and intellectual
authority and the language, form, and style in which he
habitually expressed himself: a structure of thought that was
exceptionally clear and open, pungent phrasing, and a manner
which conveyed an enormous, yet suppressed impatience—
suppressed by his own recognition of the complexity of the
things he strove to simplify and by great regard for the formal
courtesies of debate. Typically, his address was more a lecture
than a speech, an attempt, as he put it, 'to clear up the "problem of culture" in the plain meaning of the term, without
introducing startling new ideas or over-subtle refinements'.[25]
He would try to pull the subject out of the cloud of heat, debate,
and recrimination in which it had been enveloped by political
and religious zealots alike and bring it back into the light for all
to see it in its simplicity.

The idea that Zionism could be concerned exclusively with
diplomacy and financial transactions was false and dangerous,
said Aḥad Ha-'Am. In the sense that its ends and hopes were
political, Zionism had always been 'political'. And since the
prospects of the new Zionism were no brighter than those of
the old, its political content too was reducible to the matter of
its ultimate ends and to hope. On the other hand, unlike the
old, the new Zionism was narrowly conceived: a 'mere romance
of diplomatic embassies, interviews with high personages [, and]
promises, such as leaves no room for the creative work which
alone can slake the thirst for activity . . . of those who detest
waste of time and idle talk'. In practice, therefore, the new
Zionism, like the old, relied on cultural work to satisfy the
minds, and provide an outlet for the energies, of its adherents.
This was as it should be, but a great deal more was needed.
Aḥad Ha-'Am rehearsed his established theme: the national
spirit was perishing. The Jews' feeling for themselves in their
collective aspect, the value they attached to their nationhood
and to their native intellectual and artistic heritage, and the

---

[25] Aḥ ad Ha-'Am's address was published with some corrections and additions as
'Teḥiat ha-ru'aḥ', in *Ha-Shilo'aḥ*, November-December 1902, and included in his
collected writings, *Kol kitvei Aḥad Ha-'Am* (Tel-Aviv, 1947), pp. 173–86. An English
version by Leon Simon, somewhat abridged, but checked by Aḥad Ha-'Am himself,
appears as 'The Spiritual Revival' in *Selected Essays* (Philadelphia, 1912), pp. 253–305.

role it played in their lives—all these were wasting away under the eroding forces of a petrified tradition and the pull of foreign cultures. It was within this arena that the fate and quality of the Jewish people would be determined and it was here, therefore, that the greatest and most urgent of the problems of the Jews lay. Certainly, the question of the national culture, any national culture, was complex. But one crucial distinction had to be drawn, between culture in its 'objective' and in its 'subjective' aspects. The former was the expression and product of the best minds of a nation through time and tended to take on an existence that was independent both of its creators and of the nation itself, as with the wisdom of the Greek philosophers, for example. The latter was a close reflection of the condition of the entire nation at a particular moment and therefore fluctuated in depth and quality from time to time. The two aspects or levels, the high and the popular, had no necessary connection one with the other. The high 'objective' culture of England in the sixteenth to eighteenth centuries, represented by the work of Shakespeare, Bacon, Locke, Hume, and other members of what was relatively speaking a large body of men, belonged in time to a period when 'the great mass of the English people was . . . in a low state of culture which did not by any means correspond to the level reached by these giants'. Of the modern Swiss, in contrast, it could be said that their schools were excellent and that 'in many departments of the national life they show a high, perhaps unequalled level of culture. But from the point of view of *objective* culture, Switzerland is unproductive: as yet there has arisen no great creative intellect, capable of embodying the Swiss spirit in an original national culture.'

So with the Jews. There were the undoubted great and original creations of the past; and there was the problem of the state of the people as a whole, today, in relation to the past. The culture of the Jews in both its aspects, the objective and the subjective, was in profound crisis. The high culture was not dead, but it stood urgently in need of reinvigoration. First, it had undergone great and violent changes upon the removal of the Jews from that land in which the 'national creative power . . . [had grown] naturally and freely . . . [to] a strange soil where [perforce] it was preserved by artificial

means'. Now, as a consequence of Emancipation, it bore no
fruit at all. The most talented sons of the Jewish people
employed the languages, symbols, and idioms of other nations.
What they created therefore accrued to other cultures and, in
that sense, constituted a loss to the culture of the Jews—for
there could be no national literature, to take the crucial
example, except in the national language. And the national
language of the Jews was, and could only be, Hebrew. Not even
Yiddish could replace or even coexist with it. There could be
only one national language, Aḥad Ha-ʿAm maintained, warm-
ing to a theme which he pursued unvaryingly throughout his
life. The attempt to establish Yiddish ran counter to all the
nation's experience and was, in any event, doomed to failure.
Even if Hebrew were abandoned, the reign of Yiddish would be
short. This was already evident. Everywhere it was being
driven to the wall by the languages of the countries in which
the Jews lived, as much in its 'native' countries of Russia,
Galicia, and Romania as in the United States. 'The labours
performed in the service of Yiddish can lead to only one result:
that after two or three generations we shall have *two* dead
literary languages, instead of one, as at present.' There was no
substitute for Hebrew. But nor could there be a future for it
except in its native habitat, in Ereẓ-Israel. Yet 'to lay the
foundations of a spiritual "refuge" for our national culture
demands, perhaps, preparations no less elaborate and resources
no less extensive than to lay the foundations of a material
refuge for persecuted Jews.' *This* was the long and arduous
task which Zionism must undertake.

Every atom of [national creative] power which is severed from its
original source and floats away into a strange world is an irreparable
loss to the nation. To gather these atoms together and keep them in
our own world for the benefit of our own national culture is essentially
Zionist work because it adds to our spiritual wealth in the present
and prepares the way for the greater cultural work that is to come
after the establishment of the centre in Ereẓ-Israel.

What was needed therefore was 'a powerful and well-knit
organization' to gather the necessary resources, to keep watch
over the 'errant atoms' of spiritual force, and to support every
achievement and creation of promise. The Zionist Organiza-

tion, 'with all its faults', was the only Jewish institution concerned with Jewish national revival. But it could not be burdened with the task of reviving the national culture as well.
As it stood, it was ill suited to the selective advancement of
modern Jewish, especially Hebrew, literary culture. Its proper
tasks were already beyond its strength; there could be no
question of it pursuing other objects related to, yet distinct
from those for which it had been designed. A second, parallel
organization had therefore to be set up, with men who were
fully dedicated to these other ends, with their own machinery
and their own autonomous understanding of what had to be
done for the revival of Israel, yet working in parallel and in
harmony with the first, the political Organization.

The other aspect of the question, that of popular culture
and of mass education, was simpler, in his view. The free man's
ideal, properly, was to go as far and as high as his own powers
enabled him; and by this standard, the condition of the Jewish
people was unsatisfactory both in absolute terms and relative
to the condition of other nations. The progress of the Jews
was blocked on every side by every kind of obstacle. They were
compelled to fight at every turn for things and opportunities
which the members of other nations obtained without a
struggle. But the fact that

we see, that in spite of all, we are not inferior to other nations and
need not be ashamed of ourselves, should not console us; on the
contrary, it ought to be galling to us to consider how much further
we might rise if we too could use our powers without hindrance and
if each of us could develop in the way best suited to him—as other
men do. None but a slave could fail to feel, or could deny, the national
tragedy involved in an inability to rise to the level of culture for
which we are in fact fitted by our inherent powers. Beyond doubt,
therefore, there is an urgent need to improve our position . . .

None the less, this was not *in itself* a task for Zionism.
Enlightenment, and, indeed, education in general, had no
necessary connection with Zionism. On the other hand, what
was not being done, and would not be done, *without* the Zionists
was their diffusion on a national basis and in a national spirit.
Modern secular education *per se*, devoid of an infusion of
national cultural content, only accelerated the decline of the

national spirit. The Zionists, therefore, could not allow them-selves to exclude popular education from their proper sphere of activity. The Zionists, Aḥad Ha-ʿAm was saying in effect, had to take charge of education among the Jews as the only reliable means of fighting the forces of assimilation. This was much more important than the collection of subscriptions to Herzl's Bank with which so many occupied their time. And it was not so much the communities and the synagogues that had to be won for the movement as the schools—the modern ones in the first place, but the traditional ones as well. Thus to the problem of religion.

He was far from claiming, he explained, that the traditional system of schooling was in any sense opposed to the national spirit, least of all in the sense that so much of the modern schooling was. A sense of the community of Israel and a love for the nation did work themselves ineradicably into the minds of the children of the *ḥeder*. None the less

it is obvious and undeniable, however extraordinary, that most orthodox Jews who have been trained in this system, for all their devotion to the *community* of Israel, are unable to understand the ideal of the regeneration of Israel as a *people*. The masses stand aloof and regard the new movement with complete indifference; their leaders are mostly opposed to it and try, by every means that jealousy and hatred can suggest, to put obstacles in its path.

Yet it was for the *orthodox* Zionists themselves to deal with the orthodox branch of Jewry. The modernists had no more right to demand of the orthodox that they entrust the education of their children to other hands than the orthodox had the right to claim the education of all Jewish children for their own. Thus there were points of union and points of difference between the two varieties of Zionists and these had to be recognized. 'Zionism must demand from both sections—and both must obey implicitly and without reserve—that each shall make the ideal of national revival, in the modern sense, the basis of education; but on this foundation each is at liberty to erect its own superstructure in its own way, without hind-rance or interference from outside.' There therefore had to be two separate but parallel systems, one for the orthodox, the other for modernists. The attempt to find a compromise common denominator had failed, as had, inevitably, the attempt to gloss over the differences between the two sectors. Once again, these should be recognized. And if his proposal were followed, then at least

the orthodox could not complain of their adversaries wishing to infringe their liberties. They would then have to admit that the reason for their cry of alarm at the conjunction of 'culture' with Zionism was nothing less than *their own* intolerance, their desire to have all the nation's education for their own, while the 'freedom' they claimed for themselves only meant—as was usually the case with religious zealots—freedom to enslave others to do their own will . . . If the interests of the orthodox party are dearer to them than the general national goal, it behoves them to leave the company of the [modernist] Zionists entirely, as do the other [anti-Zionist, members of the orthodox camp].[26]

iv

The orthodox wing of Russian Zionism to which Aḥad Ha-ʿAm addressed himself at Minsk had greatly changed in character and composition in the time that had elapsed since the foundation of the reformed and reinvigorated movement under Herzl five years earlier. With the death of Rabbi Shemu'el Mohilever in 1898 its members had lost their leader and their protector from critics both within and without orthodoxy. Mohilever had been a considerable figure within eastern European orthodoxy in his own right and in orthodoxy's own rabbinical and communal terms—the only such figure to have been an open, active, and fully committed Zionist from the very beginning in the 1880s. After his death, when the argument between the orthodox and the secularists within the movement became very heated, notably at the pre-Congress meeting in Warsaw in the summer of 1898,[27] and especially when it ended with a plain rejection of orthodox pretensions to special lines and areas of authority, they suffered a serious loss of forces as the more rigid among them changed sides. The remaining loyalists then underwent the pain and embarrassment of an attack, long sustained and of

---

[26] Ibid. Emphases in text.
[27] See above, pp. 41–3.

unprecedented ferocity, on Zionism in general and upon themselves in particular, an attack led by the defectors, but backed by some of the most prestigious figures in the orthodox world. And meanwhile, on their other front, within the movement, they faced the continual pressure of the secularists and modernists to finally commit the Organization to 'cultural' work—which was to them, in every sense, anathema.

The hostility of the main body of orthodoxy to Zionism would be easier to explain had the Zionist position on religion—and, more generally, on the Jewish tradition—been better defined and more uniform than it was in fact. There had always been some impatience, even anger, at repeated attempts by leading orthodox figures within the movement, from Mohilever[28] onwards, to impose their views, to introduce constraints, and, finally, to take the movement into their own hands. There had been a sensational public attack by Mandelstamm (in 1899) in which he had argued that Jews who were not Zionists were—at least in principle—not Jews at all but merely *goyim* (gentiles) who observed religious injunctions; that the orthodox who opposed Zionism were more at fault than Jews who left their people altogether; and that Moses would assuredly have had them condemned to death for false prophecy.[29] Nordau, at the Third Congress (1899), was more moderate. Why was it, he asked, that millions of Jews who longed for Jerusalem were unaware that their longing had been embodied in a political programme? It was, he thought, because the Zionists could not get through to them: they read no papers, they attended no meetings, the struggle for existence robbed them of all their leisure.

But these millions go to the synagogue, most of them daily, and all of them on the Sabbath and on holidays. They regard their rabbis as their appointed teachers. The rabbis have their ear—they have the duty to proclaim the joyful message of the new Zionism. Why have they not fulfilled that duty?

---

[28] See *Origins*, pp. 174–5.

[29] *Ha-Meliz*, 24 March 1899. 'I threw a stone into a swamp and now the frogs are beginning to croak', Mandelstamm wrote to Herzl. 'I've raised a question which was long overdue and have injected new life into the movement . . . For all that they are nullities, the jesuitical orthodox do us great harm and it is about time their wings were clipped.' 18 May 1899. CZA, H VIII/541.

It is well understood that I do not speak of the so-called *Protest-rabbiner* of the West.[30] With them we have already settled [accounts] and hope that the Jewish people will soon settle with them too. It is the orthodox [*glaubenstreuen*] rabbis of the East I have in mind, whose Jewish sentiment no one doubts.

We ask those rabbis, 'Why do you hold yourselves aloof? Why do you keep silent? Why do you not lead your community . . . with the banner of David unfurled into the Zionist camp?'

We are told that they mistrust us, that they fear an attack of I do not know what nature on the faith. How can that be? We have repeatedly and publicly declared that we do not touch the faith, that within Zionism everyone is guaranteed full freedom to live according to his religious convictions! And if this declaration fails to satisfy, then think of this: You hold your fate in your own hands! For we do not have the possibility of imposing our will on you if it happens to be different from yours! Come to us, all of you, you the pious, you the mistrusting. We are hundreds of thousands, you will then number millions and it will be the will of millions, not ours, that will be done.

You, in a single day, with a single blow, can turn nine-tenths of the Jewish people, who are already Zionists in word and deed, into Zionists in heart and mind.

We, with our means, through secular propaganda, the press, travelling speakers, and meetings, can only do so slowly and laboriously. We shall do it in the end none the less, while you could do it immediately. But when we will have brought it to completion, then the Jewish people, having finally informed itself, will call its rabbis who now keep silent to render a strict account.[31]

Still, the general mood was conciliatory. At meetings held in Minsk and Vilna before the Third Congress the secularists had gone out of their way to avoid a break and the response of the rabbis who were in attendance was not unfavourable.[32] At the Congress itself Tchlenov drew what he believed to be an important distinction between concern with culture proper, as comprehending matters of language, history, and literature, of which he approved, and with matters relating

[30] A reference to a public protest and condemnation of Zionism issued by the executive committee of the German rabbinate on the eve of the First Congress. See *Origins*, p. 336.

[31] *Protokoll III*, pp. 20–2.

[32] Y. Salmon, ''Emdata shel ha-ḥevra ha-ḥaredit be-rusiya-polin la-ẓionut ba-shanim 1898–1900', *Eshel Beer-Shev'a*, i (Beer-Shev'a, 1976), pp. 409–10.

to religion, which he thought 'dangerous', and of which he wanted no part.[33] Others were less precise. But most speakers were at pains, like Nordau, to emphasize that the orthodox had nothing to fear. In this spirit, thanks partly to the secularists' own fear of the consequences of all-out opposition by the orthodox, partly to a reluctance to probe too deeply into the issues involved, and partly too to Herzl's steady opposition to the pressure to take up what was so evidently a highly controversial and divisive question which, to his mind, was nothing but a distraction from the movement's main political business, matters were prevented from coming to a head—until the Fifth Congress of 1901, as we have seen.[34] Why did the dam burst then?

The answer, in part, is that Herzl himself never entirely grasped the nature of the issues at stake for either side. His thinking on religion in general, but more especially on the Jewish religion and its past, present, and future role in the social and political affairs of the Jewish people, did not go deeper than a simplistic application of decent liberal views in the contemporary west European, notably French mould to the very different context of Jewry and Judaism. The categories of Church and State and the separation of one from the other, resistance to anything that smacked of ultramontanism, romantic notions of the clergy in their pastoral role along with an axiomatic belief in their hold over the multitude, and, perhaps, a deep-seated feeling that the question could not really be of great consequence *per se*— all these seemed to have danced in his mind whenever he, with scarcely disguised weariness, addressed himself to the problem.

Shall we end by having a theocracy? [he had asked in his original, programmatic *Der Judenstaat*] No, indeed. Faith unites us, knowledge gives us freedom. We shall therefore prevent any theocratic tendencies from coming to the fore on the part of our priesthood. We shall keep our priests within the confines of their temples in the same way as we shall keep our professional army within the confines of their barracks. Army and priesthood shall receive honours as high as their valuable functions deserve. But they must not interfere

---

[33] *Protokoll III*, p. 100.
[34] See above, pp. 193-5.

in the administration of the state which confers distinction upon them, else they will conjure up difficulties without and within.[35]

Six years after writing that passage he had advanced so little in his grasp of the problem that he could tell the Fifth Congress, as he had told the First, 'I can assure you that Zionism intends nothing that could offend the religious convictions of any school of thought within Judaism.'[36] And that on the other hand

Just as our proceedings have always had an element of modern culture by virtue of the speeches you have heard here and the speakers who have taken part, so—I must say—it is inconceivable that it should even be supposed of such people as are members of the Actions Committee that they are against culture . . .

But rather than dwell on these divisive matters, we should always seek to bring out only that which unites us. That is how our movement has managed in so few years to become one which not only unites people from various places, but also people of different outlooks. That is perhaps what is highest and most important in this movement.[37]

But in any event, the essential locus of the quarrel was not at Basel or in Vienna. It was in the Pale of Settlement; and there, the fire of argument and deed and counter-deed had been smouldering steadily. The conflict was a complex one and not without ambivalence. At certain points, orthodoxy and the majority of Zionists were at one. Both wished to avoid trouble with the Russian state. Both feared that social and political radicalism among the Jews would play into the hands of the official anti-Semites. Both tended to oppose the Bund for this reason—as for others, notably the Bund's contempt for the Jewish tradition as much in its literary aspect as in the theological. Some orthodox leaders were moved by sympathy for the common folk of Russian Jewry to be somewhat less hostile to the radicals than were the majority of their colleagues and almost all Zionists. Rabbi Mohilever is said to have gone so far as to accept the Bund as the legitimate champion

---

[35] *Der Judenstaat*, Chapt. V.
[36] *Protokoll V*, p. 424.
[37] Ibid., p. 425.

of the Jewish proletariat.[38] And while there were few prominent Zionists so frank in their secularism as to express their hostility publicly and without inhibition, as Mandelstamm had done, there were younger men who were: Democrats and such socialists as had, exceptionally, placed themselves within the Zionist camp and were to be a growing force within it.[39] But besides, there was in this conflict a fundamental asymmetry. At bottom, most varieties and intensities of Zionist opposition to orthodoxy had this in common, that there was less concern with doctrine than with freedom of action. Refusal to brook more than a very modest degree of rabbinical interference in the affairs of the movement was generally firm, but initially the underlying approach to the orthodox had been one of tolerance bordering on disregard. Even later, when the pressure mounted, few Zionists in leading positions in the movement ever went further than requiring of the orthodox that their participation in the Zionist enterprise—if any—be on an equal footing with others; or, failing that, that they stand aside. Some had taken Herzl's call at the Second Congress for a 'conquest of the communities'[40] seriously. But they had never conceived of it as an attack on religion or the rabbinate as such. What they chiefly aimed for was free access to the synagogues (as meeting houses) and a share in control of communal institutions. The leaders of orthodoxy had resisted furiously none the less, having correctly judged the campaign to be a threat to the primacy which was the basis of the rabbinate's formal authority. Moreover, their opposition to Zionism ran far deeper than merely political antagonism. The demands the orthodox made of the Zionists initially were, as we have seen, severe and sharply defined. The fight against Zionism upon which they, in their great majority, eventually embarked aimed at the destruction or, at the very least, the crippling of the movement. It was maintained with great fixity of purpose and it was informed by deep, undisguised, and at times venomous hostility.

---

[38] Ezra Mendelsohn, *Class Struggle in the Pale* (Cambridge, 1970), p. 107; and pp. 105–7.
[39] See below, pp. 391–411.
[40] See above, p. 66.

Orthodoxy's fundamental objection to Zionism was theological. It followed from the Zionists' intention to reverse the
course of Jewish history and remake the Jewish people—in
effect, to redeem them—through mere human agency. It
was the settled orthodox view that the condition of the Jews
in their Exile, with its attendant miseries, had been divinely
ordained and that to seek to alter it without divine sanction
was blasphemous and, of course, futile. The Jews were, on the
contrary, under a primary religious obligation to await
Redemption at the hands of the Messiah, in God's good time,
with patience and submission. For them to presume to take the
national destiny into their own hands was to call its special
character and the unique relationship between God and his
People—the Covenant from which all else flowed—into
question. To go so far as to seek to re-establish a state, or even
some lesser, but still political presence in the Holy Land,
when the destruction of the Second Commonwealth (and the
Temple) was to be regarded first and foremost as a sign of
God's great wrath, was plainly to compound the profanation.

There were other, somewhat subtler problems. The system
of obligations under which the Jews lived in their Exile was
a dual one: they saw themselves as bound by the law of the
land (*dina demalkhuta*) in their mundane affairs and by the
law of God (*Torah*) in their inner, spiritual, and private
affairs. The prescriptions of the *Torah* in the sphere of the
mundane—civil, criminal, and constitutional law, and the law
of war and peace—were either in abeyance, or narrowly
limited to the law of personal status, or else maintained on a
purely voluntary and often secret basis within the local community. All this by *force majeure*, as a consequence of the Exile.
But the *Torah* knew nothing of the separation *in principle* of
the spiritual from the temporal, of Church from State—or,
as the sages had put it, of those matters that were between
man and man from those matters that were between man and
God. The re-establishment of a Jewish state had therefore to
mean either the reinstitution of the *Torah* as a single system of
universal applicability (and incontrovertible authority) or
else a drastic and revolutionary restriction of its compass. To
the orthodox mind, the latter possibility was unthinkable,
while the former smacked of the Latter Day: for was it con-

ceivable that such a state should come into being except as the product of a Messianic Redemption of the Jews and as part of a reordering of the affairs of all mankind by Providential will and grace?

Besides, who were these people who claimed leadership of Jewry? Most were free thinkers in one degree or another, unlettered (in the Law), and defiant of rabbinical authority, who called openly for the 'conquest of the communities'—and conquest from whom, if not from the rabbinate itself? That they were dedicated to the reform of the traditional and auto-nomous system of education, particularly at the elementary level, there was no doubt. That some were political radicals and therefore liable to enmesh the Jews still deeper in their conflict with the Russian state was probable. That they were in the tradition of the secularist Jewish Enlightenment (*haskala*) was a certainty. The ancient objection to joining the ungodly in a common enterprise[41] was still alive. To enter a movement which was of their creation and which they would clearly continue to lead was doubly objectionable. In sum, the more closely the orthodox examined Zionism, the less like a vehicle even of secular rescue of the Jews it appeared to be and the more dangerous an agent of apostasy and disaffection—by its message, by its deed, and by the living example and subtle influence of its members. From which conclusion it was a short step, soon taken, to a view of Zionism and of the Zionists that was stoked by the fire of high hostile emotion. It was a mood to which several factors contributed, but do not, perhaps, entirely explain: wariness of yet another force come to sap at the foundations of the Law and of its, and of their own, authority; a certain caution and conservatism bred into them by their calling and by the antiquity of the tradition which they upheld; and, not least, simple *odium theologicum*.

Yes, I have read what you have had to say about the Zionists who have come together so strongly now [wrote R. Ḥayyim Soloveichik

---

[41] Cf. 'And after this did Jehoshafat king of Judah join himself with Ahaziah king of Israel, who did very wickedly: And he joined himself with him to make ships to go to Tarshish: and they made the ships in Ezion-geber. Then Eliezer the son of Dodavah of Mareshah prophesied against Jehoshafat, saying, Because thou hast joined thyself with Ahaziah, the Lord hath broken thy works. And the ships were broken, that they were not able to go to Tarshish.' 2 Chr. 20:35–7.

of Brisk (Brest-Litovsk), possibly the most eminent figure in non-Hasidic Jewry of his time] and I am not afraid to say that I just do not know how I might best set at them. For each and every one of them is of an evil reputation in his own locality . . . And their purpose, as they have already announced and published it, is the uprooting of the foundations of the religion and, to that end, the conquest of all the communities of Israel . . .[42]

The Zionists, it was stated in a formal rabbinical proclamation of the time, were

new deceivers who had arisen amongst us . . . And the core of the Zionist idea was no less than the uprooting of the religion of Moses and Israel; and, moreover, as any one who looks with open eyes at the national pride and the gross impertinence that Zionism has taught its innocent followers, and at the licentiousness and insolence that have maddened ignorant boys and girls . . . will see clearly that Zionism is liable too to bring upon our nation a greater material disaster than all the disasters brought upon the people by false prophets and disseminators of lies about the Redemption of Israel [in the past].[43]

Herzl was empty-headed, vain, and irresponsible and his followers were worse, argued the author of an orthodox, anti-Zionist tract entitled *The Book of Herzl's Dream and its Interpretation*. Some were unemployed and venal office-seekers, some were simply after public honours, and some, the worst of the lot, sought religious reform and, having failed by other means, were intent on injecting heresy directly into the body of the nation.[44] In sum, the Zionists, as the *rebbe* of Gur (Gora Kalwaria, near Warsaw), one of the principal leaders of Hasidic Jewry, put it, were a band of evil-doers and of such as they no good could come.[45]

[42] Letter to R. Ya'akov Moshe Karpas, 25 August 1899. CZA, A 9/154/13.
[43] 'Kol kore [el aheinu benei Yisrael]', in Barukh Steinberg (ed.), *Sefer da'at ha-rabbanim* (Warsaw, 1902), p. 104. After the Second World War an extreme and consistent opponent of the Zionist movement, R. Joel Teitelbaum, the Szatmár *rebbe*, went so far as to argue that, indeed, by the heresy inherent in it, Zionism had helped to bring about the destruction of European Jewry at the hands of the Germans.
[44] Shelomo Teplitzki, *Sefer halom Herzl u-fitrono* (Warsaw, 1899), pp. 15–21.
[45] Yizhak Nissenboim, *'Alei heldi* (Warsaw, 1929), p. 171. Herzl's response to the *rebbe*'s criticism was to write to him directly (in extremely courteous terms, his letter being specially translated for him into the old-fashioned and ornate Hebrew in which

In the haste with which such conclusions were drawn, in the ease with which base motives and vast designs were ascribed to the movement and its leader, in the tendency not merely to denigrate, but to simplify the Zionist phenomenon and impute a monolithic character to it, and in the confidence with which it was placed in the succession of heretical movements which had afflicted orthodox Judaism in the course of the centuries, notably the Karaites, the Sabbatianists, the Frankists, and the modern Reformists—in all this there are unmistakable signs of fear. The fear was of a challenge of unprecedented strength, effective precisely because it did indeed call into question the structure of belief and practice that had been built up so carefully in the course of close to twenty centuries of Exile, in a manner in which the heretical movements, old and new, but all being, each in its way, religious, never did. And this, of course, in times when the hold of traditional Judaism was plainly waning and Jewry was in a state of social, political, and migratory flux. The main orthodox judgement on Zionism, as it crystallized in the years 1898–1901, was more intuitive than systematic or founded on evidence. The great force of the intuition lay in its penetration—deeper and surer than the leaders of east European orthodoxy seem to have realized, to say nothing of the Zionists themselves. Yet while preponderant, it was not the judgement of all the orthodox. 'Unbelievably', Rabbi Soloveichik had written, 'even after the revelation of their [the Zionists'] evil intent, there are still some among the righteous who continue to be associated with them.'[46] It is therefore appropriate to consider the important exceptions to the general rule before returning to the fundamental problem.

v

Not all the orthodox teachers were quick to read ulterior

---

the rabbis generally conducted their correspondence). He drew attention to the fact that the Jewish people were under pressure from a common enemy and that many of those who opposed Zionism opposed orthodoxy in all its varieties as well. He appealed to the *rebbe*, in the name of great multitudes of hungry, poor, and distressed Jews, to make whatever charges he had against Zionism openly, rather than secretly. The Zionists might then be able to consider them and either see the error of their ways or, conceivably, find that they could justify themselves. (2 April 1900. CZA, HB 312–15.) Herzl does not seem to have received a reply.

[46] Letter to R. Karpas, loc. cit.

motives into the policies and purposes of the new movement. Nor were all unalterably opposed to change in the curriculum of the *ḥadarim* and the *yeshivot*, or even to presenting a friendlier, if still very cautious face to the *haskala* generally. Nor was the reluctance to have anything to do with men and women who had broken with orthodox practice and had already gone a fair way towards assimilation into gentile society (for fear of implicitly condoning apostasy and of suffering some kind of moral and intellectual contamination) a universal one. To some it made sense to argue, as Mohilever had done, that, on balance, the return of the prodigals to Jewry was to be welcomed and encouraged, and that in their return lay much of the value of Zionism itself.[47] And lastly, and perhaps of most consequence, there were the inroads on orthodox thinking made by the growing, if still largely mute pressures of the faithful themselves, by the rise of a movement like the Bund that, unlike Zionism, was opposed to orthodoxy and hotly so to the rabbinate in particular, by the great migration of the Jews to the West and largely away from the sphere of effective rabbinical influence, and, finally, by the disastrous material condition of Russo-Polish Jewry in general. The effect upon those leaders of orthodoxy who were disposed to try to meet the great changes now under way in the condition and the mores of the Jews was to weaken the stoicism and resignation in the face of disaster that were integral to their tradition. There were not great numbers of them. But to this minority, at one and the same time less alarmed than the majority of their fellows by the still limited phenomenon of modernism among the Jews and a great deal more agitated by the misery that was the lot of the greater part of eastern European Jewry, Zionism could not but appear attractive. Provided, that is, answers could be found to two questions: how this essentially secular organization was to be made tolerable for them; and how they were to justify themselves theologically.

The Warsaw conference of the summer of 1898[48] had taught the lesson, which succeeding Congresses had confirmed, that

---

[47] On the views of the Lithuanian rabbi R. Shemuel Ya'akov Rabinowitz, a noted moderate and a member for some years of the GAC, see G. Kressel, 'Ha-rav mi-sopotz-kin', *Kazir* [i] (Tel-Aviv, 1964), pp. 122–39.

[48] See above, pp. 36–43.

the modernist majority would never accept orthodox control of any major Zionist activity or enterprise. The best the orthodox could hope for was some mild and embarrassed sympathy. Mostly, they found they were faced with a mixture of tolerance and indifference which changed rapidly into hostility when they pitched their demands too high. But dared they pitch them lower? Was compromise permissible where matters of such fundamental principle were at issue? And if it was, what was its proper political expression? How should orthodox Jews seek to function within the larger Zionist camp? For and against what should they strive? With whom might they ally themselves? What should be the sticking-points? It was in the nature of things that these were questions to which absolutely clear and lasting answers could not be found; and the religious Zionists were perhaps no more than consistent in their traditionalism in being reluctant to seek them—until the attack mounted upon Zionism in general and upon them in particular from within the inner bastions of east European orthodoxy forced their pace and the formal triumph of the secularists at the Fifth Congress left them virtually no choice but to make a stab at a solution. Early in 1902, with Herzl's secret encouragement, as we shall see, the man who had been slowly emerging as Mohilever's heir to the leadership of the orthodox loyalists within the movement took the plunge and called a conference of his fellows to consider their position and chart a course of action—in effect, although not yet in name, to follow the example of the Democrats and found a party.

Rabbi Yizḥak Ya'akov Reines (1839–1915) was in most respects a lesser man than Mohilever. He had little of Mohilever's public eminence in Russia and abroad, or of his standing within the inner world of orthodoxy, or of his drive and strength and decisiveness. Reines was essentially a local, if not undistinguished figure, paler and less independent in character, more accommodating, more prudent, much less wilful than Mohilever, and also less clear- and single-minded. On the other hand, in his hesitant and sometimes muddle-minded way, Reines was a man of his times, which the older Mohilever, in his decline, was not. Reines was less confident than his seniors in the ability of the orthodox leadership to retain their world

intact and impervious to the inroads of secular learning. He
was willing, as the common run of his colleagues were not, to
distinguish between those modernists and apostates who were
moving steadily away from Judaism and those who, by their
adherence to Zionism, appeared to be coming nearer again and
to be demonstrating their devotion to their people as well as
any. He was therefore readier than most to co-operate with
the non-religious and to refrain from seeking to rule them:
conceivably because, in his caution and realism, he had never
thought the prospects of re-establishing the supremacy of
orthodoxy in Jewish public life to be anything but poor—
except perhaps in the still remote future when the restorative
effects of Zionism would have waned. But above all, he had
something of that sense of an impending catastrophe which lay
at the origin of the thinking of some of the progenitors of
Ḥibbat Ẕion, notably Lilienblum, Pinsker, and Mandelstamm
(as opposed to Aḥad Ha-ʿAm and his school), and at the origin
of the thinking of Herzl himself, of course—even if it took a
form that was less ·intense than theirs and was also clearly
limited and inhibited by his own faith and training. At all
events, it was on the poverty and misery and physical danger
with which the life of the commonalty of Jewry in eastern Europe
was bound up that Reines's thinking turned and that his
argument that religion and Zionism were not incompatible
after all was largely based.

At the heart of Reines's apologia for an orthodox presence
in the Zionist movement lay the distinction he drew between
the Messianic Redemption of the Jews by divine authority and
intention (simultaneously, of necessity, with that of all other
peoples) and the mere rescue of the Jews from their present
straits.[49] He does not in any way question orthodox belief
in the unique cosmological role of the Jewish people, or the
view that their Exile is a punishment for sin and, at the same
time, an integral and essential part of the divine scheme. The
Exile will come to its *decisive* end and the Jews will return to
dwell in their Land eternally and unconditionally only

---

[49] The most thorough review (unfortunately still unpublished) of Reines's views and
writings on public and political affairs is an extended essay by E. Don-Yihye, 'Dat
u-leʾom be-mishnat ha-rav Reines' (Jerusalem, 1970). I am grateful to the author for
permission to consult it.

upon the fulfilment of their special role, when utter unity of faith and religion under God pervades the world and the Temple will have been rebuilt. All is therefore dependent on divine will; and the onset of the millennium cannot be hastened by human agency, nor may men presume to try to do so. None the less, there is in Reines a parallel—and, in a sense, a contradictory—emphasis on the pain and bitterness that is, meanwhile, the lot of the individual. 'Not a day has passed in all the days of the Exile on which the blood of Israel was not spilt', he writes; 'and there is not a place on earth where the Jews have trodden that was not nourished by their blood.' And elsewhere the Exile is epitomized as 'A terrible night of darkness and gloom in which great stormy winds blow on the frail bark of Israel to sink it and destroy it utterly.'[50]

May one then attempt at least to ameliorate the Jewish condition—the *material* condition of the Jews—and save them, as far as possible, from persecution and humiliation at the hands of their enemies in the meanwhile? Reines believes that it is permissible to do so and argues that that is precisely what the Zionists intend. They cannot in any event touch upon the matter of the greater, the true, the chiliastic, and the divine Redemption of the Jewish people; nor do they seek to do so. The Zionists, he believes, are concerned with limited and entirely mundane reconstruction and rehabilitation. They do not even seek to encompass all Jewry; whereas divine Redemption plainly implies the gathering in of all the Jews from all the lands of their Dispersion. Zionist purposes are thus irrelevant to religious principle and belief. And it follows that the judgement of Zionism by strictly theological criteria is misplaced. Nor need the fact that so many of its members and leaders are free thinkers necessarily be a source of concern. On the contrary, since their commitment to the national cause is likely, in his view, to restore them eventually to the fold of the observant, the orthodox have grounds for welcoming them. True, it would be well if the orthodox were to strengthen their presence within, and their influence over, the movement. And certainly they should not tolerate activities that work directly against the interests and purposes of religion,

[50] *Or ḥadash ʿal zion* (Vilna, 1902), p. 124; and *Nod shel demaʿot* (Jerusalem, 1934), p. 10. Quoted in Don-Yihye, ibid., p. 7.

that would delay, let alone interrupt the process of reconciliation with the religious tradition and blur the distinction between the sphere that is properly the Zionists' and that which
is not. Whence Reines's fierce opposition to 'cultural' activities
under Zionist auspices and his willingness to go further than
the mere making of speeches in an effort to reverse the Democrats' success and assert the orthodox view in a fresh and more
powerful way.

Food was what the people needed most urgently, not 'culture', Reines had argued at the Fourth Congress (London,
1900).[51] He was defending the orthodox position against
fierce attack, notably by Sokolov, who argued for pluralism
and humanism, asserted that the question of the 'modern
development' of the Jewish people was one of the 'most radical
and far-reaching problems of Zionism', and was, at one point,
so bold as to tell the Congress that the Hasidic *rebbes* wanted
war with Zionism and that they could have it.[52] To which the
rabbi's response was that the sole object of the movement was
the Return to Erez-Israel; and that those gentlemen who
insisted on bringing up the question of culture either did not
understand Zionism or else understood it and were under-
mining it.[53]

Matters must be judged by what was specifically relevant
to them, according to the region in question, and with reference
to the people directly concerned, he told the Fifth Congress
two years later as the fight moved to its climax. 'Everyone
knows that it is with our poor Jews that the Basel Programme
is concerned. And for us the culture question is a misfortune.
It will smash everything to pieces. Our part of the world is
entirely orthodox. Culture will lose it to [Zionism].'[54] Reines's
partner in the debate, R. Shemu'el Ya'akov Rabinowitz,
a more experienced and articulate parliamentarian, his senior
in the movement by virtue of his membership of the GAC,[55]

---

[51] *Protokoll IV*, pp. 212, 221, 281. Reines spoke in Hebrew and Yiddish and his
addresses to the Congress were not recorded verbatim by the German-language stenographer. The record suggests confusion at some points as to what he actually said.

[52] Ibid., pp. 196–210.

[53] Ibid., p. 221.

[54] *Protokoll V*, p. 395.

[55] Reines was of greater rabbinical eminence than his colleague S. Y. Rabinowitz.
He was therefore a natural candidate for election as one of the twelve Russian members

and able and willing to speak German (and so, incidentally, be well reported), put the objections of the orthodox-within-the-camp more elaborately and in more accommodating terms.

I could show you statistically [said Rabinowitz] that I have done more for culture in my region [of Russia], where some people think I am against it, than has been done for culture in other regions. But the question . . . is whether the Congress should order us to concern ourselves with [it] or whether it should be dropped from the agenda and left for each of us to do as he thinks fit.

It is possible that the word 'culture' has become a bogy [*Schreck-bilde*] to many of the orthodox. We can explain to them that they have no cause to be alarmed; but if they are frightened none the less, that which worries them must be avoided; and, indeed, the orthodox do have grounds for concern . . .

Yesterday, for example, one speaker argued to the effect that Zionism should now be for us what religion was [in the past]. He said in passing that until now we had only religion, but that now Zionism would rule. That is a false principle: religion has not come to an end and will not come to an end . . . Religion unites the Jews and Zionism unites them too. But it is false to say that as religion once united us, so Zionism unites us now. Religion united us [in the past] and unites us now. We consider Zionism a means whereby our religion may be strengthened and vice versa . . .

We lose the people when the root dries up.[56]

But Reines and Rabinowitz were defeated, as we have seen, and with them Herzl and those of his supporters who had joined him in objecting to the involvement of the movement in activities and controversies they judged extraneous to its main political purpose. On the surface, Herzl appeared to have accepted defeat with grace. Privately he fumed. He was increasingly dissatisfied and irritated by the leadership of Zionism's eastern wing: he thought them unco-operative, unreasonable, and dogmatic; and it occurred to him that they

---

of the GAC. But Rabinowitz had preceded him into the movement and was already a member of the Actions Committee. Moreover, he was popular and known to be devoted to the cause. The Russian caucus wanted neither to replace him nor to have two rabbis on the Committee. So Reines went home from his first Congress, the Third, 'as he had come: a simple Zionist soldier'. Nissenboim, op. cit., p. 157.

[56] *Protokoll V*, pp. 393–5.

might have become an obstacle to the entry of fresh blood into the movement. He resolved to pay more attention to matters of organization and to 'break the iron rings which are already forming in some countries'.[57] And he did so, even though he was chiefly absorbed in the months that followed by his negotiations with the Turks. It had always been his instinct when disappointed by those whom he had marked down as allies to look for new ones to play against the old. So now with the orthodox. The details are obscure, but it is evident that at some point early in 1902 he gave positive encouragement, both directly and through intermediaries in Russia, to Reines and his colleagues to strike out on their own, along with the funds to get started.[58]

Thereafter things moved rapidly. Reines needed little encouragement and aided, principally, by Avraham Slutski, a journalist of some note who had long been trying to find a counter to orthodox opposition to Zionism, he managed to convene a conference of interested notables in Vilna on 4–5 March 1902. There were 72 in attendance, 24 of whom were rabbis. Not all were orthodox; some were 'politicals' anxious to promote a general realignment of forces. The specific grievances of the orthodox were reviewed, however, all the way from the central problem of 'culture' and education down to the vexatious matter of the presence of women at Zionist social and political gatherings. The conference then turned to its main business which was to resolve how to proceed in the future. Should an independent 'federation' or party be set up within the larger movement? Should they rather limit themselves to some looser institutional form, with restricted independence and limited aims, a 'centre' of some kind, following, perhaps, the example of the body Mohilever had formed in the Hibbat Zion period? To whom should they appeal? To observant Jews alone, or to all Zionists—provided the purposes of the new association were subscribed to? Should they, in other words, found a society of *political* Zionists dedicated

[57] *Diaries*, iii, p. 1191.
[58] The evidence that the basic initiative for the establishment of a party of the orthodox was Herzl's, while not absolutely conclusive, is more than merely circumstantial. See Nissenboim, op. cit., p. 178; Y. L. Fishman [Maimon], 'Herzl ve-ha-mizrahi', *Ha-Tor*, xli-xlii (1921), pp. 3–5; and Joseph Adler, 'Religion and Herzl: Fact and Fable', *Herzl Year Book*, iv (1962), p. 299.

principally to the removal of 'culture' from the agenda of the movement, the religious character of which would follow naturally from the fact that the majority of its members and leaders would be orthodox Jews? This would offer a chance of rapid growth and corresponding influence, but was liable to raise all the problems consequent upon the different patterns of life and thought that distinguished the observant from the secular. Or should they aim at a tighter, necessarily smaller movement of homogeneous membership and therefore able to engage in (appropriate) activities beyond the narrow limits of the 'political'? The decision at Vilna was that the new association, *Mizrahi*, would be loose in structure and such as to appeal to a wide and varied audience (except for Social Democrats, who would be excluded, and the fact that there would be a separate formation for women). It would concern itself principally with the recruitment of new members to the Zionist movement and with putting the case for a political Zionism unmixed with extraneous ingredients. It would be careful to treat those (by implication, those in the orthodox camp) who opposed Zionism with the respect that was their due. Reines was to be chairman of the new 'centre'. The Russian GAC members and Vienna were to be officially informed.[59] And the business of the conference was concluded with a public call

to all our God-fearing brethren whose hearts beat with love for their faith and their people to join us in support of the Zionist idea, now that a centre and a firm base have been established for the God-fearing and they need no longer fear lest they be swept away (Heaven forfend!) in the stream of false ideas and foreign manners.[60]

To which Reines added a particular appeal to the orthodox rabbinate to associate themselves with the Mizrahi, not least in order to safeguard their reputation—it being said of them,

[59] Resolutions adopted at Vilna in Israel Klausner, 'Be-reshit yesud ha-mizrahi 'al-yedei ha-rav Y. Y. Reines', *Sefer ha-zionut ha-datit*, i (Jerusalem, 1977), p. 346. At a subsequent conference at Lida, 24–6 February 1903, the fundamental decision taken at Vilna was reversed and a tighter organization, with a clear orthodox orientation, was decided upon instead, upon which the non-orthodox politicals left.

[60] *Mizrahi, kovez yovel li-melot 25 shana le-kiyuma* (New York, 1936), pp. 33–7. *Ha-Zefira*, 13 April 1902.

he pointed out, that they were insensitive to the condition of the people.[61]

By the summer of 1902 the new party had done well enough to lay claim to the loyalty of about a quarter of the some 650 fully active Zionist societies in Russia and to be able to send about 150 delegates to the conference at Minsk, or somewhat less than a third of the total.[62] (The Democratic Party was represented by 54.) They met in caucus before the formal opening of the conference to co-ordinate their position, and they had their collective status confirmed by being seated together (on the right of the hall) and by being allotted three of the nine seats on the conference steering committee. In the great debate on culture, the conference's central event, as we have seen, Reines expounded the orthodox case, warning his listeners against a decision unacceptable to orthodoxy. Certainly, he argued, there was much to be done in the *ḥadarim* and the *yeshivot*; but it had to be done by believers; and none of it was the concern of the Zionist Organization. Matters of culture and education were matters of the heart and it was for each to do what his own heart dictated and as best he understood. What must be entirely avoided, said the rabbi, were binding, *general* decisions. But since this was not wholly incompatible with Aḥad Ha-ʿAm's view—in that, as we have seen, Aḥad Ha-ʿAm himself was far from thinking the Zionist Organization a proper vehicle for mass education and was prepared to concede that in these matters orthodox and modernists could not but be expected to follow separate, if parallel, paths—the way to compromise was open. Tchlenov's suggestion that Reines and Aḥad Ha-ʿAm both be co-opted onto the committee that was to draft the resolution on culture and education was accepted. And the upshot was the formulation of a new approach—or doctrine—completing the process by which the new, orthodox variant of Zionism was accepted and legitimized. The Fifth Congress's peremptory resolution on culture laying down that it was 'the duty of all Zionists to

[61] Klausner, 'ha-mizraḥi', pp. 347–8.

[62] This was probably disproportionate to their true strength in the country and there were complaints that the Mizraḥi had been less than scrupulous in their elections practice (*Ha-Ẓefira*, 7 September 1902). But it was a considerable achievement none the less.

contribute' to the 'education of the Jewish people in a national sense' was qualified by an explicit recognition of 'the fact that there were two streams with equal rights—the traditional and the progressive'—and by a corresponding decision to set up *two* committees to consider how the original resolution should be implemented: one termed 'national-progressive', the other 'national-traditional'. Membership of the respective committees would be according to the beliefs and practices of those concerned and each would conduct its affairs 'independently and freely'.[63]

The immediate practical outcome of this new formulation was virtually nil. All the complex and sensitive questions of implementation were left to the two committees to deal with; but the committees never got off the ground. By April of the following year Aḥad Ha-ʿAm, the most passionately concerned of all, had given up hope of concrete accomplishment.[64] None the less, the change in approach and doctrine marked by the resolution was crucial. Henceforth parity and compartmentalization were the order of the day and were to remain the enshrined principles on which the issues of education, culture, and religion itself would be tackled—or circumvented. The orthodox had implicitly given up their original demand for a commanding voice in these matters. The secularists had concluded that they dare not push their views too hard lest they push the orthodox out of the movement altogether. In the debate on culture Motzkin and Weizmann had spoken against Aḥad Ha-ʿAm's idea of a separate organization for these matters, to operate independently of the Zionist movement; but they had agreed to his alternative suggestion that there be two parallel systems. Weizmann had approached the conference at Minsk with little but dark thoughts about the Mizraḥi ('The Rabbinical party is organizing itself in Jesuit fashion, and I think of their machinations with disgust.'[65] 'So many Mizraḥi people will be assembling, there will be so much ignorance, that in such a concentration the putrefying

---

[63] Conference at Minsk, Resolution IV 'On National Education'. *Kazir* [i] (Tel-Aviv, 1964), p. 74. Aḥad Ha-ʿAm, Bialik, Bernstein-Kohan, and Sokolov were among the members of the 'national-progressive' committee. The 'national-traditional' committee was composed mostly of rabbis, led by Reines and S. Y. Rabinowitz.

[64] Letter to Victor Jacobson, 17 April 1903. *Igrot AH*, iii, p. 236.

[65] To Vera Khatzman, 25 August 1902. *Weizmann Letters*, i, no. 297, p. 379.

bacilli of reason and culture will not be able to survive.'[66]).
But in the general atmosphere of elation and goodwill with
which the debate was concluded, he finally embraced Rabbi
Reines publicly. However, for the true politicals, the compromise resolution was a defeat. The Mizraḥi had failed to support
them. The matter of culture, in principle, if not yet in practice,
and with a new gloss, had been confirmed as a major item of
business for the movement after all—at least so far as the greater
part of its membership was concerned.

The broader consequence was that the orthodox Zionists
(not all of whom adhered formally to the Mizraḥi) had now
to bend their minds principally to the maintenance of their
own corporate identity, their own institutions, their inner
and particular life (much in the manner of their fellows outside
the movement), and to the elaboration and justification of
religious Zionism as a legitimate and constituent branch
of Jewish orthodoxy. As before, their great problem was that
of setting the terms on which they might participate in the
movement's affairs without violence to their special needs.
But its dimensions and intensity were much reduced by the
acceptance of the principle of parity in the specific context of
culture and a disposition to be flexible where matters that did
not touch on that context and, generally, on their special and
recognized requirements, were concerned. Thus for their part
in the political and institutional life of the Zionist movement.
Meanwhile, the issues of fundamental principle and ideology
which were at the bottom of the conflict remained unresolved—but alive, and so many sources of silent irritation
and unease.

vi

The leaders of the inner world of orthodoxy remained unmoved
by the establishment of the Mizraḥi, except that their fear of
the inroads Zionism might make among the faithful (unless
fought very hard) appeared to have been confirmed and that
their opposition to the movement hardened. It may be true
that had the religious party within the Zionist movement not

---

[66] To Catherine Dorfman, 27 August 1902. Ibid., no. 300, p. 384.

now been given permanent, institutional form—had it remained, that is to say, essentially a tendency, visible, but less
than entirely coherent, without established leaders and without
a fixed and wholly identifiable membership—then moderate
and intermediate positions between the old tradition and the
new movement might have remained comparatively tenable
and respectable. But the line drawn between old and new was
henceforth to be sharper than ever: precisely what Herzl and
his fellow politicals had always wanted to avoid. To which
there can be added the further, subtler irony that it was a
line that was a great deal more visible and significant to those
stationed on the orthodox side of the divide than to those
stationed on the other, the Zionist. In a matter such as this,
everything inevitably depended on how closely one chose to
examine the issues involved. The orthodox thought them
immensely serious. The secular Zionists, with rare exceptions,
were less concerned.

The central question at issue was that of the nature and
special, cosmological role (if any) of the Jewish people. Were
they to be seen primarily in theological or in historical terms?
Granted that Judaism the religion and Jewry the people were
in original conception and circumstance so intertwined as to
be inseparable in the past age of faith, must they so continue
in the modern age of doubt? Was it *religion* that was to be seen
primarily in functional terms, as the great mechanism whereby
the Jewish people had accomplished the unique feat of preserving their social and cultural identity during twenty
centuries of Exile? Or was the relationship to be seen in reverse
order if it was to be properly understood: namely, that it was
the function of the people to serve and preserve the ends and
content of their religion? To the orthodox mind the truth of
the latter proposition was beyond question. The world's
order and purposes were fundamentally divine. To deprive
the Jews of their primordial role in that order was to render
their collective existence, to say nothing of the pain they had
suffered, meaningless. Zionism, by substituting history and
sociology for theology and metaphysics, and by concerning
itself with man rather than with Providence, was far worse
than heretical; it was profoundly materialistic and wholly
and unalterably profane.

Even if secular Zionism does not conflict with any single one of Maimonides' Thirteen Principles [of the Jewish faith], it does conflict with a principle that is prior to the Thirteen Principles of Maimonides both in time and in quality: I mean the principle laid down for us as far back as the days of R. Sa‘adiya Ga’on, namely that 'It is through our Law alone that our people are a people' [*Ein umateinu uma ela be-torata*].

For it was for the individual in Israel that Maimonides laid down [his] principles, whereas R. Sa‘adiya Ga’on's principle concerns the very soul of the people of Israel as such, *as a people . . .*

Zionism announces a Jewish state in Erez-Israel that will treat our Law in a neutral mode . . . [and] will tolerate each individual who wishes to observe it; this in itself is a denial of the quintessence of Judaism, that 'It is through our Law alone that our people are a people.'[67]

Thus Rabbi M. A. ‘Amiel, a man of a later generation of the Mizrahi, but worth quoting because he was exceptionally rare in his party for his incisiveness and for his refusal to burke these issues. His solution was, somehow, to revive the ties with the main body of orthodoxy and to redefine his party's central aim as that of working for the absolute primacy of religion within the movement after all—in effect to revert to the purposes that had come to light so vividly at the Warsaw conference in the summer of 1898 and which had thereupon precipitated the great explosion. Secular Zionism, ‘Amiel argued, sought to remove precisely that which was the peculiar quality of the Jewish people—its sacred role—and 'to leave us no more than a nation like all other nations', and Zionism would be 'satisfied with a little state like any one of the miserable little states that the lesser nations are possessed of'. The task of the Mizrahi was to restore the *status quo ante*[68]—back, it could be said, to the position as Mohilever had defined it in his last published statement: 'The foundation of our national work must be our Holy Law' (*Yesod ‘avodateinu ha-leumit zarikh lihyot torateinu ha-kedosha*)[69]. For insight of comparable clarity one must recross the divide.

[67] Rabbi Moshe Avigdor ‘Amiel, *Ha-yesodot ha-idi‘ologiim shel ha-mizrahi* (Warsaw, 1934), pp. 9–10.

[68] Ibid., p. 13.

[69] 'Divrei ha-gershom ha-aharonim', *Ha-Meliz*, 9 July 1898.

Aḥad Ha-ʿAm's position was the reverse of ʿAmiel's: religion was not autonomous, but a form of culture; and the Jewish religion was the form the Jewish national culture had largely taken in the past. What form it would take in the future was, indeed, an open question.[70] But it was with this that Zionism was properly and essentially concerned. There were, of course, the learned attempts to show that Zionism was compatible with Scripture and the Talmud after all.[71] But they failed to impress him.

A generation ago too, when the controversy centred on the question of 'faith and the enlightenment', there had been writers and men of learning who had repeatedly brought evidence from the Talmud and from the later Sages to the effect that there was no incompatibility between the faith and the enlightenment and that the two could coexist. But experience has shown that matters are otherwise. For there can be a contradiction hidden deep within the soul which leads one ultimately to reject the demands of faith even when, on a superficial view, no contradiction is apparent. So with Zionism—in so far as it encompasses the entire question of Judaism as a comprehensive doctrine and is not merely support for the settlement of Ereẓ-Israel.[72]

But there was no one of ʿAmiel's stature and clarity of mind in the Mizraḥi in its early years, nor, it may be supposed, could there have been: for, at the time, the logic of his position would surely have pulled him back into the world of orthodoxy proper. Nor was there anyone on the secular side of the divide comparable to Aḥad Ha-ʿAm in his determination to get to the root of the matter in hand. But nor was Aḥad Ha-ʿAm himself disposed (even if he had been able) to bring the issue publicly to a head. He said his piece and then he too fell in with the

---

[70] Cf. Letter to Israel Abrahams, Cambridge, 30 March 1913. *Igrot AH*, v, p. 104. The Zionist position was fundamentally historical, he wrote on another occasion, and the Zionists, as nationalists, 'whether believers or apostates, might not simply cross the religious element out with our pens and consider it inexistent. If we regard our nationhood with love and respect, religion cannot be excluded. But we do not see it as the be-all; only as *part* of the spirit of the people as it evolves through life and over time.' Letter to Shmarya Levin, 27 February 1908. Ibid., iv, p. 117. Emphasis in text.

[71] Such as had been collected by Avraham Slutski in his *Shivat Ẓion* (2nd edn, Warsaw, 1899).

[72] Letter to R. Ḥayyim Halberstamm, 5 April 1905. *Igrot AH*, iii, pp. 342–3.

mood in the Russian wing of the movement as it had revealed itself at Minsk, a mood that was not conducive to the paring of issues down to the bone, even the issue of the fundamental nature and purposes of Zionism itself. Was the enterprise they were embarked upon that of the secular rehabilitation of the Jewish people, in the course of which its historical baggage was to be rigorously searched for what was worth salvaging and the rest jettisoned? Was the Jewish past one from which, broadly speaking, the Jews should be liberated? Was it solely with their condition and destiny in this, the knowable world that the movement was concerned, and was it this that the movement had taken it upon itself to change? And did Zionism therefore have a notion of what would ultimately constitute a satisfactory condition, such that its mission, when that condition had been attained, could be said to have been accomplished? Or, on the contrary, were there elements of the past that were inviolable, that it was impermissible to inquire into, and that had at all costs to be preserved? Did Zionism therefore comprehend—or was it linked to—purposes which were sacred, which it had not itself determined, nor might determine, but were none the less the terms in which its accomplishment would be measured? Was the intent of Zionism therefore no more than ameliorative; or was it truly revolutionary? No clear answers to these questions were forthcoming. Such questions were hardly put—except, of course, among the sternly and undeviatingly orthodox who remained outside the camp and in dedicated opposition to it. Within the movement the strongest tendency was towards compromise and eclecticism and—when formulations were unavoidable—towards trimming, and, more generally, towards drawing back from the brink when fundamental issues arose and were glimpsed in all their gravity. There was impatience with the orthodox view and resentment of Herzl's attempt to use the Mizraḥi. There was anticlericalism. There was irreligion. The past was rummaged continually for what it might hold for the present: language, literature, pre-Exile history, figures of heroic dimensions, models, metaphors, names, subjects of study, whole worlds to which the schoolchild must be introduced because they were uniquely, organically his own. But there was little or no outright rejection. Matters were passed by, or deliberately overlooked, or put aside for further thought, or were refashioned for modern purposes, but never—except in the rarest of cases, on the very fringes of the movement— jettisoned. The past weighed upon all, orthodox and secular alike, and drew them together in spite of themselves. There was no disposition—perhaps no capacity—to disengage from it. In sum, the preponderant tendency in the movement was to look forwards to the future and backwards to the past simul- taneously and with feelings that were equally strong: it was not to consider how the Jews might best travel light and arrive with the greatest possible speed at some appointed destination. In temperament and general outlook and in conception of what it was Zionists should concern themselves with, the activists of the great eastern branch (with such exceptions as we shall note) were thus moving ever more rapidly away from their elected leader and the *raison d'être* of the movement as he conceived it and back towards positions in which they were more comfortable and which were much more like their own before he had appeared on their horizon—all this with fateful consequences for themselves, for him, and above all for the quality and policy of the movement that he and they had formed.

8

The Autocracy as Foe;
the Autocracy as Friend

i

For the Russian Zionists Russia itself was, as ever, 'this miserable country' by which 'we have been sold and betrayed':[1] vast, cruel, brutalized, and still firmly in the grip of a state machine whose chiefs and functionaries were by and large undeviating in their hostility to the Jews. For the Zionists Russia was therefore a land without hope, a land to be evacuated sooner rather than later if the last vestiges of the Jews' *élan vital* and self-respect were not to be ground away. No doubt the state machine had to be accommodated to in the meanwhile and its functionaries treated with; but only out of necessity and for specific and limited purposes and the business then done with a silent apology and warily, as with an enemy. For the rest, they, the Zionists—as, indeed, virtually all of Russia's Jews—wanted chiefly to be left alone and unhindered in their private and communal affairs. To that end some of them retained a mild interest in the regularization of their status *vis-à-vis* the authorities and the great majority consistently avoided involvement in the revolutionary movement. The Government, for its part, whether in response to this restraint or not no one could be sure, interfered only mildly and intermittently in the movement's affairs. And, as it happened, had refrained for over a decade from massive attack (after the model of the great expulsion from Moscow in 1891) on its Jewish subjects. Thus a *modus vivendi* of sorts was in force, one of the effects of which was somewhat to dull the Zionists' political senses. Their eyes were now set mainly on the short-term bene-

[1] Emmanuel Mandelstamm in 1881. See *Origins*, pp. 71–2.

fits of the *modus vivendi* and their minds on the simple logic of what had come to be their established position, without much considering the contingency of a fresh hardening of official policy towards the Jews in general or a new and a severer attitude to the illegal Zionist movement itself and how, in that event, they should respond. Nor did they stop more than fleetingly to think of the impact their own words and deeds might be having on the view the state's functionaries took of *them* from time to time. Apart from their avoidance of revolutionary activity proper, there is nothing to suggest that they ever took fully into account what they knew well enough, namely that their letters were often opened, that their press was read, that informers were not unknown, and that, as a national movement with strong foreign connections, they were an inevitable object of suspicion and regular attention by the political (or 'higher') police. In fact, the Russian authorities had been watching the Zionists ever more closely since the founding of the new movement in 1897, their approach to the questions it raised in their minds was a good deal broader and more subtle than most Zionists seem to have realized, and they had been in two minds all along as to whether toleration of the movement was a wise policy after all.

Mandelstamm, in charge of finance and with general responsibility for the promotion of the sales of Jewish Colonial Trust shares in Russia, was much the most alert of his colleagues to the fragility of their situation. This may well have been because his activities encountered official dislike on economic and fiscal as well as political grounds.

Up to now the regime has left us unmolested [he wrote to Herzl in June 1899], in spite of being fully informed about our movement. What will come later I do not know . . . Everything depends upon the whims of the officials. Yesterday I learnt, unfortunately, from a *most dependable* source that the Minister of Finance looks askance at our Colonial Bank and will not tolerate subscriptions being taken up here. That would be fatal.[2]

---

[2] Quoted in a letter from the Jewish Colonial Trust, London, to Herzl, n.d. (but evidently sent in June 1899). CZA, H VIII/541. Emphasis in original. See also Mandelstamm to Herzl, 13 June 1899, ibid. On that occasion he wrote to Herzl: 'One must keep in mind that Zionism in Russia can be paralysed for years with a single stroke

The crisis died away and a year later he was writing to Herzl that 'We have no reason to complain of the Government *just now*, considering that it *tolerates* our movement and that suffices.'[3] But towards the end of October 1902 he was extremely worried once again.

Yesterday, the local censor, a patient of mine,[4] told me in confidence . . . that the censors would *probably* soon be receiving orders to allow nothing of a Zionist nature to be printed or to cross the frontier . . . This could be the beginning of our end in Russia . . . From the beginning of our movement I have been worried about the attitude of our Government; and I had begun to believe in wonders when I saw that we were left alone for so long. Now the people [of the Government] think they sniff something dangerous: our organization frightens them.[5]

This time Mandelstamm's concern was well founded. A decision to prohibit the import of Bank share certificates had indeed been taken on 25 August 1902 and made public at the beginning of October. More serious still, the Ministry of the Interior decided to address itself to the entire question early in 1903 and to lay down clear policy on the Zionist movement once and for all. First, a review of the nature, history, structure, and leading personalities in the movement and of some of its implications for Russian state security was ordered. Later, a detailed preliminary instruction was issued by the Minister to all governors and to the principal chiefs of police in the Empire.

Zionism: a Historical Review of its Development[6] is a detailed report, 149 printed pages long, in large format, submitted to the Minister of the Interior (possibly for onward transmission to the Tsar) by the Ministry's Police Department some time towards the middle of 1903. The origins, structure, leading

of a pen by the whim of some drunken bureaucrat in the Ministry of the Interior; and if Witte only knits his brows much could happen to us. In this country we are at everyone's mercy.'

[3] Mandelstamm to Herzl, 13 November 1900. Ibid.

[4] Mandelstamm was an eminent ophthalmologist.

[5] Mandelstamm to Herzl, 27 October 1902. CZA, H VIII/541.

[6] *Sionizm. Istorichesky ocherk ego razvitiya. Zapiska, sostavlennaya v departamente politsii* (St. Petersburg, 1903). CZA, K 14 a/13.

ideas and personalities, primary activities, membership, and finances of the movement are all dealt with in turn and in detail, as are the five Congresses held between 1897 and 1901 and the Minsk conference of 1902. The most important trends in Zionism (defined as political, practical-cultural, Democratic, socialist, and religious) are distinguished and analysed. Aspects of Zionism which are, or might become, relevant to Russian state security are considered in depth. And the general direction in which the movement appeared to be moving and the balance of forces within it are estimated. The tone is cool, matter-of-fact, devoid of animus. The compilers, obviously with access to a mass of material collected through intercepted correspondence and informers[7] as well as through normal and overt observation by local police, were evidently at pains to understand the nature of the phenomenon they were studying and to provide their superiors with a reliable basis for the formulation of policy. There are minor errors of fact, notably in the account of the early origins of the movement. The treatment of Herzl's diplomacy is perfunctory and superficial and shows no signs of the compilers having seen more than a handful of newspaper clippings on that subject, nor indeed of having taken that aspect of the movement's work seriously. Their grasp of Jewish mores and culture is sometimes shaky. There is an excessive natural tendency to rely on the judgement of established official sources such as district police commanders. Topics of special interest, such as Zionism's links with socialism, receive a degree of attention which is out of proportion to their actual significance on the ground at the time. But the picture, broadly, is not an inaccurate one and the job done by A. A. Lopukhin (the director of the Police Department in the Ministry, who signed the report) and his men may be rated workmanlike—useful to the Minister then and valuable to the historian today.

The two (linked) questions which most concerned the compilers were the degree to which Zionism was compatible with law and order as they understood it and Zionism's role, actual and potential, in the revolutionary movement proper. They noted the Zionists' practice of holding frequent secret meetings —'where matters not exclusively Zionist are discussed'.

[7] There are, for example, frequent quotations from private internal correspondence.

They noted and reckoned up their collection of 'substantial sums of money'. They were disturbed by Zionism's 'cohesive' effect on 'the Jewish masses'.[8] They observed that by presenting a vision of a better existence elsewhere and in the future Zionism tended to breed unrest here and now, especially among the young. All these phenomena were undesirable; but they were not—so the compilers seem to have wanted to imply, without having to say so explicitly—dangerous.

The more serious question was the degree of involvement of the Zionists in the revolutionary movement proper and of their likely (even if unintended) contribution to revolutionary unrest in the future. The compilers drew a clear distinction between revolutionary Jewish Social Democracy (notably the Bund) and Zionism, but were aware of certain radical tendencies and personalities within the Zionist movement. Bernstein-Kohan was an inevitable and obvious object of special inquiry, as much by virtue of his function for some years as master of the internal communications network as of his private opinions and past political connections. They seem to have regarded the rise of the Democratic Party as ominous, although they were careful to point out that the Democrats were competitors of the Bund, not allies. They come to grips with the problem they had set themselves most clearly in the course of their analysis of the growing attachment of Russian Zionists to the question of 'culture'.

When one considers the development of the Zionist movement in Russia during this period, especially in the St. Petersburg and Moscow regions, one is instantly impressed by the fact that the movement, which appeared to be expiring after the Fourth Congress, seems to have undergone a surge of energy and to have grown stronger. The reasons for this revitalization undoubtedly lie in the so-called 'cultural questions' which the cautious Herzl had avoided. The opportunity to work in a broad, almost unlimited arena of activity for the benefit of the cultural development of the Jews—conceived in a rather special way—attracted a new element to Zionism, namely the students.

Zionist ranks began to fill up with the so-called young Jewish intelligentsia of both sexes and beginning with the fifth class of the *gymnasium*. Obviously, this new source of energy has set the movement

[8] Ibid., p. 126.

in a new direction; the aims and ideals of its proponents do not fit into the framework of the original Zionist programme. Palestine has been forgotten, politics have taken second place. The first concern of these new Zionists has turned out to be the education of the popular masses in accordance with extremely varied programmes. Without renouncing, on the one hand, the mystical conception of the Zionist idea and the study of ancient Jewish history as the foundation of their activities, the Zionists have now begun, on the other hand, to introduce into their programmes of study the most modern political economy, sociology, and law . . .

Thus the original circles of 'practical' Zionists, which formerly had kept away from contemporary political tendencies on the grounds that they were harmful to the Jewish people, have in the course of time, through the gradual, covert spreading of so-called 'theoretical' circles of a definite political character, been imperceptibly preparing themselves for amalgamation with the Social-Democratic factions. For their part, the Jewish socialists, despite their hostility to Zionism as a national movement, regard the Zionist organizations as fertile ground for the spreading of their beliefs and have begun to join the ranks of the theoretical circles with the aim of guiding them in the socialist direction.[9]

Study of the question was followed by the formulation of policy. At the beginning of July 1903 a letter of instruction was issued to all provincial governors and senior police commanders over Plehve's signature. It began by contrasting the initial position of the Zionists, 'who had set themselves as their object the promotion of Jewish emigration to Palestine for the foundation there of an independent Jewish state', with their present purposes. They had now

postponed to the distant future the realization of that thought and they direct their efforts to the development and strengthening of *the Jewish national idea*, advocating the uniting of the Jews in closed organizations in the places of their present habitation. This direction, given that it is *inimical to the assimilation* of the Jews into the other nationalities and that it aggravates ethnic dissension, runs counter to the bases of the Russian state idea and thus, for that reason, cannot be tolerated.[10]

[9] Ibid., pp. 82–3.
[10] Ministry of the Interior, Police Department. Circular No. 6142. 24 June 1903 (O.S.) (7 July N.S.). *Evreiskaya Starina*, vii, 3–4 (1915), pp. 412–14. Emphases in original.

Provincial authorities were therefore instructed to collect all relevant information on the Zionist societies and to submit their own views on the question. Meanwhile, pending a final solution to the question, they were to take certain immediate countermeasures. The public propagation of Zionism, particularly among the lower orders, was to be forbidden. All Zionist associations which showed signs of public activity by holding meetings and conferences were to be closed down. Representatives and other activists of the Zionist organizations in Russia were to be forbidden to travel abroad on the business of the movement. The sale of shares of the Jewish Colonial Trust and the collection of money for the Jewish National Fund were to be stopped. Elementary schools, reading-rooms and libraries, Sabbath schools for adults, public lectures on Jewish history, and the like were to be put under special surveillance and prevented from being used to encourage national separatism under Zionist guidance. Candidates for communal office, especially rabbis, were to be vetted for possible Zionist affiliation.[11]

The timing of these events and, to some extent, the actual content of the Ministry's report suggest that the proceedings at the Minsk conference had done much to precipitate the change. Minsk reflected to a high degree the Government's original uncertainty about Zionism and its readiness to consider whether the movement could not be turned to uses of its own—after the model, more or less, of Zubatovite police socialism.[12] But so extreme was the concession that once the unprecedented permit to hold such a conference had been granted, its proceedings and results were bound to be examined with care. What the Minister and his advisors in the 'higher police' had then seen was not to their liking; and in the meanwhile, the strongest proponent of a friendlier attitude to such trends in Russian Jewry that were socially and intellectually radical without necessarily being politically subversive, Zubatov himself, was increasingly out of favour. In August 1903

---

[11] Ibid.

[12] Another gesture was the grant at this time of licences to publish periodicals in Hebrew and Yiddish. No new licences had been granted to publish in Yiddish since 1882 or in Hebrew since 1886. Ben-Zion Katz, 'Yahadut rusiya lifnei ḥamishim shana', *He-'Avar*, i (1953), pp. 8–10. Cf. Schneiderman, *Sergei Zubatov*, p. 237.

Zubatov was dismissed—probably for having been openly critical of his Minister,[13] but in any event in the wake of the evident failure of his method.

The years 1902 and 1903 were the culmination of a period of economic depression and of a sharp rise in social tension: student disaffection, peasant revolts in the countryside in the provinces of Kharkov and Poltava, extensive strikes with a pronounced political flavour in certain towns, notably Rostov-on-Don, and later in Baku, Tiflis, and Batum, Ekaterinoslav, Kiev, Nikolaev, and Odessa. The holding of great meetings of workers, the spread of strikes within a given locality from one factory to another, and the large-scale use of troops to put them down all enhanced the political quality of the unrest and of the actual clashes. Lastly, with the rise in general social and political tension came a recrudescence of political terror. In 1901 the Minister of Education, Bogolepov, was shot. In 1902 the populists, having re-formed as the Socialist Revolutionary Party, set up a 'fighting organization'. In April 1902 they engineered the assassination of the Minister of the Interior, Sipyagin (who, as it had happened, had proposed to the Council of Ministers only a month earlier some softening of the 'Temporary (May) Laws' that had been enacted against the Jews twenty years earlier).[14] When Sipyagin was replaced by V. K. Plehve the fight against the revolutionary forces took on new strength and a great governmental campaign to batten down the hatches all round was inaugurated in turn. Plehve was a senior policeman of immense experience, cool, supple, clever, and pitiless in his defence of the Autocracy and of the principle of uniform, bureaucratic control of the country from the centre. The system of special political security (*Okhrana*) sections of police in the three major cities of the Empire, St. Petersburg, Moscow, and Warsaw, was now extended to other towns.[15] Zubatov was first brought to the capital to run all political investigation; and then dismissed upon what was taken to be the failure of his policy. The emasculation of Finnish autonomy (over which Plehve had presided in person before his appointment as Minister) was

[13] Ibid., pp. 350–4.
[14] Mishkinsky, art. cit., p. 241.
[15] Ronald Hingley, *The Russian Secret Police* (London, 1970), p. 89.

confirmed. The effort to stamp out national feeling and institutions among the Armenians was intensified. Provincial governors were given a freer hand in their handling of social and political unrest. And the effort to reduce the organized revolutionary movement by penetration and manipulation from the inside was more than maintained. It was under Plehve that the *Okhrana*'s double agent Yevno Azef replaced the dedicated Gregori Gershuni as chief of the Socialist Revolutionaries' 'fighting organization' (upon the latter's betrayal and arrest); and the consequent misting-over of the line dividing action in the interests of the revolution from action in the interests of preserving police agents' cover was finally epitomized in Plehve's own assassination in July 1904 at the hands of people whom Azef, his own 'secret assistant' (as the *Okhrana* liked to denote its *agents provocateurs*), had led.

The honest Gershuni and the venal Azef were both Jews. A negligible fraction of the revolutionary movement in all its forms before 1881, Jews now comprised a very large proportion of the most active and devoted—and therefore, from the state's viewpoint, most dangerous—of the dissidents. Out of 5,426 political exiles under surveillance in Siberia 1,676 were Jews: 31 per cent.[16] These were the abundant fruits of official hostility and oppression and of the steady growth of national sentiment which ever more frequently took the form of great personal daring and of a refusal to be cowed— well illustrated by the affair of one Hirsch Lekert, a twenty-two-year-old shoemaker in Vilna, a member of the Bund, who shot the governor in 1902 because the latter had ordered a group of demonstrators, most of whom were Jews, to be *flogged*. The Social-Democratic Bund had always been opposed to terror on general principles, but the deed was greatly applauded by the public at large as a striking defence of Jewish honour. Lekert was promptly hanged (although the governor had only been wounded) and became something of a folk-hero after his death. There was a similar act of defiance after the Kishinev pogrom of April 1903 when one of its principal instigators was shot and wounded. And the Kishinev pogrom, first of a long series, was followed by the first systematic (and,

---

[16] Richard Charques, *The Twilight of Imperial Russia* (London, 1965), p. 82. The Jews accounted for approximately 4 per cent of the total population of the country.

in the event, fairly successful) plan for local Jewish self-defence against *pogromshchiki* at Gomel in September 1903. Old hostility to the Jews and uncertainty about how to handle them, renewed impatience with non-Russian peoples generally, and a fresh bout of fear of revolution in which the Jews, once again, seemed to be emerging as an important and dangerous force—all these feelings now brought relations between the Jews and their rulers to the point of explosion.

The two-day-long anti-Jewish riot in Kishinev, the capital of Bessarabia (19–20 April 1903), can perhaps best be seen as one of those events which rapidly take on a symbolic quality, which serve as archetypes for a great number of lesser incidents, and are soon taken, well nigh without question, as valid epitomes for whole, complex states of affairs. With Kishinev this was the case for contemporary Jewry, beyond Russia no less than within it. To a milder, but not insignificant extent, it was the case for liberal opinion generally—in Russia as much as outside it. To cite no more than two examples: the pogrom was the subject of a great deal of what would now be called 'investigative reporting' by foreign, notably American, journalists in unprecedented depth and extension; and Leo Tolstoy, who had kept silent during the great wave of pogroms between 1881 and 1884, now spoke out in clear (if idiosyncratic[17]) condemnation.

Some of the elements of the pogrom were classic: the ground prepared by poisonous anti-Semitic agitation in the press and by word of mouth, an Easter-time blood libel, shadowy ties between the agitators and the authorities, repeated refusals by the local governor to use police and troops to restore order until specifically instructed to do so from St. Petersburg, but immediate intervention by the police on the side of the

[17] 'If you ask me what, in my opinion, the Jews ought to do', Tolstoy added to his forthright denunciation of the Government, 'my answer in that case, as in others, is the logical outcome of that Christian teaching which I strive to understand and to follow. For the Jews, as for all men, one thing, and one thing only, is necessary for salvation: to follow as closely as may be the universal rule, "Do unto others as you would that others should do unto you." They should fight the Government not by violence—that weapon should be left to the Government—but by virtuous living to the exclusion not only of all violence towards their neighbours, but of all participation in violence, even when called upon by Government instruments of violence for their own advantage. This is all that I can say with regard to the horrible events in Kishinev; all this is very old and is well known.'

rioters whenever the Jews sought to defend themselves actively and succeeded in doing so to some effect, ambiguous statements from St. Petersburg after the event, mass trials of rioters and looters ending, for the most part, with mild sentences or acquittals, and, in the aftermath, the slow effort by the immediate victims to pick up the pieces, while the most alert and public-minded members of Russian Jewry raged at the Government, at the *goyim*, and above all at themselves for the humiliation of it all.

In cold figures, and by the standards of our times, the Kishinev pogrom was a nasty, but not outstanding case of licensed brutality: 32 men, 6 women, and 3 children killed outright, 8 persons who later died of wounds, 495 injured, of whom 95 heavily, many (mostly unreported) cases of rape, some mutilation of individual victims, some desecration of sacred objects, much blood and gore, innumerable roving and ecstatic mobs forming and re-forming continuously, and vast heaps of debris and filth left over to be cleaned up after the troops had finally moved in and peace had descended on the streets. Damage to property was in due proportion: some 1,500 homes, workshops, and stores looted and destroyed and a large proportion, possibly a fifth of the city's Jewish population, rendered homeless and destitute. There were too some touches of that blocking-off of moral sensitivity which typically accompanies a hammering of the Jews.

The better class of the Christian public behaved disgracefully [the semi-official *St. Petersburgskiye Vedomosti* reported]. They did not raise a finger to put a stop to the plunder and assaults. They walked calmly along and gazed at these horrible spectacles with the utmost indifference. Many of them even rode through the streets in their carriages in holiday attire in order to witness the cruelties that were being perpetrated.[18]

In all this there was nothing fundamentally new, nothing that had not been seen in the major pogroms of the 1881–4 wave.[19] Such differences as there were lay in what might be termed the outer circumstances of the pogrom and in the

---

[18] Quoted in *Jewish Chronicle*, 8 May 1903, p. 7.
[19] See *Origins*, Chapter Three, *passim*.

effects that the passage of time had had. For close to twenty years the persecution of Russian Jewry had been carried out almost exclusively through the legally established institutions of the state and in accordance with regular proceedings, not by ruffians in the street and by criminal violence directed at individuals on a random basis. Russia's reputation as a *Rechtsstaat*—however imperfect—had been more or less restored after the damage done to it a generation before. Now, therefore, shock and surprise doubled the sense of outrage. There was novelty too in the appearance of a fresh type of anti-Jewish agitator and a new form of anti-Semitic slander: the scurrilous P. Krushevan, editor of an arch-reactionary local newspaper (and of another in St. Petersburg), who enjoyed official protection and was free to put about not only versions of the ancient blood libel against the Jews accompanied by advice that Christians would be permitted to 'execute bloody justice on the Jews' during the approaching Easter, but also the modern invention of Jewish world conspiracy. In its early version, printed and circulated in Kishinev before the pogrom, this was *The Rabbi's Speech*. In its more elaborate version, soon to be published under more distinguished auspices, it was the infamous *Protocols of the Elders of Zion*. The *Protocols*, as has been shown conclusively, were a fabrication of the Russian secret police; their operative use in an effort to induce the Russian public at large to trace the troubles of their country to a hidden, infinitely nefarious Jewish hand was inaugurated at Kishinev.[20]

Finally, there was the question of official connivance. It went beyond the official protection extended to professional agitators like Krushevan and refusal by the local governor and police commander to enforce the law and maintain order until the killers and plunderers had had their fill and were on the point of getting totally out of hand. That much had been seen in the early 1880s. And at the time it had been accepted that it was right to distinguish between the Russian Government at its highest reaches and the conduct of some (not all) of its officials in the provinces: between passive approval and sympathy by the ruler of Russia and his entourage for the *pogromshchiki* and the aid and comfort given them on the ground

[20] Norman Cohn, *Warrant for Genocide* (London, 1967), pp. 108–9 and *passim*.

In the public mind, especially abroad, the Russian Government appeared in a poor light, but the light being poor there was much uncertainty.[21] Now, in 1903, things looked different and the result was in the nature of a public scandal too great to be shrugged off. This was partly owing to the well-publicized, contemptuous refusal of the governor to do his duty either before the riots, when well-founded information suggesting what was in store was brought to his attention, or while they were in progress. But more because, soon after the pogrom, while descriptions and analyses of the event were still flooding the press in Russia and abroad, a document directly incriminating the Minister of the Interior Plehve was published in *The Times*. It purported to be a secret instruction from Plehve to the Governor of Bessarabia, dated twelve days before the outbreak, informing him that attacks were being prepared against the Jews, hinting broadly that the future rioters merited sympathy, and warning the governor against taking strong measures against them, specifically against recourse to arms. This, of course, was a clear recipe for giving the *pogromshchiki* a free hand. The Government denounced the document as a forgery and expelled the correspondent of *The Times* in reprisal. But the denial had a feeble impact and the damage had been done. The wording of Plehve's supposed instruction rang true, its oblique terms seemed in character. If it was a forgery, it was a very good one.[22] At all events, the belief that Plehve carried a heavy and direct responsibility for Kishinev was never erased, least of all among the Jews of Russia. Neither the disgrace and dismissal of the Governor of Bessarabia, nor the appointment of an unusually fair and well-disposed official (Prince Urusoff) in his stead changed it. As Kishinev became the archetype of the twentieth-century pogrom, so Plehve became the man of Kishinev. It was to meet this man that Herzl travelled to Russia in August of that same year.

[21] See *Origins*, pp. 53–6.

[22] The question whether Plehve's instruction to von Raaben, the Governor of Bessarabia, was genuine is still open. A careful modern study of the evidence suggests that much of the supporting testimony has to be dismissed as extremely unreliable or plainly false and that the circumstantial evidence either weakens the case against Plehve or else leaves it inconclusive. See Eliyahu Feldman, 'Plehve ve-ha-pogrom be-kishinov be-1903', *He-'Avar*, xvii (1970), pp. 137–50.

ii

Herzl's approach to Russia had always been fundamentally political and, by deliberate choice, hard-headed—hardly different, except in emphases, from his approach to Germany or Great Britain. Russia was a Great Power and Russia was a neighbour of Turkey with a standing interest in the Near East. These were reasons enough to seek Russia's support. Russia had a ruler who wished to cut a figure in the world as a bene-volent, far-seeing statesman (witness his sponsorship of the World Peace Conference at The Hague in 1899) and Russian Jewry constituted a social and political problem of the first order for the Russian state. These, to Herzl's mind, were reasons enough for the Tsar and his Government to take an interest in Zionism. A little thought would show them that persecution of the Jews did nothing for their reputation abroad, that periodic eruptions of violence were dangerous at home, and that emigration of the poorer Jews from Russia and the deflec-tion of Jewish 'students and workmen away from socialism and nihilism by setting a purer national ideal before them'[23] were all to be welcomed. Thus, Herzl reasoned, there was a strong basis for co-operation between Russia and the Zionists; and true to his method, he had tried repeatedly to gain an audience with the Tsar to convince him of this—through Bertha von Suttner of the World Peace Movement and the Grand Duke of Baden,[24] who were both well disposed, and through the Grand Duke of Hesse (the Tsar's brother-in-law), who was indifferent. He had tried to develop a contact with an official of the Russian Foreign Ministry, a Polish Jew who had converted to Christianity, and he had tried too to reach one of the Russian Grand Dukes who was reputed to be com-paratively well disposed to the Jews. But he had achieved nothing; and successive failures, his primary concentration of attention on his negotiations first with the Turks and then with

[23] Herzl to Bertha von Suttner, 16 January 1899. *Igrot Herzl*, iii, no. 717, p. 251.

[24] The Tsar's polite response (25 December 1899) to the Grand Duke of Baden's intercessions was that 'The theory of "Zionism" could certainly be an important factor in regard to furthering internal peace in Europe, but I myself doubt that any practical application of this theory is possible, even in the distant future.' 'Herzl, Hechler, the Grand Duke of Baden and the German Emperor', translated by Harry Zohn, *Herzl Year Book*, iv (1962), p. 257.

the British, and, no doubt, his growing reluctance to stir up more trouble for himself than was absolutely necessary in the Russian wing of the movement had all led to a decline of activity on this, his eastern front. Then came the Kishinev pogrom in which, true again to form, he saw both a resounding confirmation of his fundamental view of the Jewish condition and an opportunity to renew the attack, a crack in the Russian wall through which he might just manage to break.

Herzl's response to Kishinev was not instantaneous. The pogrom occurred just as the negotiations over El Arish had reached their climax. Not until shortly after his conclusion in the middle of May 1903 that 'it is simply all over' in Egypt[25] do we find him applying his mind to the possibility of a fresh approach to St. Petersburg. Meanwhile, the international row over Kishinev had grown to its unprecedented proportions, the embarrassment of the Russian Government was evident, and the shattering of Jewish morale in Russia unmistakable. At this point, about a month after the event, he wrote a formal letter of condolence to the Kishinev community (19 May), following it up shortly with letters to Plehve and Pobedonostsev (23 May) in which he asked for an audience with the Tsar and with a request to Bertha von Suttner to write directly to the Autocrat himself. Herzl's tone was carefully restrained; the horrors in Bessarabia are reviewed briefly, and, as it were, from afar.

The deplorable events at Kishinev force the pen into my hand—[he wrote to Plehve] but not to bemoan what is irrevocable.

I hear from reliable sources that despair is beginning to take hold of the Jews in Russia. They feel that they are being delivered up to the evil instincts of the mob without protection. In consequence elderly people are being seized by paralyzing fear in the activities of their livelihood, and the younger people are beginning to listen to the doctrines of revolution. Fifteen- and sixteen-year-old children, who don't even understand the revolutionary madness preached to them, are letting themselves be deluded by theories of violence.

An audience would calm the Jews, he argued. It would be one of a series that he had had with other potentates. Discretion was assured.[26] And to Pobedonostsev he added, in a

---

[25] *Diaries*, iv, p. 1486.
[26] *Diaries*, iv, pp. 1493–5.

reference to official Russian anti-Semitism, that it was his belief that 'Russian statesmen are up against one of the most complicated problems of government and they would probably prefer it if it could be solved without cruelty.'[27] There was no direct reply. Baroness von Suttner was informed by Lamsdorff, the Russian Foreign Minister, that Herzl would not be received. And there the matter rested until reports of the Ministry of the Interior's planned onslaught on the Zionist movement began circulating.

'Our movement in Russia is menaced by the danger of prohibition', Tchlenov informed Vienna at the end of June. What the consequences would be he could not predict. It might be too late to do anything. The situation was very serious: if the edict of prohibition came into force before the Congress (due for the end of August) there might be no Russian delegation present.[28]

Tchlenov was speaking for a group of leading activists who were meeting in St. Petersburg to consider what might be done. His letter was followed up by the dispatch of one of their number, Jasinowski, the GAC member for Warsaw, to report to Herzl directly and seek his help.

Herzl's initial response was to advise the Russian Zionists to act somewhat along the lines he had intended for himself, as indicated in his own letter to Plehve of the month before. Someone must be found, he wrote to them—someone 'who would speak not as our friend, but as a friend of the Russian Government'—who could reach the Tsar or Plehve, show them how explosive was the situation of the Jews, point to the weight of international opinion, and argue the advantages that would accrue to Russia from a resettlement of the Jews in Erez-Israel. Once that person had been heard, the banning of Zionism would be impossible 'for it would be seen as a remedy; while a petition for further toleration would be counter-productive. What we must do is extract an advantage out of the impending calamity.'[29]

Later there was much dispute about the precise content of

[27] Ibid., p. 1495.
[28] Tchlenov to EAC, Vienna. 25 June 1903. CZA, Z 1/275. Heymann, i, no. 48, p. 86.
[29] Herzl to Katzenelsohn, 30 June 1903. CZA, H III/A3.

Jasinowski's brief.[30] Had it been agreed in St. Petersburg that Jasinowski should ask Herzl to intervene personally and seek to be received in St. Petersburg, specifically by Plehve himself? Or was the messenger's business limited to briefing the leader and announcing the imminent arrival of a somewhat more important and better-informed member of the GAC, the resident member in St. Petersburg, Belkowsky? Or was the row that was soon to follow between Herzl and an important group of Russian Zionists no more than a further consequence of his consistent refusal to consult his colleagues, even on important and delicate matters which concerned them directly and on which they were sure to be better informed than himself? From Herzl's point of view the decisive fact, no doubt, was that Jasinowski had a channel to Paulina Corwin-Piatrowska, an elderly Polish lady of letters living in St. Petersburg, well-disposed to the Jewish national cause, but also a good friend of Plehve's, and possibly his agent. The conjunction of Jasinowski's arrival in Austria, the almost certain fact that the *possibility* of an appeal by Herzl to Plehve was discussed by the Zionist leaders at St. Petersburg and the high probability that Jasinowski mentioned it to Herzl, the arrival of news of Lamsdorff's refusal to consider an audience with the Tsar, and finally, the general sense of urgency, if not desperation, engendered first by Kishinev and then the prospect of paralysing restrictions being imposed on the movement —all these taken together make Herzl's decision to try a new tack seem all but inevitable. The upshot, in any case, was a request to Paulina Corwin to arrange a meeting for him with Plehve. He could not bring himself to approach the Minister directly, Herzl wrote to her, having been turned down so recently. But he did much want to see him: partly because, as before, there was a need to 'soothe our poor excited people a bit'. But also because he had hoped

to take this opportunity to present to Minister von Plehve a plan for organized emigration without re-entry and to request his cooperation. You see, I am firmly convinced that he would understand me. I can see from everything, even from the contradictory and unreliable newspaper reports, that he is worried about the situation of

[30] Admirably summed up by Heymann, pp. 29–33.

the Jews and that he would very much like to find a solution with good grace.

He wanted, he repeated, 'to have a thorough discussion with von Plehve about starting emigration and getting him, the most powerful man in Russia, interested in it—something that would be felt as a relief on all sides'.[31]

Paulina Corwin was prompt to respond. She saw Plehve within a day of hearing from Herzl and Jasinowski and gained Plehve's consent to an interview on the spot. 'He told me', she reported, 'that to emigration without return he would have agreed and that such a Zionism he himself would have supported.' (*Er sagte mir dass eine Emigration ohne Rückkehr würde er einverstanden gewesen sein und für einen solchen Zionismus ist er selbst gewesen.*) He would be glad to meet Herzl and, such was the clear implication, do business with him.[32]

'Emigration without return' had been Herzl's own phrase. This time he had hit the mark. In a last minute flurry of contradictory advice on all sides—protest and non-co-operation from Belkowsky (who had refused to wait for him in St. Petersburg) and encouragement from Mandelstamm (if Plehve's instructions finally became law, he wrote to Herzl, the movement would be paralysed for years: nothing was more difficult than to have such an *ukase* repealed, particularly when it concerned the Jews[33])—and after some further difficulty over dates because he was due in Basel on 20 August for the Congress, Herzl finally departed on 5 August for Russia. The frontier (where he was searched) was crossed on 6 August; he arrived in St. Petersburg on 7 August; ten days later, after a brief stay in Vilna, he returned.

Herzl's visit to Russia was the last moment of his supremacy in Zionism. And it is perhaps not too much to say that in that brief journey there were encapsulated too all the main elements of the matter of Zionism and of the state of the movement: the condition and mood of the Jews, the policy of Russia towards them, the conflicting currents within the movement,

[31] Herzl to Paulina Corwin-Piatrowska, 8 July 1903. *Diaries*, iv, pp. 1509–10.
[32] Paulina Corwin to Jasinowski, 18 July 1903. CZA, H VIII/397. Heymann, i, no. 52, pp. 88–9.
[33] Mandelstamm to Herzl, 2 August 1903. CZA, H VIII/541.

Herzl's own position, at once supreme, unique, and fragile, and finally, the weakness and isolation of the Jews, the root causes of their troubles, in one degree or another, everywhere. 'I wish you a very good journey and, if possible, success', Mandelstamm, Herzl's greatest and most loyal supporter in Russia, had written to him. 'God! how unhappy is our unhappy people!'[34]

iii

In St. Petersburg Herzl saw S. Iu. Witte, the Minister of Finance, who was both unctuous and disagreeable. The Minister proclaimed himself a 'friend of the Jews'. He also related to Herzl how he had told Alexander III that he had 'absolutely no objection' to the drowning of the 'six or seven million Jews [of Russia] in the Black Sea' if only it were possible. But it was not, in his view; hence his more liberal approach. He had something too to say about Jews being reprehensible, mostly dirty, and wont to engage in 'nasty pursuits like pimping and usury'. None the less, it was his practice, Witte assured Herzl, to stand up for the Jews; and since to do so was to incur both hostility and doubts as to the honesty of one's intentions, he judged himself a brave man for doing so. Herzl kept his temper and steered the conversation to the matters in hand: a new policy towards the Zionist movement by the Government in general and by the Minister of Finance in particular, namely withdrawal of the ban on the sale of shares in the Jewish Colonial Trust. Witte expressed no opposition to Herzl's general ideas and agreed explicitly to the sale of shares being continued, provided only a branch of the Bank were established in Russia. This being exactly what Herzl had wanted, the results of the meeting were more satisfactory than the tone in which it had been conducted.[35]

He also had an interview, 'brief but full of substance' (*inhaltsreiche*) with the head of the Asian Department in the Foreign Ministry. Herzl outlined his ideas, discovered that the official knew something, but not much, about Zionism and its affairs, and obtained a promise that the question of Russian

---

[34] Ibid.
[35] *Diaries*, iv, pp. 1528–32.

diplomatic intervention in Constantinople on behalf of the Zionists would be looked into.[36]

But it was on his two lengthy interviews with Plehve on 8 and 13 August that everything turned and he had looked forward to meeting the Minister of the Interior as 'the most powerful man in Russia'[37] much as he had looked forward to meeting the 'master of England', Chamberlain.[38] Herzl was a great deal more impressed by Plehve than he had been by his rival, Witte. He found him intelligent, well-informed, self-confident, and in a mood which appeared to suggest a will to come to terms on a matter-of-fact basis. There was a harsh edge to the language in which Plehve referred to the Jews of Russia; but he was not offensive. He was prepared to listen.[39] His attitude to Herzl personally—such was Herzl's impression —was friendly. He was certainly polite. Even his French (unlike Witte's) was passable. Plehve's opening, as Herzl recorded it,[40] set the tone.

I have granted you this interview which you have requested, doctor, in order to come to an understanding with you in regard to the Zionist movement, of which you are the leader. The relationship which will be established between the Imperial Government and Zionism—and which can become, I will not say amicable, but in the nature of an understanding—will depend on you.[41]

Plehve then went on to state the Russian attitude towards minorities. The Russians wanted homogeneity; they also realized that they could not 'obliterate all differences of creed

[36] Ibid., pp. 1541–2. *Tagebücher*, iii, p. 485.

[37] *Diaries*, iv, p. 1510.

[38] See above, p. 143.

[39] Plehve made much the same impression on Lucien Wolf who interviewed him on the Jewish Question in Russia, two months later, and knew a great deal more about the subject than did Herzl: 'The impression he [Plehve] made upon me was, I am bound to say, exceedingly favourable. He has nothing of the typical Russian politician about him. In appearance he is almost English. Tall and massive, with short-cropped iron-grey whiskers and moustache, he looks something like Sir Henry Campbell-Bannerman writ large. He speaks slowly and deliberately, without a touch of the cynicism usually affected by the polished Russian. Though a somewhat impassive listener, he readily responds to any touch of humour . . . He is a strong man, and I should imagine an honest one, conscientious and inflexible as an administrator, but with little taste for experimental or constructive statesmanship.' *The Times*, 6 February 1904.

[40] He took notes during the talk.

[41] *Diaries*, iv, pp. 1522–3.

or language'. On the other hand, all subjects had to take 'a patriotic view of the Russian state as an actuality'. The Russian Government wanted to assimilate the Jews and believed that the two methods by which that end could be achieved were education and economic betterment. Fear of excessive competition being created for the Russian Christians limited what could be done through education; and objective conditions in the Pale limited the prospects of economic betterment. Besides, the Jews had been joining the revolutionary parties in significant numbers and their patriotic sentiment was to that extent in question. What was therefore favoured was the emigration of the Jews; and 'as long as it worked towards emigration we used to be sympathetic to your Zionist movement'. But, said Plehve,

ever since the Minsk conference we have noticed *un changement des gros bonnets* [a change of bigwigs]. There is less talk now of Palestinian Zionism than there is about culture, organization, and Jewish nationalism. This doesn't suit us. We have noticed in particular that your leaders in Russia—who are highly respected persons in their own circles—do not really obey your Vienna Committee.

This was Herzl's opening. He argued that his difficulties with the Russian Zionists, of which Plehve seemed so well informed, and the inroads which revolutionary socialism was making in the Pale both followed from the failure of Zionism thus far to attain its goal. Let the Russians then help; the sooner Zionism succeeded, the sooner things would be mended.

He asked for direct help in three directions. First, diplomatic pressure on the Turks; second, a Russian state subsidy for emigration out of taxes collected from Russian Jews; third, freedom to organize within Russia. The basis for this help would be a clear decision by the Russian Government to 'resolve the Jewish Question in a humane manner, out of consideration for the demands of the Russian state as much as for the needs of the Jewish people'. Such a decision could be conveniently announced at the coming Congress, along with a promise of an easing of the restrictions on Jewish residence within Russia as an earnest of Russian goodwill and in the interests of those who would not wish to emigrate. All this was acceptable to Plehve. It was therefore agreed that Herzl would work up an appropriate memorandum for formal consideration by the Government as well as a draft of proposed by-laws for the Zionist Organization within Russia, and that there would be a second meeting.[42]

The formal Russian response took the form of a letter (in Plehve's own hand) in which the terms on which the Russian Government was prepared to tolerate the Zionist movement were summed up, a warning against what was taken to be the new direction in which Zionism was moving was issued, and a promise of diplomatic support conditional on the Zionists returning to their original policy was made. There was also a reference to a recent decision to ease the residence restrictions to which Russian Jews were subject. The letter itself was for publication.

You have expressed the desire to retain a record of our conversation. I accede to it willingly so as to set aside anything that might give rise to excessive hopes or disquieting doubts.

I had the opportunity to inform you of the view the Russian Government takes of Zionism at present. It is a view which may indeed easily lead it to consider the necessity of exchanging its policy of toleration for measures dictated by national safety. So long as Zionism consisted of wanting to create an independent state in Palestine and promised to organize the emigration from Russia of a certain number of her subjects, the Russian Government could be entirely favourable to it.

But once this principal aim of Zionism is dropped and replaced by simple propaganda in favour of Jewish national concentration in Russia, the Government naturally can under no circumstances tolerate this new Zionist course. Its sole result would be the creation of groups of individuals who are entirely unacquainted with, and even hostile to, the patriotic feelings which are the strength of every state.

It is for this reason that trust in Zionism is conditional on its returning to its former programme of action. Were it to do so, it could count on moral and material support, so long as the measures it took in practice served to reduce the Jewish population in Russia. Such support could consist in backing the Zionist representatives at the Ottoman Government [protéger les mandataires sionistes près du gouvernement ottoman], facilitating the work of the emigration

---

[42] *Diaries*, iv, pp. 1520-7.

societies, and even making provision for their financial needs—not out of the resources of the state, of course, but by means of contributions levied on the Jews. I believe it necessary to add, that the Russian Government, while obliged to shape its actions on the Jewish Question in accordance with the interests of the state, has none the less never deviated from the great principles of morality and humanity. Only very recently, it has extended rights of residence in those areas which are intended for the Jewish population and there is nothing to prevent hope that the growth of these measures will serve to improve the conditions under which the Russian Jews live, especially if emigration reduces their number.[43]

The second meeting with the Minister, Herzl thought, went even better than the first. Plehve told him that the Tsar's approval for the declaration embodied in his letter had been obtained. He dwelt on the offence that had been given by the public attacks abroad on the Russian Tsar and Government and once again on Russian policy towards the Jews. His approach was fatalistic. Considering the numbers of the Jews, the Russians, said Plehve, could hardly be blamed for treating them with severity; but considering their condition, it was not unnatural that they were hostile to the Russian state. 'Therefore the creation of an independent Jewish State, capable of absorbing several million Jews, would suit us best of all.'[44] He would not promise to go as far towards easing the restrictive laws as Herzl wanted him to, but he would keep the possibility in view and would discuss it further with any representative Herzl sent him. He would not promise to arrange an audience with the Tsar for Herzl, but he would reconsider the request after the coming Zionist Congress. Glancing at the draft set of by-laws for the Zionist Organization in Russia, which he agreed to study, Plehve observed that Herzl wanted the Jews to be granted permission to do things that were forbidden to the Christians, when he had just been about to recommend to the Cabinet that the Zionist movement be suppressed altogether. The two men stated and restated their chief concerns: Herzl, that the main thing was for the Russians to bring pressure on the Turks; Plehve, that the moral attack on Russia

---

[43] CZA, H VI/D4. Published in the original French with a German translation in *Die Welt*, 25 August 1903, on the eve of the Fifth Congress.
[44] *Diaries*, iv, p. 1535.

be moderated and that the Zionists revert to past positions. And each promised to try to accommodate to the other. When it was all over Herzl summed up his conclusions: 'Either help, administrative and financial, as well as intervention with the Sultan. Or the prohibition of the movement. Thus everything depends upon our people doing nothing foolish.'[45]

It is probable that these were the conclusions that Plehve had wished him to draw.

iv

Herzl rated the results of his talks in St. Petersburg (along with those of his negotiations with the British) as the 'greatest of all [his] accomplishments to date'.[46] On the face of it, they were indeed of the first order. He had been well received, notably by Plehve. Respectfully received, it might be added: no small thing for a Jewish leader in Russia. An outline of an agreement between the Zionist movement and the Russian Government had been reached with speed. A promise of support for the movement going well beyond mere toleration had been conceded and, remarkably, an undertaking, in writing and for public announcement, to take up the Zionist cause with the Turkish Government. This was substantially more than Herzl had obtained either from the Germans in 1898 or from the British more recently. Moreover, it was unprecedented for a Russian government to join with Jews in negotiations which were so clearly political (as opposed to intercessionary) in character—in precisely that give-and-take sense that was central to Herzl's political philosophy. The evidence for the validity of his old thesis that it was where the Jews and the Jewish Problem loomed largest that the Zionists would eventually find their most useful allies seemed abundant. His strategy, he could feel, had been vindicated.

Or had he been gulled? Had he, as his critics in Russia were quick to point out, disgraced them all by treating with the unscrupulous policeman-minister, the man linked in all minds with darkest reaction, the man of Kishinev? Worse, had he played into Plehve's hands by undertaking to help still the criticism at home and abroad to which the regime was now

[45] Ibid., p. 1540.
[46] Ibid., p. 1547.

subject and help present Russia to the world with a better, cleaner face? And in exchange for what? True, Plehve had promised to ease the restrictions on Zionist activities in Russia and perhaps, ultimately, abolish them. He had also promised to intercede with the Turks. But what were his promises worth? 'Most of the Russian members of the GAC were sceptical about Plehve's promises', it was recorded in the minutes of the Greater Actions Committee when Herzl reported to it on his journey, just prior to the opening of the Sixth Congress.[47] To revulsion against Plehve and to their long-standing resentment of Herzl's refusal to brook interference or take advice, even here, on his colleagues' home ground and on matters which concerned them personally and directly, there was added the scepticism of those who knew their Russia and were more familiar than Herzl could ever hope to be with that special combination of low cunning and ruthless brutality that was the salient characteristic of Russia's 'higher' (or political) police.

Subsequent events point to no clear conclusion. The ban on Zionism envisaged in Plehve's circular of 7 July 1903 (24 June O.S.) was never fully implemented. On the other hand, the harassment of Zionists on a local, and more or less random, basis never quite ceased. The promise to intercede in Constantinople was not broken. But nor was it kept. Instructions to make an appropriate *démarche* were duly issued (after Herzl had reminded Plehve of his promise), but not so forcefully as to require the Ambassador to move against his own judgement or even, perhaps, his inclination. Moreover, the terms of the proposed *démarche* were altered: no mention of an 'independent state in Palestine'; and the promise to provide 'backing [for] the Zionist representatives' in Constantinople was reduced to one of informing the Sublime Porte of 'the sympathetic reception which the Imperial Government has given the Zionists' project to return their co-religionists to Palestine'. The Ambassador was also authorized to state that a show of goodwill to the Zionists would be taken as a gesture of Turkish friendship for Russia.[48] This was not what Herzl had had in mind; nothing but a 'personal act' of the Tsar

---

[47] 21 August 1903. CZA, Z 1/193. Heymann, i, p. 102.
[48] Plehve to Herzl, 6 December 1903. CZA, H VI/D4.

would make the Sultan take the matter seriously, he explained to Plehve.[49] But in any case, the Ambassador failed to move. 'They have written to me about it from St. Petersburg', he told one of Herzl's contacts in Constantinople, 'but up to now I have not done anything and it will not be easy to do anything.'[50] No explanation was forthcoming directly. Russia and Austria had just agreed, as the 'mandatories of Europe', to impose a form of supervision over Turkish rule in Macedonia[51] and at such a time, when, as Paulina Corwin wrote to Herzl, 'on est tellement agresseur envers Constantinople'.[52] the Ambassador may simply have been unwilling to add to his troubles.

It is likely too that the Russian Foreign Ministry's outlook on the project differed from that of the Ministry of the Interior. For the latter the Jews were an important and troublesome element of the scene with which they were professionally concerned. For the Foreign Ministry, in its sphere, they were negligible. The police function of the Ministry of the Interior inclined its people to deal with matters pragmatically and with a view to the best possible defence of the status quo. In the making of Russian foreign policy there was a large element of the ideological, the sentimental, and—in the case of the Near East, at any rate—the religious. N. G. von Hartwig, the head of the Asian Department of the Foreign Ministry, whom Herzl had seen at the end of his visit to St. Petersburg, doubled as president of the Russian Palestine Society, an organization devoted to the establishment of a Russian presence in Palestine through churchly means: monasteries, convents, pilgrimages, and missionary activities among the local population. In such eyes, the idea of the reintroduction of the Jews into the Holy Land was bound to appear retrogressive. In his conversation with Herzl, von Hartwig had made no secret of his reservations, nor of his special concern for the Holy Places. It is possible that Plehve's great prestige within the Government and the fact that Herzl had been given a clear and public

---

[49] Herzl to Plehve, 11[?] December 1903. *Diaries*, iv, pp. 1573-4.

[50] Herzl to Plehve, 4 January 1904. Ibid., pp. 1587-8.

[51] This was in accordance with the so-called Mürzsteg Programme of October 1903. It followed a brutal suppression by the Turks of increasingly violent and daring Macedonian insurrectionaries.

[52] Paulina Corwin to Herzl, 8 January 1904. Heymann, ii, no. 95, p. 220.

undertaking obliged the Foreign Minister, Count Nicholas Lamsdorff, to go part of the way with his colleague. But he might well have insisted on the undertaking being watered down and he would surely have seen no reason to regret the project being pigeon-holed subsequently in Constantinople. In any event, upon the outbreak of the war with Japan in February 1904, Russia ceased to be in a position to bring pressure to bear in Constantinople even had it truly wanted to. And with the defeat and humiliation of Russia in that war came a violent change for the worse in the regime's attitude to the Jews epitomized by the growing tendency in official circles to ascribe Russia's defeat to their machinations.[53]

In the end, however, everything turned on the question of emigration. That had been made clear to Herzl by the very terms of his invitation to Russia. It was repeated to him again and again during his stay there and once more in the letter of intent with which Plehve had provided him. It was re-affirmed when Lucien Wolf saw Plehve on 23 October and in

---

[53] Early in 1906 Lamsdorff submitted a position-paper to the Tsar in which he pressed for a Russo-German-Vatican alliance against the Jews. He argued, and the wording of the document suggests, that he genuinely believed, that 'our revolutionary movement is being actively supported and partly directed by the forces of universal Jewry' centred in 'the famous pan-Jewish universal union established in the year 1860, the "Alliance Israélite Universelle", with a Central Committee in Paris, which possesses gigantic pecuniary means, disposes of enormous membership, and is supported by the Masonic lodges of every description (according to some reports, they have again been carried into Russia in recent years), which represent the obedient organs of that universal organization. The principal aim of the "Alliance Israélite Universelle"— the all-round triumph of anti-Christian and anti-monarchist Jewry (which has already taken practical possession of France) by means of Socialism which is to serve as a bait for the ignorant masses—could not but find the State system of Russia—a land of peasants, Orthodoxy and monarchism—as obstacle in its path.' Text in Lucien Wolf (ed.), *Notes on the Diplomatic History of the Jewish Question* (London, 1919), pp. 59–60. The memorandum was thus entirely in the spirit of the *Protocols of the Elders of Zion*, the first full edition of which had just been published in Russia. Meanwhile there were changes in the Ministry of the Interior. The Russian official who was most probably the instigator of that famous forgery was P. Rachkovsky, head of the foreign arm of the *Okhrana* in Paris. He had been recalled by Plehve in 1902 (in connection with another intrigue) and subsequently dismissed without a pension. In 1905 (after Plehve's death) he was reinstated, however, and appointed to the post of assistant director of the Police Department in the Ministry of the Interior. Other anti-Semitic forgeries followed and it was during Rachkovsky's tenure that the Union of the Russian People was founded under official auspices as the spearhead of the new campaign against the Jews. But while the men of the Ministry of the Interior uttered forgeries, they did not often believe them.

very precise terms which Wolf took down during the interview and then submitted for confirmation and comment by the Minister before releasing them for publication. After reviewing the condition of the Jews and admitting that much had to be done to ease it, the Minister came to emigration as 'another remedy' for the great ill.

Hitherto emigration had been prohibited, [Wolf recorded,] but he believed a modification of the law in that respect was necessary. Perhaps other reforms might also be possible.

Apropos of emigration, M. de Plehve told me that the Russian Government would welcome permission granted by the Ottoman Government to Jews to enter Palestine. Hence he was not an adversary of pure Zionism; but he had begun to fear that political Zionism was no more than a chimera. Nevertheless he would not oppose the encouragement of Zionist ideas in Russia provided they favoured emigration. Besides, within Russia itself the Zionist ideas were perhaps useful in fighting those of socialism.[54]

Here at least Plehve's words have a sound and authentic ring. The evacuation of the Jews from Russia was a cause to which the regime had subscribed whole-heartedly for close to twenty years. It alone rendered legitimate the unprecedented (and surely controversial) decision to treat with the Zionists and grant them what were in effect special privileges. No doubt, as a good policeman, Plehve could see other advantages in his policy of informal toleration. By direct contact with the Zionists and by allowing much of their activity to surface, he and his men had already gained further insight into the affairs and mood of Russian Jewry. This would continue. Then, helping the Zionists was likely to speed up the separation of peaceful sheep from revolutionary goats. Thirdly, by linking minor relaxation of the May Laws to Herzl's intercession,[55] they may have hoped to strengthen the Zionist

---

[54] Text (of French original) in *Evreiskaya Starina*, ix (1916), pp. 123–5.

[55] Plehve's promise to Herzl and Wolf was made good in June 1904 when a bill redefining the permitted residential zone for Jews was extended right up to the frontier. Previously it had stopped 50 kilometres short of it. The main provisions of the May Laws and their subsequent amendments remained unchanged, however, as did the fundamental rule restricting the Jews to the ten provinces of Russian Poland and the 15 provinces of the Pale of Settlement.

hand within the community and the hands of the political Zionists specifically within the movement. One way or another it would all help to teach Russian Jews where their interests lay. In brief, there was here a logical and promising extension of the Zubatovite principle of moderate support for classes of the population which were potential reservoirs of revolutionaries. In it larger public purposes, the satisfaction of normal police requirements, and opportunities for political manipulation were all nicely combined.

Of course, there remained the large question of the direction that the Russian Zionists would eventually adopt. Would they finally follow Herzl's lead; or would they maintain the tendency that had been manifest at Minsk and concern themselves less and less directly and explicitly with the evacuation of the Jews in the shortest possible term and the greatest possible numbers and more and more with what, in the eyes of the *Okhrana*, was the cultivation of national feeling within an already dangerously self-conscious, unhappy, and politically turbulent minority? But large-scale emigration, as Herzl repeatedly reminded the Russians, was conditional in turn on a concession being granted by the Sultan.[56] Failure by the Russians to press 'Abd al-Ḥamid to grant the Zionists a Charter for Erez-Israel was self-defeating from their point of view; and it cut the ground from under Herzl himself in his dispute with the Russian practical-cultural school within the movement.

In July 1904 the two principals upon whom so much depended died: Herzl at the beginning of the month, Plehve (assassinated) at its end. The chapter in Russo-Jewish relations which had opened with the decision to permit the convening of the conference at Minsk ended inconclusively.

v

Herzl had two meetings with his followers while in Russia. The first was in St. Petersburg at the end of his stay there: a private meeting with a select group in the form of a banquet held in his honour. It was not in any sense a consultation. He did not report to them on his talks with Plehve and Witte. He did not ask for their advice; it was too late to hear it to any

[56] e.g. Herzl to Plehve, 24 October 1903. *Diaries*, iv, pp. 1568–70.

practical purpose anyway. Besides, no local leaders of the first rank were present.

What occurred, apart from an exchange of compliments, was a frank and sharp exchange of general views. Herzl warned his colleagues against following the example of the western Jews who had joined the fight for social progress and sacrificed much in the common cause—only to find in the end that they had helped to make one anti-Semite mayor of Vienna and another anti-Semite president of the Reichstag and had to live with the knowledge that in any conflict between Jew and non-Jew it was the latter who had the upper hand. The Jews, he told them, would do better to refrain from ploughing the fields of others. They should concern themselves with their own affairs. And there the only road was that of the Zionist *pur et dur*. It was not the case, he said, that one could be a Zionist and something else besides. A political movement must know its own limitations. To blur them was to inspire distrust. The Basel Programme was a clear and sufficient guide for all the purposes of *Zionism*. It should not be used by others as a cover for matters extraneous to those purposes. Once we were in our own country, an extreme socialist party could properly be established. When the time came he himself would take up a position in that respect. 'Those who say that my own views are very far from progressive, socialist ideas do me an injustice', Herzl said. 'But here, in present conditions, it is too early to be concerned with their realization.'[57]

Another source of confusion and weakness lay in Aḥad Ha-ʿAm's approach. Aḥad Ha-ʿAm, Herzl argued, was opposed to a Jewish state. He disbelieved in a territorial solution to the Jewish Problem in Erez-Israel and thought that the Jews would remain in the Diaspora and must make their social dispositions accordingly. Aḥad Ha-ʿAm did not subscribe to the *shekel* and was not a member of the Zionist movement. In all that he was consistent. But those who followed him and did adhere to the movement were confusing one doctrine with another, that of Zionism with something else.

The strongest spokesman for opposing views was Dr Julius Brutzkus, a leading member of the St. Petersburg Zionist

[57] *Die Neue Welt*, Vienna, 26 July 1929. Alex Bein and others (eds.), *Theodor Herzl; Ne'umim u-maʾamarim zioniim*, ii (Jerusalem, 1976), pp. 215–16.

circle, shortly to replace Belkowsky as GAC member for the capital. Brutzkus had been an early and fervent supporter of Herzl and of the political approach. But his confidence in the policy pursued from Vienna was tempered now by ever greater anxiety about the present state of Russian Jewry and by a desire to act positively and immediately to help and protect them. Since Kishinev he had been involved with others (among them non-Zionists) in the systematic collection of reliable information about the plight of the Jews and the behaviour of the Russian authorities and in its transmission to the West for publication. 'We cannot ignore present, day-to-day realities', he told Herzl. 'One cannot look without emotion at the terrible conditions in which our brethren live. I myself am now involved in current work [on their behalf]; but I am a Zionist none the less.'

Herzl stuck to his guns. 'For the present', he told Brutzkus and his friends, 'the Zionist's duty is the propagation of Zionism. So long as there is a Jew who is not a Zionist, we have our work to do—to turn him into one. Nothing that we may do to improve conditions in the Diaspora will end up bearing fruit.'[58]

Herzl's second meeting was of a different order. In Russia, thus far, he had met ministers, officials of the Government and of the court, various intermediaries, and members of the Zionist intelligentsia. With plain folk he had had no contact at all, only glimpses of them from the train on his journey to the capital. But on his way back to Austria he stopped in Vilna for some fourteen hours, 'the day of Vilna', as he called it in his diary, which he was sure would 'live in my memory forever', adding, for further emphasis, that this was 'no phrase from an after-dinner speech' (*keine Bankettphrase*).[59]

Over the years, Herzl had recorded a number of moments of high, private emotion in his diary: the first explosion of ideas for a solution to the Problem of the Jews, his first meeting with the miserable emigrants from eastern Europe in the East End of London, his thoughts in the immediate aftermath of the

[58] *Ha-Ẓeman* (St. Petersburg, 58, 13 August (26 August N.S.) 1903. Heymann, i, no. 61, pp. 95–8; S. Gepstein, 'Dr. Yulius Brutzkus', *Kazir* [i] (Tel-Aviv, 1964), pp. 200–6.
[59] *Diaries*, iv, p. 1543. *Tagebücher*, iii, p. 487.

foundation Congress in 1897.[60] But there is perhaps no passage in that extraordinary document quite as powerful as the record of his visit to Vilna: a few pages of fine, spare writing, the evidently intense feelings of brotherly pity for the wretched Jewish subjects of the Tsar carefully reined in, the scrupulously accurate descriptive detail.[61]

Vilna, the 'Jerusalem of Lithuania', had long been among the most prestigious of the great centres of rabbinical learning in the east European Diaspora, and latterly one of the great centres of the Jewish Enlightenment. It was one of the cities of the Empire in which Hibbat Zion had taken strong root. More recently, it had become the particular stronghold of the Bund as well. Its Jewish population was large, politically alert, and much of it, as we have seen, exceptionally poor. Communal organization and national feeling were strong. The Russian police authorities did not forbid Herzl to stop off at Vilna, but they did what could be done within the bounds of decorum to restrict their minister's guest in his contact with Vilna's Jewry. They rejected the local Zionist leaders' 'humble request' to entertain Herzl at a lunch for eighty people.[62] They took down the names of all those who came to call on Herzl at his hotel.[63] They eavesdropped on local Zionists' telephone calls.[64] They consistently broke up and dispersed the crowds of hundreds and then thousands that collected to catch a sight of Herzl. And from time to time they forced changes in his itinerary of visits, cutting out all direct communication with the Jewish working population.[65] Even a visit to one of the great synagogues was forbidden.[66]

Before leaving St. Petersburg Herzl had been warned by Zevi Bruck, the GAC member for Vitebsk, against going to Vilna, on the grounds that he would be given 'a bad time'

[60] See *Origins*, pp. 305–7.

[61] Herzl's account (*Diaries*, iv, pp. 1543–5) can be compared, for example, with a series of Russian police reports written during and immediately after his visit by officers of the middle rank of *pristav* (district inspector) (*Mi-Yamim Rishonim*, i (1935), pp. 63–72) and with a rare account by one of the young local Zionists invited to meet Herzl (Shemu'el Fishel Fronman, 'Herzl be-vilna' (Haifa, n.d.), unpublished).

[62] *Mi-Yamim Rishonim*, i, p. 63.

[63] Ibid., p. 65.

[64] Ibid., p. 66.

[65] Ibid., pp. 65–8 and *passim*; *Diaries*, iv, p. 1543.

[66] *Mi-Yamim Rishonim*, i, p. 65.

there in revenge for his having seen Plehve and spoken against the Bund. There was no knowing whether Bruck's warning had any foundation. Herzl ignored it anyway on the characteristic grounds that 'I wouldn't make myself so ridiculous as not to go to Vilna now that I had already announced it.'[67] In fact, the crowds came to cheer Herzl and were, as the police did not fail to remark in their reports with barely concealed surprise, entirely peaceful.

Meanwhile [reads a passage in the report submitted by *pristav* Vassilevich of Vilna's third quarter to the city's police commander], a rumour spread that Herzl would come to the great synagogue at two o'clock and also visit the synagogue library. I therefore hurried there with the officers under my command. Within minutes the synagogue courtyard had filled with Jews who had assembled from all parts of the city, especially young men, and when no room was left in the courtyard the Jews filled the neighbouring streets—Street of the Germans and Street of the Jews. There were about three thousand people in the crowd. They behaved politely, they did not disobey the police when ordered to disperse, but they came back again. Actually, they were, it seems, in a state of great emotion. When it was learned that Herzl would not visit the synagogue[68] . . . [and later] that he had returned to his hotel, the crowd refused to believe the news, and went away unwillingly, some back to work and some to the Georgy Hotel where Herzl was staying.[69]

The high point of the visit was a dinner-party at a summer-house some distance outside Vilna: fifty carefully selected guests within, an uninvited group of youths from Vilna who had walked all the way to see Herzl (and some detectives) outside. As *pristav* Vassilevich had noted earlier in the day, all were in a state of great emotion.

We walked about in the garden in the afternoon waiting for Herzl [recalled one of the guests]. Three o'clock already, then half past three. Still no Herzl. Then four o'clock. The suspense grows; then tension: a minute is like an hour, an hour like a day. We watch all the paths in the forest leading to Verki.

Suddenly, at about half past five, Herzl appears among the trees, alone—he had gone on ahead of his group and the trees had hidden

[67] Ibid., p. 1541.
[68] The police had forbidden him to do so.
[69] *Mi-Yamim Rishonim*, i, p. 67.

his companions. Herzl, straight and tall, magnificent to see as he approaches the first line of trees against the background of nature, a picture of glory that lasts a few instants until his companions emerged from the forest to join him, but which I shall never forget.[70]

Then dinner, speeches, Hebrew songs, a talk with the leader of the young Zionist workmen who had organized the deputation in defiance of the Bund, toasts in his honour, and finally back to Vilna. At one o'clock in the morning he was driven to the station.

The town was awake [Herzl wrote], awaiting my departure. The people stood and walked in the streets through which we had to pass, crying *hedad!* [hurrah!] as soon as they recognized me. The same from the balconies. But near the railroad station, where the crowds got denser, unfortunately there were clashes with the brutal police who had instructions to keep the station clear. It was a regulation Russian police manoeuvre which I saw with horror as my carriage rolled towards the station with increasing speed. Cries of *hedad*, brutal shouts of the policemen as they hurled themselves at intervals at the running crowd, and my driver lashing his horses.

At the station entrance, which was roped off, stood three police officers. The eldest, a white-bearded man, greeted me with submissive politeness.

A small group of people, about 50–60 of my friends, had nevertheless managed to smuggle themselves into the station. I was standing there quietly talking to them, when a police captain, followed by a sergeant, came through the restaurant with a great clanking of spurs. He occupied an observation post at a table behind us. When presently I took off my hat to bid my friends goodbye, he respectfully joined in the greeting.

Was this to be attributed to an order from St. Petersburg to protect me, or to the police officers' secret fear of the crowd?

Early in the morning at Eydtkuhnen I was met by a group of Zionists from the Russian frontier town.

One more speech, and a bouquet.

That was Russia.[71]

A little less than a year later, in May 1904, a police officer of the rank of colonel summed up the affair for the benefit of the governor of Vilna and looked a little way beyond it.

---

[70] Fronman, p. 3.

[71] *Diaries*, iv, pp. 1544–5.

The influence the doctrine of Zionism has had on the Jewish people was plain to see during the brief stay here in Vilna of Dr Herzl. For Vilna, in which there are 100,000 Jews,[72] it was a holiday: crowds of Jews in their holiday clothes received him as a king would be received, and it was necessary for the police to take particularly cunning steps to prevent the visit from leading to nationalist demonstrations on the Jews' part. The police now find it very difficult to keep track of Zionist propaganda. A great many charitable institutions are available to the Zionists, a great many trading enterprises, and a great many closed schools for beginners ('Talmudei-tora') over which the authorities have no control in practice. They are therefore able to propagate Zionism without recourse to secret meetings, more particularly because the gendarmerie has paid no attention thus far to the Zionist movement.[73] Given these conditions, Zionism has been absorbed into the consciousness of the people to such a degree that the police can no longer fight it; and moreover, to fight Zionism is to fight Jewry itself and would make relations between this people and the institutions of government very difficult.[74]

---

[72] The 1897 census put the number at about 60,000, and the total number of Jews for the province of Vilna at about 200,000.

[73] This was not true, as has been seen, although it may reflect local conditions in Vilna where the Bund was correctly seen as a much more serious and direct threat to the regime, and little energy was left for surveillance of the Zionists. That the Zionists were under some surveillance even in Vilna is attested to by many sources.

[74] *Mi-Yamim Rishonim*, i, p. 72.

PART THREE

Dissension

9

The Great Quarrel

By taking up Chamberlain's idea of a semi-autonomous Jewish settlement in East Africa Herzl drew the Zionist movement into a huge internal crisis—the first such, and arguably the greatest, it was to suffer. By the time it had died down some two years later the Zionist movement stood transformed: its leadership changed, its centre of gravity shifted, its purposes redefined, and, above all, its ethos and quality subtly, but crucially, altered. Much as Herzl had refashioned Hibbat Zion, so the crisis which he brought upon his own creation led to his work being remade; and thus it is only in the course of the so-called 'Uganda' affair and in its aftermath that the Zionist movement in its definitive form begins truly to be recognizable.

The surface events of the 'Uganda' affair are recounted in the present Chapter Nine. The underlying issues and their larger significance, grasped by the protagonists only imperfectly, if at all, are discussed in Chapter Ten. The concluding chapters of this book consider the consolidation of the new, post-Herzlian tendencies.

i

Herzl's decision to allow Greenberg to explore Chamberlain's proposal[1] was true to his set method. As the prospect of gaining British approval for the El Arish project faded, he would himself, no doubt, have sought a means of keeping the line to London open—by modifying the original idea or offering a new one, or by introducing mere trivia to keep a conversation going until something of substance turned up and the other side was induced to reconsider, or better still, moved to seriously examine the case for providing the Zionists with direct aid in their central endeavour. Only here, miraculously, even before the need to do any one of those things was un-

[1] See above, pp. 160–62.

mistakable and urgent, the great Joe Chamberlain himself had tossed something fresh on to the table; and if the Colonial Secretary's notion of what might serve as a 'beginning' for that territorial centre of which the Jews were clearly in need carried certain problems with it, he had met Herzl's immediate tactical requirements to perfection.

There were other grounds for following up Chamberlain's ideas, all soon adduced either by Greenberg or by Herzl himself. The Colonial Secretary was a powerful, but also a capricious man; there was the risk of offending him if his ideas were not taken to kindly. The Sixth Congress was due in August and with it the need to show progress. 'We have been beating the drum for four years in a row and we must now attain something positive if we are not to suffer the curse of ridiculousness', Mandelstamm had written in anticipation of the last Congress two years earlier where things had not gone too well.[2] Would they go better this time? What, apart from the collapse of the El Arish project, would there be to show for all the energy expended in the meanwhile. East Africa was not Erez-Israel; not (like El Arish) even remotely so. Whether it could truly serve the immediate needs of migrants from eastern Europe as a refuge and a source of livelihood—quite apart from their national aspirations—was still to be determined. But it was a *British* idea, and it did imply, as Greenberg pointed out, 'recognition of the necessity for aiding our people as a whole . . . and hence', he concluded, it would 'be the first recognition of our people as a Nation'. Indeed, seen in that light, it might not matter if nothing ever came of it. The main thing was that a form of recognition had been granted, following which the British might eventually make 'a further suggestion, and this, it is possible, will gradually and surely lead us to Palestine'.[3] Defeat over El Arish had not yet been openly conceded by the Zionists and a talk with Sanderson at the Foreign Office in June showed that that scheme was not entirely dead on the British side either.[4] Still, it was plain that nothing was likely to come of it for a long time, probably for

[2] To Herzl, 5 May 1901. CZA, H VIII/541.

[3] Greenberg to Herzl, 1 June 1903. Oskar K. Rabinowicz, 'New Light on the East Africa Scheme', in Israel Cohen (ed.), *The Rebirth of Israel* (London, 1952), p. 78.

[4] Robert G. Weisbord, *African Zion* (Philadelphia, 1968), pp. 70–1.

years. So if in the meanwhile here was Chamberlain 'offering us an area for colonization large enough for a million souls, with *local self-government*',[5] the upshot, perhaps inevitably, was a decision to take it up. Herzl authorized Greenberg to provide the British with a draft agreement to serve as a basis for discussion with the Foreign Office (still responsible for the African protectorates) and the services of David Lloyd George, Member of Parliament, as a solicitor who was at home in the world of politics and reputedly knew a good deal about East Africa, were obtained to help draw it up. It took some weeks for the document to be prepared. In its final form, it was submitted to Chamberlain on 13 July and transferred by him to the Foreign Office for action. The Greenberg-Lloyd George draft contained a long preamble setting out the general principles and purposes of the scheme, provision for an expedition to make a survey of the proposed territory, rules for the control and management of lands within the territory, and fourteen separate clauses regulating its internal regime—the first of which laid down that there would be established 'a form of popular government in the territory which shall be Jewish in character and with a Jewish Governor to be appointed by His Majesty in Council'.[6] The proposal was examined by the Foreign Secretary Lord Lansdowne, Sir Clement Hill, Superintendent of African Protectorates, and C. J. B. Hurst, Assistant Legal Advisor to the Foreign Office.

The response of the Foreign Office was cool. They were quick to see it as a 'scheme which appears . . . to contemplate the creation of an *imperium in imperio* which would be anomalous and, to say the least, inconvenient'.[7] Hurst summed up their findings:

There would, I suppose, be no objection to a Jewish colony, if it was subject to the ordinary laws of the Protectorate. Those laws provide power to confer upon a settlement sufficient autonomy to enable its inhabitants, if they were all Jews, to live their own life and develop

---

[5] *Diaries*, iv, p. 1498. Emphasis in text.

[6] 'Jewish Colonization Scheme, Terms and Conditions of Concessions to be granted by His Majesty's Government to the Jewish Colonial Trust (Juedische Colonialbank) Limited for the establishment of a Jewish Settlement in British East Africa'. Rabinowicz, 'New Light etc.', pp. 81–91.

[7] Minute by Hill, 20 July 1903. Rabinowicz, 'New Light etc.', p. 91.

their national characteristics without being troubled by outsiders.

If the promoters are looking for more than this and want a petty State of their own, something more than townships or municipalities, the scheme would, I think, be open to great objection . . .

The scheme they have sent in seems to me to go further than is reasonable, and I should have thought, further than was necessary for their purposes.[8]

None the less, when Greenberg was called in and shown these comments he made no attempt to fight them directly, for all that he saw a danger of the plan being reduced to 'a small piddling scheme of a few settlements each with a municipality'.[9] He preferred to rely on Chamberlain to keep to the original general conception—and not unreasonably: for Chamberlain continued to assure the Zionists of his goodwill and the Foreign Office, for its part, saw the project throughout as something fathered by the Colonial Secretary. Besides, Greenberg's immediate concern, as he explained, was to get a statement of British intent soon enough for the forthcoming Congress, due to convene on 23 August. But this was far too soon for the bureaucracy to work out all the details and for a firm commitment to be made by the Government. Sir Charles Eliot, Commissioner in Mombasa, still had to be consulted. The general location of the territory to be made available still had to be decided upon. Even its optimum extent had not been fixed. 'The idea suggested by Mr. Chamberlain was a district near the Mau escarpment of about 200 miles square [i.e. 40,000 squares miles]. It might not be advisable to take so great an area at once', Lansdowne's Private Secretary noted, 'but the colony should have the power of spreading to that extent.'[10] But the Foreign Office was not inflexible. There was no objection to a formal promise of assistance to any survey party that might be sent out, nor, after further pressure by Greenberg, to the formulation of a 'contingent agreement', that is to say, a general statement of what the British Government was prepared to envisage in principle, subject to a suitable site being found and to the method of its administra-

[8] Minute by Hurst, 23 July. Ibid., pp. 91–2.
[9] Greenberg to Herzl, 9 August 1903. Ibid., p. 93.
[10] Minute by Sir Eric Barrington, 6 August 1903. Ibid., p. 92.

tion being agreed upon. The result was a formal letter of 14 August from Hill to Greenberg, along lines proposed by Hurst and amended by Lansdowne, and a copy was sent to Chamberlain on Sir Eric Barrington's instruction 'so that he may see that his wishes have been carried out'.[11]

I am now directed by [the Marquis of Lansdowne] to say that he has studied the question with the interest which His Majesty's Government must always take in any well-considered scheme for the amelioration of the position of the Jewish Race. The time at his disposal has been too short to enable him to go fully into the details of the plan or to discuss it with His Majesty's Commissioner for the East Africa Protectorate, and he regrets that he is therefore unable to pronounce any definite opinion in the matter.

He understands that the Jewish Colonial Trust desire to send some gentlemen to the East Africa Protectorate, who may ascertain personally whether there are any vacant lands suitable for the purposes in question, and, if this is so, he will be happy to give them every facility . . .

If a site can be found which the Trust and His Majesty's Commissioner consider suitable and which commends itself to His Majesty's Government, Lord Lansdowne will be prepared to entertain favourably proposals for the establishment of a Jewish colony or settlement, on conditions which will enable the members to observe their National customs. For this purpose he would be prepared to discuss . . . the details of a scheme comprising as its main features: the grant of a considerable area of land, the appointment of a Jewish Official as chief of the local administration, and permission to the Colony to have a free hand in regard to municipal legislation and as to the management of religious and purely domestic matters, such Local Autonomy being conditional upon the right of His Majesty's Government to exercise general control.[12]

With Hill's letter in his pocket Greenberg arrived in Basel in good time for the Congress. He had built on Herzl's meetings with Chamberlain and had had Herzl's approval for all his moves. Still, it was his energy and his person that had now been applied and had brought forth this result. But Herzl himself, remote from London and always quick to question Greenberg's judgement and the accuracy of his reporting, had

[11] Minute by Barrington, 18 August 1903. Ibid., p. 96.
[12] Sir Clement Hill to Leopold Greenberg, 14 August 1903. *Protokoll VI*, pp. 215–16.

been throughout somewhat less sanguine about the scheme. He had been slower than Greenberg to begin to regard it as a truly useful measure in its own right, rather than as yet another lever to slip into the larger, vastly more intricate mechanism by which the Jews were to be enabled to enter Erez-Israel in mass and as of right. As the negotiations with the Foreign Office proceeded and the project took on a life (of sorts) of its own, he had begun, moreover, to dimly anticipate the objections, misunderstandings, and general trouble it might bring in its wake. In June, when the members of the GAC were finally informed (in confidence) that 'efforts to acquire Egyptian Palestine were at an end for the time being, unfortunately with negative results', he told them nothing of what was in store, only that there would be a report on current 'efforts' (their nature unspecified) at the regular meeting to be convened just prior to the Congress.[13] With Nordau Herzl was more forthcoming, although, even with him, reluctantly and by stages. At first he asked Nordau to devote his regular address to the Congress to the matter of migration in general— evidently to prepare the ground at the Congress for what was to follow—but without explaining his intention. Nordau refused. Migration was the greatest and most urgent of the problems of modern Jewry, he replied, but he knew nothing about it in detail and mere rhetoric on the subject would bring only discredit to Herzl and himself. To deal with it adequately one had to provide answers to certain questions. Should the impoverished Jew stay put, or should he migrate? If so, where to? Should he set off alone and have his dependants follow after, or should he take them with him? Who was to advise him? Who was to pay his passage? Who was to lead him on his way? Who was to receive him upon arrival at his destination? Who was to put him in touch with the local community? 'I have no answer to a single one of these incisive [*einschneidenden*] questions; and yet I am supposed to be so unworthily frivolous as to make a speech about them.'[14]

Herzl replied that the Sultan had to be shown that the Jews would and could go elsewhere if Erez-Israel was finally forbidden them; and beyond that, the Zionists had to come to

[13] EAC circular to GAC, 12 June 1903. CZA, Z 1/212.
[14] Nordau to Herzl, 2 July 1903. CZA, H VIII/615.

grips with the question of migration one way or another, because of its immensity, because the Jews were desperate for relief, because an answer to Kishinev had to be given.[15] But Nordau was unconvinced. Are we supposed to say, he retorted, 'Brothers, you must emigrate!' and then remain speechless when asked, 'Where to?' As for dropping Erez-Israel as an immediate goal of emigration, of that he thought poorly too. It would make no impression on the Sultan. And the impression on the Zionist Organization would be disastrous. The result would be disruption within the movement and a triumph for its enemies.[16]

When Herzl now stated the facts of the East Africa case[17] the response—the first reaction to the scheme from someone outside the tiny circle of those directly involved in the negotiations—was of extreme severity, evidently written at white heat by a man who could scarcely contain himself for outrage and disapproval. It would be a tremendous error, Nordau wrote, to obtain a Charter for 'Uganda'. The Jewish people would not follow Herzl there, however much they might be tempted by a blue-and-white flag. If they could not go to Erez-Israel and if they could not remain in the countries of their persecution, it was to England, America, or Australia, not tropical Africa, they would seek to go. The land in question was unsuitable for settlement except in the manner that Chamberlain evidently envisaged, by planters and overseers of black labour, by people who returned to Europe at regular intervals and who exploited it, rather than made it their true home. As such the tract in question would serve ten thousand families at most. Besides, it was inhabited by 'warlike Negro tribes' which neither the English nor the Germans had succeeded in overcoming to this day and the mortality rate there was likely to be high. In short, as a temporary haven 'Uganda' was valueless, while as a land of permanent settlement it would be disastrous for the Jews and for Zionism. Far from serving as a school for their re-education as a political nation, it would be, at best, a club, albeit with an emblem of its own and with just such internal autonomy as any club or limited company might

[15] Alex Bein, *Theodore Herzl* (Philadelphia, 1940), pp. 443–4.

[16] Nordau to Herzl, 10 July 1903. CZA, H VIII/615.

[17] Herzl to Nordau, 13 July 1903. CZA, HB/10.

enjoy. There remained the argument that it would provide
Zionism with some practical result to show for all the expenditure of effort over the years. But that argument was hollow too,
wrote Nordau, an argument for the impatient and the panic-
stricken. For the result of it all would be that nothing of value
would have been done for the Jews and the Zionist movement
would be destroyed.

Nine-tenths or ninety-nine-hundredths would leave. Some would
become Hovevei Zion, others Aḥad Ha-ʾAmites or Weizmannite
culture-Zionists; and all would be over with the political Zionism of
the Basel Programme, the Congress, and the Actions-Committee. . . .
You have already seen that your original plan for a Jewish state,
which suited me well, had to be transformed into the Basel Zionist
plan because the Jewish people was not to be had for it. The Jewish
people will show even less enthusiasm for the new plan for an equa-
torial Charter.

It was true that there had been no progress with the Turks, but
that was not reason to despair. What were a mere six years of
political Zionism when the Exile had lasted nineteen centuries?
He, Nordau, would say not a word against the plan publicly;
but, 'For Heaven's sake', he pleaded, 'let us have no acts of
panic, nothing precipitate or rash, nothing done in a spasm
under the compulsion of an idea.'[18]

   Herzl's answer to Nordau's blast of disapproval was mild,
apologetic, intensely personal, in places even tender in tone,
and a great deal less orderly in composition than was usual
for him—evidence perhaps of his weariness and steadily
declining health. But on the central issue he was unyielding.
It was impossible to reject Chamberlain's offer out of hand.
It had been years since the movement had acquired so powerful
a friend. The Charter itself had not yet been granted, still
less had it been accepted. If and when it was accepted it would
be possible to determine precisely who went to Africa and
how much or how little it was advisable to do there. If it turned
out (contrary to Nordau's supposition) that the territory was
suitable for large-scale settlement after all, the movement
would 'have achieved a worthy power-base' and be strengthened

[18] Nordau to Herzl, 17 July 1903. CZA, H VIII/615.

thereby. If it was found to be unsuitable, there would still have been achieved

that which we had not had before: a Charter! which is to say, recognition! Our road to Zion will have to be paved with Charters. And I can then present this *state treaty* as a model—particularly [to the] Sultan!—and that will carry enormous weight. Rulers too are snobs. [Thus] we shall have ceased to be lepers.[19]

For Herzl this was the nub of the matter: a tract of land in East Africa as a moral and political—and only incidentally an actual and material—staging post on the way to Erez-Israel. The need to meet and counter Nordau's criticism may have forced him to define his views somewhat more precisely and fortified him in his determination to pursue them. But Herzl had been thinking for some time that it might be well to seek a series of 'power-bases' [*Kraftstationen*] as a temporary substitute for the Turkish Charter and, cumulatively, as a means of gaining international status for Zionism and for the Jews in general. Desultory exchanges with the Portuguese were in progress; the possibility of an arrangement with King Leopold of the Belgians for a tract in the Congo was looked into and then hastily dropped. The East Africa project, apart from its other attractions, was in line with these two and much more promising. But it is worth noting too that these were matters—even that of East Africa, to some extent—which he tended to handle in a somewhat routine, not to say offhand manner or to leave partly in the hands of others. This was uncharacteristic. There may be read in it a sign of his declining health. No doubt, in the case of contacts with the British, the barriers of language and distance and his obligation to be in the editorial offices of the *Neue Freie Presse* for the better part of the year helped to keep him away from London. Partly too, it may be surmised, the scope of projects such as these was inherently too limited to fire him. But chiefly, as the summer of 1903 drew on, it was Russia that increasingly absorbed him—

---

[19] Herzl to Nordau, 19 July 1903. CZA, H III/A3. Emphasis in text. Nordau remained unconvinced, repeated his promise not to oppose Herzl in public, and left the question of the address to the Congress that Herzl had planned for him in abeyance. Nordau to Herzl, 22 July 1903. CZA, H VIII/615.

by the end of July of that year completely so. At that point
his diary, his letters, the energy and certainty of mind with
which he conducted his talks with the Russian ministers, the
composure with which he met both his supporters and his
critics inside Russia—in sum, all the evidence—testify to the
absolute moral and intellectual confidence with which he set
about to attack the *Judenfrage* at its contemporary geographical
and political centre and in what he had always believed to be
the sole mode likely to bring lasting results. In contrast, in the
matter of East Africa, with its instrumental rather than direct
rationale, his touch throughout is somewhat less sure, his mind
a shade less resolute. When the GAC met for its first pre-
Congress session on 21 August it was on his journey to Russia
that Herzl first reported and in most detail. He then spoke on
the El Arish scheme, its objective possibilities, the effort to
gain acceptance for it, and the reasons for its collapse. Only
at the end of his presentation did he come to East Africa—
briefly, if the minutes can be taken as an accurate reflection
of the course of the proceedings, even cursorily, if Tchlenov,
a critical, yet not totally unfriendly witness, is to be believed.[20]
Was this a sign that he had taken Nordau's objections to
heart after all? Was he consciously or unconsciously playing
down East Africa in anticipation of trouble ahead? Or was he
merely waiting for the full Congress to assemble before bringing
the matter to a head, so as to have before him a forum in which
the weight of his actual and potential critics would be greatly
reduced, if not dissipated? Meanwhile, the immediate
reaction at the GAC itself was too mixed to point the way.
There seems to have been an exchange of comments, rather
than anything resembling a debate, in which some approved
without reserve and some objected. But no lines were drawn
and there was no real hostility, no real indicators of what was
to follow. Herzl complained in his diary that 'I presented
England and Russia. And it didn't occur to any of them for
even a single moment that for these greatest of all accomplishments to date I deserved a word, or even a smile, of thanks.'[21]
But that with Plehve's and Hill's letters in his hand he could

---

[20] 'Protokoll der Sitzung des grossen A.C.' (Friday, 21 August 1903). CZA, Z 1/193.
In Heymann, i, pp. 101–4; and p. 103, fn. 4.

[21] *Diaries*, iv, p. 1547.

enter the Congress hall in triumph he did not doubt. Not one of the preceding Congresses had begun so auspiciously. Never before had he come so close to meeting that 'lack of inner satisfaction due to an urge to positive action' of which one of his supporters had written to him a few days earlier.[22]

ii

The great irony about the Sixth Congress of Zionists (at Basel, 23–8 August 1903) was that it was the occasion both of a defeat for Herzl and of a triumph for his child, the Zionist Congress itself. The Congress was confirmed as the autonomous parliament of the Jewish Risorgimento and Herzl's discomfiture served to prove the validity of the event. Yet there had been nothing in the preliminaries leading up to the Congress, nor in its composition, nor in its internal arrangements, to suggest that it was likely to be remarkable in any way. It was planned as the longest (six days) held thus far; but that was coincidental. It was in fact the largest held during the first fifty years of the life of the movement (1,100 delegates elected, some 600 actually present), but that was a fluke—a consequence of a failure to change the constituency rules with the growth of the Organization.[23] The published agenda was bland and routine. Several well-known figures stayed away, among them Gaster, Motzkin, and Ussishkin. The press (with the

---

[22] E. S. Soskin to Herzl, 16 August 1903. CZA, H VIII/755. Soskin, a trained agronomist, had been a member of the committee of inquiry to El Arish. His idea (like that of Ussishkin and many others) was that the 'urge to positive action' should be satisfied by settlement work in Erez-Israel.

[23] Figures for the early years of the movement were notoriously imprecise: partly because many elected delegates failed to attend (usually because they could not afford to make the long journey), partly because particularly well-known figures were often elected for more than one constituency (Herzl and Nordau, for example, had both been elected by a Russian (more strictly, Bessarabian) constituency, Kishinev), but also because of minor administrative disorder. In round numbers, between 200 and 250 delegates attended the First Congress, 350 the Second, 150 the Third, 500 the Fourth, and 350 the Fifth. The figure usually quoted for the Sixth is 592, while Georg Herlitz, *Das Jahr der Zionisten* (Jerusalem-Luzern, 1949), p. 139, gives 571. But it is reasonably certain that over 600 participated in the roll-call vote or were present at Basel but abstained from voting on the fourth day of that Congress. In any event, it was a very large number and it was therefore decided towards the end of the Sixth Congress to double the size of the single-member constituency (hitherto 100 delegates). Some 500 delegates attended the Seventh Congress, 300 the Eighth. On attendance at the Sixth Congress and the voting, see Appendix, pp. 479–94.

single exception of the *Jewish Chronicle*[24]) carried no hint of
what would prove to be the chief business of the Congress. It
was generally known that the negotiations at Constantinople
the year before had failed and that the more recent ones in
London on El Arish had not, at any rate, succeeded. It was
expected that reports on these matters would be forthcoming.
But for the rest, it was far from clear to what precisely the
Congress was expected to address itself, apart from routine
business—unless it was to those matters that the opposition,
particularly the Russian opposition, had been calling for ever
more loudly: to cultural and educational activities, to settlement work in Erez-Israel, and to the here and now of distressed
Jewry *in the Diaspora*, as opposed to the radical, speculative,
and distant solutions to which Herzl bent his energies. Such,
at all events, seem to have been the common expectations in the
Russian wing.[25]

In the event, it was to the unanticipated and unannounced
item of business, the East Africa scheme, on which all attention
was riveted as soon as the word went out of what was in the
offing. Even the matter of Herzl's journey to Russia, topped
by the publication in *Die Welt* of the full text of Plehve's
letter, was eclipsed. The Congress's planned agenda was not
abandoned; but interest in the items composing it dwindled
rapidly, the sessions devoted to them being reduced to little
more than entr'actes providing some release of tension between
the bits of furious action through which the central plot un-
folded and a means of keeping the rank and file decently

---

[24] In a report date-lined Basel, 18 August (two days before Herzl arrived) and published 21 August, the *Jewish Chronicle*'s special correspondent at the Congress wrote:
'The Actions Committee have, however, a "clou", as the French call it, and this is
being kept a secret, for if it is made public at all it will be in the shape of official dispatches, "sealed, signed and delivered". I would, however, not be surprised if, should
a definite statement be made, it takes the form of the recognition of the Zionist movement by one of the greatest of the Great Powers and an independent offer to help in
the solution of the Jewish Question. Since it will take all the statesmanship in Zionism
to reject or accept such an offer, the whole affair may be buried in Committee. And
yet this is hardly possible, and so the Congress may witness some remarkable passages.
Much will depend upon the situation in Russia. Should it prove so intense as to demand
immediate action, the Zionist movement may take some rapid strides.' The most
probable source of the leak was Greenberg.

[25] Cf. Naḥum Slouschz, 'Hashkafa'al ha-kongres ha-shishi', i, *Ha-Meliz*, 9 September
1903.

occupied while further battles were fought between the major protagonists off-stage.

The managers of the Congress, with Herzl at their head, had not expected this shift of attention. They had not anticipated the intensity of the reaction to the new scheme and had made no appropriate dispositions. They had therefore to improvise. In practice, Herzl and his friends first had to understand that a large opposition had formed and then had to recognize its true weight and grasp its likely influence. They then had to seek to reduce it—or, alternatively, to meet it—by argument, by manœuvre, and, when absolutely necessary, by compromise. All this took time and, on the whole, events outpaced their understanding. Meanwhile tension mounted and tempers rose on all sides and the opposition consolidated further. The speed with which it was pulled together in defiance of Herzl accorded, of course, with the intensity of the reaction to what Herzl was proposing. But it was primarily fruit of the long, slow build-up of inimical ideological and political positions that had been in progress, as we have seen, from the moment the curtain was rung down on the inaugural Congress six years earlier. It is also important to note that the protagonists were differently placed and the fight between them distinctly asymmetrical.

Within the great body of men and women gathered at the Congress two circles of substantial political influence obtained. One was made up of Herzl's loyal following: his friends, his immediate collaborators, his original supporters. In their case, criticism of Herzl, when there was criticism, tended strongly and rapidly to be offset by sentiment, by gratitude and appreciation for what he had done, by the feeling that he deserved the benefit of the doubt, and, in the last resort, by the conviction that he was plainly and literally irreplaceable. But however strong the feelings that pervaded Herzl's following, it itself remained devoid of set structure, let alone formal, institutional foundation. It was not a party, or a caucus, or even a cabal. Its members would not have recognized themselves as belonging to a distinctive *group*. Their background was diverse: Mandelstamm and Avinovitzky were from Russia, Greenberg and Cowan from England, Bodenheimer from Germany, Nordau's origins were much like Herzl's.

They were men of varied stature and influence: Nordau was a giant compared with Avinovitzky or even Bodenheimer. None had a significant following of his own. In a separate category there was Rabbi Reines and his following in the Mizraḥi; but he and it were immiscible with the rest.

In contrast, the opposition to Herzl, at all events that part of it that was active and resolute, was largely (not exclusively) Russian. It was therefore possessed of certain common social and historical characteristics. It had been taking shape ever more clearly over half a decade or so—a substantial period of time for so young a movement. Its more distant origins were in Ḥibbat Ẓion; its present posture owed much to the exhilarating experience of repeated opposition itself, ever more conscious and articulate as time went by. Moreover, the Russian opposition, unlike the established leadership, did have a recognized institutional base in the *Landsmannschaft* or caucus, the country delegation—in their case the largest, most coherent, and most effective of such delegations. Its individual members were used to meeting together to consider policy in advance of the Congresses as well, of course, as during them. The sense of common identity and common destiny was very strong and had been immensely fortified by the Minsk conference the year before. The easy and comparatively intimate atmosphere of the caucus was conducive to matters being thrashed out more freely, less temperately, but also more throughly than in the dignified plenum of the Congress. It was therefore in caucus that the lines were most tightly drawn and the fundamental and seemingly irrevocable commitments tended to be made. It was also in caucus that the bolder spirits moved most easily to the fore and the timid and hesitant learned to follow their example. In sum, it was within the Russian caucus that the opposition to Herzl was strongest and loudest and had the greatest capacity to mobilize support. The opposition differed from the circle of loyalists around Herzl in two further, cardinal respects. It had no acknowledged and truly effective leader. The perennial aspirant to its leadership, Ussishkin, was absent, moreover, on the present occasion. Nor had any of its principal members much influence outside the Russian delegation.

All these circumstances lent visible coherence to the opposition, while keeping it short of the capacity actually to have its own way. For the rest, the upshot was that the great issue on which the Congress was to be divided thus came to be articulated in, and mediated through, a variety of formal and informal forums: the Congress plenum itself, the full GAC, the country delegations (or caucuses), and *ad hoc* gatherings of Herzl's closest collaborators, of the Russian members of the GAC, and of a special committee formed out of the full Russian caucus and reporting to it among others. And in that variety may be seen two of the salient characteristics of the Zionist movement at the time. One was the pre-eminence of Herzl the individual as evinced in the contrast between the solitary figure of the true maker of the movement's policy up to that point and the *group* of militants of the second rank arrayed against him. The other was the final coming into its own of the Congress as a parliament, as that supreme legislator of the movement that Herzl had envisaged from the first. For throughout the whole extended and convoluted debate, what appeared to most of those present to matter in the end was the vote taken in the plenum. Indeed, not the least of the pointers to the seriousness with which the delegates approached the question that had been put before them and the political institution of which they formed the membership was the fact that virtually the entire body participated in the final vote. In this sense Herzl's unique creation now came fully to life.

Initially, as has been suggested, Herzl does not seem to have doubted that he would gain what he wanted at the Congress, namely a free hand to explore the East Africa scheme, provided only it was presented with care. It was at the Congress that he was most powerful and could play the solo role in which he was most comfortable. In the GAC, which was not a Cabinet under his leadership, but a parliament in little composed mostly of leaders in their own right—even if all on a lesser scale than he—he was a good deal weaker. *Care* in presentation meant both gaining a proper show of support for the scheme from the notables of the movement and maintaining a line of argument at all levels that would make crystal-clear what was at issue and, more particularly, what was not. But once the advantage of surprise—as at the first meeting of the GAC on Friday 21 August—had been lost, and the members of the inner circle had had time to collect their thoughts and to enter into formal and informal consultations (with and without Herzl himself), it became evident to him that too few of the leading personalities were sufficiently receptive to his central argument for the notables as a class to be relied upon. It became equally evident to the objectors— in some cases to their surprise—that Herzl was not to be moved by what they had to say to him. So when the Congress opened on Sunday morning (23 August), although the great majority of the delegates were still ignorant of what was in the offing, the ground for the fight to come had already been largely staked out.

Herzl's opening speech was a masterly précis of his case cast in the terms he thought appropriate for public consumption: relatively brief, devoid of rhetoric (except where he referred to Kishinev), clear in internal logic—namely, that everything must be tried and something must be done— guarded only when touching on the details of negotiations, and a little less than frank when referring directly to foreign governments ('His Majesty the Sultan continues to be kindly disposed to the Jewish people.'). But its underlying tone was apologetic; and the crux of his argument was that hard times dictated fresh thought and, possibly, unanticipated measures, and that the Congress would have to address itself to the resulting dilemmas. If the situation of the Jews had changed, he began, it was for the worse. The people were in danger, helpless in the face of massacre. There had been Kishinev and there were other Kishinevs, in Russia and outside it. 'Kishinev exists wherever Jews undergo bodily or spiritual torture, wherever their self-respect is injured and their property despoiled because they are Jews. Let us save those who can still be saved!' For twenty years it had been thought that the panacea for these ills was emigration. But now the receiving countries were 'beginning to resist . . . *because* the misery of east European Jewry is increasing' and with it the flow of migrants. Now England too, the last refuge to be open unconditionally, had begun to cast about for a method of stemming that flow. And therein, with its greater appreciation of the problem, had lain the basis in England for a fuller understanding of the Zionist purpose.

As the present Congress approached, things had looked dark. The talks in Constantinople had not succeeded. The fresh departure taken in London when the proposal that a concession be granted in the Sinai peninsula was put before 'several members of the British Cabinet' in October of the previous year 'had been well received'. Yet in the end, for all the goodwill and the help offered by the British and Egyptian Governments to the commission of inquiry sent to Sinai, the project had been turned down. At that point, Herzl continued, the British officials with whom he had been in touch proposed another tract of land for Jewish settlement.

The new territory does not have the historic, poetical-religious, and Zionist value that even the Sinai Peninsula would have had, but I do not doubt that the Congress, acting as the representative of the entire Jewish people, will receive the new offer with the warmest gratitude . . . Considering the plight of Jewry and the immediate necessity of finding some way to ameliorate this plight as much as possible, I did not feel justified, when this proposal was made, in doing other than obtaining permission to submit it to the Congress.

For the Congress to consider it, the matter had to be put in a suitably precise and concrete form. And there had been discussions with British officials to that end.

I do not want to anticipate the views of the Congress on the policy which the Zionist movement wishes to pursue with respect to these proposals. However, although it is evident that the Jewish people can have no ultimate goal other than Palestine, and although our views on the land of our fathers are and must remain unchangeable whatever the fate of this proposal may be, the Congress will recognize the extraordinary progress that our movement has made through the negotiations with the British government . . . I believe the Congress can find a way to make use of this offer. The way in which this offer was made to us is bound to help, improve and alleviate the situation of the Jewish people without our abandoning any of the great principles on which our movement was founded.

He then expressed the gratitude that he was sure all felt 'for the statesmanlike benevolence which Great Britain has

evinced toward the Jewish people', at which point the applause
which had interrupted him from time to time during his
speech doubled and redoubled on the floor and in the gallery
and the stenographer reported Zangwill calling out, 'Three
cheers for England!' and the Congress responding enthusias-
tically, hats and handkerchiefs waving, and the entire assembly
rising to its feet.

Herzl then went on to deal with his journey to Russia, the
other new development. He had spoken there, he told the
Congress, not for the Zionists alone, but for all the Jews in
Russia. He had been at pains to press for an alleviation of
their plight and had received some assurances in that respect.
Of yet greater importance were the assurances he had received
in respect of the Zionist movement directly: the Russian
Government would place no obstacles in its path 'provided
the movement retains its customary quiet and lawful character'; the Government would co-operate in the raising of
funds for 'emigration directed by the Zionists'; and finally,
and most important of all, 'the Russian government is willing
to use its influence with H.M. the Sultan in supporting our
efforts to obtain Palestine.' Once again: thunderous applause,
the entire assembly rising to its feet. '[Thus] not only has a
tremendous obstacle been removed', Herzl concluded, 'but
powerful aid is at hand. Its effects, to be sure, are yet to be
seen, but now we can continue to strive for Ereẓ-Israel with
renewed courage and with brighter prospects than ever
before.'[26]

Herzl refrained from mentioning by name any of the British
ministers and civil servants he and Greenberg had talked to.
Nor did he refer to Hill's letter or to any of the specific points
raised in the talks in London except to remark that 'the proposal involves an autonomous Jewish settlement in East
Africa with a Jewish administration, Jewish local government
headed by a Jewish senior official, everything, of course,
under the sovereign jurisdiction of Great Britain.' Such was
the case with Russia too, with which he dealt briefly anyway.
Plehve was not mentioned nor (as yet) was Plehve's letter.

[26] *Protokoll VI*, pp. 3–10. The English translation used here, with minor modifica-
tions, is in Theodor Herzl, *Zionist Writings* (trans. Harry Zohn, New York, 1975),
ii, pp. 221–30.

But then, he was only reporting on his efforts in St. Petersburg as he had reported from time to time on his efforts in Constantinople and Berlin. He did not ask for approval. East Africa was in a different category. He had put the matter to the Congress and his specific request was for the election of 'a small committee to deal with the entire matter'.

There was no sign that Herzl was aware of the apparent contradiction between the proposed departure from all previous thinking and planning in Zionism which was implicit in the East Africa project and the fresh hopes for progress over Erez-Israel raised by the prospect of Russian support. Or if he was, he did not think it a true contradiction. For, the one he presented as a short-term expedient with undoubted long-term implications and the other as pertaining to the permanent, long-term ends for which Zionists were duty-bound to strive. In tandem, they were characteristic of his political method: try everything within reason, advance on as broad a front as possible, seek to turn every gain, no matter how minute or peripheral, to advantage, and keep your eyes throughout on that central purpose which the Foreign Office had just defined as 'the amelioration of the position of the Jewish Race'.

However, no formal resolution was put before the Congress as yet and the East Africa question, along with Herzl's request for a select committee to deal with it, was now taken up informally in the lobbies and formally in the principal country delegations.[27] Except among the Russians, the tendency was to agree to a committee being formed, if only because it fell a great deal short of a commitment one way or the other. Within the Russian caucus it was opposed because the identical judgement led, in their eyes, to the opposite conclusion, namely that the appointment of such a committee implied a kind of neutrality or indifference on the matter of Erez-Israel and that such neutrality was impermissible. There followed a succession of immensely long, fatiguing, and often very noisy[28] private debates over which Tchlenov did his best to preside and out of which he sought to distil agreement—more in the

---

[27] The intricate course of events during the Congress and after is analysed admirably in Heymann, ii, pp. 5–61.

[28] The caucus had to be warned at least twice against disturbing the sleep of the citizens of Basel.

style of a foreman of a jury than a political leader in his own right.[29] First it was decided to reserve judgement, to refuse meanwhile to discuss the proposal with other country delegations, and, following Tchlenov's characteristic advice, to choose a committee of representatives of the various tendencies within the caucus to go over the whole of the ground and report back to the full delegation. The committee duly met that night and sat from nine in the evening till two o'clock in the morning, and its twenty-two members were soon divided into three loose parts: two small, but roughly equal groups, consisting of those, on the one hand, who were prepared to go along with Herzl—some on certain conditions, some on no conditions at all—and of those, on the other hand, who were dead set against the project from the start; and a third, larger group that disliked the proposal, regretted its having been put before them, but did accept Herzl's argument that the tactical position in which he had been placed required that the negotiations be pursued. Tchlenov thereupon drafted a resolution, intended ultimately for submission to the full Congress, into which, with some ingenuity, *all* views were incorporated, or at least hinted at, but which tended, with many reservations, in Herzl's direction after all. The British Government was to be most warmly thanked, but at the same time informed that what was proposed could not constitute a solution to the full problem. That could be only Erez-Israel, as laid down in the Basel Programme, to which ultimate purpose, it was hoped, the British would agree to lend their support. The operative clauses were two: the British proposal had none the less to be examined carefully and the Congress ought therefore to appoint a committee to do so and report back to the Actions Committee on whatever practical steps ('such as an expedition') it believed advisable; and 'the Congress should put it to the Actions Committee that it should make all efforts to

[29] It is legitimate to speculate how things might have gone had either or both of the two strongest and most forthright of the Russian Zionist leaders been present at this Congress. Ussishkin, no doubt, would have wanted to plunge into a fight with Herzl without delay. Motzkin, always more sensitive to the demand for the immediate relief of the distress of east European Jewry, would probably have been readier to listen to Herzl's and Nordau's arguments. Unlike Ussishkin and unlike most of his associates in the Democratic Party, Motzkin did not join the anti-Herzl/anti-East Africa forces in the aftermath of the Sixth Congress.

eliminate the technical obstacles to the settlement of Wadi
El Arish.'[30] The latter requirement was meaningless and
inexplicable, since it had been explained very thoroughly
that no progress there was possible. The former was close to
what Herzl had asked for, except that it was not specified
whether it referred to the Smaller Actions Committee which
(as was very well known) he controlled fully, or the Greater
Actions Committee which he did not. Moreover, the preamble
and the key operative clause stood in obvious contradiction to
each other. But either because the hour was late or because
Tchlenov's moderating influence was at work, or because
there were so many different voices to be heard (old-style
Hovevei Zion, new-style Herzlian politicals, the Mizrahi, the
Ahad Ha-'Amists, radical Democrats, and plain, undefined
Zionists), or because the debate was still in too early a stage
for what might be termed natural polarization to set in, or
for all these reasons together, Tchlenov's draft scraped through
by a vote of nine to six. None the less, when the caucus met the
following morning it was immediately evident that Tchlenov
was in trouble and that the vote in committee the night before
bore no relation to the division of opinion in the full delegation.
Thirty delegates promptly put their names down to speak,
there was a row, and a full explosion was only forestalled by a
decision to restrict participation in the debate to three speakers
for Tchlenov's draft and three against and to postpone the
debate itself until the evening. Meanwhile the delegates were
free to attend the morning and afternoon sessions of the Congress plenum where the topic, although declared out of order,
kept cropping up. Only Nordau, who had decided to back
Herzl after all, was accorded the privilege of taking up the
subject at length (and incidentally adding to the agitation of
the opposition).

Nordau's speech on the morning of the second day of the
Congress was one of the finest (to many minds, the most
notorious[31]) of his career. It was a solid structure of argument

---

[30] Text in Heymann, ii, no.-148, p. 288.

[31] It is perhaps characteristic of the ambivalence towards Nordau even many years
after his death that a memorial collection of his Congress speeches published under the
auspices of the 'Nordau Zionist Society', *Max Nordau to his People* (introduction by
B. Netanyahu) (New York, 1941), should have so thoroughly emasculated this, the
most famous of the series, that its central argument is absent.

founded on an as good an exposition of the rationale of political Zionism as the movement had ever heard and on a review of the current state of the movement. By matching one to the other Nordau sought to show that certain operative conclusions followed. The result was the case for Herzl—Aaron as a mouth to Moses, as one observer put it[32]—all without a hint of Nordau's private reservations, but without hypocrisy either. Herzl had a case, Nordau can be taken as saying; he deserved to have it put as powerfully as possible.

Precisely why and at what stage Nordau changed his mind and decided to rally to Herzl's support after all is unclear. He was not a member of the Actions Committee. He seems to have taken no part in the confidential discussions which preceded the Congress, nor those which took place while the Congress ran its course. He spent much of his time in the plenum as Vice-President of the Congress, presiding over its sessions, often taking over from Herzl to free him for private talks or for direct participation in the debates. Yet since the two men were obviously co-operating closely, the basis for that co-operation must have been laid down tête-à-tête. If so, it would have been entirely appropriate. In the world of Jewish national politics in which they had come together their relationship was unique. So far as Nordau was concerned, it can be said with confidence that for some years now loyalty had played a role, along with the guilt that a stay-at-home feels when confronted with a friend who consistently acts on the precepts to which both subscribe. There was in Nordau much of that deep uncertainty about everything that is of a manifestly positive and relatively simple character that an intellectual and, more particularly, a professional analyst of social and historical trends is likely to feel. Recognizing this in himself, he was, perhaps, the more inclined to bow to the man who was prepared to take responsibility.

Nordau began by recalling and analysing the promises of British and Russian support which had so recently been obtained and by reminding the Congress of the *fourth* clause of the Basel Programme which laid down that efforts to gain the support of the Powers were to be made. The implication was clear: Herzl's diplomatic campaign was both mandatory and

[32] Naḥum Slouschz, *Ha-Meliz*, 11 September 1903. The allusion is to Exod. 4:10–16.

legitimate. Moreover, it was necessary—necessary not only because there would be little chance of an agreement with Turkey if the other Powers were opposed, but also because the Jews had once and for all to make clear to the governments of the world what their situation was and what it was they demanded. This the Zionists were able to do because 'all serious people [now] recognize that we are the . . . legitimate custodians of the Jewish people'. Consider the change that had been wrought, said Nordau. When the representatives of the Jews met their rulers

it was always the same song: 'We are happy under your government . . . we are deeply grateful for the gracious protection you grant us; we shall humbly endeavour to continue to deserve your grace and favour . . .'

I claim it as a great credit to Zionism that it has put an end to this humbug about being happy and contented and to the comedy of gratitude . . . From the beginning we [Zionists] boldly and distinctly said, we are not contented, we consider our situation very bad, we regard our treatment as undignified and undeserved, we hold a fundamental change in our situation to be vitally necessary. After the humiliating experience of the attempt to assimilate us into other peoples we took counsel with ourselves and we resolved to live in our own way, in our own right, on our own soil . . . and we ask the governments to help us attain this goal.

Some might think it a small matter *to have asked*. In fact, said Nordau, it was a turning-point in the history of the Jewish people. Since the world began there were, he said, two ways of obtaining anything: one was to take it, the other was to ask for it. The Jews were in no position to take anything, nor did they want to. But nor had they asked for anything hitherto. The Jewish people were in chaos, they were unorganized, they were 'human dust' [*ein Menschenstaub*]. They did not know what they wanted. They had none to speak for them. All that had now changed; and that was a very great deal, even if it did not mean that what they asked for they would receive immediately. If, despite the support of the Powers, it was the Sultan's 'unbending will to shut us out of Palestine, then, still solemnly asserting our undying historical claims to the Land of our fathers, firmly and resolutely adhering to the

Basel Programme, we should have to be patient and wait.
We can wait.'

But the Zionists could afford to wait only on certain conditions: that they did not cease to insist before the world on
the urgency of the Jewish Question; that they continued to
reinforce the Zionist movement and its institutions; that they
extended the influence of the movement through the Jewish
world and did so so decisively that the minority which opposed
Zionism 'recognized itself as an alien body within the living
Jewish organism'; and that they formulated and executed a
Jewish national policy for the interim period. The Congress,
Nordau repeated, was 'the authorized, legitimate, representative [assembly] of the Jewish people'. It was therefore its duty
to make national policy. And what was required was a co-
ordinated plan of defence for the entire Jewish people. The
Zionists, Nordau was saying, had to concern themselves with
the full range of problems besetting the Jews, especially with
the fate of those who had begun to move from their old homes
and had been refused access to new ones, and who were now
being tossed like shuttlecocks from one continent to another,
and 'who would perish if we did not do something to save
them. For these hundreds of thousands we must at the same
time, before we can provide them with a permanent home,
open a temporary refuge [*ein Nachtasyl*].' Such a refuge could
be set up on the land that the British Government was prepared,
under certain conditions, to grant the Zionists. It would be a
very unusual refuge, Nordau emphasized. For it would provide
not only shelter, but political education, accustoming the Jews
and the world to the idea—repugnant to many—that we Jews
are a people, a people competent, willing, and ready to fulfil
all the obligations of a civilized, independent nation.[33]

He was loudly cheered. The term *Nachtasyl* with its suggestion
of a doss-house caused offence, some of it genuine, some of it
convenient, and became notorious. A heated debate was
under way immediately until stopped short by Herzl. The
locus of the argument—increasingly a quarrel—then moved
back to the Russian caucus.

The set-piece debate in the Russian caucus began at nine in

[33] *Protokoll VI*, pp. 62–72.

the evening and continued until midnight. At issue, technically, was Tchlenov's attempt to meet Herzl a good deal more than half way in practice (by agreeding to a committee to handle the East Africa project), while stressing powerful disapproval of the scheme in principle. To most minds, however, the real issue was that of a choice between a Jewish state and Erez-Israel; and since there were none who were prepared to say that a state in hand in Africa or anywhere else was worth Erez-Israel in the bush, the contest was unequal and the conclusion as good as foregone. Besides, the champions of the respective positions were badly matched. Rabbi Shemu'el Rabinowitz, speaking for and largely to the orthodox,[34] but with evident embarrassment, supported Herzl, principally on the grounds that unorganized emigration led rapidly to assimilation. Weizmann, ranged for once on Herzl's side, stressed the need to deal directly with the migratory flow and echoed Nordau's point about the educative value of autonomy in East Africa for those enjoying it. But of the political value of the scheme— that which no one else denied—he himself thought little. Only the remaining speaker, Feibush Avinovitzky of Odessa, a pure 'political', was whole-heartedly and unreservedly in favour, but neither he nor what he had to say carried much weight.

Two of the three speakers against the Tchlenov draft were, by comparison, very powerful indeed. Victor Jacobson and Shemarya Levin[35] were both excellent speakers, the latter especially, and considerable personalities in their own right. They took their stand squarely on what they judged to be one of the great imperatives of Jewish history: that the Jews could not, dare not, disengage from Erez-Israel and that nothing but confusion and damage to the Zionist cause would result if they did so. There could not be two lands of settlement, two states, either in principle, or in practice—for if one suc- ceeded, what hope was there of rallying support for another,

---

[34] The attendance of the Mizrahi at meetings of the Russian caucus was generally poor. Tchlenov believed this was because they were already set on forming a separate party (or 'federation'). See his remark on p. 196 of his essay on the East Africa affair, published originally in Russian as *Sion i afrika na shestom kongresse* (Moscow, 1905) and in Hebrew translation as 'Zion ve-afrika' in S. Eisenstadt (ed.), *Yehiel Tchlenov* (Tel-Aviv, 1937), pp. 170–302. The references here and below to Tchlenov's essay are to the Hebrew edition.

[35] The third was Dov Gissin, a lawyer from Mogilev.

least of all from the Powers? The Zionists must not deviate
from their declared purposes. They must resist temptation.[36]

When the caucus resumed its deliberations the following
morning (Wednesday) several alternatives to Tchlenov's
original draft resolution were before it. One provided for the
simple removal of the East Africa issue from the agenda of the
Congress on the grounds that the Congress had no authority to
deal with such a plan in the first place. Another provided for
the matter to be tucked away under some such innocuous
rubric as 'migration' or 'settlement'. But since the mood of
the meeting favoured dealing with the issue and dealing with
it head-on, and it was also felt that it would be wrong and
feeble to shy away from the bitter confrontation that was in
the offing, neither alternative was acceptable.[37] The fate of
Tchlenov's own draft resolution was decided when he himself
withdrew it—to leave no doubt, as he later explained, where
he himself stood:

I, who opposed the slightest deviation from the road to Zion with all
my heart and soul . . . I might have been instrumental in approval
being gained for a resolution that could have been interpreted as
support for the Africa programme. That could have been the result
of my enthusiasm for diplomacy![38]

With Tchlenov's retreat compromise and moderation lost
their only important champion and the way was clear for the
triumphant rebels to drive their victory home. A fresh draft,
awkwardly phrased, but washed clean of all equivocation,
was put before the caucus. It stated that the Congress was
bound to thank the British Government in the warmest possible
terms; but it went on to lay down that, given its continuing
loyalty to the Zionist programme and the fact that it sees 'the
establishment of a home secured by public law only in Palestine
as the aim of the movement, the Congress is unable to include
the realization of this proposal in the programme of the work
of the Zionist organization'.[39] It was then adopted by a majority

[36] Heymann, ii, pp. 10–12.
[37] Tchlenov, p. 195.
[38] Ibid., p. 194.
[39] Text in Heymann, ii, no. 149, p. 289.

of slightly under 5:3 (146 ayes, 84 noes)—a clear majority, if not a resounding one, for the members of which 'this was', Tchlenov later recorded, 'the finest and happiest hour of all those hard days at the Congress'.[40]

Meanwhile Herzl had clashed with the Russians on another front, the Russian home front itself. There had been an argument in the GAC on Monday about Plehve's letter. Herzl wanted to publish it; the opposition, profoundly suspicious of Plehve and all his works, did not. There seems to have been a question of timing too: was it to be published before the debate in the Congress on the East Africa scheme or after? The minutes (if taken) have not survived; other sources on the course of the argument are scrappy and contradictory. Herzl may have wanted Plehve's letter published before the main debate on the East Africa project in order to show his fundamental loyalty to the Erez-Israel orientation;[41] or, somewhat more probably, he may have wanted to postpone publication, lest it be argued on the evidence of Plehve's undertaking that hope of a rapid breakthrough in Constantinople need not yet be abandoned.[42] In any event, the upshot was that the letter was published in a special Congress edition of *Die Welt* on Tuesday, 25 August, in advance, that is, of the first full debate on East Africa later that same day. It is also certain that whatever the content of the argument tempers had run very high.[43]

There were further meetings of the GAC on Wednesday at which the resolution Herzl proposed to bring before the Congress was laid before the members and the argument concentrated on its precise content and wording: on whether there was to be an *expedition* to Africa as well as a committee to consider the scheme, and if so, how it was to be financed; on precisely how, if at all, the GAC was to be brought into the

---

[40] Tchlenov, p. 196.

[46] See Heymann, ii, p. 15.

[42] Max Bodenheimer, *Darki le-zion* (Jerusalem, 1952), p. 111.

[43] Bodenheimer, not always reliable on details, writes that he had 'seldom seen Herzl so angry as he was on that evening when he was defeated by a vote [in the GAC]. He very nearly lost his usual dignified self-control.' Ibid. In his diary, Herzl writes of having 'forced' the measure through. *Diaries*, iv, p. 1550. Most probably, there were two stages. At the first, on the question of publication, Herzl had his way. At the second, on the question of timing, he did not.

process of consultation and decision while the inquiry was in progress; on whether the vote on the resolution by the members of the GAC in the plenum was to be free, or whether they were bound by a form of collective responsibility; and whether the Congress, before it voted, was to be informed of the disagreement within the Actions Committee. Seven of the fourteen Russian GAC members stuck to their guns throughout. Two (one of them Ussishkin) were absent. Four (including the two ultra-loyalists Mandelstamm and Jasinowski) supported Herzl from the first. But the rest too backed Herzl in the final showdown; and, after some haggling, the majority being with him, he had his way on all major points: the resolution would provide for an expedition (although it could not be financed by the Bank), the further role of the GAC would be extremely limited, its members would all abstain from voting in the plenum, and the dissenters were to keep their opinions to themselves until after the Congress had voted.

Herzl had been a great deal more confident and tough at these meetings of the GAC on Wednesday than he had been earlier in the week.

Despite my deep depression at seeing the ruin of all I held dear . . . [Tchlenov related] I was unable to free myself of the impression made upon me by the creator of this entire enterprise. He both enchanted and infuriated. He had the power to oppress and to subdue without regard for others and at the same time, in his faith and perfection of spirit, the power to attract and inspire. His entire being—the look in his eyes, the concentration of his expression, every muscle, his quickened breathing . . .—all draw the weak and the doubtful after him. He walked into the hall, followed by all the others, members of the Actions Committee, some downcast, some head held high, with confidence that, 'we will win'.[44]

But the main arena was now the Congress itself. The debate on East Africa began late on Tuesday afternoon and ran for seven hours; it was resumed for another three hours the following morning. It was an intense and passionate debate and attracted an unprecedented number of speakers and would-be speakers: it was hardly under way when there were over seventy on the list; half way through there were over a hundred.

[44] Tchlenov, pp. 201–2.

The numbers had therefore to be cut down, chiefly by selecting key speakers for each side and by having them speak alternately. Cheering, booing, and other interruptions from the floor and the gallery were frequent and the chairmen (Herzl, Nordau, and Bodenheimer for the most part) repeatedly had to cut speakers down to their allotted time. All this was natural enough, as the effect of the opposition's approach had been to make it a debate on *principles* from the very beginning. And for that same reason much of it, perhaps inevitably, was in the nature of a dialogue of the deaf—a tendency enhanced by the fact that, with interest and passions so aroused, the number of speeches in languages other than the customary lingua franca of the Congress (German, often imperfect German) was unusually large and the consecutive translation provided generally poor. Herzl himself did not speak, except to call delegates who had overstepped the mark of parliamentary courtesy to order and then, at the end, immediately before the vote, briefly to restate the issue and point to the gravity of the decision that was to be taken. But he was, of course, the focus of attention and the centre of the storm throughout. It was his policy, his *modus operandi*, his conception of the Zionist—and, beyond that, the Jewish—ethos that were at issue. The rapidity with which the opposition had formed up and taken a stand owed as much to the steady growth of resistance to the general style and direction of his leadership as to the objection to the East Africa scheme specifically. It would be equally true to say that the East Africa scheme was the precipitating agent that had called forth and also—and in the mind of the opposition—had finally legitimized full, public opposition to his leadership, now unprecedented in clarity and force and virtually devoid of apology and saving Aesopic language. Hence even though the debate touched on many more—and wider—matters than Herzl's leadership, or Herzl personally, the vote towards which it led was clearly to be a vote of confidence.

The speakers all circled and recircled around a few salient issues. There were the questions of constitutional form and propriety. Was the very idea of settlement in East Africa compatible with the letter, let alone the spirit, of the Basel Programme and if not, ought the Congress to agree to consider it at all? Ought there perhaps to be a referendum among the full membership of the movement and if so, at what stage; or should there be a special Congress to deal with it? Was not the argument that all that was asked of the Congress was a semi-technical decision (appointment of a commission of inquiry) specious? And, generally, why should it be the function of the Zionists to deal with matters which were not provided for in their Programme, no matter how grave? On all these questions opinion was divided, but by and large it was, of course, opponents of the scheme who were most concerned to raise questions of form and propriety—one of them going so far as to speak of 'betrayal'.[45] Then there was the issue of expediency and the likely effect of such a departure on the movement. Supporters followed Herzl's and Nordau's argument that the movement could only benefit. Opponents offered a variety of counter-theses. Belkowsky, for example, feared dissipation of energy;[46] Tchlenov feared yet another illusion, like the Emancipation, come to tease and confuse the people, the illusion that through Africa the Jewish Question would be solved—whereas Zionism wanted to free the Jews of illusions;[47] Rabbi R. Borischansky of Gomel argued that Zionism had been precipitated by the sufferings of the Jews and that where the Jews were comfortable there was no Zionism: did we therefore want the Jews who went to Africa to be wretched?[48] Some accepted that it might be awkward for Herzl if he turned down the British offer out of hand, but insisted on his doing so, arguing he would surely find a way that would cause no damage or offence.

But the central issue was that of the role of the movement in respect of the contemporary Jewish condition—and, by extension, the relationship in which the Zionists stood, or ought to stand, towards the Jewish people as a whole. What of the great flow of migrants? What of the dangers threatening the Jews? What were the corresponding duties and responsibilities of the Zionists?

The harshest and most vociferous of Herzl's critics in the present debate, Shimshon Rosenbaum,[49] charged that the

[45] Ch. Wortsmann. *Protokoll VI*, p. 154.   [46] Ibid., p. 159.
[47] Ibid., p. 162.   [48] Ibid., p. 176.
[49] One of the organizers and leading spirits of the Minsk conference and a sometime member of the GAC.

project smacked of mere philanthropy. The philanthropists, typically, dealt with the problem piecemeal and often for unworthy reasons: rich Jews who sought to arrange for the settlement of poor Jews because they could not stand the sight of their suffering. But the purposes of the Zionists were larger: not merely to arrange for a refuge for a group of the poor, but to cause the Jews to move *en masse* to Erez-Israel. And so far as the political obstacles were concerned, he had this to say, that Erez-Israel would and could be regained because the will of a nation of twelve million people was a factor with which the practical politicians would have to reckon eventually.[50]

For Cyrus L. Sulzberger, a New York philanthropist himself, the higher aims of Zionism were all very well and commanded loyalty, but the martyrs of Kishinev were dead and the river of refugees was growing. Where would they go? There were now 1,000,000 in the United States, 600,000 in New York alone, 300,000 in one square mile of the city. What would have happened to them had they not been admitted? But could their number be increased? And with what consequences? The doors of America might close. What then? So when an offer such as this was made it ought not to be refused. How would other governments react if Great Britain's offer was turned down? Who would help a people who declined to help themselves? He was a Jew, Sulzberger told the Congress, even more than a Zionist.[51]

Others were less alarmed.

It will be asserted [said Heinrich Rosenbaum of Jassy later in the debate]: yes, there is great danger, we cannot continue to wait, the Jewish people are perishing. But is that really so? Is the Jewish people really in danger of extermination in the foreseeable future? (A shout: Yes!) Will the modern Hamans and Torquemadas really succeed in annihilating Israel? No, gentlemen, the Jewish people has too solid and healthy a constitution, even if it looks sickly; a people whom pressure and misery have so tempered must and will live, must and will survive the hard times.[52]

---

[50] *Protokoll VI*, p. 147.
[51] *Jewish Chronicle*, 28 August 1903, p. vii.
[52] *Protokoll VI*, pp. 206–7.

Was it the function and responsibility of the Zionist movement to deal with the *immediate* symptoms of distress? When
he had first heard of the scheme, Bernstein-Kohan said, he
had jumped at it, feeling as any hungry and thirsty man might
feel when offered food and drink. But now he would speak from
a properly political, rather than a sentimental point of view.
In the first place, the Congress had no authority to take a
decision of this kind, to determine the entire people's destiny.
And if it be said in answer then let us ask the people in Russia
directly and find out what it is they wish for themselves, then
the reply must be that we are not only representatives of the
people, we are their physicians. We must concern ourselves
with what is good for the organism, rather than with opinion.
You don't ask a sick man what you should prescribe for him.
He may be crying out for bread and water when a hunger cure
would do him more good. We Zionists must therefore stick to
our ideals: they are good for the people, they are the proper
prescription.[53]

Nachman Syrkin, a more explicit and radical socialist than
Bernstein-Kohan, thought otherwise. It was possible and it
was right to distinguish between the set, long-term purposes
of the movement and the immediate problem of the migrants.
There was no doubt in his mind but that the Zionists had to
try to tackle it: the gates were closing all round, the loss to the
nation of great numbers of its people through scatter and
assimilation was severe. And *there* was the danger, not in some
loss of zeal and loyalty for Erez-Israel as other speakers had
warned. Who, if not the Zionists, should and would deal with
this? The East Africa project would not affect hopes for
Erez-Israel, for in the former case only social and economic
factors operated, while in the latter spiritual and moral factors
operated as well. There was thus no cause to fear that East
Africa would diminish national feeling.[54]

But even leaving aside the ideological difficulties and assuming the obligation to deal with the contemporary distress,
could a settlement in East Africa really contribute to its relief?
Supporters of the scheme, said Brutzkus, frequently charged its
opponents with appealing to sentiment rather than reason.

[53] Ibid., pp. 165–6.
[54] Ibid., pp. 177–9.

But the supporters did the same. They spoke wildly of thousands and tens of thousands of hungry men and women, when East Africa could absorb a few thousands at the most and there were forty to fifty thousands migrating from eastern Europe every year. At best, the East Africa project might be incorporated into the movement's *Gegenwartsprogramm* [i.e. programme of current tasks within and for Diaspora Jewry, in contradistinction to tasks in and for Erez-Israel]; but the *Gegenwartsprogramm* had not even come up for debate.[55]

All told, the opposition did better than the loyalists: they had more and better speakers, they hammered away at a limited number of targets, and their case, relying on high principle and a few brute facts, was more amenable to parliamentary treatment. The loyalists were more numerous on the floor, but fewer spoke from the rostrum and few of those who did were impressive. There were not many who were capable of putting their case in general and semi-theoretical terms— Syrkin was one of the exceptions—rather than in those of the political constraints and possibilities which were the true basis of Herzl's policy, but which only he could present authoritatively. This was a price paid for lack of organization in the loyalist camp and for the absence of a caucus to compete with the Russian opposition. The opposition had a number of leaders and almost all of them spoke. The loyalists had only Herzl and his inner circle—his court, some would say—and Nordau. Only at the end of the debate, conceivably because Herzl had felt that it had gone none too well for him, were two of his best men put forward deliberately to conclude it.

Greenberg, the very last speaker, assured the Congress of the loyalty of all concerned to the absolute primacy of Erez-Israel and pressed it to remember that 'the way to Palestine need not necessarily be only the geographical way'. The political road ought never to be lost sight of. But his main task was to report on the negotiations in London and to read out Hill's letter in full.[56] The true concluding speech was Nordau's, who spoke just before him.

There were three separate questions at issue, said Nordau, and they were not to be confused one with the other. First,

[55] Ibid., pp. 198–9.
[56] Ibid., p. 215. *Jewish Chronicle*, 4 September 1903, p. 12. See above, p. 271.

there was the question whether a commission of inquiry should be set up without further commitment to the scheme; second, there was the larger question whether the movement should take up the matter of East Africa at all; the third question was whether it was proper and necessary for the movement to tackle the problem of refuge for the migrants in the first place. There was also the question of trust: all the speakers, even the most fervent spokesmen for the opposition, had expressed their confidence in Herzl personally, but had charged the movement's leader again and again with wishing to deviate from the Basel Programme. This had been denied and loyalty to the Programme had been affirmed and reaffirmed. What further proof would satisfy the critics? Was Herzl's own conduct, by burning his boats and turning Zionist, not proof enough?

He, Nordau, could say nothing in favour of East Africa specifically: he had no knowledge of it, beyond the most superficial. But he could see no reason why it should not be examined. If the country was bad, we should have nothing to do with it. But if it was good, we were then obliged, he thought, to consider the question whether the Zionist movement should seek a temporary refuge for its people there. And his answer, in that case, was positive. The uses of the settlement to the Jewish national cause would be educational, 'the nomads would be trained to be citizens, Jewish citizens—but not for East Africa itself, if East Africa it is to be, not for another country, but for Zion.'

What is it that you do now anyway? In what does your entire Zionist agitation consist? In your coming here and making a noise? Is that all? (Protests [in the hall].) I shall say even harder things to you if necessary! You labour in all the countries of the world to educate Jews as Zionists. You labour to educate a formless, chaotic mass as citizens. Will you be doing otherwise if you found settlements and conduct the education there without interference, more thoroughly, more efficaciously, and more completely?

One of the speakers, Mr Dizengoff,[57] whom, personally, I like very much, used the phrase that I know so well, 'What matters to us is not the Jews, but Judaism.' 'Judaism without Jews'. Oh, yes . . .

[57] Meir Dizengoff's own speech was not recorded. The stenographers merely stated that he spoke (in French) against the East Africa project. *Protokoll VI*, p. 170.

we know all about that. You can use that phrase at a gathering of spiritualists. Among the living, who want the flow of life about them, you will get nowhere.[58]

What was at risk? No decision was contemplated, only an inquiry; and a special Congress could be convened to decide so great a matter. Finally, he did not ask, he said, for an expression of confidence in himself personally; but he did believe that the Congress owed that much to Herzl. It also owed the British the courtesy of an inquiry for having had the generosity to make the offer in the first place. It was absurd to say, as had the previous speaker,[59] that our good leader would know well enough how to handle the matter. First the china was to be smashed, then 'our good Herzl' would be expected to stick all the pieces together?![60]

The debate ended just before three in the afternoon (Wednesday, 26 August). After an interval of about an hour the Congress reassembled to vote, Herzl presiding. There was last-minute consultation on the draft resolution, a protest (by one of Herzl's supporters) that the translation of Herzl's presentation into Russian (by Bernstein-Kohan) had been faulty, a request (by Herzl) to abstain from greeting the votes of individual delegates with any kind of demonstration, and a last procedural wrangle. Then the voting began. It was by roll-call and it took over two hours to complete, virtually the entire Congress participating. The question before it was approval of the proposal presented on behalf of the GAC.[61] The draft resolution agreed upon in the Russian caucus and presented by Bernstein-Kohan the day before was not put

---

[58] Ibid., pp. 211–12.
[59] Heinrich Rosenbaum.
[60] *Protokoll VI*, p. 213.
[61] The full text was as follows: 'The Congress resolves to appoint a Commission to examine the question of the settlement of the territory which the English Government has so generously offered. The Commission will consist of nine members and it will be its duty to assist the Smaller Actions Committee, in a consultative capacity only, in the dispatch of an expedition to the territories to be investigated. It is understood that the cost of the expedition will not be borne either by the Jewish Colonial Trust, or by the Anglo-Palestine Company, or by the Jewish National Fund. The Finance Committee of the Congress will consult with the Smaller Actions Committee on obtaining the means. The decision on the settlement of East Africa is reserved to a Congress specially convened for that purpose.' Ibid., pp. 222–3. On the supplementary resolutions which slightly modified this basic text, see below, p. 306.

to the vote, probably lost sight of in the general excitement.

The result, on the face of things, was a clear victory for Herzl. Of the 468 delegates who voted, 292 (62·4 per cent) voted 'aye', 176 (37·6 per cent) voted 'no'. But 143 delegates almost a quarter of the total, had abstained—or been prevented for one reason or another, by sickness, for example—from casting a vote.[62] Many of those abstaining disapproved of the project, while reluctant to vote against Herzl. Herbert Bentwich and Heinrich Loewe, for example, had both spoken against it in the plenum, but had abstained from voting against it none the less. There were other reasons; at all events, other reasons were given. Sokolov did not participate in the great debate at all and later justified his abstention on the grounds that the Congress should never have considered the project in the first place, but should have left it to a philanthropic organization such as the Hirsch fund (ICA) to make what it could of it.[63] But Sokolov had always been reluctant to rebel against accepted leadership; so it had been at the outset of Ḥibbat Ẓion, so it had been on Herzl's first appearance, and so, one may conclude, was it now. Reines abstained too, but was in a different category. Tchlenov records that he had been surprised to find Reines's name down to speak *in favour* of the East Africa resolution and, as the rabbi moved to the rostrum, had asked him if it was not in error. Reines's reply was that he was still undecided. In fact he went on immediately to support Herzl warmly and to beg the Congress to think mercifully of the poor and the wretched seeking refuge.[64] This was thoroughly consistent, of course, with Reines's fundamental approach to the problem of the material condition of Jewry[65] and the greater interest of the little incident lies in Tchlenov's failure to understand it. Reines's abstention would be consistent with the desire of the orthodox minority to burn no bridges to the other camp. But however they may be interpreted—whether as signs of respect, or doubt, or simple cowardice—the abstentions[66] did add up

[62] Cf. detailed analysis, Appendix, pp. 479 ff.

[63] O. K. Rabinowicz, *Fifty Years of Zionism* (London, 1952), p. 62.

[64] Tchlenov, p. 196.

[65] See above, pp. 216–18.

[66] There are no certain figures for those who simply failed to register as abstainers by absenting themselves from the hall or through error or indisposition.

to a massive proportion of the total. Whereupon the victory of the Herzlians necessarily pales: leaving aside the forced, *en bloc* abstention of the GAC, of the delegates present at Basel and free to vote 50·6 per cent voted 'aye', 30·5 per cent voted 'no', and 18·9 per cent abstained; 'noes' and abstentions together: 49·4 per cent. Hence only the barest majority of those present on the floor were prepared to commit themselves in favour. In addition there were the thirty-four members of the GAC whom Herzl had compelled to abstain *en bloc*. Seven of these were firmly opposed to the resolution and had had their names read out in the Congress after the vote;[67] but there were others, Richard Gottheil of the United States and Alexander Marmorek of Paris among them, who had disapproved of the project in private, but had bowed to Herzl's authority in the end.

If the abstentions reduced the victory, the composition of the 'no' vote vitiated it. Not all the 'ayes' were from central and western Europe or North America, nor all the 'noes' from the East: Nachman Syrkin was a notable 'aye', Martin Buber, Berthold Feiwel, and Heinrich Loewe[68] notable 'noes'. But the 'noes' were mostly eastern, Russian especially, and the Russians, in their majority, had voted 'no'.[69] Moreover, those who had done so had done so as a group, leaving three main classes of exceptions: Herzlian loyalists, socialists, and the Mizrahi, each class being peripheral in one degree or another to the Russian Zionists of the mainstream who had voted overwhelmingly against the resolution. It followed that the alliance between Herzl and the heirs of Ḥibbat Zion had now snapped and that differences among the latter (such as those out of which the Democratic Party had sprung) were now largely dissolved. When the results were announced amid cheers and counter-cheers and general uproar and Tchlenov and his companions got up and walked out of the hall, followed by most of the 'noes' and leaving a pale and shaken Herzl at the rostrum, the break seemed absolute.

[67] Ẓevi Gregory Belkowsky, Yaʿakov Bernstein-Kohan, Ẓevi G. Bruck, Yiẓḥak L. Goldberg, Victor Jacobson, Zeʾev Tiomkin, and Yeḥiel Tchlenov.

[68] Loewe was first listed among the abstainers, but declared there had been a misunderstanding and asked to be recorded as a 'no'. *Protokoll VI*, p. 236.

[69] See Appendix, pp. 479 ff.

'The Congress', a journalist wrote, '. . . suddenly dissolved.'[70]

iii

The walk-out of the larger part of the delegation from Russia was followed, right up to the end of the Congress and for a day or two after it, by further scenes of distress, hurt, and dismay in which the 'noes' stoked the fires of indignation in each other's breasts and kept their distance from the movement's leader. Some wept, it was reported. Some spoke and behaved as if the Temple had been destroyed once again. And while the elements of genuine pain and those of self-induced and self-righteous hysteria are impossible to disentangle at this remove in time, the effect, it is clear, was to envelop everyone and everything in a tickening mist of strong feeling. The intricate political calculations which were at the bottom of it all receded from most minds and all but vanished from the agenda of the continuing debate. The fact that at no time had the Congress been asked to consider more than a *contingent* acceptance of the plan was forgotten. There was a tendency abroad to pull out the stops and disburden oneself of normal parliamentary inhibitions. The debate was shot through with generalities, *idées fixes*, false assumptions, and statements of credo. Gestures charged with emotion of one kind or another were indulged in on all sides: as when Herzl was treated with deliberate discourtesy when he came to appease the wrath of the opposition within the Russian caucus in the evening after the vote; and as when he himself, at the close of the Congress, raised his right hand and solemnly intoned, 'If I forget thee, O Jerusalem, let my right hand forget her cunning!'[71] Throughout, harsh thoughts were expressed in harsh

---

[70] *Jewish Chronicle*, 4 September 1903, p. 12. It appears that Tchlenov had not at first intended a demonstration. Victor Jacobson is recorded as having explained that after the results had been announced, Tchlenov, who had been sitting next to him, said, 'What's the use! Let's go and have lunch.' When they got up to go the other Russian members of the GAC followed and their supporters in the hall, thinking it was a demonstration, followed in turn. Julius Simon, *Certain Days* (Jerusalem, 1971), p. 48. What is wrong with the story is that it was about seven o'clock in the evening at the time and very late for lunch. Otherwise, it rings true. Simon himself was a delegate. He himself had voted with the 'ayes'. For Tchlenov's own account, see op. cit., p. 203.

[71] Ps. 137:5.

language, for all the world as if in that harshness lay proof of the speaker's integrity.

The meetings held since the African project was approved all make a depressing impression [said Weizmann to a gathering of the 'noes' held in Basel immediately after the Congress]. A man comes along and transforms our entire programme at one go and here we are, all confused, devising stratagems to escape from the predicament. Before the content of the project had been made clear to me I supported it; but in the course of the debate I discovered that it was of its essence that [through it] Zionism was to be transmuted. Then I turned into an opponent, for all that I am in favour of [planned and directed] emigration . . .

Herzl's influence on the people is very great. Even the 'noes' have been unable to free themselves of [his] influence—so much so that they hesitated to state in their [draft] resolution whether [the East Africa] project was compatible with the Basel Programme or not.

The truth is that Herzl is not a nationalist, but a promoter of projects. He came across the Ḥibbat Ẓion idea and aligned himself with [the movement] for a period. Then when it failed, he reversed himself. He only takes external conditions into account, whereas the power on which we rely is the psychology of the people and its living desires. We, for our part, [always] knew that we were incapable of gaining Palestine in the short term and were therefore not discouraged when this or that attempt had failed. It is the people's consciousness that has [now] to be bolstered. There must be established a society to propagate the Zionist idea in its national form . . . Cultural work must be put before all else.[72]

Still, Herzl was heard out by the 'noes'. His greatest critics, those of the Democratic Party, were as conscious as any of his personal prestige and popularity: 'We have made a God of him', one of them complained after the Congress. And there was the concomitant fear that they had manoeuvred themselves into a false position: 'Our propagandists habitually put the [Zionist] case in terms of bread and empty stomachs and the masses, having no higher ideals, follow them.'[73] So while they seemed to have remained unmoved by Herzl's central argument at this stage, namely that he would be placed in an impossible situation *vis-à-vis* the British or any other

[72] *Ha-Ẓofe* (Warsaw), 3 September 1903, p. 836.
[73] Heilpern, ibid., pp. 835–6.

political force if the Congress refused even to consider what he put before it,[74] they did soften—at least to the extent of trooping back into the Congress hall the following morning.

The price Herzl paid for this surface restoration of unity was a change in the terms on which the East Africa question would be handled by the Zionist institutions. One of the demands of the opposition was that no Zionist funds proper, namely those deriving from the *shekel* membership-fee, would be used to cover the costs of the expedition. Their more important demand was that the GAC should have a continuing and active role in the mounting of the expedition and in the further management of the issue upon its return. The first was granted without reservation. The second was granted in principle, but later vitiated by a further resolution restoring effective, as opposed to nominal, powers to the EAC (over which Herzl ruled unopposed). In the event, the financial concession made readily enough by Herzl led to a delay in the dispatch of the expedition until the end of 1904, while the political concession which he fought to circumvent, so as to leave matters in his own hands, was without practical effect: he died before the crucial point of decision was reached. But for the time being, at any rate, the hands of those in the Russian wing of the GAC who called for moderation were strengthened. Chief among the moderates was still Tchlenov. Summing up at the end of the meeting at which Weizmann had called Herzl a 'promoter of projects', Tchlenov asked for care to be taken lest the movement break up. He also leaned the other way by arguing that the oppositions' main purpose now should be to induce the Seventh Congress (due in 1905) to drop the Herzlian concept of a Charter altogether and attend to practical work in Erez-Israel on the old model. The meeting ended on an uncertain, milder note with a resolution to make it known that the walk-out from the Congress hall had not been intended as a 'demonstration'.[75]

In their own way, the loyalists were divided too. Greenberg took the East Africa resolution as a mandate to plunge ahead, but was now entirely alert to the obstacles. Nordau told an interviewer that he thought the resolution 'not an error, but a

[74] Vladimir Jabotinsky, 'Herzl bei den Neinsagern', *Die Welt*, 3 July 1914.
[75] *Ha-Zofe*, loc. cit.

disaster' because it would inevitably be misinterpreted 'by our
enemies'. Herzl, he went on, had had no choice but to take up
the offer, but he himself would have nothing to do with the
actual settlement of East Africa with Jews.[76] Only the very
closest to Herzl, loyalists to his person, like Mandelstamm,
seem to have been reasonably content.

Herzl's own feelings at the Congress's end were appropriately grim. On the surface he had reason to be satisfied.
He had not had his way on all matters: apart from the ruling
that *shekel* funds were not to be used to finance the expedition
to East Africa, there had been an attempt by his collaborators
to bring Reines on to the Greater Actions Committee (to
strengthen the pro-Herzl contingent in Russia) which had
failed. But in the main he had done well. Nominally, he had
retained a free hand to pursue his political aims and an
advisory committee on East Africa,[77] such as had been originally
proposed, was duly elected on the last day to serve at least as
further evidence of his parliamentary mastery of the Congress.
Moreover, he was quick to see that the opposition to the East
Africa scheme could be turned to advantage in his running
dialogue with the Russian Government (because it could be
taken as demonstrating that if the Jews were ever to leave
Russia in large numbers and of their free will, there would
have to be support for the Zionists in Constantinople); and
with the Turks too (because it could be shown that there were
alternatives to Erez-Israel after all). On the other hand, the
unexpected fury of his opponents and the distrust and hostility
with which they had treated him left a deeper wound than
was generally suspected or could be discerned behind the
avuncular mask which he assumed as he came to reason with
them in their caucus just when their paroxysm of indignation
was at its peak.[78] Only in private, when it was all over, did he
lower it to the extent of telling Nordau, Zangwill, and Cowen
that he recognized that he would have to tell the next Congress
that he and the movement could not go on as before. Erez-
Israel would either have been obtained by the coming Con-

[76] Ibid., p. 835.
[77] On which Weizmann, for all his brave words, agreed to serve.
[78] No minutes were kept, but Jabotinsky recorded the meeting in convincing detail.
See *Die Welt*, 3 July 1914.

gress, or else he, at any rate, would have realized the futility of further efforts. In the latter case 'a decisive split in our movement' would have been produced, a 'rift [that] centred about my own person'. Originally, he had been a Jewish-state man, he said; only later had he become a Lover of Zion himself.[79] But whereas Erez-Israel was the only land where the Jews could finally come to rest, hundreds of thousands needed immediate help. He did not believe that the Zionists had the right to withhold such relief; and that being so, 'there was only one way to resolve this conflict: I must resign my leadership.'[80] Later, in November of that year, he wrote out a draft of a letter of resignation from the leadership of the movement in the form of a 'Letter to the Jewish People'.[81] It was not the first time that he had thought very seriously of stepping down.[82] But plainly it was more than hurt and weariness that now affected him. He had begun not to believe that he would succeed. Only his daemon pushed him on to act as if he would, and meantime to continue.

Herzl was now a very sick man. Bernstein-Kohan, a physician, relates that twice during the Congress he observed symptoms of a heart attack and that he was among the doctors present who went to Herzl's aid.[83] Even allowing for possible exaggeration (there is no other source and Bernstein-Kohan seems to have been at pains to emphasize the leader's weakness as a clue to his declining judgement), it remains true that within a couple of days of the Congress Herzl was back at his usual summer resort, Aussee, to recuperate and that he did not return to Vienna until late in October. Thereafter he must be seen as conducting his affairs in bouts of furious activity of the old kind, each promptly followed, however, by exhaustion and periods of forced rest, convalesence, and

---

[79] The distinction was between priorities. In the jargon of the movement a 'Jewish-state man' (*Judenstaatler*) was one whose prime concern was to obtain political autonomy in a defined territory, the question of its location being important, but secondary. For the Lover of Zion (Hovev Zion) the re-establishment of the Jews in Erez-Israel was the *conditio sine qua non* of the entire enterprise. See also below, p. 345, p. 395, n. 31.

[80] *Diaries*, iv, pp. 1547–8.

[81] Text in *Zionist Writings*, ii, pp. 238–9.

[82] See, for example, Herzl to Mandelstamm, 13 March 1901, *Igrot Herzl*, iv: 'I am almost exhausted. Soon you will have to find another leader.'

[83] *Sefer Bernstein-Kohan* (Tel-Aviv, 1946), p. 140.

depression. The great displays (and certainly the greater resources) of energy are henceforward all on the side of the opposition. And with the return of Ussishkin from Erez-Israel in October the opposition had a leader as well.

Ussishkin had gone to Erez-Israel in the spring of 1903 to give a push to what he had always felt must be at the centre of the entire Zionist enterprise, the settlement work in Erez-Israel. In Ussishkin the original, simple creed of the Odessa Committee[84] still burned strong, unaffected by Ahad Ha-'Am's scepticism and everyone else's weariness. In frank defiance of Herzl and as a form of protest against the failure of the regular institutions of the movement to act effectively, he had himself mounted a settlement land company, *Ge'ula*, in 1902. He had then had the satisfaction of obtaining Herzl's reluctant, but not ungracious approval as part of the latter's effort to appease the Russian opposition as the tension mounted in the course of the spring and summer of that year. The two men met in Vienna in May 1903 and parted on good terms.[85] Ussishkin then went on to Erez-Israel. He stayed for three months, moving from settlement to settlement with his customary display of energy laced with self-importance. But it was more than any other prominent leader of the movement had done for many years and he was well received. At Zikhron Ya'akov, towards the end, just as the Congress was getting under way at Basel, he helped organize a representative assembly of the new *yishuv* (*ha-kenesiya ha-rishona li-venei Israel be-Erez-Israel*, 24–6 August 1903) over which he himself presided and which he plainly regarded as his very own constituency. Its declared purpose was the founding of a permanent representative institution for the Jews of the country.[86]

Ussishkin and his friends and allies in Erez-Israel seem to have believed that the *yishuv*, provided it was organized, could take a lead in the movement, at least as a model and example, but perhaps directly and politically too. The assembly in Zikhron Ya'akov was to be a Zionist Congress in miniature,

---

[84] See *Origins*, p. 165.

[85] Schwartz, *Ussishkin be-igrotav*, pp. 73–4.

[86] Ussishkin to the EAC, 26 July 1903. Ibid., p. 77.

virtually a counter-Congress.[87] And the idea was carefully
encapsulated in a telegram of greeting sent from 'the representatives of the Jewish people in Erez-Israel' to 'the representatives of the Jewish people in the Dispersion'—that is, the Zionist
Congress. Herzl shrugged the challenge off with the cool
reply that the Congress in Basel thanked 'the brethren already
settled in Erez-Israel for their good wishes'.[88] But Ussishkin
returned to Russia undaunted and immensely fortified both
in his original convictions and in his determination to continue
to press in the same direction.

Back in Russia, he got his first full account of what had
happened at the Congress. He could see for himself that the
leading figures of the movement in Russia were divided and
that, on the whole, since the Congress it was the waverers
who were in the ascendant after all. For example, it was
symptomatic of his colleagues' loss of nerve that in their
subsidiary row with Herzl over the question of direct contact
with the Russian authorities to follow up Herzl's own talks
with Plehve in August, it was Herzl who was having his own
way. Herzl had his own preferred and trusted representative,
Nissan Katzenelsohn of Libau, and wanted the Russian
authorities to accept him as uniquely qualified to speak to
them on the movement's behalf. Initially, the leading Russian
Zionists had objected. But now the growing tendency was to
give in to Herzl's admittedly peremptory demand to leave
all but questions of purely local interest in his, and Katzenelsohn's, hands. More serious still, from Ussishkin's point of
view, was the fact that the leaders were increasingly mindful
of the common tendency in the lower ranks of the movement
to sympathize with Herzl outright—certainly, in the last
resort, to be guided by him—and, in the main, to regard the
East Africa project as not unreasonable in the circumstances.

That the leaders of the opposition so judged the mood among
the rank and file is attested to abundantly by their own
statements. The question what the true state of opinion within
the movement and on its periphery was is more difficult to

---

[87] *Ha-Zefira*, 25 September 1903; Hillel Joffe to A. Meyersohn, 19 January 1904,
Hillel Joffe, *Dor ma'apilim* (2nd edn., Jerusalem, 1971), p. 250. On Joffe, see below,
p. 368, n. 1.
[88] Schwartz, *Ussishkin*, p. 78.

answer. The evidence on which to base anything like a reliable
account of Jewish public opinion in general and Zionist public
opinion in particular is patchy. Editorial opinion in the
Jewish, pro-Zionist press cannot be taken as in any way representative: it was formed in much the same circles of middle-
class *maskilim* to which many of the Zionist leaders belonged;
but reports of outlying correspondents are more valuable.
There are also bits and pieces of random testimony in memoirs,
contemporary letters, memoranda, and the like, extending
over the period from the end of the Sixth Congress to Herzl's
death, which help to put the general picture into focus[89] and
which may be summed up as follows: loyalty to the axiom of
the primacy of Erez-Israel *in principle*; but a concomitant will
to have the East Africa project looked at with the greatest
seriousness and interest; great concern about the migratory
tide; some wonder and some irritation at the conduct of the
'noes'; and, broadly speaking, undiminished confidence in
Herzl, somewhat more pronounced in the Polish provinces of
the Empire than in those of Russia proper.

On the matter of East Africa [reported a certain Isaacson of Lodz]
almost all Zionists in our city, a few exceptions apart, support the
decision of the Congress. At the same time they are glad that sharp
protests were made by the minority to the effect that the matter of
East Africa will not have the slightest effect on the longing for Zion,
nor weaken the determination of those who press for it to achieve their
goal in the Land of our fathers.[90]

Meanwhile, greater matters were in the foreground of the
consciousness of Russo-Polish Jewry. The oppressive tension
to which they had been subject continually since the Kishinev
pogrom was raised anew by a second large-scale pogrom in
Gomel on 11 and (after a tense interlude) 14 September. In
pattern and origins it was much like the one in Kishinev; but it
differed in results because for the first time a systematic

---

[89] For example: *Jewish Chronicle*, 2 October 1903, p. 12; Weizmann to Aberson,
3 April 1904. *Weizmann Letters*, iii, no. 212, p. 233; Tchlenov's account, 'Zion ve-afrika',
Yehiel Tchlenov, p. 191; and the reports of Nissan Katzenelsohn to Herzl, 1 January and
12 March 1904, CZA H VIII/432.
[90] *Ha-Zefira*, 6 September 1903.

attempt was made by local Jews to organize their own defence. On the face of it, this might have been expected: 55 per cent of the population of the town was Jewish and it was intolerable that they, as Bialik wrote of the Jews of Kishinev in his great and terrible poem *Be-'ir ha-harega* ('In the City of Slaughter'), 'flee like mice and hide like beetles and die like dogs wherever they be found'. But the Jews of Europe, like their brothers of the Levant, had taught themselves over the centuries to abstain from active and systematic self-defence against the violence of the surrounding population, notably and necessarily when it was committed with the sanction and support of the authorities. There had been exceptions, usually *in extremis*. But the price paid, almost invariably, was horrific. The effect of the departure in Gomel in the summer of 1903 from this ancient rule was therefore electric, for all that it incorporated a partial demonstration of the rule's validity. The *pogromshchiki* were scattered by the Jews wherever they were met in force and the Russian police and troops were thereupon turned against the Jewish defenders.[91] Still, a new standard of behaviour had been set for the Jews of the Pale—the more so, perhaps, because while Kishinev, coming after a generation of relative physical security, caused shock, Gomel marked the establishment of the pogrom as a regular weapon of state against the Jews. In the aftermath, the conflict between the Jews of Russia and their rulers was thus further exacerbated and the alienation of the former from the latter became virtually complete. Inevitably, the impatience of the Jewish lower orders with their condition and their drive to change or escape it mounted. In 1903 the river of Jewish migrants to the west rose steeply; within three years it had almost trebled.[92] In brief, a period of enormous agitation and turmoil was now inaugurated.

All this stood in contrast, however, to the caution and self-control generally displayed by leading figures in the community, Zionist no less than non-Zionist and—so far as the

[91] There is a vivid account in Dubnov's *History of the Jews in Russia and Poland*, iii (Philadelphia, 1920), pp. 86–90. For a collection of contemporary press dispatches, see *Jewish Chronicle*, 2 October 1903.

[92] Figures for Jewish immigrants into the United States, some 70 per cent of whom were from Russia: 58,000 (1901), 58,000 (1902), 76,000 (1903), 106,000 (1904), 130,000 (1905), 154,000 (1906). Source: I. M. Rubinow, op. cit. Chapter 6, note 3, p. 504.

Zionist leaders in particular were concerned—their current absorption in matters of high principle on the one hand and short-term tactics on the other. The fight between Herzl and the opposition was played out above the ever more agitated heads of those for whom both sides claimed to speak and on whose behalf all wished to act, with the opposition inside Russia less distracted, in the main, by the fresh deterioration in the material condition and physical security of those around them than were Herzl and his supporters from a distance.

In the middle of October Ussishkin attacked. He issued an 'open letter'—in effect, a personal statement—to the delegates of the Sixth Congress and had it circulated to the Zionist press for publication. He had been prevented from attending the Congress by his work in Erez-Israel, he said, and had learned of his election to the GAC only upon his return. He would, of course, work untiringly for the renaissance of the Jewish people along such lines as the Congress and the GAC determined.

But, so far as the principal decision of the Congress was concerned, to send an expedition to Africa, that [was a decision] I am not prepared to undertake to comply with. I oppose it with all my being and will seek to upset it with all my power. A majority of the Congress may decide questions of ways and means, but not of principles and ideals. And just as no majority in the world can cause me to apostatize from the faith of Israel or the Law of Israel, so no numerical majority . . . at the Congress will detach me from the Land of Israel.[93]

Ussishkin's intention was now plainly to bring matters to a head and the fight into the open. The challenge to Herzl's authority, no less than his policy, was rendered clear and public; and coming as it did from a major figure in Russian Zionism, it was without precedent. It could be ignored neither by the trimmers and compromise-seekers within Ussishkin's own country organization, nor by Herzl himself. Within days Ussishkin was duly denounced in the pages of *Die Welt* under the heading 'An Answer from Dr Herzl', but where Ussishkin's open letter was brief and declarative and, in its way, passionate, Herzl's was long and expository and at the same time rough in tone. It was evidently intended to bring Ussishkin down to

[93] 16 October 1903. *Ha-Zofe*, 20 October 1903.

size—with much play on 'Mr Ussishkin of Ekaterinoslav', what 'every first-year student of law could assure Mr Ussishkin', remarks on the 'amusing side of the matter', and the fact that for all his evident good intentions, his purposes (and those of his friends) would be better advanced by one 'less noisy and conspicuous'. For the rest, it was a sharp restatement of the case for political Zionism: notably the arguments that one did not obtain national, political rights to a country through the private purchase of land (Mr Ussishkin might buy up the whole of Ekaterinoslav, yet the authority of the Russian Autocracy over the city would remain unimpaired); and that it was ill-informed and simplistic to think that political ends could be attained by other than political and diplomatic means. Ussishkin was also scolded for convening what was, in effect, a secret gathering at Zikhron Ya'akov, giving it the pretentious title of 'Palestinian Congress', and thereby, most probably, drawing the unwelcome attention of the Turkish authorities to the *yishuv*. It was to be hoped that the settlers would suffer no harm.

So far as Ereẓ-Israel was concerned, Herzl wanted no lessons in devotion to it from Ussishkin. Ussishkin was entitled to argue his case within the movement and within the Actions Committee. But he must accept the ruling of the majority. He was free of course to go his own way if he did not want to continue to accept 'party-discipline'. But in that case it was his duty to resign his office. Finally, wrote Herzl,

There are two possibilities. Either Mr Ussishkin knows a shorter and better way to gain possession of Ereẓ-Israel for the Jewish people under public law—in which case, good Zionist that he is, it is hardly proper for him to refrain from revealing it to us with all speed. Or else he knows no such way—in which case it were better if he did not disturb the unity of Zionism, which was worth more than a few plots of land in Palestine, by uttering empty phrases.[94]

Ussishkin's reply was longer and angrier than his first sally. Its main points were two: there was small chance of a political arrangement (specifically a Charter) without a foothold in the country *first* and in any case it would avail

[94] *Die Welt*, 30 October 1903.

the Zionists nothing if they did not acquire land by private purchase; the second point was that Herzl himself had not invariably abided by resolutions of the Congress. He, Ussishkin, had therefore said to himself, perhaps I, as his 'faithful pupil in matters of Zionist leadership and the tactics of infighting', might be permitted as much.[95] There the argument lapsed for a while: *Die Welt* refused to publish Ussishkin's reply and it took some time for the text to percolate westwards out of the Hebrew and Russian-language press in eastern Europe. But in any event, led by Ussishkin, the attack on the East Africa project and on Herzl personally was taking on new forms meanwhile and new force. The dissatisfaction with the internal organization of the movement in Russia that had been voiced at Minsk[96] was now the basis for a drive by the opposition to take their branch of the movement under a tighter and more independent rein, a matter as close to Ussishkin's heart as any.

The Russian caucus at Basel had considered the question of organization. It had taken no positive decisions, but it had authorized the Russian members of the GAC, the country authority under the old dispensation, to propose and (although this was later disputed) to make changes.[97] These now resolved to form a permanent steering committee out of their own number (a *Landes-Comité* in the terminology of the movement at the time), and to redefine and re-allot certain of their functional responsibilities. Structurally, the Russian branch would now be somewhat closer to the model of a vertical, well-disciplined organization that Ussishkin had adumbrated at Minsk.[98] Politically, the most striking change was to put the day-to-day responsibility for the movement's affairs wholly in the hands of the opposition. Herzl's close friend and supporter Mandelstamm was divested of his responsibility for the branch's finances, which were now transferred to J. L. Goldberg, a wealthy business man in Vilna. Goldberg was probably better suited to the function of treasurer, but the effect was deeper than administrative. Mandelstamm was one

---

[95] *Ha-Zofe*, 10 November 1903.
[96] See above, pp. 185–9.
[97] See Heymann, ii, pp. 28–9.
[98] See above, pp. 187–8.

of the last of the original founders of Ḥibbat Zion to survive[99] and after Mohilever's death in 1898 had been the only one to retain both influence and office in the new movement. But at sixty-five he was an old man by the standards of the times and a good twenty years older than most of his colleagues. The arrest of his daughter for revolutionary activities had hit him hard. He himself had been harassed by the police (as had been other delegates) upon his return from the Congress. There is an increasingly pathetic tone to his letters at this time;[100] and in the transaction of political business and the conduct of the continuing debate some loss of grip and some loss of interest were beginning to be evident. In brief, he was a tired man who was losing stomach for the fight. But Mandelstamm was the one major figure in the Russian movement who was entirely devoted to Herzl and the pro-Herzl rump which now began to coalesce was left with no one of comparable prestige to lead it. The upshot was that in short order the institutional and political base from which the opposition operated became a great deal firmer and their self-confidence increased immeasurably. 'I have been elected from among my colleagues to direct the affairs of the *Landes-Comité*', Ussishkin informed Vienna, 'and so from now on you are to apply to me in all matters pertaining to our general organization, propaganda, finances, etc.'[101]

Within the new *Landes-Comité* Ussishkin was far and away the strongest figure; and therefore, for the time being, *de facto* leader of Russian Zionism. Determined to press Herzl to the wall, he lost no time in making the most of his position—and, as was his nature, making that position clear. He wanted the relevant issues brought into the public domain. (Some, like Goldberg, were appalled by the washing of so much linen in the open,[102] But Ussishkin took no notice.) He was determined to carry the fight into the western sector of the movement too and was delighted when Herzl's opponents in the West responded to his challenge. Soon he was planning a

---

[99] See *Origins*, pp. 71–2, 141–3.
[100] For example, Mandelstamm to Herzl, 5 October and 24 December 1903. CZA, H VIII/541.
[101] Ussishkin to EAC, 16 November 1903. Text in Heymann, ii, no. 47, p. 165.
[102] Goldberg to Ussishkin, 4 November 1903. Heymann, ii, no. 41, p. 157.

journey to Vienna, Berlin, Paris, and London to rally support for 'our war against Uganda and the beginning of *Realpolitik* [*sic*] in Ereẓ-Israel'.[103]

In the West his ablest and most enthusiastic ally was Weizmann, who had been quick to offer his services in the common cause against the 'African fever' of Herzl's Russian supporters and 'the solid block of *Mizraḥi* and western Zionists who, in the name of "the Jewish people", will say that Palestine cannot be had, that the people are starving, and [that] therefore we must grab Africa!'[104] The Democratic Party was now dying or dead; and it was clear to Weizmann that here was a greater cause to fight for, one with a lower common denominator, one in the interests of which all the 'national Zionists', as he thought of them, could unite, and in which there would be a greater role for him to play than any he could find elsewhere. Ussishkin took Weizmann slightly less seriously than Weizmann would have liked him to and refused to treat him as an equal. But Weizmann was useful to the great *intransigeant* of Ekaterinoslav, primarily by supplying him with detailed and often perceptive reports on opinion in circles that were geographically and culturally remote from his own. After a journey to Paris and London in October, he wrote to Ussishkin that he had the feeling that Nordau had been 'marched in much against his will' to support the East Africa project and that 'the true ideologist of East Africa' was Zangwill, who 'went much further than Herzl would approve'; that Herzl's closest collaborators in London were divided, while in Paris the non-Zionist Jewish leaders, pressed by Lord Rothschild from London, tended to support Herzl for reasons of their own. All this was correct. True, wrote Weizmann,

The Jewish masses in London are in the throes of an African fever, but they are so unenlightened that tomorrow they might just as easily be fired with enthusiasm for America and the day after for Palestine. If this is the so-called voice of the people that our [pro-]

---

[103] Ussishkin to Gaster (the Sephardi Ḥakham, or Chief Rabbi, in London and one of Herzl's original supporters), 8 November 1903. Heymann, ii, no. 45, p. 163.

[104] Weizmann to Ussishkin, 16 September 1903. *Weizmann Letters*, iii, no. 10, pp. 10–13.

Africans speak so vociferously about, one can ignore it with a clear conscience.[105]

This first stage of the 'war against Uganda' ended with a full, four-day conference of the Russian members of the GAC and their deputies at Kharkov, 11–14 November 1903. All but one (or possibly two) turned up. The first issue, raised by Mandelstamm, was the propriety of discussing ways and means of nullifying a decision of the Congress. Having been voted down on this and having failed, as he wrote to Herzl, to calm 'the *Orlando furioso* of Ekaterinoslav',[106] Mandelstamm immediately took himself off, leaving behind the only other completely loyal Herzlian, Jasinowski, to 'observe'.[107] But most of the others stayed the course and the result was a triumph for Ussishkin. The formation of the four-man steering committee with Ussishkin as its chairman and Bernstein-Kohan, Jacobson, and Tiomkin as members—all, but especially the first two, being determined members of the opposition— was soon confirmed. The main business of the conference was, of course, the East Africa project.

The hard-liners, led by Ussishkin, made all the running. Their purpose, once the conference was under way, crystallized as a plan to force Herzl to change course under threat of all-out 'war' against him. He was to be presented with a series of explicit demands in the form of 'a final warning . . . (an ultimatum)'. These chiefly comprised: a promise to refrain from raising further territorial projects other than such as related to Erez-Israel; a promise to withdraw the East Africa project 'totally' and no later than the Seventh Congress; a promise to convene the GAC before the planned expedition was dispatched; and a promise to advance the work of settlement in Erez-Israel. These demands were to be delivered by a special delegation and Herzl was to be required to undertake to comply with them 'in writing'. If he refused, the following 'means of warfare' were contemplated: the remittance of

---

[105] Ibid., no. 60, pp. 61–8. In the event, the Parisians refused to co-operate with Herzl. Weizmann sent copies of the letter to Tchlenov and Jacobson too and to a host of minor figures. Ibid., p. 60, n. 1 to document no. 59.

[106] Mandelstamm to Herzl [18 November 1903]. CZA, H VIII/541.

[107] Jasinowski to Herzl, 17 November 1903. CZA, H VIII/397.

funds to Vienna would be stopped; the fight would be made public by way of written and signed declarations, agitation in print and by word of mouth, dispatch of representatives to the chief centres of Europe and America 'to organize the opposition to Dr Herzl's method', and a general conference; and 'steps to set up an independent Zionist Organization without Dr Herzl' would be taken.[108]

The hard-liners got their way at Kharkov because the rest were divided. Herzl's true and consistent supporters Mandelstamm and Jasinowski having withdrawn early, there remained only those (like Tchlenov and Goldberg) who disliked the harsh and peremptory character of the ultimatum and were not at all sure the movement could dispense with Herzl, but who broadly approved the philosophy behind the plan none the less. Whether the hard-liners seriously expected Herzl to yield is less clear. They did proceed with caution. Pending the dispatch of the delegation to Herzl the terms of the decision were to be kept secret; only the remittance of funds to Vienna was to be stopped forthwith. However, the latter provision may not have been of much immediate practical significance because funds, which derived from the sale of the *shekel*, accumulated chiefly in the period immediately prior to a Congress; and the former was soon vitiated when the Kharkov resolutions were leaked to the press and finally published in full within six weeks or so of their having been made. Mandelstamm, at all events, seems to have thought Ussishkin and his friends bent on full rebellion. Reporting the gist of the resolutions he warned of a deep rift in the making, but nevertheless advised Herzl to stick to his guns and to let it happen, if necessary.[109] And indeed, when the relevant entry in Herzl's diary appears on 4 December it shows a thoroughly characteristic initial reaction: the major points are grasped, questionable motives are imputed, and the first thought is for a counterweight and for countermeasures:

The Russian members of the A.C., particularly Ussishkin, Jacobson, etc., are in open rebellion. They want to give me an ultimatum . . .

[108] *Ha-Zefira*, 29 December 1903.
[109] Mandelstamm to Herzl [18 November 1903]. CZA, H VIII/541.

They have first acquired all the bad characteristics of professional politicians. I shall first of all mobilize the lower masses against these inciters to rebellion . . . In addition, I shall cut off their supply of money, etc.[110]

On 16 December he noted that he would not let himself 'be intimidated by demonstrations, whether they come from Gaster or from Ussishkin'.[111] The great row he had precipitated had at first unnerved and depressed him; on 11 November, as we have seen, he had drafted his 'Letter [of resignation] to the Jewish People'. But he was not yet done. The Kharkov rebellion revived him; and his mood (as distinct from his ultimate purposes) now changed again.

iv

Negotiations with the British Government entered a fresh stage after the Congress—a tortuous one to some extent, in which it is not entirely fanciful to see a certain parallel between the Zionists and the British. On both sides there were second thoughts from time to time, an awakened sensitivity to un-anticipated counter-pressures, and, before long, a submerged wish to retreat, provided retreat with honour was possible and provided the advantages believed to lie in the East Africa scheme could be obtained by other means.

In East Africa itself the Settlers' Association at Nairobi headed by Lord Delamere protested and the Bishop of Mombasa voiced his reservations. While in favour of a generous scheme of help for the Jews, he preferred it to be mounted in such a way and in such a place as to do no damage to the Christian missionary campaign for which he was responsible. The Commissioner, Sir Charles Eliot, complained of not having been officially informed, but on the assumption that the unofficial 'reports cannot be wholly unfounded', made the preliminary observation that 'if the settlement is made . . . it would be advantageous to have it at some distance from the [railway] line for I anticipate friction between the Jews and

---

[110] *Diaries*, iv, pp. 1571–2.

[111] Ibid., p. 1580. Gaster was a notable opponent of the East Africa scheme in the West.

the other European settlers.'[112] The local press was divided.
One newspaper took a hard line from the first, charging Lansdowne with a sell-out of the interests of the English farmer,
protesting against the plan to 'dump down some 15,000 to
20,000 alien Jews on what is practically the only white man's
portion of this country', and ridiculing the Foreign Office for
making an offer which the Jews themselves were thinking of
turning down.[113] The other local newspaper was enthusiastic.
The territory would surely prosper when the Jews settled and
it was to be hoped that the Zionists, following the biblical
example of Caleb and Joshua, would in the end tell their
people that it was indeed 'a land flowing with milk and
honey'.[114]

At home, the topic was duly taken up in the correspondence
columns of *The Times*, most correspondents being opposed to
the project and the topic being discussed in a long and thoughtful leading article. Where (as in England) the Jews have enjoyed
liberty and equality, argued *The Times*, there has been 'no
diminution of their traditional aptitudes, or of the very large
proportion of men of more than average ability which they
have produced'. Moreover, there has been a tendency towards
'amalgamation with their neighbours and towards what may
be described as a softening down of the salient points of their
national character'. This, thought *The Times*, was all to the
good. However—

A little Jewish State in East Africa, restrained within certain limits
of action by the British Government, but in many respects self-
controlled, would either succeed or fail in bringing within its borders
a fair proportion of the ability by which the Jews have always, and in
all countries, been distinguished. Failure in this respect would
produce a set of conditions in which any ability born in the country
would be compelled to seek a field for its activity elsewhere; and
success would mean that men worthy to take part in the councils of
Empires would be compelled to confine their attention to matters
of a comparatively trivial character . . .

If the projected State were constituted, the Jew of Uganda would

---

[112] Eliot to Lansdowne, 10 September 1903. PRO, FO 2/785.
[113] *African Standard*, 29 August; 28 November 1903.
[114] *East Africa and Uganda Mail*, 5 September; 21 November 1903.

be almost certain, before very long, to regard himself as the sole heir of the promises made to his fathers, and would regard the cosmopolitan financier, or the great musician, or the great statesman, as one who had fallen from his first love and had ceased to do his first works. The narrowness of a *quasi*-provincialism would be likely to become predominant in the infant State; and the experience of two thousand years has shown that the Jew, in circumstances which promote narrowness, becomes not only narrow, but intolerant and persecuting. His desire for a more permanent establishment in Palestine would be likely, moreover, to make him chafe at the control exercised by the British Government over his external relations, and to feel towards that government much as the Jews of Jerusalem felt towards the supremacy of the Caesars.[115]

In the Foreign Office itself the approach had rapidly become more cautious: there was 'much to be said for [the] view' expressed by Eliot and the Bishop [of Mombasa] deprecating 'the grant of extensive tracts of land to alien Jews, probably on a low level of civilization, in the most favourable part of the protectorate'.[116] But there was no question yet of a retreat. Privately, Lansdowne agreed with Eliot

that these people do not as a rule make good agriculturalists. Our experience of them all over the world is that they take to 'les petits metiers' but not to farming. In this case, however, other considerations were involved and it would have been difficult to decline the overture which was made to us with much influential support. Moreover there would clearly be some advantage to the Protectorate in bringing into it at once so large a sum of money and many human beings.[117]

Formally, Eliot was informed that no final commitment or decision had been made and that meanwhile the Commissioner was asked to receive and assist a Jewish delegate who would be going out to study the matter on the spot.[118]

There were thus three issues before the British Government: where precisely in the Protectorate the Jews were to settle,

---

[115] *The Times*, 7 September 1903.
[116] Minute to Eliot's letter of 10 September 1903.
[117] Lansdowne to Eliot, 5 October 1903. PRO, FO 800/146.
[118] Lansdowne to Eliot, 15 October 1903. PRO, FO 2/785.

how they were to be organized, and finally, whether, on balance, the advantages of the project outweighed the drawbacks. Eliot, in his vigorous way, took them all up in a major dispatch, immediately printed and circulated by the Foreign Office for wide distribution. The region he recommended for settlement was the Gwas Ngishu plateau,

a grassy plain, well watered, and possessing a temperate climate . . . surrounded by forests which yield good timber, and . . . practically uninhabited owing . . . to tribal wars, not to any defect . . . If the settlement proved a success, it could extend further to the North East. This would bring the colonists into contact and perhaps collision with the little known but troublesome Turkhana. I do not however anticipate that they would give any serious trouble to a modern Joshua.

So far as internal administration was concerned, he favoured a combination of elements of the Turkish *millet* system, one of 'easy tolerance', as he put it, complete communal autonomy in matters of religion, personal status, and education, and straightforward municipal autonomy. This should 'amply satisfy oriental Jews'. As for others,

It is not likely that non-Jews would much frequent the Jewish settlement, but their rights should be carefully preserved. When circumstances permit the persecuted to become persecutors, they are apt to find the change very enjoyable, and it would not be convenient for Christians if they were compelled to observe the Jewish Sabbath.

As for the scheme itself, while he was

not actively opposed to [it], it does not inspire me with the least confidence or enthusiasm. Though I have often heard it stated that the Jews make good agriculturalists, I have never seen the part of the world where they do so . . . In South and West Russia Jews follow such agricultural pursuits as dealing in mortgages and buying up grain, but I know of no case where they live by manual labour if they can help it. In the few instances where they do so live (e.g. most of the boatmen at Salonica are Jews) the fact seems attributable to the large numbers of Greeks and Armenians who can beat the Jews at their favourite occupations . . .

Again, though wealthy Jews are very wealthy, poor Jews are very poor, and a visit to the Jewish parts of Russia and Poland produces a most disagreeable impression of dirt and squalor. Whole towns look as if they had been bought up second hand and never properly repaired. Is it in these surroundings that promising settlers will be obtained?

He was not blind, he summed up, to the advantages of the scheme. It was necessary to encourage an influx of settlers. The existing East Africa Syndicate had disappointed. And 'This being so, I do not think we can afford to reject the Jewish scheme, but I deeply regret that His Majesty's Government do not see their way to initiate or actively patronize some plan for peopling the Protectorate with British colonists.'[119] The aspect of all this which particularly caught the official eye in London was Eliot's insistence on the difficulties that would arise out of the fact that it was a settlement of *Jews* that was proposed. Wherever Jews settled in large numbers, ran the minute to his dispatch, there 'a Jewish Question with its attending evils of Anti-Semitism' arose. There was not much of that yet in England, 'not so much I imagine in virtue of the larger spirit of toleration in this country—although, this must also be a factor in the case—but mainly because the number of Jews here is insignificant'. But there was now a large influx of Jews into Great Britain and there might follow 'our Jewish Question and a British species of Anti-Semitism. This danger may not be insuperable, but it should not be overlooked in the consideration of the scheme.'[120] This of course was the point at which the scheme had originated, but the dilemma was only compounded thereby. At all events, when Greenberg came to the Foreign Office a few weeks later and it was concluded at the Foreign Office (somewhat too hastily) that the Zionists might themselves give up the scheme, Lansdowne summed up what seems to have been the prevailing mood with the observation, 'We shall probably be well out of it!', adding, 'but it was right to treat the application considerately.'[121]

The British knew of the opposition to the East Africa project

---

[119] Eliot to Lansdowne, 4 November 1903. PRO, FO 2/785.
[120] 26 November 1903. Ibid.
[121] Minute to Hill's memorandum of 14 December 1903. PRO, FO 2/785.

within the movement; but they could also see for themselves
that Herzl and Greenberg, his principal representative in
London, had generally stuck to their guns thus far, and that
there was no cause to question their authority as spokesmen
for Zionism. The uncertainty about Zionist policy emerged
only in the course of the exchanges on the first question at
issue, namely that of the territory to which the settlers would
be channelled and its precise extent. Various proposals had
been aired by the British in a non-committal way, the Zionists
insisting all the while that wherever it was to be, the region had
to be truly suitable for the potential settlers and sufficiently
large to serve as a convincing basis for a substantial autonomous
settlement. But as the talks proceeded and as the Zionists
sensed the hesitations of the British, their own purposes became
more intricate. For it had occurred to Herzl and to Greenberg
that, on balance, it might be no bad thing if in the end the
British reversed themselves and withdrew the offer entirely.
Whitehall would then be under some sort of obligation—moral,
if no other—to offer help in another form or in another quarter,
and it might even be possible to resurrect the El Arish project
and that in much more favourable circumstances. In the
event, however, the British, as Greenberg discovered, were not
disposed to withdraw their offer publicly and go on to consider
an alternative: that would have meant a shift in what was now
more or less settled policy. When Greenberg told them at the
Foreign Office, as he wrote to Herzl, that 'we ought to be off
with the old love before we were on with the new . . . they then
said the matter would have to go before [Lansdowne] and
possibly the [Cabinet].'[122] The implication that this was
virtually out of the question was clear. It was therefore equally
clear and vitally important, Herzl reckoned, and Greenberg
urged, for the Zionists to pursue the East Africa project as
far as it would take them—firstly, because they could not
afford to appear as anything but serious and consistent
negotiators; and secondly, because if they hesitated they
might end up with no bird in hand at all. And then again, if
the British did finally make a really good and definite offer,
Herzl was sure that he, for his part, would want to go all out

[122] Greenberg to Herzl, 7 January 1904. CZA, H VIII/294.

for it despite the opposition that acceptance would arouse. So he assured Greenberg towards the end of 1903.[123]

These were the views and considerations, each in some degree incompatible with the other, that appear to have weighed with Herzl at this time, the relative balance between them shifting from moment to moment with events, and resolution being postponed virtually to the end. On the whole, however, the rows and tensions which the East Africa scheme had precipitated within the movement led him to take a harder line on what was at issue with the British, to be more reserved in public about East Africa than he might otherwise have been had he been determined to push the movement towards it, and to be less than frank with his associates about the state of the negotiations. How all this could be squared with the paramount aim of maintaining the friendliest possible relationship with the British and making the best possible impression on them remains an open question. In this winter of 1903/4 Herzl seems to have been steadily losing his grip even on this tactical problem—perhaps because the difficulties were made more severe for him by his being forced to work through a representative, Greenberg. Herzl was never once able to visit London in this, the final year of his life, and his last great diplomatic exercise was shot through with flashes of uncertainty, with irritation, misunderstanding, and un-friendly argument with the loyal, but far from subservient Greenberg.

This turmoil was at its peak at the end of 1903 and early in 1904. First, there was a public statement by Herzl in the form of a letter to Sir Francis Montefiore, drafted for him, after much argument, by Greenberg, and published for the record in the *Jewish Chronicle* on 25 December. The Jewish Question could only be settled in Erez-Israel, he asserted, 'but the British government, having, in terms of singular generosity and consideration, proposed to us the offer of an autonomous settlement, it was surely not possible in reason to do otherwise than extend to such [an] offer our most careful thought.' However, for it to be within 'the range of practical politics', four conditions had to be satisfied: the territory had to be large enough to provide real relief for east European Jewry;

[123] Greenberg to Herzl, 8 February 1904. Ibid.

It had to be one that could be effectively settled by European Jews; it had to be invested with autonomous rights; and 'the enthusiasm of our own people in respect to the offer had to be of such a nature as would overcome all the obvious difficulties which [even] under [the] most favourable conditions would be bound to arise in the creation of the settlement.' It was the fourth condition, he continued, that had been 'to some extent, absent'. He believed it had been his duty to submit the proposal to the movement; but it was 'with no small satisfaction' that he noted the opposition to it. The implication could not have been clearer: there might well be a retreat from the East Africa project, not least because his heart was no longer in it—but only provided the retreat was orderly and to a prepared position. This was a fair reflection of the posture he had now come to adopt in the expectation, encouraged by Greenberg, that the British would in the end make an obviously unsatisfactory offer, upon which it might be possible to revert to El Arish.[124]

In January 1904 there was a further round of talks for Greenberg and the Foreign Office. In a meeting with Sir Eric Barrington, Lansdowne's Private Secretary, and Eyre Crowe, at this time Clerk in the Foreign Office, he brought up El Arish once more as the desirable alternative, and when, once again, the British referred to what they took to be the insuperable obstacles to it,[125] he went on to insist that they then put the East Africa project in specific and concrete terms, in consultation with Eliot if necessary, before it be taken any further. There had at least to be a prima-facie chance of success, Greenberg argued, for a journey by a delegate to East Africa to see Eliot in person to be justified—upon which Crowe said he thought the stipulation reasonable and Barrington promised to put the point before Lansdowne.[126] This was done, Eliot's consent was obtained by telegram, and the decision taken. On 25 January Sir Clement Hill made a definite offer: some 5,000 square miles on the Gwas Ngishu

---

[124] Greenberg to Herzl, 13, 15, and 17 December 1903 and 7 January 1904. CZA, H VIII/293-4; and Herzl's two telegrams to Greenberg, 22 December 1903. CZA, H VIII/293.

[125] Weisbord, p. 170.

[126] Greenberg to Herzl, 14 January 1904. CZA, H VIII/294.

plateau north of Nandi, south-east of Mount Elgon, a territory with its southern border just five miles distant from the railway and on the south-west border near enough to Lake Victoria for an extension to allow a port on the lake to be envisaged from the start. This was substantially what Eliot had recommended in November. It was land that was suitable for settlement: reputedly good and attractive farming country and virtually unpopulated. The Charter, Greenberg reported, would be approximately upon the lines of the draft drawn up by Lloyd George the previous summer, adjusted to meet the terms laid down in Hill's formal letter of 14 August 1903, as read out at the Congress.

Greenberg counselled immediate acceptance. The expedition should be organized without delay. A Congress could be called for June or July *in London* [Greenberg's emphasis]. A company could then be formed to deal with the entire project and the Zionist movement as such, having brought it into being, would then be free to detach itself and go on to other things, retaining just enough control to ensure that the settlement did proceed along 'national lines'.[127] Herzl hesitated. Greenberg insisted. For the present, there was no hope of reviving the El Arish scheme, he wrote. Chamberlain, who favoured it, had told him as much when they had met in December. For one thing, Cromer was dead against it; besides, Chamberlain himself was no longer in the Government. The present British offer was an excellent one—better than any of those that had been discussed; unless Herzl had something else in mind of which Greenberg knew nothing, there were no objective grounds for rejecting it. And the crowning argument was that having pressed the British for a clear undertaking, it was 'most embarrassing to find now . . . you are holding back'.

Why? [Greenberg pressed.] Is it because you have gone back [on] your policy and want to back out of [East Africa]? If so I can give you fifty reasons against such a course and fifty others for your going on

---

[127] Greenberg to Herzl, 29 January 1904. Ibid. Greenberg's habit of excessive capitalization, apparently for emphasis, has been ignored in the transcription of passages from his letters.

with [it]. You will lay yourself at the mercy of the rebels—Every wild Louban [*sic*][128] will think he has only to invest in a pistol to dictate to you the policy of the movement and the Gasters and Ussischkins [*sic*] while conniving at this anarchism will crow out that they have beaten you. Those outside the movement will believe it and say it or at least that we are an impracticable gang unable to cope with practical work.

He had seen Wolffsohn, who agreed with him. The chief thing now was to send out a delegate—borrowing money for the purpose if none was available. The British Government 'have been too good and we have done too well with them for us to play double with them or to risk annoying them . . . I hold our movement can stand equivocations, misunderstandings and conflicting policies no longer.'[129]

A day later, Greenberg telephoned Herzl that there was real danger of the weak Unionist Government of the day falling, in which case all would be lost.[130] Herzl dithered. First he agreed and wired his consent, subject to secrecy being maintained and approval of the terms of the Charter and the report of the expedition being reserved.[131] Then he reversed himself and ordered Greenberg to take no steps until additional instructions had been sent.[132] Later, when it turned out that Greenberg had already acted—on the very night of the receipt of Herzl's first telegram—he acquiesced, only reiterating his demand for secrecy[133] and noting in his diary after the event that, 'Nevertheless I will not let Greenberg force my hand.'[134] At this last moment there was some argument in Vienna whether the British proposal was identical with the original proposal as put before the Congress or not. If not, there would have been grounds of a sort for rejecting it. If it was in line

---

[128] Hayyim Luban, a Russian-Jewish student, shot at Nordau on a Paris street on the night of 19/20 December 1903 crying, 'Death to Nordau, the East African.' Luban was later found unbalanced and unfit to stand trial.

[129] Greenberg to Herzl, 8 February 1904. CZA, H VIII/294.

[130] 9 February 1904. Ibid.

[131] [9 February 1904.] *Diaries*, iv, p. 1611. Cf. Greenberg to Herzl, 11 February 1904. CZA, H VIII/294.

[132] 9 February 1904. CZA, H VIII/294.

[133] 11 February 1904. Ibid.

[134] *Diaries*, iv, p. 1612.

with the original offer, the dilemma was entire. But Herzl and Greenberg themselves had no doubt that what was now proposed was fully in line with what had been suggested in August and Herzl consoled himself with the thought that he was therefore 'entitled and obligated [by the terms of the Congress resolution on East Africa] to accept it'.[135] It was the evident logic of the relationship that had been built up with the British Government, not Greenberg, that had forced his hand. It continued to do so. Even the injunction of secrecy could not be maintained for long. At the end of 1903 a confidential circular had been sent to members of the GAC on the strength of Greenberg's impressions at the time (but in stronger language than his reports really warranted) that the British were withdrawing their offer.[136] Now this had to be corrected. The language chosen was grudging and the content terse to the point of being misleading. Greenberg was cited as the source of the original report that the British wished to withdraw. But, Herzl stated, 'We have now received fresh reports, to the effect that the British government still maintains its proposal.' No details were given and there was no reference to Greenberg's negotiations in January, let alone their outcome. The circular announced briefly that the entire question would be thrashed out at the coming meeting of the GAC.[137]

v

By early January, when the delegation which was to present the Kharkov 'ultimatum' to Herzl arrived in Vienna as planned, the tension and irritation that had been building up on all sides were at their height. A number of minor rows and fortuitous incidents had helped to push things to the point of explosion. There had been the affair of Luban's attack on Nordau. Nordau himself had emerged unhurt, although profoundly shaken, but the scandal was immense. *Die Welt* promptly traced the incident to the influence of Kharkov. Herzl, in an interview with a Vienna newspaper, said he thought the affair of small significance in itself, but wondered aloud at the curious spectacle of Russian delegates at the

[135] Ibid.
[136] 27 December 1903. Text in Heymann, ii, no. 80, pp. 199–200.
[137] 1 March 1904. Ibid., no. 128, p. 271.

Congress, representing those most in need of refuge, opposing the East Africa scheme. A partial explanation to the phenomenon might lie, he thought, in the fact that most of the delegates were of the middle classes who suffered less at the hands of the Russian authorities and population than the poor of Jewry. They could therefore afford to cleave to their ideals. Those directly representing the Russian-Jewish proletariat had voted for the dispatch of the expedition.[138] On 21 December Herzl's preferred legate, Katzenelsohn, was received by Plehve. The meeting went well enough: Plehve seems to have reiterated his promise of diplomatic assistance at Constantinople. But the Zionist opposition in Russia was furious and their fury had something to bite on when it emerged that Herzl had followed up the interview granted Katzenelsohn with a select list of Zionist dignitaries in Russia for Plehve's information. The intention may have been innocent in its origins: to indicate who might serve as directors of the proposed Russian branch of the Bank which both Plehve and Witte had promised to approve. But it was composed of his own loyalists and showed plainly enough whom he wished the Government to deal with, who were sheep and who were goats.[139] It was an unmistakable blow at the autonomy of the movement's Russian branch.

On 24 December a 'League for the Defence of the Organization' was set up in Warsaw by Jasinowski and Jelski as a countermove to Kharkov and a counter-centre to Ussishkin's new *Landes-Comité*. But it was more an act of defiance and loyalty than a move to precipitate a reversal of the tide of opinion in the upper echelons of the movement.[140] On 29 December the new League made the full text of the Kharkov resolutions public with a long commentary of their own, the nub of which was that the resolutions were provocative and unconstitutional and signalled a desire to force a reversion from political Zionism to the methods and ethos of Ḥibbat Zion.[141] But by then Kharkov's two delegates, Belkowsky

---

[138] *Illustriertes Wiener Extrablatt*, 22 December 1903. Text in Bein et al. (eds.), *Theodor Herzl: ne'umim u-ma'amarim zioniim*, ii (Jerusalem, 1976), pp. 375–6.

[139] Herzl to Plehve, 27 December 1903. *Diaries*, iv, pp. 1584–5.

[140] Jasinowski to Herzl, 9 and 25 December 1903. CZA, H VIII/397.

[141] *Ha-Ẓefira*, 29 December 1903.

and Rosenbaum, were on their way to Vienna to present their ultimatum. Kremenetzky, one of the EAC members in Vienna, acting under Herzl's direction, had informed Ussishkin on 21 December that Herzl had been profoundly hurt and would 'in no circumstances' receive them. But the telegram appears to have reached Ekaterinoslav only on 3 January 1904, too late to delay them.[142] A final piece of tinder for the coming explosion was supplied by the choice of the delegates to Herzl. Belkowsky had been one of Herzl's original recruits and his first champion among the easterners.[143] But that had all been swept away in the mounting oppositional storm. It had been Belkowsky who had snubbed Herzl by absenting himself from St. Petersburg (where he lived and which he represented as member of the GAC) when Herzl travelled there in August. Belkowsky had spoken firmly against the East Africa project in the great debate at the recent Congress. It was Belkowsky again who, having met Herzl in Austria early in November just before the Kharkov conference and having already argued most of the points at issue, contributed heavily to the outcome at Kharkov by his account of what had transpired and what was taken as Herzl's intransigence. 'The olive branch you wanted to send us through Belkowsky became in his hands a burning brand', Mandelstamm had written.[144] And it was Belkowsky, directly and indirectly, with whom Herzl came into conflict in his effort to keep the lines to St. Petersburg in his own hands, when Belkowsky, as the man on the spot, had a natural interest in transferring them to his own. As for Rosenbaum, he, as we have seen, was the most vociferous and abrasive, not to say impertinent, of all Herzl's opponents, saying in public the sort of thing that even Weizmann, a man of roughly similar views, usually restricted to his private correspondence.

However, to the delegates' surprise and confusion, Herzl met them head-on. He was cordial, but also undeviating in his refusal to accept them as a 'delegation' at all, or to recognize

---

[142] Heymann, ii, no. 88, p. 208. Why the telegram should have taken a fortnight to reach Ussishkin is a mystery. European telegraphic and postal services at the turn of the century were generally excellent.

[143] See *Origins*, pp. 278–9.

[144] To Herzl, 18 November 1903. CZA, H VIII/541.

the group they spoke for as one that was properly constituted and representative. Instead, after considerable movement of intermediaries to and fro,[145] he invited them to attend what was nominally a regular meeting of the EAC and there, seemingly refreshed and confident,[146] Herzl opened the session by laying down that Belkowsky and Rosenbaum were present solely in their capacity of members of the GAC and that 'of course they were not delivering an ultimatum or anything of that nature'.[147] That done, he launched into a report on the state of the negotiations with the British and the Turks interlaced with comments on the internal fight within the movement. Then, in short order, the session became an argument, fierce at times, between Herzl and the visitors, especially Rosenbaum. The ground was gone over once again and newly accumulated complaints, large and small, were aired by each side as proof of the other's wrong and uncomradely conduct. The major issue of principle the Russians raised was that the Congress and Herzl had put themselves out of court by violating the terms of the Basel Programme. This, they said, was in the nature of a contract. It was pointless to argue for or against any particular variety of Zionism; there had been an agreement and it had been broken. Herzl's retort was that the Congress was a sovereign institution. No one Congress was entitled to bind its successors. Each was free to make policy according to circumstances.[148]

Herzl had the advantage of being on home ground and in the chair and took it to the full. He repeatedly put the visitors down; and as a final shot, ended the meeting abruptly by solemnly and somewhat inaccurately reciting the Latin tag,

---

[145] Admirably summarized by Heymann, ii, pp. 51–2.

[146] His good mood and high spirits may be judged by the language in which he indulged. Reporting his failure to persuade the managers of the Hirsch Fund (ICA) to finance the expedition to East Africa, he told his committee, 'Die Herren haben sich da in einer Lage befunden, wo sie weder ja noch nein sagen konnten, und wenn Sie diese berühmte Anekdote kennen, "Ja habe ich nicht sagen wollen, Nein habe ich nicht sagen wollen, habe ich gesagt, Lecken Sie mich im Arsch." Sie wollen weder Ja noch nein sagen, haben sie zurückgeschrieben, sie acceptieren unter der Bedingung, dass die Sache nicht politisch sei. Darauf habe ich ihn geschrieben, indem ich mir die Hosen heruntergelassen habe.' EAC meeting, 6 January 1904. CZA, Z 1/178, pp. 2–3.

[147] Ibid., p. 1.

[148] Ibid., pp. 12–13, 18–19.

Gracchi de seditione querentes.[149] He cowed Belkowsky and Rosenbaum somewhat; but there had been no meeting of minds; and no attempt by either party to conciliate the other. Herzl's main concern had been to assert his authority, not to debate the rights and wrongs of the East Africa project. That effort, so far as it went, had succeeded. But so far as the substantive issues were concerned, nothing had been settled. Belkowsky and Rosenbaum soon hurried away to St. Petersburg to attend a new conference of the Russian GAC members, a follow-up to Kharkov. Herzl pursued them briefly with shots in the press and in confidential letters of inquiry and remonstrance to friends and foes alike, in which he restated his refusal to accede to pressure and his protest against those who had come seeking quarrels. Then he turned to other things. A fortnight later he travelled to Rome for the penultimate of his personal confrontations with the great and powerful of his times.

vi

Herzl set off for Italy on 17 January 1904 to be received in audience by King Victor Emmanuel III. The audience had been applied for on his behalf by the Chief Rabbi of Florence, Dr S. H. Margulies, in October of the previous year. Knowing of the Italian interest in Tripolitania, it seems to have occurred to Herzl that if and when the Italians took control of the territory, there might be the making there of a settlement on the model of the one that had been proposed for El Arish. But chiefly, he wished to enlarge the circle of his contacts, to make the subject of Zionism known at the higher reaches of the Italian state, and, if possible, to enlist Italy for possible intercession or pressure at Constantinople. The King had been very willing to receive him and the audience itself (23 January) went well—the conversation, as Herzl recorded, being 'animated' and Victor Emmanuel ready enough to promise Herzl that 'whenever I meet a Turk, I will bring up your cause.' Meanwhile, the King wished him to see the Foreign Minister, Tittoni.[150] Herzl saw both Tittoni and

---

[149] Juvenal, *Satires*, II.24: *Quis tulerit Gracchos de seditione querentes?* ('Who could endure the Gracchi railing at sedition?'; i.e. here was the pot calling the kettle black.)

[150] *Diaries*, iv, pp. 1595–1600.

Giacomo Malvano, the Secretary-General at the Foreign Ministry. Malvano, a Jew, was entirely unhelpful. Tittoni was polite and non-committal and asked for a memorandum. A meeting with the Prime Minister, Giolitti, could not be arranged, but was promised for Herzl's next visit to Rome. On departure, Herzl judged the 'balance-sheet for Rome— good'; but, in the event, the results proved negligible. In his memorandum to Tittoni, written after his return to Vienna, he restated the Zionists' central aim of a Charter specifying rights of settlement in Ereẓ-Israel, but limited in practice to the northern part of the country (the *sanjak* of Acre) and granted against a pledge of an annual tribute to the Ottoman treasury of £T100,000. The tone and content were carefully moderate. An 'independent Jewish state in Palestine' was not asked for in view 'of the difficulties which such an objective would encounter'. And, 'in deference to the sensibilities of all believers, the Holy Places are to be exempted and to receive the character of extraterritoriality forever.' What the Zionists did want urgently was help in persuading the Ottoman Government to reopen negotiations. To that end, a letter from the King of Italy to the Sultan 'recommending our proposals and giving friendly counsel that they be taken into consideration would have a decisive effect'.[151] Herzl's very tentative notion about Tripolitania, which the King had laughed off, was forgotten.

Tittoni's reply was prompt, but it was a refusal in all but name. 'I appreciate the humanitarian purpose which the Zionist Committee has assumed to provide comfort for poor Jews whose condition in a number of countries is a sad one. But as for the approach you would wish His Majesty the King to make to the Sultan, I can only rely on my august sovereign's superior wisdom.'[152] However, the highlight of Herzl's journey to Rome had not been the audience with the King, but a wholly unplanned—although long-desired—meeting with the Pope.

Herzl had concluded as early as 1896, correctly as it turned out, that 'Rome will be against us'[153] and nothing had occurred since to alter that judgement. A year later, on the convening of

---

[151] Ibid., pp. 1610–11.
[152] Tittoni to Herzl, 16 March 1904. CZA, H VI/66.
[153] *Origins*, p. 268.

the First Congress, there had been signs of mild concern in the Vatican. One press report spoke of the Pope writing to the Sultan to ask him 'not to cede Palestine to the Jews . . . lest [doing so he] give the lie to the prophecy according to which they were to be dispersed throughout the world and incapable of forming a nation'. Another spoke of the apostolic delegate in Constantinople being recalled to Rome to consult on measures to be taken against the Zionist movement and of the Pope applying for help to France as the protector of the Christians in the Orient.[154] When Herzl then made a fresh attempt to explain the purposes of Zionism to the papal nuncio in Vienna and was not even received, and with Pope Leo XIII hostile to the Jews as the bearers of the germ of liberalism and the Church backing the anti-Dreyfus camp in France with all its might, there seemed little point in pursuing the issue further. Thereafter, except for a flicker of interest from time to time when coming across someone with access to the Pope or the Curia, the matter seems to have dropped from his mind. Only in August 1903, upon the death of Leo XIII and the election of Giuseppe Sarto, Patriarch of Venice, in his place, did it occur to Herzl that a fresh attempt might succeed.

There had been a delegate to the Sixth Congress from Venice, Angelo Sullam, who, he thought, might be useful and there were, by now, other friends in Italy, notably the leader of the Italian Zionists, Felice Ravenna, a lawyer in Ferrara. Herzl, in his impulsive way, seems suddenly to have been fired by the prospect. 'I must see the Pope as soon as possible', he wrote to Ravenna, pressing him to seek out Sullam, or any other potential intermediary he might know of. Then, his mind

---

[154] *Le Temps*, 8 September 1897; *Daily News*, 7 September 1897. It should be noted, however, that a search by the author in the files preserved in the Vatican Archives of regular correspondence for the period between the Secretariat of State in Rome and the missions in Vienna, Paris, and Constantinople revealed no trace of the subject of Zionism, nor any mention of Herzl. Nor did a search through the private papers of Mgr. Bonetti, the apostolic delegate in Constantinople, kindly conducted for me by the Vice-Prefect of the Archives, reveal any reference to the subject, let alone to his reported recall to Rome to discuss it. Conceivably, the matter was not handled by the Secretariat of State at all, but by another office in the Vatican. Equally, it may be that nothing was committed to paper. All that is really clear is that the entire subject of the Vatican's approach to the Jewish Question in its modern form and to Zionism in particular is ripe for thorough and comprehensive investigation.

shooting ahead to the substance of any talk he might have with the Pope, he briefed Ravenna on the basis on which he thought the Church might be induced to moderate its hostility.

This is what I want of the Pope and what you may say, but only to people whom you are sure you can trust: It is only secular land [*terre profane*] that we want in Palestine. We have no intention of touching the Holy Places, even from afar. The Holy Places must be permanently extraterritorialized, *res sacrae extra commercium* of the law of nations. This is the proposition I want accepted and protected by the Pope as the spiritual sovereign respected and recognized even by Christians of other churches.[155]

An ostensibly promising potential intermediary was soon found: Leone Romanin Jacur, a leading Italian politician and a member of a prominent Jewish family in Padua, who knew the new Pope well enough to put a request for an audience directly to him and was, in fact, received at the Vatican a short time later. But Romanin Jacur refused to help or even to meet Herzl when the latter passed through northern Italy on his way to Rome for his audience with the King[156] and the prospect of a meeting at the Vatican then receded once more—until a chance encounter with one Berthold Lippay, an Austrian painter whom the Pope had appointed to serve him professionally and had created a papal count, unexpectedly revived it.

Herzl had stopped off in Venice for a 'breathing spell'[157] of a day and a night. Lippay recognized him in a restaurant, attached himself to the weary and initially reluctant Herzl, and in a rush of chatter—presumably to impress him, and certainly to Herzl's great astonishment—offered to present him to the Pope. The man struck Herzl as a gossip and a name-dropper, over-anxious to play a role on a greater stage than any offered by his art—on a political one, if possible. (Later it

---

[155] Herzl to Ravenna, 5 and 10 September 1903. CZA, H III/A3. See also Umberto Nahon, 'Le lettere di Teodoro Herzl a Felice Ravenna', in N. Goldmann et al., *Nel Centenario della Nascita di Teodoro Herzl* (Venice-Rome, 1961), pp. 33–4.

[156] Ravenna to Herzl, 12 October 1903. CZA, H VIII/669a; and Romanin Jacur to Ravenna, 15 January 1904. Nahon, pp. 39–40.

[157] *Diaries*, iv, p. 1589. Herzl's health was now failing rapidly and he was husbanding his remaining reserves of strength with unprecedented care.

turned out that he was heavily in debt and wanted Herzl to
help him procure a loan from the 'Jews'.) But the fact remained
that he evidently knew the Pope well and that he seemed to
mean what he said; and the offer was accepted. Lippay was
indeed as good as his word and everything went forward with
great speed. A few days later, on 22 January (a day before his
audience with the King), Herzl was ushered in to see the
Secretary of State, Cardinal Merry del Val.

Herzl found the atmosphere pleasant and the conversation
earnest. At the same time, the extreme reluctance of the
Church to consider any question relating to the Jews in other
than traditional terms was plain from the start. The goodwill
of the Holy See for the cause of Zionism was what was requested
of it, Herzl told the Cardinal. The response was, that 'as long
as the Jews deny the divinity of Christ, we certainly cannot
make a declaration in their favour.' The Jews, the prelate
explained, were 'the indispensable witnesses to the phenomenon
of God's term on earth. But they deny the divine nature of
Christ. How then can we, without abandoning our own highest
principles, agree to their being given possession of the Holy
Land again?' But the Zionists did not want the Holy Places,
Herzl countered: they could be extraterritorialized. No, said
Merry del Val, 'it won't do to imagine them in an enclave of
that sort.' It would be something, said Herzl, if the Church did
no more than make clear that it did not oppose us. 'The history
of Israel', replied the Cardinal, 'is our heritage, it is our foundation. But in order for us to come out for the Jewish people in
the way you desire, they would first have to be converted.'
Herzl then went as far as he could: 'Think of the wanderer
and his cloak, Your Eminence. The wind couldn't take it
away from him, but the sun smiled it away from him. We have
withstood the persecutions, we are still here today.' Merry del
Val would promise only to consider the request—and to
recommend that the audience with the Pope be granted.[158]

---

[158] Ibid., pp. 1593–5. The only source available (and possibly the only source in
existence) for this conversation, as for the conversation with the Pope that followed, is
Herzl's own record in his diary. However, Herzl was always scrupulous in his setting
down of the bare facts of whatever it was that he was dealing with and his record can
always be trusted. (His understanding and interpretation of events, on the other hand,
are often open to question even if they are, of course, of great intrinsic interest.) And

Three days later Herzl was received by Pius X. 'A good, coarse-grained village priest', Herzl described him, 'to whom Christianity has remained a living thing even in the Vatican.' He too was not unfriendly, although put out—so Herzl judged—by the Jew's refusal to kiss his hand, and the message was the same. The Church could not prevent the Jews from returning to Jerusalem, but could never sanction it, Herzl was told. 'The Jews have not recognized our Lord, therefore we cannot recognize the Jewish people.' The extraterritorialization of the Holy Places did not interest him. Jerusalem, he repeated firmly, must not fall into the hands of the Jews. But the Zionists' point of departure, Herzl insisted, was the Jews' distress and they wished to avoid religious issues. 'Yes', retorted the Pope, 'but we, and I as head of the Church, cannot.' There were therefore two possibilities, said Pius. If the Jews continued to cling to their faith and deny the divinity of Jesus, the Church was unable to help them; if they went to Palestine 'without any religion' the Church would be still less favourable to them. 'This very day', the Pope concluded, 'the Church is celebrating the feast of the unbeliever who, on the road to Damascus, became miraculously converted to the true faith. And so, if you come to Palestine and settle your people there, we shall have churches and priests ready to baptize all of you.'[159]

Back in Vienna, Herzl was swept up once more into the storm over the East Africa project.

---

indeed, it is noteworthy, in this particular case, that when Merry del Val granted an interview to a representative of *Die Welt* some months later, the substance of his response was much the same. 'How, for example, can we deliver up the country of our Redeemer to a people of a different faith?', he expostulated. The Cardinal then went on to stress a point which had not been raised in Herzl's presence, the frequent membership of Jews 'in the camp of our opponents. Whenever a bad book appears, or an ugly picture which mocks us, or a newspaper which defames us—then, when we examine the affair with precision, we find the Israelite behind it.' Finally, softening slightly, Merry del Val stressed that the Church, notwithstanding, would do nothing to impede the Zionists' effort to obtain 'a home in Palestine secured by public law'. For that, he said, 'is quite another matter . . . If the Jews believe that they can ease their lot in the Land of their fathers, that is a humanitarian question in our view. The foundation of the Holy See is apostolic; it will never oppose an undertaking that alleviates human misery.' *Die Welt*, 1 April 1904.

[159] *Diaries*, iv, pp. 1601–5.

vii

At the St. Petersburg meeting of the Russian members of the GAC (13–15 January 1904) the rebels were in a commanding majority. None of the loyalists attended and of the moderates only two. Tchlenov was absent. The Kharkov resolutions were reconfirmed easily and it was agreed that they should now be published 'officially'—with language and tone softened somewhat, but with the substance as before. Elaborate plans were then made to carry on the fight for the hearts and minds of the Zionists both in the East and the West and a fortnight later Ussishkin travelled to Germany to that end. But there was less steam behind all this than there had been at Kharkov. Herzl had held firm. Support for him in the East and the West, irrespective of views on his policy and on political Zionism in general, was unmistakably strong. It had proved impossible to disentangle the campaign against East Africa from the campaign to depose him and equally impossible to pursue the campaign against him without a violent schism in the movement. This had now been grasped fully and at that point the men of Kharkov, not excluding 'the man of Ekaterinoslav' himself, had finally drawn back after all—much as Herzl himself, while pushing the 'Gracchi' hard, had refrained from forcing an explosion and had, as we have seen, been reconsidering his policy.

In March Herzl tried once again to start up conversations with the Turks, this time on the restricted basis of Jewish settlement in the *sanjak* of Acre alone. But all concerned ran true to form. The Zionists[160] lost their bearings in the labyrinth of the high Ottoman bureaucracy and the Turkish response, as before, was that Jews could settle in Mesopotamia, but not in Palestine—which *might* come later. Herzl's motive for reapplying to Constantinople is obscure. He may have intended no more than to provide himself, and his opponents, with evidence of his own good intentions and of the hopelessness

---

[160] Herzl did not go to Constantinople himself. By this time he was far too sick for such a journey; besides he could hardly have believed it was likely to succeed. His emissaries were Leopold Kahn, a member of the EAC and a lawyer, and Zalman Levontin, one of the founders of Rishon le-Zion (see *Origins*, pp. 98–190) and newly established as manager of the Jaffa branch of the Bank.

of an acceptable deal with the Turks being concluded. He may have wished to test the water: to see whether knowledge of his negotiations with the British had led them to consider things afresh. In any event, while harsh things were still being said between January and April, there was somewhat less acrimony in the air and more thought of peacemaking (though not compromise) on both sides when the full GAC assembled in Vienna for its regular meeting on 11 April with almost all of the most articulate advocates of the alternative policies for the movement present.[161]

The Greater Actions Committee sat in Vienna for the better part of five days (11–15 April 1904). About half of the time was devoted to the crisis of the movement, the rest—no mean gesture on Herzl's part—mostly to matters of settlement and development in Erez-Israel. It was, of course, the first half of the session, nominally in the form of a debate on Herzl's report as president, actually an exercise in reconciliation in which all participated, that counted for most. None thought it was anything but overdue. All were anxious to come to terms with their respective opponents. But none had finally modified their position on fundamentals; nor was there a disposition to listen to opponents with a genuinely open mind; nor, indeed, given the depth of the divide between the parties, could this have been expected. The result was an immensely long, but almost consistently lively debate in which the speakers were torn between a desire to promote goodwill (sometimes grudging, sometimes dissolved for a moment by flashes of irritation) and what seemed to them to be dictated by their particular approach to the Jewish Question. So once again there was no real meeting of minds and once again the main arguments for and against Herzl's policy were heard and much past history was brought up: that it was not the task of the Zionists to seek immediate relief for all Jews in their distress, nor should the programme and policy of the movement

---

[161] But it is worth noting leading figures of the Zionist movement (all with much to say on the subject) who were not members of the GAC and were therefore absent: Aḥad Ha-'Am, Bialik, Bodenheimer, Gaster, Motzkin, Nordau, Reines, Wolffsohn, and Zangwill.

be determined by 'the people' (Bernstein-Kohan);[162] that the East African project, being on too small a scale to provide relief for more than a handful, would lead nowhere, that it would therefore only harm and confuse a movement which had been founded from the first on the absolute primacy of Erez-Israel—so much so that it would be an enormous success for the movement if the project were rejected and a disaster if it were accepted (Jacobson);[163] that, on the contrary, one could be entirely loyal to Erez-Israel while seeing East Africa as a stepping-stone to it, a basis for continuous contact with the British Government, a far better prospect for the migrants concerned than their dispersal in the ghettos of America, and a future show-piece that would stand the future Jewish state in Erez-Israel in good stead (Greenberg);[164] and the equally fundamental question of method—as it emerged, for example, when Ussishkin charged Herzl with mere talk for Erez-Israel as opposed to deeds for East Africa:

HERZL. I told you: I negotiated with the Russian Government, the Turkish and Italian, and with the English Government too: for Palestine. Yes, gentlemen, if we are to call negotiating for 1,000 dunams[165] and buying 500 'deeds' for Palestine, why then we are on different planets . . . and do not understand each other. Palestine is not this [particular] plot of land, it is this [particular] country. I have tried hard in this matter; to my regret I have achieved nothing yet. Had I achieved it, you would have thrown me out already . . . Mr Ussishkin says too that in the matter of East Africa I have perpetrated a *coup d'état* . . .

USSISHKIN. The Congress itself perpetrated a *coup d'état*.

HERZL. Mr Ussishkin, do you know what the Congress is? Why, the Congress is the organized representation of the people.

USSISHKIN. No, of Zionism. (Commotion.)

HERZL. Mr Ussishkin, we want the growth of Zionism and we want

---

[162] 'Grosses Aktions-Comité, Sitzung in Wien, 11–15 April 1904.' CZA, Z 1/195–9, pp. 81–5 (51–4). 'It's hard to discover the truth', Herzl said to Bernstein-Kohan at one point in the debate, 'if we assume there is a truth—if there is a truth at all, I don't know—if your view is right. Who is to warrant that your political conception is the most advantageous and correct for the people?' 'That is the affair of History', Bernstein-Kohan retorted. Ibid., pp. 412–13 (231–2).

[163] Ibid., pp. 302–14 (165–73).

[164] Ibid., pp. 389–91 (216–18).

[165] 1 dunam = 1,000 square metres (approx. ¼ acre).

Zionism to be the representation of the people. Why do we want that? Because we believe that in order to attain this great objective we need great strength and that that great strength will not be found in an association of conventicles. That is what you had twenty years ago. You say: we were Zionists twenty and twenty-five years ago. That is your reproach. That is what you always say to me. Yes, but what do you prove thereby? What could you do so long as you lacked this formula, so long as you lacked political Zionism? You lived in little circles and met in little rooms and you collected money. Your purpose was splendid. Your idealism was beyond question. But you could do nothing because you did not know the way, and that is the organizing of the nation, the instrument being the Congress. That is why you must submit to it, even if you are enraged by its decisions.

USSISHKIN. In that case the greatest anti-Zionists can enter [the movement].

HERZL. But Ussishkin, surely you know that people come to the Congress as the greatest of anti-Zionists and leave as Zionists?

USSISHKIN. I have seen the opposite too.

HERZL. You refuse to be persuaded, I can see that.

USSISHKIN. No.

HERZL. . . . . That secret meeting at Zikhron Ya'akov (as long as we are not yet doing battle, permit me a blunt word) was a great piece of foolishness, my dear Ussishkin. You go to Erez-Israel, ruled by a Pasha, and you do a thing the like of which has never been seen in Turkey, a political meeting.

USSISHKIN. It was a non-political meeting.

HERZL. Just as at Minsk. You [people] really do not understand that there are certain things that can be said at Basel, but that perhaps even in Zürich or Luzern cannot be . . . It was a mistake, an incautious act. First of all, there is only a single Congress, which is at Basel. And if a congress is held in Palestine it is not more Zionist or Jewish than the one at Basel. The Zionist Congress is there where the organized will of the people resides, and that is our Congress. And you convene congresses in Minsk and Zikhron Ya'akov![166]

Still, the meeting was distinguished by a marked desire on all sides to burn no bridges and by the sharper, neater, and more explicit terms in which each case was put. And once again, in parallel with the debate on policy, there was a

---

[166] Ibid., pp. 454–64 (254–9).

debate on Herzl—Herzl the maker of policy, Herzl the leader, Herzl the indispensable man of the movement and, perhaps, of the people. Some of this was by way of allusion; quite a lot was straight talk in which Herzl himself took part. Generally, Herzl dominated the meeting as he had always dominated the Congresses. In one respect more so and more easily, because he was both its hub, its principal participant, and also its underlying subject. Besides, he was in excellent form throughout: always alert, always ready to question, rebut, interrupt, fully in control of his tongue, sharp, conciliatory, kind, patronizing, witty, courteous, and crushing in turn. 'You have a hard skull', he told Ussishkin; 'So have I. Perhaps that is the reason that I have such a liking for you.' 'And I [for you]', Ussishkin replied. 'But now I want to tell you something', Herzl went on. 'Believe me: I am stronger than you. That is why I am conciliatory, because I know that if we fight I shall win.'[167] There were none to compete with him. His chief opponent, the recognized champion for the opposition, was Ussishkin, naturally. He opened the debate after Herzl's statement and there were repeated exchanges between the two as the debate wore on. But Ussishkin was too solid and heavy and blunt to shine in such circumstances and he was isolated somewhat in his absolute refusal to yield. His colleagues were not at their best either. Tchlenov was weak, Bernstein-Kohan unconvincing, Rosenbaum comparatively subdued. The opposition's star in debate was Jacobson, but even he was unable to dent Herzl's devastating combination of unquestioned personal authority, clarity of exposition, and a readiness to make concessions in practice while beating down all the arguments raised against him as matters of theory. It was Herzl at his strongest and most impressive. For a man dying of heart disease it was a last, extraordinary performance.

But Herzl was defeated: not on the issue of his own leadership and authority, nor on the question of the 'sovereignty' of the Congress and its ancillary institutions, but on the central issue of policy under debate and on the matter of the ethos of the movement that was implicit in it. For he now conceded without argument the principle that Zionism had to do essentially and necessarily, perhaps exclusively, with Zion—

[167] Ibid., pp. 475–6 (266).

with Erez-Israel. He allowed the ideological board to be
swept clean and tidy, leaving the arguments justifying the
indirect approach to statehood and to Erez-Israel itself
unspoken. He was content to insist that decisions of the Congress had to be respected, that the expedition had to be dispatched, and the fight fought within the movement and
along parliamentary lines. For the rest, what his colleagues
heard was an apologia. The question that had been before the
GAC in August, he said in his opening statement, was

whether we should inform the Congress, or hide from it, the fact
that the English Government had offered us a territory for our suffering masses. My personal view was and still is that we have no right
simply to reject such a proposal, to toss it off the table, without asking
the people if it does or does not want to accept it.

I shall not refer to this proposal by the very controversial term
Nachtasyl, but I will say, a piece of bread. I, who perhaps have cake to
eat, at any rate my bread, have no right to refuse a slice of bread
offered to the poor because I do not want it or because I do not need
it. I may perhaps be enchanted and inspired if even in their misery
and hunger, impelled by ideals, they reply: 'No, we do not want this
bread.' But I must put the question.[168]

'You are mistaken', he told the Committee at one point,

if you think that I shall press hard for [East Africa] at the [Seventh]
Congress. I shall not press hard for anything. What I shall say is,
that I have no scheme or position to defend, nothing of that kind.
What I want is to have the true will [of the Congress] revealed on the
basis of true facts—the facts which we wish to explore.[169]

Later in the debate he said,

No one could rightly reproach me with disloyalty to Zionism were I
to say: I am going to Uganda. It was as a Jewish-state man [*Judenstaatler*] that I had [originally] presented myself to you. I gave you
my card: Herzl, *Judenstaatler*. I learned a great deal in the course of
time. I got to know Jews—and sometimes it was a pleasure. But,
gentlemen, I also learned that the solution for us lies only in Palestine.[170]

[168] Ibid., pp. 24–6 (18–19).
[169] Ibid., p. 411 (230–1).
[170] Ibid., p. 472 (263–4.

At the end he was rewarded with a statement by Tchlenov that his faith in Herzl and in the Smaller Actions Committee had been restored, that it was clear that Herzl's promise of loyalty to Zion at the end of the recent Congress was entirely sincere, and that Herzl was indeed working 'systematically and energetically and wisely for Zion'.[171] A subcommittee of which both Tchlenov and Ussishkin were members drew up a resolution in that spirit. It also specifically sanctioned the expedition to East Africa, leaving the decision on the scheme itself to the next Congress and the debate on it, in the interim, open. It declared the extended row over the previous seven months at an end.

A second resolution, submitted by Herzl himself, touched explicitly on the matter of discipline:

The East African scheme may be freely discussed by all. At the same time, every member of the Actions Committee pledges himself to avoid all personal attacks not only in official circulars, but as far as possible to exercise his influence to guard against such attacks and, generally, against the discussion assuming a harmful form.[172]

Both resolutions were carried by large majorities. Two of Herzl's supporters (Cowen and Jasinowski) voted against the first; a third, Greenberg, abstained. Mandelstamm and Friedemann joined them to vote against the second resolution, Greenberg abstaining once more.[173] Ussishkin went along with the majority, but did not really believe what he had seen and heard. 'Territorialism' was gathering force all the time, he wrote to a friend after the conference, and 'we must defend ourselves with all our power.'[174] But he was wrong. The outcome was not, as he had feared before the conference and still suspected at its end, a victory for Herzl. If there was a victory, it was for mildness, and if there was a victor, it was Tchlenov.

---

[171] Ibid., pp. 944–5 (549–50).

[172] *Die Welt*, 15 April 1904.

[173] The loyalists, among them Mandelstamm, Jasinowski, and Alexander Marmorek, had favoured a straightforward vote of confidence in Herzl and Cowen had proposed simply to proceed to the next item on the agenda, presumably as a deliberate snub to the opposition.

[174] Letter to Barzilay, Schwartz, *Ussishkin*, p. 85.

viii

After the GAC there was time for one last exercise in personal diplomacy: a long talk at the end of April with the Austrian Foreign Minister Count Goluchowski. This was Herzl's first serious attempt to enlist the state of which he himself was a subject in the Zionist cause. It was a good talk and Herzl heard a strong expression of sympathy. But no promises were made. It was a beginning, or so, at any rate, Goluchowski and Herzl agreed.

Early in May Herzl was sent by his doctors to a watering-place for six weeks. In the middle of the month members of the movement were requested to refrain from writing to him. Early in June, after returning briefly to Vienna he went to Edlach, another resort, now very ill indeed. Thereafter work virtually ceased. His health now deteriorated rapidly. A month later, on 3 July 1904, he died.

Theodor Herzl was just forty-four years old at his death. Only nine years had passed since, in isolation in Paris, he had thought out his formulation of 'a modern solution to the Jewish Question', seven years since in a single stroke he had made himself the most considerable public figure in contemporary Jewry.

He had no true successor and no competitors. He left no heirs. He had few true followers. He was, it seems true to say, unique.

Looking Back and
Thinking Forward

Such was the debate on the East Africa project—harsh, convoluted, and unamenable to resolution. For when all the surface layers of the quarrel have been allowed for—the genuine differences on strategy, the play of personalities and temperament, the private hurts, grudges, and jealousies, the competition for place and influence, and the friction that could not but arise between men of different culture and social experience—there was here a clash of ideologies, of conflicting principles, and incompatible prescriptions for the ills of Jewry. And far from mitigating or deflecting the debate on ideology, the political fight for supremacy in the movement only intensified it—no doubt because in these the formative years of the Zionist movement ideology was all. The movement had no *material* power; it was a voluntary association within the larger society of Jewry that was itself devoid of any but the most tenuous centres of formal and truly enforceable authority. The influence and moral authority of Zionism was therefore a function of its power to move men's minds; and any such power as it had to do so turned on the force and conviction carried by its doctrines. Unfortunately, one of its besetting problems was that these doctrines were (and have remained) very imperfectly defined. The Jewish national revival lacked figures comparable to, say, John Locke, or the American Federalists Hamilton, Madison, and Jay; it had no great doctrinaire historian like Macaulay, no social and political theoreticians of the quality of Mosca, Pareto, or Weber, let alone Marx. It is true that the question whether the history and sociology of Jewry are amenable to all-encompassing treatment is one of exceptional difficulty; and of the handful of scholars who have attempted to answer it in the grand manner none has completely succeeded. There was, of course, Aḥad Ha-ʿAm—a great mind and one that was at its best on great public affairs. Yet, in the last resort, what Aḥad Ha-ʿAm provided was a continuing critique of the activities of others. His splendid essays highlighted the great issues of the day as turned over in a superior, if idiosyncratic mind. At best, they were guides to the inner logic and essential nature of the movement as he understood it—or, alternatively, prescriptions for the handling of specific and immediate problems in public policy. Their most powerful ideological influence was upon the minds of members of his own, numerically limited class, the intelligentsia. They were not expositions of doctrine for all. In so far as they could be said to imply a programme, it was not one for a large mass movement. The Zionists, it may be said, articulated their doctrine by stages, by trial and error, by periodic debate on matters of practical policy in so far as, and provided that, these forced them to consider fundamentals. None did this so well as Aḥad Ha-ʿAm; but what he did was in accord with general practice, rather than in contrast to it: the unspoken rule was that action taken or action proposed led to the consideration and formulation of doctrine rather than that consideration of doctrine led to the taking of action. It is not surprising, therefore, that so far as doctrine is concerned, Zionism presents a patchy and unsystematic appearance. So it was in this, perhaps the greatest of the movement's debates, the debate with the most far-reaching consequences for the evolution of the movement, in regard to both doctrine and action.

On some points there was full agreement: that the Emancipation had failed to liberate the Jews; that, accordingly, the course of Jewish history must be reversed; that the *rule* of Exile must be ended and the Diaspora—all or most of it—wound up; and that, finally, by one great stroke—by the setting apart of a defined territory into which the Jews would gather and in which, as a majority people, they would govern themselves—the scales of the Exile would be made to drop away, its social, psychological, and intellectual distortions eliminated, its physical miseries and its humiliations ended, and a whole new range of mental and social activity opened up as much for the Jews as a people as for Jews as individuals. This much was common ground for virtually all Zionists; this was the message and the prospect which they held out to their actual and potential adherents; and to argue otherwise was simply to put oneself outside any recognizable class of Zionists at all.

But these were very general propositions and in practice, as we have seen, there were different schools, each with its distinct interpretation, none capable of squaring its differences with the others or redefining the common ground so as to minimize them. They could only fight their differences out, or suppress the intramural argument in the common interest, or retire. But to fight, in such circumstances, was to fight to win; and to win support for a particular interpretation of the common programme or for a particular strategy for making that programme effective was, in effect, to win the leadership of the movement. This was what leadership of the movement *meant*; and there was no other way of winning it.

Two linked questions had always been at issue and were now to the fore throughout the debate on East Africa: what was the true and desirable relationship between the Jewish people and other nations; and what was the true and desirable relationship between the Jews and their own historic past? The starting-point for the Zionists' view of these matters had been the question of the *individual* Jew and on this there had indeed been loose agreement all along. Thus all Zionists rejected assimilation—in part because it carried with it the taint of surrender and self-abnegation, but more significantly on the pragmatic grounds that the painless, lasting, and self-induced absorption of Jews in large numbers into the surrounding population was simply not feasible. As the early literature shows clearly enough, this denial of the feasibility of assimilation relied on no more than extremely simple and unsystematic social observation, often no more than a modest extension of personal experience.[1] But the precise terms of

[1] For example: M. L. Lilienblum's classic 'Obshcheyevreiski vopros i Palestina', *Razsvet*, xli, 9 October 1881 (O.S.), pp. 1597 ff. See *Origins*, pp. 117–19; or Herzl's views as set out before the Royal Commission on Alien Immigration in London in 1902—poor sociology, very bad history, but genuine fruit of personal experience:

the analysis hardly mattered, because the evidence for the failure of the Emancipation to resolve the tension between the Jew and the gentile in the West was so abundant and because for the overwhelming majority of east European Jews assimilation was in any case not only impracticable, but literally unthinkable. In this respect, namely that of the assimilation of individual Jews into their immediate non-Jewish environment, the consensus could therefore be strong and complete. But so far as what might be termed the *collective* assimilation of the Jews was concerned, namely the absorption (or reabsorption) of the Jewish people as such into the society of nations, the terms on which it was to take place, and the problems it would raise, matters were otherwise. There was no clear or authorized doctrine here either; but nor was there, except rarely, explicit recognition that there was here an issue with which the movement was properly concerned. Least of all was there anything like consensus.

Broadly, there were two schools of thought and their classic exponents were those two somewhat eccentric figures on the institutional fringes of the movement, Zangwill and Aḥad Ha-'Am. Strikingly different in background and views, they had this in common that both were intellectuals of independent mind and independent prestige whose thinking revolved consistently around general, relatively abstract categories, and who granted or withheld their support in the fulfilment of solemn acts of moral and social judgement.

Herzl and his closest followers—Zangwill among them—had always taken it as a matter of course that Zionism would

---

MR NORMAN. With regard to assimilation as a remedy for anti-Semitism, as I gather from you, it neither could be expected nor, from the Jewish point of view, is it desired?

DR HERZL. I myself was an assimilated Jew, and I speak from experience. I think the Jews have rather a tendency to assimilate, they have a natural tendency to assimilate; but there comes the moment when they are in a very good way on the road to assimilation, and then just at that moment comes anti-Semitism. The whole of history has taught us that never have Jews been in a happier condition than they were in Spain before events which led up to the Inquisition and Expulsion of the fifteenth century; they were to Spain all they could be, and they had all they could have.'

Royal Commission on Alien Immigration, ii, *Minutes of Evidence*, p. 214.

bring peace[2] between the Jews and other peoples, upon which the Jews would enter the ranks of the nations on a basis of equality and benefit for all. Like Pinsker before them, they had seen no reason to reject the non-Jewish world *as such*. Their criticism of non-Jewish society had been precipitated by, and then been formulated in, the particular contemporary context of the disastrous relations between it and the Jews. But the brunt of their social and cultural criticism was directed *inwards* at Jewry itself. And the particular force and originality in what Pinsker and Herzl and, later, Zangwill had to say lay in the combination of these two logically distinct strains of criticism: for they argued for radical and linked changes both in the relations between Jewry and other societies and in the structure and nature of Jewish society itself. Indeed, their primary reference all the while was rather to society at large, as they understood it, than to Jewry or Judaism. Aḥad Ha-ʿAm had good cause therefore to pounce on Herzl's fantasy *Altneuland*[3] (in which he portrayed a Jewish state-to-be in Erez-Israel of superior social and political standards and great economic prosperity) and dismiss it on the grounds that there was nothing immediately recognizable as *Jewish* in it. Indeed there was not. If anything, it was Viennese. *Altneuland* was poor literature: crudely constructed, of wooden characterization, psychologically superficial. It was also politically and sociologically naïve. Relations between Arabs and Jews, for example, are envisaged in outrageously optimistic terms on the basis of nothing firmer than Herzl's own *a priori* view of the way in which 'peace' between the Jews and their former enemies should work out and the social and economic benefits the Jews of Europe would bring to the Levant and impinge on Arab and Moslem consciousness. And, more directly to the present point, the immensely complex and important matter of the interconnection between Jewish religious orthodoxy and Jewish national political renewal

[2] 'If we only begin to carry out the plan, anti-Semitism would stop at once and for ever. For it is the conclusion of peace.' *Der Judenstaat*, Chapter VI, Conclusion.

[3] Theodor Herzl, *Altneuland* (Leipzig, 1902). Herzl described it on the title page as a novel (*Roman*). Naḥum Sokolov translated it into Hebrew as *Tel-Aviv: sipur* [*sipur* = a story] (Warsaw, 1902). The page references here are to the most recent English translation by Paula Arnold, *Altneuland, Old-New Land* (Haifa, 1960).

is disposed of in four brief sentences: 'The New Society was the last to favour obscurantism among its people', Herzl wrote, 'even though everyone was allowed his own opinions. Questions of faith were definitely excluded from all influence in public affairs. Whether you prayed in a synagogue, a church, or a mosque, in a museum or at a philharmonic concert—it was all one to the New Society. How you sought to get in touch with the Eternal was your own affair.'[4] What emerges clearly, in any case, is that *Altneuland* is represented as a *new* society, one which had broken away from tradition, one in which the Jews are at last a people like other peoples in all significant respects, and in which the newly gained territorial concentration and political autonomy are the basis for an internal social revolution. And it is this which permits their collective assimilation into the general society of nations on terms of equality and no greater specificity than is commonly tolerated and generally understood by all its other members.

However, nothing could be further from this than the ancient and profoundly ingrained notion of the uniqueness of the Jews: of their being a people eternally set apart and of their being a people profoundly and rightfully dedicated to the preservation of their special character and role above all else. It is true that in Herzl himself and in those who modelled themselves after him most closely there is a certain ambivalence from time to time on this point, a lack of ease. Every so often there is a relapse, so to speak, into the set and traditional mode of thought in which particularity and specificity are celebrated as a matter of course. Such, it may be argued, is the very representation of the future Jewish state as an *old-new* land and one in which the political and social order is *uniquely* decent, reasonable, and progressive—so much so that the non-Jewish observer in the story is moved again and again to comment on the Jews' qualities and sums up jocularly by saying, 'You know, to be frank, there was this and that in your New Society that seemed too good to be true—I suspected you in spite of what I saw with my own eyes. But now that I see what bastards you have, in addition to your angels and heroes, I begin to believe you. Even I, old cynic that I am, believe you implicitly, in fact!'[5]

<hr>

[4] *Altneuland*, p. 192. [5] Ibid., p. 190.

In Zangwill, however, a man free of the political pressures to which Herzl was subject and more than anxious to follow his private inclinations wherever they might lead him and to set out his views in the clearest language of which he was capable, there is no ambiguity at all, and no reluctance to make a break from the traditional mode of thought. When he embarrassed his fellow Zionists in 1903 by marrying a non-Jew and was thereupon asked to 'lie low' for a while, he wrote indignantly to Herzl that that

would be an admission of crime and my own attitude is that this superstition should be swept away, and Jews must become a people like any other. It is a positive duty to 'marry out'. Much as I value my Zionist activity, I cannot allow it to dwarf my larger sense of what the world needs, and what perhaps I exist to help to teach. It was for this reason, in my distrust of the fanatics, that I stood aside for some years from the movement. I do not care to help it except as a political movement: on the religious side I have a great deal to say, which I have for some years suppressed, for fear of hurting it. I am not sure, however, that the movement did not make a mistake in allowing itself almost to be captured by the religious party—you lose thousands of the most intelligent men in Judea, who are frightened away by the idea that Zionism is a movement of fanatics. All that large cultur-element [*sic*] would find a place in the nation, that element which in Germany baptised, could find a place in the movement.[6]

Later, after Herzl's death, as the retreat from Herzl's positions gathered speed and force, Zangwill tried hard to block it by founding a Jewish Territorial Organization (ITO) to pursue the now fading prospect of an East African province for the Jews.[7] As always with the Pinsker-Herzlian school, his starting-point was the current scene: 'the vital needs of the masses of the Jewish people at the present time', the gross inadequacy of such machinery as existed for alleviating these needs and for dealing with the great stream of Jewish migrants from

---

[6] Zangwill to Herzl, 21 December 1903. CZA, H VIII/946. Concerning his marriage directly, he had written to Herzl earlier: 'Joe [Cowen] tells me you think my future wife should become a Jewess and should make this sacrifice for our cause. She is ready to make any sacrifice—but not of conscience. The gates of Judaism are kept by cleri-calism and she could no more become a Jewess than I could become a Jew.' 5 November 1903. CZA, H VIII/946.

[7] See below, pp. 435–9.

Russia, and the inappropriateness of customary attitudes to the problem. But the pain and gloom which infuse Pinsker's *Autoemancipation!*, which the Territorialist manifesto so closely resembles in its approach, are replaced by a note, deliberately struck, of brisk and even cheerful pragmatism. ITO, Zangwill proclaims, is 'business-like in anticipation of the inevitable'.[8] Again, unlike the more circumspect Pinsker and Herzl, there is, along with the pragmatism, a great undisguised impatience with the hopeless conservatism, the pathetic absurdities, the internal contradictions, the humiliations—in a word, with the failure of Jewish life, public and private.

We are approaching the season [Zangwill told his listeners as he launched his movement] when the pious Russian Jew, sitting at the Passover table, rejoices at his redemption from slavery . . . A few months ago you might have seen our prisoners of the Pale celebrate their feast of Chanucah, their Thanksgiving or Independence Day. The irony of it! These downtrodden, cringing victims of the Ghetto celebrating the victories of Judas Maccabaeus! The poor, peaceful slum dwellers, who have never known a fatherland, singing paeans of triumph at having won back their Holy Land and Temple from the ancient Syro-Greeks over two thousand years ago! What a shadow-world the Jew lives in! Is it not about time Rip Van Winkle woke up and took stock of things and himself? We have not had a stocktaking for nearly two thousand years. It is eighteen hundred and thirty-five years since we lost our fatherland, and the period of mourning should be about over. We have either got to reconcile ourselves to our loss or set about recovering it. But to choose clearly between one alternative or the other is a faculty the Jew has lost.[9]

There followed a renewed plea for Zionism; and all Herzl's main arguments were rehearsed, except that since Erez-Israel was unobtainable and, on the other hand, 'Zion without Zionism' (that is, a return to the small-scale methods and the humble purposes of Ḥibbat Ẓion) 'is a hollow mockery', then 'better Zionism without Zion'. Better, said Zangwill, 'a Provisional Palestine'. 'Any territory which was Jewish,

---

[8] Maurice Simon (ed.), *Speeches, Articles and Letters of Israel Zangwill* (London, 1937), pp. 231–3.
[9] Speech at Derby Hall, Manchester, April 1905. Ibid., p. 198.

[and] under a Jewish flag', be believed, 'would save the Jew's
body and the Jew's soul.'[10]

It is plain that what Zangwill was after was not so much the
end of the Jewish people, once and for all, even with dignity
preserved, at high noon and with church bells ringing, as in
Herzl's celebrated first fantasy,[11] as the end of Jewry as a
Peculiar People. If elements of the past could be preserved
without too much trouble and, above all, without impeding
progress towards Redemption through Normalcy, as it might
be termed, well and good. On the other hand, whatever
threatened to impede such progress had to be jettisoned;
and this sloughing-off of ancient burdens could be done, he
thought, with a good conscience, to say nothing of some not
unjustified relief.

It is precisely this that the other school denied. For them the
ancient burdens—the past itself—were of the essence, central
and indispensable to their national feeling. Perhaps not all
of it was to be preserved intact: this was where the whole-
hearted traditionalists and these Zionists, like all others, differed. There was to be selection: and on the criteria the
Zionists of the school opposing Herzl were themselves divided.
There had always been some who were more aware than
others of the pitfalls that awaited them in the event of a
Return engineered by man rather than by Providence. But
so far as solutions and the philosophy in terms of which solutions would be formulated were concerned, very little had been
spelt out. 'We remain [in the movement] to defend Zionism',
wrote Yiẓhak Gruenbaum in a typical protest against the
Herzlian approach. 'Not the Zionism of diplomacy and charity
for the impoverished of the East, but the Zionism that is the
full renaissance of the Jewish people in Ereẓ-Israel.'[12] Just
what 'full renaissance' was to mean he did not say. However,
what united the anti-Herzlians was that all thought that
continuity was crucial: the Jewish society at which they
aimed, however vague and badly focused their picture of it,
had to contain within it the major elements of the Jewish

---

[10] Ibid., p. 212.

[11] *Diaries*, i, p. 7; see *Origins*, p. 239.

[12] Yiẓhak Gruenbaum, 'Letter to the editor of *Ha-Ẓefira* (1904), in Gruenbaum,
Dor be-mivḥan (Jerusalem, 1951), p. 36.

heritage—language, culture, history, and (with reservations) faith. Like the Herzlians, they wanted to reform Jewry and alter the Jewish condition, but the target that presented itself to them was the Diaspora, which, with its familiar ills and distortions, was distinguishable in their minds from Jewry and Judaism in their proper, unencumbered, pristine state. Thus in this, the largely east European Zionism, there was a touch of the romantic too. The original Odessa Lovers of Zion, the Aḥad Ha-'Amist moralists, the Ussishkinite settlement-first men, and the other subcategories of the genus, were all, each group in its way, creatures of the *haskala*, the Jewish Enlighten-ment.[13] All looked forward to a reform of the Jewish condition, but at the same time backward for the elements out of which to reconstruct it. And since the return to the cultivation of land was an essential part of their prescription for the restoration of social health in the future, and since the Land of Israel specifically was, of course, central to past Jewish history and belief, they inevitably saw Erez-Israel as the pivot on which all would turn. To do without it was to lose an indispensable source of strength, a force for renewal as powerful as it was indefinable.

There were difficulties. The true Zionists had always known, wrote Aḥad Ha-'Am, that the enterprise on which they had embarked would take generations to accomplish and that they could only approach their target very slowly and gradually. The Zionists

were, indeed, divided, both in respect of the target and in respect of the means. The majority believed that the result of their labours would be the ingathering of all our Exiles into Erez-Israel and an end to the afflictions of our people, material as well as spiritual. The minority said that in the nature of things that was too much to hope for and that the purpose for which we laboured was only this: the gathering into Erez-Israel of a *certain part* of the people, a part that, when in the course of time it had attained a natural and free life there, would constitute a *centre* for our national life as a whole and exert a *spiritual* influence on all other parts of the people, those who would remain in foreign lands, to cleanse them of the filth of their inner slavery and to unite them into a single national body with a single spirit . . . But both parties stood on a common, rock-solid base:

[13] See *Origins*, pp. 43–8.

belief in the power of the historic bond between the people and the
land to reawaken our people to *self-recognition* and to stir them to
fight for strength until such time as the conditions necessary for their
free development had been established.[14]

This was why they had never had any interest in plans to
resettle the Jews elsewhere, even in the United States, not even
when twenty years ago it was commonly argued that if only
a sufficient number of Jews, perhaps 60,000, gathered in a
designated territory of the United States, they would have the
right to petition the Congress to agree to the foundation of a
distinct State within the Union.

Yes, there in America there is everything—everything except one
thing: the historic base that alone is capable of accomplishing the
great feat of binding tens of thousands of pedlars and middlemen to
the land and renewing a proper national spirit in the heart of a
scattered and divided people.[15]

What had happened, Aḥad Ha-ʿAm argued, was that Herzl
and the politicals had bemused the true Zionists by holding
out the prospect of the end being attained with speed, with
relatively little effort or preliminary preparation, but rather
by a single, great, and adventurous leap. The politicals, who
seemed to think that a nation-state for the Jews could be
established anywhere if only the necessary land and rights
were available, might indeed be proper Jews, perhaps even
proper nationalists, but they could not be *Zionists*.[16] In any
case, Zionism in the form it had assumed at Basel was now
bankrupt. There remained only 'historic' Zionism. And as
for it,

---

[14] 'Ha-bokhim' [The Weepers], first published in *Ha-Shiloʾaḥ*, August/September
1903. *Kol kitvei Aḥad Ha-ʿAm*, p. 337. (Emphases in text.) It is interesting to compare
Herzl's view on what was best calculated to sustain national consciousness. Asked
whether for him 'Zion' (i.e. Erez-Israel) was no more than the means by which he
hoped to arouse Jewish national sentiment, whereas his real and sole purpose was a
Jewish state, he replied, 'Not at all; on the contrary. It is East Africa that is the means
by which we will be brought nearer to Zion.' Interview with Moshe Naḥum Syrkin,
Ha-Zefira, 25 September 1903.
[15] 'Ha-bokhim', *Kol kitvei Aḥad Ha-ʿAm*, p. 338.
[16] Ibid., p. 340.

Do not concern yourselfs [Aḥad Ha-'Am wrote]. It can wait. Some time will elapse, the African dream will recede into the past along with the other political dreams that had preceded it and one more drop of bitterness will have been added to the sea of affliction that is 'the history of Israel'. In due course, new people will appear and raise the eternal banner of Zionism again, to carry it with all their might, with all their heart, as you yourselves did before them. Then if a new political wise man emerges and seeks to lead you to Zion by a short, political route, the book of history will be opened and the chapter on 'Political Zionism' up to and including Uganda shown him . . . 'We shall manage our affairs slowly, by the long route', he will be told; 'we shall not hasten the end.'[17]

In both schools' thinking diagnosis and prescription were thus inextricable. If you were prepared to 'manage . . . affairs slowly' and to give the *yishuv* in Ereẓ-Israel all the time it needed to develop organically and if, above all, you accepted with more or less equanimity that the immediate, material problems of the bulk of Jewry could only be alleviated by other, that is, non-Zionist, non-territorial means and elsewhere, that is, in the Diaspora itself—then the proper concerns of the Zionists did, not unreasonably, boil down to care for a small, very superior community in Ereẓ-Israel whose essential role within the nation was educative and inspirational, an example, rather than an instrument; and then the East African (or any other territorialist) project was an obvious monstrosity, a perversion of the original ideas. The effect on this school of the renewal of the pogroms in 1903 as an instrument—or at the very least the salient feature—of Russian state policy towards the Jews was therefore less to spur them to a greater effort to rescue Russo-Polish Jewry than to induce concern lest others seek at all costs to 'hasten the end'. Ussishkin simply concluded that 'the events at Kishinev have entirely confirmed my old view that the *centre of gravity* of all our activity must be in Ereẓ-Israel and not in the Diaspora, that the preparation of the Land must come before the preparation of the people: the purchase of land by the Jewish National Fund and *Ge 'ula*, the economic development of the country by the Anglo-Palestine Company [that is, the Bank], self-government in the

[17] Ibid., p. 341.

settlements initiated by the [Odessa] Hovevei Zion Committee, and finally Jewish youth in Erez-Israel who are imbued with idealism and will strive for liberty.'[18]

But the hard-pressed Jews of eastern Europe, and the rank and file of the movement among them, were not disposed to wait. They did wish to 'hasten the end'. They did believe—at all events, and as Aḥad Ha-ʿAm and most of his disciples had always recognized, they did *wish* to believe—in 'a speedy Salvation' (*yeshuʿa kerova*).[19] And they were drawn to Herzl because he did appear to offer—manifestly he was working for—a rapid release from an intolerable situation. The fundamental diagnostic question, therefore, was whether their situation did allow for delay. Just how intolerable was the present condition; and how intolerable was it likely to become in any foreseeable, let alone the still unforeseeable, future? How urgent was the treatment? On this the followers of Herzl and Zangwill on the one hand and the followers of Aḥad Ha-ʿAm and Ussishkin on the other hand were profoundly divided.[20]

But perhaps the schools were divided more deeply still by their fundamental approach to questions of public policy. For Herzl and Zangwill and their school these were the questions that were always uppermost. Herzl was somewhat more attached to the past than Zangwill, more in awe of it, more fearful of the inestimable, certainly revolutionary consequences of cutting the umbilical cord, and more sensitive to the sensibilities of others on all these scores. Zangwill was somewhat less concerned about the inner life of the Jews, less repelled or intimidated by the imperfectly understood life and culture of the gentiles, and, because even more offended than Herzl by the dualities and timidities which life in the Diaspora entailed, more anxious to break free of them, once and for all,

---

[18] Schwartz, *Ussishkin be-igrotav*, p. 76. Emphasis in text.

[19] Letter to S. Bernfeld, 8 March 1899. *Igrot AH*, ii, p. 250.

[20] One of this great quarrel's ironies was the alignment of the small *orthodox* contingent within the movement with Herzl. The Mizraḥi had 'agreed to Africa', it was explained, 'because we hoped it would be the means of saving a substantial part of our people and making it whole in body and spirit . . . If there is no Israel [i.e. Jewish people], there is no Zion. So long as Israel lives, so long the hope for Zion will be sustained.' Reines to Herzl, 9 December 1903. Heymann, ii, no. 61, p. 180.

and at whatever the cost. But for both tendencies, the moderate Herzlian and the radical Zangwillian, within what might be called the ultra-revolutionary party in Zionism, a great deal turned on what might and might not be accomplished in actual practice. And it was decisive for their attitude to the tradition. The tradition had its undeniable value, but it was not to preserve the tradition, even a modified tradition, that the Zionists had formed their movement; and therefore one could not make it the touchstone, let alone the corner-stone, of policy. For if one did so, in the manner the opposition had made their own, one had necessarily to readjust—in practice, diminish—one's purposes; whereas for Herzl and Zangwill it was the purposes that were the true and necessary corner-stones of policy and whatever impeded progress towards them had to be jettisoned or circumvented. To the question what would befall the Jews who could not be encompassed by his 'centre' in Erez-Israel Aḥad Ha-'Am answered, essentially, with a shrug: in his view Erez-Israel could hold out no salvation for them in any event. Herzl was concerned with all Jewry. The opposition was not.

We must tell the Government of England plainly [wrote Lilienblum] that the Zionists are not the representatives of all the Jewish people and that the settlement of Uganda cannot be encompassed within our activities. If all our wealthy people, those who oppose Zion and the ICA, wish to deal with it, that is their affair. But we Zionists cannot deal with it, for we have another purpose . . . We must not cut our life's thread with our own hands, for Uganda will not deprive the Jewish people of Zion, but rather Zion of the Jewish people. It will be the last Destruction, the absolute separation of the nation from its country.[21]

The views and programme propounded by Herzl and Zangwill were thus *political* in type—both in the obvious and straightforward sense that they aimed at providing the Jews with national political institutions and that they sought to obtain them by political means, but also in a broader and perhaps deeper sense. Herzl's outstanding and most original quality as a leader of Jewry lay in his effort, from the very first,

[21] Moshe Leib Lilienblum, 'Mi-ẓion le-uganda', *Ha-Magid*, 24 September 1903.

to confront and assess such forces at large in the world as were relevant, for good or for ill, to his purposes and to seek to deflect or neutralize those forces that were hostile to them. This could only be done, he thought, by some adjustment of policy and by seeking allies in his cause—which required further adjustment and readjustment of policy in turn. There were limits. These limits were so severe that in the end little was accomplished. Thus compromise, manœuvre, and indirection were all of the essence in the Herzlian approach. It also followed that his ultimate purposes could only be of the simplest character and cast in the most general terms.

Aḥad Ha-ʿAm and his school (and, in this respect, the greater part of the opposition) were, by the same token, and in contrast, essentially non-political in their approach. The principles to which they cleaved were absolute, allowing of no argument or compromise. 'The Ereẓ-Israel Zionists fight Territorialism', ran the key sentence in an anti-Herzl manifesto, 'not only because it is contrary to the Basel Programme, but because it is contrary to the Jewish national idea.'[22] At the same time, the concrete ends towards which they strove were both more complex and clearer and better thought out than Herzl's. Aḥad Ha-ʿAm's 'centre' for Jewry, whatever its other failings, made a lot more sense as a practical and practicable proposition than Herzl's New Society. Yet, for these very reasons, the opposition was under heavier constraints. Their ability to adjust and modify in the light of circumstances and operative forces was still more severely limited than the politicals'. Their ability to manœuvre, to form alliances, to *alter*, however slightly, the structure of power in Europe and the Levant in a direction more favourable to themselves was therefore— even if they had been so minded—so circumscribed as virtually to be nil. And indeed they were not so minded. They hardly thought in such terms. They did not seek to precipitate change; they awaited it, doing whatever could be done in the meantime. Thus there was much in their approach to public affairs that partook of the religious: quite clearly-articulated principles, severe rules of conduct, firm beliefs, faith, some fatalism, diffidence, a certain passivity, and considerable patience. It was an approach that accorded with the Jewish

[22] From a manifesto 'To Ereẓ-Israel Zionists', in *Ha-Ẓefira*, 276, 5 December 1904.

tradition a great deal more smoothly than did Herzl's—which may help account for the rage with which Herzl and his works, but above all the support given him by those of the old guard who had gone over to his side or the performance of those who had been less than firm in their opposition to him, were met by the purists. 'I tell you, the deed you have done at Basel is no less in my eyes than a public change of religion', wrote a furious Aḥad Ha-ʿAm.[23]

These antitheses were still unresolved at Herzl's death, much as the question of East Africa as a formal issue remained unsettled. The Congress's resolution to send an expedition of inquiry stood. The expedition was dispatched eventually, as we shall see, and the report was duly taken up at a Special Congress, as had been provided for.[24] But the reality was that Herzl himself, just before his death, at the grand confrontation of April 1904, had already conceded crucial points to the opposition and so caused the balance to shift. Had he lived and sought to restore it, he would first have had to restore his authority to the full and to that end he would have had to find fresh allies. He might have resolved to throw over the old guard of Ḥovevei Zion altogether. The alliance concluded in 1897[25] to make the First Congress, and then the movement itself, possible seemed, in any case, to be breaking up. Herzl might then have appealed to the silent rank and file, to such people as had cheered him in Vilna and still looked to him to release them from their misery. It would have been in character and in accord with past precedent, as when, having failed to gain the support of the millionaire notables of western Jewry, he originally resolved on the creation of a popular movement.[26] But if he had lived, he would still have been an extremely tired and disappointed man and possibly too weak in body to precipitate and carry through a fresh upheaval. Besides which, he himself, as we have seen, had become increasingly uncertain and ambivalent in his own attitude to the tradition and had assured the opposition that in certain respects he would uphold

[23] Letter to A. L., 31 August 1903. *Igrot AH*, iii, p. 265.
[24] See below, pp. 425–34.
[25] See *Origins*, pp. 339–53.
[26] See *Origins*, pp. 307–8.

it. He was always a man of his word. In any event, Herzl's
death rendered the shift irreversible. Zionism became identified
exclusively with Ereẓ-Israel once more. And, by necessary
extension, there ensued both a long retreat from true political
action and a massive blocking-off of anything like the call
for radical national renewal and reform which the East
Africa affair had brought to the surface of public consciousness
and, in a limited way and for a brief moment, into the arena
of open debate.

PART FOUR

Displacement

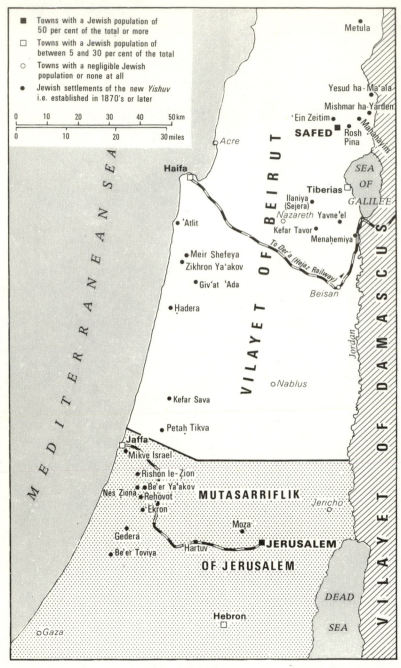

Legend:

■ Towns with a Jewish population of 50 per cent of the total or more

□ Towns with a Jewish population of between 5 and 30 per cent of the total

○ Towns with a negligible Jewish population or none at all

● Jewish settlements of the new *Yishuv* i.e. established in 1870's or later

Scale: 0 10 20 30 40 50 km
0 10 20 30 miles

MEDITERRANEAN SEA

○ *Acre*

Metula ○

Yesud ha-Ma'ala ●

Mishmar ha-Yarden ●

'Ein Zeitim ●   ● *Maḥanaim*

SAFED ■   Rosh Pina ●

Haifa □

SEA OF GALILEE

Tiberias □

Ilaniya (Sejera) ●

Nazareth ○   Yavne'el ●

Kefar Tavor ●

Menaḥemiya ●

● 'Atlit

To Der'a (Hejaz Railway)

● Meir Shefeya

● Zikhron Ya'akov

Beisan ○

● Giv'at 'Ada

● Ḥadera

VILAYET OF BEIRUT

Jordan

VILAYET OF DAMASCUS

○ *Nablus*

● Kefar Sava

● Petaḥ Tikva

Jaffa □

● Mikve Israel

● Rishon le-Zion

Nes Ziona ●   ● Be'er Ya'akov

● Reḥovot

● Ekron

MUTASARRIFLIK

Jericho ○

● Gedera

Moza ●

● Be'er Toviya

Ḥartuv ●

■ **JERUSALEM**

OF JERUSALEM

DEAD SEA

Hebron □

○ *Gaza*

B. Erez-Israel in 1907.

11

New Blood

i

The death of Herzl deprived the movement not only of a leader, but of a natural centre to which all eyes were accustomed to turn. Herzl not only propounded, but in a sense embodied a set of ideas and attitudes on which other Zionists sharpened their own and which they were free to applaud or reject, but could not ignore. Upon his death, the Zionist movement, hitherto so different from most other contemporary Jewish movements and tendencies by virtue of the coherence which he imposed on it, came somewhat to resemble its rivals. Its central institutions weakened; its branches took on additional strength—and, at the same time, became increasingly subject to local influences and considerations. The result was much separate development, an upsurge of new forces and personalities, a corresponding loss of cohesion, and a blurring of the targets to which the movement as a whole, and as such, aspired. With Herzl dead and his successors (as we shall see) unable, and in the final analysis unwilling, to continue fighting the dead man's battles, Zionism's internal political centre of gravity began to shift back to what might be termed— given the sheer numbers involved and the actual locus of the most acute problems of contemporary Jewry—its proper place, in eastern Europe, especially in Russia. And there the processes of change and separate development were much accelerated and intensified by the dramatic events of 1904–6 which of course had no parallel elsewhere. One effect of this partial (and temporary) disintegration was to bring Erez-Israel and its resettlement once more to the fore and for reasons additional to, and distinct from, the upshot of the great debate on the East Africa project. It was not simply

that the settlement-men under the leadership of Ussishkin
and others now began to move much closer to the commanding
heights of the movement. The effects of the changes in leadership and in the official policy of the movement after Herzl's
death, while real, were, as we shall see, gradual. It was rather
that interest in Erez-Israel as a *pays réel* of immigration and
settlement began to grow once more and to extend a little
beyond the tiny circle of enthusiasts that had been attracted
to it in the course of the past two decades. It was still the case
that for most members of the movement (and certainly for
most other Jews) Erez-Israel did not then (or later) present
itself as an object of immediate desire, still less a land of
immediate settlement. The more common tendency was to
see it in symbolic terms, or vaguely as a distant target, or (as
the critics of the movement would have it) as a figment of
romantic imagination. In this sense, its role in the Zionist
mind was not unlike its role in the mind of the orthodox: a
destination towards which you travelled, as opposed to one at
which you yourself unequivocally intended to arrive.

I know you have great influence [complained the resident physician
in Zikhron Ya'akov to a prominent member of the Odessa Commit-
tee] . . . that is why your Platonic love for Zion angers me so. True,
you are a great enthusiast and you are ready to sacrifice your health
on the altar of debate, but you do not wish to do anything real.[1]

Indeed, even for those who did mean to arrive and who did
eventually settle in it, the enterprise on which they had embarked was normally shot through for them with symbolic
and romantic significance and associations; and in many such
cases the flame of their dedication burned with a heat and a
zeal which can only be described as religious. For such men
and women the contrast with the Land as they wished it to

---

[1] Hillel Joffe to Mordekhai Ben-'Ami, February 1894. Hillel Joffe, *Dor ma'apilim*
(2nd edn., Jerusalem, 1971), pp. 82–3. Joffe (1864–1936), an early member of Ḥibbat
Ẓion in Russia, left for Erez-Israel soon after qualifying as a physician in Geneva. He
practised in Tiberias, Zikhron Ya'akov, Ḥadera, and Haifa and played an important
role in the campaign to eradicate malaria in the northern part of the country. He served
as chairman of the Ḥibbat Ẓion committee in Jaffa and was a member of the commission sent out in 1903 to investigate the El Arish region in northern Sinai as a possible
site for Jewish settlement. See above, pp. 151 ff.

be or fancied it had been in the distant past was therefore at once painful and challenging; as was the contrast between the dream of its repossession and mastery and the actual, inferior, and diminished status of the Jews within it in their own times. Similarly acute, but infinitely encouraging, was the contrast constantly before their eyes between the largely derelict country which they now inhabited and through which they moved from time to time and the picture presented at least by the more successful of the new Jewish villages. Here is one of the early settlers, a member of BILU[2] in his time, describing a journey from Jaffa to the Jewish farming village of Rosh Pina in Galilee in 1903:

Soon marvellous Mount Carmel will be before us, the mountain of which our prophets sang and upon which Elijah fought his great battle with the priests of Ba'al, now desolate and abandoned . . . Here and there there are to be seen a Carmelite monastery, English summer-houses, German buildings . . . but its *sons*—its sons have left it for the Alps and the Tyrol . . . [Further on to the east and north, in the valley] there is the same oppressive wilderness. Only a poor, unfortunate fellah is to be seen scratching the land with his ante-diluvian plough, a camel harnessed to it with ropes of straw and a naked and barefoot boy driving it . . .
  'Is this land yours?', I ask him. 'No', replies Hamdan . . . 'All this land, far into the distance, belongs to an effendi in Beirut.'
  At which I am reminded of how we talk of the redemption of this valley right up to the foot of Mount Carmel, perpetually arguing and quarrelling among ourselves while the day approaches when this land of ours will fall into the possession of strangers! . . . [Then on to Tiberias, then north, then west again.] No road, not even a path: only waste land pitted with black lumps of basalt. The heart is oppressed more than ever in among those black rocks, burnt seemingly by the heat of the sun . . . until after a long and tiring climb we breathe the wind on the plateau . . . and can continue our journey northwards. We make our way across the barren plain for more than an hour until suddenly a marvellous picture of an enchanting village unfolds before our eyes! The white houses with their red roofs that we see through the orchards and the eucalyptus trees positively gladden the heart. There are wagons loaded with crops being driven through the fields; there is ploughing and there is the harvesting of the last of the wheat too . . . The almond harvest is being gathered in

[2] See *Origins*, pp. 80–8.

the orchards and in the tobacco fields women and children are gathering the leaves. Throughout—there is the joy of life, labour, and hope! These are our Jewish farmers, only recently settled here, the pioneers of national revival, the first of the builders who have arisen and returned to their country and their motherland![3]

But such moments of exhilaration were fleeting even for the greatest of Ereẓ-Israel loyalists. For the unorganized, unindoctrinated migrant from the Pale whose overwhelming and immediate urge was to escape the endemic misery of eastern Europe and improve his own individual condition, there was not enough here to counteract the pull of the classic countries of immigration in North America and the Antipodes and the grim and depressing realities of his own ancestral land—the more so as the official Zionist movement itself neither would nor could do much for him when he arrived there, nor even encourage him to try his luck there before he set out on his migration overseas. Ereẓ-Israel/Palestine at the turn of the century was a backwater of the Ottoman Empire devoid of clear political identity and of administrative unity and only barely beginning to come to economic life. Most of the region which later comprised the territory defined as 'Palestine' and ruled by Britain under a League of Nations mandate was generally, if loosely, thought of as part of Syria both by the great majority of its inhabitants and by its rulers. The northern part of the country was administratively an integral part of the Ottoman *vilayet* of Beirut; most of the south comprised the so-called 'independent' governorate (*mutasarrıflık*) of Jerusalem which came directly under the authority of the Ministry of the Interior in Constantinople; part of the far south and all the land to the east of the Jordan River belonged to the *vilayet* of Syria. The border with British-controlled Egypt was not finally agreed upon until 1906, prior to which it was generally taken as running through western Sinai, rather than to the east of the peninsula. But however defined, it was a poor and uninviting place, small in territory and population (some 25,000 square kilometres and between 500,000 and 600,000 inhabitants all told)[4] and vir-

---

[3] 'Mi-ziknei ha-yishuv' [Menashe Meirovitch], *Lifnei sheloshim shana* [Tel-Aviv], 1933; facsimile edn, Jerusalem, 1976. Emphasis in text.

[4] Official Ottoman population figures for the 1880s give a total of 425,966 for the

tually devoid of commercially exploitable natural resources, apart (potentially) from the minerals of the Dead Sea. Some 70 per cent of the population lived off agriculture, but poorly. Little of the land was cultivable, at any rate above subsistence level; most of it was either rocky terrain, or semi-desert, or swamp. Much of it was owned by absentee landlords, or by the state, or by religious and philanthropic institutions, notably the Moslem *waqf*. There was no industry, except of the most elementary kind (soap production in Nablus, for example). The supply of drinking-water was inadequate and much of what was supplied impure, notoriously so in Jerusalem. Roads were extremely poor. The harbours were open roadsteads. Commerce was local and primitive. Banking was extremely limited; much of what would pass for normal banking business in Europe was in the hands of private and usurious money-lenders. A further difficulty was that, in effect, there was no standard currency. Education—apart from what was provided privately within the Jewish sector and by the Christian missionary societies—was abysmal. The population was plagued by diseases typical of a warm climate and a land where virtually no attention was paid to public health either in the strictly medical context or in that of civil engineering: dysentery, malaria, trachoma, typhoid, and, periodically, cholera (of which there were severe epidemics in the winter of 1902/3 and in 1910).

It is true that a moderate economic change came over the country in the course of the last quarter of the century.[5] The railway finally made its appearance in 1892 when a line

---

three districts of Jerusalem, Nablus, and Acre. (See Kemal H. Karpat, 'Ottoman Population Records and the Census of 1881/82–1893'. *International Journal of Middle East Studies*, 9 (1978), tables, pp. 258–74.) These census figures are to be treated with caution. The figures for the Jews—7,000 all told for Jerusalem and its immediate environment, for example (instead of 17–20,000)—are wildly inaccurate. But the figures for the Moslem population are within reasonable distance of the best modern estimates.

[5] Admirably summed up by Nachum Gross in his contribution to *Banka'i le-uma be-hithadshuta; toldot bank le'umi le-Israel* (Tel-Aviv, 1977), part I, chapter 2, pp. 24–63. For a contemporary survey see Leo Motzkin's report to the Zionist Congress made at Herzl's request, *Die Juden in Palästina* (Berlin, 1898); Hebrew: 'Ha-yehudim be-Erez-Israel', in Alex Bein (ed.), *Sefer Motzkin* (Jerusalem, 1939), pp. 17–48; also, in somewhat different form, in *Protokoll II*, pp. 99–127.

between Jaffa and Jerusalem was inaugurated. This did
something to ease passenger travel (notably of pilgrims)
between the coast of Jerusalem, even if little for the general
economic development of the region through which it passed.
Another line was built in 1903–5 from Haifa through the
Jezreel Valley and up into Transjordan as far as Derʿa,
where it joined the main Hejaz Railway from Damascus to
Medina which it had been designed to feed. Its contribution
to the country at large, even to the areas through which it
passed, was small; but it did have a marked effect on Haifa
itself which thenceforward developed as a port and eventually
as a centre of industry. Foreign trade rose fairly steadily,
particularly after the turn of the century: exports, notably
with the firm establishment of citrus fruit as the country's
best-known quality product; and imports, the rise in demand
directly traceable to the new Jewish immigrant community.
Indeed, the most important factor for change was now the
country's Jewish population, for even though it remained of
very moderate size in absolute terms, it was much the most
dynamic in character and was, of course, itself during all this
period in process of striking transformation.

The *yishuv* doubled in size from an estimated 24,000 in
1881/2 (as the first members of the First ʿAliya, or wave of
modern Jewish immigration, began to arrive) to some 50,000
in 1900, two-thirds of the rise being commonly attributed to
immigration, one-third to natural increase. The great qualitative change lay in the altered composition, distribution, and
prevailing social functions of the country's Jewish population,
best illustrated by the steady rise in the fraction living in the
countryside, in the new settlements, and therefore outside the
ambit of the old, traditionally-minded *yishuv* and implicitly
in opposition to it: none in 1880; some 3,000 settlers by 1890
(6 per cent of the entire Jewish population); 5,000 by 1900
(10·5 per cent). Within the *yishuv* as a whole, the settlements,
along with their growing hinterland of the like-minded,
non-farming immigrants in the towns, notably in Jaffa,
constituted the modern, active sector. And, of course, it was
in the settlements, moreover, that the Zionist tendency was
seen by all to be embodied—both because they had been
organized and populated from the start by the Zionists and

because the resettlement of Erez-Israel in the spirit of Zionism and in line with its long-term purposes was still conceived of almost exclusively in agricultural terms. It was in the settlements, it could be argued, that a new society had been formed: it was these new immigrants to Erez-Israel and they alone— of all the vast crowd moving out of eastern Europe—who had broken with precedent and had not replicated in the country of their new residence even approximately the social and economic conditions prevalent in the old. Their purposes and motivation were not exclusively private. They all in one degree or another had national, as well as personal salvation in mind. They identified themselves and were identified by others as Jews unencumbered by the attributes of other nations. The language of instruction in their schools was commonly Hebrew. They were to all intents and purposes self-governing. And, gradually and most significantly, they were impelled to add defence to the burdens of local, limited, municipal government.

None the less, the scale of settlement was exceedingly small. The sum of it all, measured against the magnitude of the human problem of east European Jewry and the great, continuing migratory flow, was risible; and the new *yishuv*'s likely future rate of increase was no more encouraging. Barely twenty settlements all told in 1903, with landholdings totalling some 200,000 dunams (with about a third again east of the Jordan), or somewhat less than 1 per cent of the area of the country. The holdings of the various settlements were very unevenly distributed. Many of the villages were entirely isolated—from the towns and markets and from each other— and travel was difficult and long. There were hard cases of settlements being comparatively distant from their lands. And for all, the process of setting them up as going concerns, clearing and preparing the land, acquiring tools, farm animals, housing, elementary skills, and taking in a first, often pitiful harvest, could last for as long as four years. By and large, a generation and more after the start, the settlements were still not self-sustaining economically. The vast sums that had been poured into them to keep them alive, notably by Baron Edmond de Rothschild, had not always been wisely invested, nor had the social effects of continued support from the outside been for the good. The Baron's intentions were excellent;[6] those of his officials were generally (but by no means exclusively) good. The importance of his aid for the sheer survival of at least half of the new *yishuv* cannot be overstated: without it much would almost certainly have gone under. But serious mistakes had been made, as is often the case where centralized and imperious planning (to say nothing of an impulse to social engineering) obtains. Most notably there had been his and his experts' insistence on plantation farming, as opposed to field crops and mixed farming.[7] The settlers who were in receipt of the Baron's support and whom he tried so hard to fashion into communities after his own heart had perforce become protégés of a distant master and benefactor and, more immediately, the wards of the officials whom Rothschild had appointed to administer his great philanthropic enterprise on the spot. Tension between the officials and the settlers was endemic; habits of dependence, not to say mendacity and petty corruption took root. And the larger social, and the ultimate political purposes that lay behind the revival of Jewish settlement in the country tended to erode under the twin pressures of the struggle to promote it on economically viable lines and Rothschild's own disbelief and distrust in Zionism as an organized national *movement*, particularly in its Herzlian form. Besides, Rothschild was unwilling to countenance a marked expansion of the *yishuv*—of that part of it, at all events, for which he was prepared to accept responsibility. In 1900 he gave up direct management of 'his' settlements. Supervision passed to the independent Jewish Colonization Association (ICA) founded by Baron Maurice de Hirsch in 1891. The system of aid and training was rationalized and made less personal; and types of farming that were more in keeping with the conditions of the country and the social needs of the settlers were encouraged. But the ICA was in no sense a Zionist organization: it remained devoted to its original, manifestly philanthropic purposes and it chose to regard its activities in Erez-Israel in much the same way as it did parallel good works

---

[6] See *Origins*, pp. 212–18.

[7] Only when Jewish farmers, following Arab example, took up citrus fruit as a major product did plantation farming in the Jewish agricultural sector begin to prosper.

in Argentina, Brazil, Canada, and the United States.

But nor was the internal structure of the new *yishuv* appropriate to the task of bridgehead for such large-scale migration as might follow. While it was well in tune with most contemporary Zionist (especially Russian Zionist) notions of what a new society of Jews in the Land—and on the land—should look like, the accepted pattern of smallholding, if it was to be frequently replicated, required substantial investment. However, few immigrants had adequate capital; and the Zionist institutions were too poor to provide real support, even if (under Herzl) they had wanted to. Motzkin reported in 1898 that it could cost 250,000 francs to set up twelve new families and complete the settlement of thirteen existing ones in the single village of Mishmar ha-Yarden.[8] This was about as much as the total income of the Zionist Organization at the time.

There was not much room for Jewish immigrants as landless farm-labourers either. The common and not inaccurate assumption was that the labour of experienced Arab peasants—readily available and cheap—was much superior to that of Jews, tailors' apprentices or students or whatever they might be, freshly out of Europe. Besides, farm-labour tended to be seasonal and the wages offered Jews, even if marginally higher in some cases than those offered Arab labourers, were still below subsistence level as they understood it. And, once again, the *scale* was very small. Normally, all the Jewish settlements together probably employed no more than 2,000, or at the most 3,000 labourers.[9] The number of openings for artisans, shopkeepers, and such employees of the community as school-teachers was smaller still. Clearly, if there was to be rapid absorption of large numbers of immigrants, industry was required. But there was no industry to speak of, little or no thought of systematically promoting it, and much influential opinion against it—or rather, in favour of relying principally on agriculture. The arguments were partly ideological, as we shall see; in part, ostensibly practical. What raw materials would feed such industry? How could a vast investment in

[8] 'Ha-yehudim be-Erez-Israel', p. 33.

[9] In 1912, when the new *yishuv* was roughly double its size in 1900, 5,000 Arab farm-labourers were employed in the Jewish villages. Gross, *Banka'i*, p. 43.

imported machinery be sustained? What market would there be for a local product inevitably more costly than any available from foreign producers? And if industry at all, then, as the most sophisticated proponent of intensive and systematic agricultural development, Yizhak Wilkansky, was later to argue,[10] surely superimposed on a firm agricultural base.

Beyond all these intrinsic weaknesses there were the external circumstances of the new *yishuv*; a strange and for the most part unfriendly general population and a politically hostile administration. Given the depth, intractability, and sheer violence of the Arab–Jewish conflict as it was later to develop and is now so familiar, there is a natural impulse to search for early manifestations of it in the *yishuv*'s foundation years. Certainly there was tension and friction between Jews and Arabs. Some of the land purchased by and for the settlers was unoccupied and uncultivated. But some was not. When it was not, a deal between unwitting settlers and absentee landlords or local money-lenders to whom the land had gone forfeit—all over the heads of uncomprehending and outraged fellahin— could easily lead to endless altercation. So could and did quarrels over grazing rights, watering rights, and the precise demarcation of boundaries, all of which were frequent and endemic. The Jewish settlements and settlers, in their isolation and initial disorientation, were the natural prey of would-be extortioners, thieves, and bullies of all kinds from neighbouring villages and bedouin encampments, the more so as they were long dependent on their neighbours for farm-labour, for such services as transport, and, so long as the cash-crop system preponderated, for a good part of their supplies for their own consumption and for all the manure they needed for their vineyards and plantations. Pressure and provocation and low-level injury led in turn to resistance and counter-pressure, ugly incidents, and occasional counter-brutality as the settlers found their feet and gained in self-confidence. But the broad

---

[10] 'Megamat yishuvenu u-te'udato' (1913?), in his *Ba-Derekh* (Jaffa, 1918), pp. 17–25. Yizhak Wilkansky [Elazari-Volcani] (1880–1955) was a professional agronomist of the highest order whose influence on the economic and technological development of the *yishuv* is apparent to this day. However, he was also a leading member of *Ha-Po'el ha-Zair* (see below, pp. 407–10) and his science cannot always be disentangled from his politics and *Weltanschauung*.

tendency in a virtually unpoliced countryside, particularly
of the recognized leaders of the communities, was to damp
down conflict as it arose, and to settle disputes by negotiation
as far as possible. Given the ease and speed with which an
opponent is identified in the Levant in primarily ascriptive
terms, namely as a member of a particular ethnic and/or
religious group, and the relatively high degree of responsibility
for his actions which is imputed to his fellows, the importance
of group discipline and good behaviour all round is soon
learned, if not always successfully practised. The Jews learned
it;[11] and as they consolidated their settlements the Arabs
began to practise it too. In time, a *modus vivendi* of sorts obtained
(somewhat more firmly in the south of the country than in the
north). Where it obtained it tended to be reinforced by
the discovery of common or complementary *economic* interests,
even by occasional partnerships and by the simple effects of
time and familiarity, by more numerous efforts by some
Jews to learn Arabic, by a growing, if grudging respect on the
Arab side for Jewish industry and economic and social reliabi-
lity, and by similar manifestations of general stock-taking
all round and a common interest in a peaceful life for all.
The tensions and frictions in the countryside were, after all,
local and direct in origin—exacerbated, it is true, by profound
ethnic and cultural differences, but sporadic and spontaneous
and (for the time being) still unorchestrated. The Jews in
question were only a minute fraction of the total population
that lived on the land (roughly 1 per cent). They were isolated
and obviously vulnerable and for long they were dependent
on their neighbours in various ways, as we have seen. No
doubt to some they were a source of annoyance; to others a
source of competition; to others again a source of plunder.
But in no sense could they be, nor indeed were they, construed
as a threat.

In the towns of Palestine matters were different. The Jews,
new and old *yishuvim* together, were much more numerous.
In Jerusalem they had formed the majority of the city's

[11] On the efforts of the Rehovot village council to cope with the pressures and
depredations of their neighbours and to impose a code of firm, but decent conduct
on their members, see Ya'akov Ro'i, 'Yahasei Rehovot 'im shekheneiha ha-'aravim',
Ha-Zionut, i (1970), pp. 150–203.

population, at least since 1860. The flow of immigrants, while small in absolute terms, was very noticeable, especially in Jaffa. The dangers of competition from Jews naturally loomed large in the eyes of the Arab merchants and artisans. And the townsfolk were much more open to foreign influence and ideas, among which must be counted modern anti-Semitism in its contemporary European forms, advanced widely and propagated successfully by many of the Christian missionaries, expatriates, and consular representatives with which the country teemed, most notably the French and the Russians. European anti-Semitism thus came to be superimposed on and intermingled with anti-Jewish attitudes and beliefs of the indigenous Moslem variety which were of much longer standing, but hardly of greater virulence. In this climate, resistance in the towns to the entry and settlement of Jews, when it occurred at all, took on forms that were less violent physically (at this stage) and less frequent, but more coherent and more reasoned and above all more political than in the country. An early manifestation was a petition to the Grand Vizier in 1891 in which a group of Moslem and Christian notables in Jerusalem asked for the entry of Jews into the country to be prohibited and the sale of land to them forbidden. The occasion was a report of an impending increase in the rate of immigration; its origins lay in the fear of commercial competition. Some Moslem notables refused to co-operate on the grounds that, in their judgement, the Jews *were* of benefit to the country.[12] But the pattern remained the characteristic one for some time: opposition to Zionism, such as it was, was addressed to the Ottoman authorities. Turkish rule was still largely unquestioned; the Turks were of fixed mind in their hostility to a Jewish national movement intent on striking roots in their territories; and it was they who could determine how fiercely the Zionists would be fought and by what means in practice. In 1899, when the Mufti of Jerusalem ('our implacable enemy', as a well-placed Jewish observer in that city described him) proposed in the Jerusalem Administrative Council that new Jewish immigrants be set upon and terrorized as a preliminary to the expulsion of all Jews who had been

[12] N. J. Mandel, 'Turks, Arabs and Jewish Immigration into Palestine: 1882–1914' (D.Phil. thesis, Oxford, 1965), pp. 44–5.

allowed to enter in the past eight years, the Turkish governor rejected the idea and no more was heard of it.[13] Not until 1908, upon the collapse of the Sultanate and the release of new forces, some of them genuinely popular, but all vying in one degree or another for popular support, was resistance to the advent of Jews taken up by Palestinian and other Arabs on large enough a scale and with sufficient intensity to begin to be of real consequence and, incidentally, to begin to be taken note of by the Zionists themselves.

A few exceptionally perceptive observers in the Zionist camp had sensed long before that there was trouble in store for the movement from that quarter.[14] But on the whole, the leadership in the period prior to the Young Turks' revolution of 1908 (when ʿAbd al-Hamid was deposed and power assumed by new, ostensibly modern men) was sanguine and uncomprehending. It was remote in space and thinking from the real Erez-Israel; there was very little in the lives of the notables —whether in Vienna or Ekaterinoslav—to disturb their essentially theoretical and schematic outlook on the country and its problems. The settlers themselves knew better, and later, especially after 1908, the twin effects of frequent alerts sounded by them and the official resumption of interest in settlement in the last decade or so before the Great War would bring the leadership to seek a productive and friendly relationship with the Arabs. But for the time being, minds were turned overwhelmingly to other things and even Herzl, in his supremacy, was for once fully representative of his colleagues.

In March 1899, Yusuf al-Khalidi, an elderly Jerusalem notable with a distinguished record of public service and a reputation for comparatively liberal views and plain speaking, took up the subject of Zionism. He wrote on the subject to Zadoc Kahn, Grand Rabbi of France. Kahn passed his letter on to Herzl for a reply. Al-Khalidi accepted that the Zionist

[13] Albert Antébi, Jewish Colonization Association (ICA) representative in Jerusalem, to ICA head office, London, 23 October 1899. ICA Archives, 263/17. The Mufti of Jerusalem at the time was Muhammad Tahir al-Husseini, father of a later, well-known holder of that office under British rule, Haj Amin al-Husseini.

[14] For Aḥad Ha-ʿAm's premonitions in 1891 see *Origins*, pp. 195–6. See also Yosef Gorni, 'Shorsheiha shel todaʿat ha-ʿimut ha-leumi ha-yehudi-ʿaravi ve-hishtakfuta ba-ʿitonut ha-ʿivrit ba-shanim 1900–1918', *Ha-Zionut*, iv (1975), pp. 72–113.

idea, in principle, was natural and just. He asked who could challenge the rights of the Jews in Palestine. 'Good Lord', he wrote, 'historically it is really your country.' But reality was brutal. Palestine was part of the Ottoman Empire and by virtue of its Holy Places a subject of interest to hundreds of millions of Moslems and hundreds of millions more of Christians. The Holy Places could not be acquired without 'cannons and battleships'; but the Jews were weak and there were none to fight for them. Within the country itself, while the Turks and the Arabs were generally friendly to the Jews, some had been infected by racial hatred, as in Europe. There were Christian fanatics, especially Catholic and Orthodox, who overlooked no opportunity to further excite Moslem hatred against Jews. In the end, if the Jews persisted, there would be a popular movement against them which nothing, not even the Ottoman Government, could put down. Thus the Jews could never become masters of Palestine and would do better to look for an uninhabited country elsewhere

where millions of poor Jews could be settled and perhaps be happy and some day constitute a nation. That would be the best, the most rational solution to the Jewish Question [al-Khalidi concluded]. But in the name of God, let Palestine be left in peace.[15]

Herzl's response was calm and friendly. He restated his established position, namely that the Zionists wished the Ottomans no harm, but on the contrary believed they could help them and the country in question. It was perfectly true that the Jews were supported by none of the Powers; nor had they military intentions of their own. All the less reason to fear them. As for the Holy Places on which al-Khalidi had put such stress, there was no intention of touching them. In any case they were now precious to all three religions; hardly the exclusive possession of any one of them. Nor did he see any difficulty with the local population. None sought to remove non-Jews. The local population's private circumstances would only be improved by the prosperity the Jews would bring in their wake.

[15] Al-Khalidi to Kahn, 1 March 1899. CZA, H III d. 14. Mandel, 'Turks, Arabs and Jewish Immigration', pp. 95–7.

Do you believe that an Arab who has a house or land in Palestine whose value is three or four thousand francs will greatly regret seeing the price of his land rise five- or tenfold? For that is necessarily what will happen as the Jews come; and this is what must be explained to the inhabitants of the country. They will acquire excellent brothers, just as the Sultan will acquire loyal and good subjects, who will cause the region, their historic motherland, to flourish.[16]

But in any case, meanwhile, in the eyes of all concerned—Jews, Arabs, and the Turks themselves—it was Turkish policy that formed the most formidable obstacle to the progress of the *yishuv*, which to its cost, remained devoid of political rights and status, an object of the administration's continuing hostility and of frequent, if irregular harassment at its hands. The Turks' fundamental opposition to Zionism had not abated one whit over the years. Immigration was still illegal in principle and heavily circumscribed in practice, the purchase of land was subject to severe restrictions, as was even the erection of buildings for housing and farming purposes, which could be delayed for years at a time. And the effect of thus being perpetually at odds with the Ottoman administration was to cloud the new *yishuv* and all its works with elements of uncertainty, fragility, and doubt.

It's very hard going in our country. So far we have neither [real] villages nor farmers, for all that so much wealth, life, and labour have been invested. The Baron's settlements too have failed to bear fruit in due proportion to what has been put into them. Gedera manages with difficulty, in Reḥovot there is only hope for the future, Mishmar ha-Yarden does not exist in actual practice and will soon disappear in principle too, for it does not even own its land. The landlord threatens to cancel the purchase if [the Odessa Committee] does not hurry up and pay him his price. Ḥadera just agonizes.

I take a great deal of interest in [Ḥadera] and an active part in all its affairs—to such an extent that they have turned me into a farmer and elected me head of the committee. To this day they remain without a permit even to build a cow-shed. They all live in one old building resembling a small fortress with an inner courtyard, all crowded together and in filth. It used to be a khan. They are devastated by disease. The authorities fleece them like bandits. Not long

16 Herzl to al-Khalidi, 19 March 1899. *Igrot Herzl*, iii, no. 809, pp. 309–10.

ago the local governor came along with fifty horsemen and informed
them that the land they were working was his. A committee of
inquiry was formed. The committee duly recognized that the people
of Ḥadera did have a just claim (besides, it received 400 francs),
but in the meantime sown fields and planted groves were trampled
over. And after the committee's decision, that same *kaymakam*'s
deputy turned up with seventy horsemen and demanded a 'tax'
on the grounds, he said, that the land was his anyway and that he
cared nothing for the decision handed down by the committee. So
now we have to submit a complaint, to act—but you can't act without
money . . .

Some work has been done this year in spite of all the difficulties.
The farmers have planted almond trees, vines, and mulberries. They
have also begun to graft. But there is no order or system in their work.
It would be very desirable if an expert gardener were to draw up a
plan suited to the climate, the types of soil, and the capabilities of the
farmers.[17]

All told, then, there was little or nothing to warrant belief
that there was being actively prepared in Erez-Israel, and
on an adequate scale and with appropriate speed, the groundwork for a great Return of the Jews to the Land of their fathers.
But nor were the circumstances and quality of the new *yishuv*
such as to suggest that the chances were great of its evolving
into the 'spiritual centre' which would, by virtue of its social
qualities, spearhead the cultural renaissance of the Jewish
people in the manner outlined by Aḥad Ha-ʿAm. The *yishuv*
could not manage without consistent support from outside.
Even Aḥad Ha-ʿAm, a fierce critic of the philanthropic system
that had evolved over the years and a believer in the need to
inculcate self-reliance into the settlers for their own good and
everyone else's, even he recognized that there were obstacles
they could not be expected to overcome without assistance.

There was indeed a special kind of permanent aid without which
the *yishuv* could not survive, even in the future, so long as its external
circumstances had undergone no fundamental change: this was the
removal of general obstacles whose roots lay in the *political order*
and the great neglect to which the country was subject, obstacles
which the farmers themselves were powerless to overcome. But this

[17] Hillel Joffe, Zikhron Yaʿakov, to Vladimir Rozenstein, Montpellier, 2 February
1894. *Dor maʿapilim*, pp. 77–8.

aid could not be characterized as philanthropic guardianship, for it had nothing to do directly with the labour and life of the farmers, but was limited to removing very great stumbling-blocks, the like of which are unknown in other countries and have no natural connection with the work of settlement. Aid of this kind would properly stem from love of the Land and have as its purpose the easing of those of the country's afflictions that were peculiar to it *alone* and so create for the settlers there such natural conditions as settlers in other countries face without external aid.[18]

In sum, being too small and weak to sustain itself economically and politically and having already set in a socio-economic mould that did little to facilitate and encourage the arrival and integration of reinforcements, the impetus to both qualitative and quantitative change within the new *yishuv* could only come (like the semi-political aid Aḥad Ha-ʿAm had in mind) from the outside. The locus of all the main motive forces of Zionism was still Europe.

ii

There are, none the less, important respects in which the growth and development of the *yishuv* were autonomous and its human and material evolution the unplanned work of its members. At no point prior to the Great War did the Zionist movement systematically encourage, let alone organize, large-scale immigration into Erez-Israel—as opposed to modest and occasional assistance to individuals travelling on their own initiative. At no time did it assume, or claim, full practical responsibility for the enterprise—as opposed to sporadic support for it spread very thin. Even the most ardent 'settlement-men' were appalled at the prospect of anything like a mass movement of people—necessarily, in their view, uncontrolled and uncontrollable, unprovided for, and therefore doomed to fail and to redound to Zionism's discredit. That had been the reaction in Odessa in the 1890s. This was the characteristic reaction in Kharkov in the late spring of 1903, soon after the Kishinev pogrom, as the greatest of all the migratory waves out of Russia gathered force and Ussishkin,

[18] 'Ha-yishuv ve-apitropsav', *Ha-Shiloʾaḥ*, March–June 1902. *Kol kitvei Aḥad Ha-ʿAm*, p. 214. Emphases in text.

Bernstein-Kohan, and some other Russian GAC members issued a warning against a rush to Erez-Israel on the explicit grounds that a repetition of the experience of the 1880s and the 1890s had to be avoided.

On the other hand, once immigrants arrived there they were entitled, in the view of all the various schools of thought within the movement, to sympathy, attention, and, within the limits of the movement's means and its order of priorities, some material support as well. It was around the need to assist the early, struggling settlements that Hibbat Zion itself had taken shape in the early 1880s. And while other, financially stronger sources of assistance were repeatedly appealed to, practical concern with the settlements as communities which it was the duty of good people back in the Diaspora to sustain remained a central preoccupation of the movement. Such had been the case before Herzl, but it was also true of parts of the movement in Herzl's time and later. The larger the new *yishuv* grew and the stronger it became, the more directly the line of its development came to be dictated by its own evolving character and its immediate, locally defined needs. In parallel, the official movement's moral authority over the *yishuv* began slowly, and at this stage virtually imperceptibly, to erode, much as its own centre of gravity and its main subject of concern began to move from the Diaspora to Erez-Israel itself, each increment to the *yishuv*, each band or party of migrants contributing its mite.

This simple but important feature of the slow shift in the balance of prestige and power away from organized Zionism abroad to that of the *yishuv*—a process that was to take a generation and more to be completed—is reflected in the convention whereby the ups and downs of the migratory flow into the country are seen as successive waves, the *ʿAliyot*, in each of which it is customary to discern certain typical, salient characteristics.[19] Of the *ʿAliyot* none had so profound an impact on the *yishuv* (and through the *yishuv*, by virtue of the command-ing position that some of its members would attain within it) and on Zionism as a whole as the Second.

---

[19] For a critique of this convention see Nachum Gross, *A Note on the Periodization of the Yishuv's History during the Mandatory Period*, Falk Institute discussion paper, no. 801 (Jerusalem, 1980).

Strictly speaking, there is a distinction to be drawn between the 30,000–40,000 immigrants of all sorts and all motivations, modernists and orthodox, settlers-to-be and plain unthinking refugees, who reached Ereẓ-Israel between 1904 and 1914 and a class of perhaps 2,000 young people among them, all of high political and social motivation, who were, as a group and as a type, to make a distinctive mark on the country and to whom the term 'Second *ʿAliya*' is most commonly applied as a generic term. Of neither the larger group, nor of what might be called its inner core, did more than a fraction remain at the end of the period. Many failed to strike roots and having moved on to North America, South Africa, Australia, or back to Europe, left little trace or influence behind them. But of the inner core a great deal is known and the grounds for treating them as a coherent group are good.

The great rise in the Jewish migratory wave which occurred in the early years of the present century—of which the Second *ʿAliya* (in the broad sense) was an organic part—owed everything to precisely those trends and circumstances which had combined to bring the social ferment in all of Russia, and for all Russians, to boiling-point and the Autocracy to momentary collapse between two great bouts of repression. 'It was only world-upheavals such as there were in 1905–6, shaking and boiling the ice-age formations of our Pale of Settlement and throwing tens of thousands of our people overseas at a single blow', wrote Y. H. Brenner, the most perceptive writer-member of the group, 'that led to some bits and pieces being cast up on Ereẓ-Israel itself.'[20]

The precipitant of the crisis of the regime was the war with Japan which broke out early in 1904 and lasted until the middle of the following year. Huge military disasters, repeated displays of incompetence in high places, the misery inflicted upon men in the ranks of both the standing army and of the reserves called up to fight (a disproportionately high number of whom were Jews), and the civil unrest caused directly by the act of mobilization of unwilling and disaffected reservists—all these factors helped to unnerve the regime and to discredit it. Revolutionary terror struck harder and deeper than at any

[20] 'Aliyot vi-ridot', in Berakha Ḥabas (ed.), *Sefer ha-ʿaliya ha-sheniya* (Tel-Aviv, 1947), p. 21.

time since the assassination of Alexander II. Milder elements pressed for reform as never before. And three stunning blows to the moral authority of the Autocracy in quick succession—the fall of Port Arthur to the Japanese in December 1904, a great strike in St. Petersburg, and the stupid gunning-down of a vast, but peaceful and fundamentally loyal demonstration of workers before the Tsar's Winter Palace in the capital—finally broke the dam. Strikes and riots spread throughout the Empire and after a period of uncertainty the Autocracy caved in. On 17 October 1905 the Tsar issued a manifesto in which constitutional concessions were explicitly promised and in April 1906, following country-wide elections, a Duma, or parliament, began to sit, ostensibly inaugurating a new form of government for Russia. However, since almost immediately a contrary trend was equally in evidence and there began a process whereby slowly, but effectively, bits and pieces of constitutionality were chipped away and the old regime restored in all but name, taken as a whole it was a period of extraordinary turmoil and uncertainty, rather than of fundamental, let alone lasting change. Spasms of extreme radicalization and bitter reaction, of fury, violence, hope, and despair convulsed great parts of the population in turn, fuelled in all cases by a general sense that the fate of all the subjects of the Tsar, high and low, was bound up in one way or another with the outcome of these great events. So for all the inhabitants of Russia; so *a fortiori* for the Jews.

Never, on the face of it, had Russian Jewry had such good cause to hope for the better; but never had it been punished so hard by either the state or the populace as it was to be at this time. The Passover of 1904 passed safely enough without attacks by mob or discontented soldiery. In August some minor reforms in their legal status were granted the Jews, as had been promised earlier by Plehve. But in the same month of August pogroms broke out afresh in the southern and western provinces; again in September; and then in October. In the course of the following year, as the Government cast about for means of recovering social control (and, presumably, its own nerve), it chose once again to try to deflect dissidence and unrest away from itself and on to other targets. A vast campaign of co-ordinated violence was now launched against all classes of subjects deemed hostile to the Autocracy and to the Russian Church, but chiefly against the Jews, in parallel with, but separately from, the regular, but now greatly intensified effort to suppress the revolutionary movements proper through the established state machinery of police, army, and courts. No secret was made of the policy that informed the campaign or of the auspices under which it was being waged. Its chief political instrument, the Union of the Russian People, enjoyed the open patronage of the Court. It stood for a sharp reversal of the liberal course on which the regime was ostensibly embarked and, so far as the Jews were concerned, demanded harsher treatment than ever. The Union's (and therefore, for these particular purposes, the Autocracy's) fighting arm was the Black Hundreds movement, which gathered and fielded the mobs which did the actual killing, beating, rape, pillage, and arson by which the declared enemies of Russia were to be punished.

The Autocracy's new war against its Jewish subjects opened with full force on the day after the Tsar's promise of a constitution and civil rights was proclaimed and in its first stage, which lasted for 11 days, from 18 to 29 October, the Jewish quarters of 660 cities, towns, and townlets in 8 of the provinces of southern Russia were sacked under the benevolent eyes of the official and uniformed forces of law and order. Over 800 people were killed, 130 of them in active self-defence, leaving 300 widows and some 1,300 orphans; and the property of almost 200,000 inhabitants, over 10 per cent of the total Jewish population of the region, was destroyed or severely damaged, to a total cost of 55,000,000 roubles. The greatest of these pogroms, in Odessa, left 302 dead (of whom 55 were killed in active self-defence), some 5,000 wounded, 1,400 ruined business enterprises, 3,000 self-employed craftsmen reduced to beggary by the destruction of their workshops, and the homes and property of tens of thousands of others destroyed or damaged.

For almost four days and four nights blood flowed in Odessa as on a battlefield [wrote Leo Motzkin, the author of the most thorough and detailed compilation of data on the entire campaign], but without the generally valid laws of war prevailing. There rushed through the streets tens of thousands of soldiers, policemen in and out of uniform, government officials of all sorts, and the blind civilian troops of Reaction [ranging] from householders . . . to aimless companies of workmen and peasants, and all these elements robbed, stole, raped, and killed until Jewish Odessa was like a field of rubble strewn with corpses.[21]

It was the early 1880s over again. In some ways it was worse. In the background there was the same fear in St. Petersburg of a peasant rebellion and the same effort to deflect it from the institutions and beneficiaries of the state. But the mood in high places was closer to the pathological than it had been a generation earlier. There was less shame at the execution of the intent, less embarrassment in retrospective contemplation of the result. The whole dark business was more central to the purposes of the Government. Above all, it was bloodier and, unlike that of the 1880s, the campaign was *not* brought to an end and followed by an extended period of civil peace. For all these reasons the chief response of the Jews themselves was swifter this time and on a greater scale. There was a giant rise in the panic flow of emigrants. After running at about 50,000 a year for some time at the turn of the century, it jumped to double that figure in 1905 and by 1907 had trebled.[22] Millions now accounted Russia a country to be abandoned, not to be lived in, if one could only get away from it.

Yet it was equally true—at all events, it was arguable— that the regime was visibly weakening and in retreat and that the forces attacking it above ground and sapping it below were more varied and powerful than at any earlier stage of the interminable struggle to liberalize Russia; that the Jews were now less isolated; that they had allies who were willing to stand by them, not only accepting them as individuals, but even—some, at all events, if then very gingerly—conceding to the Jews collectively something like the status of a legitimate constituent of the multinational Russian scheme. In the fever of the summer of 1905 even the Polish revolutionaries, always

---

[21] [Leo Motzkin], *Die Judenpogrome in Russland*, i (Cologne and Leipzig, 1910), p. 195. On the genesis of Motzkin's report, see below, p. 444.

[22] Based on figures in Rubinow, op. cit. Chapter 6, note 3, pp. 503–4; and A. Ginzburg, 'Emigratsiya evreev iz Rossii', *Evreiskaya Entsiklopediya*, xvi (1913), cols. 264–5.

foremost in their resentment of Jewish claims to a particular
and separate status, had been prepared (briefly) to co-operate
with independently organized Jews—specifically the Bund.[23]
The October programme of the liberal Constitutional Democratic Party (Kadets) demanded unequivocally that 'all
Russian citizens, irrespective of sex, religion, or nationality,
are to be equal before the law' and that 'all class distinctions
and all limitations on the personal and property rights of
Poles, Jews, and all other groups of the population must be
abolished, without exception.'[24] The Tsar's own October
Manifesto, announcing what appeared to be a constitutional
regime, declared that it was his will 'to grant the people the
unshakeable foundations of civic freedom on the basis of genuine
personal inviolability, freedom of conscience, speech, assembly,
and association';[25] and it was a fact, remarkably, that for the
elections that followed the Jews received the franchise along
with all others and that a handful of their number were
elected to the Duma. Undeniably, it was a time of movement.
Hence the grounds for optimism, if one was inclined to it,
whatever one's precise philosophy—that is, whether one
sought no more for the Jews than for them to be left alone
and in peace, or whether one wished them to emerge, emanci-
pated, into the new, liberal, perhaps even socialist Russia
now presumably opening up before all eyes, or whether it was
acceptance of the Jews *collectively* as a constituent nation of a
multinational state that one insisted on. In March 1905
representatives of a large group of Jewish communities went
so far as to formally petition the Government for equality with
the other peoples of Russia; and in the same month a League
for the Attainment of Complete Equality for Russian Jewry
was publicly established. Even in the aftermath of the October
pogroms, even after the crushing of the St. Petersburg Soviet
at the end of 1905, it was not implausible to argue that things
could now never be the same, or as bad, again. Even after the
dissolution of the First Duma and the final descent into the
long, dark corridor of obscurantist repression and revolutionary
terror that followed, and in the face of the reduction of the

[23] Sidney Harcave, *First Blood* (New York, 1964), pp. 155–6.
[24] Text ibid., pp. 292 ff.
[25] Text ibid., pp. 195–7.

hammering of the Jews to a ritual and a routine, it was still possible and never wholly unreasonable to regard the first Russian revolution as a sort of proof that a second must follow and that there could be light at the end of the journey. But then it was a time when all arguments were plausible: for the uncertainties were enormous and all, ultimately, was speculation.

This then was the climate in which the ethos and cadres of the inner, politically and ideologically motivated core of the Second *'Aliya* were formed. These were young people (some 75 per cent were under the age of twenty-five),[26] and mostly alone upon arrival in Erez-Israel (being unmarried and having left their parents behind). A relatively high proportion had undergone some kind of secondary and higher education, if only as 'external' students (25 and 8 per cent respectively, not counting some who had been briefly trained in traditional Jewish secondary schools or *yeshivot*). But about two-thirds were without any profession or settled occupation of their own. Within the minority that had had an occupation in their countries of origin the skilled artisans (14·5 per cent) and the schoolteachers (7·5 per cent) stood out. The social origins of these young people were predominantly lower middle-class: well over half being sons of 'merchants' (a term encompassing shopkeepers as well as 'merchants of the First Guild', with many more of the former than of the latter), skilled craftsmen, teachers, clerks, rabbis, ritual slaughterers and other communal functionaries, and independent farmers. Only a handful were sons or daughters of modern professionals, that is to say, physicians, lawyers, pharmacists, and the like, or of labourers and of such as could be classed with the army of the truly indigent and the virtually unemployed who were such a considerable component of east European Jewry as a whole. Sociologically, they were thus much like the common run of young recruits to the general revolutionary movements of the day, populist as well as Marxist. And, indeed, a high proportion of the future members of the hard core of

[26] For the figures that follow see Yosef Gorni, 'Ha-shinu'im ba-mivne ha-hevrati ve-ha-politi shel "ha-'aliya ha-sheniya" ba-shanim 1904–1914', *Ha-Ẕionut*, i (1970), pp. 204–46.

the Second ʿ*Aliya* (some three-quarters of all male adults of
that category at the time of arrival in Ereẓ-Israel) had already
been involved in political activity in one form or another in
the Diaspora. A small, but still substantial proportion (16 per
cent) had joined actively in the revolutionary turbulence.
Five per cent had been gaoled for revolutionary activities and
a further 9 per cent had been under arrest for Zionist connections. Seven and a half per cent had joined self-defence
groups organized to resist *pogromshchiki*. Finally, a fifth of
all of the approximately 1,000 members of the Second ʿ*Aliya*
on whom the relevant data is available had been members
of the major Zionist socialist trend in Russia, Poʿalei Ẓion
('Workers of Zion').[27] This was the largest single category of
its kind. In it were reflected vividly the continuing drawing-
powers of Marxism along with a primary identification with
Jewry, but on terms which entailed a rejection of the now
well-established Bundist recipe for a synthesis of the two.

Poʿalei Ẓion, which later took shape as an established party
or federation of parties within the Zionist movement, was
at this early stage (1901–6) no more than a generic term
for a set of small, local groups, chiefly in Byelorussia and the
Ukraine. These had sprung up spontaneously, much in the
manner that the local Ḥibbat Ẓion associations had originated
twenty years earlier, under the twin influences of Herzl's
new movement and the spread of Marxist socialism throughout
Europe. They were devoid of any country-wide organizational
tie (until 1906); and for all their common ground, there
remained much to divide them. Not all were convinced that
they themselves should venture into politics (some, that
is, were not bent on revolution at all, but, in the jargon of
the Social Democrats of the time, were 'economists' who
wanted to concentrate on the socio-economic needs of the
workers);[28] some favoured Yiddish, some Hebrew; some,

---

[27] Ibid., pp. 229–30.

[28] The three stated purposes of the Poʿalei Ẓion society, most moderate of all,
founded in Minsk in 1901, were: a) to help propagate the Zionist idea as expressed in
the Basel Programme; b) to strengthen Jewish national sentiment among Jewish
workers; and c) 'raising the spiritual-cultural condition [*oifheyben dem geystigen zustand*]
and improving the material state of the Jewish workers'. B. Locker (ed.), *Idisher
arbeyter yarbuch un almanach* (New York, 1928), p. 186.

when the East Africa affair broke, sided with the old guard of
Russian Zionism, some with Herzl; and there was the fundamental, if still barely visible division between those who,
consistent with their mode of social analysis, relied on great
underlying impersonal forces apparently at work on the Jews
to move them bodily and in the mass to the 'territory' they
so badly needed and those, in contrast, who wished to act
for themselves and without delay. All, however, can be seen
as latter-day children of Leo Pinsker in the sense that they
believed that it was futile for the Jews to rely on others, even
other socialists, for their emancipation; and all, in one degree
or another, had taken in the fact that the general socialist
movement was hostile to Jewish particularism. To join the
general socialist parties was therefore, in the view of many
of the Poʿalei Zion, an act akin to assimilation, a denial of
origins. So while all welcomed the revolution of 1905, its
effect in many cases was to induce discomfort and to bring
their latent sense of alienation out into the open and in a
fresh and unexpected context. In this discomfort and in this
alienation lay the basis for the power of Zionism to draw
them.

[In October 1905] all the revolutionary parties emerged from the
underground and appeared *for the first time* in public with their flags
and slogans. A giant mass meeting convened 'spontaneously';
thousands upon thousands—Russians, Ukrainians, and Jews—
streamed without hindrance to the broad square near the new theatre
in my city of Poltava. Speakers of each trend and party got up to
speak to the public; representatives of *Iskra* (the Social Democrats),
the Socialist Revolutionaries, and the Ukrainian Socialist Party.
It goes without saying that there were Jews among the speakers for
the 'general' parties, but they did not come to speak as Jews, but as
Russians or Ukrainians. We, the Poʿalei Zion, demanded a place for
a Jewish speaker who would speak in the name of the Jews. Our
request was granted; and it was I who spoke to the crowd of ten
thousand souls—in Russian, of course. I spoke as a Jew—on the
Russian revolution, on the participation of the Jews, and on our own
aspirations to the life of a free nation in Zion. But then, as I was
speaking from the theatre balcony, I saw in my mind's eye a living
image of the holy city of Jerusalem, in its ruins, empty of its sons, as I
had seen it a year earlier on my first visit to the Land in the summer of

1904. And I asked myself: *to whom am I speaking?* Will my listeners here in Poltava understand me, will they believe? Are we the Jews *true partners* in this revolution and in this victory? Will this revolution which heralds salvation for the Russians bring the hoped-for salvation to us Jews as well? Why am I here and not there? Why are we all here and not there? And once these questions had sprung to my mind I was unable to shake free of them; and when I had finished speaking my thoughts were not on the demonstration and on the victory of the Russian revolution, but on *our own Jerusalem*. I decided absolutely that my place was in Erez-Israel and that it was for me to go there and to dedicate my life to its reconstruction, and without delay.[29]

In these circumstances both a sudden switch midway from one course and transfer of allegiance to another were as common as the yearning for firm ground, fixed purposes, and a rational plan of action. It was not the least of the characteristics of such young people as have been described, caught up as they were in a period of unprecedented upheaval and uncertainty, that they felt free—but also obliged—to make a clear-cut choice of political and social direction. They could plunge into the thick of the fight in Russia itself; they could turn away from Russia altogether. They could choose the greater, all-Russian political arena; they could limit themselves to the Jewish sector within it. Each possibility broke down into further sets of alternatives. Each had its *rationale*, each its specific attraction. Each offered, or seemed to offer release from some burning pressure or doubt. In the event, what an alert, politically minded, moderately educated, half- (or entirely) secularized young Jew living through these tumultuous times actually decided upon was likely to depend more on chance factors than on a process of careful study and rational judgement. For in case after case, by hundreds and by thousands, the decision turned on personal temperament, or on the colour of what happened to be the local political group or discussion circle, or on the chance of already being known to, and sought after by the police, or on some bitter personal experience in the army, or on the desire to escape it

---

[29] Yizḥak Ben-Ẓvi, *Po ʿalei ẓion ba-ʿaliya ha-sheniya* (Tel-Aviv, 1950), p. 15. Emphases in text.

altogether, and perhaps most often on the direct influence of a single powerful personality in the young person's vicinity.

There is no evidence of a general rule; there appears to be no clear pattern. What is clear is that, so far as the circumstances impelling or drawing him to this or that political commitment were concerned, the young Zionist socialist of the first decade and a half of the century had a great deal more in common with his contemporaries in the (all-Russian) Social-Democratic and Socialist-Revolutionary Parties than with his own 'bourgeois' seniors in the Zionist movement itself—even radicals like Bernstein-Kohan or like the first outright socialist of real note in the Zionist camp, Syrkin.

Nachman Syrkin (1868–1924), for some years the chief proponent of socialism within the official Zionist movement, was a familiar, because independent and turbulent figure at the early Congresses. He was of the class and type of the leading members of the Democratic Party: born in Byelorussia, educated at western universities, a founder-member with Motzkin of the pre-Herzlian, proto-Zionist 'Russian-Jewish Scientific Society[30] in Berlin, and both an immediate adherent to the new Zionist movement and a consistent critic of Herzl thereafter, like Motzkin, on radical-political and anti-authoritarian grounds. He was not a Marxist properly speaking; nor was he in any real, active sense a revolutionary, although he had had an early, moderately serious brush with the Russian police and later, in 1904, had had his socialism taken sufficiently seriously by the German police for it to result in his expulsion from the country. But he took class-categories to be of fundamental importance and at the centre of his concern was, consistently, the wretched Jewish commonalty of eastern Europe. The result was a fierce criticism of all the conservative forces in Jewry, notably of 'the bourgeoisie' and of 'the synagogue', but also of the non-political strains in Zionism itself; and with this criticism went an emphasis (foreign to the political strain in the movement) on the form the Jewish state-to-be should take. There were aspects of the Jewish condition, Syrkin believed, which socialism could not deal with: the socio-economic imbalance within Jewry itself, the lack of political rights, its isolation within society at large.

[30] See *Origins*, pp. 224–5.

The Zionist-territorial solution to the problem was therefore indispensable. But it was unthinkable and impracticable that a state based on social inequality be founded for the Jews and by them: it would be absurd, because it would entail a social contract of servitude; it would fail, because a *laissez-faire* economy would, among other things, encourage the recruitment of cheap native labour and discourage the employment (and therefore the immigration) of Jews; and it would be a gigantic missed opportunity, because the Jews had never entirely abandoned Messianic hopes and it was socialism alone that could now provide them with a vision.

Because the Jews are forced to find a homeland and establish a state, they therefore have the opportunity to be the first to realize the socialist vision. This is the tragic element of their historic fate, but it is also a unique historic mission. What is generally the vision of a few will become a great national movement among the Jews; what is Utopian in other contexts is a necessity for the Jews.

The Jews were historically the nation which caused division and strife; it will now become the most revolutionary of all nations. From the humblest and most oppressed of all peoples it will be transformed into the proudest and greatest. The Jews will derive their moral stature from their travail and out of the pain of their existence will come a pattern of noble living. The Jew is small, ugly, servile and debased when he forgets and denies himself. He becomes strong, noble and socially aware when he returns to his true nature.[31]

There was much in Syrkin that was Herzl writ very large, written, in fact, in letters of fire: his contempt for the Jewish bourgeoisie, his restricted kind of nationalism, his secularism, his notion that a Jewish national revival would be in the interests of, and be applauded by, all civilized and progressive forces, his utopianism, his attention to organizational

---

[31] *Die Judenfrage und der sozialistische Judenstaat* (Berne, 1898). English translation as 'The Jewish Question and the Socialist Jewish State' in Marie Syrkin, *Nachman Syrkin* (New York, 1961), p. 285. Strictly speaking, a *Judenstaat* is a state of Jews, not a Jewish state; namely, a state inhabited and governed chiefly by Jews, but like all or most others in its salient features, as opposed to one whose socio-political order would differ from the norm in certain significant respects. A more precise translation of the title than the customary one given above would therefore be *The Jewish Question and the Jews' Socialist State*. The same distinction applies to Herzl's *Der Judenstaat*, commonly, but incorrectly translated as *The Jewish State*.

details, and, and, above all, his compassion for the 'wretched Jewish masses . . . doomed to destruction both by government pressure and by social anti-Semitism which deprives them of all means of livelihood'[32] which led him to support Herzl over East Africa.

But Syrkin, in style and comportment, in breadth of interests and culture, was as fair a representative of the educated Russian-Jewish bourgeoisie as Leo Motzkin, or Shmarya Levin, or Julius Brutzkus, or Victor Jacobson. This was precisely what the typical member of the *new* crop of Zionist socialists was not—not in social origins, not in superior formal education, and not in intellectual and cultural propensities, but chiefly not, because the temperament of the new man was in a true and important sense revolutionary. His hatred of the Russian state specifically and his suspicion of the State as such, as an institution, were both profound. He knew the State to be evil, or at the very least to be an instrument of evil; and always—perhaps by its nature—it was 'theirs', never 'ours'. Therefore no real and lasting reforms *from above* were to be expected, no truck with authority could be entirely proper. Its minions were to be despised, its embrace avoided, and the authority of its institutions rejected. And as a corollary to the rejection of publicly instituted authority and to the value attached to the rules of voluntary personal commitment and self-discipline, there was an absolute devotion to equality as a cardinal virtue in itself and as the fundamental principle of justice. In all this, the views of the young Zionist socialist of the day were therefore much like those of the Russian populists of the latter half of the nineteenth century and their successors among the revolutionaries of his own times— only held, if anything, more bitterly and tenaciously and subject to daily reinforcement under the impact of the measures taken by the Russian state against its Jewish subjects. At the same time, this was a respect in which his views were significantly different from those prevalent among the older generation of Russian Zionists. They had always craved official regularization of their status and, for all their loathing of the Autocracy, wanted no quarrel with it, but only, in the

---

[32] *Vozzvaniye evreiskoi molodezhi* [Berlin], 1901. English translation: 'Call to Jewish Youth', in Syrkin, p. 295.

final analysis, to be left alone. As for the Herzlian school, which wished positive co-operation with all states, including the Russian, and was very far from seeing the State as such as an instrument of evil, but wished, on the contrary, to replicate it for the Jews themselves—an entire culture separated him from it.

The Zionist socialists, but especially that significant part of the Second *'Aliya* that stood the course and remained to have so great an impact on the country, were like their revolutionary contemporaries also in that they were, perhaps above all, intensely serious people. They reckoned social responsibility and social commitment cardinal virtues and tended to judge themselves and others by the degree to which these were assumed and acted upon. They tried hard and continually to look at the world around them with clear, cold eyes so as to recognize the forces—particularly the impersonal forces—operating within it. But such understanding was meant to lead to doctrine and doctrine, in their view, entailed practice. Reason and social action had always to be linked, and rightly so, to their minds, else what was the use of reason? Thus their outlook, their method, and their standards, no less than what they actually saw around them, all impelled them to severity of judgement, to the drawing of sharp distinctions, to the anticipation of sweeping change, to a constant effort to work out their proper location and direction on the sea of events, and to correspondingly bold and often harsh personal decisions. This was very much in the spirit and teaching of Chernyshevsky and his heirs. It was very unlike the meeker, prudential habits of mind of their own ancestors or, by and large, of their non-socialist fellow Zionists.

But there were differences. Unlike most Russian populists, they had no clear—certainly no commonly held—idea where they and the activities they were embarked upon stood in relation to 'the people': that is to say, to Russian Jewry in the mass. They were not out to educate or organize them. In fact, they were leaving them behind. It could only be very distantly that they could hope to influence and stimulate them by example. They were far more intent (in so far as they had clear views) on building, from the ground up, a wholly new society which would indeed be properly ordered, unlike that hopeless one which they were abandoning because there was nothing they could do and nothing worth doing in or for it. And thus there was a sense in which they were at least as much concerned with their private destinies as with those of their people. Certainly, they were intent upon change, but on a reduced scale and at a level of quality and intensity superior to anything they thought could be accomplished in Europe, because only outside Europe could the contradictory pulls of socialism and nationalism be satisfactorily resolved.

But again, unlike so many Russian populists and other revolutionaries, they were not destructive. They were not so set, as were the others, upon a great clearing of the ground as a prelude to building something better to replace it with, the great, immediate emphasis being on sweeping away the old, rather than on the contours and content of the new. Their fervour and their rationalism were streaked with restraint after all. They were not brutal like the revolutionaries of the day of whom the fine Yiddish writer Y. L. Peretz wrote 'My heart is with you . . . but I fear you. I fear the enslaved when they turn victorious.'[33] They were not wholly and implacably sure of themselves—at all events in these early years. Bakunin (his anti-Semitism apart) would have thought little of them. Herzen might have approved.

That said, it is not immediately clear how this relative, and for their class and general tendency, uncharacteristic mildness may be accounted for. It may perhaps be ascribed to their fundamental concern with their own people, at least in the abstract, with action within and on behalf of Jewry. It had never seemed to the Jews in any of the lands of their Dispersion that they as a collectivity were capable of inducing a change in society at large. They might seek to influence, to deflect, to induce marginal alteration. They might as individuals seek more—but then as part of, and on behalf of all the people (or peoples) of the state. Taking up the cause of the Jews directly and explicitly and with radical intent had always meant tacit acceptance of the existing political and social order, or at the very most only very moderate, almost unexceptionable social purposes to be pursued with

---

[33] 'Tikvah va-faḥad' ['Hope and fear'], *Kol kitvei Y. L. Peretz* (trans. and ed. Shimshon Meltzer), viii (Tel-Aviv, 1962), p. 228.

extreme caution and in close alliance with other, like-minded, but non-Jewish forces.

Their mildness may owe something too the fact that, while it was their judgement and their impulse to write Russia off—and the Diaspora in Russia and elsewhere with it—it was not part of their purpose to change it. Those who wished for change, there *in situ*, stayed on. Those who left sought to work change elsewhere: in practice in Erez-Israel—and *there* the slate was (or was thought to be) clean. In Erez-Israel there was nothing to destroy; everything was to be built, everything was for the future.

Finally, where the decision to leave Russia was a decision to leave for Erez-Israel it was radical and brave and difficult; it was heterodox; it was highly unusual and it was dramatic; but it was not denying 'everything' in the manner of Turgenev's prototype 'nihilist', Bazarov,[34] and not even to the extent that a decision to make for America was. There was in it an element of preservation and of retreat, partly to a mythic past. This last was not noticeably rational. Nor was it obviously consistent with any of the accepted principles and modes of socialist analysis. And thus the Zionist socialists (most of whom never got so far as leaving Russia at all, while many of those who did made for America, in the event, not Erez-Israel) had a great deal to explain to themselves and to other radicals and were under an inescapable impulsion not only to accommodate their Zionism to their socialism theoretically, but also to rediscover as rapidly as possible—and if necessary to encourage—within Erez-Israel a state of affairs which was amenable to Marxist class-analysis and to their own participation in the social struggle along doctrinally acceptable lines.

Their hardest problem was to decide whether socialism, as a system of beliefs and ideas which tended strongly to reduce the problem of nationalities into what purported to be its fundamental socio-economic components, was indeed applicable to the particular and, on the face of it, abnormal case of the Jews; and if not, whether it was useful and legitimate for Jews to profess it. In part, the problem was intellectual and amenable (or so it appeared) to rational analysis and argu-

---

[34] *Fathers and Sons* (trans. Rosemary Edmonds, London, 1971), p. 65. Cf. Isaiah Berlin, *Fathers and Children* (Oxford, 1972), pp. 24–8.

ment. In part, the more important part, it was inevitably linked to the greater, classic problem of identity—the problem of the obligation and pull of loyalty towards Jewry encountered by just such Jews as had distanced themselves from the Jewish tradition (notably in its religious aspect) and who insisted on considering all questions, not least the Jewish Question itself, in strictly universal terms. The great number of young Jewish members of the *intelligentsia* who flocked to the Social-Democratic and Socialist-Revolutionary Parties (Jewish workmen tended more to the Bund) can be taken as a measure of the force and attraction of universalist creeds and ostensibly universalist movements, part evidence of the onset of decomposition within hitherto virtually monolithic east European Jewry. Many were satisfied with what they found, or smothered their lingering reservations. Some took a harsh line with the Jews themselves. 'Why do you come to me with your special Jewish sorrows', Rosa Luxemburg once complained. 'I feel just as sorry for the wretched Indian victims in Putamayo, the negroes in Africa . . . I cannot find a special corner in my heart for the ghetto. I feel at home in the entire world wherever there are clouds and birds and human tears.'[35] But there were always such as were unable to totally sink themselves and their people in a wider movement. These either moved away from it or else sought a synthesis: either of a rigorous, theoretical kind, or in action, or both. Finally, some of these, after a period, eventually abandoned the particular cause of the Jews after all and merged, or sought to merge, in the general current —to the great initial advantage of the revolutionary movement in Russia, but to their own great personal cost in the prisons and slave-labour camps with which that country was soon lavishly provided.

Neither the decision to leave Russia for Erez-Israel, nor the press of life within the new-old country ever erased all sensitivity to the terms of the problem set in the Diaspora. There had been, and there remained, no single, acceptable formula for the mixture of a 'class' outlook with a national one. Each component was available in a variety of doses and types and the number of possible combinations was very high: more or less rigour in Marxist analysis; more or less attachment

[35] Quoted in J. P. Nettl, *Rosa Luxemburg*, ii (London, 1966), p. 860.

to the Jewish tradition in its secular manifestations—or even, in some rare cases, in its religious manifestations as well; more or less emphasis on actual, personal involvement in the necessary and immediate conflict or struggle, once that conflict or struggle had been identified; more or less discipline and 'centralism' within the chosen group; more or less interest in co-operation with other groups, Zionist and non-Zionist, Jewish and non-Jewish; and more or less concern with one's own moral and social development, more or less concern with the moral and social development of society as a whole—at all events, that part of society to which one was addressing oneself. But throughout, among these people, the standards by which behaviour was judged and by which it was intended to be ruled were the highest: truth, equality, self-effacement, dedication; and for long, power was neither understood nor discussed and violence was unknown. The result was something like a church—or perhaps a cluster of churches, each perpetually liable to be rent by schism, no such schism ever being amenable to repair except tediously and imperfectly. Certainly, as in other churches, the business of internal government was destined in time to become of absorbing interest to those who applied themselves to it; while on the other hand, given the strict norms of private egalitarian conduct, such internal government had to be engaged in with much indirection and discretion. At the same time, because beliefs were strongly held and expected to be acted on, the internal cohesion of the Zionist socialist groups, so long as they lasted, was immensely strong; and authority within and over them, as exercised by those who emerged in the course of time to seek and attain it, was particularly potent. But again, because the ultimate source of this internal strength was moral and non-coercive, and a frank striving for and exercise of power was out of the question, their business came to be enveloped from time to time in a cloud of casuistry and hypocrisy. Here too, however, the measure varied from group to group and of course from individual to individual. The end-result almost defies generalization.

Broadly, however, two strains are detectable. In one the emphasis is on the great social forces and categories, on the impersonal and the elemental, on (to use a favourite term) the 'stoicheiological'. For the adepts of this approach theory counted for at least as much as practice and tended to be rigorous. In debate and in action they were somewhat less tolerant and more aggressive and, in the long run, more interested in power and better at acquiring and wielding it. They were interested in organization and institutions. They were more urban in character and outlook, more inclined to gravitate back to the town even in Ereẓ-Israel itself, more sympathetic to the traditional Marxist view of the central role and importance of the proletariat, and more wary of the romantic and the sentimental. They were firmly anticlerical. For all these reasons they had a great deal in common with the Russian Social Democrats and, indeed, with the Bundists, especially in their final years in Russia and their early years in Ereẓ-Israel, when they still paid enormous attention to the theoretical problem (academic on the face of it, but loaded with political and emotional meaning) of reconciling Marxist socialism with Zionism. Accordingly they held Borochov, the man whose effort to arrive at such a reconciliation was the most ambitious, in particular esteem. And they continued to hold him in posthumous, somewhat awkward respect even long after, when they had been caught up in affairs around them and their interest in the speculative and the theoretical had largely waned.

Ber Borochov (1881–1917) himself was not quite one of their number. He had good revolutionary credentials: he had been a member of the Russian Social-Democratic Party (until expelled from it in 1901 for, in his own words, having had 'a bad influence on the workers—I was teaching them to think for themselves'[36]); he had taken part in Jewish self-defence against the *pogromshchiki*; he had been on the run from the police; he had been in prison. But he was a man of ideas and theory, a figure much like Syrkin, neither a latter-day populist goer-to-the people, nor a man of direct, personal revolutionary action; and, like Syrkin, he put his very considerable intellectual gifts and his (largely self-taught, but substantial) learning to the service of the political and social

---

[36] 'At the Cradle of Socialist Zionism', *Die Wahrheit* (New York), 13 March 1916, quoted in Ber Borochov, *Nationalism and the Class Struggle*, ed. Abraham G. Duker (New York, 1937, reprinted Westport, Conn, 1972), p. 180.

cause which absorbed him, as it did so many others of his type and generation, to the exclusion of all else: the wretched mass of Russian Jewry. His life was the life of the agitator and the polemicist, the editor and publicist, the talented but amateur sociologist, the inventor and expounder of formulae and political programmes, and the critic—but virtually all his works centred, in the final analysis, on Russia and Russian Jewry. He was compelled to live abroad after 1907, in central Europe and in the United States. He did not go to Erez-Israel; he did not make *that* break. And upon the collapse of the Autocracy in February 1917 he promptly returned to Russia. None the less, Borochov—with the notable exception of Aḥad Ha-ʿAm—was the most distinguished and systematic Zionist theoretician of his day. Compared with his essays on the subject, the pamphlets and articles of Lilienblum, Pinsker, Herzl, or even Nordau—judged for their intellectual quality, rather than for their undoubted historical importance— border on the mediocre, not to say the rudimentary. There is a great deal of scholastic Marxism in Borochov and a lot of juggling with fashionable terms and constructs. But he escapes the charge of sophistry by virtue of his transparent seriousness and sincerity of intention.

Borochov was convinced that the Marxist class-analysis of society was correct and that the future lay with the proletariat. The Jews' problem was that they did not constitute (or include among their numbers) a true proletariat and that their alien social status, their lack of a territory of their own, and their consequent economic and political weakness all effectively prevented them from becoming one and so merging, ulti- mately, in the great march towards a just, universal, socialist society. Where they were employed in industry it was only in the light and marginal sectors which were weak and largely irrelevant to the main struggle. In any case, a very large pro- portion were effectively outside industry altogether. Worse still, the new, objectively progressive forces would, when they had won their battles, press on the Jews as hard as the forces of reaction. Salvation therefore lay in the proletarianization of Jewry and in good time. How was this to be accomplished? As things were, this necessary socio-economic conversion was bound to be impeded by the local forces and instincts of nationalism. And these could not be mitigated. The Jews had to leave. Indeed, the Jews were leaving. But it would do them no good to leave for countries where the same conditions were repeated or repeatable. In the end, the proletarianization of Jewry was therefore conditional on the acquisition of a territory in which the Jews, because they formed a majority of the population and would not be alien from it, would no longer be impeded from occupying the key strata of the economy, either as bourgeois or as proletarians. 'The first and most important question, therefore, the one which anyone who saw himself as a true friend of the Jewish people had to answer was: what is the place where the Jews would be able to achieve normal proletarianization?'[37]

Unlike Syrkin, and many other Zionist socialists, Borochov was not a Territorialist.[38] 'The well-being of the people in Erez-Israel is dearer to us than the well-being of the people outside Erez-Israel', he wrote, admittedly adding the qualification that, 'none the less, the people without Erez-Israel is dearer to us than Erez-Israel without the people.'[39] At the height of the battle over the East Africa proposal in the aftermath of the Sixth Congress he sided with the opposition and became one of Ussishkin's most energetic and effective agitators, travelling through the provinces of the Pale and pleading the cause of Erez-Israel with success—much of that success lying in the fact (as Ussishkin appears to have understood very well[40]) that he could speak to his contemporaries in the class-analytical terms that most impressed them. It is curious that, given his outlook, this talented man should have espoused Ussishkin's cause. Few of the movement's leaders fitted the outline of the stereotype 'bourgeois' Zionist better than Ussishkin. None of the Po'alei Zion to whom Borochov was now increasingly drawn was as well-versed and earnest a Marxist as he. That he should have been drawn to a view of the Problem of the Jews as a distinctive one, and as one requir-

---

[37] 'Li-she'elat zion ve-teritoria', B. Borochov, *Ketavim* (eds. L. Levite et al.), i (Tel-Aviv, 1955), pp. 145–6.
[38] Syrkin too eventually changed his mind and rejoined the fold.
[39] Ibid., p. 93.
[40] Matityahu Mintz, 'Igrot Borochov le-Ussishkin', *Ha-Zionut*, ii (1971), p. 242 and *passim*.

ing a differentiated solution, is readily understandable in the light of the events around him, which hit him emotionally and intellectually quite as hard as they hit other Zionists and Zionists-to-be.[41] The further step, the insistence on Erez-Israel, is less easily understood and the elaborate argument which he developed in 1905 in its favour is less than entirely convincing—partly, no doubt, because it purports to be rigorous and rational throughout.[42]

In a series of articles headed 'On the Question of Zion and Territory',[43] Borochov lays down what he takes to be the conditions that must be satisfied if a given territory is to answer to the needs of the Jews and not contain within itself the seeds of a repetition of the ancient pattern of social alienation and economic imbalance and powerlessness. Ideally, it must be remote from centres of power and civilization, and a relatively poor, unpopulated, and underdeveloped country—else there would be no chance of the Jews forming its proletariat: non-Jewish capital and non-Jewish labour would shoulder the Jews aside, if they were already in place. Ideally, such population as it has must be nomadic: capable of moving elsewhere; and the country itself sufficiently inhospitable in climate to deter the common run of immigrants from Europe, but not Jews who need it badly. A static population would be agricultural, and an agricultural population, Borochov thought (evidently with the European experience in mind), could always compete for jobs in industry more effectively than the Jews. A territory of no importance and little value to anyone, remote, but not inaccessible—that was what was wanted. Where was there such a land? The only one he knew of was Wadi al-'Arish. But that was out.

So, what of lands with a settled population? In such a case, at the very least, the sovereign Power must not itself be

---

[41] Matityahu Mintz, *Ber Borochov; ha-ma'agal ha-rishon (1900–1906)* (Tel-Aviv, 1976), p. 62.

[42] Yizhak Ben-Zvi thought that the decisive influence on Borochov may have been a series of talks in Poltava in the summer of 1904 in which both young men participated and in which Ben-Zvi, recently having returned from his first visit to Erez-Israel, played a central role. *Kitvei Yizhak Ben-Zvi*, i (Tel-Aviv, 1936), pp. 19–20.

[43] Originally published as a series of articles in *Evreiskaya Zhizn*, June–October, 1905. The quotations that follow are based on the Hebrew version, 'Li-she'elat zion veteritoria', Borochov, op. cit., pp. 18–153.

possessed of an advanced capitalist economy; the territory itself must be comparatively remote from foreign centres of capitalism; there must be an existing Jewish element in the population ready for proletarianization; and 'the ethnic composition and mental disposition of the [non-Jewish] local population must be sufficiently close to our own for it to be possible, with proper management of the process of settlement and of the economy, for them to adapt to our culture so as to be indistinguishable from us in every respect.'[44]

The only land that answered to these requirements was Erez-Israel. The Ottoman regime was indeed weak; its economy, let alone that of Erez-Israel itself, was not of the advanced capitalist kind; there already was a substantial number of Jews there, many of whom, notably the members of the Sephardi and Yemeni communities, were already potential members of a proletariat; and

a most important thing: the local population of Erez-Israel is nearer to the Jews in its ethnic composition than any other people, nearer even than the 'Semitic' peoples. It is a very reasonable assumption that the fellahin in Erez-Israel are the direct descendants of the remnants of the Jewish and Canaanite agricultural population, with a very slight admixture of Arab blood; for, as is well known, the Arabs, proud conquerors, mixed very little with the mass of the people in the lands which they conquered, especially in Erez-Israel which was conquered as early as the time of Omar. In any event, all travellers to the country confirm that apart from the Arabic speech, it is impossible to distinguish in any respect between a Sephardi porter and a simple labourer and fellah. And such an external similarity is important . . . for it is on a difference of appearance, in the absence of differences of custom and manner, that all sorts of 'hatreds' depend. Thus the ethnic difference between the Jews of the Diaspora and the fellahin of Erez-Israel is no greater than the difference between the Ashkenazi and the Sephardi Jews. The local people are neither Arabs nor Turks . . . They assimilate willingly into any higher culture. And in the vicinity of the Jewish settlements they acquire the Hebrew culture, send their sons to Hebrew schools to learn to speak a Hebrew that is no less fluent than that of the Jewish children.[45]

In sum, Borochov argued, Erez-Israel was a genuine possibility in the sense that if there was a territory anywhere that satisfied

---

[44] Ibid., p. 147.　　　　　[45] Ibid., p. 148.

the needs of the Jews, it was the one; while he, for his part, knew of no other. And that being the case, the elemental forces driving the people would in the end drive them there. His operative conclusion, like Ussishkin's, was therefore to do everything to strengthen the existing Jewish base—and notably, the potential Jewish proletariat. That was the function of the Zionist movement as an institution; and that was the task of Zionist socialists as individuals and as a group.

Borochov's views on the common ethnic origins of Palestinian Arabs and Jews may have some small basis in fact. His views on the cultural affinity between them had (and have) hardly any. Of the supposed propensity of the Arab villagers to assimilate to Jewish society and culture, even in its modern form, there was (and is) little evidence. Borochov's own disciples soon learned the facts of the matter and his well-meaning, but uncharacteristically wild thesis on the subject soon faded from their minds. What remained was the example he set. Like the Ussishkins of the movement, he was convinced beyond argument that it was to Erez-Israel that Jews would eventually go and that nowhere else would they prosper. Unlike the 'bourgeois' of the movement, he evidently held that it was not enough to state and restate the proposition as a self-evident truth. It had to be explicated rationally; and it had to be integrated into a complete and watertight system, the terms of which were of universal and objective validity. Only thus would the young people to whom he addressed himself be fortified intellectually to do what their hearts dictated.

The other strain among the core members of the Second *Aliya* was, by analogy (in nineteenth-century Russian—and therefore already somewhat old-fashioned—terms), populist. They were on the whole less doctrinaire than the others, more varied in their subsidiary opinions,[46] more innocent, more passionate, more libertarian, and slower to learn the realities

[46] A notable figure among them was the A. D. Gordon who tended to religious mysticism and saw working the land as a form of worship; and on the other hand, there were free thinkers whom even Ahad Ha-'Am, who was closer to them in his conception of a Jewish society in Erez-Israel than he seems to have realized, found offensive in their blasphemous 'impertinence'. Letter to Ledizhinsky, 14 December 1910. *Igrot AH*, iv, p. 324.

of power. There was among them a somewhat lesser emphasis
on universal categories (but not values), and a greater, at any
rate more direct, emphasis on the particular, the Jewish.
They tended too to lay great stress on the individual—not,
as among the Marxists, on duty and internal discipline and on
the individual's paramount need to align himself with the
great, impersonal social forces if he was not to be chaff in the
wind of history, but rather more on the individual's destiny
and moral standing and on the imperative need for him to act
on behalf of society and in accordance with his view of it.
Certainly, by so acting, one might serve as an example and so
generate further movement. But even if none followed, it was
still incumbent upon one to play out one's beliefs. And at
the centre of these beliefs, as with the Russian populists and
as with the first, proto-Zionist offshoot of Russian populism,
the BILU movement,[47] there was the notion that there was
virtue in the country as opposed to the town, in the peasant
as opposed to the town-dweller, and in working the land as
opposed to all other occupations. The culture of the city was
'false' and 'artificial', life within it impersonal, competitive,
uncreative. Accordingly, since the Jewish populist had no
peasants of his own to go to, or fight for, let alone emulate, and
the Jews were predominantly a landless, urban, non-agri-
cultural people, the ultimate moral and social salvation of the
Jews had to take the form of a great conversion of this people of
petty tradesmen and craftsmen into men of the land. It was
therefore the duty of the Jewish socialist, and his private road
to salvation, to become a peasant himself. In Russia this was
out of the question, even if there had been a disposition to
attempt it. Neither the state nor society, least of all Russian
peasant society, would have tolerated it. The arena had to be
elsewhere. For the young men and women drawn by the mystique of the earth and the plough, the mystique of the Land of
Israel formed a perfect fit. And there the key was labour.

Only labour can spin the threads that will bind us intimately and
truly to the country. It alone will give us that profound and spiritual
relationship that obtains between the artist and the picture he has
painted, as opposed to the superficial, legalistic relationship that
obtains between the buyer and the picture he has bought.

[47] See *Origins*, pp. 78–88.

Yes, everything that is to be created in the country we must create ourselves: every tree, every vegetable, every house, every fence; every thing that makes man a partner of nature. Every line, every inscription on the unfolding roll of our future—everything, every-thing must be our handiwork. Only with our sweat must our land be watered. Our hands alone must bring its soil to life.[48]

For it was not to be the labour of *others*, as with so many of the members of the First *'Aliya*, or, for that matter, as with most European settlers in non-European lands, the British and the Germans, notably.[49] It had to be the labour of the new Jewish agricultural proletariat itself—although not, as they were to decide after bitter experience and heavy losses, a proletariat in the strictest sense, namely one of landless, largely casual farm-labour to be employed for the most part in the plantations of the landed 'bourgeoisie' of the farmers of the First *'Aliya*. These did not want them: the socialists, of all varieties, were too free in their behaviour and their thinking; they were less efficient in their work because less experienced and less hardy than the Arab villagers; and they had to be paid somewhat better wages. Besides, they were resented because the more doctrinaire among them now seized upon the smallholders of the First *'Aliya*, themselves only just, or still not firmly established, as if they were an oppressor class[50]— when in fact they would have achieved nothing, would have been so much flotsam washed upon the eastern shore of the Mediterranean Sea, had it not been for the base provided by the previous generation. In any event, in their (the populists of the Second *'Aliya*) view, the notion of an agricultural prole-tariat did not work at all. The results were hope- and soul-destroying. Moreover, as some realized after a while, it was notorious that it was the fate of landless peasants to be drawn sooner or later to the towns.[51]

[48] Eli'ezer Shohat, 'Yezira le'umit ve-heshbonot' (1911), part 3, in Eli'ezer Shohat and Hayim Shurer (eds.), *Pirkei ha-po'el ha-za'ir*, iii (Tel-Aviv, 1935), p. 19.

[49] Thus Eli'ezer Shohat. See Israel Kolatt, 'Eli'ezer Shohat ve-"ha-po'el ha-za'ir"', *Avot u-meyasdim* (Jerusalem, 1975), p. 123.

[50] On very early talk (1905) of a Jewish state being founded on socialist principles through 'class warfare', see Yizhak Ben-Zvi, *Po'alei zion ba-'aliya ha-sheniya* (Tel-Aviv, 1950), p. 33 fn.

[51] Yosef Vitkin, 'Kibbush ha-kark'a ve-khibbush ha'avoda' (1908), in *Pirkei ha-po'el ha-za'ir*, viii, part 2 (1936), p. 12.

The solution they hit on was to form a class of self-employed farmers who were neither landed in the classic sense, nor landless, neither masters nor servants, who preferred field crops to plantations because ploughing and sowing and reaping the harvest brought them closer to the soil than they could otherwise ever be, who were of the land, but civilized and modern, and who, in difficult circumstances, could find strength and solace in numbers. Their solution, their invention, in due course, was the *kevuza*,[52] the agricultural commune: voluntary, rigorously egalitarian, socially stable, possessed of real economic promise, and (despite a shadowy resemblance to the Russian *artel*) brilliantly original.

iii

The immediate significance of the Second *'Aliya*—and, more generally, of the rise of the socialist trend within Zionism—was in its internal effect on the movement. It helped destroy the monolithic character which Herzl had wanted to assure for it and to establish a sort of antechamber through which disappointed revolutionaries on the one hand and impatient potential revolutionaries on the other would pass each other, either way, into and out of the Zionist movement. So doing, it opened up a whole range of fresh ideas and influences. It signalled a somewhat different, but at all events reinvigorated approach to Erez-Israel and its settlement. And there, indeed, the impact of the socialists was to be remarkable. In the course of time, they were to provide the major leaders of the *yishuv* and, later, of the movement as a whole. Their people were to invent and manage its central political, economic, and military institutions and were, to a considerable extent, to set the *yishuv*'s norms of conduct, private as well as public and collective. It would be under their hegemony that the *yishuv* would become the politically preponderant component of Jewry after the Second World War.

But on the condition of Jewry as a whole, and more particularly on that of east European Jewry, the Zionist socialists

---

[52] *Kevuza* (=group) was the term first used. It denoted a commune that was relatively small and intimate (often under a score of young men and women) and loosely structured. In the early 1920s, as much larger and somewhat more tightly structured groups became the rule, the term *kibbuz* (=collective or collectivity) came into use.

were to have virtually no impact at all. Like all Zionists, they had begun by being obsessed by the problem of east European Jewry; and their own rise owed everything to peculiarities that were specific to that vast community. But as with most immigrants to the Land, but particularly the toughest and strongest-minded of them—which is what the core members of the Second *'Aliya* certainly were—they were subject to a characteristic change of perspective, values, and priorities. The bitter and intractable problem of the Jews in their Dispersion receded; the difficult, but seemingly manageable, even surmountable problems of the *yishuv* moved to the forefront—in their case, the tendency being reinforced by their own genuine (and entirely justifiable) sense of constituting an élite and a vanguard whose concerns, despite the minuteness of the scale, were properly the concerns of all Jewry and hence their great and special responsibility.

Thus the socialist Zionists were at one with the political Zionists in wanting a revolution in the life and conditions of the Jews. But the revolution they were working for (whether they realized it nor not), while in its way as radical qualitatively as any which Herzl and his friends had in mind, was drastically reduced in scope—applicable in practice to no more than a tiny fraction of the Jewish people, with the greater part left in a conceptual (and in the event actual) limbo, being neither capable of incorporation into the new society to be constructed in Erez-Israel, nor candidates for safety from the ravages of poverty and persecution overseas.

12

Transition and Deviation

i

The Zionist movement changed direction after Herzl's death, but Herzl's death alone cannot be made to account for the profundity of the displacement. Whatever Zionism owed to Herzl, it was before all else a movement born of specific circumstances and none of those aspects of the condition of Jewry that had given rise to it altered fundamentally in kind or diminished in intensity after 1904. The movement did not grow dramatically in public standing and in numbers not at all[1] until after the First World War. But no significant source of support which had accrued to it over the years crumbled or was withdrawn. As an organization, it was confirmed as a going concern capable (as we shall see) of surviving internal stress and surviving the loss of its creator too. Certainly, a marginal change of policy, a fresh tack, a new style, and, in

[1] No accurate membership figures seem ever to have been kept in these early years. But there are adequate indicators of the general trend. The number of Zionist associations in the various countries of the Jewish Dispersion rose from 900 in 1898 to 1,600 in 1903. In Russia alone the number rose in the same period from 370 to over 1,000. Recorded income from *shekel* membership-fees rose from Kr. 80,000 for 1897/8 to Kr. 220,000 for 1902/3. Income figures recorded in francs, collated by Georg Herlitz, were 114,370 fr. (1899), 96,434 fr. (1900), 96,626 fr. (1901), 232,645 fr. (1903), and 137,071 fr. (1905). The sum for each year can be taken as an approximate figure for actual membership; and what is clear is that the peak year was 1903. After Herzl's death there was a sharp drop, membership picking up slowly up to the Great War, but not exceeding the figure for 1903 until 1921. The great weight of the Russian wing of the movement is indicated by the figures for income from the *shekel*. Of the Kr. 220,000 paid in in 1902/3, Kr. 157,000 — 71 per cent — came from Russia. Yet even this large proportion probably understates the true measure of support for Zionism within Russian Jewry because even the small *shekel* fee (40 copecks) was beyond the means of so many Russian Jews. Sources: CZA, Z 1/444; *Protokoll II*, p. 47; *IV*, p. 71; *V*, p. 12; *VI*, p. 16, pp. 22–8; Georg Herlitz, *Das Jahr der Zionisten* (Jerusalem-Luzern, 1949), p. 139; Nordau, in an interview with *The Times*, 14 August 1911 and *Ketavim Zioniim*, iii (1960), p. 122.

the long term, broad shifts of emphasis were all to be expected after 1904. Cracks in the structure were already in evidence before Herzl's death. The pressure of the opposition to him personally and to his purposes was strong and growing in his lifetime; and when the fort collapsed the opposition was free to pour over its ruins and did precisely that. But what followed was much more than a change of tack or tactic, rather a *deviation*; and this, his sudden death, let alone his weakening in the last year of his life, are inadequate to explain.

All are agreed that Herzl's dominance over the movement and, indeed, the ease and speed with which he had formed it out of the bits and pieces of Ḥibbat Zion owed a great deal to his personal gifts, his 'charisma'. Still, even at its peak, his authority never stemmed exclusively or even predominantly from his persona and cannot be understood at all except in the context of the specific circumstances of eastern (and to a lesser extent western) European Jewry and what he stood for in that particular context. In the final analysis, Herzl had gained acceptance not by virtue of his eloquence, or appearance, or any other such personal characteristics—for all their importance—but as a figure who seemed to be pointing a way to deliverance from misery, fear, and indignity. In a sense he was pre-eminently a symbol and his great power as a symbol was no more than a measure of the depth of the misery and degradation of the Jews. Yet since misery and degradation were as much cardinal features of Jewish life after his death as before; and since the longing for deliverance did not diminish; it would follow that had only Herzl the individual been lost to the movement, or been found to have failed it, there would still have been ample room after his death for a successor offering identical or analogous ideas, or even quite fresh ideas and other plans, provided only they continued to point *grosso modo* in the same direction—or, at all events, if pointing elsewhere, then at least with the same promise of fundamental deliverance. But this did not occur. For a decade and a little more after 1904 Zionism ceased, in effect, to concern itself with the deliverance of the Jews in the terms which had been the basis for Herzl's rise, except in a form so reduced, and with purposes so dwindled, as to constitute for all intents and purposes a programme as different from the

Zionism of which Herzl had been the great proponent, and to a large extent the inventor, as was his political Zionism—Zionism writ large—from the proto-Zionism of Ḥibbat Zion. Moreover, the deviation from the path that had been set between 1896 and 1904 occurred very rapidly. The Herzlian loyalists led by his nominal successor as leader of the movement failed signally to maintain political (as opposed to mere formal, institutional) continuity; and the erstwhile opposition, now released from the obstacle to its progress offered by the movement's unquestioned leader in his lifetime, moved promptly to the fore and was in occupation of places of influence in a matter of months. Certainly, this was no more than the culminating stage of a long-standing process of rejection of what Herzl stood for by the largest and most coherent wing of the movement. And certainly, by the last years of Herzl's life this process was already well advanced, as we have seen, and his death undoubtedly eased and hastened it. Yet there still remains the question how this can have been possible if the power of the ideas for which Herzl was taken to stand had indeed been so great and the misery of the Jews had continued unabated.

The answer, broadly, is fivefold. It lies in the intrinsic weakness of his immediate successors; in the undeniably enormous objective obstacles to visible progress along the Herzlian 'political' road; in the social structure and composition of the movement; in the ever firmer refusal of his old opponents, as they moved to the fore in his stead, to conceive of Zionism in terms of massive national deliverance; and, lastly, in intervening circumstances which greatly helped the old opposition to shift the movement away from Herzlian Zionism by providing Zionists who were minded to reconsider their over-all strategy with ostensibly valid grounds for doing so.

The change which came over the movement in the years 1904–6 may be looked at too in its institutional aspect. The Zionist Organization had been set up with a particular problem in mind and as an instrument to further its solution. The problem had been defined by Herzl; the institution had been built to his specifications. However, once built it came to be inhabited by a great many other people; and as the prospect of a swift solution to the problem originally set them dwindled and the institution's effective and successful employ-ment in its primary task was delayed, questions which related to the continuity and survival of the institution itself and of those inhabiting it loomed the larger. All public institutions are subject to a shift of emphasis and concern of this kind; but it tends to be particularly acute in those whose primary and explicit task is to engineer change, yet which lack the means, or at any rate the immediate prospect, of accomplishing it. What happened to the Zionist movement in these years was that it ceased to know how it proposed to deal with the problem which it had been created to solve and that this loss of confi-dence in the original programme of action, already evident in the last years of Herzl's life, was almost complete after his death. Naturally and almost imperceptibly, the question what was to be done for the Jews became transmuted into the question what *the Zionist movement* was to do about the Jews, the Zionist movement having meanwhile taken on a life of its own which all concerned with it wished instinctively to preserve. The fact that the arrival of Zionism on the Jewish public scene was not promptly followed by its rapid departure once some of the steam had gone out of the mechanism was in itself a sign of strength. It marked the fact that Zionism, as an approach and a set of ideas and as an organized body, had become a permanent element of Jewish public life. However, once the intractability of Zionism's primary task had been generally recognized and a variety of methods came to be proposed for dealing with its secondary tasks, the internal cohesion of the movement became a great deal more difficult to maintain. On that count alone, therefore, attention to these secondary tasks took on some urgency. The result was further to accelerate the change in the order of priorities. Among the consequences of this change were the withdrawal from the centre of affairs of those whose minds were concen-trated essentially on Zionism's original and primary task, as they had understood it, and a corresponding enhancement of the role of those who were less single-minded and whose thinking was less strictly ideological and programmatic, and who had a taste and a talent for management.

ii

The Zionist Organization's internal, administrative, and constitutional arrangements, as Herzl left them, were simple. The statutes of the movement approved by the Fifth Congress in 1901 had reconfirmed (with minor changes) the structure instituted at the very beginning. It had been laid down that the Smaller Actions Committee (EAC) 'shall conduct the affairs of the Zionist movement',[2] subject to consultation with the Greater Actions Committee (GAC) on 'important matters' at least once a year. Formally, the chairman of the EAC possessed no social rights or privileges; in practice, everything rested on the fact that the chairman was Herzl and his four colleagues on the Committee were men of the second and third rank. From Herzl's point of view this was an excellent arrangement, tailor-made to his needs and *modus operandi*. It had the further advantage that upon his death the formal structure of the movement remained intact. Its disadvantage was that in the absence of anyone else at the movement's institutional centre who was of anything like Herzl's calibre, every line of activity, except the entirely routine, promptly fell slack. Accordingly, upon his death the question how the vacuum was to be filled and *by whom* moved instantly to the top of the movement's agenda. But only nominally. The role Herzl played had been so overwhelming and the shock of his sudden death so great that it was a long time before the principal figures in the movement could bring themselves to provide an answer. Their first real concern was only to stifle any attempt by the four remaining members of Herzl's Executive to take over the leadership of the movement in anything more than name, but to do so without breaking the surface continuity of things or the statutes of the movement. The difficulty lay in the fact that while such leading personalities as Nordau, Ussishkin, Greenberg, Warburg, and Wolffsohn did possess considerable moral authority, not all were even elected members of the GAC and collectively they had no formal standing whatsoever. At the leaders' gathering in Vienna for Herzl's funeral it was therefore resolved to push forward only slowly; and meeting

---

[2] 'Das engere A.-C. leitet die Geschäfte der zionistische Bewegung . . .' *Protokoll V*, Appendix C, Section IV, 24, p. 455.

formally later in the summer (17–19 August 1904), it was agreed to do no more than stiffen and broaden the rump of the EAC by the formation of an *ad hoc* steering committee made up of the EAC's four members and five more members of the GAC—Tchlenov, Ussishkin, and Greenberg among them. This group of nine was then to be reinforced by the co-optation of four more people, none of whom were members of the GAC enjoying official sanction by the Congress, but all prominent in the movement: Nordau, Wolffsohn, Warburg, and Katzenelsohn. Herzl's old Executive had thus been dissolved into a larger, more prestigious, and more representative group; and an important precedent had been set; for what resulted was a strong collective Executive into which the old opposition to Herzl and to 'Vienna' generally had been smoothly incorporated. The antithesis between the movement's organizational centre and its outlying branches was thus diminished and the influence of the latter enhanced. And the path was now clear for the establishment before all eyes of a wholly new balance of forces within the movement in which the intrinsic strength of the branch in eastern Europe relative to the contingent strength of the centre would be much more accurately reflected.

The problem of the official leadership had still to be settled, however, and in retrospect three aspects of it may be detected. One was the issue of professionalism—common to all political movements, but liable to be acute in those which are remote from state power. The amateur, voluntary, part-time activist can rarely be relied upon to perform the major functions, but the full-time, paid, professional activist is expensive; he is also likely to be feared, or resented, or disparaged. Herzl in his time had consistently rejected all suggestions that he leave the *Neue Freie Presse* and take a salary from the movement; and it was the common (and reasonable) belief of his friends that his tremendous effort to maintain himself in independence and his family in style, while never allowing his political activity to abate, had sapped his strength and helped shorten his life. Yet it was the prevailing view that Herzl's example was the proper one to follow none the less. This narrowed the field considerably; and since, as a rule of conduct, it was also applicable to lesser, if still important elective posts in the movement's hierarchy, it helped prevent potential candidates for the highest posts from moving nearer to the seat of power, so becoming actual candidates for it in due course. For example, arrangements made after the Seventh Congress provided for the eastern representation on the new, enlarged EAC to be strengthened by the addition of Ussishkin and Bernstein-Kohan. These broke down, partly because of the disinclination to break the precedent of wholly unpaid work by people in authority. (Paid functionaries were in a different class and regarded by some with mild contempt for that reason.) Bernstein-Kohan had no private means and could not move to Berlin without abandoning his medical practice, in which he was doing none too well anyway. Ussishkin was better placed, but he too seems to have reckoned that he would have to take a salary and was reluctant to do so. The argument that the Organization's limited resources should not be put to such use was a hard one to answer in any event and the upshot was that it was impossible to persuade all concerned to agree on what to do. Time passed and meanwhile, as conditions in Russia deteriorated, Ussishkin felt it would be wrong to leave for the safety of Berlin. When he was elected to the chairmanship of the Odessa Committee the plan fell through entirely.[3] It is clear that he had been afraid all along of isolation from his true constituency and much preferred to operate on home ground, but also that these were second thoughts and that what had precipitated the failure to move to Berlin was the problem of finance. So not the least of the reasons why, in the end, Wolffsohn found himself virtually alone in the field and, indeed, why *his* successor, Otto Warburg, followed smoothly in his wake was that both were wealthy men, free to devote a great deal of time and considerable private resources to the cause. They could also make demands. Wolffsohn insisted on the Zionist offices being moved to Cologne where he lived and ran his timber business, rather than to Berlin, which was the city most Zionists at the time thought appropriate as the seat of the movement. (Vienna had never been a deliberate choice; it was the city in which Herzl lived and the Central Zionist Office had simply grown around him.)

The second difficulty stemmed from the impossibility of

[3] Schwartz, *Ussishkin be-igrotav*, pp. 118–20.

maintaining the functioning, institutional centre of the movement in Russia where its true centre of gravity lay and where,
upon Herzl's death, the most ambitious, energetic, and powerful
personalities lived. There could be informal consultations in
Russia. There could be local offices, more or less disguised.
But there could be no question of the Central Zionist Office
(*Zionistisches Centralbureau*), complete with clerks, archives,
streams of incoming and outgoing letters and telegrams, the
official weekly, financial records, and the other paraphernalia
of organization, being maintained in good order inside the
borders of the imperial Russian police state. The Russian
authorities would not permit the Zionists to function entirely
openly; the Zionists knew that they could not conceivably
function wholly in secret—even if they succeeded in getting
away with it—without instantly losing the public, open character that had been intended for the movement from the first.
Besides, there would have been great organizational difficulties.
The revolutionaries of Russia too had discovered in the course of
time that even their necessarily and deliberately conspiratorial
organizations had to maintain centres outside Russia if they
were to survive and operate to good effect inside it. For the
Zionists, who by and large had no taste for conspiracy and
no more desire to go further underground than was absolutely
necessary, the need to maintain the seat of the EAC and the
Central Office in the west was thus never at issue. But its
corollary seemed at the time to be that the leader of the movement must himself be a man of western Europe.

This drastic narrowing and—having in mind the distribution of the membership on the ground—distortion of the field
set the terms of the third aspect of the problem, that of personalities. The failure of Zionism to strike deep roots in western
Europe was evident. It was not a movement of masses there or
even of large numbers, but of individuals, all sparsely scattered
in the communities or living on their margin. There were
men of standing with the general public among them, even
some of prominence. Of these a few had a measure of influence
in the movement and were listened to with respect; others,
like Sir Francis Montefiore of England, merely adorned it.
But for very few of the western Zionists did Zionism occupy
more than a fraction of their time or, it seems, of their thoughts.

And of the handful of whom it may be said that Zionism was a major, if never exclusive element in their lives—Nordau, Greenberg, Wolffsohn, Bodenheimer, and the Marmorek brothers among them—all had been heavily associated with Herzl and none except Nordau were possessed of sufficient personal prestige either in the world at large or within the movement to override the distrust of the old opposition on that score and so seem fit and proper candidates for the succession none the less. So, initially, all eyes turned and turned again to Nordau.

Nordau, however, was consistent in his refusal to accept office. He was a sick man, he told those who pressed him (true, but an overstatement of a kind common enough in his milieu). He had married a non-Jewish woman and thought (as did many others) that that was a serious failing in a candidate for national Jewish leadership. He recognized (but again, probably overstated) the strength of the opposition to him and to what he was thought to represent. But, in any event, he had no stomach for what would plainly be a long and bitter fight with 'the Russians'[4] and with others. He was, as he said, a poor man who lived by his pen; and he 'would die', he said, 'rather than receive a single pfennig' of support from public or other funds.[5] But finally and perhaps decisively, there were reasons of temperament. Nordau was continually torn between, on the one hand, his posthumous loyalty to Herzl and what he took Herzl to stand for, 'the Zionism of decent and sensible men',[6] and, on the other hand, his growing scepticism amounting, in moments of particular depression, to disbelief in the entire enterprise. He was, after all, nothing if not a habitual critic of his environment, a restless, sharp-eyed, somewhat sour intellectual who loathed humbug and was never less at ease than when confronted by simple,

[4] The young Russian Jews 'are people without discipline or modesty', he wrote to Mandelstamm after Luban's attack on him, 'who, on the one hand, respect only what they see respected by the Christians, but, on the other hand, have no confidence in those few Jews they do respect—because they think they are bad Jews. I told Herzl more than once: our Russians will only follow Russian leaders; they tolerate us for the time being, but secretly they clench their fists behind our backs.' Schwartz, *Nordau be-igrotav* (Jerusalem, 1944), p. 185.

[5] Nordau to Mandelstamm, 21 May 1905. CZA, A 3a/11.

[6] Nordau to Mandelstamm, 21 July 1905. Schwartz, *Nordau*, p. 187.

unwarranted faith. Herzl had employed him as an advisor, even as a mentor, and—on great occasions—as a decoration or, as in the Sixth Congress, as a reinforcement; but no more. This had allowed Nordau to help Herzl and publicly identify himself with his cause while yet retaining a certain distance and freedom from total inner commitment. It suited him, for he did not always agree with Herzl (as we have seen). He never had Herzl's faith.

Herzl could build up a façade without an edifice, believing that it would not occur to anyone to look behind it to see whether anything was there [Weizmann reported him as saying a few days after Herzl's death]. Herzl acted like this because he had immense faith in his personality. I am not a man of such deeds. I am of the view that one must first have the people, then build up the façade. Do you believe a leader can now come to the Jews and tell them: 'You should expect nothing new, but create an iron organization, gather strength, and then success will follow'? I cannot speak to the people otherwise.[7]

Weizmann's judgement was that now, after Herzl's death, Nordau considered 'everything that has been done as undone, and worthless' and he took him to be saying that everything had now to be begun 'afresh'.[8] But certainly Nordau saw the main task before the movement to be one of internal consolidation with no room left for the time being for fresh political initiatives. There might be something to do if a conference of the Powers were convened in the wake of the Russo-Japanese war. In that event the Zionists could try to bring their case before it and he, for his part, would do all he could to assist. But in the meantime, the Zionists, he thought, should attend first to the internal state of the movement, to the gathering of their forces.[9] And for such purposes and in such matters he saw no role for himself. Later, he agreed to preside at the coming Congress and, under pressure, to join Wolffsohn and Warburg in a triumvirate to run the movement. He kept the first part of the undertaking, but not the second. Years after, in another bout of depression, he wrote to Mandelstamm:

---

[7] Weizmann to Ussishkin, 14 July 1904. *Weizmann Letters*, iii, no. 264, p. 281.
[8] Ibid.
[9] Letter to Wolffsohn, 26 September 1904. Schwartz, *Nordau*, p. 123.

Our people is divided and disunited, impractical and devoid of will.
Capable only of passive resistance without positive efforts. That is
the misfortune. Our masses tremble, wail, and frequently rush off
panic-struck in all directions. What they do not have is the capacity
to set down a unified plan, to gather together in support of common
action, to submit to discipline, to have confidence in their elected
leaders and to follow them. What then can the individual, however
strong and wise, do with a people with such hopeless characteristics?
. . . Still, we shall not cease to work and sacrifice ourselves for our
unfortunate people. Perhaps we shall serve as an example.[10]

Once Nordau had put himself out of the running the idea
of a triumvirate was dropped and the search for a single
leader resumed. The only serious candidate was Wolffsohn.
Otto Warburg, a distinguished academic scientist and a
member of a prominent German-Jewish family, would have
enhanced the triumvirate had it been formed and his talents
and inclinations were well suited to the diminished horizons
of the movement in the post-Herzlian years. 'There was
nothing in Warburg . . . to suggest a politician', wrote one who
knew him. 'He was mild and courteous, but at the same time
impatient of all utopian and irrational thought, typically
an intellectual pioneer rather than a political leader . . . In
his Zionist work he preferred deeds to words, constructive
work to influence.'[11] But it was still too early for the break
with the Herzlian tradition to be so vividly confirmed, even
by those who wished the break to be made. Wolffsohn was a
better man for the new season. He was not of either Nordau's
or Warburg's breed or quality.[12] He was simpler than Nordau,
more self-confident, less tormented, more modest. He was
quite as loyal to Herzl and to Herzl's memory as Nordau,
if not more so, but with a narrower perspective and a lower
horizon; a man of strong feelings, but little imagination and
with few ideas of his own to offer except in the specific respect
of organization. Unlike Warburg, he was a self-taught, self-
made man (and for that very reason looked at askance by a
great many of his colleagues who wanted someone of more

---

[10] Letter to Mandelstamm, 26 October 1909. Schwartz, *Nordau*, p. 188.
[11] Professor Hellmut Pappé, in a letter to the author.
[12] On Wolffsohn, see *Origins*, pp. 271–2.

distinguished intellectual and academic attainment to lead and represent them). Wolffsohn's close personal relationship with Herzl (extending, it might be said, after Herzl's death, by virtue of his function as Herzl's executor and his assumption of responsibility for the dead man's children, especially after the death of Herzl's widow Julia in 1907) was offset by his being an *Ostjude* (east European Jew) from Lithuania and so possibly a man to help heal the rift between the Herzlian loyalists and the old opposition. Wolffsohn's main function in the movement thus far had been as chairman of the board of directors of the Bank. As such he was in his element and he had stood up to Herzl whenever he thought his leader's political purposes were getting in the way of sound business practice. On purely political issues, on the other hand, he had always deferred to Herzl. So on the East Africa project, of which he had disapproved, but silently, out of loyalty. After his friend's death and when confronted by a question for which there was no ready answer, he tended to ask himself what Herzl would have done had he still been alive. Posthumous judgements on Wolffsohn are mostly harsh or patronizing. Bodenheimer, who knew him well, summed him up as a 'cautious merchant'.[13] He was 'the President whose great inheritance from Herzl was more than he had the spiritual power to sustain', said Ussishkin, '. . . and under whom the movement shrivelled and dwindled and nearly gave up its ghost.'[14] But at the time, after a full year of patched-up interim arrangements and almost desperate casting-about for a leader, his formal assumption of office at the Seventh Congress was a source of relief to all. Reviewing the period many years later, Bodenheimer remarked, shrewdly enough, that 'there should [have been] no need to search for a leader. The day comes when he simply appears.'[15] Bodenheimer was thinking explicitly of the man who turns up, points the way, and induces people to follow after him, 'like Herzl'.[16] Wolffsohn was not like that at all. He had not put himself forward and there is no doubting his reluctance to take on the task. Doing so he helped to keep the

---

[13] *Darki le-Zion* (Jerusalem, 1952), p. 124.
[14] 'Shelosha' (1923), *Sefer Ussishkin* (Jerusalem, 1934), p. 361.
[15] *Darki le-Zion*, p. 119.
[16] Ibid.

movement going; therein lay his service to it. Greater things were beyond him.

Wolffsohn's first independent move was to transfer the Central Zionist Office to Cologne and to reorganize it on more business-like lines. He brought in new men, all of a higher calibre than had been usual there and in some ways of a higher calibre than his own, but also of a different school. The most notable of the new functionaries was Naḥum Sokolov, former editor of the Warsaw Hebrew daily *Ha-Ẓefira*. Sokolov had had high regard for Herzl and had served him by translating Herzl's Utopian novella *Altneuland* into Hebrew. But he was nothing if not a man of the east European Jewish Enlightenment (*haskala*), most contemporary adepts of which followed Ahad Ha-'Am in their rejection of what Herzl stood for and Wolffsohn still represented. Precisely where Sokolov himself stood in that debate it is hard to say. He was not a strong man, nor consistent in his views, nor a man of much originality. 'He envisaged all life, but he did not penetrate it', wrote Shmarya Levin. 'He was witty, learned, intellectual and intelligent—but not passionate.'[17] But Sokolov was a man of ability, notably in those verbal and literary spheres in which Wolffsohn was notoriously weak, with a positive forte for the fluent, long-winded, learned, middle-brow journalism that was then in vogue in the Jewish press. He had a marked talent for languages too and—unusually for his class—cosmopolitan manners and tastes which seemed to mark him out for 'diplomacy'. In 1931, when Weizmann was forced to resign the presidency of the World Zionist Organization and the movement was once more at a loss for a successor, it was Sokolov who was elected to replace him. Then, as earlier, as Wolffsohn's chief official, he left no mark.

The last bit of business to be disposed of before the Seventh Congress could assemble to inaugurate the new era was to provide the East Africa scheme with a decent burial. That it was up for slaughter had hardly been in doubt after the ostensibly inconclusive, but actually decisive conference of the GAC over which Herzl had presided in April 1904.[18] Certainly,

[17] Shmarya Levin, *Youth in Revolt* (London, 1930), p. 216.
[18] See above, pp. 341–6.

such was the common view after his death, the out-and-out loyalists and 'Ugandists' being forced to fight a losing, rear-guard battle from then on. The long-term outcome was obscured momentarily by a small tactical victory when the efforts of Ussishkin and his friends to prevent the commission of inquiry from being formed and dispatched to East Africa, as resolved by the Congress, were rejected. The loyalists had no difficulty in insisting on the proprieties being observed. It was harder, however, to get the expedition off. It was particularly hard to find the money, the Congress having laid down that no internal resources be used for the purpose. But eventually an expert commission was formed and money for its expenses found after all; and at the end of December 1905, sixteen months after the formal decision to send it out had been taken, the expedition set off for Mombasa.

iii

The expedition to East Africa was a modest affair. There were three members in all, an Englishman with experience of African exploration, Major A. St. Hill Gibbons, as the leader, a Swiss naturalist, Alfred Kaiser, a convert to Islam, and a Russian-Jewish engineer, Naḥum Wilbush, who was in the process of settling in Erez-Israel. Gibbons was Greenberg's choice; Kaiser was Warburg's; Wilbush, who was Warburg's too, was an afterthought when it was realized that the group might be sent off without a single Jew, let alone a Zionist, within it. A plan to include a physician fell through. There was not enough money for more than six weeks in East Africa itself. (Gibbons and Kaiser were paid for their services; Wilbush was not.) There were mishaps and difficulties: some of the equipment failed to reach them on time, a part of their stores was stolen, and the guides were often unreliable. Gibbons's relations with his two companions, especially with Wilbush, were poor; and Gibbons himself proved to be an incompetent organizer. Thanks to him a great deal of valuable time appears to have been wasted in marching to and fro across the savannah to insufficient purpose.[19] Later there were stories (and some evidence) that local white settlers had done what they could to

[19] Naḥum Wilbush, *Ha-mas'a le-uganda* (Jerusalem, 1963), based on the author's notes and diary, is a reliable and lively account of the journey.

mislead and frighten off the members of the expedition. But the authorities appear to have behaved correctly and given them all necessary facilities, including somewhat obsolete arms; and there is nothing to suggest that the three explorers were in any way discountenanced (or if at all, then not for long) either by the growls of the white settlers, which they certainly heard, or by brushes with wild animals, or by an unferocious attack on them towards the end of their journey by native blacks bent on plunder.[20] Whether they saw enough of the area they were supposed to investigate (some 90 miles long and 70 miles wide) in the time available to them, considering that all their movements were on foot and that they, with the help of their bearers, had to carry all their provisions with them—this is a question to which there can now be no clear answer. But what they did see of it led all three to conclude that the land was good for very little else except pasture: there was insufficient water and insufficiently good soil for regular cultivation; there were no raw materials or fuel supplies on which to base industry. And it was far from ideal even for pasture so that, if allowance was made for the large areas that could be put to no agricultural purpose whatsoever, a very large allocation of land (perhaps 5,000 acres) would be required for each family if the basic farming unit was to be viable. On the specific question of the area's suitability for Jewish settlement each member of the expedition struck a different note in his analysis of the evidence. Gibbons's conclusions were fairly favourable and optimistic. Kaiser was sceptical:

That the Jews would be able to colonise a country if they were able to carefully select the persons who would carry out their scheme of immigration, is beyond all doubt, and I even believe that they could once more become a real pastoral people . . . However, economic conditions on the Guas Ngishu Plateau are so unfavourable that a

[20] Cf. Robert G. Weisbord, *African Zion* (Philadelphia, 1968), pp. 210–12. Professor James Barber, who worked in the official archives in Entebbe in 1960, recalls documents indicating that 'the local officials were not keen to see the [Jewish] settlement as it would change the nature of the development of East Africa and the sort of jobs they had been doing, and therefore they emphasized [in contacts with the commission] the roughness and toughness of living in East Africa. Again, trusting my memory, I think that one official wrote that he had taken the Zionists on a very long, tough walk which would discourage them.' (Private letter to the author.)

portion of the immigrants would certainly leave the country again, and there would thus never be a real colonising association which could work successfully. The immigration would cost millions, and the actual usefulness of the whole scheme would be totally out of proportion to the labour expended . . . If Jewish capital, Jewish labour and Jewish blood is to serve the Zionist idea, a more promising country must be found, not a land that is so remote from all communi-cation with the rest of the world, that makes such heavy demands on the settlers, and is so little fitted to consolidate the bonds uniting Jews.[21]

Wilbush was derisive. The tracts of land surveyed would 'neither now nor at any future time be of use to us for the development of industry or any form of agriculture'.[22] Of course, it was possible for the Jewish settlers to adapt to a nomadic mode, living in tents and moving to distant places in the dry season. But this, Wilbush observed, was fantastic.

The crucial question was that of numbers. If pasture were the economic basis of settlement, the numbers could only be very small, perhaps no more than 1,000 families in all, even by Gibbons's calculation. If the best reading of the evidence was relied on and hopes were pinned on crop farming after all, there was still no more than about a sixth of the area in question considered more or less suitable to the purpose and that could mean a working population of 15,000 to 20,000 at most. But it would be a risky, unprecedented venture, similar land in South Africa having been used for pasture only, it was pointed out. The conclusion was that even in the best of cases a good deal of additional research and calculation would have to be done before a really substantial movement of settlers could be mounted and the prospects of success still remained doubtful.

After all this, the idea of East Africa as an actual place of mass settlement for east European Jewry (at all events, within the territorial limits set by the British Government) was dead. Those who had originally argued for its consideration on pragmatic grounds, as a place of refuge, fell silent. Only those

[21] *Report on the Work of the Commission sent out by the Zionist Organization to examine the Territory offered by H.M. Government to the Organization for the Purpose of a Jewish Settlement in East Africa* (London, May 1905), p. 56.
[22] Ibid., p. 68.

who had favoured it for the issues of principle which it raised and for the strategic options it appeared to open continued to press their respective arguments. But they had never been more than a handful and if their numbers were now not further diminished, their morale, at all events, was lowered. Those who had opposed the scheme most vigorously had done so as a matter of principle and general outlook from the start. From their point of view, its collapse as a practical proposition was a windfall. Some evidently regarded it as a sign as well— conclusive proof of the validity of their position, as in a trial by ordeal. All of Herzl's late opponents were vastly encouraged, their spirits boosted, their confidence restored. They had waged a hard campaign and with the balance now tipped visibly in their favour they had every reason to feel that it only remained for the Seventh Congress to confirm their victory. Meanwhile, the GAC, when it met in May to consider the commission's report, resolved that no action should be taken, but that other Jewish organizations should be invited to follow it up for their explicitly philanthropic purposes if they wished.

At its opening, the fact uppermost in the minds of the some 500 delegates attending the Seventh Congress of Zionists (Basel, 27 July–2 August 1905) was the absence of the founder of the Congress. It was therefore a solemn affair to begin with, Nordau delivering a eulogy of Herzl and then the presidential address in Herzl's place. Oscar Marmorek (for the EAC) reviewed the affairs of the movement in their organizational and financial aspect and the Seventh Congress was then adjourned and the Special Congress, with an identical membership, called to order to consider the East Africa proposal for the last time. This was in accord with what had been laid down at Basel two years earlier. Ussishkin, characteristically, was now all for dispensing with the formality and having the business over and done with as soon as possible. But he did not get his own way: it would have seemed too sharp a posthumous rebuff to Herzl.

The debate on the East Africa project was long (almost two days), undistinguished, and noisy. Few of the leading figures participated. Nordau had referred to the issue in his inaugural speech as President of the Congress the day before, only very obliquely. The movement should not fall back on the old methods of 'petty colonization' of Erez-Israel as practised in the 1880s, he said, vast efforts on the part of all Jewry having yielded no more than a handful of subsidized farmers. The Zionists should continue to follow Herzl's lead. They should seek to form a great international political movement that would not rest until normal conditions of existence had been created for the entire Jewish people with the consent and co-operation of the Powers. Nordau proceeded to illustrate what this could mean in practice. It would be well to note, he told the Congress, that the interests of the Jewish people in Erez-Israel might be affected by the nationalist movement beginning to engulf the Arab world and liable to sweep Erez-Israel back into the centre of international political concern. For Turkey might then be impelled to stand and defend itself from its own subjects. The consequent value to the Turks of the presence in Erez-Israel of a strong, highly organized people which, while respecting the rights of the country's earlier inhabitants, could be relied upon to resist all damage to the Sultan's authority would be apparent and the European Powers too would welcome the peaceful re-entry of the Jews into Erez-Israel if it ensured stability and obviated the need to intervene. But to that end the confidence of the Turks and Europeans alike in the Jews' will and ability must be aroused. The Zionists must therefore remain united and must improve and strengthen their movement. 'No man can peep at the cards of Providence. History may suddenly provide an opportunity which must immediately be seized.'[23]

There was not a word about East Africa specifically. But Nordau's resurrection of Herzl's pre-1902 approach, in which Turkey as the sovereign Power in Erez-Israel was firmly in the centre of the Zionist scheme of things, carried its own message. Otherwise he took no part in the proceedings. Reported to be slightly indisposed, he only presided over their beginning and their end—conceivably because the rowdiness that accompanied much of the debate so offended him that he preferred to keep away. At one point the gallery had to be cleared because of interruptions by (pro-East Africa) visitors;

[23] *Protokoll VII*, pp. 22–6.

and when it was suspected that interlopers had infiltrated the hall, authorized delegates were supplied with fresh tickets of identification. Wolffsohn and Ussishkin kept silent too. Warburg, as chairman of the Congress's East Africa Committee, confined himself to a factual report on the commission's formation and dispatch. Greenberg's presentation was mostly a cool political-historical review of the matter. He did observe, however, that he thought it had been a mistake to have insisted on the British Government defining the area before the expedition set out rather than to have employed the commission of inquiry to help determine the area to be selected for settlement.

The outcome could not have been in doubt to any of those present. Led by Ussishkin, the old opposition had been working hard all year to marshal their forces and ensure success for their school at the elections to the Congress. Their some 200 delegates, meeting at Freiburg just prior to the main Congress to co-ordinate action, formed a party in all but name. Some wanted a hard line, drawn so as to extirpate all traces of territorialism in the movement. Others argued for a measure of tolerance so as to keep the erring brothers within the fold if it were only possible. But all were agreed that the Congress must reassert the movement's exclusive concern with Erez-Israel as an article of absolute faith and consistent practice. When the full Russian caucus met at Basel on the eve of the Congress, it was clear that anti-territorialists would be in the overwhelming majority and that the only question still open, as at Freiburg, was that of the severity of the terms in which the Congress would be asked to uphold the strict construction of the Basel Programme. None the less, over 100 delegates put their names down for the full-dress debate in the Congress and the presidium had recourse, once again, to representative 'main speakers'. Of these only Zangwill, the opening speaker, and Tchlenov were of note. Zangwill's speech was passionate without being fierce. He spoke in English, however, and some of the force of his speech was evidently lost in the course of its translation, sentence by sentence, into German.

Zangwill recognized that nearly everyone present had already made up his mind on the subject. He had conceded as much in a speech in London earlier in the month and said so, plainly,

now. He agreed with Ussishkin that to the question that was
before the Congress there could only be a straight answer, yes or
no. He agreed too that the 'yes' could not be unconditional.
The commission's report was too unfavourable. On the other
hand, to say 'no' was to risk striking a blow at all Jewry. It
would be said of the Jews that just when the gates were being
shut in their faces, they 'had been offered a large and fertile
territory, [but that] they will not go there—[so] then let them
go to the devil!' The scheme's opponents might say, of course,
that none of this had anything to do with *Zionism*: 'what have
these wandering masses who had, perhaps, never paid a single
shekel to do with us?' Well, he would tell the Congress: a
great deal! The British Government had recognized the Zionists
as the trustees of the Jewish people. Were the Zionists to
take a lesser view of themselves? 'We are more than a parliament of Zionists; we are a parliament of Jews' and bore a
corresponding responsibility for all the people. It was in this
light that the actions of the Zionists had to be guided. So while
it was perfectly true that the area in question was not the
'large and fertile territory' of which Balfour had recently
spoken in the House of Commons, it was impossible to reply
to the British Government with a bare 'no'. The answer had
at least to be a reasoned one. Two years earlier, at the Sixth
Congress, the reason could have been the plain one that East
Africa was not Erez-Israel. But then the commission should
never have been sent out. It was too late for that. What could
be said now was only that the offer was not good enough. And
that, in fact, was what the Actions Committee had said in its
report to the Congress. But if the offer was not good enough,
it could be *improved*. There was nothing to prevent the British
Government from doing so; and if it did improve its offer,
what then? What response would be made? The issue could
not be dodged. Ussishkin was right. But his operative conclusion was wrong. The approach should be positive. The report
of the commission should be the basis for negotiations aimed
at something better suited to Jewish needs. Zangwill moved
accordingly

That the Congress resolves gratefully to accept the magnanimous
offer of the British Government to put at the disposal of the Jewish

people a large and fertile territory for colonisation, with autonomous rights under British suzerainty; but with the expectation that the Guas Ngishu Plateau, the particular territory at present under consideration, shall be supplemented or replaced by other territories, inasmuch as according to the report of our Commission this Plateau does not correspond to the intention of the British Government to afford very large numbers of Jewish emigrants the possibility of gaining a livelihood in British colonial territory.

Two purposes, he argued, would be served by such a resolution. Firstly, the world would be informed that the territory in question was indeed entirely inadequate to solve the problem of the Jews. Thus, if the British Government failed to offer an alternative, at least the onus for inaction would not fall on the Jews themselves. Secondly, the way would be open to revive the project for El Arish. That, he thought, was what Herzl would have done.

The rest was a recapitulation of the argument for going ahead in East Africa as 'a means to Palestine' and an attack on the old opposition, Ussishkin principally, for their failure to think their own policy through. There was, notably, their apparent assumption

that the Sultan of Turkey is a fool. Do you think that the Sultan of Turkey will fold his hands and let us take something that he refuses to give us? Why all Europe cannot get the better of the Sultan. Do you know that our Anglo-Palestine Company's building in Jerusalem could be invaded by Turkish soldiers had we not put up the British flag? There are not wanting sneers and criticisms anent our Jewish-British alliance, but do not forget that only as a British institution can Zionism work in Palestine at all. To make a Talmudic argument, small colonisation or industrial work in Palestine must either be supplemented by political and diplomatic action, or not. If only temporary, still it will make later political and diplomatic action far more difficult, since the Sultan has nothing further to gain from us. If, on the other hand, as the [anti-Territorialists] and others recommend, parallel with work in Palestine goes diplomacy, it must be remembered there are two ways in which forces may be parallel. They may go the same way, or they may go opposite ways. I may either increase my speed by driving two parallel horses abreast, or I may be tied to two horses going in parallel directions, and torn to pieces between them. This is unfortunately the position in Palestine—work is opposed to diplomacy: diplomacy is opposed to work. In this dilemma our poor Herzl had to make his choice, and his political instinct decided to shut out work in Palestine, and continue on the high political road. For Herzl had by now learnt what Ussishkin and, I fear, the majority of Zionists, have not yet learnt—that the object of Zionism is to create, not things, but conditions.[24]

Tchlenov, the main speaker for the other school of thought, countered Zangwill's remark about Herzl by pointing out, correctly, that in April 1904, at the GAC, Herzl had told them that he had first come before them as a Jewish-state man (*als Judenstaatler*), but had changed his mind and now believed that the Problem of the Jewish people was soluble only in Erez-Israel. But Tchlenov, as usual, took a moderate line. Like Zangwill, like almost everyone present, he knew that most minds had been made up. His speech, as spokesman for his faction, was a confident, in some ways smug review of the case against Territorialism, hinging on Ahad Ha-'Am's now classic distinction between the two afflictions which beset the Jewish people: the material and the moral.[25] So far as the material affliction of the Jews was concerned, it was in any case beyond the power of the movement to deal with more than a fraction of Jewry and so matters would remain for a long time. On the other hand, it was to be expected that the establishment of a safe refuge even for a fraction of the whole would fundamentally alter the condition of the rest in all parts of the Dispersion. But as for the moral and spiritual affliction of the Jews, there was no question in the minds of the majority of Zionists but that its cure was possible only in Erez-Israel. Indeed, given the enormous effort needed to work any change, however small, success was unthinkable unless the drawing-power of the ancestral country was harnessed to the enterprise. He would not deny that even then it would be exceedingly hard to succeed and that much patience would be required, nor that not everyone shared the hopes of the members of his camp and their conviction of ultimate success. None the less, it was pointless for Zangwill to talk of organized settlement in

---

[24] *Jewish Chronicle*, 4 August 1905, pp. 19–20. The official record of Zangwill's speech and draft resolution (in German) is in *Protokoll VII*, pp. 70–5.

[25] See *Origins*, pp. 199–200.

countries other than Erez-Israel. The goal of Zionism was
tied up with one country alone. It was not attainable elsewhere.
For the rest, said Tchlenov, if 'the Territorialists say, no, we
neither wish to go and lead the way to Palestine, nor are we
able to [because] the land is poor and the conditions very
unfavourable, [why] we Zionists compel no one to go with us.
You are free to go to Uganda. Go there!'[26]

The sole effect of the debate, such as it was, was to make
the division of opinion sharper than ever. 'Zion-Zionists'
(*Zionei-Zion*) and 'Territorialists' were now distinct categories.
When the GAC's proposal (the composite work of Greenberg
and Ussishkin) to thank the British Government for its goodwill, but reaffirm the movement's exclusive devotion to Erez-
Israel, was put to the vote, the Territorialists abstained and
allowed it to be carried by acclamation. There was then a
minor row when, Zangwill's proposal not having been put to
the vote at all (on the not unreasonable grounds that the
matter had been settled by the acceptance of the GAC's
draft resolution), he lost his temper and charged Nordau
before 'the bar of history' with 'treason against the Jewish
people'.[27] And there was a last-minute statement by Syrkin
on behalf of the 28-man-strong Zionist-socialist group[28]
condemning the decision taken as an injury to the Jewish
people, and as 'detracting from the meaning and content of
our liberation movement and standing in profound contradiction to the interests of the Jewish proletariat and the
broad Jewish masses'. The socialists recommended to all 'true
and consistent Zionist-Territorialists to follow our example
and leave the Congress hall'.[29] The Special Congress was
then ended. The 'Zion-Zionists', severely restrained by their
leaders up to this point, were free to celebrate. Later in the

[26] *Protokoll VII*, pp. 111–16.

[27] Thus according to the *Jewish Chronicle*, 4 August 1904, p. 21. The official verbatim
report of the proceedings gives a slightly different version: 'You will be charged before
the bar of history with juggling with me and the resolutions of the congress.' *Protokoll
VII*, p. 134. As Zangwill spoke in English, the *Jewish Chronicle* reporter is probably the
more reliable source in this case.

[28] Some socialists, Borochov among them, *supported* Ussishkin and his friends in this
matter. Matityahu Mintz, 'Ber Borochov ba-kongress ha-zioni ha-shevi'i be-bazel',
Zion, iv (1976), pp. 9–43.

[29] *Protokoll VII*, pp. 135–6.

day the regular Seventh Congress reconvened and the delegates turned to matters of routine.

iv

Zangwill and some thirty other delegates, mostly socialists, left the Congress and lost no time in consolidating their views and making them public. A preliminary meeting was held at Basel while the Zionist Congress proper was still sitting. Zangwill's new creation, the Jewish Territorial Organization (ITO), was established formally a fortnight later. In September he approached the Colonial Office in London, seeking to keep the East Africa project alive despite its rejection by the official Zionist Organization. And when all hope of doing so finally flickered and died in the course of the following year, he applied elsewhere, as we shall see. It was an effort reminiscent, in some ways, of Herzl's—imbued with the same urgency and restlessness, the same impatience, the same clear and simple (and simplified) view of the condition of the Jews and what had to be done to correct it, and the same detachment and independence from traditional Jewish thinking on public affairs, stronger, if anything, in Zangwill's case even though he was vastly more learned in the Jewish tradition and more comfortable with it than Herzl had ever been. But then Zangwill, more than Herzl—and certainly more explicitly and consciously than Herzl—was in rebellion against the tradition. It was not, as Lucien Wolf pointed out many years later, a rebellion with an extrinsic base as with Heine, 'who brought to the gates of the Ghetto the culture he had acquired at Bonn and Göttingen and for a brief moment dreamt of opening a new epoch in Hebrew history . . . Zangwill was a *revolté* on the ground of Jewish idealism against the Philistinism of one half of Jewry and the pathetic stagnation of the other half.'[30] He owed to Herzl not so much his views on the Jewish national Question as their crystallization; and he had always given them a sharper, more provocative edge than had Herzl or any other member of the 'political' school.

---

[30] Lucien Wolf, 'Israel Zangwill', memorial address before the Jewish Historical Society of England, 26 October 1926, p. 4. Unpublished typescript, YIVO Archives, Mowshowitch Collection, File 205.

Bonnie Prince Charlie, the Stuart pretender, scribbled upon a paper preserved at Windsor: 'To live and not to live is worse than to die.' That is our position. I had rather we died, and were done with. I thank Heaven that ten tribes at least were lost. What our preachers and teachers really preach is that the mission of Israel is *sub*mission, for never do they set up our own ideal—our supposed mission of Peace and Brotherhood upon earth. Let war break out, and we are the noisiest singers of war-songs. The poor people of Kischineff tried to save themselves by putting in their windows sacred Russian images. It is our history in a nutshell. In moments of danger we put up the flag of the enemy. And it avails nothing in the long run—the image-imitators at Kischineff were the people particularly chosen for crucifixion . . .

When we have a country of our own, we can begin to talk brotherhood. It comes too suspiciously from a people without one. It is like a *Schnorrer* [beggar] talking socialism . . . 'Be at the tail of the lions rather than at the head of the foxes', said the Rabbis. Be at the tail of the nations rather than at the head of the gypsies. We stand for Peace—but a proposal of universal disarmament would have more weight coming from Germany than from Monaco. Let Park Lane preach against luxurious dinner parties, and Society may listen. But the gospel of plain living and high thinking cannot be effectively proclaimed from Rowton House[31] by tramps cooking their own bloaters. If we want the nations to listen to us, we must first get them to respect us. To fulfil the ideals of our prophets we must have a soil of our own.[32]

Zangwill's new organization—it never became, nor was it intended to be a popular *movement*—had some initial success. Several members of Herzl's old guard, Mandelstamm and Jasinowski notably, joined him. So did some of the socialists, under Syrkin. He gained the guarded support of the German-Jewish philanthropic organization the Hilfsverein der deutschen Juden and of its founders Paul Nathan and James Simon. Lucien Wolf, the best mind and the sharpest pen in Anglo-Jewish public affairs, promised cordial co-operation (specifying that his objections to Zionism remained unaltered, as did his view that the Jewish Question in Russia as a whole could *not* be solved by emigration). Lord Rothschild, the most influential Jew in Great Britain, opposed Zangwill at

---

[31] A lodging-house for the very poor in Vauxhall, London.
[32] Speech in 1903. Israel Zangwill, *The Voice of Jerusalem* (London, 1920), p. 85.

first, but later softened and agreed to join ITO's 'Geographical Commission' in whose hands the choice of the alternative to Erez-Israel was to be placed. He was joined on the Commission by Mandelstamm and Paul Nathan and three Americans: Oscar Straus (later Theodore Roosevelt's Secretary of Commerce and Labour, the first Jew to attain Cabinet rank in the United States), Daniel Guggenheim (the mining magnate), and Judge Meyer Sulzberger of Philadelphia (a founder and the first president of the American Jewish Committee). None of these people played a role of real consequence in ITO.[33] None the less, it was a more impressive group than Herzl had ever managed to enlist and with Zangwill himself at the head there was enough in ITO to worry the Zionists, particularly in England where ITO was strongest and was in competition with them for the ear of Whitehall and to some extent of Westminster too. All in all it was, at least, a good start.

The reasons for Zangwill's initial success, especially with the magnates whom Herzl in his time had so badly wanted to enlist, are clear, if paradoxical. The paradox is in the fact that Zangwill's ITO, more than Herzl's Zionist movement, emphasized the territorial-political solution to the Problem of the Jews. The first article of ITO's constitution opened with the plain statement that 'The object of the Organization is to procure a territory upon an autonomous basis for those Jews who cannot or will not remain in the land in which they at present live' and concluded with the explanation that 'the expression "autonomous basis" means and implies that the territory shall be one in which autonomy shall be attainable, and in which the predominant majority of the population shall be Jewish.' This was a lot more radical than the circumlocution of the Basel Programme: 'Zionism aims at the creation of a home for the Jewish people in Palestine to be secured by public law.' But the magnates' friendly attitude to ITO had its logic. What Zangwill could be taken as aiming for, at all events initially, was, as Lucien Wolf noted,

---

[33] However, Lord Rothschild (with Jacob Schiff, the investment banker) did back ITO's Galveston Plan, a project designed to channel immigrants to the United States away from New York and other cities on the eastern seaboard by shipping them to the Texas port of Galveston instead. In this Zangwill had some success, but it was irrelevant to the central aim of a Jewish self-governing territory.

to found a new Self-governing Colony in the vast waste lands of the British Empire. You are perfectly willing [Wolf wrote to Zangwill] that such a Colony should fulfil all the conditions of political evolution by which the Over-Sea Dependencies of the Crown have hitherto progressed towards self-government, and that in all political and municipal respects it should be assimilated to existing Colonies. Such a Colony would be politically Jewish only through the pre-ponderance of its Jewish population. It would have no established Church, no religious tests or disabilities, but it would be free to make holiday and other municipal arrangements to suit the peculiar circumstances of the Colonists, while due exemptions would be granted to the strangers within its gates . . . You hope, by the com-bination of these two classes of Colonists [a 'better class' of emigrants attracted by the idea of self-government and a 'working population' drawn to a home where anti-Jewish prejudice would be unknown] to make and administer on British lines a model British Colony.[34]

Even if this did not reflect Zangwill's thinking with absolute precision, it was not an unreasonable or unfair reading of what he was saying and certainly it was compatible with the way in which a Jewish autonomous province in the British (or any other) Empire, as perceived by Zangwill and his friends, was likely to develop, if ever one was established. On this reading, Zangwill's plan could be taken to be no more than a severely practical but also attractive attempt to do something for east European Jewry in the immediate future, something that would draw them away from the crowded cities of western Europe and North America. True, it was equally possible to read into it the basis for a state of (and for) the Jews not unlike that which Herzl had originally envisaged. Yet there was a difference. It was plain it would be a state of the Jews, rather than a Jewish state; it would be— at all events it could turn out to be—a state of the Jews denuded of any Jewish national principle or purpose or of any repre-sentative or symbolic character. In this respect it went con-siderably beyond Herzl's amalgam of a society and polity that partook equally, but selectively, of western European liberal civilization and of the Jewish historical tradition. And it was, of course, a very far cry from the distinctive, parti-

---

[34] Wolf to Zangwill, 1 September 1905. *Jewish Territorial Organization*, ITO Pamphlet Number One (London, 1905).

cularist society wanted by the adepts of the Jewish Enlightenment who had adopted Zionism.

Zangwill's ITO was in this respect a further, internally
consistent step down the road along which Herzl had travelled
—only, in the end, to turn back. Through it and its rivalry
with the Zionist movement proper the debate between Herzl
and his opponents was pursued and intensified after his death,
the remaining traces of Herzl's ideological and conceptual
influence within mainstream Zionism being drawn off and
killed in the process. Had ITO achieved anything of substance
in the realm of the practical, its heresy might have had a
better hearing. It did not; and ITO's failure requires an
explanation, if only as the sharpest possible illustration of the
disabilities under which the Jewish national revival laboured
even in its most self-denying and accommodating form.

What Zangwill had asked of the British Colonial Secretary[35]
after the foundation meeting of ITO in the summer of 1905
was to leave the question of the ultimate disposal of the Gwas
Ngishu plateau in the East Africa Protectorate open despite the
negative decision of the Zionist Congress. The Colonial
Secretary's refusal to do so was point-blank. In the first place,
Lyttelton wrote, having 'understood . . . that it was not likely
that [Zangwill's] secession movement would assume important
dimensions' and having received Greenberg's notification
that the Zionists at Basel were not interested, he had already
informed the Commissioner for the East Africa Protectorate
that the land need not be reserved any longer. Secondly,
he had noted that Zangwill himself was 'not by any means
assured' that the land in question was suitable. Accordingly,
the most he was prepared to say was that the decision taken
would 'be no obstacle to the consideration by His Majesty's
Government of any well-considered proposals which you
may hereafter feel yourself in a position to make'.[36] To this
formula of a will to look at 'any well-considered proposals'
that ITO (or the Zionists too, for that matter) might make
the Colonial Office adhered, both while the Unionists remained

[35] British East Africa passed from the jurisdiction of the Foreign Office to that of the
Colonial Office in April 1905.
[36] Alfred Lyttelton to Zangwill, 16 September 1905. Ibid., p. 5.

in power and, after December 1905, when the Liberals replaced them and installed the Earl of Elgin in the Colonial Office with Winston Churchill as his Parliamentary Under-Secretary. It was a polite response, not unreasonable in the circumstances. It promised nothing and it both epitomized and veiled what was now the set thinking on the matter among the civil servants concerned in both the Foreign and Colonial Offices. These, with their eyes mostly on the practical side of things in Africa itself, had been immensely relieved by the decision of the Congress. A troublesome and eccentric scheme could now be filed away and forgotten with a minimum of fuss and without the British Government having to do more than register the scheme's rejection by those for whom it had originally been intended. The Foreign Office had long since been instructed (by Weizmann, among others[37]) that many Zionists were bitterly opposed to it. 'There are two factions in this movement', Sir Clement Hill noted in August 1904, when, a year after the Sixth Congress, it was still not clear what the Zionists were doing about the projected expedition to East Africa. 'I think we might take this opportunity of saying that the promise of HMG was given in the belief that the Zionist Congress were united in their wish for a settlement and that we must now reserve the right to reconsider our position if that belief should prove to have been ill founded. (I believe this is also Lord Percy's view.)' But the Government's decision was to hold its hand for the time being. Lord Lansdowne minuted: 'But we must be careful not to say anything which might lead the two factions to join hands and present a solid front.'[38] In the Colonial Office there were now none who thought the scheme workable except at great cost in money,

[37] Weizmann met Lord Percy, Parliamentary Under-Secretary at the Foreign Office, and Sir Clement Hill, the official responsible for the Protectorate at the time, on 25 July 1904. This was a few weeks after Herzl's death and not 'shortly after the sixth congress' as he wrote in his memoirs. (*Trial and Error* (London, 1949), p. 117.) It is improbable that he would have dared to do so behind Herzl's back in the latter's lifetime. The meetings were not a success for Weizmann personally because he irritated the two men by sending them formal résumés of his conversations (in French). 'I did not know I was being interviewed', Hill minuted. Nor did Percy. But Weizmann's point was taken and British distaste for the commitment into which Chamberlain had entered grew a little stronger. Lansdowne read through the file observing, 'We shall be fortunate if the project falls through.' PRO, FO 2/848 283–92.

[38] Ibid., 448–9.

energy, and goodwill in the Protectorate. Some thought it 'fantastic and impracticable to the last degree'.[39] No one throught Zangwill would ever gain the necessary support or funds. By 1906 it was accepted that, as one official minuted, 'even if the scheme were one which it was desirable to promote, there is no territory at our disposal.'[40] Lastly, and decisively, it was agreed that 'to grant a territory in which a Jewish State can be formed under the protection of the British Govt.' was 'to form an *imperium in imperio*' and that that was not 'desirable'.[41]

But these were views and comments reserved for internal consumption. There was no need to be so blunt with Zangwill himself. It was enough to set certain conditions for the resumption of discussions, namely that 'responsible men, adequate capital and a workable plan' were all to be available, and leave it to him to satisfy them. When Zangwill pressed for a statement by Elgin to the effect that *if* his conditions were satisfied, then 'the Government would view favourably the development of the East Africa Protectorate as a British Jewish Colony', the refusal to do so was absolute.[42] And thus there was repeated for Zangwill with uncanny precision the predicament in which Herzl believed he had been placed by the Turks: there could be no serious negotiations with the imperial Power until the Jews negotiating with it had displayed their financial resources; but there could be no hope of extracting such resources for the purpose of display from those who possessed them until the imperial Power had gone some way to demonstrate its fundamental goodwill. Briefly, in the summer of 1903, the British Government had made that demonstration. That moment had come and gone. As further argument and feeling and second thoughts came crowding in, and in the absence of a powerful figure like Chamberlain with an independent mind and adequate political muscle to keep them at

[39] 27 June 1906. PRO, CO 533/26 529.

[40] 3 April 1906. PRO, CO 533/24 137.

[41] 21 June 1906. PRO, CO 533/26 528. The *imperium in imperio* theme had been aired publicly by opponents of the plan at least as early as two years before. See *Jewish Chronicle*, 21 June 1904, p. 13.

[42] Zangwill to the Colonial Office, 20 June 1906; Colonial Office to Zangwill, 7 July 1906. Ibid., 530–1.

bay, the obstacles to a revival of the plan became ever steeper.
Here and there there was a kindlier voice.

I should gladly help forward any practicable scheme [wrote Winston
Churchill], but the more I examine the question the more oppressed
I am by consciousness of the serious, and in some cases, growing obstacles, which stand in the path of action. Since the Colonial Office
offer was first made to your people, much land has been occupied in
the East African Protectorate and the Guasau Gishu [*sic*] Plateau
is no longer an unoccupied table land . . . The enquiries I have made
of local feeling fill me with apprehension at the violence of the local
opposition which will certainly be offered by the existing settlers
and by the whole official world. Further, there is the undoubted
division among the Jews themselves, which seems to have impressed
itself even upon some of those, who, like Lord Percy, were strenuous
in your support. Lord Elgin is quite resolute in his decision that he
can do nothing until and unless you are able to present him with a
definite scheme, adequately supported by persons of wealth and
influence in the Jewish world. Surely this is not an unreasonable
position for the head of a Public Department to assume. If you were
able to come to us with a long list of powerful names guaranteeing a
great sum of money, I would do my very best to further your wishes,
though, even then, I cannot command success. But it seems to me that
nothing else than a definite detailed plan sustained by ample funds
and personalities would have any chance against the obstacles to
which I have referred.
     Believe me, your letter touches responsive chords.[43]

But it was to no avail. The bureaucracy's mind was made up.
The new Liberal ministers were a lot less interested in imperial
development and expansion than their predecessors had
been. Domestic affairs were at the centre of their concern.
Besides, an Aliens [Immigration] Act had been passed after
all (in December 1905) and the problem posed by the influx
of east European Jews seemed less urgent—even though in
practice immigration continued at a high rate. Zangwill,
in any event, was forced to turn elsewhere. He applied successively to the governments of Canada and Australia, to the
Canadian province of Ontario, to the Australian state-

[43] Letter to Zangwill. Text in D. Y. Marmor, 'Ha-masa u-matan ha-diplomati shel
ha-histadrut ha-teritorialistit ha-yehudit ITO u-mesibot kishlono, *Zion*, xi, 4 (1946),
p. 201.

governments of South Australia and Western Australia, and to Portugal with a plan to settle Jews in Angola. The possibilities of settlement in Cyrenaica and Mesopotamia were investigated too. In each case there was some measure of reluctance to receive Jews (difficult to estimate because it was rarely expressed in explicit terms) and, in contrast, an entirely frank objection to anything that smacked of a *corpus separatum*, let alone political autonomy. 'The government [of Ontario]', Zangwill was informed, 'could not entertain any proposition that contemplated the allotment of land in large tracts to the people of any distinct nationality and religion, as it is not deemed desirable, looking to the future interests of the province, to adopt any system of settlement which tends to perpetuate racial and religious differences.'[44] The Portuguese went so far as to pass a Bill through their lower house of Parliament in 1912 to promote the settlement of Jews in Angola as had been proposed to them, but they were careful to offer no municipal or political privileges at all and to specify that the language of instruction in the public primary schools to be established in the colonies the Jews were to inhabit would be exclusively Portuguese.[45] This was not even remotely the 'Zionism without Zion' that Zangwill had been prepared to make do with. And thus, in the end, nothing was achieved. Zangwill and his friends—and it was mostly Zangwill alone— were no more successful in laying the basis of a territorial state for the Jews than the Zionists of the mainstream. The political mode of Zionism in its purest form appeared to have reached a dead end. The appeal to the Powers had failed. None were prepared to help the Jews break out of the strait-jacket of their exile, except, at best, on terms that effectively nullified whatever national, collective significance the change might have.

v

Almost four months passed between the Seventh Congress and the first regular meeting in November 1905 of the new,

---

[44] Department of Agriculture, Ontario, to Zangwill, October 1906. Marmor, art. cit., p. 205.

[45] Text of Act of Portuguese Parliament. Ibid., pp. 205–7.

strengthened Zionist Executive (EAC) which it had elected.[46] By then, for all intents and purposes, East Africa was out of sight and out of mind and the great question was what to do next. Greenberg was instructed, somewhat half-heartedly, to see if the British Government could be induced to look again at the idea of a Jewish settlement in El Arish. This was roughly in line with Herzl's thinking towards the end of his life—the difference being that he had thought of the revival of El Arish as conditional on a *British* decision to scrap the East Africa plan. For then they would have been under a moral obligation—mild, no doubt, but not entirely insignificant—to suggest an alternative, or at the very least to listen to whatever fresh ideas the Zionists might have, even fresh ideas about old projects. But since in practice it was the Zionists who had made the decisive move, no such obligation existed and the prospect of any kind of arrangement being concluded after two years of tedious negotiations was poorer than ever. The effort duly failed and it was finally recognized in the course of the following year that the subject had to be dropped. But the great development since the Congress had of course been the revolution in Russia and its concomitant, the ghastly hammering of Russia's Jews.

The scale of events and the helplessness of Russian Jewry were numbing; but the theses of Zionism, it could be argued, had been borne out once more and, it seemed too, the Zionist Executive, if it had any claim to leadership, had to act. But how? A little money was allocated for relief. A thorough inquiry into the pogroms (to be conducted by Motzkin)[47] was ordered with a view to wide publication of the facts. Lastly, but less readily, after much argument and by a vote of four to three, it was resolved to call a general Jewish conference to consider the problem of Russian Jewry in the broadest possible terms. All major Jewish philanthropic and communal organizations in Europe and North America were to be invited and in order to fulfil the purpose of the conference, it was to be stipulated that nothing would be done or said that might

---

[46] Wolffsohn (chairman), Bernstein-Kohan, Greenberg, Kann, A. Marmorek, Ussishkin, Warburg.

[47] This resulted in a massive report, [Leo Motzkin,] *Die Judenpogrome in Russland*, 2 vols. (Cologne and Leipzig, 1910).

harm the Jews of Russia and that no plan or concept, Zionist or other, was to be either pre-ordained or ruled out. It was to be a conference called by the Zionists; it was not to be a Zionist conference. But for those who favoured it, Greenberg before all others, there was here 'an opportunity we ought under no circumstances to miss. It is the one thing that it is now possible for us to do[:] to show that we are working and doing something tangible. Even if the other people refuse to come to the Conference we shall have shown to the World that we are alive and that we are taking the lead in Jüdische Weltfrage [*sic*].'[48]

The response of the now dominant 'practical' wing among the Russian Zionists was generally cool, when it was not suspicious. It was plain to them not only that this was an initiative of the 'politicals', Herzl's heirs, but also that, by the emphasis on the immediate, bitter conditions of the Jews, it could indirectly strengthen the case for a territorialist approach. Much as the Kishinev pogrom had contributed to the mood in which the masses sought ever more desperately to escape from Russia and in which the East Africa project made sense, so the new, greater wave of pogroms was liable to drive Jewish opinion further towards the point where it was on migration and resettlement that everything was taken to hinge, not on national renaissance and rehabilitation.[49] Besides, they were only too well aware, as Tchlenov pointed out to Wolffsohn, of the helplessness of Jewry, and of Russian Jewry specifically, in the face of catastrophe. It was hard for him to understand, he wrote, what 'we *as Zionists*'—post-Herzlian Zionists, he might have said—could propose to safeguard Russian Jewry.[50] Still the Russian Zionists could not object to a well-intentioned effort to come to the aid of their own people and the final verdict of the Russian members of the GAC was therefore reluctant, if extremely sceptical, agreement.

Aḥad Ha-ʿAm, as so often, put the matter in the sharpest light. He had decided not to attend, he explained, partly

---

[48] Greenberg to Wolffsohn, 27 November 1905. CZA, W 78.

[49] Cf. Paul A. Alsberg, 'Documents on the Brussels Conference of 1906', *Michael*, ii (1973), pp. 147–8.

[50] Tchlenov to Wolffsohn, 27 December 1905. CZA, W 59/II. Emphasis in original.

because he did not think that in such a time of transition and tumult in Russia it was possible to draw up plans—not that plans or proposals of any kind had been put forward; only the question what could be done to save Russian Jewry had been posed. But did anyone know the answer to it? He, for his part, did not and he could see no purpose in travelling all the way to Brussels to say so. In any event, he did not expect the majority of Jewish organizations to agree to attend. If the Zionists had wanted a better attendance and a conference fully representative of Jewry, they would have been wiser to try to persuade one of the *non*-Zionist organizations, such as the Anglo-Jewish Association or the B'nai B'rith, to act as conveners. *Their* initiative only frightened away their opponents—and, in a sense, Aḥad Ha-'Am observed, who could blame the opponents of Zionism for fighting shy of a movement that was bound, in one way or another, to inject an element of nationalism into the debates and resolutions or, at the very least, to seek to do so. It was true that Wolffsohn and his colleagues had announced that it would not be a 'Zionist' conference. But so doing

they had denied any possibility of considering the Jewish Question in all its aspects and of offering *fundamental* proposals for the not-so-immediate future. After all, such proposals would necessarily touch, somehow, positively or negatively, on the matter of Zionism. If, on the other hand, [as had been reported,] the conference was to deal exclusively with 'current tasks' [*'avodat ha-reg'a*], then it would be of no real benefit. 'Current tasks' could only mean support for the plundered, support for exiles, and the like, which is to say, just what is being done now, before and without the conference.[51]

Warburg too thought little of the initiative and tried to dissuade Wolffsohn from going through with it,[52] agreeing only reluctantly to attend. Nordau was equally sceptical and stayed away. He sympathized with the urge to act, he wrote to Wolffsohn; and he agreed there were occasions on which it was a mistake to be inactive. But to set out for great

---

[51] Letter to Sh. Barabash, 23 January 1906. *Igrot AH*, iv, pp. 6–7. Emphasis in original.

[52] Warburg to Wolffsohn, 3 January 1906. Jacob Thon, *Sefer Warburg* [Tel-Aviv], 1948, pp. 90–1.

things and achieve nothing, that was always a greater error. He did not see what the Jews could do. He did not think the Russian Government was susceptible to pressure from the outside.[53] In the end, probably as a conscious act of loyalty, he offered Wolffsohn detailed advice: the Jews of Russia must be encouraged to organize; a central clearing-house for information about their condition and the war being waged against them must be set up under unofficial Zionist auspices; the campaign for equal rights for Russian Jews must be pursued in co-operation with liberal groups within Russia; and system and organization must be introduced into the unending river of migrants. They must be assisted on their way with guides and information. They must be met and assisted once more on arrival at their destinations. That was as much as could be done 'outside Zionism'.[54]

Wolffsohn's conference was a failure. The non-Zionist organizations and communal representatives stayed away in droves—even the Chief Rabbi of Brussels refused to attend.[55] Only the Anglo-Jewish Association and the German-Jewish charitable society, the Hilfsverein, turned up, the latter having been secretly deputed to participate by a council of major philanthropic organizations (the Alliance Israélite Universelle and the ICA among them), so as to ensure, by its presence, that nothing embarrassing emerged from under the hands of the irresponsible and clamorous Zionists.[56] Representatives of Zangwill's ITO attended too, but that was hardly an achievement and served only to increase the suspicions of the dominant 'practical' wing in the movement, particularly in Russia. Nothing of the kind of action Nordau had recommended was resolved on. There was a pious call for 'constant co-operation' between all Jewish organizations and for a commission to study 'various countries, particularly the Orient', with the settlement of Russian Jews there in mind. But equally it was 'noted' (without further comment) that it was the view of the Jewish relief organizations that they could not undertake

---

[53] Nordau to Wolffsohn, 29 November 1905. Mordechai Eliav, *David Wolffsohn; ha-Ish u-Zemano (Jerusalem, 1977)*, p. 71 and pp. 338–9, fn. 26.

[54] Nordau to Wolffsohn, 26 January 1906. Schwartz, *Nordau be-igrotav*, pp. 130–1.

[55] CZA, Z 2/23.

[56] Alsberg, art. cit., pp. 150–2. Cf. I. Halpern, 'Nisayon shel intervenzia politit le-maʿan yehudei rusiya aharei peraʿot oktober', *Zion*, xx, 3–4 (1955), pp. 163–74.

to 'promote' emigration from Russia.[57] Since this latter resolution was precisely in line with the decision taken by the non-
Zionist relief organizations at their own gathering at Frankfurt earlier in the month to actively discourage the continual
migration of the Jews and to seek to assure their welfare by
means of economic assistance in the lands of their present
dispersion,[58] Aḥad Ha-ʿAm's sour prognosis was entirely
borne out. It is hard to see on what grounds (other than to
keep Wolffsohn's spirits up) Greenberg maintained that the
conference had been a success after all.[59]

The sequel was of the same kind: after the conference
Greenberg and Meyer Spielmann (a Home Office official
much devoted to Jewish charitable work and prominent in the
Anglo-Jewish Association) issued a call for the formation of a
'General Jewish Organization . . . [to] deal with such problems
as confront our brothers in Russia, [to] regulate so far as
practicable the migration of Jews from land to land, and . . .
when requested so to do, by any of the delegated bodies,
undertake such work as can be better done by a general than
by any individual organization'.[60] But nothing came of it.
No General Jewish Organization was ever brought into being.
Nor were the prospects for one ever serious—least of all, by
a grim irony, a *philanthropic* one with nothing more daring
than the amelioration of the condition of Russian Jewry as its
central object. It was out of the question for the predominantly
French Alliance Israélite Universelle, the most important of
contemporary Jewish philanthropic organizations, to co-
operate publicly with German Jewish organizations (in
which class French officialdom seems to have included the
Zionists) in a project which implied public criticism of France's
ally Russia.[61] It was out of the question too for non-Zionists

[57] *Die Welt*, 2 February 1906. A detailed proposal to organize a 'Jewish emigration
fleet' to evacuate large numbers of Russian Jews under the protection of a friendly
European Power, setting them down temporarily in camps on the Anatolian Black
Sea coast, was submitted to the conference but not considered. CZA, Z 2/24.

[58] Alsberg, p. 152.

[59] Letter to Wolffsohn, 4 February 1906. CZA, W 79/I.

[60] Typewritten text headed 'General Jewish Organization', n.d. (probably mid-
February 1906). CZA, W 79/I.

[61] Paul A. Alsberg, 'Mediniyut ha-hanhala ha-ẓionit mi-moto shel Herzl veʿad
milḥemet haʿolam ha-rishona', unpublished doctoral dissertation (Jerusalem, 1958),

and Zionists to bury their differences. The concessions Wolff-sohn and Greenberg had made to the non-Zionists to induce them to enter into a form of co-operation had yielded no results, except to make the Zionists themselves more inward-looking in the aftermath and to provide ammunition for the 'politicals' ' opponents to attack them. Under these two men, Weizmann observed, the 'old delusion . . . that it is possible or desirable to cooperate with partly or wholly assimilated bodies' was persisting. Under 'Zionists of the brand of Green-berg, Wolffsohn, I mean the opportunists . . . [Zionism was] becoming estranged, shallow and insensitive, descending from its democratic eminence to the baize-green table of plutocratic philanthropists, and perhaps as low as to the back-door of the elements dead to Judaism'.[62] Hope of co-operation with ITO even on this limited front fizzled out too within a few months.[63]

The origins of the Brussels conference had lain in an anxiety to do something, anything for Russian Jewry. Its lesson was twofold, part old, part new. There was a display, once again, of the terrible weakness and disunity of Jewry and the feebleness of those who sought to lead it, Zionists and others, even—perhaps especially—when they set out to deal directly with the greatest of the problems confronting them.

It was a sort of cruel mockery of 'Providence' that a pogrom took place in Gomel as the conference was in session—as if a divine voice had spoken to tell the good people sitting there and taking counsel to save us: 'Behold a new form of pogrom, not at the hands of "hooli-gans" and not at the hands of *provocateurs*, but the army itself, openly and undisguised, setting the houses on fire and killing the inhabitants —now go and fight it with resolutions and protestations!'[64]

The other part of the lesson was that once the Zionists turned away, even temporarily, from their original, *radical*

---

p. 16. The Hilfsverein der deutschen Juden had in fact been originally established (1901) as a German-Jewish organization in implicit competition with the *Franco*-Jewish Alliance Israélite Universelle.

[62] Weizmann to Magnes, 13–17 February 1906, *Weizmann Letters*, iv, p. 241. Weiz-mann had wanted to go to Brussels, but had been prevented by injury as a result of an accident in his laboratory in Manchester.

[63] Greenberg to Wolffsohn, 3 June 1906. CZA, W 79/I.

[64] Aḥad Ha-'Am to Eisenstadt, 4 February 1906. *Igrot AH*, iv, p. 10.

position on what needed to be done and concern themselves with 'current tasks', namely with the amelioration of the condition of the Jews in the Dispersion, the distinction in practice between them and other trends in Jewry necessarily dwindled and the fundamental, qualitative difference in principle between their approach to the problems of the nation and those of all the others began to fade from sight. This was the case regardless of whether they did so of set purpose or as a tactic, and whether as a major sphere of activity or a minor one. And it was a natural and necessary consequence of the decision the movement had taken on the East Africa project and the mood and principles underlying it, which the remaining 'politicals' under Wolffsohn, with the best will in the world, were unable to reverse. In fact they were now swept up in the new wave themselves—more so, it seems, than they realized.

The Brussels conference had been presented as a means of reasserting the 'political' line. Greenberg, in his effort to keep up Wolffsohn's spirits, had argued that it would be held for an object that was very different from the frankly philanthropic gathering in Frankfurt. The latter was being held, he argued,

to concert measures for dealing with the Emigration from Russia—to see that the burden of the trouble is fairly distributed and that some means is taken for guiding the poor people. This is a most necessary and laudable object. But the object of the Brussels Conference is something far different. It is to take into consideration the condition of the Jews who are remaining in Russia, and is thus not remedial so much as preventive work. The Frankfort Conference is like one called together to see how best to deal with a number of victims of some plague that has broken out in a town—what hospitals they shall be sent to and what sanatoria are available. The Brussels Conference is to see whether something might not be done to the drains and waterworks of the town, so that further plague ravages should be prevented or at least guarded against.[65]

Whatever merit the distinction Greenberg was drawing between the two conferences might have had, it remained true that the themes to which the people gathered at Brussels

[65] Greenberg to Wolffsohn, 30 December 1905. CZA, W 78.

were supposed to address themselves were a far cry from the classic themes of Zionism—of any variety. They were indeed the themes which came under the increasingly familiar label of 'current tasks' (*Gegenwartsarbeit*). The future was impenetrable, the afflictions of Jewry intense, the Zionists, it was felt on all sides, must lower their sights and apply themselves to less fundamental, less dramatic purposes than had preoccupied them thus far. Yet what the central spokesmen and leaders of the movement had demonstrated by holding the Brussels conference was that there might not be anything of consequence that they could do in this lesser sphere either. They had thus opened the way still further for the people on the spot to take the initiative as much in the realm of ideas as in that of action.

vi

Triumph at the Seventh Congress did nothing to help solve the dilemma in which the leading 'practical' Zionists found themselves in Russia, where they were now plunged, like all the thinking inhabitants of the Empire, into the ferment of the revolution. In very strict principle they could argue (and some, as we shall see, did argue) that it was not their concern. On the one hand, it had been Pinsker's teaching[66] that it was a mistake to rely on the tide of European liberalism to wash the Jews of eastern Europe to safety and freedom. On the other hand, unlike the territorialists, they had eschewed responsibility for the deliverance of Russian Jewry in the mass. Yet the effect of the great upheaval in Russia was to modify the views of a great number of leading Zionist activities on both counts: towards a more optimistic (and therefore less strictly Zionist) view of the general trend of European events and towards more thought for what Aḥad Ha-ʿAm had called the afflictions of Jewry (as opposed to those of Judaism). Why should this have been so? And how, for that matter, is the ease with which Aḥad Ha-ʿAm's famous distinction between the needs and troubles of the Jews as individual people and the needs and troubles of Judaism as a culture had come to be accepted and to have so large an influence to be explained?

[66] See *Origins*, Chapter 5.

Part of the answer, at least, appears to lie in the social characteristics of the principal activists and ideologues of the movement taken as a group. It can be shown[67] that they were predominantly in their middle years; that a high proportion were professionals (physicians, lawyers, pharmacists, engineers) and other university graduates, teachers, business men, and communal officials and employees of various kinds (rabbis, cantors, teachers again), and that among the younger people most were students. They were, in a word, overwhelmingly middle-class. Moreover, they tended strongly to be modernists and modernized: even the rabbis were often 'Crown rabbis', that is, state appointees, usually with a secular as well as traditional education. These were therefore people who for the most part were family men and appropriately cautious, settled, and law-abiding; many were (in the terms the Russian Government had once favoured) 'useful' Jews; and a comparatively high proportion was accordingly privileged to live outside the Pale, notably in Moscow and St. Petersburg. For all these reasons, their private circumstances, as individuals, set them apart somewhat from the common people of Russian Jewry. For the class to which they belonged was rather more protected from persecution by the authorities and depredation by the mob (which is not to say they were at peace with the former or safe from the latter) than were the petty traders, the artisans, the factory-hands, the waggoners, and day-labourers and the outright paupers who formed the bulk of Russian Jewry. As possibly the surest measure of the somewhat more comfortable situation in which the Russian-Jewish, non-traditional, middle-class intelligentsia was placed, it may be noted that their rate of emigration was half that of the commonalty.[68]

It must be conceded that Exilic Jewry cannot be efficiently divided into strict socio-economic classes on any of the models

---

[67] See Appendix, pp. 479–94.

[68] According to the Russian census of 1897, 5·8 per cent of Jewish males gainfully employed belonged to the professional classes. Of the Jews immigrating into the United States in the years 1901–6 (over 70 per cent of whom were from Russia) 1·3 per cent were of that category. The corresponding figures for Jews engaged in 'manufacturing and mechanical pursuits' were 38 per cent of the Jewish population of Russia and 63 per cent of those arriving in the United States. Rubinow, op. cit. Chapter 6, note 3, pp. 500–4.

commonly thought appropriate to other nations. (It is even possible, at the cost of some terminological distortion, to conceive of Jewry *as a whole* as constituting a 'class' in itself, or, more strictly, as a 'caste', as did Max Weber.)[69] In its internal stratification it has never had much in common with other European and Near Eastern peoples. Since ancient times the Jews have had no land-owning class, neither magnates nor gentry, no class or caste of warriors, and no peasantry. The prime determinants of individual status within Jewry have been learning, wealth (irrespective of its nature or source), professional skills, and (but more shakily) the degree of involvement in (and, in recent times, adaptation to) the outside world. None of these have been hereditary, at all events in principle.

It follows, particularly—and increasingly—in modern times, that as *individuals* Jews possessing relatively high social status within a given Jewish community have tended to be members of the middle, and even the higher, rungs of the society at large in which the community is embedded. Or if not members in the full, organic sense, then at the very least possessed of the salient qualities by which membership in those classes is normally detected: wealth, education, and skills. It was these middle and higher classes in Jewry and outside it which were most attentive to the latest events in the Russian political arena, who found the prospect of non-violent evolution towards a liberal, constitutional regime immensely attractive, had the most to gain from it, and were most easily recruited to support it. It was also from this class that the leading members of the Zionist movement—with insignificant exceptions—were drawn.[70]

The point here is not that the roots of Zionist policy are traceable simply and directly to the socio-economic characteristics of those most involved in its formulation and propagation. It is rather, on the contrary, that the principal activists in the movement were comparatively free to hold views and take steps which were *not* overwhelmingly determined by their pri-

---

[69] 'Class, Status, Party', *From Max Weber: Essays in Sociology* (New York, 1958), p. 189.

[70] See Appendix.

vate circumstances because, by and large, these were not as harsh as those of most Jews in Russia, notably in the Pale of Settlement. And further, by virtue of their easier circumstances, their education, their habits of mind, and the tremendous impact upon them of influences from outside Jewry—in brief, as members *par excellence* of the modern Jewish intelligentsia— they tended to attach more weight than other sectors of the Jewish population to matters of principle, to argue social issues on an *a priori* basis, and, so far as the world of action was con-cerned, to wish it to reflect their ideas and principles with the greatest possible accuracy.

It is useful to recall in this connection one of the small but nagging sources of tension between Herzl and the opposition in the year before his death.

Herzl's journey to Russia and his talks with Plehve had outraged a great many of those Russian Jews who tended to be prominent in the Zionist movement: middle-class liberals, all intensely hostile to the regime in mind (rather than in deed), to whom the St. Petersburg bureaucracy—and the police above all—was the epitome of all that was wrong and hateful in Russia. Plehve was one of the masters of that bureau-cracy. Worse, he was the master of the police. To these good people he was therefore the personification of the enemy. This was the case before the Kishinev pogrom occurred and would have remained the case had it never happened. But the pogrom, especially after twenty years or so of comparative safety from police-protected mobs, and the popular conviction that Russia's chief policeman had personally and specifically connived in its eruption, doubled the general indignation and focused it upon him. So over and above their underlying scepticism in regard to the wisdom and utility of dealing with the man, the response of most leading Zionist activists in Russia was moral outrage. How could Herzl treat with such a man? How could he, how dare he, see in the undoubted enemy a potential ally?

To the rising tension between Herzl and so many of his leading colleagues in Russia there was thus added a new strain: conflict between a morally neutral conception of politics and a morally positive one. And the dilemma for Zionism as a whole was classic: were moral dictates and

political imperatives compatible? Must means, no less than
ends, be chosen in the light of clear moral principles? Were the
principles by which private conduct was properly governed
relevant to behaviour in the public sphere? Herzl, who had
from the first slipped easily into the mode of high, international
politics, thought not. That much was implied in all he said
and did. So far as political relations with forces that were
external to Jewry were concerned, the affairs of the Jewish
state-in-the-making must be ordered as if it were a state-in-
being. This was as much to impress upon his interlocutors
that his movement was a fit partner for negotiations as for
reasons of expediency. It also owed a great deal to Herzl's
single-mindedness. The mode of thought and action most
characteristic of the Tchlenovs, Belkowskys, and Bernstein-
Kohans, on the other hand, was *domestic*, rather than diplomatic. They knew the State as an evil; they did not see themselves as acting for one. They were more comfortable standing
apart from great affairs and subjecting them to strict and
somewhat prudish judgement: authentic heirs to a national
tradition that had long been drained of political thought and
experience. They were willing to seek out Russia's policemen,
as Bernstein-Kohan did in the aftermath of the Kishinev
pogrom,[71] in the role of aggrieved subjects remonstrating
with the oppressors. It was quite another matter to seek to
treat with them as potential allies and on a basis of give and
take. They were also less single-minded than Herzl, more
sensitive to the reverberations their actions (and actions taken
in their name) might have in their own domestic arena. All
told, their Zionism had always been more complex in content
than was Herzl's. So it remained. And after Herzl's death it
was of course they who made all the running. In May 1905
the Russian members of the GAC, as a body, went so far as to
publicly align themselves with the opponents of the regime by
proclaiming their support for the fight for democracy and civil
liberties and rights. They did not totally abandon caution: it
would be well, they thought, if individual members of the
movement joined in the fight, each according to his outlook;

[71] See his autobiography, 'Zikhronot', *Sefer Bernstein-Kohan* (Tel-Aviv, 1946), pp.
133–5.

they did not think it right for Zionists to enter it collectively and as such.[72]

After the Tsar's Manifesto and the great hammering of the Jews in October 1905 it was more difficult than ever for sensitive men and women to cleave to the old posture of non-involvement and to stand aside. When the Autocracy, with characteristic inconsistency, granted Jews the right to elect and to be elected to the Duma along with all other Russian peoples, while refusing to change any of the restrictive laws to which they were subject and by which they were set apart, the dilemma became acute. Russian Jews individually and even Russian Jewry collectively did appear to be moving, however slowly, towards a form of integration into Russian society and it was hard not to reach out and grasp the straw and make the most of it. Indeed there was more than one straw in the wind. When the new Imperial Duma was urged by its Jewish members to inquire into the great pogrom of Bialystok of 14–16 June 1906 (which had left some 80 dead) it promptly agreed to do so. It sent out a three-man commission, one member of which was himself a Jew (Victor Jacobson, a member of the Zionist GAC). The commission had a free hand, as reflected in its report which stated flatly that the pogrom had been 'previously planned and prepared by the administration and that the local population was quite cognizant of such preparation'; and it recommended the dismissal or removal of 'all the members of

---

[72] It is fair to add, however, that in this particular regard Herzl's presumed ideological legatee was in agreement with them. In the summer of 1905, at Basel, Nordan too had been moved to depart from the established Herzlian position of political caution and non-involvement, declaring that

'The profound changes towards which Russia is moving will have an enormous influence on the fate of six million Jews. Zionism, the meaning of which is freedom, self-determination, renaissance, and resurgence, would be denying its own principles were it not to support popular sovereignty and enlightenment against absolutism, repression, and the forces of darkness with conviction and determination.

It is true that the Zionists do not believe for one moment that upon the attainment of freedom and equal rights by the Jews in Russia the Jewish Question in general or the Jewish Question in Russia alone will finally be solved. The ideal of Zionist Jews in Russia as in other lands remains the renaissance of the nation in the Land of the Fathers. But nothing will prevent the Jews in Russia from fighting with the best elements of the Russian people for a progressive constitution that will assure them too full equality of rights. For only free Jews can train themselves to be effective citizens of the future land of the Jews.'

Protokoll VII, pp. 23–40.

the local civil and military administration'. There followed an extended debate in the Duma, with the whole House rising to honour the memory of the victims and Jacobson and the most eminent of the Jewish deputies, Maxim Vinaver, attacking the Government in forthright terms. 'The Government', said Jacobson, in his address, 'had acted like a thief who was wanted by the police and in order to divert attention from its own crimes, had pointed to the Jews, crying "Stop, thief!" It had provoked bloodshed and organized bands [of hooligans] ... The Minister of the Interior was either a criminal or a helpless weakling.' And the debate ended with the Duma resolving (on 20 July) that the situation was 'unparalleled in the history of civilised countries', that there must be an immediate judicial investigation, that officials responsible for the pogrom should be punished regardless of rank, and that the Ministry should be dismissed.[73] All this was totally, startlingly, without precedent. Even the immediate aftermath, despite the dissolution of the Duma two days later, was encouraging. P. A. Stolypin, the Minister of the Interior, who had been present throughout the debate, and was appointed Prime Minister several days later, conceded to Paul Nathan of the Hilfsverein that the Problem of the Jews was indeed among the most urgent of the Government's tasks and before two months had passed his Government proclaimed formally that 'regarding the Jewish question ... those restrictions which only produce irritation and which can be immediately removed will be considered, together with those which fundamentally affect the relations between the Jews and the Russian nation.'[74]

Yet on the other hand, there were ample grounds too for dismissing the entire exercise in constitutional government, the use of softer language, and the making of imprecise promises to the Jews as a delusion and snare. That was how most of the left-wing forces in Russia, the Bund among them, had seen it from the first and it was not long before events seemed to be bearing them out. The Bill providing for civil equality for the Jews was never passed because the First Duma was dissolved before this could be done. The composition

[73] 'Report of the Duma Commission on the Bialystok Massacre', *American Jewish Year Book, 1906/7* (Philadelphia, 1906), pp. 84–9.
[74] *Jewish Chronicle*, 31 August and 14 September 1906.

of subsequent Dumas was markedly less liberal, the Jewish representation in them smaller and less distinguished. (The Jewish members of the First Duma had all joined the liberals in signing the Vyborg declaration of protest against the dissolution and had joined in the call for passive resistance to the Government which accompanied it. They were therefore barred with the rest from re-election. Changes in electoral procedure then worked against the election of Jewish deputies.) Debates were less friendly to the Jews, anti-Semitic tones and arguments were more strident.[75] Of Stolypin's promise of progress towards emancipation no more was heard. The hammering of the Jews continued—virtually as a matter of routine.

Thus in the realm of the concrete. In the realm of ideas the promise the electoral franchise and the convening of the Duma seemed to hold out posed questions for which none of the Jews of Russia—but the Zionists least of all—were able to provide persuasive answers. It therefore continued to trouble them long after hope that it be met had evaporated. In the first place, there was the question whether the interests of the Jews were best pursued by the alignment of Jewish voters and Jewish candidates and deputies with all-Russian parties in or out of Parliament. The Zionists were divided, but on the whole thought not. The non-Zionists were in favour. In the event, of the 12 Jewish deputies in the First Duma, 9 were elected as liberal Kadets, 3 as more radical Trudoviki. None were elected explicitly as representatives of a Jewish constituency, although 5 of the 12 were Zionists.[76] The Zionist deputies favoured the formation of a Jewish parliamentary bloc, but the others were opposed. Led by Maxim Vinaver, who was himself a prominent member of the Kadet Party, they would agree only to informal consultations and co-operation on specifically Jewish issues as they arose.[77] Then there was the question should the target be the civil emancipation of the Jews as individuals on the western model, or should it be the

[75] See Sidney Harcave, 'The Jewish Question in the First Russian Duma', *Jewish Social Studies*, vi (1944), pp. 155–76.

[76] Gregory (Zevi) Bruck, Victor Jacobson, Nissan Katzenelsohn, Shemarya Levin, and Shimshon Rosenbaum.

[77] *Die Welt*, 1 June 1906.

acquisition of national rights and a measure of autonomous, internal self-government such as the Poles in the Russian Empire and the Slavs of the Austrian-Hungarian Empire demanded; and if so, on what (non-territorial) basis? The Russian parliamentary experience was too brief and too marginal to the deeper and more decisive political and social processes in Russia for answers to such questions as these to be acted upon. But posing them forced everyone concerned— Zionists as well as others—back to a reconsideration of basic views on the elements of the Jewish Problem. For the non-Zionists the process was educative. For the Zionists it was profoundly disturbing. It put the fragile *modus vivendi* with the Russian state authorities which Herzl had achieved for them at risk; it implicitly called some of their established, common beliefs into question; and it precipitated fresh divisions in their ranks, even within the ranks of the up to now coherent group of 'practicals'.

vii

In the course of the spring and summer of 1906 two broad trends in Russian Zionism emerged. The first, led by Ussishkin, drew its strength from the stalwarts of Hibbat Zion. Its centre was Odessa which was turning into a bastion of 'practical' Zionism *pur et dur*. In July, Avraham Greenberg, Pinsker's timid but reputable successor as chairman of the Society for the Support of Jewish Farmers and Artisans in Syria and Palestine (the Odessa Committee), retired and Ussishkin was elected in his stead. It was an office entirely to his liking and in which he was to consolidate his position as the leader *par excellence* of 'practical' Zionism and, in some ways, as the major figure in the movement as a whole until the Great War shut him out of the decisive political arena. He began his reign confidently.

It has been agreed, [he commented soon after,] that there be founded here the centre for the Zionists of Russia and to choose as its members: me, Bernstein-Kohan, [Menahem] Sheinkin, and [Yosef] Sapir. The 'Ge'ula' [land] company will be here and of course the centre of the [Hibbat Zion] society. Thus I shall have achieved what I have wanted for years—to concentrate all the Zionist work and all the practical work for Ereẓ-Israel in one place.[78]

The other school, less clear-cut in its composition and point of view, but much more inclined to accommodate its thinking to the new circumstances, was led chiefly from Vilna (the seat of the new Central Zionist Office for Russia) by the more important of Ussishkin's fellow members for Russia on the GAC and by a number of younger men who were now coming to the fore and on the point of making their mark. Neither group was blind to the contest for the leadership of the movement in Russia—and ultimately of the movement as a whole—that underlay the argument over policy. But at no time was there a will to bring the argument to a head in the manner in which representatives of both schools, as one, had brought their argument and contest with Herzl to a head three years earlier. This was a family disagreement; it was hardly a quarrel at all. When Ussishkin, in the first flush of his election into Pinsker's seat, convened a large conference in Odessa at the end of July explicitly to formulate policy for the movement in Russia and to consolidate his position, most of the members of the GAC for Russia stayed away. In August, at the full GAC's meeting at Cologne, the members for Russia, as a body, determined that the Odessa conference had been irregular and that its resolutions were not binding. But there was no great confrontation, no drawing-together of ranks. Some of the wind had been taken out of Ussishkin's sails; otherwise he was free to pursue his purposes to the best of his ability. It was also decided at Cologne that a regular, properly elected conference of the Russian Zionists would be held at the end of the year. When it convened at Helsingfors (Helsinki) in December Ussishkin, for his part, sent a message of polite greeting and stayed away.

But while the argument was mild, the outcome was important. Discussions in Odessa and Vilna, particularly the latter, facilitated the articulation and ventilation of a host of ideas, some old, some new, some stale, some fresh, pre-Herzlian and post-Herzlian, all with energy and all against the background of the great and terrible events of the time. The effect was to

[78] Letter to Yehoshu'a Barzilai, [mid-?] July 1906. Schwartz, *Ussishkin*, p. 121.

create an unusually uninhibited climate of discussion and further to ease the way to the final dissipation of Herzl's ideological and conceptual legacy.

The view advanced by the Odessa school had two prongs. The events in Russia were regarded with a profoundly sceptical eye. Pinsker's analysis of the Jewish condition, set out a quarter of a century earlier, the common doctrinal starting-point for all schools of thought within the movement, still ruled. Put briefly, Pinsker had held that there was nothing to be hoped for from the tide of liberalism in any part of Europe, that the true and final Emancipation of the Jews would never come as a free gift but rather as the outcome of the Jews' own efforts, and, finally, that true emancipation was conditional on the evacuation of Russia and the resettlement of the Jews elsewhere as a *majority* in whatever territory they occupied.[79] It was in this spirit that the Jews, Ussishkin told a public meeting at St. Petersburg at the end of 1905, should refrain from looking to the all-Russian progressive forces for salvation because 'the followers of Marx and Lassalle will forget the sufferings of the people of whom they were born as easily as the disciples of Jesus of Nazareth and Paul the Apostle forgot their origins.' He was hooted down;[80] but he was being true to the established teaching of Zionism when all around him people were under the sway of other theses.

The other prong of the approach of the Odessa school was its minimalism and austerity of purpose as epitomized in the teaching of Aḥad Ha-'Am and owing much to his direct influence. 'The day is not far off', Aḥad Ha-'Am had written with satisfaction in mid-October 1905, just before the onset of the pogroms, 'when Zionism will once more be a movement of *national-historical revival* and for that very reason a movement of limited *numbers*; for, being incapable of responding to their economic needs, the masses will have no interest in it.'[81] A year later his views, in all essentials, were the same.

---

[79] See *Origins*, pp. 126–32.

[80] Joseph B. Schechtman, *Ze'ev Jabotinsky*, i (Tel-Aviv, 1957), p. 84.

[81] Letter to Klausner, 16 October 1905. *Igrot AH*, iii, p. 354. Emphases in original. Aḥad Ha-'Am regarded the optimistic and enthusiastic reaction of the Jewish intelligentsia to the outbreak of revolution in Russia even more sourly than Ussishkin. See his letter to Dubnov, 3 April 1905. Ibid., pp. 340–2.

Whatever was done in Erez-Israel, he wrote to his son, the masses will always see that they should not look to it for full and immediate salvation; and it was better that way if disappointment was to be avoided.[82]

Thus it was agreed at Ussishkin's conference in Odessa in July that the main concerns of the movement should remain the 'practical' work in Erez-Israel and education and culture in the Diaspora: the purchase and settlement of land in Erez-Israel was therefore of highest priority; political arrangements, if and when feasible, would only follow (and rely on) practical achievement, not precede it; a land-bank should be set up; Hebrew education ought to be greatly expanded and popular understanding and feeling for the national enterprise increased. All this was consistent with Ussishkin's own definitive contribution to the debate between 'politicals' and 'practicals' when it had been at its height two years earlier—'Our Programme', a carefully thought-out, detailed, somewhat intricate plan of campaign. Its heart was the proposition that since only a handful of men, perhaps one alone, sufficed for 'diplomacy', a strong commitment to political work left the question of what the *others* were to do and on what *they* were to be nourished in the meanwhile entirely open.[83]

Still, even in Odessa, none could be entirely insensitive to the prospect of civil rights and freedom of political action for the Jews, nor to the attraction of a good fight to be fought. It was therefore resolved that it was legitimate for the Zionists to participate in Russian political affairs, provided they did so *independently*. How this was to be accomplished in practice was not spelt out, however. Nor were the members of the Odessa school quick to note the fresh dilemma they had created for themselves: if the East Africa project and other territorialist schemes were rejected on general principles along with all those exercises in 'politics' and 'diplomacy' which they scorned as futile and premature, what precisely were they left with to fuel the movement and occupy its members? Settlement work in Erez-Israel could only be a

---

[82] Letter to his son Sh. Ginsberg, 2 December 1906. Ibid., iv, p. 72.
[83] Text in *Sefer Ussishkin*, pp. 97–125. Originally published in *Evreiskaya Zhizn*, 11–12 (1904).

small affair at best, a matter for a limited number of dedicated people in Europe to concern themselves with, and still more highly dedicated, but not much more numerous people in Erez-Israel, while all the rest (as with Herzlian diplomacy) were left to watch them from afar. Once again, the Zionists *in the mass* were invited to be bystanders at a small, if exceptionally important arena. Set against what appeared to be at stake in Russia itself, the matter of Zionism as conceived in Odessa seemed small beer.

The Vilna school, as it might be termed, took shape as a more precise, more hopeful, and, at the same time, more self-questioning response to the first Russian revolution and its immediate aftermath. Its origins were in the period of greatest confusion, just prior to the elections to the First Duma, when those Zionists who were prepared to make common cause with the liberal, non-revolutionary, non-nationalist forces in Jewry learned that they would have to compromise. It had done them no good to outvote Vinaver and his Kadet friends on the steering committee of the League for Attainment of Equal Rights for Jewish People in Russia— the one forum within which they had come together thus far and within which an effort to work out a common stand had been made. The non-Zionists would not agree to an uncompromisingly *national* stand. For the Zionists to have insisted on fighting the elections as a body and setting up a formal Jewish bloc in the Duma would have been to forgo even minimal parliamentary co-operation. They therefore bowed to necessity and reluctantly accepted Vinaver's leadership. Clearly, the moment they ventured into the wider, all-Russian arena they had to take account of other forces and new rules.

But should they? How far might they retreat from set and strict *Zionist* positions? Was there a way in which the dictates of the immediate political struggle in Russia could be squared with, or even related to, the practical work of settlement and construction in Erez-Israel? Was there not implicit in their participation in Russian politics a retraction of the Zionists' fundamental article of faith, namely that the Exile was a misfortune and that a cure to any of the ills and afflictions of Jewry was conditional on its rejection in principle and its termination in practice?

The institutional base of the Vilna school was the Central Office for the Russian branch of the movement set up in that city by the GAC members for Russia following the Seventh Congress. In retrospect, it would seem to have had great political possibilities. In the hands of a man like Ussishkin it could probably have become a powerful engine for new (or even old) ideas and fresh forms of organization. In the event, Ussishkin preferred his bastion in Odessa; and the Vilna office, like the EAC in Cologne, had to be made up of the best men available. These were worthy, but weaker (or less power-hungry) men, the stronger figures remaining as remote 'advisors'; and the Central Office never went beyond the immediate purposes set for it. These were to help steady Russian Zionism on its new, semi-independent course and to improve internal administration—filling gaps left by defecting territorialists, for example. (Mandelstamm, it will be recalled, had been responsible for the finances of the movement in Russia and it was urgent to replace him.) The task of formulating and rationalizing a new policy for the new circumstances was assumed by newer men still, initially unsanctioned by the movement's institutions and acting outside its formal ambit.

Chief among these were editors and writers for the principal Zionist weekly journals published in St. Petersburg, Vilna, Warsaw, and Odessa. Avraham Idelson (1865–1921), editor of the St. Petersburg *Khronika Evreskoi Zhizni* (later *Razsvet*), was the moving spirit of the group. He had been a member of the Aḥad Ha-ʿAmian Benei Moshe Society and later a leading member of the Democratic Party. Yizḥak Gruenbaum (1879–1970) too had had a connection with the Democratic Party, but his outlook, unusually for a Zionist activist in the Russian Empire, had a Polish edge to it. He was thoroughly conversant with Polish politics and his views on Jewish affairs bore traces of their influence upon him and of his belief that the Jews could and should find a place in Poland as one of that country's constituent national groups. The journal of which he was just about to become editor (*Glos Zydowski*) was published in the Polish language. Ze'ev Vladimir Jabotinsky (1880–1940), a staff member of Idelson's *Razsvet*, was—at first sight—more in the established mould of the Russian-Jewish intelligentsia with a better Russian-secular than Jewish-traditional education and, like so many key figures in the early years of the movement, he was from Odessa. But Jabotinsky was unusual among Russian-Jewish journalists in that it was as a contributor to the non-Jewish press that he had first made a name for himself. He was in fact a man of striking linguistic and literary talent—brilliant in quality, rather than profound—with a superlative gift for oratory.[84] He was also a man who knew the world outside Russia a great deal better than did most of his fellows and had a particular feeling for Italy, where he had studied and whence he had written for the Russian press, bearing traces of Italian culture, manners, and political ideas in his thought and conduct to the end of his days. He differed from most of his contemporaries in Russian Zionism in one other respect: he owed nothing to institutional position or status or the support of his fellows and everything to manifest personal ability. He was not, nor did he really ever become, an organization-man. He was a star, from the first.

The issues on which the movement had to take a stand were thrashed out by these three men and some others at two extended meetings in Vilna (20–22 July and 17–20 October 1906). The sessions were private and appear to have been marked by a rare lack of ideological inhibition. The principle that the national revival and the national *rights* of the Jews had to be conceived of and worked for under two heads, the long-term Zionist and the short- and middle-term Russian, was admitted and laid down. 'Zionism, which seeks the Return of the nation to its historic homeland and its Redemption as a self-governing people, proclaims . . . its refusal to be denied a national life [for Jewry] in its Exile so far as that might be obtainable'[85]—so Gruenbaum, in retrospect, defined the central theme. It was an attempt to square the principles of

---

[84] Jabotinsky's own account of these events is typically brilliant, if overcharged, writing. See his autobiography, *Sippur yamai* (Jerusalem, 1958), pp. 64–72; and his tribute to Idelson, ''Al 'arisato shel tokhnit helsingfors', A. Goldstein et al. (eds.), *Sefer Idelson* (Tel-Aviv, 1946), pp. 83–8.

[85] Yiẓḥak Gruenbaum, *Ha-tenu'a ha-ẓionit be-hitpaṭḥuta*, iii (Jerusalem, 1949), p. 54.

pristine Hibbat Zion both with the needs of the Jews of contemporary Russia (as the participants understood them) and with the needs of a movement endangered by a shift of attention away from the affairs of the Jews strictly conceived and the prospect of a massive flight of its constituents to the radical and revolutionary parties. Accordingly, a great deal more attention was paid to the Russian side of the newly struck coin than to the Zionist one. This was partly because the general lines of Zionist policy as laid down at the Seventh Congress were not at issue and partly because there was no evident answer to the question how Jewish national rights were to be interpreted and maintained if ever they were granted. It was precisely this that had to be explored.

Equal rights for Jews as individuals presented no problem in theory. But what did national rights for the Jews as a people mean in practice? Increased authority to the Jewish community over its members? A national council or a form of parliament for all Russian Jewry? Was the Council of the Four Lands which had provided the Jews of Poland-Lithuania with a measure of self-government from the middle of the sixteenth century to the middle of the eighteenth to be brought up to date? What were the terms and limits of Jewish self-rule? What was to be the national language: Hebrew or Yiddish? How fierce was the opposition of other peoples in the Empire, notably the Poles, to recognition of Jewish *national* rights side by side with their own likely to be? There could be no clear and agreed answers to such questions, not even to that of the language[86]—not within and for Russian Jewry as a whole, not even for the Zionists as a group. And beyond all these consequences of the anomalies and incongruencies of the Dispersion, there was the problem that Zionism in either of its established forms had always sought to break away from them—Hibbat Zion by shifting the moral and cultural centre of the Jewish life back to Erez-Israel, the Herzlians by evacuating and resettling the Jews themselves. To look at the Dispersion afresh and with a less negative and certainly more attentive eye was both to introduce a contradictory element into the relatively straightforward Zionist conception of the Jewish

[86] Yizhak Gruenbaum, 'Ha-pegishot shel ha-'itonut ha-zionit', *Dor be-mivḥan* (Jerusalem, 1951), pp. 64–70.

predicament and to plunge the Zionists themselves into just
those dilemmas by which all other contemporary movements
of modern Jewish opinion were baffled and from which the
Zionists up to now had been free. Still, thinking along such
lines as these was a great deal more in tune with the times and
the immediate circumstances of Russian Jewry than anything
emanating out of Odessa, let alone Cologne, and it was on the
basis of the journalists' discussions and proposals that a full-
dress debate on policy for Russian Zionism was ordered by its
established and elected leaders. It took the form of a formally
convened, all-Russian conference of Zionists, the third in the
series, following the first held in Warsaw (1898) and the
second held in Minsk (1902). It opened in Helsingfors (where,
exceptionally, permission to hold it had been granted by the
Finnish authorities) on 4 December 1904 and lasted for a
week. Over 100 delegates were elected. Some 80 attended.
Lapsed (territorialist) Zionists like Mandelstamm and Jasinowski were absent, of course. Aḥad Ha-'Am, Ussishkin, and
Bernstein-Kohan stayed away. The Mizraḥi were not represented; nor were the socialists. Only a handful of the GAC
members for Russia attended. Still, it was a fair gathering,
considering that it was held in the winter, to say nothing of it
being a time of great political uncertainty. The mainstream
(with Tchlenov in the chair) was much in evidence, along
with members of the now defunct Democratic Party (Motzkin,
notably) and the new men who had done so much to bring it
about (Gruenbaum and Jabotinsky). Idelson, in trouble
with the censorship, had been prevented from attending by a
police order.

The conference at Helsingfors was not such a scene of
heated conflict as had been the first (at Warsaw), nor was it
as well attended and as impressive a demonstration of the
strength of the movement as the second (at Minsk). But it was
by far the best prepared, the most homogeneous in composition,
and its participants were never in doubt nor disagreement
about the chief issue to be discussed. Tchlenov, as chairman,
opened with a conciliatory, Panglossian speech in which he
tried to draw all the threads together—the varying tendencies
in Zionism, territorialism and 'Palestinocentrism', left and
right, 'politicals' and 'practicals'—to show that in its gradualist,

self-correcting, dialectical way, the movement was continually moving forward in the right direction, no one school of thought having failed to contribute its ideas and energy, all modes of action having their due place and role, good sense and realism always triumphant at each fight's end. Like the German Social Democrats when they lost their belief in the imminence of revolution and turned to 'current tasks', so the Zionists, said Tchlenov, having realized that a rapid 'political' solution to the problem of Erez-Israel was not feasible, had now turned most properly to 'practical' work in and for Erez-Israel in the expectation that 'sooner or later, in this way or that, the country will be ours'. To this 'practical' work it is 'the evolution of Zionism·that has opened the door'. That issue was now settled, although there still remained the question of the present condition of the Jews in their Dispersion and the loss of 'proletarian Zionists' who were exceptionally subject to the pull of circumstances and tended to a materialistic view of things. No doubt they would return to the fold. They would realize that the social and national questions were indissolubly connected. It was a question of time. And meanwhile, because events in Russia were compelling the Zionists to revise their attitude to subjects which were not directly connected with their own ultimate and well-defined purposes, they too were changing positions. For the problem of the coexistence of nations in Russia, a hard problem for all, but hardest for us, was moving towards solution. It was clear that the day was coming when the Jews of Russia would be freed of their shackles and could set about treating their wounds. Zionism, Tchlenov concluded, had passed into a new phase. It had become more complex and its tasks more numerous. There would be plenty to do.[87]

Three main topics were before the conference. First, there were matters of organization: the weakness of the central institutions of the movement in Russia and the indiscipline of the outlying branches and their members, all old subjects for complaint, but somewhat sharpened by the dislocation caused by the defection of the territorialists. Criticism was

---

[87] *Die Welt*, 14 December 1906; 'Hitpathut ha-zionut ha-medinit ve-te'udot ha-sha'a', *Yehiel Tchlenov*, pp. 339–53; A. Rafa'eli, 'Ve'idot arziot shel zionei rusiya', *Kazir* [i] (Tel-Aviv, 1964), pp. 78–9.

voiced, correction was demanded, and detailed resolutions were passed whose chief effect, if implemented, would be to strengthen the authority and improve the practice of the new Central Office of the movement in Vilna.

The second topic before the conference was Zionist policy proper. All those present conceived of it in terms of the promotion of settlement in Erez-Israel in the spirit of the decisions taken at Basel the year before, for there were no territorialists to argue for an alternative, nor any true and consistent Herzlian 'politicals'. But nor was there anybody who ruled out 'politics' and 'diplomacy' entirely. The question in most minds, as it emerged in the course of debate, was partly one of procedure and partly one of emphasis or balance. The favoured formulation, originally advanced by Idelson, was that of *synthesis*: in the evolution of the movement, it was suggested, the 'thesis' of Hibbat Zion had been followed by the 'anti-thesis' of Herzlian politics; and this in turn was now to be followed (and the contradiction resolved) by 'synthetic Zionism' in which elements of both conceptions would be commingled. But how, in what proportions, and to what precise effect? Much of the debate in which the participants sought to grapple with these questions revolved around the issue of 'Charterism', a reference to what was still the nominal policy of the movement as laid down by Herzl at the Third Congress. The Zionists' basic and explicit demand was for a 'Charter' in Erez-Israel, namely an agreement with the sovereign Power whereby certain rights of settlement and self-government in a designated part of the country would be conceded to them. But since it had now been accepted all round that there was no prospect of such a Charter being granted by the Turkish Government in the foreseeable future, there arose the question whether the Zionists should not aim at something less comprehensive in scope, less binding formally on the Turks, and *ipso facto* more attractive to them because it would then be, so it was argued, without international political content and significance.

One's answer to the question depended to no small degree on one's conception of the purposes and nature of the movement. If what Gruenbaum called the 'catastrophic' mode of Zionism, that which rested on a belief in the absolute need and the real feasibility of solving the Problem of the Jews at a single, great revolutionary stroke, was ruled out, then the sense of urgency which underlay the push towards a 'Charter' fell away and more moderate targets came into view. These would have as their common denominator no more than general aid and encouragement to settlement work in the *yishuv* and, being of limited scope, would have a better chance of being agreed to by the Ottoman authorities. Of course, the Turks would have to be spoken to and negotiated with. In that sense political work of a sort would still have to be undertaken. In fact, it would be well if a Zionist office were set up in Constantinople to that end. But this new Zionist diplomacy would be in a lower key; and being in a lower key and having more limited aims, was more likely to succeed. And that being the case, Herzl's argument against unauthorized settlement work, lest it interfere with the diplomatic effort, fell away as well. Here, then, were the terms of the 'synthesis': carefully limited political activity pursued side by side with stepped-up (but still limited) settlement work; 'diplomacy' limited by deliberate design to match settlement limited by resources and the facts of the environment.[88]

What then of the bulk of Jewry at whose deliverance 'catastrophic Zionism' had been aimed, but who would be beyond the scope of the infinitely more modest 'synthetic Zionism'? They, so Idelson's preparatory committee of journalists had proposed, and the Helsingfors conference finally determined, were properly the subject of Zionism's 'current tasks' and of the conference's chief concern, which was the ways and means of integrating Zionism (Russian Zionism, at all events) with the great movement for political and social reform in Russia as a whole. And to this, the third topic debated by the conference, most of the second half of the conference and all of the best minds present were devoted. The immediacy and urgency of the issue and the delegates' familiarity with the matter at hand lent this part of the proceedings a more authentic, less scholastic flavour than the debate held on the settlement of Ereẓ-Israel. Once again,

---

[88] *Die Welt*, 14, 21 December 1906; Rafa'eli, pp. 82–5.

there were no sharp differences. Hardly anyone—and no one of influence—disputed the propriety of assuming current *political* tasks in Russia. That issue had already been settled for good or ill by the fact that the majority of Zionists were already involved in Russian politics in one way or another. What was at issue was the question of the form future participation would take, whether under a specifically Zionist 'flag' or with the Zionists integrated with other forces. This was a practical matter on which a decision had to be taken; it was also one which raised a profound issue of principle. If the Zionists were to participate in Russian politics, they would have to formulate a clear approach to the problems on which all who claimed to speak and act for Russian Jewry had to take a stand; but to take a stand on them was to propose policy for all Russian Jewry. In what way, then, would Zionists *acting in the context of Russian-Jewish affairs* remain distinguishable from non-Zionists? And if the Russian Zionists concerned themselves with these matters—all of which were of the greatest importance, but none of which were specific to Zionism—how was this activity related to what *was* specific to Zionism? Thus, to debate 'current tasks' in their local political connection was necessarily to reconsider the Zionist approach to the problems of Jewry and the Zionist programme as a whole.

Gruenbaum, the leading figure in the debate, put the case for 'current political tasks' in the clearest, but also the most general terms. The Zionists' abstention from the political struggle in Russia and their belief in the feasibility of attaining their goals by a unique and final act had led nowhere and caused them nothing but harm. Under the pressure of events, they had indeed been changing course, but incompletely and unsystematically.

Life assaulted us [he said]. We gave half-answers, surrogates of solutions. First the cultural and then the economic questions were taken up in our programme, forgetting that culture and economics are closely connected with politics. But the deeper we penetrated real life, the more difficult became our position *vis-à-vis* the masses. For the masses wanted an answer to the questions of the day.[89]

[89] *Die Welt*, 28 December 1906.

The central thing to grasp, Gruenbaum argued, was that while Zionism was indeed a movement of national renaissance directed towards Erez-Israel, its starting-point was in the Diaspora and the question of what was likely to further Zionism and what might hamper it in the Diaspora itself was paramount. It was vital to distinguish between the 'real, deep condition of Jewish misery which could not be removed by Emancipation, namely the lack of [national] territory', and pressures of the State upon the Jews and the consequent 'misery which was not organically connected with the [fundamental] Jewish Question as such' and which only dammed up national energies. The proper outlet for these energies was the fight for a national home. It was therefore as much the business of the Zionists as anybody else's to seek to release the Jews from the legal pressures to which they were subject. It was their business too, to that same end, to help develop a communal life that was as free as circumstances allowed and which went beyond the narrow religious sphere to which it was now largely restricted. Accordingly, the Zionists in Russia should join the 'territorial [i.e. majoritarian] peoples' of the Empire in the general demand for a democratic constitution, for civil rights, for freedom of speech and assembly, for the separation of Church from State, for national regional autonomy as well as autonomy for the minorities, and for the other essential elements of a 'complete democracy'; for these were the necessary conditions of the organization of the Jewish population and their free development as well.[90]

To Gruenbaum's notion that the removal of the legal restrictions and pressures would help free the Jews to move faster towards their own national renascence there came the inevitable retort (from Daniel Pasmanik) that the example of western Europe demonstrated otherwise and that the key to change and improvement remained emigration. Another delegate (Noaḥ Bass) argued that the Zionists could not assume *two* immensely ambitious programmes of action and that it was not right or sensible to demand of those who supported the primary programme the acceptance of the terms of the secondary one as well. Several delegates put the question whether the Jews could hope for co-operation from

90 Ibid.; Rafa'eli, p. 86.

other national and political groups in a common effort. On
this all were sceptical. Motzkin alone took Gruenbaum's
thesis to its logical conclusion, dissolving Zionism into Jewish
nationalism pure and simple, where other speakers had
sought hard to retain a distinction. Motzkin argued that the
reincorporation of the Jews into a *territory* of their own—the
central and distinctive aim of Zionism—was no more than
a means to a larger national end. That end was the revivific-
tion of the nation. But the fact was that the Jewish people as
a whole did not now tend notably to nationalism and the
national sentiments of the Jewish masses would not be affected
one way or another by a handful of settlements in Erez-Israel,
least of all when the prospects for the future growth of the
yishuv remained so poor. Thus what counted was the Diaspora
after all. It was there that the fight for national survival
would be waged; and there it was circumstances—not principles, as Gruenbaum had asserted—that had changed. How
then were the Jews to comport themselves in their Diaspora?
The Democratic Party, said Motzkin, had said from the first
that the Jews must join the revolutionary movement—provided
only that they were not the instigators of the revolution and
that the result was not to drive the masses further towards
assimilation. Now too there was no question in his mind but
that they must be with the progressive and democratic
forces. The Jews dare not pursue particularist interests
which ran counter to what humane and ethical principles
of a general character prescribed. Even strong nations
might not do so for long. Weak nations, if they did, condemned themselves to destruction. Even where progressive
measures were not initially advantageous to most Jews because
of their special needs and customs, it was wrong to oppose them
—the more so since in the course of time things were bound
to even out. It was true that the democratic forces were
slow to understand the needs of the Jews and slower still to
recognize them and think of them as a nation. But that too
would come in time; and it depended more than anything
on the distinctiveness of the Jews' own way of life, above all
on their language. Language, thought Motzkin, was the key
to the future of the Jews as a people, particularly in view of the
powerful contemporary tendency to assimilate. The Jews

must therefore look to their culture, to their language, and to their internal organization. The function of the Zionists was to make of (and for) Jewry a powerful, disciplined force—at all events in Russia, if nowhere else. Only thus would the ultimate aims of Zionism be achieved and respect for the Jewish people ensured both in the eyes of the world outside and in their own.[91]

None were prepared to go so far as Motzkin and in any case the question whether the Jews could find an honourable place for themselves within the 'camp of the progressive forces' was not one that could be settled in the abstract; nor could the question how far the Zionists dare go in co-operating with other Jewish tendencies and organizations in the common interest; nor could there be agreement on the major issue that had emerged: how a shift of attention to the political and social turmoil in Russia could fail not merely to distract the Zionists from the established aims of the Zionist movement as seen by all its component schools of thought, but to diminish these aims. The first two matters, however, related to tactics at least as much as to principle; and as the facts were either in dispute, or unknown, or unknowable because they lay in the future, a detailed plan of campaign was out of the question. What could be agreed upon was a common view of what had already occurred and of what might reasonably be anticipated in the future. The conference approved *a posteriori* of

the natural entry of the Zionist masses into the liberation movement of the territorial nations of Russia and, given the change being undergone by the imperial regime in Russia, considers necessary the union of Russian Jewry for the attainment of recognition of Jewish nationhood and legally established self-government in all matters relating to Jewish national life.

And it listed a number of specific political demands in the interests of Jewish self-government and recognized national status and rights.[92]

On the larger issue Gruenbaum wound up by saying frankly

---

[91] Ibid.; Rafa'eli, pp. 89–90; *Sefer Motzkin*, pp. 74–5.

[92] The specific demands were:

1. The democratization of the regime on a strict parliamentary basis, broad political freedom, autonomy for national territories, and guarantees for national minorities.

that indeed the departure he and his fellows had in mind could not be squared with the bare text of the Basel Programme. But Zionism had to be seen as an *evolutionary* movement and the Zionists as bent on a national revival and on the self-determination of national destiny here and now in the Diaspora as well as in Erez-Israel in the future. Those who were sure that the Jews would never prosper in their Dispersion, must say, as Herzl had said, that *die Juden sind im Wege* (the Jews are on the move) and set up tents for the people, not houses. But he, Gruenbaum, did not believe that a great movement of evacuation was really in the making. It therefore followed, in his view, that the Jews had to demand their rights as a nation, and in the countries of their Exile. 'There is no future', said Gruenbaum, 'without a present.'

On this keynote all were agreed. For some it entailed a very proper lowering of the sights after the heady years of 'catastrophic Zionism'. For others it signified a widening of scope: 'The masses must understand that Zionism as such provides an answer to all the questions of their lives.'[93] At the conference's end Tchlenov, characteristically, summed up saying that there had been no intention to induce change in the foundations of Zionism at all. There had only been an adjustment to changed circumstances. Had any of the founda-tion-stones laid by the creator of political Zionism been moved, he asked. 'I say clearly and firmly, No! We have moved nothing. The wide horizons that he opened and the paths he paved are as fixed in our work as ever before.' Herzl, if he were alive, said Tchlenov, would surely have approved of all that they had done. Few could have agreed with him.

---

2. Complete and absolute equality of rights for the Jewish population.

3. Assured representation of national minorities in state and local elections to be conducted by universal, equal, direct, and secret ballot irrespective of sex.

4. The recognition of Jewish nationality as an entity with the rights of self-govern-ment in all spheres of national life.

5. The convening of an all-Russian Jewish national assembly to lay the bases for the national organization.

6. National-language rights in the schools, in the courts, and in public life.

7. The right to substitute the Sabbath for Sunday as a day of rest in all parts of the country.

Sources: Rafa'eli, pp. 98–9; *Die Welt*, 28 December 1906.

[93] *Die Welt*, 28 December 1906.

Postscript

Why Tchlenov should have thought it useful to assert that Herzl would have given his blessing to the Helsingfors Programme is obscure. It contained all the elements to which Herzl in his lifetime had been most strongly opposed and paid little more than lip-service to that conception of things and politics which he himself had formulated and represented. But in any case, no one followed Tchlenov in his assessment. Nobody then or later thought that Helsingfors signified anything but a departure—the final departure from Herzlian teaching and Herzlian practice.

Yet that said, there was a respect in which the departure turned out to be less sharp than it had at first appeared and was intended to be and therefore a respect in which Tchlenov spoke somewhat truer than he knew. On strict construction, Helsingfors in its main aspect—the decision to plunge with full force into the Russian political mêlée—led nowhere and the good intention to be left behind neither by events nor by the 'masses' turned to ashes. The resurgence of the Autocracy was already in progress and if there is no evidence that at the time of the conference the participants were really aware of what was afoot, it was not long before matters were as clear to them as to others. Moderate, liberal, non-violent, non-revolutionary opposition to the régime made less and less sense—at all events held out less and less hope. So far as the Jews of Russia were concerned, the old alternatives (self-abnegation and immobilism apart) regained their credibility: all-out revolutionary action or final withdrawal from Russia in mind and body. The former led away from a collective and specific solution to the afflictions of Jewry. The latter meant migration, actual or eventual, and a further choice: either the extension and perpetuation of the Exile in new parts or its winding-up, if only fractionally, as the Zionists had always proposed.

True, the benefits likely to accrue from the strict Zionist course were only hypothetical. Its achievements thus far were very small. But it could not be said of it, as it could be said of all other courses of *collective* action by the Jews, that it was founded on an optimistic view of the prospects of European Jewry, nor that it led necessarily to a national dead end. Except that now, in the course of the years 1905–6, Zionism had been revised. There had been a fresh attempt to put Zionism and the general Jewish condition into a single perspective by looking at the real, but only partly Zionist and nationalist world of the Jews, accepting the divisions within it, and accepting too that all parts of it had an equal—or almost equal— right to attention. In practice, this reformulation of the Zionist programme had proceeded as an effort to suit the purposes of the movement to the particular circumstances of Russian Jewry as the leading Russian Zionists in their majority understood them. However, since the circumstances of Russian Jewry had been at the roots and origins of the movement anyway, and since the Russian branch, by virtue of its numbers and by its seizure of the commanding heights of the movement in all but name after Herzl's death, was preponderant, the result for the entire movement was portentous. Naturally and perhaps inevitably, the views expounded and adopted at Helsingfors reappeared and were readopted at the Eighth Congress of Zionists in the following year.

Herzlian Zionism too had followed from an attempt to look at the real world of the Jews and to prescribe for all parts of it, but particularly for the Russian part. In contrast, the proto-Zionists of Hibbat Zion had always had a more limited perspective. Yet the effect of Helsingfors was to complete the demolition of Herzlian Zionism that had been in progress since the beginning of 1904 and to resuscitate Hibbat Zion. It did so in two ways: firstly, by proposing to modify the strict, rigorous, and admittedly grim analysis of (and prognosis for) Jewry that had been the foundation of Zionism of all schools, thereby diverting from it just that increment of thought and energy that had accrued to it upon its consolidation by Herzl in 1897; secondly, at the end of the day, when all hope of

making headway with the Helsingfors Programme had
dissolved, by leaving the Odessa school (with its allies in
western Europe, especially Germany) virtually unchallenge-
able in its preponderance—the reward for its doggedness and
self-confidence. Henceforth, albeit with drastically reduced
intentions, the mind of the movement would be almost
exclusively on Erez-Israel and the Jewish national principle, in
something much more like its ancient form, would have an
acknowledged champion and a plan to safeguard it. On the
other hand, how the Jews themselves would fare there were
now none who would say.

Appendix

General

THE Sixth Congress of Zionists (Basel, 23–8 August 1903) was the largest ever to assemble between 1897 and 1948. While the First, foundation Congress was a unique *event*, having regard to the movement's later political history and evolution, there are grounds for judging the Sixth to have been the most important of the series—certainly so for the period leading up to the Great War; but arguably so for the entire span as well. The account given of it in this book has therefore been a detailed one.

However, over and beyond the importance of the Congresses —and of the Sixth Congress in particular— as arenas of debate and political action and, on occasion, as turning-points in the movement's history, they are rewarding subjects of study simply as gatherings of its leading activists. No freely and democratically elected parliament—let alone a bogus, undemocratic one—can ever be a true microcosm of the entire body of its constituents. So with the Zionist Congresses. But the Congresses, as other parliaments, do tell us much that is of interest about the movement, above all about its activists and leaders, small and great.

What follows here are the main results of an attempt to analyse the body of delegates to the Sixth Congress in elementary sociological terms and with particular reference to the vote on the East Africa resolution.

Three preliminary remarks are in order. The first is that the data for an entirely complete and thorough examination of the delegates are not available. A great deal is known about some delegates. Virtually nothing—in some cases, nothing at all beyond the bare fact of election—is known about others. Much of what is 'known' (in the sense that there is ostensibly reliable documentary evidence for assertions about individual delegates) is, in fact, uncertain. Attendance- and voting-lists have proved, on examination, to be faulty. Biographical details such as are given in the records and in standard books of reference are often incomplete and, in some cases, mutually contradictory or demonstrably false. Generally, while the search for data to compile this analysis extended to a great variety of sources, the results were often disappointing. For example, it was necessary to make do with a great deal of *uneven* data: to know the age of one delegate, but not his place of birth, or the occupation of another, but nothing else about him, or not even to be entirely certain that, having been elected, he did in fact make the journey to Basel. Where the uncertainty was very great—where, for example, nothing but the bare fact that a certain man or woman had been elected was known, but no other particular, neither basic biographical data, nor the fact of attendance at the Congress, let alone his or her vote on the East Africa resolution—there the case was eliminated from the working list entirely. So while it is likely that the number of those elected reached as many as 1,000 (and very probably 1,100), the working list of elected delegates used for this compilation was made up of only some three-quarters of that number. On the other hand, it was possible to revise some of the figures that have become standard in the literature and some of the figures in the Congress's own records as well. For example, a commonly accepted figure for attendance at the Congress, 592, proved to be incorrect. It is virtually certain that at least 611 delegates showed up at Basel, although not all voted or even appeared on the list of formal abstainers.

The second remark concerns the division of the delegates into three political, or institutional-functional (as opposed to sociological), categories. The statutes of the movement provided for two classes: rank-and-file delegates on the one hand and elected members of the Greater Actions Committee (GAC) on the other. The latter, by definition, formed the formal and authorized, or primary, leadership. But clearly there were a great many others who fell naturally into an informal, intermediate class consisting of men and women of undoubted influence, or high repute, or such as were particularly active and energetic Zionists (Brutzkus, Reines, Weizmann, Zangwill, and, of course, Nordau—to name a handful). They were not members of the GAC, but they may be properly distinguished from a third class consisting of the relatively anonymous delegates, whose participation in the movement's affairs was limited or intermittent. For present purposes, the line between members of this secondary leadership level and the true rank-and-file delegates was drawn by the application of two simple tests. Personalities for whom *all* basic biographical data were available were placed in this, the secondary category on the grounds that, generally speaking, the relevant records tend to completeness and accuracy *pari passu* with the degree of prominence of those concerned. On the other hand, where the individual was none the less known to have played a notable role in the movement, he has been included in this category even if one or two biographical particulars were lacking.

Thirdly, nothing is easier than to feed data of this kind into a computer and, choosing an appropriate programme, subject the material to comparatively sophisticated statistical analysis. This has not been done—chiefly because the results obtained after a trial run seemed tenuous and intricate out of all proportion to the plain purposes I had set myself. These were: (a) to establish in deliberately *broad* terms the general character or common features of the leading members of the movement; and so doing, to see whether the impression of that general character which I (and, no doubt, other students of the subject) had gained over the years was borne out by the ascertainable facts; (b) to see whether the East–West, young–old, modernist–traditionalist divides which have occurred and reoccurred as themes in this book and as correlates of political behaviour and opinion tended to reappear in—and so, to some extent, to be substantiated by—the figures. It seemed undeniable that whatever answers one got, they were bound to be imprecise ones, evidence of certain tendencies and so, at best, so many legitimate, but marginal, additional touches to the general picture this book has sought to convey. But not more. To ask for more would be to ask for conclusions that evidence of this kind in this form provides too fragile a foundation to bear.

Tables

Table 1 : Attendance

	Present at Basel		Absent from Basel		Total for group	
	number	per cent	number	per cent	number	per cent
Formal or primary leadership (GAC)	34	5·6	15	10·3	49	6·5
Secondary leadership	135	22·1	19	13·0	154	20·3
Rank-and-file	442	72·3	112*	76·7	554	73·2
Total for all groups	611	100·0	146	100·0	757	100·0

* Rank-and-file delegates absent from Congress, but included in the survey. It is probable that 200 or more other delegates were elected to the Congress, but did not show up at Basel and have not been adequately identified for inclusion in this survey.

Table 2: Countries of Origin/Countries of Residence

Leadership group	GAC		Secondary leadership		Rank-and-file	
	number	per cent	number	per cent	number	per cent
Western Europe and North America	6/13	15·0/26·5	8/30	5·3/19·6	1/53	3·3/15·1
Central Europe	8/14	20·0/28·6	35/47	23·2/30·7	5/102	16·7/29·1
'The West'	14/27	35·0/55·1	43/77	28·5/50·3	6/155	20·0/44·2
Austrian-ruled Poland	7/3	17·5/6·1	7/4	4·6/2·6	6/20	20·0/5·7
Russian-ruled Poland	3/2	7·5/4·1	18/16	11·9/10·5	5/40	16·7/11·4
Russian Pale of Settlement	14/9	35·0/18·4	75/36	49·7/23·5	10/109	33·3/31·1
Inner Russia	—/2	—/4·1	4/10	2·6/6·5	2/15	6·7/4·3
Balkans	2/6	5·0/12·2	4/4	2·6/2·6	1/10	3·3/2·8
'The East'	26/22	65·0/44·9	108/70	71·5/45·8	24/194	80·0/55·3
Erez-Israel	—/—	—/—	—/6	—/3·9	—/2	—/0·6
Total	40/49	100·0/100·0	151/153	100·0	30/351	100·0
Unknown	9/—	—	3/1	—	524/203	—

Table 3: Age*

	GAC		Secondary leadership	
	number	per cent	number	per cent
years				
0–24	—	—	16	10·5
25–29	2	5·0	34	22·2
30–34	5	12·5	36	23·5
under 35	*7*	*17·5*	*86*	*56·2*
35–39	9	22·5	18	11·8
40–44	15	37·5	26	17·0
45–49	3	7·5	9	5·9
50–54	2	5·0	3	2·0
55–59	—	—	6	3·9
60–	4	10·0	5	3·3
Total	40	100·0	153	100·0
Unknown	9	—	1	—

* Data on rank-and-file delegates were too sparse for a comparison to be significant.

Table 3a

	GAC	Secondary leadership
Mean	42·2 years	35·8 years
Median	41·3 years	33·7 years

Table 4: *Occupations*

	GAC		Secondary leadership		Rank-and-file		All groups	
	number	per cent	number	per cent	number	per cent	number	per cent
Professionals, university graduates	31	68·9	52	34·4	106	26·4	189	31·7
Rabbis and other traditional communal office-holders	3	6·7	15	9·9	31	7·7	49	8·2
Writers, artists	3	6·7	29	19·2	10	2·5	42	7·0
Merchants, manufacturers	6	13·3	24	15·9	174	43·4	204	34·2
Schoolmasters	—	—	4	2·6	15	3·7	19	3·2
Students	—	—	20	13·2	43	10·7	63	10·6
Others	2	4·4	7	4·6	22	5·5	31	5·2
Total	45	100·0	151	100·0	401	100·0	597	100·0
Unknown	4	—	3	—	153	—	160	—

Table 5: Cross-tabulation: Occupation by Country of Residence

	Western Europe and North America		Central Europe		'The West'		Austrian Poland		Russian Poland		Pale of Settlement		Inner Russia		Balkans		'The East'		Erez-Israel		All Countries	
	no.	%	no.	%	no.	%	no.	%	no.	%	no.	%	no.	%	no.	%	no.	%	no.	%	no.	%
Professionals, university graduates	21	14·3	50	34·0	71	48·3	12	8·2	11	7·5	31	21·1	12	8·2	8	5·4	74	50·4	2	1·4	147	100·0
Rabbis and other communal office-holders	11	27·5	7	17·5	18	45·0	—	—	5	12·5	13	32·5	1	2·5	3	7·5	22	55·0	—	—	40	100·0
Writers, Artists	11	28·2	10	25·6	21	53·8	1	2·6	4	10·3	10	25·6	2	5·1	1	2·6	18	46·2	—	—	39	100·0
Merchants, manufacturers	17	14·0	34	28·1	51	42·1	4	3·3	19	15·7	40	33·1	4	3·3	2	1·7	69	57·1	1	0·8	121	100·0
Schoolmasters	1	6·3	3	18·8	4	25·0	—	—	4	25·0	5	31·3	—	—	1	6·3	10	62·5	2	12·5	16	100·0
Students	5	11·4	17	38·6	22	50·0	—	—	2	4·5	17	38·6	3	6·8	—	—	22	50·0	—	—	44	100·0
Others	2	8·0	4	16·0	6	24·0	8	32·0	1	4·0	5	20·0	1	4·0	2	8·0	17	68·0	2	8·0	25	100·0

Total number of delegates whose occupation and country of residence are both known: 432

Table 6: *The Vote on the East Africa Resolution*

	Number	As per cent of votes cast	As per cent of all present at Basel (less GAC members)
Ayes	292	62·4	50·6
Noes	176	37·6	30·5
Votes cast	*468*	*100·0*	—
Abstentions (declared and undeclared)*	109	—	18·9
Noes + abstentions	285	—	49·4
GAC members present at Basel†	34	—	—
Total present at Basel	*611*	—	—
Total present at Basel less GAC members	*577*		*100·0*
Delegates (including GAC members) absent from Basel	156	—	—
Total	757	—	—

* Delegates known to have declared their abstention: 99; delegates known to have been at Basel, but not appearing on any list—and presumed to have been absent from the hall at the time of the vote: 10.

† Herzl insisted on the GAC abstaining *en bloc*. Opinion within it was divided. A strong minority would undoubtedly have voted against the resolution had they been free to do so.

Table 7: *The Vote on the East Africa Resolution by Group*

	Primary leadership (GAC)		Secondary leadership		Rank-and-file	
	number	per cent	number	per cent	number	per cent
Ayes	—		48	37·8	244	55·5
Noes	—		59	46·5	117	26·6
Abstentions	34	100·0	20	15·7	79	18·0
Noes + abstentions			79	62·2	196	44·6

* Delegates present at Basel only.

Table 8: Secondary Leadership Group: the Vote by age*

	Ayes		Noes		Abstentions		Noes + abstentions		Total in age group
	number	per cent of age group	number	per cent of age group	number	per cent of age group	number	per cent of age group	
Under 35 years	23	31·5	39	53·4	11	15·1	50	68·5	73
35 years and over	25	47·2	19	35·8	9	17·0	28	52·8	53

* For a total of 126 cases whose vote and age are both known. Parallel data on the rank-and-file were too sparse for a significant comparison to be made. The primary group (GAC) was not allowed a free vote.

Table 9 : The Vote by Country of Residence*

		Secondary leadership		Rank-and-file		Total	
		number	per cent	number	per cent	number	per cent
Ayes	{'The West'†	36	29·5	65	27·1	101	27·9
	{'The East'‡	12	9·8	59	24·6	71	19·6
Noes	{'The West'	21	17·2	14	5·8	35	9·7
	{'The East'	34	27·9	58	24·2	92	25·4
Abstentions	{'The West'	10	8·2	26	10·8	36	9·9
	{'The East'	9	7·4	18	7·5	27	7·5
Total		122	100·0	240	100·0	362	100·0

* Excluding primary leadership group (GAC) and delegates from Erez-Israel.
† Western Europe, central Europe.
‡ Austrian-ruled Poland, Russian-ruled Poland, Russian Pale of Settlement, Inner Russia, the Balkans.

*Table 10: The Vote by Occupation**

	Professionals, university graduates		Rabbis and other communal office-holders		Writers, artists		Merchants, manufacturers		Schoolmasters		Students		Others		Total	
	number	per cent	number	per cent	number	per cent	number	per cent	number	per cent	number	per cent	number	per cent	number	per cent
Ayes	68	52·7	24	63·1	13	40·6	108	57·1	7	38·9	15	26·8	9	42·9	244	50·5
Noes	40	31·0	9	23·7	13	40·6	48	25·4	7	38·9	28	50·0	10	47·6	155	32·1
Abstentions	21	16·3	5	13·2	6	18·8	33	17·5	4	22·2	13	23·2	2	9·5	84	17·4
Total	129	100·0	38	100·0	32	100·0	189	100·0	18	100·0	56	100·0	21	100·0	483	100·0

* All delegates (less members of GAC) for whom relevant data are available.

Table 11: The Vote by Principal Occupations: Secondary Leadership

	Professionals, university graduates		Students		Professionals, university graduates + students		Merchants, manufacturers		Total	
	number	per cent	number	per cent	number	per cent	number	per cent	number	per cent
Ayes	19	43·2	3	15·8	22	34·9	10	55·6	32	39·5
Noes	19	43·2	12	63·2	31	49·2	7	38·9	38	46·9
Abstentions	6	13·6	4	21·0	10	15·9	1	5·5	11	13·6
Noes + abstentions	25	56·8	16	84·2	41	65·1	8	44·4	49	60·5
Total	44	100·0	19	100·0	63	100·0	18	100·0	81	100·0

Table 12: The Vote by Principal Occupations : Rank-and-file Delegates

	Professionals, university graduates		Students		Professionals, university graduates + students		Merchants, manufacturers		Total	
	number	per cent	number	per cent	number	per cent	number	per cent	number	per cent
Ayes	49	57·7	12	32·4	61	50·0	98	57·3	159	54·3
Noes	21	24·7	16	43·2	37	30·3	41	24·0	78	26·6
Abstentions	15	17·6	9	24·3	24	19·7	32	18·7	56	19·1
Noes + abstentions	36	42·3	25	67·6	61	50·0	73	42·7	134	45·7
Total	85	100·0	37	100·0	122	100·0	171	100·0	293	100·0

Observations

a. The pattern of Jewish migration at the end of the nineteenth century and the beginning of the twentieth is evident when delegates' countries of origin and countries of residence are compared: out of the heartland of Jewry (Poland and the Pale of Settlement) and into western and central Europe and, to a lesser extent, into the Russian areas normally forbidden to Jews. (Table 2)

b. 'Eastern' and 'western' Jews are fairly evenly distributed at all ranges of the movement's leadership, but western Jews marginally outnumber the easterners at the higher ranges, while easterners marginally outnumber westerners at the lower ranges. (Table 2)

c. The Zionist movement in this period is led by comparatively young men: well over half of the intermediate range is under the age of 35. Even of the small primary leadership group, two-fifths are under 40. (Table 3)

d. The leading members of the Zionist movement at this time were overwhelmingly middle-class. Professionals (physicians, lawyers, engineers, pharmacists, academics) and other university graduates account for about a third; together with tomorrow's professionals—the students—they account for two-fifths of all delegates whose occupations are known. Merchants and manufacturers account for another third. As one goes up the hierarchy, the entirely modern (university-trained) middle-class Jew tends increasingly to predominate, the generally less well-educated, more traditional type of Jewish bourgeois being somewhat more in evidence at the lower reaches. All in all, the evidence suggests that, broadly, the higher ranges were somewhat more modern—in these specific senses of occupation and education—than the lower ranges, but that, as a class, the group of university-trained was about equally composed of western and eastern Jews. (Tables 4 and 5)

e. Delegates present at Basel: 611; delegates casting a vote: 468; delegates abstaining *en bloc* by Herzl's instruction: 34; delegates abstaining by choice: 109. Accordingly, while Herzl gained a handsome majority of the votes cast (62·4 per cent), he gained only the slimmest of majorities (50·6 per cent) of the potential free vote. (Table 6)

f. The difference in pattern of voting between the secondary and tertiary leadership groups is striking: only 37·8 per cent of the former, as opposed to 55·5 per cent of the latter, voted 'aye'. (Table 7)

g. Younger delegates tended to be less inclined to support Herzl on the major issue before the Congress than older delegates. (Table 8)

h. Delegates from western countries tended strongly to vote with Herzl. Delegates from eastern countries at the more senior level tended strongly to vote against him; but at the more junior level to be evenly divided between 'aye' and 'no'. (Table 9)

i. Members of the intermediate (or secondary) leadership with a modern, university background tended to support Herzl less strongly than delegates with less formal modern education (Table 11); but at the rank-and-file level of delegates, there was no appreciable difference between the two classes.

Select Bibliography

The difference between proto-Zionism and Zionism proper is reflected in the contrast between the nature of the resources available respectively for their study. The bulk of the usable material relating to the earlier period[1] consists of private papers and memoirs and the files of the loosely federated and widely scattered local associations of which the proto-Zionist movement was largely composed. Some of this material has been published, but not much. A good deal of it is trivial in content. Certainly it does not add up in any immediately obvious way to the basis for a coherent picture of the subject and the precise relevance of much of it to the central concerns of historians of the modern Jewish revival must often be in question. But upon the advent of Herzl, and with the successful consolidation of the movement, a dramatic change occurs—reflected neatly in the sources. The movement is now provided with a central political focus, with established leaders—and rivals for their places—and with an orderly, functioning bureaucracy. Internal debate is conducted either within the well-defined parliamentary and executive structures with which the Zionists are now equipped, or with reference to them. And there is a powerful effort to gain a place for the Zionists—and indeed for Jewry as a whole—in the international political arena. One minor and incidental result on the ground, at the time, but a crucial one for the later historiography of the movement, is the steady production and accumulation of documentary evidence on its affairs. Most of it is internal to the movement in origin; but some of it is external to it—and external to Jewry too: a consequence of the Zionists having entered into political relations

---

[1] Reviewed in the Select Bibliography appended to the present author's *The Origins of Zionism*, pp. 377–85. It has not been possible to avoid some overlap between that review of the sources and this one. On the other hand the present review provides an opportunity to call attention to some useful additions to the relevant literature which appeared too late for mention in the first book. One such work which merits special mention is a comprehensive bibliography of the literature on Zionism by Israel Klausner, *Toldot ha-Zionut* (Jerusalem, 1975), published under the auspices of the Historical Society of Israel. Its only serious flaw is that it omits works in the Russian language.

with, or come under observation by, some of the contemporary governments of Europe. Taken together, along with the private correspondence of the major figures in the movement, these are the means by which the central threads of the story can be plotted with considerable confidence, often in great detail, and the chief issues of policy analysed and their outcomes accounted for.

However, it is equally the case that with the change in structure and pace that was precipitated in 1897 and with the movement's entry into a greater arena than its forerunners had ever envisaged as appropriate, its affairs soon became very complex—so much so that if they are to be understood in all their major ramifications and if, particularly, the interplay of endogenous and exogenous forces is to be charted with any accuracy, a range of sources wider than the specifically Zionist and the specifically Jewish must be tapped. There has perhaps never been any real justification for Jewish history, no matter how limited the period in question or narrow the aspect under review, in which the Jews are conceived essentially in isolation from the world around them. In any event, a restricted, inward-looking view is least appropriate in the case of a movement within Jewry which sought explicitly to reorder the relations between the Jews and other nations, and to do so on a basis that was unprecedented for the radical and forthright terms in which its proponents conceived of it.

THE HERZLIAN SUPREMACY

The essential materials for the study and reconstruction of the Herzlian period can be divided into five groups, of which the chief primary sources form three. First in order, but not necessarily in importance, are the minutes (some verbatim, some in summary form) of the formal institutions of the movement over which Herzl presided and through which much, not all, of his activities were ventilated. The minutes of the Smaller Actions Committee (EAC) are the least interesting intrinsically, but give a good notion of what the routine of the movement at its centre consisted of. In contrast, the minutes of the Greater Actions Committee (GAC), which met more rarely, usually twice a year, and was the scene of ever more tension and plain speaking as time went by, are the records of a body whose discussions reward close study. The minutes of the EAC and GAC are to be found (in the original German, partly in manuscript, partly typewritten) in the Central Zionist Archives (CZA), Jerusalem. Some notable passages (statements by Herzl, for the most part) have found their way into print (for example, in the collection of Herzl's speeches and articles edited by Alex Bein, Moshe Schaerf, and Yosef Wenkert, *Theodor Herzl, bifnei ʿam ve-ʿolam* (2nd edn, 2 vols, Jerusalem, 1976), and the parallel, abridged English version, *Zionist Writings* (trans. Harry Zohn, 2 vols, New York, 1973–5). But apart from one excellent treatment of the documents relating to the East African issue—and to the connected tension between Herzl and his opponents generally (see below)—namely, Michael Heymann (ed.), *The Minutes of the Zionist General Council [GAC]; the Uganda Controversy* (2 vols in print, Jerusalem, 1970, 1977, a 3rd in preparation), recourse must be had to the originals. The verbatim reports of the debates at the Congresses (in German, until the 1930s, then in Hebrew) were all printed and published, usually within months of a Congress being held, under the standard title *Stenographisches Protokoll der Verhandlungen des I. (II., III., etc.) Zionisten-Kongresses*. The debates were very uneven in quality. Statements and declarations were more common than genuine argument designed to convince. Moments of excitement and 'truth' were infrequent. But the major speeches by Nordau and Herzl are of lasting interest and importance; and all currents of opinion tended to be reflected in the debates in one way or another, sooner or later. The material as a whole is indispensable.

The major European newspapers tended to report briefly on the Congresses, but extensive summaries of the debates will be found in *Die Welt*, the official organ of the movement, published in Vienna; in the *Jewish Chronicle* (London), the coverage and analyses of which were particularly good; in *L'Écho Sioniste* (Paris); and in the Hebrew newspapers published in Poland and Russia, especially in *Ha-Meliz* (St. Petersburg) and *Ha-Zefira* (Warsaw). Eye-witness reports by delegates and onlookers are often illuminating, e.g. Leib Jaffe, *Be-Shelihut ʿam: mikhtavim u-teʿudot 1892–1948* (ed. Benjamin Jaffe, Jerusalem, 1968).

The second class of primary sources comprises Herzl's correspondence and other writings. A fully annotated edition of his letters was initiated a generation ago with two volumes, Alex Bein et al. (eds), *Igrot Herzl*, ii (1895–7) (Jerusalem, 1958); iii (1897–9) (Jerusalem, 1957). (It verges on the scandalous that although much of the remaining material has been in an advanced state of preparation for years there is still no certain news (in 1980) of the other volumes going to press.) Almost as important are the letters and reports of Herzl's formal and informal representatives in Russia, England, Germany, Italy, the United States, and so forth, which, with his own responses and instructions to them, provide an unrivalled map of his activities and thinking and of the reactions to both through much of the movement and European Jewry. Of particular note are the exchanges with his intimates, Nordau before all others, but also Mandelstamm, for example. Part of Nordau's correspondence has been summarized, with extensive quotations, in S. Schwartz, *Nordau be-igrotav* (Jerusalem, 1944); but for Mandelstamm (Kiev) there is no alternative to recourse to the Central Zionist Archives; nor for Herzl's important correspondence with Leopold Greenberg (London). Zangwill's correspondence with Herzl has not been published either, but his chief writings on the Jewish national Question can be found in his own collection, *The Voice of Jerusalem* (London, 1920), and in Maurice Simon (ed.), *The Speeches, Articles and Letters of Israel Zangwill* (London, 1937). Herzl's correspondence with Bodenheimer is to be found in an untidy, but useful collection, Henriette Hannah Bodenheimer (ed.), *Be-reishit ha-tenuʿa* (Jerusalem, 1965) (German edition: *Im Anfang der zionistischen Bewegung* (Frankfurt a.M., 1965)).

Of Herzl's other published writings far and away the most important is his diary, the best edition of which is the English, Raphael Patai (ed.), *The Complete Diaries of Theodor Herzl* (trans. Harry Zohn, 5 vols, New York, 1960). The German, *Theodor Herzls Tagebücher* (3 vols, Berlin, 1922–3), has the virtue of being the original, but is incomplete. The Hebrew is also incomplete and further marred by poor translation. Herzl's Utopian novella *Altneuland* is inferior as literature, but very revealing for his social thinking; it exists in a multitude of editions, the best in English being *Altneuland, Old-New Land* (trans. Paula Arnold, Haifa, 1960).

The third class of primary sources for the Herzlian period, and, more specifically, for political Zionism as Herzl understood and practised it, comprises the material on Zionism (and on Herzl himself) that accumulated in the archives of the governments with which he sought to deal. Easiest of access, because its bureaucratic and archival routines were among the smoothest, is the British. Most of the Foreign and Colonial Offices' files on the East Africa project at the Public Record Office seem to have been read for the preparation of Robert G. Weisbord, *African Zion* (Philadelphia, 1968), but they still repay examination at first hand. Other (primary and secondary) material on the first phase of official British involvement with Zionism will be found in Julian Amery, *The Life of Joseph Chamberlain*, iv (London, 1951); in Bernard Gainer, *The Alien Invasion* (London, 1972) and Lloyd P. Gartner, *The Jewish Immigrant in England, 1870–1914* (Detroit, 1960), on the domestic background to British interest in the Jewish Problem; and in D. A. Low, *Lion Rampant* (London, 1973), an excellent introduction and bibliographical guide to contemporary British thinking on imperial questions. The most comprehensive and systematic collection of data on Jewish immigration into Great Britain and the reactions to it (including Herzl's) remains the Royal Commission on Alien Immigration [of 1902], *Report, Minutes of Evidence, Appendix, Index and Analysis to Minutes of Evidence* (4 vols, Cds 1741–3, London, 1903–4).

Virtually untapped, but potentially of the utmost importance, are the Turkish archives. Unfortunately, they are still all but inaccessible. Bits and pieces of Ottoman documentation have turned up, however, and, while rarely of major significance in themselves, have helped to establish the outlines of Ottoman policy on Zionism and the growth of the new *yishuv* in Erez-Israel. These seem firm, but it must be said that a major revision is always possible—if and when access to the archives in Istanbul is made free. Meanwhile, a pioneering study, based partly on Ottoman documents and incorporating extensive transcriptions from the originals, deserves special mention: Bülent Mim Kemal Öke, 'Ottoman Policies towards Zionism (1880–1908)' (unpublished M.Phil. thesis, Cambridge University, 1979).

German archives too contain material of value, a good part of which has been published in specialist journals and year-books. Two noteworthy sets are Alex Bein, 'Zikhronot u-te'udot 'al pegishato shel Herzl 'im Wilhelm ha-sheini' ['Memoirs and Documents on Herzl's Meeting with Wilhelm II'], *Sefer ha-yovel li-khvod N. M. Gelber* (Tel-Aviv, 1963), pp. 13–28, comprising 13 documents among which are the Kaiser's letters to the Grand Duke of Baden on the subject of Zionism and Philipp Eulenburg's letters of 27 and 28 September 1898 to Herzl; and 'Herzl, Hechler, the Grand Duke of Baden and the German Emperor', translated by Harry Zohn, in *Herzl Year Book*, iv (New York, 1961–2), pp. 297–70.

French diplomatic archives yield their mite, but—for this period, at any rate—are ultimately disappointing. Whether because they were weeded at some stage, or because the subject had not yet emerged as one meriting more than routine reporting by French officials, or, finally, because the files that contain the sort of material the historian of the movement most wishes to see have not yet been identified, remains an open question. In Rome, a search of the Secretariat of State's files in the Vatican Archives for the years 1895–1903 by the present author was still more disappointing. Not a single reference to the subject was found. Yet the evidence that the Curia was troubled by the advent of Herzlian Zionism is persuasive. One way or another, there are grounds for thinking that there is a lot of archival territory in Europe that deserves further exploration.

Of the two additional groups of sources (chiefly secondary) for the Herzlian period, one comprises the material which centres on Herzl himself, the other studies and documents which deal with, or have emanated from, his opponents. Alex Bein's *Theodore Herzl* (trans. Maurice Samuel, Philadelphia, 1940) still holds its ground as the best political biography and much the most meticulous one in its use of the primary data. It should be said too that no study of the movement at this period is possible without recourse at some point to Bein's work—a pioneering contribution to the historiography of Zionism, particularly in its application of rigorous, scholarly standards. For a bibliography of Bein's *œuvre* complete to 1973, see Haim Golan, 'Kitvei Alex Bein', *Ha-Ẓionut*, iii (1973), pp. 558–95. Bein's biography apart, the only attempt at a full treatment of political Zionism under Herzl, M. Medzini, *Ha-mediniut ha-zionit me-reishita ve-ʿad moto shel Herzl* (Jerusalem, 1934), is now seriously out of date.

For the internal politics of the movement under Herzl and his relations with the (preponderantly Russian) opposition to him and, ultimately, to most of his works, Michael Heymann, 'Herzl ve-zionei rusiya' ['Herzl and the Russian Zionists'], *Ha-Ẓionut*, iii (1973), pp. 56–99, is a good introduction; Israel Klausner, *Opozizia le-Herzl* [*Opposition to Herzl*] (Jerusalem, 1960) covers some of the ground too; and there is much instruction to be dervied from the documents and, still more, from the apparatus incorporated in the first three volumes of *The Letters and Papers of Chaim Weizmann*, Series A, *Letters*, general editor Meyer W. Weisgal (London, 1968–72). One of the young Weizmann's main political concerns was Herzl the leader and Herzlian Zionism generally, with both of which he was increasingly at odds. Through Weizmann, at the time no more than a figure of the third rank, but in whose letters the debate between Herzl and his eastern European opponents is well reflected, there is a virtually unique means of grasping the irritation and tension that informed its extreme fringes. Weizmann's autobiography, *Trial and Error* (London, 1949; and other editions), deals with these matters at some length in its initial chapters, but in a form that is instructive chiefly for Weizmann's past as contemplated in his own old age. It is therefore best read in conjunction with the close (if pitiless) analysis of *Trial and Error* by Oskar K. Rabinowicz, *Fifty Years of Ẓionism* (London, 1952).

RUSSIA, RUSSIAN JEWRY, AND THE RUSSIAN ZIONISTS

The literature on pre-revolutionary and revolutionary Russia is so large and the role in its affairs played by the Jews of the Empire as a class, and by Jews individually, was so great (relative to their numbers) that a proper guide to essential reading on Russo-Polish Jewry in this period would be unmanageably large. Among the best scholarly introductions to Russian society and politics as a whole are Hugh Seton-Watson, *The Russian Empire 1801–1917* (Oxford, 1967); and Richard Pipes, *Russia under the Old Regime* (London, 1974). Richard Charques, *The Twilight of Imperial Russia* (London, 1965) and Harrison E. Salisbury, *Black Night, White Snow; Russia's Revolution 1905–1917* (New York, 1978) are among the other studies that stand out in the multitude. Sidney Harcave, *First Blood* (New York, 1964) is a first-rate account of the revolution of 1905. On the role of the political police in Russian policy towards the Jews see Norman Cohn, *Warrant for Genocide* (London, 1967) (for a specific reference to its most famous fabrication, 'The Protocols of the Elders of Zion'); Ronald Hingley, *The Russian Secret Police* (London, 1970); Moshe Mishkinsky, 'Ha-"sozialism ha-mishtarti" u-megamot ba-mediniut ha-shilton ha-zaari le-gabei ha-yehudim (1900–1903)' ['"Police Socialism" and Tendencies in the Tsarist Government's Policy towards the Jews (1900–1903)'], *Zion*, xxv, 3–4 (1960); and Jeremiah Schneiderman, *Sergei Zubatov and Revolutionary Marxism* (Ithaca, N.Y., 1976). For studies of two major figures in the revolutionary movement who in their careers and positions go far towards epitomizing the intellectual and political predicament in which forward-looking members of the Russian-Jewish intelligentsia were placed, see Isaac Deutscher, *The Prophet Armed; Trotsky: 1879–1921* (New York, 1954); and Israel Getzler, *Martov* (Cambridge and Melbourne, 1967). See also, Robert S. Wistrich, *Revolutionary Jews from Marx to Trotsky* (London, 1976). On revolutionary ferment in the Jewish working class, see Ezra Mendelsohn, *Class Struggle in the Pale* (Cambridge, 1970); Henry J. Tobias, *The Jewish Bund in Russia* (Stanford, Calif., 1972); and essays on the subject collected in Moshe Mishkinsky (ed.), *Sozialism yehudi u-tenu'at ha-po'alim ha-yehudit ba-me'a ha-19* [*Jewish Socialism and the Jewish Workers' Movement in the Nineteenth Century*] (Jerusalem, 1975).

On Russian Jewry as a whole (in this period) the best introductions are still the second volume of S. M. Dubnov's *History of the Jews in Russia and Poland* (Philadelphia, 1920) and the second volume of Louis Greenberg's *The Jews in Russia* (New Haven, Conn., 1951). Salo W. Baron, *The Russian Jew under Tsars and Soviets* (2nd edn, New York, 1976) is less satisfactory, but its extensive notes provide an excellent guide to the sources. The Russian-Jewish encyclopaedia, *Evreiskaya Entsiklopediya* (16 vols, St. Petersburg, 1906–13) is a mine of information and a monument to the community at its most distinguished before the flood. Similarly representative of the high intellectual and scholarly standards to which some of the best minds in the Russian-Jewish community were committed is Dubnov's historical quarterly, *Evreiskaya Starina* (published in St. Petersburg, 1909–18), much of the material in which is of abiding interest. A modern periodical devoted to the history of Russian Jewry, *He-ʿAvar* [*The Past*] (published in Tel-Aviv since 1952), while uneven in quality, is indispensable for further study. The most thorough and detailed compilation of data on the great wave of pogroms that battered Russian Jewry in 1905 and never really subsided while the Autocracy lasted is [Leo Motzkin,] *Die Judenpogrome in Russland* (2 vols, Cologne and Leipzig, 1910), and since the campaign waged by the Russian Government was among the key determinants of the Jewish condition in Russia, the insight into that condition which it provides is unique. H. Shurrer (ed.), *Ha-pogrom be-kishinov* (Tel-Aviv, 1963) comprises contemporary reports and other documents on the great pogrom at Kishinev in 1903. Two other contemporary compilations of data on pre-revolutionary Russian Jewry deserve special mention: the material collected in the course of the investigations of the Royal Commission on Alien Immigration [of 1902], *Minutes of Evidence*, Cd. 1742 and *Appendix to Minutes of Evidence*, Cd. 1741–I (London, 1903); and a report prepared for the United States Bureau of Labor (for analogous reasons) by I. M. Rubinow, *Economic Condition of the Jews in Russia* (Washington, D.C., 1907, reprinted New York, 1975). To this must be added the regular, detailed, and generally very accurate reporting from Russia in the *Jewish Chronicle* (London) for the entire period.

The only modern, full-length study of the Zionist movement itself in Russia, Izhak Maʾor, *Ha-tenuʿa ha-zionit be-rusiya* (Jerusalem, 1973), is not without value as an introduction, but of limited use as a guide to further study. The two volumes of *Kazir* (Tel-Aviv, 1964, 1972) contain useful material, notably A. Rafaʾeli's extended article, with accompanying documents, on conferences of the Zionist movement in Russia held between 1898 and 1917 (*Kazir* [i], pp. 43–102; ii, pp. 235–93). Yizhak Gruenbaum's history of the Zionist movement, *Ha-tenuʿa ha-zionit be-hitpathuta* (iv parts (but particularly parts ii and iii), Jerusalem, 1942–54), is strongest on Zionism in the Russian Empire and may be read principally for what the author, as a prominent participant, had to say about it. Otherwise, the published sources—material in scholarly journals apart—are chiefly the contemporary Jewish periodical press in Russia, especially *Ha-Meliz* (St. Petersburg), *Ha-Zefira* (Warsaw), and *Ha-Zeman*

(Vilna), the official organ of the movement in Vienna, *Die Welt*, and, again, the *Jewish Chronicle* (London), along with the memoirs, biographies, and published letters of prominent figures in the movement.

In the latter class the outstanding personality, but equally the observer whose writings are unique both for their contemporary influence and for what they can still teach us is, of course, Aḥad Ha-ʿAm. His published articles appeared regularly in the monthly *Ha-Shiloʾaḥ* (Cracow and Odessa) which he founded and which, for some years, he edited; but they are most accessible in his collected writings, *Kol kitvei Aḥad Ha-ʿAm* (Tel-Aviv, 1947). A large selection of his letters (mostly chosen and edited by himself) have been published as *Igrot Aḥad Ha-ʿAm* (2nd edn, ed. Arye [Leon] Simon with Yoḥanan Pograbinsky, 6 vols, Tel-Aviv, 1956–60). There are several collections of his essays in English, the most recent, edited and introduced by Hans Kohn, is *Nationalism and the Jewish Ethic; Basic Writings of Aḥad Ha-ʿAm* (New York, 1962). The standard biography and discussion of his work is Arye [Leon] Simon and Yosef Heller, *Aḥad Ha-ʿAm: ha-ish, poʿolo ve-torato* (Jerusalem, 1955). Its purely biographical part by Simon is available in English as *Ahad Ha-am; Asher Ginzberg* (Philadelphia, 1960). The literature on the man and his ideas is generally unambitious in scale and marked by the awe in which he has commonly been held. A study that is instructive for his views on Zionism, by taking them in conjunction with those of two other great contemporaries, is S. Breiman, *Ha-pulmus bein Lilienblum le-vein Aḥad Ha-ʿAm ve-Dubnov ve-ha-rekʿa shelo* [*The Debate between Lilienblum and Aḥad Ha-ʿAm and Dubnov and its Background*] (Jerusalem, 1951). All in all, a review of his role and ideas in a properly open and critical frame of mind is long overdue.

Other figures in the mainstream of Russian Zionism who may be glimpsed through selections of their writings or speeches, or through memorial volumes containing biographical or autobiographical sketches and other papers are: Bernstein-Kohan—Miriam Bernstein-Kohan and Y. Korn (eds), *Sefer Bernstein-Kohan* (Tel-Aviv, 1946); Bialik, remote from great affairs, but an acute observer—P. Lahover (ed.), *Igrot Hayyim Naḥman Bialik* [*The letters of Hayyim Naḥman Bialik*] (5 vols, Tel-Aviv, 1937–9); Gruenbaum—Yizḥak Gruenbaum, *Dor be-mivḥan* (Jerusalem, 1951); Idelson—A. Goldstein et al. (eds), *Sefer Idelson* (Tel-Aviv, 1946); Jabotinsky—the official full-length biography: Joseph B. Schechtman, *Zeʾev Jabotinsky; parashat ḥayyav* (3 vols, Tel-Aviv, 1957–9) (in English: *Rebel and Statesman; the Vladimir Jabotinsky Story*, 2 vols, New York, 1956–61); Jabotinsky's autobiography *Sippur Yamai* [*The Story of my Days*] (Jerusalem, 1958); and his journalism and recollections on the period, as for example, in the volume *Uma ve-ḥevra* [*Nation and Society*] (Jerusalem, 1950); Motzkin— Alex Bein (ed.), *Sefer Motzkin* (Jerusalem, 1939); Sokolov—S. Rawidowicz (ed.), *Sefer Sokolov* (Jerusalem, 1943); Tchlenov— S. Eisenstadt (ed.), *Yeḥiel Tchlenov; pirkei ḥayyav u-feʿulato* (Tel-Aviv, 1937); Ussishkin—S. Schwartz, *Ussishkin be-igrotav* [*Ussishkin through his letters*] (Jerusalem, 1949); and *Sefer Ussishkin* (Jerusalem, 1934); Weizmann—no full-length biography has yet been written (several have been promised), but a careful reading of Weizmann's *Letters* (see above, p. 500) can be rewarding.

For the socialist strain in Russian Zionism in its early form, the basic contemporary writings are by Nachman Syrkin—in *Kitvei Naḥman Syrkin*, edited by Berl Katznelson and Yehuda Kaufman (Tel-Aviv, 1939), with a long and valuable introductory essay by Katznelson; and by Ber Borochov—in the full edition of his works, *Ketavim*, edited by L. Levite, D. Ben-Naḥum, and Sh. Rehav (3 vols, Tel-Aviv, 1955–66); Matityahu Mintz, *Ber Borochov; ha-maʿagal ha-rishon (1900–1906)* (Tel-Aviv, 1976) is a detailed study of the first stage of Borochov's career. For an English edition of Syrkin's main texts, see Marie Syrkin, *Nachman Syrkin; Socialist Zionist* (New York, 1961); for some of Borochov's texts in English, see Ber Borochov, *Nationalism and the Class Struggle* (New York, 1937, reprinted Westport, Conn., 1972). Y. Petrazil, *Yalkutei poʿalei zion, i, ha-mahapekha ha-rishona ve-ha-sheniya be-rusiya* (Tel-Aviv, 1947) has some material on the Zionist socialists at the time of the revolution of 1905. But chiefly the sources, such as they are, on the early Zionist socialists tend to merge with those for the Second ʿAliya. On the latter, there are vivid, first-hand accounts in Yiẓhak Ben-Ẓvi, *Poʿalei zion ba-ʿaliya ha-sheniya* (Tel-Aviv, 1950); S. H. Bergmann and E. Shoḥat (eds), *Kitvei A. D. Gordon* (3 vols, Jerusalem, 1951–4); Berakha Ḥabas (ed.), *Sefer ha-ʿaliya ha-sheniya* (Tel-Aviv, 1947); Yaʿakov Sharett and Naḥman Tamir (eds), *Anshei ha-ʿaliya ha-sheniya; pirkei zikhronot* (2 vols, Tel-Aviv, 1970); Yehuda Sharett (ed.), *Igrot B. Katznelson 1900–1914* (Tel-Aviv, 1961); and E. Shoḥat and Ḥ. Shurer (eds), *Pirkei ha-poʿel ha-ẓair* (Tel-Aviv, 1931–9). For general surveys of the socialist strain in Zionism as it took shape in Ereẓ-Israel in the period leading up to the Great War and beyond, see Moshe Braslavsky, *Tenuʿat ha-poʿalim ha-Ereẓ-Israelit* (4 vols, Tel-Aviv, 1955–62); and Yehuda Slutski, *Mavo le-toldot tenuʿat ha-ʿavoda ha-israelit* (Tel-Aviv, 1973).

While no comprehensive study of the *yishuv* as such in its early years has yet been put together (the multi-volume, multi-authored project in preparation under the auspices of the Israel National Academy of Sciences and Humanities is unlikely to be complete and in print before the middle of the 1980s), a great deal of information on the inner life of the *yishuv* can be mined from those more narrowly conceived compilations which are already available: the work of settlement and defence organizations, celebratory in intent, often somewhat tendentious politically, but packed with generally accurate and usable data. The most distinguished example of such a series is *Sefer toldot ha-hagana* [*The History of the Hagana (defence forces)*], prepared partly under the auspices of the Israel Defence Forces (7 vols, Tel-Aviv, 1954–72), the first volume of which, edited by Ben-Zion Dinur, covers the period between the early 1880s and the end of the Great War. The first part of an official history of Bank Leumi le-Israel, the lineal descendant of Herzl's Jewish Colonial Trust, *Banka'i le-uma be-hithadshuta* [*Banker to a nation in process of renewal*] (Giv'atayim-Ramat-Gan, 1977), provides an excellent survey, by Nachum Gross, of the economy of Erez-Israel/Palestine in general, and of the *yishuv* in particular, up to 1918. For relations with the Ottoman authorities and the Arab population, see Neville J. Mandel, *The Arabs and Zionism before World War I* (Berkeley, Calif., 1976); and Moshe Ma'oz (ed.), *Studies on Palestine during the Ottoman Period* (Jerusalem, 1975). Y. Porath, *The Emergence of the Palestinian-Arab National Movement 1918–1929* (London, 1974) deals chiefly with a later period, but its initial, introductory chapters referring to the situation before the war are as good as anything that has been written on its subject. Finally, mention should be made of the study Herzl commissioned Leo Motzkin to make, published as *Die Juden in Palästina* in Berlin (1898?); the vivid contemporary writings of the physician, Hillel Joffe, *Dor ma'apilim* (2nd edn, Jerusalem, 1971); and the journal *Cathedra* (Jerusalem) which began publication in 1976, and which is devoted exclusively to the study of Erez-Israel and the *yishuv*.

For the orthodox strain in the early years of the Zionist movement, R. Yizhak Nissenboim's autobiographical *'Alei heldi* (Warsaw, 1929) is the most rewarding work. Rabbi Y. Y. Reines's views are in his books *Or hadash 'al zion* [*New Light on Zion*] (Vilna, 1902) and *Nod shel dema'ot* [*A Bottle of Tears*] (Jerusalem, 1934); the best analysis of Reines's position, E. Don-Yihye, 'Dat u-le'om be-mishnat ha-rav Reines' ['Religion and Nationhood in the Doctrine of R. Reines'] (Jerusalem, 1970), has yet to be published. Rabbi M. A. 'Amiel, *Ha-yesodot ha-idi'ologiim shel ha-mizrahi* [*The Ideological Foundations of the Mizrahi*] (Warsaw, 1934) belongs to a later period, but as the most incisive statement on the subject from the inside (before latent, sub-Messianic tendencies in the Mizrahi rose to the surface) it commands attention. A large collection, Y. Rafael and S. Z. Shragai (eds), *Sefer ha-zionut ha-datit* (2 vols, Jerusalem, 1977), has several documents of interest. Yosef Salmon, "'Emdata shel ha-hevra ha-haredit be-rusiya-polin la-zionut ba-shanim 1898–1900' ['The Attitude of Orthodox Society in Russia-Poland to Zionism in the Years 1898–1900'], *Eshel Beer-Shev'a*, i (Beer-Shev'a and Jerusalem, 1976), pp. 377–438, is a detailed account and analysis of the dilemma with which Herzlian Zionism confronted orthodoxy before it moved, in its great majority, into opposition to the Jewish Risorgimento.

Index

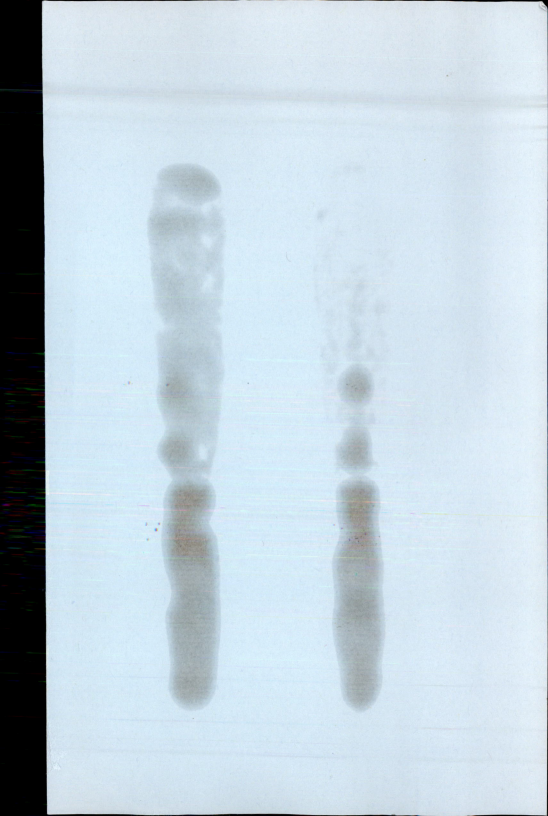